DISCOVERING
GOD

DISCOVERING
GOD

*The Origins of the Great Religions
and the Evolution of Belief*

RODNEY STARK

HarperOne
A Division of HarperCollinsPublishers

MERIDEN PUBLIC LIBRARY
Meriden, Conn.

4375111
200
St

HarperOne

DISCOVERING GOD: *The Origins of the Great Religions and the Evolution of Belief.*
Copyright © 2007 by Rodney Stark. All rights reserved. Printed in the United States of
America. No part of this book may be used or reproduced in any manner whatsoever
without written permission except in the case of brief quotations embodied in critical
articles and reviews. For information address HarperCollins Publishers, 10 East 53rd
Street, New York, NY 10022.

HarperCollins books may be purchased for educational, business, or sales promotional
use. For information please write: Special Markets Department, HarperCollins Publishers,
10 East 53rd Street, New York, NY 10022.

HarperCollins Web site: http://www.harpercollins.com

HarperCollins®, ✶ ®, and HarperOne™ are trademarks of HarperCollins Publishers.

Maps by Topaz Inc.

FIRST EDITION

Library of Congress Cataloging-in-Publication Data
   Stark, Rodney
        Discovering God : the origins of the great religions and the evolution of belief /
   Rodney Stark. — 1st ed.
        p.   cm.
   Includes bibliographical references (p. 447) and index.
   ISBN: 978-0-06-117389-9
   ISBN-10: 0-06-117389-4
   1. Religions.   I. Title.
   BL80.3.S73   2007
   200—dc22   2007018576

07 08 09 10 11   RRD(H)   10 9 8 7 6 5 4 3

CONTENTS

PREFACE

Portions of Chapters 2, 3, 4, and 7 were given as Templeton Research Lectures at Vanderbilt University in February and March 2006. I thank the Vanderbilt faculty and staff, especially Volnay Gay and Mark Justad, for their hospitality. I usually decline such invitations, but these four visits to Nashville turned out very well.

Several people were of great help on this project. Eric Brandt, my very gifted editor at HarperOne, detected many places where more needed to be said, and several where the less said, the better. I also am grateful to Anna Xiao Dong Sun for help with Chapter 6, to David Lyle Jeffrey for comments on Chapter 7, and to Laurence Iannaccone and Roger Finke for serving as general sounding boards. My friend and colleague Byron Johnson saw to it that many potential distractions never materialized.

Let me also acknowledge dozens of used book dealers affiliated with Amazon and with Barnes & Noble for providing me with several hundred books, most of them long out of print. Nearly all of these are celebrated works that, sad to say, were available at very low prices after having been discarded by college and university libraries. So, my special thanks to the librarians at the California Institute of Technology for discarding a fine unabridged, three-volume copy of *The Golden Bough* (1900), to the librarians at Loyola Seminary in New York for my copy of Wilhelm Schmidt's invaluable and rare *The Origin and Growth of Religion* (1931), to their colleagues at Albion College who sold off W. Robertson Smith's *Lectures on the Religion of the Semites* (1889), and to the staff at the University of Washington Library for scrapping J. Stuart Hay's *The Amazing Emperor Heliogabalus* (1911).

Finally, I have tried to make this book easily accessible to readers who have no background in comparative religion, while still maintaining a high level of scholarship. To that end I have set in boldface and defined important esoteric or technical terms—whether the names of Gods or of social-science concepts—as they enter the narrative, and these also appear in a glossary at the end of the book. These terms aside, I have tried to write everything else in plain English. I do not concede that this in any way compromises sophistication. What it does do is prevent me from hiding incomprehension behind a screen of academic jargon.

Corrales, New Mexico
February 2007

DISCOVERING
GOD

INTRODUCTION

REVELATION AND
CULTURAL EVOLUTION

SINCE I WAS VERY YOUNG I have often wondered about God. Does he really exist? If so, where was he before he revealed himself to Abraham? Were many generations of humans condemned to live and die in ignorance, followed by many generations during which only the Chosen Few knew God? Or could it be that from earliest times God has revealed himself often and in various places so that many different religions possess at least fragmentary knowledge of divine will? If so, why do even some very major religions seem to lack any trace of divine inspiration?

Questions such as these prompted me to fully reassess the origins and cultural evolution of the world's great religions, a topic that once attracted many distinguished philosophers, anthropologists, and sociologists, although today it is dominated by biologists and evolutionary psychologists. No matter. This entire body of recent work is remarkably inferior because so few authors could restrain their militant atheism.[1] Contempt is not a scholarly virtue, and most of these scholars openly presumed that Gods[2] exist only in the human imagination, that religion arises mainly from fear, and that faith is sustained only by ignorance and credulity. Richard Dawkins's latest title tells it all: *The God Delusion*.

Not only does the topic of religious evolution tend to attract those antagonistic to religion, but comparisons among religions can easily be corrosive to faith because one must confront the fact that, since they disagree, not all religions can be entirely true. From there it is a small step to conclude that all religions are false, that "all are refuted by all," as the renegade monk Jean Bodin put it in 1593.[3]

Ironically, the similarities among the world's religions also are taken as "proof" that they all are human inventions. The most famous proponent of this view was James Frazer (1854–1941), who published his monumental *The Golden Bough* in twelve volumes beginning in 1890. Frazer was born in Glasgow, Scotland, and spent his entire career at Trinity College, Cambridge. He worked for sixty years, with hardly ever a day off,[4] to compile an enormous set of examples in order to argue, among other things, that tales of crucifixion and resurrection are commonplace in world "mythology," and so is the notion of "a divine man . . . as a scapegoat . . . a dying god chosen to take upon himself and carry away the sins and sorrows of the people."[5] Hence, Frazer devoted considerable space to claiming that the Christian Passion Narrative derives from myths about the deaths and resurrections of Attis, Adonis, and many others, and that it is a reenactment of "the Jewish festival of Purim [which] is a continuation, under a changed name, of the Babylonian Sacaea [which is] a reminiscence of the ancient custom of crucifying or hanging a man [Haman] in the character of a god at the festival."[6] Acknowledging that Easter is a month later than Purim, Frazer proposed that "Christian tradition shifted the date of the crucifixion by a month in order to make the great sacrifice of the Lamb of God coincide with the annual sacrifice of the Passover lamb."[7] Next Frazer proposed "that the crucifixion with all its cruel mockery was not a punishment devised for Christ, but was merely the fate that annually befell the malefactor who played Haman [in the original Purim ritual]."[8] Frazer continued along these lines at great length, attempting to demonstrate that "the conception of a dying and risen god" has been popular in all the early civilizations "from time immemorial."[9] He ended by suggesting that Jesus could have been "no more than a moral teacher, whom the fortunate accident of his execution invested with the crown, not merely of a martyr, but of a god."[10]

The Golden Bough made Frazer the most admired anthropologist of his day, and he was knighted in 1914. Nevertheless, Frazer ignored the most important question raised by his huge study: *Why* is there so much similarity among religions? Aside from saying that humans are inherently gullible, Frazer was content to postulate that once someone, somewhere had made up a "myth" or a ritual, it soon spread (or diffused) to other cultures, readily crossing substantial barriers of geography, language, and time. Of course, neither Frazer nor any of his many admirers would entertain the possibility that the common source of religious culture might be spiritual.

Perhaps that is why social scientists have displayed very little interest in the remarkable fact that, although they were scattered from Southern Italy to China, many of the great religious "founders" were contemporaries. As shown on Map 1–1 on the next page, Buddha, Confucius, Lao-Tzu (Taoism), Zoroaster, Mahāvīra (Jainism), the principal authors of most of the Hindu *Upaniṣads*, Grecian innovators such as Pythagoras and the unknown founder of Orphism, even the Israelite prophets Jeremiah and Ezekiel, as well as the biblical author referred to as Second Isaiah—all lived in the sixth century BCE! Was this pure coincidence? An example of diffusion? Evidence of repeated revelations? Or what? On this, the social-scientific literature has had very little to say, and most of what has been said uniformly ignores or specifically denies any spiritual aspects.[11] Oddly enough, this literature also ignores compelling evidence of substantial diffusion—some of these founders appear to have been greatly influenced by one another, especially in India.

Instead, spurred by Frazer's example, many social scientists have continued to compile additional similarities among religions. Some have gleefully equated various forms of ritual cannibalism with the Christian sacrament of communion. Others have made much of the fact that the story of Christ's Nativity is but one of many in which a God impregnates a human female. But seldom has anyone with respectable credentials considered the rather obvious possibility that these similarities may testify that authentic revelations underlie many of the major faiths. Instead, the dominating scholarly perspective regards all revelations as purely psychological events and assumes that the answer to where God was prior to Abraham's generation is that Yahweh hadn't been invented yet. That certainly was my view early in the 1980s when I wrote a chapter on the "Evolution of the Gods."[12]

Today my answer is quite different, as should be evident from the title of this book, which refers to the *discovery*, not to the evolution of God. Of course, cultural evolution often takes the form of discovery, whether it is sharp sticks becoming flint-headed spears or alchemy becoming chemistry. In this instance, what evolved were human conceptions of God, which

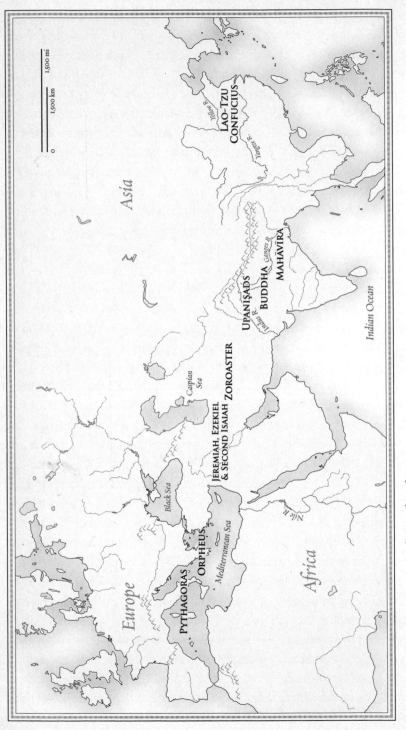

Map 1-1: Map of sixth-century BCE religious founders.

also constitutes discovery if one posits that God exists. So, as to where God was in primitive times, I shall raise the possibility that he was there all along, revealing himself within the very limited capacities of humans to understand. Even so, the chapters that follow are not significantly different from what I would have written from my earlier perspective *except* that I am careful at key points to provide alternative interpretations, one of which assumes the existence of God. Thus, when discussing revelations in Chapter 1, I suggest the recipients might either be "externalizing" the source of their own creative genius *or* that they might, in fact, be hearing God. In any event, it is impossible to analyze the discovery of God, or the evolution of our images of God, outside of specific contexts. Hence, this also is an interpretive *history* of the origins of the great religions.

REVELATION AS DIVINE ACCOMMODATION

Theology involves *formal reasoning about God.* The emphasis is on *discovering* God's nature, intentions, and demands, and on understanding how these define the relationship between human beings and God. Hence, Jewish and Christian theologians have devoted centuries to reasoning about what God may have really meant by various passages in scripture, and over time the interpretations often have "evolved" in quite dramatic and extensive ways. For example, not only does the Bible not condemn astrology, the story of the Magi following the star might seem to suggest that it is valid. However, in the fifth century Saint Augustine (354–430) *reasoned* that astrology is false because to believe that one's fate is predestined in the stars stands in opposition to God's gift of free will.[13]

In keeping with this approach, Jews and Christians have always assumed that the application of reason can yield an *increasingly more accurate* understanding of God. Augustine noted that although there were "certain matters pertaining to the doctrine of salvation that we cannot yet grasp . . . one day we shall be able to do so."[14] Of crucial importance is that their efforts to reason out God's will required that Christian theologians not always interpret the Bible literally. Instead, from earliest days it has been the conventional Christian view that although the Bible is true, its meaning often is uncertain for, as Augustine noted, "divers things may be understood under these words which yet are all true."[15]

The three Magi following the star to attend the birth of Christ are depicted on this early Christian sarcophagus. The Magi were the premier astrologers of the era, and the appearance of this story in Matthew would seem to give biblical support to astrology. Even so, the Church accepted Saint Augustine's logical rejection of astrology. (Museo Pio Cristiano, Vatican Museums, Vatican State; Photo: Scala/Art Resource, New York.)

Thus did Augustine frankly acknowledge that it is possible for a later reader, with God's help, to grasp a scriptural meaning even though the person who first wrote down the scripture "understood not this." Thus, he continued, "Let us approach together unto the words of Thy book, and seek in them Thy meaning, through the meaning of Thy servant, by whose pen Thou hast dispensed them."[16] Moreover, Augustine wrote that since God is incapable of either error or falsehood, if the Bible seems to contradict knowledge, that is because of a lack of understanding on the part of the "servant" who recorded God's words.

This line of thought is entirely consistent with one of the most fundamental, yet remarkably neglected, of all Judeo-Christian premises, that of **Divine Accommodation**, which holds that *God's revelations are always limited to the current capacity of humans to comprehend*—that in order to communicate with humans, God is forced to accommodate their incomprehension by resorting to the equivalent of "baby talk." This view is, of course, firmly rooted in scripture. In Exodus 6:2 (in the Torah), when God tells Moses that he had made himself known to Abraham, Isaac, and Jacob, not as Yahweh, but as El Shaddai,[17] presumably this was because the Patriarchs were not ready to be told more.[18] Or, when asked by his disciples why he spoke to the multitudes in parables, Jesus replied that people differed greatly in what they could comprehend: *"This is why I speak to them in parables, because seeing they do not see, and hearing they do not hear, nor do they understand."*[19]

It was in this same spirit that Irenaeus (c. 115–202) invoked the principle of divine accommodation to human limits in order to explain God's tolerance of human failings. A generation later, Origen (c. 185–251) wrote in *On First Principles* that "we teach about God both what is true and what the multitude can understand." Hence, "the written revelation in inspired scripture is a veil that must be penetrated. It is an accommodation to our present capacities . . . [that] will one day be superseded."[20]

Thomas Aquinas (1225–1274) agreed: "The things of God should be revealed to mankind only in proportion to their capacity; otherwise, they might despise what was beyond their grasp. . . . It was, therefore, better for the divine mysteries to be conveyed to an uncultured people as it were veiled . . ."[21] So, too, John Calvin (1509–1564) flatly asserted that God "reveals himself to us according to our rudeness and infirmity."[22] If scriptural comparisons, between earlier and later portions of the Bible, for example, seem to suggest that God is changeable or inconsistent, that is merely because "he accommodated diverse forms to different ages, as he knew would be expedient for each . . . he has accommodated himself to men's capacity, which is varied and changeable."[23] The same constraints applied to those who conveyed God's words. Thus, Calvin noted that in formulating Genesis, Moses "was ordained a teacher as well of the unlearned and rude as of the learned, he could not otherwise fulfill his office than by descending to this grosser method of instruction. . . . [Seeking to] be intelligible to all . . . Moses, therefore, adapts his discourse to common usage . . . such as the rude and unlearned may perceive . . . [and] he who would learn astronomy, and other recondite arts, let him go elsewhere."[24]

The principle of divine accommodation provides a truly remarkable key for completely reappraising the origins and history of religions. Calvin said straight out that *Genesis* is not a literal account of the Creation because it was directed to the unlearned and the primitive, even though, when they received it, the ancient Jews were far from being truly primitive. How much greater an accommodation would be required to enable God to reveal himself to the truly unsophisticated humans living in the Stone Age? So, it is at least plausible that many religions are based on authentic revelations as God has communicated within the limits of human comprehension and as his message has been misunderstood and erroneously transmitted. Moreover, if humans have been given free will and thereby put mostly on their own to develop their capacities and culture, that also places serious restrictions on the extent to which God will reveal himself. From this perspective, God *asks for* human assent and will not force conformity, not even in the way that extremely dramatic, general revelations would do—if, for example, he appeared in the sky each morning.

It is not illogical to argue that revelations do not occur and that *all* religions are of human origins, but it seems to me well beyond credibility to argue that *all* religions are to any significant extent true. Given the importance of religion in human cultures and the nonempirical nature of its source, it is to be assumed that many illusory or even fraudulent religious claims have been advanced. The immense and humbling challenge is to tell which ones are valid, while attempting to respect the extremely sensitive matters involved. Even so, at the end of the book I shall attempt to justify three tests of divine inspiration.

EVOLVING CONCEPTIONS OF GOD(S): A PRELIMINARY SKETCH

This book can be read either as a study of the evolution of human *images* of God, or as the evolution of the human *capacity to comprehend* God. The same theoretical model suits either interpretation.

Theories of the evolution of human culture must differ substantially from theories of biological evolution, since culture has no equivalent to genes[25] and is not transmitted in a "mechanical" way, but only imperfectly through the socialization of the young. However, both biological and cultural evolution seem to be greatly shaped by the principle of *natural selection* or *survival of the fittest*, which refers to the tendency for better-adapted organisms or cultural elements to prevail over the less well-adapted. Keep in mind that I am not referring to the evolution of new species, but to natural selection *within* the "species" known as human cultures or, to even more greatly restrict the term, I am concerned with natural selection among variations within the "species" called religion. As the pioneering anthropologist Edward Burnett Tylor wrote in 1871: "To the ethnographer the bow and arrow is a species."[26] Thus, cultural evolution examines how an overall culture is shaped by natural selection among subsidiary elements of culture (how more powerful bows supplanted less effective models) or how the array of human cultures is changed by the survival of the fittest among them (how cultures having bows eliminated those having only clubs or spears).

Remarkably, Charles Darwin[27] borrowed the phrase "survival of the fittest" from the English sociologist Herbert Spencer,[28] who coined it in 1851, applying it not to the evolution of organisms, but to the evolution of culture. As proposed by Spencer, the principle of the survival of the fittest meant that, within particular circumstances, those cultures and/or cultural elements better suited to human needs will survive and those less suited will tend to die out. This may occur because a society shifts its cultural elements accordingly, or because the society itself (and its culture) succumbs to another having a better-suited culture.

As implied above, natural selection requires two conditions that are met by both organisms and cultures: considerable variation across individual cases and a challenging environment. And just as biological survival selects for favorable variations, better-adapted cultures also enjoy a survival advantage. For example, it was only their far superior military culture that allowed the small city-states of Ancient Greece to repeatedly defeat and ultimately dominate the huge armies of Persia. Had the Greeks lacked highly disciplined phalanxes, there may never have been any Greek philosophers.

Whether or not biological evolution is guided by Intelligent Design, it is not the product of conscious selection or invention by the organisms involved. But that is very much the case with cultural evolution—its fundamental mechanisms are human creativity and evaluation. Humans constantly invent new elements of culture. Whether an element will be generally adopted or retained depends upon how it is evaluated by humans in terms of its apparent utility—the latter being broadly defined to include such things as intellectual, emotional, and artistic satisfactions, as well as more practical matters. Hence: *Humans will tend to adopt and retain those elements of culture that appear to produce "better" results, while those that appear to be less rewarding will tend to be discarded.* Thus, the Roman numerical system was discarded for the far more efficient Hindu-Arabic system, and monophonic music was superseded by polyphonic harmonies. The use of "appear" to modify the proposition is important since human evaluations often are mistaken, sometimes from faulty perceptions, sometimes because of vested interests, and sometimes due to strong attachments to tradition. Therefore, the proposition asserts only a general tendency over the long run and, as with all properly formulated theoretical propositions, it is to be assumed that it also is qualified by the phrase *other things being equal.*

Keep in mind, too, that whether it is biological or cultural, change is *neither a unilinear, nor necessarily a progressive phenomenon, at least not in the short run.* Evolution, in the sense of becoming better adapted, is not inevitable, and many changes are not in any way "favorable." Instead, regression occurs, and dead ends are frequent—consider the dinosaurs. The same occurs with cultures. This will be particularly clear in Chapter 1, where most of the information on the religions of primitive cultures comes from groups still living in the Stone Age as of the eighteenth and nineteenth centuries—cultures that obviously had long ago ceased to evolve, most of them soon to be extinct.

Moreover, from a comparative perspective, at various times religious cultures display a remarkable confusion as, for example, early trends toward monotheism are reversed and lush polytheism is reasserted, while elsewhere well-defined Gods recede into unconscious spirits, only to have both trends later be reversed. Such variability not only poses intellectual challenges, but narrative difficulties. Rather than attempt to follow a unitary time line, trying to keep track of many differing simultaneous developments, I have chosen to carve up the subject in order to follow a particular founder or faith in adequate detail before switching to another.

These matters having been clarified, let us turn to the evolution of conceptions of God(s): *Humans will tend to adopt and retain images of God(s) that appear to provide greater satisfactions, both subjective and material.* Given this master trend, it follows that *humans will prefer Gods to unconscious divine essences.* As will be pursued in various chapters, unconscious "divine" essences are not Gods. One might as well invoke Lady Luck as call upon Baruch Spinoza's (1632–1677) "Nature," since neither of them can hear, nor can they care. Hence, a major distinction: **Supernatural** refers to *somewhat mysterious forces or entities that are above, beyond, or outside nature and which may be able to influence reality.* **Gods** are *supernatural beings having consciousness and intentions.* When given the choice, humans prefer Gods.

Human images of God will tend to progress from those having smaller to those having greater scope. Scope of the Gods refers to the diversity of their powers and interests and the range of their influence. A God of weather is of greater scope than a God of rain or of wind. A God that controls the weather everywhere on earth is of greater scope than a God whose control of weather is restricted to a small tribal area. Over the long run, the trend will be toward a conception of *God(s) of infinite scope and absolute power*. However, over the shorter run, humans may shift their worship to Gods of lesser scope, but (perhaps) of greater psychological appeal—for example, from a rather distant, morally demanding High God to the quite permissive, colorful, nearby, and abundant Gods of the ancient pantheons.

In addition, humans will prefer an image of God(s) as *rational and loving*. Nothing can be done with or about irrational beings; they cannot even be propitiated. If the Gods truly are crazy, then religion is futile. But if the Gods are *rational*, there is an immense range of possibilities. However, even when dealing with Gods conceived of as conscious, rational beings, relations with Gods are contingent on another feature, whether the Gods are *loving*. As they were portrayed, the traditional Greek and Roman Gods could *hear* prayers, but it was rather uncertain whether they would care. It was wise to propitiate such Gods with periodic rituals and sacrifices, but they were not very loving and more often seem to have provoked anxiety than to have been loved. Consequently, Greco-Roman societies proved very vulnerable to an influx of loving deities from elsewhere, including Cybele (the Great Mother Goddess from Phrygia) and Isis (the Savior Goddess from Egypt). Loving Gods merit deep commitment—the term *loving* sums up a whole set of divine attributes: merciful, accessible, aware, and benign. Given the choice, humans will prefer loving Gods.

These preferences lead to a conception of God as a *loving, conscious, rational being of unlimited scope, who created and rules over the entire universe*.

However, this image of God does not necessarily imply absolute monotheism. In fact, only "Godless" religions centered on an unconscious, divine essence can easily be purely monotheistic. When God is portrayed as a conscious being, the degree of monotheism is limited by the problem of evil. If God is responsible for *everything*, evil as well as good, then God may seem to be an irrational, perverse, capricious entity who shifts intentions unpredictably and without reason. Such a conception of God was prevalent in Egypt and Mesopotamia, although it was attributed to supreme Gods such as Marduck and Amun-Re, not to an *only* God. The idea that God is inexplicable, and that divine blessings and terrible punishments occur unpredictably, may not have been so alien in cultures accustomed to rule by capricious royalty. Indeed, there are strong echoes of such a conception of God in early Judaism.[29]

To more plausibly picture God as rational and loving, it is helpful to assume the existence of other, if far lesser, divine beings. That is, *evil* supernatural creatures such as Satan are essential. In this manner Zoroastrianism, Judaism, Christianity, and Islam are *dualistic* monotheisms—each teaches that, in addition to a supreme divine being, there also exists at least one additional, if less powerful, supernatural being who is the source of evil.[30] Consequently, in each of these faiths God is not assigned the primary responsibility for evil and injustice—for example, it was Satan, not God, who heaped misfortunes upon Job.[31]

Dualistic monotheism is not symmetrical. Evil is not afforded full Godhood—Ahura Mazdā, Yahweh, Jehovah, and Allāh merely tolerate lesser evil beings and will vanquish them at the appropriate time. There is an extensive theological literature as to why God tolerates evil, mainly having to do with issues of free will. Here it is sufficient to note that the "evolution" of religion cannot achieve absolute monotheism without abandoning belief in a conscious God—an unconscious divine essence does nothing and cannot be blamed for anything.

Keep in mind, too, that monotheism is compatible with the existence of many lesser spiritual beings such as angels, demons, imps, jinns, cherubs, and saints. This does not constitute a form of polytheism because these entities are not regarded as Gods. They exist and function only within God's authority. In this sense, then, Judaism, Christianity, and Islam are correctly identified as the three great monotheisms.

The chapters that follow are shaped by the assumption that, despite its many twistings, turnings, and retracings, the path along which human cultures progressively discovered God led toward dualistic monotheism.

But, many modern social scientists would say, why all the bother about God? Surely religion is a matter of ritual, not of divinity, so why waste time on images of God? Such views reflect the fact that for much of the twentieth century, the social-scientific study of religion was essentially a Godless field. Not only because so many practitioners were nonbelievers,

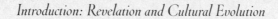

All of the great monotheisms solve the problem of evil by assuming the existence of a lesser, wicked supernatural creature. Here Satan exhorts a rebellion among the angels, as depicted by John Martin (1779–1854). (Victoria and Albert Museum, London; Photo: Victoria and Albert Museum, London/Art Resource, New York.)

but because God was banished from definitions of religion and was ignored in both research and theorizing.

In his immensely influential work, the French sociologist Emile Durkheim (1858–1917) dismissed Gods as unimportant window dressing, stressing instead that rites and rituals are the fundamental stuff of religion. In a book review written in 1886 of Herbert Spencer's *Principles of Sociology*, Durkheim[32] condemned Spencer for reducing religion "to being merely a collection of beliefs and practices relating to a supernatural agent." He continued:

> The idea of God which seemed to be the sum total of religion a short while ago, is now no more than a minor accident. It is a psychological phenomenon which has got mixed up with a whole sociological process whose importance is of quite a different order. . . . We might perhaps be able to discover what is thus hidden beneath this quite superficial phenomenon. . . .
>
> Thus the sociologist will pay scant attention to the different ways in which men and peoples have conceived the unknown cause and mysterious depth of things. He will set aside all such metaphysical speculations and will see in religion only a social discipline.[33]

Twenty-six years later Durkheim had not wavered in his conviction that Gods are peripheral to religion, noting that although the apparent purpose of rituals is "strengthening the ties between the faithful and their god," what they really do is strengthen the "ties between the individual and society . . . the god being only a figurative representation of the society."[34] Thus began a new social-science orthodoxy: Religion consists of participation in rites and rituals—*only*.

One must wonder how anyone can think it plausible that the abundance of religious rites and rituals found in all human cultures are sustained without any apparent rationale. But Durkheim and his disciples were not even content to claim that people worship illusions, for then they would have had to restore the Gods, illusory or not, to the core of religion. Instead, they even dismissed illusory Gods, thereby proposing, at least by implication, that people knowingly pray to and worship the empty void. Remarkably, when confronted with this implication of the claim that religions are Godless, some well-known social scientists have, in fact, affirmed that religious rites, including prayers, are *not* directed toward the Gods! We are asked to accept that even primitive tribal priests realize there are no Gods and are fully aware that their ritual actions are devoted merely to sustaining group solidarity.[35] Rodney Needham[36] went so far as to deny that there is any human mental state that can properly be called religious belief, and therefore that *all* religious activity is purely socio-emotional expression.

It requires a great deal of sophisticated social-scientific training for a person to accept such nonsense. People pray to *something*! To something above and beyond the material world. To something having the ability to hear prayers and having the supernatural powers needed to influence nature and events. Real or not, such "somethings" are Gods. Variations in how God or the Gods are conceived is the crucial difference among faiths and cultures, as will be demonstrated beyond question in the chapters that follow.

Nevertheless, conceptions of God are not the only major aspect of religions. Culture is not something that hovers over a society like some sort of intellectual cloud bank. Culture matters only as it is embedded in society. Hence, religion matters only as it is the focus of human activities, especially of organized activities devoted to religious purposes: the history of religion involves not only the discovery of God, but the evolution of specialized religious roles and institutions, of priests and temples, clergy and congregations.

With that in mind, I have aspired to far more than simply applying basic principles of cultural evolution to conceptions of God. What I have attempted is to more fully analyze and explain each of the great episodes in the history of the origin of religions.

PLAN OF THE BOOK

Chapter 1 examines the initial stages in religious culture. What did primitive humans believe, and why did they believe it? The four major "schools" concerning the nature and origins of primitive religions are assessed, each of them depicting primitive religions as crude mixtures of magic and superstition sustained by humans having very inferior mental capacities. These claims are dismissed in light of more recent studies showing that many of the most primitive of the known cultures had rather sophisticated notions of High Gods and extensive accounts of Creation.

The theological and social-scientific responses to these facts are examined. However, all students of primitive religions agree that religion is a universal feature of human societies. Thus the chapter summarizes and evaluates the three major contemporary approaches to explaining why all societies have religion: the biological, cultural, and theological.

Chapter 2 sketches the ascendancy of state-supported temple religions featuring priestly polytheism in the early civilizations—Sumer, Egypt, Greece, and Mesoamerica. Why did these civilizations turn from the High Gods of more primitive times and embrace idols and an image of the Gods as essentially human beings, except for being immortal and having some special powers? Why were these early professional priesthoods so opposed to all innovation? Why were they so unconcerned about the religious life of the people? And did they really believe that "idols" were alive?

Chapter 3 analyzes the relatively open religious "marketplace" that evolved in Rome and how this permitted the constant influx of new faiths, especially from Greece, Egypt, and the Near East. It examines how competition among these many religions resulted in an unusually high level of religiousness among ordinary Romans, with side effects of frequent conflicts and intermittent persecution. Particular attention will be paid to the generic basis for religious conflict in Rome: the opposition of the state to all religious movements based on highly committed congregations, as opposed to the more low-key involvement generated by the traditional temples. Thus, persecution of Christianity was preceded by persecution not only of Jews, but also of intense pagan[37] groups such as Bacchanalians and followers of Isis and Cybele. Furthermore, the chapter explores the thesis that the two major persecutions of Christians, the first under Decius and the second by Diocletian, were collateral to urgent efforts to revive traditional Roman religion in response to social crises, thus demonstrating that even Roman polytheism was more robust than that of the ancient temple societies.

Chapter 4 explores the emergence of religious movements that challenged temple establishments and offered various forms and degrees of monotheism. Starting with Pharaoh Akhenaten's efforts to force Egyptians to become monotheists, the chapter proceeds to an analysis of what may have been the appearance of the first fully developed dualistic monotheism—Zoroastrianism. This is followed by a lengthy assessment of Judaism in its various stages: how it was transformed under Solomon into an established temple religion that exhibited considerable polytheism, and how in the sixth century BCE a monotheistic sect rooted in the elite group of Jews held in Babylon returned and overthrew the remnants of polytheism, finally instituting unwavering monotheism in Israel. The next section traces the establishment of Jewish Diasporan communities around the Mediterranean and their efforts to proselytize on behalf of the One True God. Then the chapter interprets Isiacism as a pagan attempt at monotheism, and ends with imperial efforts to establish Sol Invictus as the High God of Rome, thereby forestalling conversion to the God of the Jews and the Christians.

Turning to the East, Chapter 5 is focused on the rise of religions in India, principally Hinduism and Buddhism. India has sustained a very unregulated and competitive religious economy for more than three thousand years, with the result that it abounds in "cults and sects."[38] Indeed, the density of Hindu groups has caused some to adopt extreme forms of worship and behavior in order to attract attention amid the din of competing messages. All this competition instills high levels of public commitment that is reinforced by the fact that all caste and ethnic distinctions were (are) conceived primarily in religious terms, as most of the several thousand caste sub-groups sustain their own Hindu sects. Hence, all conflicts and disputes among these caste groups take the form of religious conflicts, thus energizing the religious loyalty and participation of individual members in each group. Put another way, the primary social cleavages in this region coincide with, and give primary importance to, religious cleavages.

A central focus of the chapter will be on the sudden eruption during the sixth century BCE of a revolutionary new form of Hinduism—the Hinduism of the Upaniṣads—that introduced the notion of the transmigration of souls (reincarnation) and proposed strategies for escaping from the Wheel of Karma. At the very same time, and only several hundred miles to the east, two new faiths also appeared: Buddhism and Jainism. As for Buddhism, I shall suggest that it was simply another form of the New Hinduism—that Buddha's innovation was to reduce all of the Hindu Gods to unimportant onlookers as he retained belief in the transmigration of the soul and in meditation as the means to achieve release from the endless cycle of rebirths. Although founded on relative

"Godlessness," even the initial, elite form of Buddhism was a religion because it explicitly accepted supernatural forces and effects. One of history's great ironies is that because "Godless" religions are so unsatisfactory, Buddha was himself elevated to divinity. A second great irony is that, after a period of popularity and rapid growth, Buddhism died out so completely in India that all memory of its existence was lost until unearthed by amateur English archaeologists in the nineteenth century. Explanations of both the rise and the decline of Indian Buddhism are assessed. So, too, for Jainism. The chapter also investigates why all this new religion-founding took place in India when it did.

Chapter 6 examines the rise of Taoism and Confucianism and the arrival and growth of Buddhism in China. The basis of these faiths among upper-class intellectuals is examined to explain why they proposed relatively "Godless" religions sustained by full-time "philosopher" monks who devoted very little attention to recruiting popular followings—indeed, these were (are) classic temple religions like those in Sumer, Egypt, Greece, and Mesoamerica. How did these temple religions spread? How did Buddhism make the long journey from India to China? Why did it survive in China and the rest of Asia although it died out in India? Another important question asked in the chapter is, why did Confucianism and Taoism repeat the Buddhist pattern and also transform their founders into Gods? Indeed, in China and throughout the Far East, Buddhist, Confucian, and Taoist temples soon were stuffed with many other Gods. Why? Furthermore, why did none of these three "major" religions, nor even all of them together, actually become the religion of most Chinese? Why did most people continue to patronize the elaborate polytheism known as Folk Religion long after similar faiths had died out in the West?

Chapter 7 analyzes the rise of Christianity. It begins with the "historic" Jesus and then examines how the theological Christ effectively humanized the Jewish conception of God, thus fusing the intellectual appeal of monotheism with the emotional appeal of anthropomorphic deities. That is, Christ offered a comforting, accessible, human Son, who mitigated the difficulties in relating to an inherently far less comprehensible and very distant Father—a dualism yielding both a transcendent and an incarnate divinity. Indeed, the many similarities between the Christ story and that of major pre-Christian divinities served to greatly reassure the Greco-Roman world, easing the way to conversion. Next, the chapter assesses the bitter controversies about the origins and authenticity of the New Testament. Special attention will be given to the frequent, recent claims that many important and enlightening scriptures were wrongly excluded from the New Testament by repressive Church leaders—writings now known as Gnostic gospels. The truth is that these scriptures were properly dismissed as a last-gasp effort to incorporate Christianity within traditional polytheism.

Having examined the development of the early Jesus Movement, the chapter turns to an estimated growth curve that shows the number of Christians within the empire at various times between the years 40 and 350—a curve that is validated by comparison with known statistics such as the increases in Christian identifications on gravestones and the incidence of Christian names on contracts. The growth curve clarifies many matters, especially why Diocletian and other emperors grew fearful of Christianity and why Constantine recognized that the Christians could be vital political allies. The curve also provides a basis for asking why people became Christians. What was its appeal?

The chapter then sketches the long decline of European Christianity, beginning with Constantine's establishment of it as the subsidized state church. The empty churches in Europe today are not the recent result of modernism, for Europe's churches have been poorly attended for more than a thousand years. The final section of the chapter shows how the competitive religious economy in America reinvigorated Christianity, engendered a new sense of mission, and has led to extraordinary Christian growth in the Global "South"—that is, Latin America, Africa, and Asia.

Chapter 8 examines the explosion of Islam and the revival of theocratic states. It begins with a brief biography of Muhammad, his first visions, and his flight to Medina, and it gives extended attention to his role as a military leader and to his creation of an Arab State. Attention then turns to the religion he founded, to the Five Pillars of Islam, the origins and nature of the Qur'an, and to the Muslim conception of Allāh, addressing the issue: Do Jews, Christians, and Muslims worship the same God, known by different names? Next comes an account of the Arab conquests and their rapid creation of a Muslim Empire. It dispels the notion of mass conversions to Islam, showing that the new faith spread rapidly by treaty and conquest, but that the actual conversion of the general public in most of these satellite societies took many centuries. It also exposes the anti-Christian fabrication that Islam was very tolerant of other faiths, including Christians and Jews. Claims that Islam sustained a "Golden Age" of civilization and amity in multicultural societies such as Moorish Spain are false. Muslims were no less intolerant than Christians. Finally, the major outlines of Muslim sectarianism are sketched, demonstrating that Islam is as fractured and diverse as are Christianity and Judaism.

The Conclusion begins with the sudden appearance of a multitude of religious founders and their new faiths that took place during the sixth century BCE. Some have identified the sixth century as the **Axial Age**[39] in recognition of the pivotal shift in religious perceptions that occurred along an axis from the Mediterranean to northern China. Even more remarkable than their number, their dispersion, or even their simultaneity, is that all these new faiths discovered "sin" and the conscience, as each linked morality to transcendence.[40] Contrasted with the prevailing conceptions of immoral and amoral Gods, this was revolutionary. And with it came a universal corollary: that one must *earn* one's "salvation," whether this meant a rewarding afterlife or escape from the Wheel of Karma. How did all of this happen in so many places at once? How much of it could have been the result of diffusion, of the spread of religious ideas from one society to another? Alternatively, is it plausible that the Axial Age resulted from many revelations having occurred in many places at about the same time? Here we must recognize that only some founders of major religions claimed to have had revelations from God. Others dismissed Gods as insignificant bystanders and claimed to have discovered the spiritual workings of the universe from within themselves. Amid this diversity, can we isolate a core of divinely inspired faiths?

Thus we reach the fundamental question: *Does God exist?* That is, have we *discovered* God? Or have we *invented* him? Are there so many similarities among the great religions because God is really the product of universal wish fulfillment? Did humans everywhere create supernatural beings out of their need for comfort in the face of existential tragedy and to find purpose and significance in life? Or have people in many places, to a greater and lesser degree, actually gained glimpses of God?

· 1 ·

GODS IN PRIMITIVE
SOCIETIES

MUCH HAS BEEN SAID about the religious life of primitive[1] humans, despite the fact that very little is known about it with any certainty. We do know that for thousands of years, some human burials have included grave goods, which may be taken as evidence that our distant ancestors believed in life after death. Deep inside caves we also have found structures that might have been altars, and some caves contained collections of such things as bear skulls that might have had religious significance, too. In early Neolithic (New Stone Age) sites such as Çatalhöyük in Turkey,[2] there is some evidence that bulls may have been sacred, and here and there archaeologists have found small figurines that might have represented a very ample mother goddess, or not.[3] Beyond that, all is conjecture.[4]

These conjectures take two forms. The more reasonable of these is based on the assumption that recent observations of surviving primitive cultures can be taken as representative of those long gone. But is that true? If these cultures are not significantly different from those of early times, why did they not keep up? A common answer has been that most human progress is the result of diffusion, not independent innovation, and these particular groups failed to keep up because they were too isolated to benefit from the spread of innovations that carried other cultures forward. On these grounds it is claimed that surviving primitive cultures present a reliable image of the past. Although I am among those

This limestone scuplture is known as the "Venus of Willendorf" and is typical of female figurines that have often been found in Stone Age sites in many places. Some believe they were fertility charms. Others think them to have been Goddesses. And some think that because women in this era ate a very starchy diet and were constantly pregant, these figurines merely reflected that most women became very obese. (Naturhistoriches Museum, Vienna; Photo: Erich Lessing/ Art Resource, New York.)

who regard this as a somewhat "unsound" assumption,[5] I agree that the ethnographic accounts of the religions of these groups deserve careful analysis.

The second conjecture proposes that not too long ago humans lacked sufficient intelligence and consciousness to entertain such things as religious notions, having very little mental life of any kind. Granted that if we accept as human those creatures lacking not only stone tools, but even language, the assertion probably is justified. But many scholars have made this claim about the humans who lived during Paleolithic (Old Stone Age) times and from this have assumed that the earliest religions were extremely infantile. Surprisingly, the primary basis for claiming that Stone Age humans were dim brutes is not comparative physiology based on skulls and brain capacity, these being much less diagnostic of intelligence than might be supposed. Instead, the biology is inferred from culture—from the fact that during the Paleolithic period, "technological progress was extraordinarily slow,"[6] ergo people in those days were of low intelligence and their religions, if they had any, must have been very rudimentary.

These biological inferences are very doubtful because the technological gap between modern cultures and those of surviving "primitive" cultures is about as great as between modern cultures and those of the *Neanderthals*, despite the fact that the biological differences at issue no longer exist—today all humans are *Homo sapiens*. Nevertheless, the notion that even "modern" primitives are biologically inferior was an article of faith among nineteenth- and early twentieth-century scholars, and variations on that theme persist in some current attempts by biologists and evolutionary psychologists to predict the end of religion, claiming that faith is incompatible with the greater mental capacity of modern humans.

The first portion of this chapter examines efforts by early social scientists to use ethnographies of recent primitives to characterize and classify primitive religions of long ago. While their reconstructions differed substantially, there was consensus on two points: religion is a *universal* feature of human cultures, albeit primitive religions were *very crude*. Consequently, the chapter summarizes, compares, and evaluates three major kinds of explanations offered as to why religion is universal: biological, cultural, and theological. Next, the characterization of early religions as crude and infantile will be reconsidered in light of an abundance of later ethnographic evidence showing that many of these religions were far more sophisticated than had been supposed. Both the social-scientific and the theological implications of this discovery are considered.

RECONSTRUCTING PRIMITIVE RELIGIONS

With the advent of the Age of Exploration, many Europeans began to return with reports of the exotic religious beliefs and practices of "backward" people around the world. Some of these were pure fantasy. Some were extremely biased. Some were very unreliable, having been written by a person who could not speak the local language and who devoted little time to the study. But many were remarkably accurate, and a few were magnificent works of scholarship, such as the detailed, sixteenth-century study of Aztec religion based on careful interviews with actual priests and observations of many rites by the Franciscan missionary Bernardino

Ribeira de Sahagún (c. 1500–1590), which, sad to say, lay unnoticed in a Spanish library until 1830.[7]

As these reports piled up, some European scholars tried to use them to learn what primitive religions were actually like. Others simply mined them for examples that supported their preconceptions, and a few paid very little attention to this literature, preferring to not let facts inhibit their theorizing about primitive religions. The major pioneering efforts to reconstruct the religions of primitives fall into four approaches or "schools" of thought: Naturism, Animism, Ghost Theory, and Totemism. Although each of these approaches has many shortcomings, they serve as an effective way to begin an exploration of primitive religion and are especially useful to set the stage for a remarkable later breakthrough.

Naturism

Max Müller (1823–1900) popularized the comparative study of religions, in part by editing good English translations of Eastern scriptures. Müller was only marginally interested in primitive religions, but he proposed that *all* religions, primitive or otherwise, arise because from earliest times humans have always been awed by the grandeur of nature. **Naturism** proposes that *religions have their origins in the personification of natural forces and objects and the "myths" that arise from these personifications.* Hence, Müller is considered the leader of the Naturism "school."

Although most Naturists were Germans, Müller spent most of his adult life at Oxford, rising to be a Professor and Fellow of All Souls. He was perhaps "the first 'celebrity' academician,"[8] who lectured far and wide and gave many newspaper interviews—today he would be a regular on the talk shows. Much of his public prominence came from his editorship of a massive project known as *The Sacred Books of the East*, a set of fifty volumes that appeared between 1879 and 1910, most of which are still in print. The first volume in this series was Müller's own translation of the *Upaniṣads*.

Unlike others who theorized about the origins of religion, Müller paid little heed to ethnographic accounts of the religion of contemporary primitives. This was because, as Müller put it in the Hibbert Lectures of 1878, all of these reports are static and therefore yield no information about the "growth of religious ideas." Indeed, "among the savages of Africa, America, and Australia . . . it is difficult enough to know what their religion is at present; what it was in its origin, what it was even a thousand years ago, is entirely beyond our reach."⁹ Nor is it possible to see the growth of "the religion of Moses . . . [or] of Zoroaster. [These were] placed before us as a complete system from the first."¹⁰ But the surviving Sanskrit literature goes back so far "that I have selected the ancient religion of India to supply the historical illustrations of my own theory of the origin and growth of religion."¹¹ Even though his earliest information was on the religion of a literate society, Müller "certainly believed that his explanations had general validity."¹²

As noted, the fundamental premise of Naturism is that humans gain a sense of the divine from natural phenomena: sun, moon, stars, mountains, rivers, thunder and lightning, storms, the seasons, animals, and plants. Faced with such an inspiring, mysterious, frightening, and awesome natural world, humans endowed nature with supernatural qualities. Not content to leave it at that, the Naturists transformed the study of religions into a study of language, to "discovering" the basis for the evolution of religions in the personification of natural "objects" and subsequent confusions as to sacred names.

Applied to classical mythology, this approach quickly degenerated into elaborate word-games, into claims that many stories about the Gods are nothing but a "disease of language" that hides simple natural phenomena behind elaborate "myths" because people have personified what once had merely been the names of natural objects. Take the story that Apollo loved Daphne who fled from him and was changed into a laurel tree. Müller translated this by claiming that originally the word *Apollo* had merely meant "sun" and *Daphne* had meant "dawn." Having been personified, all sorts of fanciful stories were invented about Daphne dying in Apollo's arms, by people unaware that Daphne and Apollo were not beings, mythical or otherwise. Decoded according to the premises of the Naturists, these myths dissolve into the observation that dawn dies as the sun rises. Müller and his colleagues repeated this sort of decoding to the point of utter absurdity—eventually Müller claimed that the siege of Troy was merely a solar "myth."¹³ But far from being mythical, Troy existed and the names of some of the heroes that appear in Homer's accounts have been found in Mycenaean and Hittite documents.¹⁴

Müller "outlived his own reputation, and before he died, saw the almost complete collapse of the school of [Naturism]."¹⁵ It succumbed

to attacks from scholars who thought that there was far more to understanding primitive religion than could possibly be decoded from linguistic "misunderstandings" and personifications of nature. These critics
vigorously asserted that anyone presuming to reconstruct primitive religions must first master the enormous and rapidly growing ethnographic
literature on what truly primitive peoples actually believe and do. And
one thing this literature reveals is that "primitive peoples show remarkably little interest in what we may regard as the most impressive phenomena of nature—sun, moon, sky, mountains, sea, and so forth—whose
monotonous regularities they take very much for granted."[16] Of course,
primitives do attempt to utilize their religion to control nature—to cause
rain or to quiet storms. But that was a far cry from worshipping Gods of
Nature.

Not surprisingly, given it was based on the religion of Vedic India,
Naturism is a much better description of religion in similar, rather advanced cultures: those in ancient Sumer, Egypt, Greece, Rome, the Aztecs,
and the Maya—the kinds of societies in which Müller and his colleagues
were primarily interested and that left the written records on which they
chose to rely. For example, each of these societies did pay great homage
to a Sun God, and many other heavenly bodies were deified, as were other
natural phenomena and various beasts. Where the Naturists went so
wrong was to recreate primitive religions by simply projecting backward
from a later day, their assumption being that the "seeds" of the later faiths
must have consisted of crude versions of same thing—"must have" being
one of the most misleading phrases in the scholarly vocabulary. Of course,
they also erred in their decoding of the more "advanced" religions, since
there was nothing hidden about the personifications of nature in these
faiths. Any Greek who visited a temple dedicated to "Helios," or any Roman who dedicated a sacrifice to "Sol," knew these were the names of a
God who personified the Sun.

Animism

The most prominent critic of Müller and the Naturists was a man who
devoted his life to study of the ethnographic literature on the religious culture of surviving primitives: the English anthropologist Edward Burnett
Tylor (1832–1917). The son of the owner of a prosperous brass foundry,
Tylor was able to devote himself to unpaid scholarship. In his youth he

Sir Edward Burnett Tylor, the most influential anthropologist of the nineteenth century, and the chief proponent of the Animism theory of primitive religion. (*Sir Edward Burnett Tylor* by G. Bonavia; © Archivo Iconografico, S.A./CORBIS)

visited the famous Mayan and Aztec ruins of Mexico with the great archaeologist Henry Christy (1810–1865). Upon his return to England, Tylor plunged into the ethnographic literature, eventually publishing in 1871 his two-volume classic *Primitive Society*, the entire second volume being devoted to religion.[17] When he was past fifty, Tylor accepted an appointment to direct the museum at Oxford, and when he was sixty-four, he became Oxford's first-ever professor of anthropology. He was knighted in 1909.

Tylor coined the term *Animism* to distinguish primitive religions from more "advanced" forms. **Animism** *consists of the belief that literally everything is inhabited by a spirit, not only animate things, but inanimate things as well.* Tylor allowed that he would rather have used the term *spiritualism* to identify "primitive" religions, but that term had already been claimed by "a particular modern sect."[18]

According to Tylor, belief in Animism "characterizes tribes very low on the scale of humanity."[19] Theirs is a "childish" world, overwhelmingly cluttered with spirits. Every shrub, pebble, and stick, as well as created items such as each canoe, pot, and hut, and of course all the wildlife, has an individual soul and must be dealt with according to proper rituals and procedures. However, according to Tylor and most other early anthropologists, although Animism abounded in spirits, it was lacking in Gods. Tylor *defined* religion as "the belief in Spiritual Beings," but he noted that this did not require belief in "a supreme deity" or even "the adoration of idols," for if it did, "no doubt many tribes may be excluded from the category of religious."[20] Tylor was so certain that primitive peoples could not even imagine a God that he dismissed any evidence to the contrary as a cultural impurity that could only have been caused by exposure to missionaries, even if no such contacts were known.[21] Even so, Tylor was confident that religion is universal: "From the immense mass of accessible evidence, we have to admit that belief in spiritual beings appears among all the low races with whom we have attained to thoroughly intimate acquaintance."[22]

Obviously, Tylor had remarkable command of the enormous ethnographic literature on "primitive" religions. What is less certain is whether his generalizations about primitive religion arose from his reading or whether he simply mined this literature to provide examples in favor of his presuppositions and intuitions. What is certain is that Tylor filled hundreds of pages with fragmentary recitals of exotic rites, taboos, initiations, fetishes, myths, and beliefs. For example:

> It is recorded by Brebeuf that the Hurons, when a little child died, would bury them by the wayside, that their souls might enter into mothers passing by, and so be born again. In the North-West America, among the Tacullis, we hear of direct transfusion of the soul by the medicine-man, who, putting his hands on the breast of the dying or dead, then holds them over the head of a relative and blows through them; the next child born to this recipient of the departed soul is animated by it, and takes the rank and name of the deceased. The Nutka Indians not without ingenuity accounted for the existence of a distant tribe speaking the same language as themselves, by declaring them to be the spirits of their dead.[23]

And on and on and on.

Tylor attributed Animism to the severe limitations of the "primitive mind," a prejudice that was shared by nearly all scientists and scholars at that time. Charles Darwin equated the people of Tierra del Fuego with "the lower animals," Francis Galton claimed his dog had more intelligence than did the natives of South Africa, and Herbert Spencer claimed that the "primitive mind" lacks "the idea of causation" and is "without curiosity."[24] Meanwhile, in France, Lucien Levy-Bruhl agreed with Tylor that primitives don't even know where babies come from[25] and devoted several books to illustrate his claim that the "primitive mind" is "prelogical," a view emphatically endorsed by Emile Durkheim.[26] From this perspective it was impossible for primitive religions to be other than crude, implausible superstitions. Consider, too, that nearly every one of these scholars dismissed *all* religious beliefs as "absurd" and regarded primitive religions as "a weapon which could, they thought, be used with deadly effect against Christianity."[27] As Charles Darwin put it in a letter to Tylor, "It is wonderful how you trace animism from the lower races up to the religious beliefs of the higher."[28]

But at least Tylor rejected the many reports by Western observers that a number of primitive groups around the world had no religion at all. The famous English explorer Samuel Baker informed the Ethnological Society of London in 1866, that tribes living along the northern part of the Nile River were entirely "without a belief in a Supreme Being, neither have they any form of worship or idolatry; nor is the darkness of their minds enlightened by even a ray of superstition. The[ir] mind is as stagnant as the morass which forms its puny world."[29] This claim was absurd in light of existing evidence that these same people had quite extensive religions, evidence that was well known to Tylor, who also was in a position to see through the many similar reports of societies without religions that were widely circulated at the time. So, whatever the shortcomings of his reconstruction of the religious culture of primitives, Tylor was right to support what became the overwhelming consensus among social scientists, that religion is a *universal trait* of human cultures.

Ghost Theory

A severe critic of Naturism, and a strong supporter of Tylor's notions about Animism, was another Englishman, Herbert Spencer (1820–1903), who wrote an entire bookshelf of works on social and cultural evolution. He was mostly self-educated, having turned down a wealthy uncle's offer to send him to Cambridge. To support himself he worked very briefly as a schoolmaster, then as a railroad engineer, followed by three years as a sub-editor for *The Economist*. When he was just past thirty, he inherited a sufficient amount from that same uncle to permit him to be self-supporting. From then on he spent every day at his writing desk, so engrossed in his work that he never married and hardly ever saw anyone except for brief meetings with his library assistants.

Spencer pursued the origins of religion one step beyond Tylor by asking: *why* do primitive people believe they are surrounded by spirits? Where do they get the idea of spirits in the first place? He answered: *These ideas arise because primitives, lacking a proper awareness of their own mental functioning, are puzzled by the difference between the living and the dead and between when they are dreaming and when they are awake, especially when their dreams involve people who are dead. To solve these mysteries, primitive people assume that all things are dualistic and possess a sort of inner phantom that is capable of detached movement so as to appear in one's dreams. Or, as in the case of death, the spirit departs to lead an independent existence.* Spelled out and illustrated in massive detail, Spencer's notions became known as the **Ghost Theory**.

Spencer began with the assumption that a primitive "thinks without observing that he thinks" and fails, therefore, to develop any conception of the "Mind" as an internal seat of thinking. "But until there is a conception of Mind as an internal principle of activity, there can be no conception of dreams."[30] Consequently, primitives believe "that dreams are actual experiences."[31] Of course, they often dream they are elsewhere and engaged in many activities, but upon waking are reassured that they have not left their bed. What then? "The simple course is to believe both that he has remained and that he has been away—that he has two individualities, one of which leaves the other and presently comes back."[32] Hence, humans (and all other things, since they, too, appear in dreams) are believed to be inhabited by a second identity, a spirit. In the case of the dead, the separation has become permanent, the life forces having departed with the spirit, and these now disembodied spirits are ghosts. Because in dreams one often has conflicts with those already dead, there arises the belief that ghosts must be propitiated or somehow prevented from haunting the still living. Hence, the immense culture concerning burial and funeral rites. This also leads to ancestor worship, which, in

Herbert Spencer, the pro-
lific originator of the Ghost
Theory of primitive religion.
He devoted fifty years of his life
to writing every day, seldom
seeing anyone. (Courtesy of the
Library of Congress)

turn, eventually leads to the invention of Gods and the formation of religious organizations.

This, according to Spencer, is the origin of primitive religion and the
underlying cause of Animism (and accepted as such by Tylor). Given
these origins, early primitive religion *must* have been Godless, ignorant,
and childlike. Having proposed this theory, Spencer then wrote: "From
all quarters come proofs that this is the conception actually formed by
the dreams of savages, and which survives after considerable advances in
civilization have been made. Here are a few of the testimonies."[33] What
followed were many accounts gleaned from the ethnographic literature.
Remarkably, these are without documentation of any kind, and even
the writer goes unmentioned, Spencer dismissing such scholarly practices as "a waste of energy and time."[34] Perhaps, but an associate claimed
that Spencer did not base his work on his sources, but simply asserted
his views and then sent assistants to look for instances that supported
his particular claims, and to ignore anything that was discordant.[35] That

Spencer did not require these assistants to document their sources was a license for them to use creative methods.

However, sloppy research was not the primary reason scholars eventually dismissed Ghost Theory as nonsense. Spencer's fundamental errors were to offer an obvious supposition for an empirical finding and to assume that primitive people are essentially morons (albeit that view was widely held at the time). As the distinguished E. E. Evans-Pritchard (1902–1973) put it: "Spencer had got it into his head that rude peoples have no idea of natural explanation, as though they could have conducted their various practical pursuits without it!"[36] Recall that Spencer believed primitives fail to understand cause-and-effect and have no curiosity. Not surprisingly, Evans-Pritchard's judgment that Spencer's theory "is a priori speculation, sprinkled with some illustrations, and is specious"[37] has been widely ratified, which is not to say that most of his critics had better interpretations to offer.

Totemism

A fourth perspective on primitive religion is known as *Totemism*. Concern with the common practice among primitives of identifying themselves as relatives of an animal or other creature appeared in the ethnographic literature from the start. Tylor gave it sufficient importance to write a book about it: *Totemism* (1887). But Totemism was made the centerpiece of all primitive religions by a Scottish scholar, W. Robertson Smith (1846–1894), when he gave the Burnett Lectures of 1888–1889.

Smith believed that Totemism is "the most primitive stage of savage society," and, therefore, all human cultures pass through the totem stage, during which "each kinship or stock of savages believes itself to be physically akin to some natural kind of animate or inanimate things, most generally to some kind of animal. Every animal of this kind is looked upon as a brother, is treated with the same respect as a human clansman, and is believed to aid his human relations by a variety of friendly services."[38] From this obervation, Smith spun out a theory of the origins of religion. **Totemism** holds that *all religions originated in the practice of each primitive tribe, or of each clan within a tribe, to identify with a particular animal species (a totem) that is held to be sacred and not to be harmed. However, during certain festivals or at times of dire need, the group conducts a solemn rite during which the totemic animal is sacrificed and eaten. This is the ori-*

gin of all rites and practices associated with sacrifice, especially of blood sacrifices, and from these humble beginnings came all of the more advanced
religions.

Published as a book, *The Religion of the Semites* (1889), Smith's notions
about Totemism attracted a great deal of attention, particularly because
he attempted to show that all sacrifices among the Jews derived from
the primitive tradition of totemic sacrifices. However, the best anthropologists of the day, including Tylor and Sir James Frazer, and supported
later by the formidable Californian, A. L. Kroeber (1876–1960), dismissed
Smith's claims as nonsense and his theory as pure fantasy, if for no other
reason than that there was only *one* known example in the entire ethnographic literature (and it dubious) of *any* group *ever* having actually sacrificed and eaten its totemic animal.[39] But the theory flourished, in part
because it so greatly influenced, and misled, two very famous scholars
who used it as the basis for their very different reconstructions of primitive religion and the origins of religion: Emile Durkheim and Sigmund
Freud.

Durkheim's Aboriginal Religion

The sociology of religion was dominated for nearly a century by a
single volume published in French in 1912 and in English in 1915: *The Elementary Forms of the Religious Life*, by Emile Durkheim (1858–1917), a
professor at the Sorbonne in Paris. As noted earlier, Durkheim dismissed
Gods as of any real significance in religion, stressing the centrality of rites
that arouse deep emotions of belonging to something far greater than
the individual—"it is action that dominates the religious life." And behind rites and rituals lies a hidden "reality, which mythologies have represented in so many different forms, but which is the objective, universal,
and eternal cause of those . . . sensations of which religious experience is
made—[this reality] is society."[40] What Durkheim proposed is that the
hidden truth about religion is that *all religious rites constitute society worshipping itself in order to sustain social solidarity. And the most primitive
form of this collective self-worship is Totemism.*

Seeking details on the most "elementary" forms of religion, Durkheim
turned to published reports about the aboriginal peoples of Australia, on
the grounds that theirs was the most primitive of all known surviving
human cultures. This was not a happy choice because, unrecognized by

Durkheim, "the literature on [the] aboriginals was," as Evans-Pritchard explained, "by modern standards, poor and confused."[41] But finding that the aboriginal religion was totemistic prompted Durkheim to conclude that Totemism is the most primitive of all forms of religion. This is because Totemism is "closely allied with the most primitive social organization that is known and even, in all probability, that is conceivable. Therefore, to assume [Totemism] to have been preceded by another religion different from it [even if] only in degree is to leave behind the data of observation and to enter the domain of arbitrary and unverifiable conjectures."[42]

Summarizing the "data of observation," Durkheim noted that each Australian aboriginal belongs to a totem group or clan signified by some animal, reptile, or bird, representations of which serve as a "flag of the clan, the sign by which each clan is distinguished from others."[43] Members of any given band within which the individual usually lives and travels are divided among several different totem clans, and each totem clan extends beyond the band to also embrace members from among the other

The religious life of aboriginal Australians, shown here performing a sacred ritual dance, dominated the sociology of religion for nearly a century because Emile Durkheim claimed that theirs was the most primitive of all surviving cultures and thus revealed the most elementary forms of religion. Unfortunately, Durkheim got all the important facts wrong. He even claimed the Australian tribes had no conception of God, when in fact they worshipped a quite sophisticated Supreme Being. (© E.O. Hoppé/CORBIS)

groups making up the tribe. From time to time each totem clan gathers at its special sacred place and engages in extensive rites, often including initiations of the young (but *not* including a feast on their totem creature!). According to Durkheim, participation in these rites instills a strong sense of commitment to the group and causes people to fulfill their obligations to society, especially those of the moral variety.

Durkheim sometimes referred to the totem as the God of the clan, but he didn't mean what usually is understood by that word. As he explained, "Taking the word 'god' in a very broad sense, one could say that it is the god that each totemic cult worships. But it is an impersonal god, without name, without history, immanent in the world, diffused in a numberless multitude of things."[44] Eventually, Durkheim gave some credence to the reports that the aboriginals in fact worship an actual God. But he regarded this as a very late development in their Totemism, amounting to nothing more than the very modest elevation of "an ancestral spirit"[45] who ultimately "can be none other than the clan itself, but . . . transfigured and imagined."[46] It is upon this sacred totemic foundation that all of the higher religions are built. As he concluded, "There is no reason not to extend the most general results of this research [on primitives] to other religions . . . We must presume that the same explanation is valid in principle for all peoples."[47]

Although many sociologists still seem to have no inkling of any criticism of Durkheim's work on religion,[48] it justifiably came under withering attack from anthropologists and comparative religion scholars from earliest days. For one thing, Durkheim dismissed belief in the supernatural from any acceptable definition of religion on grounds that many primitive religions, as well as some advanced faiths including Buddhism and some other Eastern religions, not only are entirely Godless, but even reject the supernatural. This was a howling error. No one can credibly identify a primitive group devoid of supernaturalism. As for Buddhism, although a few Buddhist intellectuals and monks pursue a *relatively* Godless Buddhism, popular Buddhism abounds in Gods of many sizes and shapes, as a visit to any Buddhist temple reveals. These errors were pointed out in the first review of the French edition of Durkheim's book in the *American Anthropologist* by Alexander Goldenweiser in 1915. Goldenweiser (1880–1940) also pointed out, as have innumerable scholars since, the circularity involved in Durkheim having defined religion as "a unified system of beliefs and practices relative to sacred things . . . which unite into a single moral community . . . all those who adhere to them,"[49] before proceeding to "discover" that religion exists to create social solidarity. Nor has the empirical basis for Durkheim's work stood up. Not only did he rely on a very muddled literature, but Durkheim's use of it seems to have been excessively careless—he frequently claimed the opposite of what actually is reported.[50] This is not surprising given the many self-serving arithmetic errors contained in his equally long-admired study: *Suicide.*[51]

But perhaps the most remarkable shortcoming of Durkheim's thesis is that, if the function of religion is to generate and ensure social solidarity, Totemism ought to be associated with the wandering band or with the tribe as a whole, not with the widely dispersed totem clans. For, to the degree that the totem clans are the primary basis of solidarity, they threaten the unity of the actual social groups within which the aboriginals live their lives. Given that totem groups are, just as Durkheim claimed, dispersed so that members of several clans live within each band and tribe, and while these divisions might cause intragroup conflict, they certainly cannot unite the group. It must follow that either Totemism is not the basis of primitive religion, or that religion does not exist primarily to generate social solidarity—or both.

Finally, many primitive religions have no element of Totemism. Durkheim probably would argue that any group lacking Totemism is not as primitive as those with Totemism, but that would simply be unfounded special pleading.

Freud's Incestuous Approach

Sigmund Freud (1856–1939) invented the controversial practice of psychoanalysis and applied remarkably unlikely psychological notions to an array of historical and anthropological matters, most of them involving religion. In *Totem and Taboo*[52] (1913) Freud made Totemism world famous and, in doing so, concocted a version of the theory that far more closely resembles a crude, primitive "myth" than a social-scientific theory.

Freud claimed that the earliest humans lived in small groups made up of one dominant adult male and a number of women and their children. As they approached maturity, all young males were driven off by the father, who monopolized the women. Borrowing from Robertson Smith,

Freud next proposed that blood sacrifices at an altar are central to the religions of all primitives and stem from the custom of killing and eating the totem animal. To this, Freud added an Oedipal twist: that frequently some of the young males, consumed by lust for the women (their mothers), combined against their father, killed him, and ate him in true totemic style and then possessed his women. Freud was content to intuit this alleged pre-history without any supporting ethnographic evidence whatever, other than the existence of Totemism.

Freud did not claim that primitives had any conception of Gods. What he argued was that as religious culture became more sophisticated, the underlying stimulus remained guilt-rooted in the Oedipus complex— of sons lusting for their mothers and bursting with jealous rage toward their fathers. Freud claimed that God is, in fact, the father figure of all human beings, and that in totemic rites it is God himself who is killed and eaten, thus constituting the "original sin." In Christianity this blood guilt is atoned by the totemic sacrifice of Christ. Freud continued: "In the Christian doctrine, therefore, men were acknowledging in the most undisguised manner the guilty primæval deed, since they found the fullest atonement for it in the sacrifice of this one son.... As a sign of this substitution the ancient totem meal was revived in the form of communion ... the Christian Eucharist.... The Christian communion, however, is essentially a fresh elimination of the father, a repetition of the guilty deed."[53]

With the collapse of the psychoanalytic movement and revelations that Freud was a charlatan,[54] we may be spared more of this, although his "theory" of Totemism continues to receive respectful treatment in some textbooks.[55]

Freud aside, however, each of the scholars discussed above made significant contributions to our understanding of religion. Many primitives do seem to have used their religions, if not to worship nature, at least as an attempt to control it—and many of the more advanced cultures did worship Nature Gods. Many primitive people do live in a spirit-infested world. People in any era tend to connect dreams with the supernatural, and ancestor worship is common even today. Morever, many primitive cultures have Totemism, although none would appear to feast upon their totem creatures, and religious rites often do engender intense feelings of group solidarity. Finally, even Freud joined the consensus that *all human societies have religion.* Hence, the most fundamental of all questions concerning human religion is: *Why?*

ON THE UNIVERSALITY OF RELIGION

That all known societies have (or had) religion is assumed by all "schools" of social science and is asserted in every introductory sociology and anthropology textbook available. Since it is axiomatic that a universal phenomenon can only be explained by other universal phenomena, to explain why religion is universal, we must examine potential causal factors that also are universal. Through the years, three major kinds of universal factors have been proposed: biological, cultural, and theological.

Biology and Religion

Ever since Darwin equated human devotion to God with a dog's devotion to his master,[56] biologists have been postulating religious instincts and other neurological bases for religion, and their work has increasingly attracted considerable attention, especially in the popular media.

Building from Darwin's notion, various biologists have claimed that man is, in effect, God's "best friend," this thesis taking up an entire chapter in Alister Hardy's *The Biology of God*. Hardy (1896–1985) began by noting that dogs are pack animals and that the dogs in a pack instinctively bond to the pack leader. Although humans do not share a common genetic heritage with dogs and therefore do not possess the same instinct, humans emerged as a hunting pack and therefore the "*same biological principles*" apply as "the hunting hominid, is *closer* in *social behavior* to the hunting dog than he is to any other member of the animal kingdom . . . [and] the emotions that had developed originally as part of the hunting-pack system . . ."[57] were redirected toward God. He explained, "The behavioral relation of the dog to man is not just an illustrative analogy to [the human relation to God]. . . . It is a clear demonstration that the same biological factors . . . have become involved in the formation of man's images of God. . . . This is not altogether unlike the almost sudden 'conversion' that occurs in the religious life of many adolescents. . . . The faithfulness, love, and devotion of a dog for his master or mistress shows us . . . the same elements that make up the essentials of man's attitude to his personal God."[58] In addition, both dog and man are carnivores and this, too, is significant as it probably is why "in every history of man's religion . . . blood sacrifices have played their part, before being converted into less barbaric sacraments."[59] Thus does Hardy conclude that humans have a biological predisposition to believe in a divine *being*.[60]

And well they should, according to Julian Jaynes (1920–1997), because until about 3,000 years ago, everybody heard God's voice.[61] It is well known that the brain is bicameral, in that it has two hemispheres that differ in their functions. The left hemisphere is the center of language and verbal memory; the right hemisphere controls many aspects of visual and tactile abilities, including depth perception. In *The Origin of Consciousness in the Breakdown of the Bicameral Mind*, Jaynes claimed that consciousness consists of a synthesis between the left and right hemispheres of the brain that allows them to function in unison. What got Jaynes on the talk shows and made him a popular lecturer was his proposal that this synthesis is only about 3,000 years old! Before that time, he postulated, humans lacked consciousness as the two hemispheres functioned with little or no interaction, and mostly people just cruised along on autopilot as controlled by the right side, while the left side was busy hearing and talking—all of this much in the manner of a modern driver steering on instinct while gabbing away on a cell phone.

This led Jaynes to conclude that preconscious humans were utterly lacking in a sense of self-identity; they had no concept of "I." Their natural state was a sort of schizophrenia in that, at times of great stress, the left hemisphere issued verbal commands to the right hemisphere, which the individual experienced as hearing voices. These were misinterpreted as the voices of the Gods, and this was the basis of religion.

However, when humans gained consciousness, they ceased to hear these voices even at moments of great stress, except, of course, for schizophrenics. Consequently, conscious humans are inherently less religious than their preconscious ancestors, and therefore religion is doomed to eventually fade away. Jaynes drew on secularization theory to confirm this point, and cannot be blamed for overlooking the evidence that secularization was no more than a hopeful social-scientific ideology, soon to be recanted, since at the time he wrote, all the leading social scientists were overlooking this evidence, too.[62] Not that Jaynes knew much about evidence in any event. Indeed, much of his "proof" rested on his interpretation of the *Iliad* and the *Odyssey*. Jaynes's reading of the *Iliad* found a total lack of consciousness on the part of the characters and, faced with the stress of the Trojan War, each character carries on a constant "dialogue" with the Gods. However, in the *Odyssey*, which may have been written a century later, Jaynes finds the new modern human: the bicameral mind has broken down, and consciousness has emerged. As a result, according to Jaynes, by then the Gods became silent—an incomprehensible claim given the lush history of mysticism and revelation during the ensuing 3,000 years.

Given the immensity of his thesis, for Jaynes to propose that the lack of introspection by characters in the *Iliad* is firm evidence that in those days humans had yet to become conscious can only be dismissed as absurd. It utterly ignores the issue of literary conventions. It is equivalent to claiming that humans only recently became three-dimensional, since cave drawings and even the surviving early depictions of humans from Egypt show them to be only two-dimensional.

And then there is Pascal Boyer. In his book *Religion Explained: The Evolutionary Origins of Religious Thought*,[63] Boyer proposes that there is an innate predisposition, hardwired into our brains, that causes humans to *mistakenly* believe in the existence of supernatural beings. It works this way: We are extremely highly tuned to detect purposeful behavior, or "agency," in our environment. We instantly perceive that an animal, although sitting still, is not inanimate but manifests purposeful behavior, while dismissing a rolling rock as inanimate—rustling bushes demand further investigation. This ability has been vital to our survival, especially in more primitive times, enabling us to "deal with both predators and prey." Consequently, this detection system is "biased towards overdetection. . . . It is far more advantageous to overdetect agency than to underdetect it. The expense of false positives (seeing agency where there is none) is minimal" so long as we are able to "abandon these misguided intuitions quickly. In contrast, the cost of not detecting agents when they are actually around (either predator or prey) could be very high"[64] as there might be a wolf in the rustling bush. Unfortunately, a consistent false positive arises as we see agency, or purpose, in nature generally, and that mistake leads to false beliefs in the existence of supernatural agents. Religion is thus a "parasitic" rider on valuable mental circuitry that evolved for valid reasons, but has the unfortunate "side effect" of prompting supernatural beliefs, which involve "the sleep of reason" since religion is, of course, "an illusion."[65]

Ironically, Boyer's definition of religion applies to many portions of science, including to his own postulated cause of religion! His entire definition reads: "Religion is about the existence and causal powers of nonobservable entities and agencies."[66] Presumably, then, Boyer disdains religion as an illusion because it postulates unobservables. But real science embraces many unobservables—no one ever has seen gravity. Of course, Boyer would respond that gravity's *effects* are observable. But proponents of Intelligent Design would answer, so are the effects of a Creator! It must be noted, too, that the mental process for detecting agency that Boyer proposes also is an unobservable, at least by current technologies. He simply asserts that such a circuit exists. How is this more scientific than assertions about the existence of God? How is it different in form and plausibility from an assertion that some of the great mystics have had a special circuit in their brains that allowed them to be sensitive to supernatural phenomena? Boyer would, of course, ridicule such an assertion. But in doing so, he would seem to be "hoist by his own petard."

In similar fashion, Richard Dawkins has popularized the concept of "memes" as the cultural counterparts of biological genes. Dawkins's definition of the *meme* is remarkably vague in comparison with his clear expositions involving genes. Initially he defined the *meme* as "a unit of cultural transmission, or a unit of imitation" and proposed that "just as genes propagate themselves in the gene pool by leaping from body to body via sperm or eggs, so memes propagate themselves in the meme pool by leaping from brain to brain by a process which, in the broad sense of the term, can be called imitation."[67] He subsequently tried to give the meme more substance by describing it as a fundamental unit of information that gives rise to cultural artifacts and ideas.[68] Where the meme comes from, how it functions, its physical properties, and its location, all remain mysteries, and Dawkins settles for merely asserting analogies with biological genes. As to how memes are transmitted, Dawkins invokes viral infections. This allows him to reduce religions to "mind parasites" and the "God meme" to a highly infectious "virus." Indeed, he proposed that "faith is one of the world's great evils, comparable to the smallpox virus but harder to eradicate."[69]

Eventually it dawned on Dawkins that in his efforts to reduce religion and other cultural products that he dislikes to viruses, he had, by implication, also reduced all scientific ideas to viral memes. Perish the thought! Hence, he recently claimed that, of course, science is nothing of the sort, although scientific ideas "might look superficially virus-like," they are not, because scientific ideas "are not arbitrary or capricious" whereas people embrace the God meme without giving any thought to the matter,[70] thereby dismissing an enormous confessional literature. Many competent scientists have found it quite bizarre that Dawkins constantly berates the religious for believing in unobservables, when his primary line of attack involves an entirely unobservable entity imagined by him for polemical purposes.[71] Perhaps the most telling comment on Dawkins's work appears on the back of the dust jacket of his latest book, *The God Delusion* (2006). In accord with common practice, this space is devoted to blurbs praising the book by persons whose intellectual standing is such as to cast the book in a favorable light. Two of those selected to praise *The God Delusion* are the Las Vegas comedic magicians, Penn and Teller, who enlighten us all with the comment: "If this book doesn't change the world, we're all screwed."

Finally, there is Daniel Dennett, whose recent *Breaking the Spell: Religion as a Natural Phenomenon* received much favorable press attention. Indicative of his scientific objectivity, Dennett identifies irreligious people as "brights"[72] in contrast with those dullards who still cling to faith. That creative flourish aside, there is nothing particularly original in the entire book. Most of it is a rehash of Dawkins and Boyer, and Dennett makes no effort to deal with their insufficiencies. He also devotes considerable space to quoting me as a supporter of his peculiar views, a strange reading to say the least. Dennett even attempts to resuscitate "ghost theory," displaying no awareness of the serious shortcomings of Spencer's original version. But enough.

The recent popularity of evolutionary biological explanations of complex forms of human behavior is little more than a return to the "instinct theories" that dominated the social sciences at the start of the twentieth century. The leading figure back then was William McDougall (1871–1938) of Harvard, whose very influential *An Introduction to Social Psychology* (1908) attempted to explain all human behavior as produced by a blending ("compounds") of eighteen biologically given "instincts." Religiousness, according to McDougall, is caused by a blend of four instincts: curiosity, self-abasement, fear, and the protective, or parental, instinct. By the 1930s, instinct theories such as these had been laughed into oblivion, and it is high time for social scientists to laugh again! For the final insufficiency of all biological approaches to explaining religion, or any other aspects of human culture, is that they are *unnecessary*! The fundamental biological basis of all culture is general intelligence, and nothing more needs to be postulated. Of course, culture "evolves," but not via imaginary memes or viral infections. Instead, it evolves through reason and assessment: culture is discovered and refined by thinking human beings as they attempt to solve problems and satisfy their desires. To search for a religious instinct or a biological basis for faith is like searching for an algebra or a chemistry instinct—a misguided waste of time.

Culture and the Human Predicament

New culture doesn't just happen, and neither tribes nor societies invent anything. Innovations are the work of individuals, or at most, of small groups. Once something new has been developed, whether or not it is adopted can be viewed as a group phenomenon and so, too, its spread from one culture to another—a process anthropologists like to call **diffusion**. But anything new is the work of some specific person or persons. Therefore, to ask about the origins of religious culture, the focus must be on individuals. This is true whether one assumes that religion is entirely a human creation or the result of revelations—the agents of change are individuals, either as inventors or as prophets.

Because of the focus on religion as a cultural product and on the individual as its source, this approach to explaining religion is variously referred to as "cultural" or "intellectual."[73] I prefer "cultural," but whatever the label, this approach often has been angrily attacked as resting upon the "absurd" assumption that primitives are proto-theologians, concerned with the great existential questions as to the meaning of life or the origins of the universe. Thus, the anthropologists William Lessa (1908–1997) and Evon Z. Vogt (1918–2004) ridiculed those who tried to make "primitive man into a kind of rational philosopher . . . [ignoring] the prelogical and mystical character of primitive thought."[74] Lessa and Vogt assumed that to credit primitives with "philosophy" would be to suppose that whole tribes, or at least many members, engaged in this sort of thinking. That would, indeed, be an absurd assumption. Only a few people, whether ancient or modern, *initiate* inquiry about the meaning of life or the origins of the universe, let alone fashion original answers to these questions. But Lessa and Vogt's criticism loses all force when one traces primitive religious innovations to their actual source, to those rare geniuses who, in fact, *are* early theologians! Although usually we don't know who they were, or even when they lived, their sophisticated contributions have endured in the cultures of their people, prompting Paul Radin's famous collection of their work in *Primitive Man as Philosopher* (1927). As for ordinary people, primitive or otherwise, they often can quite easily be convinced of the importance of existential questions by someone filled with enthusiasm for these issues and who offers plausible answers.

That being the case, what follows is an attempt to explain the origins of religion on grounds of the universal human predicament and of the competitive advantages enjoyed by responses to these circumstances that are based on belief in the supernatural. Assuredly this approach *does assume* that human beings, even in Stone Age times, are intelligent creatures given to reflection, reason, and inspiration. This assumption seems fully warranted by the richness of their religious culture, as will be seen. In any event, religion originates with unusual individuals whom the influential anthropologist Paul Radin (1883–1959) called "religious formulators,"[75] but whom I prefer to call "innovators."

A **religious innovator** must not to be confused with a shaman or priest, although he or she may adopt one of these roles. Innovators are *very gifted individuals who appear from time to time and introduce new religious culture*—they are so rare that most cultures probably gained their religion by diffusion from a single original source. But even though innovators are scattered across time and space, their new formulations are remarkably similar, especially when comparisons are made across cultures at comparable levels of development. Perhaps new religious cultures tend to be similar because each innovator is responding to the universal human predicament. Or, perhaps, they are similar because each is responding to a revelation from the same divine source.

As to the human predicament, over the centuries, many skeptics have attributed religion to the primitive human's fear of nature—of storms, earthquakes, volcanic eruptions, floods, and fires—and of death, of sickness, of the dark, of the unknown, and so on. But having carefully surveyed the ethnographic literature, Paul Radin concluded that primitive people are only really "afraid of one thing, of the uncertainties of the struggle of life . . . of the battle for existence under the difficult conditions that prevail in simple societies." That is, primitive peoples have very practical fears: of the unsuccessful hunt, of failed crops, of sickness, of aggressive neighbors, and the like. Whenever possible, primitive people prefer direct efforts and techniques for overcoming these uncertainties. They do not call upon supernatural means to get the weeds out of their gardens, to skin a deer, or to construct a canoe. They do call upon the supernatural for rain, for help in finding game, and for safe voyages. In doing so, they acknowledge the fundamental principle that the *supernatural is the only plausible source of many things that human beings greatly desire.*

Therein lies one key to the universality of religion—its capacity to overcome the generic limitations of human power by invoking entities or forces that transcend nature. Whether it is a Bantu priest in Nigeria chanting that Awwaw grant a good harvest, or a Baptist congregation in Georgia singing, "What a friend we have in Jesus, all our sins and griefs to bear," religion offers an alternative means to achieve greatly desired ends, when direct methods fail or do not exist.

However, although this proposition identifies a basic function of religion, it *does not explain its origins.* The need to overcome nature mainly explains why most people (primitive or modern) *will accept* religious culture, not where such culture originates. While in order to be successful, religious innovators must appeal to these utilitarian desires, their personal reasons for delving into supernaturalism typically seem far more theological or philosophical—they seem driven mainly by their concern with great existential matters such as the origin of the world and the meaning of life. As a Greenland Eskimo explained: "Thou must not imagine that no Greenlander thinks about these things. . . . Certainly there must be some Being who made all these things. . . . Ah, did I but know him, how I would love and honor him."[76] Or a young Oglala Sioux recalled: "When I was 10 years of age I looked at the land and the rivers, the sky above, and the animals around me and could not fail to realize that they were made by some great power. I was so anxious to understand this power that I questioned the trees and the bushes. It seemed as though the flowers were staring at me, and I wanted to ask them 'Who made you?' . . . Then I had a dream, and in my dream one of these small round stones appeared to me and told me that the maker of all was Wakan tanka, and that in order to honor him I must honor his works in nature."[77]

Such motivations also are consistent with the fact that the "intellectual" aspects of religion come to the fore whenever religious innovators gain sufficient authority, so that they can move the community's religious life beyond the narrow appeal to practical advantages, whereupon emphasis is given to worship as an end in itself, and to thanksgiving for the gift of life and opportunity. That being the case, it will not be sufficient to define religion merely as belief in the supernatural, as Tylor and Spencer were content to do, and surely not to define it as pure ritual, as Durkheim did. A more adequate definition of religion is required.

On Religion

Religion consists of *explanations of existence (or ultimate meaning)* based on *supernatural assumptions* and including statements about the *nature of the supernatural*, which may specify *methods* or *procedures* for *exchanging* with the supernatural.

Earlier, **supernatural** was defined as *somewhat mysterious forces or entities that are above, beyond, or outside nature and which can control, suspend, alter, or ignore the natural order*. By use of the term *supernatural*, this definition of religion leaves room for Godless religions, **Gods** being defined as *supernatural beings having consciousness and intentions*. Some primitive religions may lack Gods, and relatively Godless religions also are pursued by various small groups of intellectuals, such as elite Buddhists in the East, and by those in the West (mostly seminary professors) who associate God with purely psychological constructs such as Paul Tillich's "ground of being."[78]

Measures and procedures for exchanging with the supernatural include *rites* and *rituals*. Here, too, allowance is made for relatively Godless religions, since even such a vague supernaturalism as is involved in elite forms of Confucianism can prompt rituals. The definition excludes all systems of belief that do not address the great existential questions, that offer no *explanations of existence* or statements concerning *ultimate meaning*. That is, religions answer such questions as: Why we are here? What we can hope? Can virtue triumph? Is death the end? and the like. A belief system qualifies as a religion even if its answers to these questions declare that life is meaningless and the universe is without purpose—the issue is whether such questions are *addressed* (so long as the existence of the supernatural is also postulated).

The anthropologists whose work on primitive religion was reviewed earlier in the chapter probably would complain that the inclusion of ultimate meaning in the definition of religion excludes the most primitive religions in that although all primitive cultures have some notions about the supernatural, most have no grasp whatever of ultimate questions. Perhaps, but as will be seen later in the chapter, the religions even of some of the most primitive groups were far more sophisticated and "theological" than once was recognized.

What this definition does do is separate mere magic from religion. **Magic** is limited to efforts to *manipulate the supernatural* to obtain desired outcomes, *without reference to a God or Gods* and *without general statements about existence or ultimate meaning.* Magic consists of various ritualistic practices and procedures believed able to produce particular results, but the underlying explanations of why and how these procedures work are vague almost to the point of nonexistence. As the great anthropologist Bronislaw Malinowski (1884–1942) put it, magic is "circumscribed in its beliefs, stunted in its fundamental assumptions."[79] Or, in the words of Malinowski's celebrated student Ruth Benedict (1887–1946), supernaturalism is "an attribute of objects just as color and weight are attributes of objects. There is the same reason that a stone should have supernatural power as one of its attributes as there [is] that it should have hardness. It [does] not imply the personification of the stone."[80] Thus it may be that rites and rituals often associated with relatively Godless religions are primarily acts of magic. It is possible, too, that some societies do not have religion, but only magic—I doubt it, but there is no way to be sure.

Admittedly, the most sophisticated form of magic, known as *sorcery*, sometimes involves supernatural forces a bit more animate than magic stones and the like. Sometimes, sorcerers do attempt to compel certain primitive spiritual entities, such as imps and demons, to perform certain services. Even so, it still remains possible to "distinguish magic and religion on the basis of the criterion of compulsion."[81] To quote Benedict again, "Magic is mechanical procedure, the compulsion of the supernatural," whereas religion is based on seeking "rapport" with God(s).[82]

Finally, Max Weber (1864–1920) gets the last word: "Those beings that are worshipped and entreated religiously may be termed 'gods,' in contrast to the 'demons,' which are magically coerced and charmed."[83]

Religious innovators, then, are always "theologians" in the sense that they offer answers to the most basic existential issues. Thus do the two primary questions concerning religious innovators come into view. First, how do some people "obtain" new religious culture? Second, how do they convince others to accept their new religious culture?

On Revelations

One might suppose that religious innovators "think up" their new culture in the same way that someone might write a poem or compose a song. But that doesn't fit with what many innovators seem to believe about their sources. Some claim to have discovered their ideas through intense meditation. But many claim to be no more than a channel through which the supernatural has communicated, hence theirs is a *revelation*, endowed with divine authority.

A **revelation** is a *communication believed to come from a supernatural source, usually from a God, or to be divinely inspired knowledge.*

Until recently, the very slim social-scientific literature on revelations proposed that they stem either from psychosis or fraud—that those reporting revelations are crooked or crazy. Either assumption is incompatible with the biographies of many prominent cases: most showed no indications whatever of mental illness, and most made personal sacrifices utterly incompatible with fraud. This led me to formulate a model whereby entirely normal people can, through entirely normal means, believe that they communicate with the divine.[84] Here it will suffice to summarize a few elements of that theory.

In rare instances, revelations are experienced as very direct communications involving visions and voices, as when God spoke to Moses from a burning bush, or when Jesus appeared to Paul on the road to Damascus. Far more often, revelations involve only the sudden certainty that a particular idea or interpretation is of divine origins, often based on the belief that *God placed the thought, insight, or even whole passages of scripture into one's mind.* When Spencer W. Kimball, president of the Church of Jesus Christ of Latter-day Saints, announced the revelation that persons of African ancestry should be admitted to the Mormon priesthood, he described the process by which he gained this revelation as the result of many hours of prayer that ended in the sudden, absolute certainty that this was God's will. In somewhat similar fashion, the authority of the Mishnah rests on the Jewish belief that God continues to reveal himself to scholars through their close study of the Torah.

Regardless of the form they take, most revelations are uncreative in the sense that they *do not include anything new*, but merely *confirm* the truth of the current religious culture. As Evelyn Underhill (1875–1941) explained in her classic study *Mysticism* (1911), most revelations are "founded upon the formal creed which the individual mystic accepts. . . . He is generally an acceptor not a rejector of such creeds. . . . The greatest mystics have not been heretics but Catholic saints."[85] Thus, when most people feel inspired or catch sight of divinity, it merely confirms them in their prior faith and generates no new religious culture. But religious innovators have *novel* revelations, which often leads to their being identified as heretics. More than that, new faiths are not created by the obviously uninspired "revelations" to be found in abundance in any occult bookstore. Assuming for the moment that all revelations are of human origin, how is it possible that some of them are so impressive as to seem worthy of divine sources? Enter genius.

Suppose that someone with the literary gifts of William Shakespeare underwent a series of mental events that he or she interpreted as contact with the supernatural. Would it not be likely that revelations produced by such a person would be messages of depth, beauty, and originality? The question is, of course, how can geniuses mistake the source of their revelations? How can they not know that they, not the supernatural, composed it? In fact, such a mistake is easily made by an entirely rational, honest individual.

Most composers *compose*. They write their music slowly, a few notes at a time. But that's not the way all composers work. For Mozart and Gershwin, melodies simply came to them in complete form. They did not compose tunes; they simply played what they heard or saw—of course, they often polished these melodies and then embedded them in elaborate arrangements and orchestrations. Both of them seemed to regard the sources of their music as somehow "out there," as external. In a letter to Isaac Goldberg, Gershwin described the genesis of his *Rhapsody in Blue*: "It was on that train, with its steely rhythms, its rattlety-bang that is so often stimulating to a composer—I frequently hear music in the heart of noise—I suddenly heard—even saw on paper—the complete construction of the rhapsody from beginning to end."[86]

Compare this with the account offered by the great first-century Jewish mystic Philo of Alexandria: "Sometimes when I come to my work empty, I have suddenly become full; ideas being in an invisible manner showered upon me, and implanted in me from on high; so that through the influence of divine inspiration, I have become greatly excited, and have known neither the place in which I was, nor those who were present, nor what I was saying, nor what I was writing . . ."[87]

Indeed, the similarity between artistic and religious creation has long been remarked. To quote Evelyn Underhill once more: "In all creative acts, the larger share of the work is done subconsciously: its emergence is in a sense automatic. This is equally true of mystics, artists, philosophers, [and] discoverers . . . [whose work] always owes its inception to some sudden uprush of intuitions or ideas for which the superficial self cannot account; its execution to powers so far beyond the control of the self, that they seem, as their owner sometimes says, to 'come from beyond.' "[88]

It needs to be recognized, too, that *content* will play a crucial part in determining how an individual will interpret "a sudden uprush of intuitions and ideas." There is nothing intrinsic to music to suggest that it was *sent* from beyond—no sender is implied by the material itself. But a sender *is* at least implicit in religious inspirations. So, suppose that instead of the *Rhaposody in Blue*, splendidly expressed and profound new religious truths (even scriptures) suddenly flooded into one's consciousness. How very easily one might be convinced by the quality and content of these revelations, as well as by their sudden arrival, that they could only have been sent by a supernatural source. Alternatively, we are, of course, free to assume that the revelation *was sent*, that it did come from "out there," that God does reveal himself to humans—even if it is only within the limits of their capacity to understand. It is possible, too, that some revelations are purely human creations, while others truly are communications from beyond.

Taking account of these possibilities, and stated as a theoretical proposition: *Certain rare individuals have the capacity to perceive revelations, whether this be an openness or sensitivity to real communications from the supernatural or consists of unusual creativity enabling them to create profound new religious truths and then to externalize the source of this material.*

Although the examples just cited come from modern times, there is no reason to suppose an occasional Stone Age genius did not have similar experiences. That these experiences would produce new religious culture rather than confirm the old would be maximized during times of crisis when the prevailing religious culture seemed unavailing—a phenomenon that Anthony F. C. Wallace identifies as "revitalization movements."[89] Thus, most leaders of significant uprisings by American Indians sought to revitalize or reenergize their followers to successfully resist encroachments by the white man. And they did so under the mantle of new religious revelations, beginning with the prophet Handsome Lake among the Iroquois in 1799[90] and culminating in the Ghost Shirt Dances[91] that swept through the plains Indians late in the nineteenth century. Judaism in exile, and often confronted with repression and persecution, has produced a long line of messiahs, even in recent years.[92] The same is true among groups of African ancestry in the New World.[93]

On Credibility

It is one thing to possess new religious culture, but it is something else to convince others to accept it. It is now well known that people do not initially accept a new religion because they find its doctrines especially attractive. Of course, there must be something novel about the new religion in order to justify change. But given that, people accept a new religion because their relatives, friends, and associates—people whom they trust—have accepted it. In fact, most people don't learn much about their new religious culture until after they have converted (see Chapter 4).[94] It follows that *successful* religious innovators will tend to be *well-respected members of an intense primary group.*

Imagine yourself living a life of solitary contemplation. Then one day new religious truths are revealed to you by a divine being—a revelation that doesn't merely ratify current religious conceptions, but which adds to or departs from these conceptions to a significant degree. Having imparted this revelation, the divine being directs you to communicate it to the "world." Having no close friends to reassure you or to help you spread the word, somehow you must find someone who will believe you, and then another, and another. It is a daunting prospect.

But what if, instead of leading a solitary life, you are a respected member of an intense primary group? It would seem far less difficult to share your revelation with people who love and trust you, than to convince strangers. Thus, contrary to Mark (6:4), which states that a prophet is without honor in his own country and among his own kin, the most famous prophets began by converting their immediate families and friends.[95] Consider Joseph Smith Jr., founder of Mormonism. His first twenty-two converts were his wife, his parents, his seven brothers and sisters, ten members of the neighboring Whitmer family, a teacher who roomed with Smith's parents, and a former employer. The same pattern existed among the initial converts made by Zoroaster, Moses, Buddha, Jesus, and Muhammad, all of whom began with their families, as will be discussed in the appropriate chapters.

In addition, of course, all of these famous religious innovators faced the task of eventually converting a world of strangers. But for an innovator in, say, the Stone Age, that challenge did not exist. To convert one's kinfolk and neighbors was to convert the "world." If the new religion then spread to other tribes, that was through the ordinary process of cultural diffusion.[96]

This, then, is the cultural explanation of the origin of religion. Religion is everywhere, because the needs it fulfills are everywhere. Religions are so similar because they all address the same set of existential questions and the supernatural options available are inherently limited. Alternatively, many religions come from God according to the ability of humans at a particular time and place to understand, and, of course, all revelations are subject to misunderstanding, exaggeration, and faulty transmission.

THEOLOGY AND UNIVERSALISM

As the Age of Exploration began and Europeans became increasingly familiar with other religions and noted the many "conspicuous similarities"[97] with Christianity, questions began to arise among Christian theologians as to the history of salvation. Had God condemned most human beings through most of history merely for the "sin" of ignorance? Late in the fifteenth century came a discovery that seemed to settle the matter: a revelation to Hermes the Egyptian that seemed to prophesy the birth of Christ and that long preceded the revelation given to Moses.[98] Here seemed to be proof that God spoke to pagans, too. It happened this way.

In 1460 Cosimo de'Medici, grandfather of Lorenzo and himself an avid collector of old manuscripts, bought one that came to be known as the *Corpus hermeticum*. He arranged to have it translated by Marsilio Ficino, a very eminent classical scholar. Both Ficino and his patron were thrilled by the results. The striking similarities between this revelation to the pagan Egyptians and Christianity even inspired Pope Alexander VI to commission a fresco in the Vatican teeming with Egyptian images and symbols. In the words of Mircea Eliade (1907–1986), the excitement over this discovery revealed "a profound dissatisfaction with the [provincialism of] medieval theology . . . [with a] purely *Western* Christianity; a longing for a universalistic, transhistorical, 'mythical' religion."[99] Indeed, Nicholas of Cusa (1401–1464), a distinguished scientist who became a bishop, was prompted to interpret this amazing document as proof that all religions are essentially the same: "Religion and the worship of God, in all men endowed with the spirit, are fundamentally, in all the diversity of rites, one and the same."[100] Two centuries later the *Corpus hermeticum* was revealed as a fake, written in about the third century and probably best classified as a Gnostic creation. But the enthusiasm it aroused in late medieval theological circles was entirely genuine, as witnessed by the fact that the quest for a "universal" revelation continued.

Turning to the Bible, theologians soon emphasized the first covenant made by God with Noah. From this it was reasoned, consistent with both Jewish and Christian theology, that since everyone is descended from Noah, everyone has been eligible ever after to be saved, that "the universality of salvation includ[ed] the religious development of mankind before the time of the special covenant [with the Jews] . . . [the] history of salvation being basically identical with the history of mankind and no single period of the development of mankind [is] excluded from God's love."[101]

Remarkable support for this view can be attributed to Paul. As quoted in Acts (14:16–17)[102] when he was speaking to a group of pagan priests in Lystra, and having refused their invitation to join in the sacrifice of oxen, Paul explained that this was a new day and his a new message, whereas: "*In past generations he [God] allowed all the nations to walk in their own ways; yet he did not leave himself without witness, for he did good and gave you from heaven rains and fruitful seasons, satisfying your hearts with food and gladness.*" Later, speaking to philosophers in Athens (Acts 17:29–30), Paul criticized the worship of graven images, but noted that during earlier "*times of ignorance God overlooked*" such practices (the King James Version says that "God winked at" such ignorance).

These scriptural passages prompted some theologians early in the twentieth century to propose that there had been "universal revelations." As expressed by Hugh R. Mackintosh (1870–1936) in *The American Journal of Theology*, "revelation has been going on in all places and at all times—in nature, in history, and specially in the history of religions. . . . It is not possible . . . to believe . . . that God the father . . . seduously hid himself from all but Jews and Christians." Mackintosh went on to point out that this admission does not undercut Christianity. "That God has spoken to the world through prophets, seers, saints in every clime, is no reason why he should not have spoken finally in his Son, to make an end of sin and bring everlasting righteousness. A great missionary was once heard to say that he had never preached the gospel anywhere, without finding that God had been there before him. Yet that divine presence and action did not serve to make the Christian message superfluous, but to make it appreciated when it came."[103]

Hence, it can be argued that if religions have much in common, that is to be expected because each is based on revelations, variously accommodated and interpreted, from the One True God.

That these theological views did not become more popular is due to the fact that academic theology soon was taken over by those who had no interest in the matter, having rejected revelations of *all* kinds, who disliked "God talk," and who devoted the rest of the twentieth century to exploring psychological or philosophical foundations for a kind of post-Christian religiousness. However, during this same era anthropologists had been lending even greater credibility to the idea of a universal revelation.

PRIMITIVE RELIGIONS RECONSIDERED

Durkheim claimed that the Australian aborigines had the lowest possible level of culture. Perhaps so, but their religious culture was not, as he believed, limited to crude, Godless totemism. Instead, the aborigines had quite well-developed notions about cosmology and about the existence and nature of High Gods who created the world. So did many other primitive groups, especially groups at about the same low level of culture as the aborigines: the Pygmies, the Fuegians (whom Darwin said were on a par with "the lower animals"), the Andamanese, and many others. When these facts were announced in 1898, they were hotly denied or studiously ignored. But by the 1920s the claim that many primitives believed in High Gods was accepted by the best anthropologists of the day, only to have that fact soon slip once again into relative obscurity.

This story begins with one of the most accomplished scholars of his time, Andrew Lang (1844–1912). Born in Scotland and educated at the Universities of St. Andrews and Glasgow, he then studied at Oxford, subsequently becoming a Fellow of Merton College, where he did research in anthropology until leaving for London and the literary life in 1875. Lang wrote novels and poetry and gained fame for his superb translations of Homer's *Iliad* and the *Odyssey*. He also was a student of Tylor's and wrote an acclaimed study of primitive religion, the two volume *Myth, Ritual, and Religion* (1887), a recent edition of which remains in print. However, *The Making of Religion* (1898) was by far Lang's most important scholarly book. But it no longer is in print and is not even mentioned in most of his biographical notices, such as the one in the *Encyclopaedia Britannica*. This seems to be a holdover from the period of twenty years or so after the book appeared, when the leading anthropologists were either very upset by his claims or dismissed them as rubbish. That he was subsequently fully vindicated seems not to have become well known, perhaps in part because the theological implications of his work had by then been recognized by anthropologists, who make up the most irreligious discipline of all.[104]

In his earlier *Myth, Ritual, and Religion*, Lang had supported Tylor's claims that primitive religion consisted of animism and expressed his commitment to a simple, unilinear model of cultural evolution.[105] But in *The Making of Religion*, Lang broke with Tylor and overturned all previous studies of primitive religions, which were unanimous in claiming that groups in the earliest stages of cultural development had no Gods and that belief "in a moral Supreme Being is a very late result of evolution."[106] Having carefully sifted through the most recent and reliable

Andrew Lang was a celebrated Scottish author, but he should be remembered primarily for having realized that primitive humans were not Godless savages with inane religions, but that most believed in morally concerned High Gods and had surprisingly elaborate beliefs about Creation. (Courtesy of the Library of Congress)

ethnographic accounts of religion in surviving primitive societies, Lang discovered that many of the most primitive groups, scattered in all parts of the world, believed in the existence of **High Gods:** "moral, all-seeing, directors of things and of men . . . eternal beings who made the world, and watch over morality."[107] This was not fully expressed monotheism, since the existence of subordinate Gods was accepted, too—a perspective sometimes referred to as *henotheism* (literally "one-Godism")[108] because of the emphasis on the High or primary God.

Because Lang based his work on the literature rather than on original fieldwork, obviously many had noted the existence of primitive High Gods long before Lang, but their major concern had been to deny that the High Gods represented early monotheism,[109] ignoring that the mere idea of such Gods made a shambles of all theories that characterized primitive religions as crude, Godless muddles of superstition. When Lang pointed this out, neither the message nor the messenger was well received. Instead, being committed to a simple, unilinear doctrine of "progressive evolution," all the leading anthropologists of the time, including Tylor, rejected all claims for early belief in High Gods as impossible. Such nonsense "must be got rid of," since it is obvious that the earliest stage of religion "*must have* been extremely low, not far removed from that of beasts; therefore [High Gods] must be deferred to quite late stages of development."[110]

That Lang had been trained in anthropology at Oxford and worked with Tylor was disregarded; he was treated as an amateur dilettante— "literary gifts usually arouse the scholars' suspicions."[111] So, Lang's book was carefully ignored in the leading journals, either going entirely unmentioned or dispatched with very brief notices of publication—a German editor called it an "unexpected theory" and pronounced that it "had been received with due mistrust."[112] In 1913, fifteen years after Lang had published, Elsdon Best noted, in the very prestigious British anthropology journal *Man*, that he was "not aware that any other writer has since written in favour of [Lang's thesis]" and then proceeded to inform his colleagues that, despite early reports to the contrary, the Maori of New Zealand worship a Supreme Being.[113] As Best's report and many others demonstrated, the facts were on Lang's side, and he was eventually vindicated, although posthumously.

Reading Lang's book, one must wonder how any anthropologists of the day could ignore the remarkable reports from far and wide that some of the most primitive peoples on earth acknowledged High Gods. Among the many reports utilized by Lang was a model of good anthropological fieldwork conducted by E. H. Man, an Englishman who lived among the Andaman Islanders for eleven years and took the trouble to learn their language. Man published his findings in a series of three articles in the *Journal of the Anthropological Institute of Great Britain and Ireland* in 1883. Although the Andamanese were described by Spencer as "Godless," what Man found was that they not only had Gods, but they had a High God named Puluga, who was never born, is invisible, and is immortal. Puluga created everything: "the world and all objects, animate and inanimate, were created, excepting only the powers of evil." Puluga "is regarded as omniscient . . . knowing even the thoughts of their hearts. He is angered by the commision of certain sins. . . . He is the Judge from whom each soul receives its sentence after death."[114] Man convincingly refuted the possibility that the Andamanese had learned about a High God from missionaries or other outsiders on grounds that prior to his arrival with a colonizing British force, they had been fearsome cannibals, who hated all outsiders and attacked anyone nearing their shores. As for the aboriginal peoples of

Australia, Lang reworked the somewhat muddled ethnographic accounts written by A. W. Howitt and published between 1882 and 1889 (the very ones on which Durkheim based most of his analysis of primitive religion) and concluded that they, too, celebrate an ethical Supreme Being who created all things. Eventually, Lang filled many of his 355 pages with accounts of what he called the "High Gods of Low Races." It should be noted that in those days the word *race* often carried no biological implications, but was a synonym for the word *culture*. Hence, the English often referred to the "French race," and the French to the "English race." Here the best translation would be "High Gods of Primitive Cultures."

Today we know that some of Lang's examples were wrong. But we also know of many supportive examples unknown to him, and so, by the 1920s, it no longer could be denied that many of the most primitive peoples known to anthropologists had High Gods. A milestone was the publication in 1924 of *Monotheism Among Primitive Peoples* by the distinguished Paul Radin, wherein he acknowledged that Lang's work "has been abundantly corroborated. . . . That many primitive peoples have a belief in a Supreme Creator no one today seriously denies."[115] Since then the studies have continued to accumulate. The greatly respected Chicago professor Mircea Eliade (1907–1986) confirmed that there "is a general belief among the Australians that the world, man, and various animals were created by certain Supernatural Beings. . . ."[116] He reported that "Baiame, the supreme divinity of the tribes of South-East Australia . . . dwells in the sky, beside a great stream of water (the Milky Way), and receives the souls of the innocent. He sits on a crystal throne. . . . Baiame is self-created and has created everything from nothing. . . . [He] sees and hears everything."[117] In another pair of well-known essays, Eliade went on to identify High Gods all across South America.[118] Many other scholars identified High Gods in the religions of Africa.[119] As the distinguished Ninian Smart (1927–2001) put it: "In most, if not all, of the indigenous cultures of Africa there is a belief in a supreme Spirit ruling over or informing lesser spirits and gods. He governs natural forces, dwells on high, is inexplicable, creates souls, men, and all things."[120] In similar fashion, High Gods were abundant in the religions of North American tribes.[121]

Not content to note the prevalence of High Gods, Lang proposed that because they were so often found among the least advanced peoples, High Gods would seem to represent the *earliest form* of religion and that "lower" religions, such as animism and crude idolatry, probably *devolved* from these more ethical religious beginnings. Lang's reasoning about devolution of the Gods partly anticipates the discussion in Chapters 2 and 4 of the attractions of polytheism and why there are repeated historical instances when people reverted from monotheism to idolatry—as often occurred among the ancient Jews. As Lang explained, "That god thrives best who is most suited to his environment. Whether an easy-going, hungry ghost-god . . . or a moral Creator not to be bribed, is better suited to an environment of not especially scrupulous savages, any man can decide. . . . Beyond all doubt, savages who find themselves under the watchful eye of a moral deity whom they cannot 'square' [buy off] will desert him as soon as they have evolved a practicable ghost-god . . . whom they *can* square. No less manifestly, savages, who already possess a throng of serviceable ghost-gods, will not enthusiastically evolve a moral Being who despises gifts, and only cares for obedience."[122]

There is, of course, considerable variation in the images of High Gods reported for primitive cultures. The major distinction is between active, concerned High Gods, and inactive or withdrawn High Gods.[123] Even the active High Gods are somewhat remote, presiding over lower Gods who take a more vigorous part in human affairs, as is evident in this prayer often spoken by the Pawnees,[124] transcribed and translated by the remarkable Alice C. Fletcher (1838–1923):

> *Father, thou above, father of the gods,*
> *They who can come near and touch us,*
> *Do thou bid them bring us help.*
> *Help we need. Father, hear us!*

Many other primitive people believe in a High God who created the entire universe and set everything in motion, but who then withdrew to some remote place and no longer attends to his creation (similar ideas were expressed by several Greek philosophers). The withdrawal of High Gods is so common that it has inspired various explanations, most of them echoing Lang's analysis that High Gods usually are too demanding and too abstract to satisfy ordinary people who want to be on more familiar terms with more permissive, closer, more "human" Gods, like those the Pawnees called upon their High God to motivate and direct. This matter is pursued in Chapter 2.

In any event, it no longer is necessary to compile sets of examples of beliefs about the High Gods, whether active or not, because George Peter Murdock (1897–1985) provided an impressive quantitative basis for doing so. Murdock devoted his career to organizing the ethnographic literature to the point that a large number of cultures could be coded to permit statistical analysis. In 1967 he published coding for 563 past and present cultures on dozens of variables. Many of these variables were devoted to kinship patterns, others to technology and methods of subsistence. But among them was a measure of High Gods. The codes were: 1) belief in an active High God who is supportive of human morality; 2) belief in an inactive High God; 3) no conception of a High God. The information on the religion of 136 cultures was too incomplete to permit coding. That left a total of 427 cultures for which adequate data existed. However, while all of these are pre-industrial cultures, many of them do not qualify as primitive: the ancient Egyptians, Greeks, Hebrews, and Romans, for example. Therefore, I have limited the analysis to only the most primitive groups, which can be identified in various ways. The results[125] are these:

Nomadic Groups

Believe in:

An Active High God	42%
An Inactive High God	22%
No High God	36%
	100%
Number of Cases (N) =	(36)

Use Slash and Burn Agriculture

Believe in:

An Active High God	23%
An Inactive High God	44%
No High God	33%
	100%
Number of Cases (N) =	(144)

Much Dependence on Gathering

Believe in:

An Active High God	16%
An Inactive High God	27%
No High God	57%
	100%

Number of Cases (N) = (120)

Most of the 36 nomadic tribes (64 percent) accept a High God, and nearly half regard this High God as active. Keep in mind, too, that most of the cultures coded as not having High Gods were not crude animists, but did worship Gods, albeit "lower" Gods like those of the classical civilizations. Among the 144 tribes who rely on slash and burn agriculture, two-thirds believe in a High God, but they tend to conceive of this God as inactive. Among the 120 groups who rely heavily on gathering for their subsistence, the majority of tribes do not recognize a High God, but many do. Lang's point is overwhelmingly confirmed.

The obvious question is *why weren't* primitive religions a crude muddle of superstitions just as Tylor, Spencer, and all the rest believed them to be? How is it possible that many of the earliest religions had a far more sophisticated conception of God than did far later ancient civilizations such as Egypt and Greece? The only sustained effort to provide an answer caused such widespread consternation among anthropologists that the question itself has largely been dismissed as either irrelevant or unanswerable.

A General Revelation?

At the end of his career, Paul Radin suddenly disavowed all of his previous writings on High Gods among primitive groups and reverted to an animistic conception of early religion.[126] It is surmised that he did so because he was so upset about the theological interpretation being put on the prevalence of High Gods by a group of Jesuit scholars, led by Wilhelm Schmidt (1868–1954) of the University of Vienna.

Schmidt was universally regarded as a master of the ethnographic literature and admired for his immense scholarly output, including *Der*

Ursprung der Gottesidee (The Origin of the Idea of God), published in twelve volumes from 1912 to 1955. Even a militant atheist such as the anthropologist Anthony F. C. Wallace (1923–) found "a refreshing objective quality" in Schmidt's work.[127]

Schmidt was thirty and just completing his training when Lang's book appeared. He saw at once the theological implications of the existence of High Gods in the religions of many of the most primitive tribes: "The Supreme Being of the primitive culture is really the God of monotheism."[128] The many similarities of religions around the world are not evidence that they all are human inventions, but reflect a "universal revelation" dating from earliest times. Schmidt proposed that at the dawn of humanity all religions were alike; everyone knew the same God. It is the variations from one religion to another that reveal the insertion of human inventions, of misunderstanding, and of faulty transitions across generations—an additional source of variation being subsequent revelations as humans became capable of better comprehending God. In this way, Schmidt showed how snugly the huge ethnographic literature of primitive religions fits with the account in *Genesis* of the Creation and the Fall.

Schmidt's thesis was brilliantly argued and massively documented, and it so frightened many secular-minded anthropologists that some of them, like Radin, recanted their acceptance of High Gods among the primitives. Most of the rest simply disavowed the possibility of ever explaining either the origins or the similarities of early religions. Instead, the prevailing textbook axiom became that the origins of religion are so shrouded by the clouds of pre-history that we never can know what took place—"Inevitably and forever, we are barred from obtaining the needed data," was how William J. Goode (1917–2003) put it.[129] Kingsley Davis (1908–1997) concurred, "Due to the impossibility of recovering traces of the earliest social beginnings [of religion] . . . [it is] a fruitless search."[130] Even Ninian Smart (1927–2001) could agree that "it is impossible to discuss the religion of the earliest humans except in terms of speculative theories."[131] Which is to say that if it is impossible to know what early religions were like, we need not worry about the possibility that a general revelation might actually have occurred. Thus did social scientists breathe a profound sigh of relief, even as they abandoned what they had long regarded as one of their primary reasons to study surviving primitive cultures.

CONCLUSION

Granted that our knowledge of primitive religions must remain fragmentary, there seems sufficient reason to accept that at some point many cultures abandoned belief in High Gods and embraced a flock of smaller Gods. *When* did this happen, and *why*? As to when, the change seems to have coincided with the rise of civilizations—of societies having cities and a productive agriculture. As to why, the next chapter attempts to explain the rise of elaborate polytheisms as it examines the religions of these early civilizations, including Sumer, Egypt, and Greece, as well as religion among the Aztecs and the Maya. These civilizations, separated not only by geography, but by many centuries, nevertheless sustained an amazingly similar array of Gods. These religions also were very highly controlled by priests who stressed ritual and sacrifice rather than beliefs. Housed in great temples, these all were "state" religions: fully funded by land grants or subsidies, the priests were in service to despotic rulers, some of whom presumed to be God.

· 2 ·

TEMPLE RELIGIONS OF
ANCIENT CIVILIZATIONS

Hᴉsᴛᴏʀʏ ʙᴇɢɪɴs ᴀᴛ Sᴜᴍᴇʀ."[1] Thus did the great archaeologist Samuel Noah Kramer (1897–1990) identify the collection
of city-states located around the lower Tigris and Euphrates
Rivers as the first real civilization. It is from hundreds of thousands of
surviving Sumerian tablets,[2] inscribed in cuneiform script, and from the
spectacular ruins, artifacts, frescoes, and carvings that we have our earliest information about an *organized* religion—one housed in great structures, having a specialized priesthood, elaborate rites, written scriptures,
and a multitude of Gods.

Written on hardened clay tablets, Sumerian sacred texts have survived—although even larger troves of tablets are thought to await exca-
vation[3]—while the ancient sacred texts of other Old World civilizations
were mostly written on perishable materials such as papyrus or leather
and are long lost. Consequently, we know far more about the religion
of Sumer than about the religions of such later ancient civilizations as
Egypt, Greece, or even Rome. The New World is another matter. There,
in addition to a wealth of well-preserved Aztec and Mayan "ruins" and
art, some very important sacred writings also have survived. To this may
be added some obviously authoritative, sympathetic, and lengthy reports
by Spanish missionaries, which offer firsthand accounts of things we can
only surmise about elsewhere, even in Sumer.[4]

Because so much detailed knowledge exists, the chapter begins with an extensive portrait of Sumerian religion, fleshed out with material from Egypt and Greece (Rome is taken up in the next chapter), and also from the Aztec and Mayan Empires. Along the way, it demonstrates the remarkable similarities between the religions of the early civilizations of the Old and the New World—if only because all of them were temple religions.

Temple religions are staffed by an *exclusive priesthood* and serve a *clientele* rather than a membership. Clients come to a temple to participate in periodic festivals and ceremonies and sometimes appear there in pursuit of personal spiritual, material, and social returns. But their temple activity is a relatively incidental aspect of their social relationships and their self-conceptions: people *go* to temples; they do not *belong* to them. This is

The cuneiform script on this ancient Sumerian tablet details the proper rite for an annual marriage between the king and a woman chosen to represent the Goddess of fertility. Hundreds of thousands of these tablets have been found, making Sumer the best known of all ancient cultures. (Louvre, Paris; Photo: Erich Lessing/Art Resource, New York)

in contrast with religions that are able to generate **congregations**—*communities* of religious participants whose religious life is of substantial importance for their *social relationships* and *self-conceptions*. No Sumerians referred to themselves as Enlilians, nor did Greeks claim to be Zeusians, in contrast with, say, people who proudly identified themselves as Christians, Jews, or Mithraists. Temple religions differ in their inclusiveness, but most of them limit their clientele to the social elite, although some offer limited access to the public. This exclusiveness reflects, in part, that temple religions usually are *fully subsidized state monopolies* and need not seek popular support.

In what follows, temple religions will be examined in detail, and then the descriptive material is analyzed to answer a number of questions about this "stage" in the cultural evolution of religion, including: Why, in this first era of true "civilization," did conceptions of God seem to regress? What was the appeal of extensive polytheism as opposed to the emphasis on High Gods that had dominated less advanced societies? And did anyone actually believe that "idols" were alive? Then, why did these religions endure for several millennia without any significant change? How did religion relate to the state? What prompted the incredible emphasis on monumentalism, on building gigantic temples and tombs? And, for all of their enormous temples, huge "idols," and abundance of priests (and some priestesses), why did these "state" religions seem to have been of only marginal importance to the average person? Finally, why was sacrifice so central and sometimes carried to such excessive lengths?

Everyone knows where the Egyptian, Greek, Mayan, and Aztec Empires were located, but because Sumer and Sumeria refer primarily to a language group rather than to a place, most readers will be a bit vague as to precisely where it was. Sumeria today is southern Iraq (see Map 2–1). Over the centuries, Sumer has been referred to by various other names, most often as Mesopotamia, but also (in various eras) as Assyria, Chaldea, and Babylon. So far as is known, Sumerian was the very first written language—an inscribed tablet from about 3100 BCE has survived, and experts assume that the written language goes back considerably further. In about 2000 BCE, Sumerian was largely replaced as a spoken language by the Semitic Akkadian, but it remained the written language in this region until nearly the start of the Christian era.

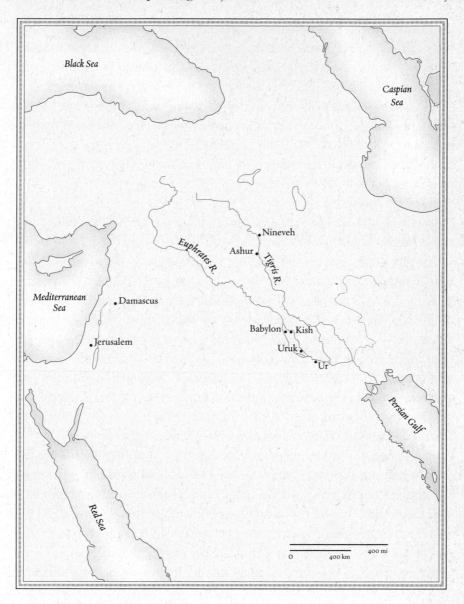

Map 2–1: Map of ancient Sumer.

Over the millennia, Sumer was associated with many successive king-doms, each including the cities that had sprung up in the region: Baby-lon, Nineveh, Kish, Ashur, Uruk, and Ur (said to have been the birthplace of Abraham). These kingdoms were ruled by such famous names as Sar-gon, Hammurabi, and Nebuchadnezzar. But although kings and ruling dynasties came and went, and cities rose and fell, the Sumerian culture was extraordinarily stable, enduring with very little change for more than four thousand years. And the most unchanging element of this culture was religion.[5]

TEMPLES AND "IDOLS"

From earliest days, the Sumerians built enormous temples. One of them, unearthed in Uruk and dating from about 3500 BCE, consists of several major buildings, the largest having nearly the area of a football field. All Sumerian buildings were constructed of baked mud bricks (similar to adobe), and the interiors were decorated with colorful frescoes. Although the floor plans of the temples always provided an area for the periodic public rites, most temple activities were closed to the public, hence many interior rooms were devoted to these more secret and sacred rites—in-cluding the holiest place of all, the sanctuary housing the God. Many ad-ditional rooms provided living quarters for the priests.

Baked mud bricks are easy to make and easy to use, but they wear out—although they were unusually durable and lasting in the dry climate of Sumer. Consequently, when a temple became too worn, the entire edi-fice was leveled and a new temple was built on the base provided by the old one. Since it was "a tenet of Mesopotamian faith that a temple should be rebuilt on the same 'consecrated' site,"[6] eventually many temples were piled one atop another and the site became higher and higher—some of the "last" temples were based fifty feet above the surrounding landscape.[7]

Even so, these were not ziggurats, the stepped temples for which the region was famous—the one at Babylon was immortalized as the Tower of Babel (the Sumerians also had a version of the "babel of tongues" nar-rative).[8] A ziggurat consisted of a set of huge square blocks (or floors) of decreasing area set one atop another, often having as many as five levels. Ascent was by an exterior stairway (or sometimes a ramp)—all religious ceremonies were held in a small shrine at the top. The lower terraces, created by the setback of each block, were often landscaped with trees and shrubs, hence the "Hanging Gardens" of Babylon.

The ruins of more than twenty ziggurats are known. But having been built anywhere from four to five thousand years ago of mud-baked brick, these ziggurats are not stately ruins like the Egyptian, Aztec, or Mayan pyramids, which were built of enduring stone. Rather, the known ziggurats long ago eroded into great heaps and now resemble hills. The largest of these is near Susa in southern Iran and is 336 feet per side at the base and is estimated to have been 174 feet tall (about seventeen stories), although the existing ruin is only about 80 feet high.[9] For a long time it was thought that the ziggurats were solid, having no internal passages or rooms. But in 1954 to 1955, Roman Ghirshman (1900–1984) excavated the ruin near Susa and discovered a stairway buried deep inside the second stage that was connected to a set of rooms. Later he found additional rooms that were walled up and not connected to a hallway. All the rooms were empty, but Ghirshman suspected that those connected to the stairway may have been intended as royal tombs, while those walled up may have been meant as symbolic tombs for the Gods.[10] No other ziggurat has been so fully excavated.

That the ziggurat included tombs for the Gods is consistent with the fact that in Sumer, as in most neolithic societies that preceded them in this region,[11] the dead usually were buried beneath their dwellings so that "their spirits continued to participate in the life of the family."[12] And a Sumerian temple was quite literally "the house of a God, the place where he [or she] has chosen to dwell . . . and for which reason it was created."[13] Consequently, the major aspect of each temple was the image of the God to whom the temple was dedicated. These were often very large and very elaborate—"most were made of precious wood and where not covered with garments were plated with gold. . . . They had the characteristic staring eyes made of precious stones inset in a naturalistic way and were clad in sumptuous garments of characteristic style, crowned with tiaras and adorned with pectorals."[14] And they were regarded as *living beings*! As the very influential Leo Oppenheim (1904–1974) pointed out, it was only in the myths that the Gods were said "to reside in cosmic localities"; in daily life the God was "considered present in the image."[15]

This aspect of ancient polytheism has often been denied or greatly downplayed by historians who have preferred to regard these as merely

The idol of Nintura, God of Storms, displays the enormous, staring eyes that were typical of depictions of the Gods in Sumer. This statue was one of many discovered buried in the ruins of an ancient temple by archaeologists from the University of Chicago. (Iraq Museum, Baghdad; Photo: Scala/Art Resource, New York)

symbols of invisible gods since it seemed obvious that even people in ancient times must have known that "idols" were not alive.[16] This view was encouraged by the fact that the Greeks paid little homage to their images of Gods,[17] and far more scholarly attention has been paid to Greek religion than to that of other ancient civilizations, despite the extreme lack of written sources. But in Sumer, Egypt, and most other ancient cultures, the "idols" clearly were thought to be fully alive (although some priests may have thought otherwise). Of course, Gods were presumed to have an independent existence, but they were believed to become resident in an idol in response to the appropriate rituals.[18] Priestly practices and duties involved not only direct worship of the "idol," but elaborate procedures for bathing, dressing, and feeding it.[19] "Idols" were offered only special foods and wines, and they "ate" behind a curtain. The construction and repair of the images of Gods involved great secrecy and a great deal of ritual—elaborate rites were required "to transform the lifeless matter into a receptacle of divine presence. During these nocturnal ceremonies they were endowed with 'life,' their eyes and mouths were 'opened' so that the images could see and eat."[20] In fact, the entire ritual used by Sumerian priests to animate the statue of a God has survived and recently was published in English.[21] It was an extremely elaborate undertaking and took many days—as one step the priests sewed a golden turtle inside a living turtle and threw it in the river. Throughout it is clear that the entire point was to bring the God to life.

Each Sumerian city-state had a temple dedicated to its own patron God, as well as temples devoted to the many other major deities, although several Gods of descending importance often occupied a single temple. This divine diversity did not reflect competing faiths—the Gods were part of a single cosmological vision, each acknowledging and interacting with each other. In similar fashion, the temples represented a "common faith," more like a set of parishes belonging to the same denomination than like a set of disputatious denominations. Although the priests of any given temple no doubt were concerned to gain adequate support, they were not embedded in an especially competitive religious marketplace. Temple communities were based on extensive land ownership and huge flocks. Financial records from excavated cuneiform tablets reveal that one temple in the Sumerian city of Uruk owned 5,000 to 7,000 cattle and 100,000 to 150,000 sheep.[22] Another temple in Uruk "possessed over 11,000 acres and [employed] 1,000 workmen."[23] Sumerian temple lands were divided three ways. Some were parceled out to commoners and was their basis of support. Another portion was rented to more affluent laypeople. The largest share was reserved for the God. This was known as *nigenna* land, and it was the basic source of support for the temple. All commoners were required to "volunteer" a specified number of days each year to cultivating *nigenna* land as well as to maintaining the dikes and irrigation system that watered it.[24] Since Gods only owned things in principle, the high priest was the real owner of a temple community, and this served as an overwhelming basis for power.

Elsewhere in the ancient civilized world, things were much the same. Huge temples housed elaborate, richly adorned images of Gods. Unlike the pyramids, the temples in Egypt were not as lofty as those of Sumer, but they covered larger areas despite not needing to provide a substantial public area. Temples in Greece were of surpassing beauty, although they seem to have served as much as monuments as they did as centers of worship. The Aztecs and Mayans also built huge temples. The Aztec Templo Mayor (known to the Aztecs as Coatepec) at Tenochtitlán (now Mexico City) was ninety-eight feet high. It consisted of a massive double pyramid, one side devoted to the God of War and the other to the God of Rain and Lightning and each ruled by a High Priest. Even larger is the Tigre Temple built by the Maya at El Mirador, which is 180 feet high (about eighteen stories). Many Mayan and Aztec temples are remarkably similar to the Sumerian ziggurats,[25] being pyramids ascended by very steep exterior steps to a shrine at the top (the Templo Mayor had two shrines on top). However, as in Egypt, these edifices were built of stone, not of mud bricks—huge sandstone blocks, held together with a very strong lime mortar.[26] As in Sumer and Egypt, these Aztec and Mayan building projects were funded by the "state" and were served by a full-time, highly trained, literate priesthood.

PRIESTS

In some ways the term *priest* (and *priestess*) referred to a different profession in ancient times than it does today, in that priests in ancient civilizations performed no pastoral functions, in part because they did not serve congregations. Instead, their focus was on performing rituals and on service to the Gods, not to humanity. However, then as now, **priests** are those who *serve in a relatively formal role as an intermediary between humans and God(s).*[27] As Plato explained, priests "understand how to offer our gifts to the gods in sacrifices in a manner pleasing to them, and they know, too, the right forms of prayer for petititioning the gods to bestow blessings on their worshippers."[28] Put another way, priests are *religious specialists.* Note that this definition excludes laity who sometimes perform acts of intercession, as when a parent leads prayers.[29]

The priests of Sumer formed a highly trained, closed professional guild. Most priests were descended from priestly families, but all underwent extensive training, nearly all of it devoted to ritual rather than to beliefs. Moreover, many priests specialized: some conducted major rituals, some fed the images of the Gods, others bathed the images, and some were exorcists who treated the ill. "All of these people formed a closed society which had its own rules, traditions and rights, lived partly from the revenues of the temple land ... partly 'from the altar' [sacrificial offerings], and played an important part in the affairs of state."[30]

Most Aztec priests and priestesses came from the nobility, but membership could not be directly hereditary as all Aztec priests and priestesses were required to be celibate.[31] The Aztecs admired rhetoric even more than did the ancient Greeks. Consequently, those most gifted in expressing wisdom were selected "to be high priests, lords, leaders, and captains, no matter how humble their estate. These ruled the states, led the armies, and presided in the temples," as Father Sahagún explained.[32] Priests and priestesses belonged to a set of "colleges," each devoted to the exclusive service of a specific God. In addition, one group of priests specialized in predicting the future by consulting the sacred texts as well as by reading signs and interpreting numbers, and their predictions controlled every facet of Aztec life.

Mayan priests and priestesses were not celibate, and most inherited their positions, although some of them came from the nobility as well.[33] In addition to performing religious rituals and divining the future, the Mayan priesthood devoted much of their effort to astronomy and to keeping the calendar.

Perhaps surprisingly, in Egypt during the Old Kingdom (c. 2686–2160 BCE), which was the era of pyramid building, the priesthood was rather small and staffed by part-time laymen. But come the Middle Kingdom (c. 2040–1786 BCE), a highly professional priesthood had developed. There is no record of a layperson ever having also been a priest during this era. "The priests now wear a costume denoting their position ... [and] the office, further, has become hereditary."[34] Rank within the priesthood, however, was appointed by the pharaoh. During the New Kingdom (c. 1570–330 BCE), priests were required to shave their heads, and five classes, or levels, of the priesthood had emerged. The High Priest, who presided over the Temple of Ammon at Thebes, had rapidly gained immense wealth and power. One pharaoh after another left long lists of enormous gifts made to this temple, until "its fortune was second only to the pharaoh's own."[35] This continued until a High Priest named Hrihor ousted Rameses XII, usurped the throne, and founded the twenty-first dynasty.

In Greece, the priesthood in many temples usually was restricted to one or two family lines, and elsewhere many priests and priestesses served only a limited term of office. In any event, only those entirely free from physical defects could serve.[36] Sexual abstinence was also often required of both priests and priestesses for a time prior to entering the temple sanctuary or serving in a particular ritual, and some temples required women to be virgins. Priests and priestesses usually "received a modest fee for their services . . . [but] there is no evidence that they were required to undergo any formal training or ordination before assuming their duties."[37] However, they were required to make an exclusive commitment to "one god or goddess [and to] one particular sanctuary."[38]

Given Greece's democratic regimes, the priesthood was not ruled by either a king or a High Priest, but nevertheless these were *polis* or city-state religions, and the priests were effectively civil servants, governed by "sacred laws" enacted by the local governing assembly.[39] Although individuals often paid for sacrifices, the temples did not depend upon donations. Most were funded from very extensive land-holdings—it is estimated that from 5 to 10 percent of all arable land belonged to the Greek temples—and this agricultural income was exceeded by regular tribute payments supplied by each city-state.[40]

RITUALS AND SACRIFICES

As to the rituals the priests conducted, we know those of Sumer in intimate detail because tablets have survived that served as textbooks to train priests in their performance. Many tablets consist mainly of prayers, but the prayers were always part of a specific ritual—"these rituals are carefully described in a section at the end of each prayer which addresses . . . the officiating priest . . . in order to regulate his movements and gestures as well as the nature of the sacrifice and the time and place it should be undertaken."[41] Perhaps remarkably, there is almost no variation in a prayer or its accompanying ritual over the centuries.

Music played a very important role in Sumerian rituals. Most of the recovered ritual poetry appears to have been hymns. Many "beautifully constructed harps and lyres [have been] excavated,"[42] and an elaborate ritual for making and consecrating new drum heads has survived.[43] Dance also seems to have played a prominent part in Sumerian worship. Many Egyptian rituals also required music, and it was provided by women of very high status who sang and played the sistrum (an early tambourine)—

most women of rank were identified as singers (*kem'at*) on their grave tablets.[44] But nowhere were music and dance of such ritual importance as among the Aztecs and Maya. Temple festivals were marked by "priests singing, drums beating in complicated rhythms, thousands of dancers circling around a central point, slowly, then with increasing speed until they whirled . . ."[45]

Most Sumerian temple rituals had very restricted audiences—only priests and, sometimes, various members of the upper nobility were admitted. Once a year each major God was treated to a feast day whereupon the statues of the Gods from other temples "visited" and gathered in the main courtyard, which was closed to the public on this occasion. There were many other special ritual days, and the new moon and full moon were always celebrated. A five-day ceremonial greeted the new year, during which the major rite enacted a holy marriage. In this ritual, the king would take the part of a major God, one of the priestesses represented Ishtar, the Goddess of Carnal Love, and the two engaged in sex in order to ensure "the fecundity and prosperity of Sumer and its people."[46] In addition were the many ceremonies held in each temple every day. As part of these activities, large amounts of food and drink were brought for the Gods and, using the proper rituals, these offerings were mostly consumed by the priests. Of course, each day also brought supplicants seeking to have special rituals done for their benefit.

Few if any of these supplicants were "ordinary" citizens. In fact, the statue of a temple's God was not visible from the public area, "as it was at a right angle with the temple doorway, or hidden behind a curtain, depending on the layout of the temple."[47] Only priests and the elite were admitted to the area from which a God could be seen. This exclusivity stemmed in part from the fact that these were "state" temples, hence the priests had no need to engender popular support, and from the disdain that the elite typically felt toward the populace. The king was the supreme priest.[48] He also built the temples and supported the priests: "The kings and rulers of the city-states . . . [believed they] could ensure long lives for themselves as well as the well-being and prosperity of their subjects by building, repairing, and furnishing the temples that were presumably the dwelling places of their gods."[49]

Temples in Egypt also limited public access. No one but priests and a few high officials (including women singers) could even enter the temples.

Perhaps because they had no lay audience, Egyptian temple rituals were standardized to the point that their performance was essentially "mind-less. . . . No spontaneous . . . behavior ever took place."[50]

Things were far more public in Greece, where the sacrifices could be seen by all, being held in the open air in front of a temple, while within Greek temples, the statue of the God or Goddess was visible within the main interior room. Indeed, anyone could enter and offer sacrifices in most Greek temples, provided he or she was ritually pure. Usually, all that was required was to wash one's hands and face in a basin provided at the entrance. Some temples were more restrictive, requiring that an entrant be morally pure, and some excluded certain groups—men were not per-mitted within sanctuaries of Demeter, and women were excluded from temples devoted to Herakles.[51] However, Greek temples had at least one inner room to which access was very restricted. Many suggestions have been made concerning rites reserved for these inner rooms, but we don't know what went on in them. A very plausible case has been made that these rooms were used merely for the safekeeping of religious valuables,[52] which is consistent with the fact that the Greek temples had abundant treasures. An inventory of valuables held by the Parthenon, conducted in 413 BCE and engraved in stone, recorded "a golden libation bowl, from which they sprinkle themselves, unweighed; 121 silver libation bowls, the weight of these 2 Talents 432 Drachmas; 3 silver drinking horns, the weight of these 528 Drachmas; 5 silver cups, the weight of these 167 Drachmas; a silver lamp, the weight of this 38 Drachmas . . ."[53]

Ritual life among the Aztecs and Maya was dominated by the calendar. The Aztecs had an accurate system divided into eighteen months, each with twenty days, and five additional, unlucky days—there were many other unlucky days, too. Each month included a feast day, which involved nonstop celebrations, parades, and ceremonies that included grisly orgies of human sacrifice.[54] All of this was entirely public, the human sacrifices being accomplished at the top of temple pyramids, the heartless bod-ies being heaved down the staircases for the edification of the spectators below. It was much the same among the Maya. A 365-day year made up of nineteen months was punctuated by a heavy schedule of rituals and ceremonies, especially if the auguries had predicted an unlucky coming year.[55] And from the Mayan pyramid temples there also came an ava-lanche of bodies.

GODS

As for the objects of all these rites and prayers, the Gods of Sumer, Egypt, Greece, and of the Aztec and Mayan Empires were conceived of as ordinary humans, aside from having some supernatural powers and (usually) being immortal. That is, most of the Gods looked like human beings, and all had human desires and defects: they thirsted, hungered, bathed, lied, stole, murdered, envied, hated, loved, and lusted.[56]

Early on, the Sumerian pantheon included hundreds of Gods, but they became considerably fewer over time with "the fusion of one divine figure into another, often with the [confusing] retention of both names."[57] At the top were three male Gods: An, Enlil, and Enki. **An** was a withdrawn High God. He had created the universe and begotten all the other Gods, but he no longer played "an important part in earthly affairs and remained aloof in the heavens as a majestic though somewhat pale figure."[58] With An having withdrawn, **Enlil** became the most important Sumerian God. Somewhat confusingly he, too, was referred to as the "father of the Gods," as well as the creator of agriculture and the God responsible for bringing forth the day. Perhaps his major role was as the source of the divine right of kings and other rulers. Paraphrasing ancient tablets, Kramer noted that "it is Enlil who has given them kingship of the land, who has made the land prosperous for them, who gave them all the lands to conquer by his strength. It is Enlil who pronounces the king's name and gives him his scepter and looks upon him with a favorable eye."[59] Enlil was believed to dwell in his temple in the city of Nippur, "the most important religious center of the Sumerians."[60]

Enki, the name also means "cunning," was the third major God of Sumer. He did the actual labor of creation, following the plans of An or Enlil (depending). Enki ruled over the abyss, located beyond the great sea. Enki was the brother of Enlil and son of An. Fourth among the Sumerian Gods, and only slightly less exalted than An, Enlil, and Enki, was the Mother Goddess, **Ninmah**. She was assumed to have been An's consort and therefore the mother of all the other Gods—sometimes referred to as Nintu, the lady who gave birth.[61]

In addition to these four, the Sumerians worshipped the usual Nature Gods, including **Nintura**, God of Storms, and **Nipper**, the God of Wind, and three "important astral deities": the Moon God, **Nanna** (or Sin);

Nanna's son, the Sun God, **Utu**; and Nanna's daughter, known as Inanna, or **Ishtar** (the Semitic form).[62] Nanna's primary duty was to light up the night, just as it was Utu's task to light up the day. But it is Ishtar who spices up many an otherwise dreary account of Sumerian religion. Not primarily because she was the Goddess of War and of Rain, but because she was the Goddess of Carnal Love and the special Goddess of Prostitutes—and for that reason is usually depicted in the nude. Ishtar is involved in many myths, usually taking and then betraying lovers. A surviving hymn reveals her to have been insatiable:

Sixty then sixty satisfy themselves in turn upon her nakedness.
Young men have tired, Ishtar will not tire.[63]

Many of the rituals enacted at Ishtar's temples involved orgies, real and simulated, and not only were prostitutes abundant among those who served her shrine, so were castrated priests. A number of figurines of couples engaged in sexual intercourse have been found in temples devoted to Ishtar, and in some of them the woman rests on a structure thought to be an altar. Some depictions of a couple having sex include other figures, suggesting a sexual rite. A number of artificial penises made of wood or clay and apparently meant to be worn and used also have been unearthed in temples of Ishtar.[64]

In addition to these nine Gods, scores of minor Gods appear in Sumerian writings—there are frequent references to the fifty "great" gods.[65] Sumerians were also believed to be afflicted by a flock of minor demons hovering everywhere, responsible for diseases and other misfortunes, and requiring exorcism.[66]

No ancient civilizations possessed a truly coherent theology like that found in the Torah, Bible, or Qur'an—although Sumer seems to have surpassed the rest in this respect. There were too many Gods, with too many proclivities, too many biases, and too many conflicting accounts. Any coherent summary of the pantheons of these cultures necessarily imposes far more system and order than is really warranted, since it cannot be derived from ancient syntheses, but must be a modern assemblage based on disparate, uncoordinated writings about this or that divine being—"to expect from Egypt a coherent body of religious doctrine means looking for a single tree where there is multifarious growth."[67] Not only that, aside from Sumer and Mesoamerica, the sources are so remarkably slim

This votive offering was mass produced from a mold and sold in large numbers to those who wished to honor Ishtar, the Sumerian Goddess of Carnal Love, by depositing the object in her temple. It was found near Susa in Iran. (Louvre, Paris; Photo: Erich Lessing/Art Resource, New York)

that some lack of coherence and system may simply reflect our ignorance. When I first ventured into religious history,[68] I was quite shocked to discover how very little we know even about Greek and Roman religions—the "mysteries" of the mystery cults remain deeply mysterious. If only everyone had used clay tablets—presuming that these things were ever written down.

What we do know of the ancient Gods is that the various pantheons were remarkably similar—perhaps due to diffusion. Indeed, the great Greek historian Herodotus (c. 484–425 BCE) claimed that the Gods of Greece had been adopted from Egypt, and many modern scholars agree.[69] There is equally strong evidence that both Greek and Egyptian religions display strong Sumerian influences. In fact, both Homer's *Iliad* and *Odyssey* display many significant similarities to the Sumerian *Epic of Gilgamesh*.[70]

In the Egyptian system, **Ra** (also Re) was the equivalent of the Sumerian An, a withdrawn Creator God. He, too, had made the universe and was the father of all the Gods, but had wearied of earth and, assisted by

Nut, he was raised into the heavens, taking on the aspect of the sun, to rise each morning and cross the sky. Depicted as a falcon-headed man, crowned with the sun disk, Ra was regarded as the chief God, although he was believed to have been replaced by **Thoth**, the Moon God, as ruler over earth.[71] A typical inconsistency in Egyptian sources is that **Amon** (or Amun, or Amen, or Ammon), not Ra, was regarded as the king of the Gods and was the patron God of the pharaohs. Some have resolved this by suggesting that Amon is simply another name for Ra, since he also was referred to as Amon-Ra. This seems unlikely since it is possible to trace the evolution of Amon from a minor, local fertility God, to the God of Agriculture, and then to the exaltation by the pharaohs as their personal divinity.[72] He was in no sense a Creator God. Indeed, aside from the creation of the Gods, Egyptian religion paid little attention to the Creation, at least in sources that have survived.

Over time, Egypt evolved an immense pantheon. Erik Hornung catalogued 104 significant Egyptian deities,[73] and in his definitive work, Richard H. Wilkinson listed more then 450.[74] Although many of these were very minor figures, more than 30 were of major significance. But even about these Gods our knowledge is very confused. **Hathor** is considered Egypt's "greatest goddess"[75] and the model for the Greek Goddess Aphrodite. But was she the mother or the wife of Horus? Was she the Goddess of Heaven or the Underworld? Was she the Moon Goddess or the Sun Goddess? Was she the Cow Goddess or the Goddess of Love and Intoxication? The answer to all these questions must be "yes." And what about **Horus**? Was he the Sky God or the Sun God? Was he even "Horus," since he seems to have been addressed by dozens of other names? Then there was **Mut** (not to be confused with Nut), the Great Mother, wife of Amon, and a member of the "Theban Triad" along with Amon and **Khonsu**, the latter being either a Moon God, the God of Healing, or "a bloodthirsty deity"[76] given to killing and eating other Gods. The Greeks renamed him Herakles. Another major God was **Min**, male God of Fertility, always depicted with an erection, and who eventually became confused with the God Amon, becoming Min-Amon. The Greeks renamed him Pan. **Montu** was the God of War, and a solar God, who sometimes was confused with Horus and sometimes with Ra. The details about **Osiris** and **Isis** also are confusing, but we meet them in Chapter 4.

Although Greece imported many, perhaps most, of its deities from Egypt, the Greek Gods were fewer in number and more clearly defined. According to Herodotus, **Zeus** was the Greek counterpart of the Egyptian God Amon.[77] But to ask just how Zeus fit into the Greek scheme of Gods brings us face-to-face with the remarkable fact that not only do no Greek "scriptures" exist, it is probable that none were ever written.[78] We have little more than literary works such as the *Iliad* and the *Odyssey*, two lengthy poems by Hesiod (*Theogony* and *Works and Days*), and commentaries by secular philosophers, plus the evidence of statues, frescoes, and temple ruins, to inform us. There must have been many oral accounts of the Gods, but none survived.

Apparently, Zeus was the son of **Cronus**, a terrible Creator God who ate his children because he feared they would overthrow him, but he was tricked by Zeus and Zeus's mother, **Rhea**, who forced Cronus to disgorge his children, then forced him into exile. Cronus's children then divided the universe by casting lots, with the underworld going to **Hades** and his wife, **Persephone**; the oceans to **Poseidon**; and the heavens and earth to Zeus. The principal Greek Gods lived on Mount Olympus and were believed to form a family, many being the sons and daughters of Zeus and his wife, **Hera**, although the exact relationships are inconsistently given across the sources (some identify Hera as Zeus's sister, for example). The twelve principal Gods on Olympus, including Zeus, Hera, and Poseidon, were **Aphrodite**, who was in charge of sex; **Apollo,** who was God of Learning, Prophecy, and the Sun; and **Artemis**, Goddess of Animals and Hunting. **Ares** and **Athena** were in charge of war; **Demeter** was the Earth Mother; **Dionysos** was God of Drunkenness; **Hephaistos** was God of Fire and of Crafts; and **Hermes** was the Divine Trickster.[79]

As depicted, Zeus was not sympathetic to humans. Hesiod tells that Zeus denied mortals even such a basic necessity as fire, and they gained it only when his cousin **Prometheus** stole it and gave it to them. Zeus then created women as punishment to men for having gained fire and proceeded to make "life hard for humans."[80] In addition, the Greeks accepted fate as the primary (if blind) moving force of life and the universe, and believed that not even Zeus could influence its workings.[81] Although even the number-one Greek God seems rather limited as to interests and activities, this may have been made up for by divine quantity—in addition to the twelve major Gods listed above, the Greeks worshipped a huge cast of minor divinities, perhaps more than three hundred.[82]

It seems obvious that many of the Gods and Goddesses of Egypt and Greece can be traced to earlier Sumerian divinities. That is not suprising, as most of the culture of *any* society, modern as well as primitive, is borrowed in the sense that most items—ideas, beliefs, and arts, as well as technology—did not originate in that culture, but somewhere else, and often in the distant past. Social scientists identify the *process by which cultural innovations spread from one society to others* as **diffusion**. Given that Sumer's pantheon evolved long before many of its Gods and Goddesses diffused to Egypt and Greece, it seems odd that the Sumerian version seems more sophisticated and coherent than either the Egyptian or Greek versions—but that may simply be due to an abundance of carefully written, detailed documentation from Sumer.

Be that as it may, the Aztec Gods are as well documented as those of Sumer, not only through the survival of sacred texts, but from the fine ethnographic studies written by Spanish missionaries, especially the extensive study by Father Bernardino de Sahagún, who arrived in Mexico in 1529 when it was still possible to interview authentic Aztec priests. Father Sahagún learned the language and produced a detailed account of Aztec beliefs and rituals.[83] He also saved several vital sacred books, including the major work now known as the *Florentine Codex*.

A revealing aspect of Aztec belief is that the chapter on the Gods in the *Florentine Codex* begins with the acknowledgment that "where the gods began is not well known."[84] In part this is because Aztec Gods did a great deal of dying, often slain by other Gods, and also because of the periodic death of the whole universe. In any event, the Aztecs believed in a semi-withdrawn Creator God named **Ometecuhtli** and his wife, **Omeciuatl**.[85] Although they were the parents of all the Gods as well as of humankind, they were thought to reign, but not to govern, having "been pushed into the background by the vigorous crowd of younger and more active Gods." However, they still fixed "the birth-date of each living being, and thus its fate."[86] The Aztecs believed that the universe periodically was destroyed by catastrophes, the current age, or "sun," being the fifth. The second sun had been ended by a hurricane that turned all men into monkeys. The third ended in a rain of fire, and the fourth was ended by a huge flood that lasted for fifty-two years and which only one man and one woman survived, only to be transformed into dogs.

The offspring of Ometecuhtli and Omeciuatl created the fifth world. But there was no sun, so all of the Gods gathered around a divine hearth where a fire was burning. After several Gods failed to summon the nerve required to do so, **Nanauatzin** (the Pimply One) "cast himself into the fire. . . . Thereupon he burned; his body crackled and sizzled,"[87] and Nanauatzin disappeared into the heavens. Then the Gods waited for the sun to rise, as eventually it did, and a new age was begun. Unfortunately, to keep the sun rising and to thereby avert the disaster of the earth going dark, it was necessary to keep feeding the sun with human blood—a belief that had extraordinary consequences, as will be seen.

As befitted their extremely warlike culture, the Aztecs' most exalted deity was **Huitzilopochtli**, God of War. He was the son of **Coatlicue**, the Mother Goddess who had borne four hundred Gods before him—his was a miraculous conception since he had no father. His birth was told in an incredibly hostile "myth" (see below), involving as it did the newborn God slaying all of his siblings—admittedly, in defense of his mother. The remainder of the Aztec pantheon is very similar to that of Egypt and Greece: **Huaxtec,** the Love Goddess; **Tlaloc**, God of Rain and of Lightning; **Itzpapalotl**, Goddess of Fertility; **Otontecuhtl**, the Fire God; **Texcatlipoca**, God of Night; and several hundred minor Gods, including **Tepoztécatl**, the God of Drunkenness.

The Mayan Gods also are well known, not only through ruins and the very detailed accounts written by Spanish priests, but by books and inscriptions actually written by Mayan priests and readable since the "decoding" of the Mayan script a generation ago.[88] Like the Aztecs, the Maya believed that the universe had been created and then destroyed several times before the current era. They expected that the current creation would end beneath a deluge. Some Maya worshipped **Hunab Ku** as the creator of the present universe, but he, too, was semi-withdrawn, and it was his son **Itzamná** who ruled the Mayan pantheon. This pantheon consisted of the usual set of "nature" Gods, including the Earthquake God, **Kisin**; the Rain God, **Chac**; the Moon Goddess, **Ixchel**; along with **Yum Kaax**, God of Corn and of the Forest; **Hurakan**, God of Lightning; **Ek Chuah**, the God of War; and **Ah Puch**, the Lord of Hell.[89]

Thus we have seen that withdrawn Creator Gods were typical of the temple religions in the ancient societies and that all of these featured a very similar set of "nature" divinities.

"MYTHS"

The word *myth* is inescapably pejorative. It identifies some narratives as false, as being fairy tales.[90] To refer to Greek "mythology" is quite different from referring to Greek "history" in that historical accounts might be true, but "myths" most certainly are not. At issue is that those narratives identified as "myths" include Gods or supernatural creatures in the account, although they may not be the central figures. Thus, to identify anything as a "myth" is often interpreted to mean that it is the product of irrational thought and probably was created in a pre-modern society—as illustrated by the contemptuous remarks of the sociologist Read Bain (1893–1972):

> The myth emerges from the uncritical verbalization of hopes and fears. It flourishes by repetition and authoritarian tradition, is sustained by coercive control, and finally dies out when science and common sense demonstrate its absurdity and harmfulness. It seldom dies a decent and definitive death, however. In subtle forms it lingers on to confuse men's minds and confound their management of practical affairs.[91]

Bain was, of course, a militant atheist, but the invidious qualities of the term *myth*, even when used by religious scholars, can be recognized in Moshe Weinfeld's conventional statement in the authoritative *Encyclopedia of Religion*, that there is no "mythology in the religion of Israel."[92] He continued: "Mythology, here defined as storytelling about the gods and their life, activities, and adventures is inconceivable in the monotheistic sphere." Granted that the Bible includes no biography of Yahweh, but it tells of purely otherworldly events such as Satan having been ejected from Heaven, as well as accounts of the Creation, the Fall, the Flood, the Parting of the Red Sea, and similar "stories" that Weinfeld and everyone else would classify as "myths" were they associated with any other religion or God.

Thus, in an early draft I suggested the term *spiritual narrative* as a more neutral substitute for *myth*. I dropped that substitution because it was cumbersome and seemed too idiosyncratic. Instead, I settled for placing quotation marks around the term *myth* and its various forms in order to indicate that I use the term in an entirely non-pejorative sense. I define a **"myth"** as an *account that may happen in this world or in "another" world, but which includes active supernatural participants.* Some "myths" involve only Gods; some tell of extensive interactions between Gods and humans; and in some the focus is on humans, with Gods in the background. A "myth" may be included in scriptures, as is the story of Noah in *Genesis*. Or it may stand alone, as with the *Epic of Gilgamesh*.

The most fundamental assumption about "myths" is not that they are incredible tales, but that they convey hidden and revealing truths about their cultures of origin. This has generated such an enormous and amazingly trivial literature of interpretation that one is tempted to agree with Leo Oppenheim, who proposed that no account of Sumerian "mythology" should be written.[93] Oppenheim was responding to the excesses of literary imagination, the "deep" interpretations, and to the truly bizarre "symbolic" decoding that so many academics have imposed on "mythology." Consider these all-too-typical examples.

A "Star-Husband" "myth" was quite common among the North American Indians. It involves two girls lying outside at night looking at the sky, who pick out two stars they would like for husbands. Having fallen asleep, they suddenly are transported into the sky, where they find themselves married to these stars, which have taken the form of men. Then the girls discover a hole in the sky and descend a rope back to earth again. According to Michael P. Carroll, a latter-day Freudian, rising and descending always refers to sexual intercourse. In addition, lowering a rope through a hole can "reasonably be interpreted as a metaphor for a penis entering a vagina."[94] In addition, since each of these girls wishes to marry a man on high, it easily can be recognized that the whole "myth" is about girls wanting to have sex with their fathers.[95]

In rather similar fashion, Joseph Campbell (1904–1987), undoubtedly the most prominent interpreter of "myths" in his time, explained to his many readers and television viewers that when Circe directed Odysseus to the underworld to find out about his journey home, she really sent him there to gain greater insight into his sexuality. Campbell was not deterred by the fact that Homer tells us that once in the underworld Odysseus did learn about the dangers he would face in attempting to journey back home, and that nothing whatever is suggested about sexuality.[96] For far too many who study "mythology," a snake, a cigar, a rope, a spear, a candle, or anything "long and narrow"[97] is really a penis and most apertures are vaginas. The notion that sometimes a story might really be about candles or even about a hole in the clouds is disdained.

Of course, some "myths" *are* about sex—those concerning the Sumerian Goddess Ishtar are about little else. But out of respect for the sources, I think we should take a "myth" to mean what it was understood to mean by those from whose culture it came. No doubt the ancient Greeks were content to believe that after many years of fighting against Troy, Odysseus just wanted to get home safely to his wife.[98] As for the Indians, it seems far more plausible that, rather than being about incest, the Star-Husband story was meant to convey the moral that one should be careful what one wishes for. Moreover, we should not assume that these narratives ever were regarded as entirely true. Most "myths" are not parts of scriptures: they do not *expound* doctrines; they *illustrate* them. Thus, most Greeks probably accepted the essential characterizations of the Gods as depicted in the *Iliad* and the *Odyssey*, but these great stories lived on, not because people thought them sacred, but because they were so entertaining—they were gripping adventure tales recited by storytellers, not expounded by priests. In this way Homer's great epics resemble the immensely popular[99] "Left Behind" novels of present times.[100] Most readers of these novels accept the underlying Christian doctrines that give plausibility of the plots, but they also remain fully aware that these are works of fiction. It is, of course, impossible to know what ordinary Greeks really thought about Homer's epics, but we do know that most Greek philosophers regarded them "as allegories revealing naturalistic and moral truths."[101] Hence, unlike scripture, the truth claims of most "myths" may be regarded as problematic.

Despite the many silly and pretentious interpretations imposed upon them, many of the surviving "myths" do help us grasp the religious character of particular cultures and so deserve study and contemplation. The Sumerians bequeathed us two of such striking quality and lasting significance that it is appropriate that they be summarized here. The first is the Sumerian account of the Flood, which closely parallels the story in Genesis. The second is the *Epic of Gilgamesh*, an early poetic masterpiece that displays many remarkable similarities to the *Iliad* and the *Odyssey*. Finally, a revealing Aztec narrative is recounted.

The Flood

Every reader will be familiar with the biblical account of Noah and the ark. Many will not know that there is an earlier and nearly identical Sumerian story. There are several versions of the Sumerian narrative, differing primarily in the name of Noah's counterpart. One version, which has come down to us on a broken tablet, begins with a summary of the Creation and then shifts to reporting that many lesser divinities were very upset about the decision by the highest Gods to bring a flood and destroy humanity. Ziusudra, "a pious, god-fearing king who is constantly watching for divine dreams and revelations"[102] is told of this plan by Enki. The next part of the story is missing, but must have included instructions for building a huge boat and surviving the deluge. When the tablet picks up again, it is in the midst of a flood that raged for seven days and nights, after which Utu, the Sun God, dries everything out. Ziusudra prostrates himself before Utu and offers him sacrificial oxen and sheep. Subsequently, Ziusudra is deified by An and Enlil (the two highest Sumerian Gods) and goes to live in Paradise.

Another, far more detailed version is included in the *Epic of Gilgamesh*. In pursuit of the secret of eternal life, Gilgamesh encounters Utnapishtim, who tells him how he alone was warned of the Flood. He was instructed to tear down his house, build a ship, and take with him "the seed of all living creatures." Soon he had a huge, seven-decked vessel, caulked and loaded with pairs of beasts, his family, some relatives, and workmen. Then came the terrible storm. Even the Gods were frightened and regretted their actions:

> *The gods cowered like dogs and crouched in distress.*
> *Ishtar cried out like a woman in travail . . .*
> *The gods sat bowed and weeping . . .*
> *Six days and six nights*
> *The wind blew, the downpour, the tempest and the flood*
> *overwhelmed the land . . .*

But on the seventh day things were quiet:

> *I opened a window and light fell upon my face.*
> *I looked upon the "sea," all was silence,*
> *And all mankind had turned to clay.*[103]

The boat landed on a mountaintop. After a week, Ut-napishtim sent out a dove, but it came back. So did a swallow. But when he sent forth a raven, it found a home. Ut-napishtim and his passengers then disembarked and offered a sacrifice to the Gods. So pleased were they that life had survived, that the Gods granted Ut-napishtim and his wife immortality.

This Sumerian account of the Flood has often been used to disparage the Bible as nothing but a compendium of "borrowed myths," while too many Jews and Christians either have dismissed this overlap as a coincidence, or have remained blissfully unaware of it. More significant is the fact that there are not merely these two very similar accounts of the Flood, but there are scores of them! The Flood is one of the most common of all "myths,"[104] found not only in cultures of the Near East, but as far away as the Maori in New Zealand,[105] the North American Indians, as well the Aztecs and the Maya.[106]

For more than a century, geologists, archaeologists, and Bible scholars searched for evidence that the Flood actually occurred. Of course, there is no scientific basis for the claim that the entire earth ever was covered with a flood, but there is evidence of an immense flood in the Near East at what would seem to be an appropriate time.[107] In addition, the Sumerian list of kings reports those who served before and after the Flood. While a huge local flood would help explain the prevalence of Flood narratives in this area, it would not explain the existence of such "myths" elsewhere, although most cultures no doubt were fully aware of severe floods. Unfortunately, the virtual universality of the Flood narratives has encouraged a great deal of interpretive nonsense, including that these stories arose from dreams based on the repressed need to urinate,[108] and (what else?) incest guilt.[109] But the edifying aspect of the narrative—that even if everyone else turns to sin, each individual retains full moral responsibility—seems of such universal value that it is theologically credible to trace the many instances of the myth to a common source, even if no actual catastrophe was involved. And it seems to me that the the purpose of myths is primarily to make and sustain an edifying moral. In this instance, the immense drama of the catastrophic flood is such a good story that it will continue to be told; hence its edifying moral concerning personal responsibility in a sinful world will continue to be heard. In that way myths resemble the parables told by Jesus to edify his hearers. Although not presented as factual accounts, the Parables of the Talents, the Good Samaritan, or the Prodigal Son are such good stories that they serve as enduring vehicles for their moral teaching. Put another way, the story of the Flood may be a compelling example of divine "baby talk," of God addressing humans in language that is comprehensible to them at a particular time.

The Epic of Gilgamesh

The heart of this great epic is a hero's desperate search for the means to avoid death. Long dismissed as a mythical figure, Gilgamesh is now believed to have been the actual king of the Sumerian city Uruk, sometime around 2600 BCE.[110] He must have been a remarkable man to have inspired such an extensive mythology, but we know nothing of him other than that his name is on a list of kings. The surviving tablets inscribed with the extraordinary poem telling his adventures date from around 1600 BCE. The account below ill-serves the poetic grace of the original.

Gilgamesh was very strong, brave, and handsome. But he was a relentless womanizer, and this became a problem for the citizens in his city-state of Uruk. So they complained to the great God Anu, who then created a wild version, or double, of Gilgamesh, called Enkidu—who could challenge Gilgamesh and distract him from pursuing everyone's daughter or wife. But Gilgamesh was too smart. He hired a comely whore to seduce and civilize Enkidu, who soon learned to bathe and anoint himself. He also learned to consume strong drink. Then, after a terrible fight, Gilgamesh and Enkidu became fast friends and soon went venturing together. After several bloody exploits, Gilgamesh encountered the Goddess Ishtar, who fell in love with him and proposed marriage. Tactlessly, Gilgamesh responded by reminding the unfaithful Ishtar of her many lovers and their unpleasant fates. For revenge, Ishtar asked the God Anu to send the Bull of Heaven to ravage Gilgamesh's kingdom of Uruk. But Enkidu grabbed the bull by the horns and Gilgamesh cut its throat. Then, as Ishtar cursed at Gilgamesh, Enkidu tore off one of the beast's legs and threw it in her face.

The Gods responded to this incredible sacrilege by causing Enkidu to die. This shook Gilgamesh. For the first time he recognized his own mortality. As the poem recounts:

> Fearing death I roam over the steppe;
> The matter of my friend rests heavy upon me.
> How can I be silent? How can I be still?
> My friend, whom I loved, has turned to clay,
> Must I, too, like him, lay me down
> Not to rise again for ever and ever?[111]

Upon hearing that Ut-napishtim, the ark-builder, knew the secret of immortality, Gilgamesh made a long, adventurous journey to him. Ut-napishtim did impart the secret to Gilgamesh—a thorny plant of life grows in the depths of the ocean. After tying heavy rocks to his feet, Gilgamesh reached the bottom, picked the plant, and survived. Then, while Gilgamesh was sleeping off his ordeal on the beach, along came a snake and stole the plant. Sadly, Gilgamesh could not escape death, and his coming to terms with his mortality is the main point of the story, as it also is the primary theme of the *Odyssey*.

In 1890, William Gladstone (1809–1898), a frequent prime minister of Great Britain, published a book in which he claimed that newly translated Sumerian texts contained many remakable similarities with Homer's epics.[112] Of course, he was immediately ridiculed by the scholarly world as an untrained "outsider." Nevertheless, today all the leading classicists not only agree that "the *Epic of Gilgamesh* combines the power and tragedy of the *Iliad* with the wanderings and marvels of the *Odyssey*,"[113] but that there are so many stylistic and substantive similarities that Homer must have been familiar with this and other Sumerian literary works.[114] What this does, of course, is give compelling evidence that not only "history," but "culture" began at Sumer—that the cultural roots of Egypt, Greece, and hence of Rome and Western civilization in general, lie deep in the "fertile crescent" formed by the Tigris and Euphrates Rivers.

But there would not seem to be any Sumerian roots to the civilizations that arose in the Western hemisphere. Aside from the Stone Age culture brought by migrants from Asia who crossed into Alaska and roamed south, it would seem that the Aztec, Mayan, and Inca cultures developed on their own. Yet they, too, evolved into temple religions and worshipped the usual set of Nature Gods. Where they mainly differed from those in the Old World was in the violent and bloody character of their major rituals (as will be seen). Perhaps that is why their myths were bloody affairs as well.

The Birth of Huitzilopochtli

The most important of all Aztec "myths" begins with the Goddess Coatlicue, mother of four hundred Gods and Goddesses, sweeping the temple on Coatepec, the Serpent Mountain. A small ball of fine feathers fell upon her. She placed it on her breast, and when it suddenly disappeared, she knew she was pregnant. When word of this reached her four hundred offspring in the south, they were insulted, and the Goddess Coyolzauhqui aroused their anger, exhorting them that "my brothers, she has dishonored us, we must kill our mother [and] what she carries in her womb."[115] Coatlicue was both saddened and frightened that her children meant to kill her. But Huitzilopochtli, who was still in her womb, calmed her by saying, "Do not be afraid, I know what I must do." Meanwhile the four hundred Gods adorned themselves "as for war. . . . Their arrows had barbed points. Then they began to move."

As the army of Gods stormed up the mountainside, Huitzilopochtli sprang from his mother's womb full grown, in full war regalia—just as the armed and armored Athena had sprung from the forehead of Zeus. Huitzilopochtli put his brothers and sisters to flight and chased them four times around the mountain. Grabbing a serpent of fire, he used it to decapitate his evil sister Coyolzauhqui with one swing, "her body went falling [down the mountain] and it went crashing to pieces in various places, her arms, her legs, her body kept falling."[116] The other Gods realized they could not defend themselves against Huitzilopochtli's wrath and begged for mercy. But Huitzilopochtli could not be satisfied, and he killed them all and stripped them of all their warrior regalia. In tribute to this great deed, more than "seven thousand ritual objects from conquered and allied communities . . . were arranged according to Aztec cosmic symbolism into the base of the Templo Mayor" dedicated to Huitzilopochtli.[117] Also in his honor, a constant stream of victims, dressed in plumes, were forced to climb the stairs up the side of the temple to the altar at the top, there to be killed and tumbled down, in a ritual reenactment of Huitzilopochtli's slaying of the four hundred Gods.

Huitzilopochtli wielding his deadly serpent of fire, as depicted by the Aztecs in a manuscript preserved by Fra Diego Durán (1537–1588), a Spanish monk who learned the Aztec language and wrote sympathetic accounts of their customs and religion. (Biblioteca Nacional, Madrid; Photo: Bildarchiv Preussischer Kulturbesitz/Art Resource, New York)

MORALITY

Of course, Sumer, Egypt, and other ancient civilizations all had moral codes that governed behavior, but morality was not rooted primarily in religious justifications.[118] Moreover, in these ancient societies the moral emphasis was collective, not individual; lapses on the part of one or several members of the community, such as failure to properly propitiate the Gods, brought punishment to all—it was cities, not individuals, that suffered for offending the Gods. But aside from requiring humans to venerate them properly, the Gods often seemed to care little about human behavior, moral or immoral. In fact, the Greeks did not regard morality as God-given, but of human origins—"Greek gods do not give laws."[119] Nor could they, since the residents of Mount Olympus were, as William Foxwell Albright (1891–1971) put it, "unedifying examples."[120] For, as Mary Lefkowitz explained, the Greek Gods "exist to please themselves, not to please or serve humanity. They offer no hope that justice will be done to any individual. . . . They do not suggest that it is easy or always possible for a mortal to distinguish right from wrong."[121]

The Aztecs and the Maya also emphasized collective guilt and punishment, but they did acknowledge that at least some Gods could know their innermost thoughts. This prayer to Texcatlipoca, the God of Night, was recorded by Father Sahagún:

"O master, O our lord . . . thou seest, thou knowest . . . that which is within us: what we say, what we think, our minds, our hearts."[122]

A major reason why the ancient temple religions played a peripheral role in sustaining individual morality was because they lacked attractive doctrines concerning individual salvation. Since, with few exceptions, humans faced a miserable afterlife whether or not they had been virtuous, there was no compelling religious reward for virtue.

THE AFTERLIFE

Sumerians expected that after death they would descend into a dismal underworld[123] to pursue an unattractive existence:

Where dust is their food, clay their sustenance;
Where they see no light and dwell in darkness . . .[124]

The Greeks also believed in a very unheavenly afterlife—that the dead endured a drab existence in an unattractive, shadowy underworld, in "the dank halls of Hades."[125] In the words of Achilles, speaking from beyond the grave to Odysseus, "I would rather be the servant of another, of a poor man who had little substance, than be lord over all the dead."[126]

The Egyptians envisioned a far more pleasant afterlife, but initially they believed that only pharaoh, being himself a God, lived on after death, and what was believed about the fate of everyone else is uncertain. But by about 2000 BCE, it was accepted that other Egyptians could enjoy an afterlife, too, if they were sufficiently wealthy to afford the necessary rituals, mummification, and an adequate tomb. The Sumerians also accepted that the afterlife could be greatly improved by proper preparations and burial practices. The result in both Egypt and Sumer was a mammoth commitment of resources to build elaborate tombs, to assemble expensive grave goods, and to provide the dead with servants and companionship.

The Aztecs and the Maya did not believe in the survival of the individual consciousness after death. Instead, they believed that after death
the energy of the human body, especially of the heart, became "deified or
grafted onto the celestial substance of a divinity,"[127] such as the sun or a
star, hence, the sacrificial practice of ripping the still-beating heart from
a victim and holding it up as a gift to the sun.

TOMBS

Egypt was unsurpassed in the construction of tombs—the enormous
pyramids rising high above the desert and the elaborate resting places
that honeycomb the Valley of the Kings. The three great pyramids at Giza
were constructed nearly five thousand years ago, but continue to amaze
us—Cheops's (Khufu's) pyramid remains among the largest buildings
ever constructed, being 775 feet per side at the base and rising to a height
of 481 feet (about fifty stories). Built of huge blocks of stone, each pyramid involved construction crews of tens of thousands laboring for many
years—most of them probably were peasants who worked on the project
during the agricultural off-season.[128]

Even the pharaohs could not continue such spectacular projects, and
soon they settled for burial in far less elaborate structures or even in
tombs cleverly hidden in the cliffs. While even these were more elaborate
than were those constructed elsewhere, all ancient civilizations paid considerable attention to proper resting places for the dead—or at least for
the powerful dead.

In Sumer, all of the dead were buried, and cremation was rejected, as
the body was essential to even an unattractive afterlife—to burn to death
was considered the worst of all fates. Most people were simply put below
ground, some in coffins, some wrapped in mats. Some were buried beneath their homes; others were placed in caves. The custom was to place
bodies in a sleeping position, legs straight and lying on their backs. Beads
and metal pins are commonly found in these graves.

Upper-class graves were another matter. The elite were entombed in
vaulted chambers built of brick and stone, some buried, some above ground.
In 1927 Sir Leonard Woolley (1880–1960) excavated about a thousand
graves in what he identified as the Royal Cemetery at Ur. Some of them
contained extraordinary grave goods, including jewelry, crowns, games,

weapons—even golden cups and eating utensils. But Woolley's most sensational finds were the bodies of servants and companions entombed to serve the dead. In one royal tomb, Woolley found eighty bodies of the royal retinue—servants, soldiers, musicians, courtiers, horse- and oxen-driven chariots, complete with drivers and grooms—all of whom had apparently been poisoned. Other tombs yielded smaller numbers of bodies, some as few as six.[129] Woolley's discovery confirmed the closing lines of the *Gilgamesh Epic*. In describing the death of Gilgamesh, the poem lists various gifts he presented to the Gods on his behalf and of those who "lay with him." Listed are "his wife, son, concubine, musician, entertainer, chief valet, and household attendants."[130] One hesitates to imagine the rites involved in such affairs.

The ancient civilizations in Mexico also built pyramids. For a long time it was believed that these Aztec and Mayan structures were only temples, not tombs, probably because they were used constantly for religious rituals— including prodigious and regular episodes of human sacrifice. But in 1951, a hidden staircase was found in the pyramid at Palenque, which led to a crypt containing a huge sarcophagus in which lay the body of a man wearing a jade face mask and ornaments. And, as with tombs in Sumer, the skeletons of six humans sent along on the journey were discovered, too.[131] Then, in 2005, archaeologists excavating a Mayan pyramid in Guatemala also found a vaulted burial chamber inside. It contained the skeleton of an elderly woman of apparent royal lineage, as well as those of two younger women, one of them having been pregnant, who appear to have died as "sacrifices in the context of a royal burial."[132]

Tombs from the first dynasty in Egypt also contain large numbers of "officials, priests, retainers, and women from the royal household . . . sacrificed to serve their king in the afterlife," and the corpses show signs of having been strangled.[133] The practice of entombing a retinue with the dead was later discontinued.

Finally, it is not coincidental that the polytheistic state religions of the early civilizations so greatly resemble one another. For one thing, there was substantial diffusion of religion, and especially of Gods, all around the Mediterranean. From time to time it has been suggested that the many similarities between the temples, as well as the pantheons of the Maya and the Aztecs and those of Egypt, might have been the result of diffusion, too—that perhaps a boatload or two of Egyptians were driven across the Atlantic by a storm, bringing pyramid-building and a set of Gods with them. However, recently a sophisticated observatory atop a pyramid dating from about 2200 BCE was discovered in the Peruvian Andes, which makes it contemporary with the Old Kingdom in Egypt and favors independent development. Indeed, since religion deals with universal human problems, this tends to result in universal solutions in that all societies confront birth, death, dawn, darkness, stars, storms, war, agriculture, and sex. Of course, there also is the possibility of inspiration and revelation from a common source, shaped to suit cultures at similar levels of sophistication. As for religious practices and organizational forms, in addition to diffusion, there are many sociological and theological principles that account for these consistent patterns.

THE ATTRACTIONS OF POLYTHEISM

Repeatedly, early religions seem to have "devolved" from a focus on High Gods into lush polytheism. In fact, although the Sumerians had two High Creator Gods, they were not content to let them reign supreme or even to conceive of them as invisible powers. Instead, even An and Enlil were "embodied" in idols along with a whole pantheon of lesser Gods and Goddesses. As Mircea Eliade noted, this marked "a victory for the dynamic, dramatic forms [of Gods], so rich in mythological meaning, over the Supreme Being of the sky.... [Thus] the supreme divinities of the sky are constantly pushed to the periphery of religious life where they are almost ignored; other sacred forces, nearer to man, fill the leading role."[134] As Eliade hinted, and as Andrew Lang asserted (see Chapter 1), people seem more comfortable with Gods that are less awe-inspiring and more human, less demanding and more permissive: Gods who are easily propitiated with sacrifices. There also seems to be some preference for specialized Gods, so that one can seek fertility from one, rain from another, and victory from still another. The logic involved seems akin to consulting specialists in various professions.

In Chapter 4 we shall see how Israel's conception of Yahweh confronted the preference for "closer" Gods by emphasizing his "human" aspects. Although it was forbidden, and theologically impossible, to depict Yahweh, the belief that humans were created in his image encouraged Jews to imagine their God as having human form. Even so, it took centuries for monotheism to be widely observed among the Israelites, and there were repeated instances of backsliding into "idolatry," even on the part of priests serving the Temple in Jerusalem. There is something very reassuring and attractive about very tangible, very "human" Gods; in contrast, monotheism is a very demanding discipline, difficult to achieve and hard to sustain. As the distinguished Denis Baly (1913–1987) put it, "Belief in only one God does not, it would seem, come easily to the human mind, for it is attended by serious intellectual problems, notably the problem of evil, and one of the most marked characteristics of a monotheistic God is his tendency to retreat into the infinite distance, and there to be completely lost to sight."[135]

ON PRIESTLY RELIGIONS

The most fundamental aspect of life in any human group is a division of labor—different people have different tasks and exchange goods or services with one another. In the primitive band, this primarily consists of differentiation on the basis of gender and age: adult males hunt and fight; adult women gather, cook, and mother; the elderly do what they can; and children are given various chores. As groups become larger and their cultures more complex, specialization appears, and seemingly the first two specialties involve leadership and religion, eventuating in the appearance of full-time rulers and priests. Often enough, as in Sumer and in Egypt, the ruler is also the chief priest. Often, too, rulers and High Priests are blood relatives, and sometimes the ruler is God. The point is that there usually is no separation of· church and state. Rather, as already noted, most ancient civilizations had state "churches."

Many consequences follow from this fact. The most obvious is the triumph of tradition. Priests in fully subsidized, monopoly religious organizations become intensely opposed to change. Ancient Sumer demonstrates this opposition. In the beginning the Sumerians built their civilization by inventing or adopting a whole series of important technologies. At the same time their religion was evolving. Once a smoothly functioning empire of city-states had been established, technological progress ceased as life in Sumer settled into "a fixed and sacred routine."[136] Each city had its own God, and "all inhabitants were his slaves." The priests taught that to ward off disasters, it was necessary to demonstrate obedience by "slavish"

MERIDEN PUBLIC LIBRARY
Meriden, Conn.

adherence to tradition and by offering extravagant sacrifices to their particular God.[137] Hence, for millennia new temples were built atop old ones,
without any change in plans. Inside these temples, the same Gods were
the objects of the same rituals, and the same prayers were recited, word
for word. Later tablets reporting the same narrative tell the same story.
For thousands of years, nothing happened! Why?

One reason that priests oppose religious innovations is because their
status rests on mastery of a relatively complex body of knowledge—
especially rituals. Once learned, it is not lightly discarded in favor of something new. In addition, their education into the priesthood is steeped in
the principle that there is a *correct* view, or a *right* way, to perform a ritual. Therefore, innovation is error. Thus, the religious culture on which
these priesthoods are based originates prior to their ascendancy and then
freezes. For example, the sacred Pyramid Texts predated the professional-
ization of the Egyptian priesthood, but once that occurred, any additions
or changes were impossible.

A second reason is that a privileged and closed priesthood tends to
drift toward cynicism and unbelief. People wish to be priests because of
the power and prestige of the priestly position, not primarily out of personal religiousness—indeed, in most of the ancient civilizations, including Sumer and Egypt, priests formed a hereditary class. As insiders they
became all too familiar with "idols" and can hardly have failed to realize
that, regardless of the many rituals conducted to bring these images to
life, quite obviously the "idols" did not see or hear any better than they ate
and swallowed—the priests knew full well who actually ate the food and
drank the wine brought to the Gods. Their cynicism made them unsus-
ceptible either to having or accepting revelations.

Because significant religious change is brought about by religious innovators, a third reason for the "stagnation" of state religions is that such
individuals are feared and disdained by the priests of state religions, and
their revelations are suppressed. Anyone outside the priesthood is denied
all religious standing, and anyone within the priesthood who begins to
innovate is subdued by whatever means necessary. Indeed, efforts to prevent or control revelations are not limited to state "churches," but arise
in all religious organizations, both ancient and modern. This is because
all religious organizations are served best by a *completed* faith; they are
unsettled by the prospect of frequent revisions in basic teachings or prac-

tices. Consequently, even in religious organizations founded on the basis of revelations, after the revelator has died or retired, those in power either declare that the "age of revelations has ended" or impose a monopoly on revelations by limiting them to the leadership. In Sumer the "king could receive divine messages of certain types, but it was not considered acceptable for a private person to approach the deity through dreams or visions."[138]

In Egypt, of course, it was Pharaoh Akhenaten who turned out to be a religious innovator and who imposed a strict form of monotheism. When he died a dozen years later, the deposed priesthood declared his vision to be "a heresy and Akhenaten was described as a criminal. His temples were demolished, his reign expunged from the records"[139] as his successor dated his reign from the end of Akhenaten's predecessor. This whole episode is reported at some length in Chapter 4.

This incident aside, in Egypt and in most ancient civilizations, as noted, there were no new, upstart faiths to challenge the established temples for public support because the combination of a strong state and a powerful temple priesthood prevented any significant challengers from making headway. Having no competititon, the official priesthood had no need to change, and if this resulted in a relatively apathetic public, so what? Subsidized temples have no need for public support.

But things were somewhat different in Greece. Having an unprofessional, part-time priesthood and with many of its city-states having far less repressive regimes, there was far more religious diversity as a number of relatively intense religious movements arose and competed with the subsidized temples. Two well-documented Greek religious movements were the Orphics and the Pythagorans, named for their "founders," Orpheus and Pythagoras.

Although historians once dismissed both as "mythical" characters, all reputable scholars now accept that Pythagoras was a real man who lived during the sixth century BCE,[140] and some suppose that Orpheus lived during that same century as well.[141] Indeed, if Orpheus did not exist, then *someone* who lived in the sixth century BCE founded a new religion in his name. Both the Orphics and the Pythagorans appealed to the upper classes. As Plato reported, their priests "come to the doors of the rich and ... offer them a bundle of books"[142] in an era when only a small number of the most privileged Greeks could read.[143]

According to tradition, Orpheus was a musician and mystic who founded a religious movement that was devoted to asceticism. The Orphics believed that the body is "the root of evil" and "a prison for the soul. The soul is punished in the body for earlier sins. If these sins are not expiated during one incarnation, the soul transmigrates to another body."[144] The solution to this problem, the way to break the cycle of deaths and rebirths, is through asceticism. Plato[145] reported that the Orphics were bound by many rules of dress and daily routine, were vegetarians, drank no wine, and encouraged celibacy, and some even became wandering beggars. Eventually the group transformed Orpheus into a God, which led many historians to believe he never existed.[146]

Pythagoras was born on the island of Samos in the middle of the sixth century BCE. After studying in Greece, Pythagoras resettled in Croton in Magna Graecia (southern Italy) where he founded a group very similar to the Orphics.[147] He, too, taught reincarnation and claimed that if the soul could be freed of "physicality," it could gain immortality in "the realm of the divine."[148] Thus, the Pythagorans also observed extensive dietary laws, followed elaborate rules concerning daily life (including an absolute prohibition on speaking in the dark), wore only white garments, and accepted many restrictions on sexual activities. Due to the many ancient writers who commented on Pythagoras's teachings, fewer scholars have ever denied his existence, and no reputable historian does today—perhaps in part, too, because Pythagoras was never made into a God.

It remains of considerable interest whether or not Pythagoras met or became a student of Zoroaster. Several ancient Greek historians reported this connection, as did some early Christians.[149] In fact, the two men were contemporaries, and there is no reason to doubt reports that Pythagoras visited the East. That may well be where Pythagoras came to believe in reincarnation, but he didn't learn that from Zoroaster, who believed, not in repeated lives, but in resurrection and eternal life, as will be discussed in Chapter 4. Instead, it is far more plausible that Pythagoras had contact with Brahman sages in India or even with Buddha, as also was reported by some early writers, including Clement of Alexandria.[150] Alfred Weber (1868–1958) was quite willing to propose that Pythagoranism was, in fact, Buddhism.[151] Whatever the case, that Pythagoras, Buddha, Zoroaster, and Orpheus (or whoever founded that faith) all lived during the remarkable sixth century BCE, when the world was so populated with famous religious founders, will be discussed in the Conclusion of this book.

In any event, groups such as these provided a religious option for Greeks seeking more intense forms of religion, options not available in Sumer or Egypt. Even so, the existence of the subsidized temples inhibited the religious diversity of Greece in comparison with Rome, where a remarkable number of religious organizations all had to attract their own support by catering to variations in public needs and tastes. That will be the primary focus of Chapter 3.

RULERS AND PRIESTS

In ancient civilizations the concept of a "state church" didn't really exist because people did not distinguish them as two institutions. Sometimes the High Priest ruled the state. Often the ruler was head of the religion, in fact as well as in name. And sometimes the ruler also was regarded as a God. Once again, it will be helpful to return to the beginning, to Sumer.

The linkage of church and state was displayed by the physical structure of most ancient cities, which usually surrounded an *acropolis*. An acropolis was a walled, fortified, and usually elevated part of an ancient city that enclosed both the temple devoted to the primary God(s) and the ruler's palace. Whenever possible, the acropolis was built on a hilltop in the midst of a city, looking down on the lower city, which often was divided into four quarters. Most Sumerian cities were built according to this plan, as were most other cities in this era and area, including in ancient Israel. Placing the house of the God(s) and the house of the king together, and set apart, not only symbolized the unity of church and state, but facilitated its reality. "Temples built by the king were state administrative places which often became financial centers," and typically the king not only built and maintained the temple, but was its protector—in Sumeria, kings often were called "the good shepherd," and "God's vicar." Thus, the people not only were the king's subjects, but God's as well. "Therefore, temple and palace should be seen as two aspects of the same phenomenon; together they constituted the essence of the state."[152]

In early days, an occasional Sumerian king attached the divinity sign to his name, but after about 1500 BCE this practice disappeared. In general, unlike Egypt where the pharaoh was regarded as a God, the Sumerians "viewed their king as a mortal endowed with a divine burden."[153] Indeed, Sumerians held that the institution of kingship had been given to humans by the Gods, as was explained in this surviving text:

> They [the Gods] had not yet set up a king for the beclouded people
> No headband and crown had been fastened . . .
> No scepter had been studded with lapis lazuli . . .
> [Then] kingship descended from heaven.[154]

Perhaps the most remarkable thing about kingship in Sumer is that although the kings were believed to have been chosen by the Gods, we don't know how this was effected—clearly it was not reliably hereditary. Like nineteenth-century American presidents, Sumerian kings liked to stress their humble origins and rise to power. Upon the death of a king, there was no settled rule of succession, and it is recorded that there often were several claimants—how one of them gained divine selection we do not know, but "each succession was essentially an *ad hoc* solution."[155]

In any event, aside from moments of democracy in Greece and Rome, all ancient rulers claimed to hold a mandate from the Gods, and some, as in the case of Alexander the Great, even asserted their divinity. Not only were ancient kings selected by the Gods, it was assumed that the Gods helped them rule. Their courts were crowded with seers and soothsayers who helped them detect and interpret the will of the Gods. Observations of the moon and stars were of great importance—eventuating in the universal practice of astrology. Sumerian tablets abound in messages informing kings of heavenly portents. One of them noted that an eclipse had occurred, but since it was not visible from the capital due to heavy cloud cover, it could have no local effects: "The great gods dwelling in the city of the king, my lord, [caused] the sky to be overshadowed and did not allow the eclipse to become visible, saying, 'Let the king know that this eclipse is not against the king and his country.' Let the king rejoice."[156] Among the Maya and the Aztecs, astrology and the calendar also provided priests with immense power, and rulers lived in fear of great catastrophes, such as the four that had previously destroyed the universe.

In these early civilizations, kings also relied on the results of priestly inspections of the internal organs of sacrificial animals in search of omens. Oracles played a very popular role, too, especially in Greece. Dreams were

another major channel of divine communication—not only dreams reported by priests, but especially the dreams of kings themselves. In times
of peril, kings often made special efforts to receive dreams, sleeping in
a temple being a common practice. In Egypt, because the pharaoh was
thought to be a God, there not only was less concern about what other
Gods might have to say, but also lacking was the fear of the Gods that was
typical of other ancient kings. During the entire succession of kingdoms
in Sumer, elaborate procedures were used to frustrate evil omens and
thwart divine wrath against the king. When enough impending peril had
been detected, a substitute king was selected and, after a brief reign (often
a hundred days), the substitute was killed in the belief that he carried
away the threatened disasters. In one famous instance, the king's chief
gardener was crowned and put on the throne, whereupon the real king
died suddenly. This was interpreted to mean that the gardener was supposed to be king, and so he reigned for some years.

Fear of the Gods reflected the fact that ancient civilizations did not
regard their Gods as necessarily just or loving. The Gods seemed often
to strike the virtuous and reward the evil. Worse yet, it was impossible to
know why. Hence, as the celebrated archaeologist Henri Frankfort (1897–
1954) explained, the numerous Sumerian "penitential psalms abound
in confessions of guilt but ignore the sense of sin; they are vibrant with
despair but not with contrition—with regret but not with repentance."
When they suffered, they assumed they had offended the Gods, and confessed even though:

> I do not know the offense against god,
> I do not know the transgression against the goddess.[157]

MONUMENTALISM

Perhaps the cuneiform tablets from Sumer never would have been translated had it not been for the egotism of King Darius of Persia (521–486
BCE) that caused him to have a huge monument 25 feet tall and 70 feet
wide carved to himself on a shear cliff face 500 feet above the ground. On
it, in addition to an elaborate bas relief of Darius overcoming his enemies,
were hundreds of lines of text recording his exploits and achievements
in three different languages. After many sessions of dangling perilously

from a rope, Sir Henry Rawlinson (1810–1895) managed to copy all three inscriptions and then used them as a key, much like that provided by the Rosetta Stone, to decipher the previously impenetrable, older Sumerian cuneiform.[158]

In commissioning this elaborate cliff carving, Darius exhibited the monumentalism so often found in despots. Keep in mind that even today most prominent leaders are concerned with their "legacy." Whatever they end up achieving, they are secure in the knowledge that their "works" will live on via written history. But the ancients could only hope to live on through monuments. And it worked. Who would remember Cheops except that his is the largest pyramid at Giza? Darius the Great was equally concerned that we all remember him.

In addition to wanting to leave a mark, monumentalism reflects an attitude toward wealth that appears very early in the human story. Beginning in the Stone Age, the primary purpose of wealth is for display in order to assert superior status.[159] Or, as Adam Smith put it even about more modern times: "The chief enjoyment of riches consists in the parade of riches."[160] Indeed, in many primitive groups the primary function of wealth not only is display, but wealth is exchanged primarily through gift-giving, not through commerce.

The potlatch activities among the Northwest Pacific Coast Indians are the most obvious, if extreme, example. Potlatch is simply the most exaggerated and ritualized form of the gift economies that are basic to all stateless societies, wherein gift-giving is the primary method of exchange. A potlatch occurred when a "big man," or chief, invited others to gather for feasting and dancing and then showered gifts upon all of the guests. The value and number of the gifts served as an index of the host's wealth and status. Guests were required to accept these gifts even though they thereby became obligated to reciprocate in the future—sometimes a "big man" would seek to ruin a rival by imposing such a high value of necessary reciprocation that the victim was thereby impoverished. Beyond giving gifts to others, potlatch also often involved the public destruction of wealth, sometimes the host even burning down his own house.

In his classic study of gift economies, Marcel Mauss[161] characterized potlatch as a "war of property"—a battle over status. To give away and to otherwise show contempt for one's possessions established one's high status. To accept and then to reciprocate preserved one's status. Since humans are not really unreasonable fools, underlying the gift economy is the brute fact that the powerful always have more wealth than they need, and there is little to do with their surplus wealth that is more satisfying than to use it to buy status and influence, which always are in short supply.

As societies become more civilized, the "big men" become rulers, adopting such titles as king, emperor, or pharaoh—all of them despots. But the tradition of regarding wealth as a prestige good continues, especially since wealth is so easily obtained by rulers. It is within this context of display that one must understand the huge temples, palaces, and tombs built by ancient rulers. It is true that the temples were built in part to please the Gods and the tombs were meant to ease a ruler's way into the hereafter. But pride and the display of wealth and power were, perhaps, even more important than religious motivations. As Plutarch (c. 46–119 CE) explained, "Most people think that to be deprived of the chance to display their wealth is to be deprived of the wealth itself."[162]

UNDERSTANDING SACRIFICE

A fundamental aspect of religion is an exchange relationship between humans and Gods. Since Gods are the only plausible source of many benefits humans greatly desire, the most basic religious questions are: What do the Gods want? And, how can one gain their favor? Not surprisingly, humans have answered that question based on their image of God(s). When people conceive of God as a being of infinite power and scope, their answer tends to emphasize morality, good works, and faith—as will be discussed at length in later chapters. But when Gods are conceived of as "humans" with superpowers, the answers tend to focus on basic human needs and desires—food, drink, wealth, sex, and deference. The point was emphasized by these instructions written for temple officials in Sumer: "Are the minds of man and the gods somehow different? No! Their minds are the same. When a servant stands up before his master ... either he gives him something to eat, or he gives him something to drink."[163]

Sacrifices are *things given up or foregone so that they may be offered to God(s).* In all religions, the exchange aspect of sacrifice is quite overt, but nowhere more so than in Rome where the formula invoked was "*do ut des* (I give that you should give)."[164] Yet, despite the obvious rational self-interest involved when humans exchange with God(s), a long tradition arose in the social sciences of regarding sacrifice as an irrational act in great need of explanation. Aghast at the "waste" involved in "blindly" bringing valuable offerings to "nonexistent" Gods, one social scientist after another has tried to understand "why they do it." This has led to the formulation of many remarkably silly "theories." As would be expected, Freud and his followers regarded sacrifice as another enactment of the Oedipus complex.[165] It is equally predictable that Durkheim found sacrifice to be one more instance of the group committing itself to solidarity via Totemism. Others traced sacrifice back to ghost religions, and still others have blamed biology. Such nonsense need not delay us, since the case for sacrifice as a highly rational economic act is overwhelming.

The rationality of sacrifice is evident in the fact that people so often approach it in the same spirit as they do mundane, practical matters: they seek to maximize gains and to minimize costs.[166] The ethnographic literature on sacrifice is filled with examples of sharp practices, haggling, and raw self-interest in setting and fulfilling the terms of exchanges with the Gods.[167] For example, among the Swazi, their priests select an especially fine cow and devote a whole series of rituals to make it *licabi*, suitable for sacrifice. Then, during the last several days, they place an old, inferior cow in the enclosure with the *licabi* cow, and when the time comes, it is the old cow that is sacrificed, since this is, in the words of the distinguished Raymond Firth (1901–2002), the "most economical way of meeting one's ritual obligations."[168] In many cultures, humans only fulfill their part of a sacrificial bargain after the God(s) have delivered. Indeed, Chinese who patronize the folk temples in modern Taiwan not only withhold their offering until after they have received the object of their petition to a God, but they often enter the temple and beat the idol with sticks when a prayer goes unanswered.

What no doubt spurred so many social scientists to attribute sacrifice to irrationality was monumentalism. Not content to build huge temples or erect imposing shrines, the wealthy and powerful have often staged immense sacrifices. This has been particularly true when temple religions were involved.

Temple Sacrifices

In Sumer the Gods ate twice a day, at dawn and again in the evening. They were served the finest wines as well as meats, vegetables, breads and cakes, prepared by highly trained chefs. What the Gods didn't eat and drink was consumed by the priests. The same was true of other offerings—of gold, jewels, robes, and other valuables—all was received on behalf of the Gods by the priesthood. Therein lies the fundamental basis of temple sacrifices: the priests lived "off the altar."[169] We need not even suspect that priests were insincere to recognize that they had every reason to maximize sacrifice since this was the means by which they, in effect, lived like Gods.

In Egypt, no sacrificial meat was offered to the Gods, either directly or in burnt form, but all was eaten by the celebrants after the ritual was complete. Since only the priests and the nobility were involved in the temples, this was not a matter of frugality—apparently spilling the sacrificial animal's blood sufficed for the Gods. In contrast, extensive and expensive offerings to the Gods were included in Egyptian tombs.[170]

Priests did not monopolize sacrifices in Greece. Instead, when there was a festival requiring the sacrifice of a substantial number of animals (sometimes a hundred), the meat was roasted and distributed, some to the priests, some to a whole host of civic officials (the costs being borne by civic tribute funds), and the remainder to citizens living in the area around the temple.[171] Cattle were the sacrifice of choice, especially at the large temples, but sheep, goats, pigs, and even chickens also were offered. There were quite elaborate rules concerning the killing and then the preparation, cooking, and distribution of an animal. Edible portions were placed on skewers and roasted over coals, and "the inedible portions were burnt for the god."[172]

Blood played a significant role in sacrifices in all of the ancient temple religions. Some have dismissed this as incidental to obtaining meat. This view is inconsistent with the many instances when meat was not an issue and blood was the focus of the ritual. For example, in the Cybelene ritual known as the *taurobolium*, a bull was slaughtered on a wooden platform under which lay new initiates who were then drenched in the bull's blood—and none of the bull was eaten. Other scholars have read very deep significance into the ritual importance of blood.[173] Although some of these interpretations strike me as quite unlikely, some of them ring true. Even very primitive people realize that blood is the stuff of life, which suggests that blood and, indeed, life itself often were the fundamental aspects of sacrifice, being the "ultimate" sacrifices, as in the case of human sacrifice.

Human Sacrifice

There is considerable dispute as to whether or not human sacrifices may have occurred in Greece and other ancient civilizations in that region.[174] Herodotus tells us that human sacrifice did take place from time to time. Archaeologists have found some very suggestive gravesites. Micah 6:7 suggests that the idea of human sacrifice was not foreign to the Israelites, and 2 Kings 3.27 reports it among the Moabites, albeit at a time of maximum danger. What everyone agrees upon is that even if some human sacrifices did occur in these societies, it was irregular, rare, and done on a very small scale. Not so across the Atlantic.

When the Spaniards arrived in Mexico, they were utterly astounded by the immense ritual slaughters that were taking place. Bernal Díaz del Castillo, who accompanied Cortez, wrote that "in the plaza [of Mexico City] where their oratories stood, there were piles of skulls so regularly arranged that one could count them, and I estimated them at more than one hundred thousand. I repeat again that there were more than one hundred thousand of them. . . . We had occasions to see many such things later on . . . for the same custom was observed in all the towns."[175] These monumental piles of skulls represented the huge numbers put to death each year atop the Aztec and Mayan temples.

For most of the twentieth century, it was claimed, especially in textbooks, that tales like that of Díaz were falsehoods, told to justify Spanish imperialism. But these Spanish reports are verified by actual Mayan and Aztec frescoes, by their sacred texts, and, most of all, by archaeology. Indeed, David Carrasco was moved to write a most remarkable book on human sacrifice among the Aztecs after viewing a ritual receptacle containing the "skeletal remains of forty-two children . . . a messy remnant of a fifteenth century, precious offering to the rain gods."[176] The victims were all around five years old and had been sacrificed, probably by having their throats cut. Carrasco noted that human sacrifices were conducted

An actual Aztec drawing of human sacrifice, the bloody, heartless bodies rolling down the pyramid. (Biblioteca Nazionale, Florence; Photo: Scala/Art Resource, New York)

in more than eighty different places in the Aztec capital and in hundreds of other ceremonial centers. As for frequency, there were eighteen major, yearly ceremonies that required extensive human sacrifices.

While most victims were men, "women and children were also sacrificed in over a third of" the ceremonies, which were "ritually choreographed" and performed before large crowds.[177] Adult male victims usually were held down on a sacrificial stone atop a pyramid, their chest was slashed open, and the priest snatched their still-beating heart from their chest and held it aloft to the sun. Then "the body, now called 'eagle man,' was rolled, flailing down the temple steps to the bottom where it was skinned and dismembered."[178] When females were sacrificed, they sometimes had their living hearts ripped out, too, but more often their necks were stretched back over the edge of the stone and then they were slowly beheaded, after which their hearts were extracted. At that point a female victim often was skinned by a priest who then wore her skin as the slaughter continued.[179]

How many victims were consumed by these ceremonies? In 1487, well before any contact with Europeans, the Aztecs inaugurated their great new Templo Mayor. The day began with four lines of victims, each line stretching for two miles. Igna Clendinnen estimated the total number sacrificed on that occasion as twenty thousand, although others have placed the number as high as eighty thousand.[180] This was, of course, a one-time occasion. During regular festivals, the numbers killed at a particular temple probably ran around two thousand a day.[181] But there were literally hundreds of sacrificial sites.

There are fierce arguments over why human sacrifice was so central to Aztec and Mayan religious practice. Of course, many social scientists cling to the doctrine that religion as such cannot be the cause of anything, since it amounts to nothing more than a set of illusions that always overlie (and often hide) material realities.[182] For these convinced skeptics it will not do to suggest that the primary reason for human sacrifice in Mesoamerica was that people wanted to make sure that the sun continued to rise. But I am certain that nearly everyone involved sincerely believed that was the reason—things are "real" to human beings if they believe them to be real! In any event, several militant materialists, including Marvin Harris, have claimed that human sacrifices were "really" a matter of proper nutrition,[183] motivated by the need to add amino acids or more protein in the Aztec diet, since the bodies were gathered up, butchered, and prime cuts passed out to people who took them home, cooked, and ate them. This ignores the fact that most other groups in that region did not sacrifice or eat humans, although their diets were otherwise the same as those of the Aztecs and Maya. Other scholars have argued that human sacrifice was "really" motivated by the need to limit population growth.[184] But human sacrifice could have had essentially no effect on the Aztec or Mayan populations since the victims usually were prisoners taken in wars and raids on other societies or were slaves purchased from other communities to provide sacrificial bodies. And therein lies a clue as to a reason for human sacrifice in addition to those of a purely religious nature: submission.

The Aztecs and the Maya were imperialists. Theirs were societies of warriors who lived off the fruits of subject peoples. These peoples not only lived in adjacent areas under the control of the Empire, but many subject "immigrants" lived in the imperial cities, including Tenochtitlán (Mexico City). The true Aztecs and Maya were members of elites, linked by ancestry, who claimed affinity with the Gods, and "like gods . . . wore cotton mantles, fine skin sandals, and jewelry, and they consumed human flesh. The [immigrant] commoners, by contrast, did not dress like the gods or share in the cannibalistic meals."[185] The institution of human sacrifice served to glorify the status of these elites and to intimidate their subjects both at home and abroad. The religious aspects of human sacrifice reinforced the status of the elites as favorites of the Gods and as those privileged to eat rather than to be eaten. The bloody reality reinforced the structure of domination and submission—any sign of resistance or even of resentment was a sure ticket up a steep temple staircase.

Two lessons are revealed by this discussion of sacrifice. One is that just because religion provides real motives and causes real things to happen, this is no reason to suppose that material factors don't impinge as well. If the Aztec and Mayan priests had selfish motives to engage in human sacrifice, so, too, the temple priests in Sumer, Egypt, and Greece had a substantial self-interest in the feasts offered to the Gods. But the second lesson is of even greater significance: without the religious reasons, no sacrifices would have occurred!

CONCLUSION

It seems likely that the small tribal societies that existed in the Tigris-Euphrates Valley prior to the rise of Sumer worshipped High Gods and had advanced a considerable distance along the path to monotheism. Thus, the significant question posed at the start of this chapter was: Why the regression? Why did the temple religions to a considerable extent "undiscover" God? Two major factors seem to have been involved. First, the temple religions offered an array of Gods because that was the easier course. Second, they were positioned to suppress challenges from anyone wishing to missionize for a more demanding faith.

The first factor already has been discussed several times: that people probably are more comfortable with the far more humanlike and far less demanding Gods of extensive polytheism—Gods whose demands can quite easily be satisfied. In comparison, monotheism is a much more demanding and far less comfortable faith. Consequently, it takes an immense amount of sustained effort to supplant polytheism with monotheism—the greater intellectual and philosophical attractions of monotheism notwithstanding. By offering many quite undemanding Gods, the temple religions chose the easy way. Not only were their Gods easily satisfied so long as they were properly tended and if the appropriate rites and rituals were perfomed in the correct way, these were chores fully satisfied by the professional priesthood. So, in return for status and luxury, the priests saw to it that others need not concern themselves much with religion. Indeed, it was better that outsiders did not concern themselves with religious matters because no competition was allowed. Probably there were people who from time to time did challenge the temple establishments, but it is unlikely that they made serious headway, and their names would not have survived. Indeed, as will be seen in subsequent chapters, even many of the famous religious innovators ran great risks.

Temple religions displayed all of the negative aspects of despotism, and for good reason. They were a leading institution of despotic states, so closely intertwined with political power that the two can be separated only crudely and with great analytic difficulty. That simple fact explains a great deal. From the perspective of the ruling elite in Sumer (throughout its many imperial manifestations), in Egypt, and in Mesoamerica, if to a lesser extent in Greece, the status quo could not be improved. So, nothing should be changed! And, at least in the religious sphere, for many centuries nothing was changed. If innovators appeared and offered new religious perspectives, they were silenced. If ordinary people gained little from the temple faith—were indeed largely excluded from it—so what? They were excluded from everything else, too—except from supporting their indolent "betters." And that's how things stood in the "civilized" world for thousands of years. Then the Romans changed everything.

∘ 3 ∘

ROME: AN ANCIENT
RELIGIOUS MARKETPLACE

ONE OF THE MOST REMARKABLE THINGS about religion in early Rome is how little we know about it. The city itself is thought to date from about 700 BCE, but no surviving accounts of religion in early Rome were written until about six hundred years later. We know the names of some major rituals, but little or nothing about what many of them meant or how they were conducted. We do not know whether the early Romans had an explanation of Creation. We are not even certain what Gods they worshipped, where their Gods came from, or what they looked like.

In the first century BCE, Marcus Terentius Varro compiled a huge manuscript on ancient Roman religions in order that the knowledge be preserved. But this great work was lost, and all we have are fragments quoted in many different sources, including in Saint Augustine's *The City of God*. Also writing in the first century BCE, the historian Livy provided some details about early Roman religion, but we know nothing of his sources and some of his claims are clearly incorrect. The truth is, we know far more about the religion of Sumer in, say, 2500 BCE than we do about religion in Rome two thousand years later.

For a long time it was believed that very early Roman religion was a purely civic faith based on Gods who so transcended material existence as to be impossible to depict—according to Varro there were no images of Gods in Rome during the city's first two centuries.[1] Much misspent effort has been devoted to trying to cram these Gods into simpleminded animism,[2] although it would seem considerably more appropriate to regard them as High Gods of a particularly abstract variety. No matter, since more recent discoveries demonstrate that even the early Romans conceived of at least some Gods as having human shapes—there were images of the several Gods in Roman temples during the sixth century BCE.[3] The best we can do is to assume that from the very start, Roman religion was an exotic mélange of Gods adopted from the Etruscans, the Greeks, other Italian cultures, and perhaps even from Carthage.[4] There were, of course, many more Gods still to come.

A remarkable feature of Roman religion was the prominence of ritual in all aspects of public life. "Every public act began with a religious ceremony, just as the agenda of every meeting of the senate was headed by religious business."[5] In effect, nothing of any significance was done in Rome without the performance of the proper rituals. As John North pointed out, when a religion places the primary emphasis on ritual acts, it becomes paramount that the "ritual should be successfully repeated."[6] For the Romans, "successfully" meant precisely, word for word. Thus, in his famous *Natural History*, Pliny the Elder (23–79 CE) noted that "a sacrifice without a prayer is thought to have no effect," but it is equally ineffective when the prayer is not the one appropriate to that occasion or when performance errors occur. Thus, Pliny continued, "someone dictates the formula from a written text to ensure that no word is omitted or spoken in the wrong order; someone else is assigned as an overseer to check [what is spoken]." He went on to warn against the often dire consequences "when the prayer has been spoken wrongly."[7] To have stumbled over a phrase or omitted a word required that one start over. Should it be discovered that a ritual done to open a municipal assembly, for example, either was not appropriate to the occasion or had been performed incorrectly, the result was that any and all decisions made by the assembly were invalidated.[8]

In addition, nothing in the way of public activities took place without recourse to divination.[9] The senate did not meet, armies did not march, and decisions, both major and minor, were postponed if the signs and portents were not favorable. The *Augures* read the signs based on observations of the flight and calls of birds and from thunder. The *Haruspices* interpreted the entrails of sacrificial animals. The *Quindecimvri* consulted the sacred books of the Sibylline Oracles. Such importance was placed on divination that, for example, if lightning were observed during the meeting of some public body, "the assembly would be dismissed, and even after the vote had been taken the college of augurs might declare it void."[10]

The ubiquity of very public rituals and the constant rescheduling of public life, including festivals and holidays, in response to the "temper of the gods," made religion an unusually prominent part of the everyday life, not only of the Roman elite, but of the general public.[11] It was this that so impressed vistors from societies where state temples prevailed. As the Greek historian Polybius (203–120 BCE) commented, "The quality in which the Roman commonwealth is most distinctly superior is, in my opinion, the nature of their religious convictions."[12]

However, the *most* unusual aspect of Roman religion is that it was relatively unregulated and little subsidized. The Roman Republic did not impose a system of state temples and allowed the evolution of a remarkably free and crowded religious marketplace wherein an amazing array of faiths jostled for popular support. Some of these faiths demanded an exclusive commitment; most did not. But all of them were at the "mercy" of the marketplace, forced to vie with one another for followers and financial support. It wasn't very important that individuals could frequent several temples devoted to different Gods; what mattered was that each temple had to attract sufficient support or close, a pattern that exists among the folk temples in China today.[13] The vigorous competition among Roman religious organizations resulted in a great deal of religious conflict and even outbursts of vicious persecution. But it also prompted constant innovation as each group sought to more effectively appeal to the general public for patronage. The collective result of these organizational efforts was to create a far higher level of religious involvement on the part of ordinary Roman citizens than ever was achieved in societies served by monopoly state temples.

Consequently, rather than move from description to analysis as in the prior chapter, here it is appropriate to begin with a theory concerning religious markets.

ON RELIGIOUS MARKETS

For centuries, all discussions of why people are more or less religious focused on variations in *demand*, on differences in individual needs. Much of this work is valid and important,[14] and it is especially appropriate to examine demand when asking such questions as why religion exists in all societies. But it is far less useful when addressing questions concerning religious *change* or about *variations in the general level of religiousness* from one society to another. For these questions, it is vital to consider *supply*, to recognize that some religious organizations (suppliers) are far more vigorous and effective than others, and that some societies sustain a far greater supply of religious options. In Sumer, Egypt, and Mesoamerica, although there were temples devoted to many different Gods, they were all part of a single organized religious option that was content to serve the elite and to largely ignore the public. Consequently, most ordinary people probably were rather uninvolved in the "official" religion, meeting their personal needs through a mixture of magic and unorganized folk religion. This result was not produced by variations in individual religious needs (demand), but by the nature and actions of the suppliers.

To shift the focus from demand to supply, the concept of a religious economy is useful: a **religious economy** consists of *all the religious activity going on in a society: a "market" of current and potential adherents, a set of one or more organizations seeking to attract or maintain adherents, and the religious culture offered by the organization(s).*

For more than twenty years, I have been refining a theory based on the concept of religious economies and have had considerable success in explaining religious variations from one contemporary society to another.[15] It is entirely appropriate to extend the application of this theory to Rome and to the ancient civilizations with temple religions.

Although the primary emphasis of the theory is on the efforts of religious suppliers, it rests upon several crucial assumptions about demand— about the nature of individual capacities and preferences.

The first of these is: *people are as rational in making religious choices as in making secular decisions.*

Claims that religion stems from ignorance or irrationality reveal more about those who make them than they do about human behavior. Two issues are involved here. The first concerns the so-called rational-choice assumption: that humans tend to seek rewards and to avoid costs. Although some social scientists imply that to make this assumption is tantamount to signing a pact with the devil,[16] it is patent that within obvious limits, humans *are reasonable beings* who act accordingly. Of course, everyone acknowledges that human behavior isn't *always* rational, being subject to error and impulse. But the best starting assumption is that behavior *is* rational in that people usually attempt to pursue what they *perceive to be the best option* for achieving their goals—and these goals need not be selfish, nor must they be admirable. Stated with proper qualifications, the rational-choice premise reads: In pursuit of things they deem desirable or valuable (rewards), people attempt to make effective and efficient (rational) choices, limited by their information, by the available options, and by their understanding of what's involved. What it is that people deem rewarding differs, being shaped by culture and socialization. Allowance also must be made for character—laziness often influences choices, impulsiveness and passion may short-circuit calculations, and moral concerns may rule out many options.

Despite the complaints by post-modernists and other opponents of reason, there is nothing radical or new about the assumption that human behavior generally makes sense and is, therefore, relatively predictable. This is the primary assumption that all humans make about others, withdrawing it only when forced to do so by clear cases of madness.[17] Were our behavior not relatively rational, not only would social science be invalid, but social life would be impossible—if the behavior of others were not fairly predictable, we could not interact. Fortunately, within the suggested limits, humans generally act in reasonable ways—*at least as they see it.* This qualifying clause reminds us that, as James Coleman (1926–1995) put it, "much of what is ordinarily described as nonrational or irrational is merely so because observers have not discovered the point of view of the actor, from which the action *is* rational."[18]

The second issue is the claim that while most kinds of human behavior meet the standard of rationality, religious behavior mostly does not, being rooted in ignorance and neurosis. Such views go back to the beginnings of social science. Thus, Thomas Hobbes (1588–1679), one of the celebrated founders, dismissed all religion as "credulity," "ignorance," and "lies," and Gods as "creatures of . . . fancy."[19] A century later, David Hume (1711–1776) echoed Hobbes, dismissing all miracles as limited to "ignorant and barbarous nations."[20] During the nineteenth century, Auguste Comte (1798–1857) coined the word *sociology* to identify a new field that would replace religious "hallucinations" as the guide to morals.[21] Then, Ludwig von Feuerbach (1804–1872) "discovered" that humans create Gods in their own image,[22] a thesis appropriated (without acknowledgment) by Emile Durkheim (1858–1917), who taught that the fundamental reality is that society itself is always the true object of religious worship: "god . . . can be nothing else than [society] itself, personified and represented to the imagination."[23] Next it was Sigmund Freud's (1856–1939) turn to tell us that religion is an "illusion," a "sweet—or bittersweet—poison," a "neurosis," an "intoxicant," and "childishness to be overcome," all on one page of his once-admired exposé of faith: *The Future of an Illusion*.[24] Nor has such militant atheism become a thing of the past. On the first page of his recent book *Mystical Experience*, Ben-Ami Scharfstein revealed that "mysticism is . . . a name for the paranoid darkness in which unbalanced people stumble so confidently" and went on to identify the supernatural as a "fairy tale."[25] And Michael P. Carroll, the same person who interpreted the "Star-Husband" "myth" as repressed incest, was permitted to fill many pages of a usually reputable journal with his claims that praying the Rosary is "a disguised gratification of repressed anal-erotic desires"—a substitute for playing "with one's feces."[26]

Research makes mockery of all such claims. A mountain of trustworthy studies reveal that religion is positively associated with good mental health—religious people are substantially less prone to neuroses, anxiety, depression, and other forms of psychological problems.[27] As for ignorance as the basis of faith, in many nations including the U.S., the more educated they are, the more likely people are to attend church, and among university faculty, those in the physical and natural sciences are more religious than are their colleagues in other fields.[28] Even very intense religious movements usually have been based primarily on the sophisticated upper classes rather than on the poor or the peasantry.[29] Finally, there is overwhelming evidence that people, in both pre-modern and modern societies, weigh their religious decisions carefully.[30]

Now, consider that: *in every society, people differ in their religious tastes.*

Were we to rank people in any society according to the intensity of their religious preferences, the result would approximate a bell-shaped curve: some people wanting high-intensity religion, some wanting little to do with religion at all, and most people wanting a faith that offers them valuable rewards in exchange for various requirements—but the latter should be moderate both in number and cost. The importance of diversity in religious tastes is that all societies, therefore, include a set of relatively stable market *niches*, sets of persons sharing distinctive religious preferences (needs, tastes, or expectations). Relatively similar sets of niches have been identified in many Western nations,[31] in Islam,[32] in China,[33] and in ancient Rome,[34] and there is no reason to suppose that they are not universal. This is to reject the frequent and facile claim that most people in most cultures have no religious choices. For example, the late H. W. F. Saggs (1920–2005) denied that the ancients had any option other than belief, since for them religion was not a matter of faith, but was perceived to be a matter of fact.[35] However, even if people perceive there to be only one religion, they still have a considerable leeway in their *degree* of commitment—even in pre-literate societies unbelief is quite common, as the prominent anthropologist Clifford Geertz (1926–2006) made abundantly clear.[36] The esteemed Mary Douglas extended that point to *all* prior eras: "Let us note at once that there is no good evidence that a high level of spirituality had generally been reached by the mass of mankind in past times."[37] This view is supported by the walls of Pompeii, which "display dozens of blasphemous graffiti, insults to Venus (patron deity of the town), or, in a tavern, an obscene painting at Isis's expense. We may take their like for granted elsewhere, if other sites were so well-preserved."[38] In similar fashion, Mesopotamian cuneiform tablets report many thefts from temples, including a remarkable caper wherein fearless burglars stole the bejeweled sun disk from the chest of a "living" idol.[39] Clearly, even in societies that appear to have but one religious option, people will be distributed across niches based on their levels of commitment: from the intensely pious to the uncommitted and unconvinced.

The existence of such niches has profound consequences for religious suppliers, including: *pluralism is the natural state of any religious economy.*

Pluralism consists of *the existence of an array of independent religious suppliers.*

No single supplier can satisfy the full array of niches in the religious market since no organization can be at once intense and lax, worldly and otherworldly. Thus, other things being equal, there will always be a variety of suppliers, each competing to attract a particular niche or narrow set of niches. These may be independent organizations within the same religious tradition, as in the case of Christian denominations. Or they may represent different traditions, as they did in ancient Rome. What is important is that they must depend upon adherents for their support. Consequently, to the extent that a religious economy is pluralistic, (1) there will be *competitive efforts to appeal to each market niche*. As a result, (2) the *overall level of public religious involvement will be maximized*. In addition, (3) *the more effective and innovative organizations will grow, and less effective organizations will decline and eventually disappear.*

These propositions greatly clarify the history of religions. Consider religious changes such as when people turn away from one religion and embrace another—when, for example, people left the Church of England to become Methodists, or left various pagan temples to become Christians. Invariably, the explanations for such shifts have been based on changes in demand, hence scholars have struggled to discover why people's religious *needs changed*. When so formulated, the answer must be sought in the rise of new, unmet religious needs or in the decline of other needs. Thus, the rise of Methodism has often been traced to growing class conflict, and the defection of pagans to Christianity has long been attributed to the arrival of an "age of anxiety."

Not only are these likely the wrong answers, they seem to answer the wrong questions. There is considerable evidence that, although it often may be somewhat latent, religious demand is quite stable and that religious change is mainly the result of supply-side transformations.[40] That is, while potential demand remains constant, suppliers rise and fall, and the overall level of public religious participation is a function of the diversity and energy of suppliers. Hence, the appropriate questions are: Why do *religious organizations change* so they no longer can attract the public? Or, why are some religious organizations *overwhelmed* by the appearance of far more *appealing and effective competitors*? In the instances above, the appropriate questions are: What went wrong with the Church of England? Why did the pagan temples not reach out more effectively, perhaps by organizing congregations and offering social services, in order to attract and hold an active membership in the face of Christian competition?

Monopoly has been the usual state of religious economies.

Notice that pluralism is identified as the *natural* state of religion in societies, not as the *usual* state. Typically, pluralism has been suppressed in favor of religious monopolies.

Religious monopolies are artificial, existing only to the extent that *coercive force* is utilized to prevent competition. That is, wherever and whenever coercion is not employed, pluralism will emerge. Coercion does not always involve naked force—during their democratic interludes, Greek city-states employed less brutal techniques to place all religious groups, other than the "state" temples, at severe disadvantages. The Greeks only admitted a new religion as an "ethnic" faith, limiting its adherents to members of that specific set of foreign residents. The Greeks also handicapped any potential competitors by providing all of the funding needed by the official temples, through land grants and by annual tribute payments. But however pluralism is impeded, the results are far-reaching, being the obverse of the benefits of pluralism: many niches will go unserved; lacking competition, religious organizations will not innovate and will not exert themselves to arouse public religious involvement. Hence: *where religious monopolies prevail, the overall level of public religious involvement will be low.*

All of this was anticipated by Adam Smith more than two centuries ago:

> [Religious leaders] may either depend altogether for their subsistence
> upon . . . voluntary contributions; or they may derive it from some
> other fund to which the law of their country may entitle them; such
> as a landed estate, a tythe or land tax, an established salary or stipend.
> Their exertion, their zeal and industry, are likely to be much greater
> in the former situation than in the latter . . . [wherein] the clergy,
> reposing themselves upon their benefices . . . neglect . . . to keep up
> the fervour of faith and devotion in the great body of the people; and
> having given themselves up to indolence . . . [are] become altogether
> incapable of making any vigorous exertion in defence even of their
> own establishment. . . . Such a clergy . . . have commonly no other
> resource than to call upon the civil magistrate to persecute, destroy,
> or to drive out their adversaries . . .[41]

Smith's description seems accurate when applied to the monopoly temple religions examined in the previous chapter. Then as later, secure state "churches" were content to live off their "benefices." Consequently, Wilhelm Schmidt proposed an inverse relationship between the splendor of state polytheism and personal piety: "Wealthy temples, shrines and groves arose; more priests and servants, more sacrifices and ceremonies were instituted. But all this cannot blind us to the fact that despite the glory and wealth of the outward form, the inner kernel of religion often disappeared and its essential strength was weakened."[42]

The weakness of the temple religions among the general public was a matter of neglect. If all significant religious rites and worship activities are hidden from public view, as they were in Egypt and Sumer, what is to inspire the people to faith?[43] Clearly, in both Egypt and Sumer the people were pretty much on their own as to a religious life. If they engaged in worship activities, they conducted them in their homes or, in the case of rituals involving rites of passage, they were performed, not even in the temple courtyards, but usually outdoors. There also were local shamen and, probably, wandering mystics to augment varieties of folk religions and practices. But these necessarily kept a low profile since had they posed any challenge to the official temples they would have been suppressed.

As for Greece, subsidization of the temples offered everyone a "free" religion, thereby setting the norm for religious commitment at a very low level of intensity—when little is asked, little is given. Thus, as a number of scholars have proposed, because of the failure of monopoly state religions to cultivate popular support, the ordinary person in these societies "lived in a quite tepid religious climate."[44] Keep in mind, too, that unbelief and skepticism are not modern phenomena. Not only were there significant numbers of doubters in these ancient civilizations,[45] but, as already noted, unbelief is not uncommon even among primitives.[46] It requires vigorous effort to produce high levels of religious commitment on the part of the general public. State churches lack that effort. Which is why Anthony Spalinger remarked that religion in ancient Egypt resembled "the Church of England . . . not Methodism."[47]

Now it is appropriate to see if Rome enjoyed the benefits predicted by the market theory of religious economies.

THE EVOLUTION OF ROMAN PLURALISM

In the beginning Rome had kings, and they built and sustained state temples. The first was dedicated to Jupiter (and contained his statue) and probably was built by King Lucius Tarquinius Priscus in the seventh century BCE. The second was a Temple of Diana, thought to have been built by King Servius Tullis a few years later. But in 509 BCE, the Romans overthrew their king and initiated a Republic ruled by an elected Senate, although it was dominated by a small group of rich and powerful families. Even so, most "citizens" had some say in the affairs of Rome, keeping in mind that eventually as many as half of the residents were not citizens, but slaves.

In the first days of the Republic, Rome was not an empire but was little more than a city, covering only about fifty square miles along the Tiber River, and holding sway over no additional territories. But the Romans soon won much more territory, initiating many centuries of almost nonstop wars of conquest. These victories brought many new Gods to the city, but not, for the most part, at public expense. Very few temples ever were built by the Senate; Roman religion depended almost entirely on private initiative, as not only the rich, but sometimes even poor people combined to finance a temple or shrine. Many temples were built by military commanders as the result of vows made prior to a victory, and the "building costs were normally met by the booty and profits of the campaign."[48] Many others were built by groups of adherents to various Gods, often by one of the many "foreign" groups residing in the city. State officials did, however, control what could be built, where, and dedicated to what God.[49]

Another aspect of the absence of a subsidized state religion in Rome is found in the priesthood. The traditional Roman temples were not served by professional, full-time priests. Of course, priests showed up to conduct festivals or supervise a major sacrifice, but most of the time the Roman temples seem to have been served only by a few caretakers who lacked any religious duties or authority. In addition, except for a very small number of priests who were advisors to the Senate and those who undertook divination, nearly all other priests were prominent citizens who served in the priestly role only part-time, and who did it for the status involved— Julius Caesar got himself elected *pontifex maximus* (a position of major religious importance) in 63 BCE. Presumably those who served as priests in Rome received some training for their duties, but it could only have been minor compared with the full-time, professional priests of Sumer, Egypt, or Mesoamerica.[50] These Romans do qualify as priests as defined in Chapter 2, in that they regularly performed their duties and had the exclusive right to do so. However, since Roman priests were in some sense amateurs, for whom being a priest was not their primary role, "Roman temples were not independent centres of power, influence, or riches. . . . They did not . . . have priestly personnel attached to them and they did not therefore provide a power base for the priests."[51]

Surviving accounts of temple funding are very fragmentary. As already noted, with very few exceptions, the temples were built from private donations and their operations were not subsidized at state expense (or by land grants given by the state). There are some records of temples being supported by endowments given by the individuals or families who had built them,[52] and many scattered references survive of individuals and families involved in maintaining or refurbishing a temple. Keep in mind that to support a traditional Roman temple did not require support of a priesthood, which was the major cost involved in sustaining temples in Sumer, Egypt, and Mesoamerica. After the Republic was replaced by emperors, some of them built temples from time to time, and remodeled others—Augustus made a great show of this. But even support from an emperor was regarded as more of a personal good deed than as a state expenditure.[53]

Perhaps the most convincing proof of how greatly Roman temples depended upon private support can be seen in the results of the widely known collapse of temple donations that began late in the third century, long before the conversion of Constantine. Suddenly, in about 270 CE, inscriptions proclaiming private gifts to various temples "wither away within a generation."[54] The reasons for the rapid decline of donations have long been debated. Many have argued that this was caused by the onset of an economic recession.[55] But by then, times had been bad for decades, and besides, that would not account for a precipitous drop in pagan inscriptions on gravestones that occurred at precisely this same time, since there was no drop in the size or expense of the gravestones. Families simply no longer identified themselves as pagans. A plausible interpretation is that by 270 the Christian populations of the major cities had become very large and increasingly influential, creating an era of religious tension and uncertainty, and people found it expedient to lower their religious profiles—Christians did not often identify themselves on their gravestones at this time either.[56] Whatever the reason, it is the results that are of interest here. Lacking donations, the temples began to deteriorate rapidly. Not only literary, but archaeological evidence confirms the decay of the temples from that time on: "roofs fallen in, votaries departed, idols missing, the whole sanctuary tumble-down."[57] The important point is, not that people stopped giving, but that when they did it became obvious that these were not state temples.

THE ARRAY OF ROMAN RELIGIONS

Romans took pride that theirs was an open city that welcomed not only people from a great many different cultures, but their Gods as well.[58] From early days this included large numbers of Greek immigrants since, prior to the rise of Rome, various Greek city-states had established many colonies on the Italian peninsula and these were soon incorporated as Rome expanded. Consequently, the Romans developed such admiration for Greek culture that they not only imported many Greek Gods, but were inclined to identify Roman Gods with Greek counterparts whether or not that had originally been the case. Furthermore, following the influx of Greek Gods, came new Gods from Egypt and from the Near East. In addition, Rome gave birth to several new religious movements and had long and transforming encounters with the first two great monotheisms: Judaism and Christianity.

It is a challenge even to list the Gods of sufficient importance to have temples in Rome, let alone the many more having shrines.

Seven major Gods were established prior to the Republic. **Jupiter** was the supreme God (also called Jove), father of the Gods, and eventually equated with Zeus. **Mars** was second only to Jupiter in the early Roman pantheon, a God of agriculture, father of Romulus, and eventually worshipped as the God of War (and equated with Ares). His priests, known as the Salii, celebrated his festival by dancing in full armor before his altar. **Quirinus** probably was adopted from the Sabines who worshipped him as a God of war, but the Romans regarded him as the ascended Romulus, legendary founder of their city. **Janus** was usually represented as two-faced and was the guardian of doorways and custodian of the universe. The gates of his temple in Rome were closed in time of peace and open in time of war—and were hardly ever closed. Three Goddesses completed the initial seven early Roman Gods: **Vesta** (identified with Hestia),

Goddess of the Hearth, served by the six Vestal Virgins; **Diana**, Goddess of the Moon and of Fertility (soon equated with Artemis); and **Fortuna**, Goddess of Luck (equated with Tyche).

Once the Republic was established, the Gods proliferated rapidly. The influx began from Greece: **Juno**, wife of Jupiter (Hera); **Minerva**, daughter of Jupiter (Athena); **Vulcan**, God of Fire and Craftsmen (Hephaistos); **Saturn**, father of Jupiter (Cronus); **Hercules**, the risen great hero (Herakles); **Ceres**, Goddess of Grain and Nature (Demeter); **Liber**, God of Fertility (Dionysos); **Mercury**, the Messenger God (Hermes); **Neptune**, God of the Sea (Poseidon); **Venus**, Goddess of Gardens and Beauty (Aphrodite); and **Apollo**, God of Prophecy, Medicine, and the Arts (known as Apollo in Greece as well). Finally, **Aesculapius**, the God of Healing, was introduced to Rome from Greece (Asklepios) in response to a plague.

This blend of Roman and Greek Gods (it seems appropriate to refer to them as Greco-Roman Gods) constituted the traditional religions of Rome. But even though this array of Gods sustained scores of temples, both in Rome and in all the other cities of the empire, somehow they didn't seem to provide enough religion. New faiths from the East and Egypt continued to arrive and to generate public enthusiasm.

One of these new faiths involved the God **Bacchus** (or Dionysos), whose mystery religion came to Rome from Greece as an intense, proselytizing group and aroused vicious persecution by the Senate, on (probably) spurious grounds that it was devoted to drunken immorality. Another of the new imported faiths was devoted to the Goddess **Cybele**, known to the Romans as Magna Mater (the Great Mother) and her consort, **Attis**. Although initially from Phrygia, Cybele was imported from Greece by an act of the Senate. The Cybelene faith stirred up considerable government concern and opposition, but to no avail. As will be seen, Cybele proved to be immensely popular, eventually having six temples in the city of Rome, compared with four devoted to Jupiter (see Table 3–1). Then from Egypt came **Serapis**, consciously created by two scholars to be a supreme God, and his female companion, **Isis**, who evolved from many centuries as Goddess of the annual inundations of the Nile to become a serious pagan candidate to be the One True God—as will be seen. Isis became so popular in Rome that eventually she had eleven temples in the city alone.

Table 3–1: Number of Known Temples Devoted Exclusively to a Major God in the City of Rome

GOD	NUMBER OF TEMPLES	GOD	NUMBER OF TEMPLES
Isis	11	Ceres	1
Cybele	6	Diana	1
Jupiter	4	Janus	1
Venus	4	Juno	1
Fortuna	3	Liber	1
Apollo	2	Mars	1
Sol Invictus	2	Neptune	1
Aesculapius	1	Quirinus	1

Source: Beard, North, and Price, *Religions of Rome*, vol. I, maps 1 and 2.

Table 3–1 reports the number of known temples in the city of Rome exclusively devoted to each major God as of about the year 200 CE. As already noted, Isis had by far the most, and Cybele was a strong second. Then came Jupiter and Venus, with four each, Fortuna with three, and Apollo and Sol Invictus each had two. Nine other Gods had a single temple in Rome. Of course, many other Gods had a niche in the pantheon, and small shrines to various Gods were abundant throughout the city. A number of temples also were devoted to "divine" emperors.

In addition to new "pagan" imports, many large Diasporan Jewish communities grew up in many parts of the empire; the one in the city of Rome was established sometime around the middle of the second century BCE.[59] In those days Judaism engaged in very active missionizing, and many scholars agree that converts made up a significant number of the Diasporan Jews.[60] And, of course, in the days of the Caesars, Christianity arrived.

The Romans also created some new religions of their own. It was in Rome, not in the Near East as was long believed, that the worship of **Mithras** was initiated and rapidly spread throughout the Roman army.[61] Finally, in 274 CE the Emperor Aurelian attempted to establish a new God, **Sol Invictus** (the invincible sun). Like Isis, Sol Invictus was another pagan reponse to monotheism, as will be seen in Chapter 4.

It is worth noting that Rome's religious history parallels the cultural evolution of religion as sketched in the Introduction. The Romans began as a tribe and worshipped tribal Gods. Then they built a city that sustained state temples on behalf of the usual array of Gods. Having created a Republic, they evolved a relatively free-market religious economy wherein religions were required to compete for popular support. This resulted in an influx of new religions, each bringing a God of increasingly greater scope, eventuating in the Christianization of the empire. This evolution was not achieved without a great deal of controversy and conflict, much of it caused by the fact that not all of the religious "firms" were equally competitive.

COMPETITIVE ADVANTAGES

Given the immensely crowded array of Gods and temples, the question arises: Why did new faiths continue to arrive in Rome from Egypt and the East? Moreover, why was it that these new faiths seemed so vigorous in comparison with the traditional temples, in terms of attracting and holding a committed following?

A very insightful analysis of why these new religions achieved great popular success in Rome was written a century ago by Franz Cumont (1868–1947), the great Belgian historian. Cumont argued that the new religions succeeded because they "gave greater satisfaction." He believed they did so in three ways, to which must be added a fourth and fifth. First, "they appealed more strongly to the senses," having a far higher content of emotionalism, especially in their worship activities. Although Cumont made no mention of it, the chief emotional ingredient lacking in the traditional Roman faiths was *love*. Romans thought the Gods might come to their aid, but they did not believe that the Gods loved them—indeed, Zeus was depicted as quite unfriendly to humans. Consequently, pagan Romans often feared the Gods, admired some of them, and envied them all, but they did not love them. Not the way that some Romans loved Isis or Christ. Second, the new faiths appealed directly to the individual rather than to the community, linking faith to the "conscience." Third, "they satisfied the intellect" by possessing written scriptures and by presenting a more potent and virtuous portrait of the gods.[62] Fourth, I would add, they were far more appealing to women, some offering them the opportunity to lead. Finally, the new religions were not content to function merely as temples to which people went from time to time, but organized their adherents into structured and very active communities that provided a deeply rewarding social as well as spiritual life.

Emotionalism

In Rome, the traditional religions mainly involved tepid, civic ceremonies and periodic feasts. They sought to enlist the traditional Gods to provide protection and prosperity both for the individual and the community. Mostly this involved public rites conducted by priests and involved little more than some chanting and a sacrifice. Even "worship" by groups devoted to a specific deity usually amounted to little more than an occasional animal sacrifice followed by a banquet[63]—inspiring the early church father Clement of Alexandria to remark: "I believe sacrifices were invented by men to be a pretext for eating meat."[64] In any event, traditional Greco-Roman religions relegated religious emotionalism "to the periphery of religious life."[65] In contrast, the new faiths stressed celebration, joy, ecstasy, and passion. Music played a leading role in their services—not only flutes and horns, but an abundance of group singing and dancing. As for ecstasy, the behavior of participants in the worship of some of these groups sounds very much like modern Pentecostalism— people going into trancelike states and speaking in unknown tongues. Writing in the second century, the physician Aretaeus of Cappadocia described worshippers of Cybele as entering a state of ecstatic madness: "This madness is divine possession. When they end the state of madness, they are in good spirits, free of sorrow, as if consecrated by initiation to the God."[66] As Cumont summed up, the new "religions touched every chord of sensibility and satisfied the thirst for religious emotion that the austere Roman creed had been unable to quench."[67]

But as noted above, the emotion most lacking in traditional Roman religion wasn't a matter of ecstasy and dancing. The Roman Gods had many shortcomings, but of greatest importance was that they were neither loving nor loveable. The traditional Roman image of a God, like those held in Greece, Sumer, Egypt, and Mesoamerica, was essentially a human being having immortality and some supernatural powers. Such Gods were very fallible and often quite lacking in morals and manners. They were afflicted with jealousy, greed, pride, and lust. They usually had little or no interest in humans or human affairs, so long as they were properly and adequately propitiated. Consequently, even in times of dire crisis, Roman efforts to enlist divine aid involved remarkably impersonal rites. In contrast, her devotees often addressed Isis in deeply emotional and loving ways, and Christians emphasized their joy at knowing the love of Christ.

Individualism and Virtue

The traditional Gods of Rome were "primarily gods of the state," not the individual.[68] As did the temple religions of Sumer, Egypt, and Mesoamerica, the traditional Roman religions pursued "salvation," not for the individual, but for the city or state. Moreover, aside from requiring humans to venerate them properly, the Greco-Roman Gods seemed to care little about human behavior, moral or immoral—"moral offences were not treated as offences against the gods."[69] Worse, these Gods set bad examples of individual morality: they lied, stole, raped, adultered, betrayed, and tortured.

In contrast, the new religions arriving in Rome were not devoted to sanctifying civic affairs, but were instead directed toward the individual's spiritual life and stressed individual morality, offering various means of atonement—it was not primarily *cities* that were punished or saved; *individuals* could "wash away the impurities of the soul . . . [and] restore lost purity."[70] Some paths to atonement were built into the initiation rites of many of these new religions, which stressed purification and the washing away of guilt—various forms of baptism were common. In addition, formal acts of confession were practiced by followers of both Isis and Cybele, but no such practices existed in the traditional temple faiths.[71] Nor was atonement achieved through rites alone; many of the new faiths required acts of self-denial and privation, sometimes even physical suffering—actions that gave credibility to doctrines of individual forgiveness.

Sophistication

Remarkably for a society abundant in historians and *written* philosophies, the traditional Roman religions had no scriptures. "They had no written works which established their tenets and doctrines, or provided explanation of their rituals or moral prescription for their adherents."[72] In contrast, the new faiths were religions of the book. Not only Judaism and

Christianity, but Bacchanalian, Cybelene, Isiaic, and Mithraic religions also offered extensive written scriptures that "captivated the cultured mind."[73] Moreover, the new faiths presented a far more plausible portrait of the Gods—even many worshippers of Cybele, Isis, Bacchus, and Mithras worshipped "no other deity but their god,"[74] and if they did not claim theirs was the *only* God, they did regard theirs as a supreme God.

As Cumont summarized, the new "religions acted upon the senses, the intellect and the conscience at the same time, and therefore gained a hold on the entire man. Compared with the ancient creeds, they appear to have offered greater beauty of ritual, greater truth of doctrine and a far superior morality. . . . The worship of the Roman gods was a civic duty, the worship of the foreign gods the expression of personal belief."[75]

But Cumont failed to recognize two additional factors that were at least as important as the three he noted, and probably even more important: gender and organization.

Gender

The situation of Roman women was abysmal. They were married off in their early teens (usually to far older men), had no legal rights except as the ward of a spouse or male relative, and wives of the wealthy were kept in virtual seclusion. As for religion, although women were permitted to attend "most religious occasions . . . they had little opportunity to take any active religious role"[76] in the traditional Greco-Roman religions. There were some priestesses in various traditional temples, but only in those dedicated to a Goddess. Worse yet, priestesses were subject to severe regulations quite unlike anything imposed on priests—Vestal Virgins were buried alive for transgressions!

In contrast, many of the new religions offered women substantial religious opportunities, as well as far greater security and status within the family. As will be seen in Chapter 7, for these reasons Roman women flocked into Christianity when it became available. But this trend began much earlier vis-à-vis other new religions. Consider the "cult" of Bacchus that developed in Rome several centuries before Christianity arrived, and which seems to have held a very strong appeal to women.[77] What this group may actually have done to bring about its vicious repression by the Senate will be discussed later. But among its alleged "sins" was that both

men and women held leadership positions within the group.[78] *Either* a
male or a female leadership would have been within Roman norms; to
have *both* was not.

Roman authorities also were deeply offended by the gender outlook
and practices that accompanied the arrival of temples dedicated to the
great female deities Cybele (Magna Mater) and Isis—both religions were
negatively portrayed by Romans as being "for" women. But this was not
so. While both drew enthusiastic female followings, they also were popular with men, and both sexes held priestly positions.[79] Nor was Diasporan Judaism wanting in this respect. Beyond the reach of patriarchs in
Israel, Jewish women held leadership roles in many synagogues, including "elder," "leader of the synagogue," "mother of the synagogue,"[80] and
"presiding officer" (*archisynagogos*), which is supported by inscriptions
found in Smyrna and elsewhere.[81]

Organization

But it wasn't only a matter of having scriptures and moral concerns,
of singing and speaking in tongues, or even a more equitable view of sex
roles that gave the new religions such an advantage. Above all else was
their capacity to mobilize a lay following by involving people in **congregations**, in *active communities of believers.*

Traditional Roman religions offered very little in the way of community. It was typical for devotees of a particular God to meet once every few
months for a sacrifice and dinner, and nothing more between times.[82] The
new religions expected their followers to worship daily on their own and
then to gather for services weekly or even more often. Sheer frequency,
let alone the intensity of these gatherings, made these religious groups
central to the lives of their adherents. This was something that had not
previously existed: "at least until the middle of the Republic, there is no
sign in Rome of any specifically religious groups: groups, that is, of men
or women who had decided to join together principally on grounds of
religious choice. . . . There were no autonomous religious groups."[83] Put
another way, the Greco-Roman Gods had only clients and festivals, not
members and regular services. It was the new religions that "offered a
new sense of community . . . a much stronger type of membership."[84] As
John North expressed it, "the degree of commitment asked of the new
member when he joins is patently far higher . . . [and involves an] inten-

sified awareness to direct personal experience of contact with the divine. The new structure corresponds to the intensification of religious life and to the new place which religious experience will occupy in the life of the initiate."[85] The esteemed Arthur Darby Nock (1902–1963) noted that weekly religious observances served as a "steady thread running through the continuity of daily life ... [and] while it might not tell with full force on the first generation of converts, was bound to make a background of otherness for their children."[86]

Thus, followers of the new religions had a singular religious identity. "They could and did identify themselves by their religion as well as by their city or their family, in a way that earlier centuries would not have understood at all.... It is hard to exaggerate the importance of this change."[87] Although not so exclusive as Judaism and Christianity, initiates into Bacchanalianism, Mithraism, Isiacism, and Cybelene worship were expected to cease temple-hopping and devote themselves fully to their respective deity. To support this commitment they adopted a clear religious identity, which required and sustained a closely knit and very active religious community—a *congregation*, not a clientele. Like Jews and Christians, followers of these pagan faiths made their religious group the focus of their social life. In doing so, not only did they strengthen their commitment, but they gained far greater rewards from being committed, as other members rewarded them for it. It is by being set apart and offering opportunities for intense interaction and the formation of close social ties that religious groups generate the highest levels of member commitment and loyalty.[88]

But it was precisely those religious groups that were set apart and strongly committed that caused so much anxiety among Roman officials and provoked official reprisals. The rulers of Rome not only feared and opposed intense or semi-secret groups, they feared *all* voluntary groups as a potential source of dissent and conspiracy. Thus, early in the first century, edicts were issued regulating the formation of all private gatherings. Under Augustus a "more extensive Law on Associations was passed which required that all associations be authorized by the senate or emperor,"[89] and such permission was seldom granted.[90] Consider that during the first decade of the second century, Pliny the Younger wrote to the Emperor Trajan asking permission to establish a company of volunteer firefighters in Nicomedia, following a serious blaze in that city. The emperor wrote back, denying his request on grounds that "it is societies like these which have been responsible for political disturbances. . . . If people assemble for a common purpose, whatever name we give them and for whatever reason, they soon turn into a political club."[91]

Thus it was that from time to time the Roman state persecuted many religious groups—not only Christians and Jews, but pagan congregations, too.

CONFLICT

There is little evidence of religious conflict in societies having state-supported, monopoly temples. Aside from the interlude when Pharaoh Akhenaten attempted to impose monotheism, and whatever conflicts occurred with the Jews, ancient Egyptian history lacks evidence of any significant religious disputes. The same is true of Sumer, Greece, and Mesoamerica. This tranquility reflected the absence of significant challenges, not tolerance—after all, in designing his ideal state, Plato recommended that anyone who did not conform to the official religion should be executed.

Things were far different in Rome. The massive immigration of Greek Gods did not please everyone. Inspired by such resentments, the first-century BCE satirist Lucian wrote a parody in which the Gods on Mount Olympus are concerned about running short of ambrosia and nectar should their numbers keep increasing—especially since the newcomers were "a riotous rabble of many tongues."[92] But really vigorous intolerance was reserved not for new Gods per se, but only for those who inspired *congregations* of highly committed believers.

In Pursuit of Bacchus

Today the term *Bacchanalian* refers to people committed to drunken orgies, because that's what the Roman Senate claimed about the group when they "ferociously suppressed"[93] the cult of Bacchus in 186 BCE—although the charges probably were false.[94] Unfortunately, many generations of historians of Roman religion based their accounts of this affair entirely on two sources. The first is Livy, whose report seems more like fiction than history: how a good boy is led by his evil mother into this dreadful group.[95] The second source is the Senatorial decree that condemned the group and laid down regulations by which it must abide. Based on Livy's account, it has been assumed that this group engaged in all manner of vile deeds: human sacrifice, rape, unrestricted sex, drunkenness, and the like. According to Livy, at least seven thousand people were involved, including "certain nobles, both men and women." Subsequently the male leaders of the group were rounded up and executed; others committed suicide, and the "women were handed over to their relatives for punishment."[96] But if these sentences were actually imposed, and if the charges brought against the group were true, then the restrictions laid down in the Senate decree were absurdly mild.

The Senate decree[97] began by prohibiting Bacchic shrines (allowing ten days from the receipt of the decree for them to be dismantled). However, the group itself was not outlawed, but was only limited as to the size and functions of its gatherings. The Senate commanded that they no longer meet in groups larger than five (no more than two of the five being male), that they could hold no funds in common, and that they not swear oaths of mutual obligations. In addition, they were forbidden to celebrate rites in secret and men were not permitted to be priests. And that was it! Nothing was said about refraining from rape, drunkenness, group sex, or human sacrifice, which makes it obvious that these claims were "fantasies" knowingly invoked by at least some senators "to provide legitimation for . . . [their] very controversial decision."[98]

Equally spurious is the assumption that this was a group that had appeared suddenly and was of Roman origins. The Bacchanalians had been in operation for a considerable time before the Senate took action, long enough to have built up a substantial following all across Italy.[99] Moreover, the cult of Bacchus did not originate in Rome; it was an "oriental" import from Greece—even Livy blames an anonymous Greek priest and missionary for bringing the cult to Rome.[100] Consequently, we don't need Roman sources to discover the group's origins, what it actually taught and practiced, why it was so attractive, and what it was that the Senate really feared. All that is required is that we turn to the many studies of the group by historians of religion in Greece. Here one finds an extensive literature on the Bacchic or Dionysiac mysteries—including recent reports of many important new discoveries.[101]

Drawing on this literature allows insight into two fundamental questions. What was the movement really like? Why did it provoke such a violent, yet limited, response from the Senate?

Specifically, the cult of Bacchus (or Dionysos) promised the initiated that they would be welcomed into a blissful life after death, enjoying the company of their fellow initiates. A recently discovered gold plate shaped in the form of an ivy leaf instructed the dead to "Tell Persephone that Bacchus himself has set you free."[102] The ordinary person need only become an initiated and committed Bacchanalian in order to escape the dreary afterlife envisioned by the traditional religions of Rome, and to gain everlasting joy: "Now you have died, and now you have been born, thrice blest, on this day."[103] This was a remarkable innovation and gave everyone, rich or poor, a substantial reason to join.

Had the promise of an attractive afterlife been the only unusual feature of Bacchanalians, it seems certain that the Roman Senate would have ignored them—as indeed it did for several generations. But of perhaps even greater importance in gaining converts, the cult of Bacchus surrounded its members with a very intense group life. Originally in Greece, it had been a group restricted to women, and subsequently there were separate male and female groups. Transplanted to Italy, the congregations became mixed. Moreover, rather than meeting several times a year, as they had in Greece and as was typical of groups devoted to other traditional pagan Gods, the Bacchanalians now met at least weekly. In order to do so without disrupting their affairs, they held their meetings at night in temples and shrines built for that purpose. To become a member required initiation into the group's mysteries and the swearing of solemn oaths of devotion and loyalty.[104]

What these facts tell us is that the Bacchanalians were not casual participants in periodic sacrificial feasts—they were closely united into intense, very self-conscious congregations. And it was this that aroused the senators against them. No doubt senatorial fears also were inflamed by stories about lurid activities (similar claims were routinely leveled at many other "unpopular" religious groups, including Christians and Jews), but what the Roman Senate actually suppressed were the *congregational features* of the group—its regular meetings, its formal organizational structure, the strong ties among members, the prominent role of women in a group including both sexes, and, most of all, the high level of member commitment. These things, not noisy revelry, were what the Senate perceived as a threat and "wished above all to destroy."[105]

Cybele Arrives

Cybele's origins are lost in unrecorded history. Many scholars believe she evolved from the generic Mother Goddess found in many primitive religions.[106] In any event, Cybele seems to have first come into her own in Phrygia in central Anatolia (modern Turkey). Archaeological evidence from as far back as the eighth century BCE establishes *Matar* (as she was known then) as "the most important cult figure in Phrygia."[107] Unfortunately, thoughts leave neither ruins nor fossils, so almost nothing is known of the "mythology" surrounding Matar. It was not until she was known as *Kybele* (in Greek) or *Cybele* (in Latin) that her story has come down to us. And clearly, much of this narrative was not of Phrygian origin. In Greek and Roman teachings, Cybele is linked to Attis, whose castration, death, and rebirth are central to her story. But Attis seems to have been unknown in Phrygia, as Matar was usually depicted alone, and any male companions were always depicted as much smaller figures, indicating that they are merely "attendants, not equals."[108]

Turning to the Greco-Roman Cybelene narratives, we read of an unusually handsome Phrygian shepherd named Attis (who, in some accounts, is of supernatural origins) with whom Cybele fell in love. Unfortunately, the young man became sexually involved with a nymph, and Cybele found out. In a fit of extreme anger, Cybele caused Attis to become insane, and in his mad frenzy he castrated himself, lay down under a pine tree, and bled to death. Cybele sorrowed and caused Attis to be reborn, and he became her companion ever after (amazingly Frazer regarded this as a major instance of a "myth" prefiguring the death and resurrection of Jesus). Attis never became a major figure, remaining only a member of his lover's supporting cast. However, his self-castration became a major feature of Cybelene worship. For one thing, the most solemn ritual of Cybelene worship was the *taurobolium*, wherein a bull was slaughtered on a wooden platform under which lay new initiates who were then drenched in the bull's blood—all in commemoration of Attis's mutilation. It was believed that the blood washed away each initiate's past, giving each a

In this sandstone relief found in
Rome, a priest sacrifices to the
Goddess Cybele. She is depicted
in a shrine at the upper left and
in front of her is a diminutive
figure of Attis. (Museo Ostiense,
Ostia, Italy; Photo: Erich Less-
ing/Art Resource, New York)

new life. But perhaps the most remarkable aspect linking the Attis story
to Cybelene worship is that all "priests of Cybele were eunuchs; self-
castration in ecstasy was part of the process of [their] initiation."[109] This
Cybelene mythology and the self-castration of her priests must have developed in Greece, because both were fully developed by the time that
Magna Mater reached Rome.

Just as Christianity gained immense influence by being credited with
bringing Constantine victory at the Battle of the Milvian Bridge, Cybele (also known to the Romans as Magna Mater, or Great Mother) was
brought to Rome by order of the Senate in 204 BCE (personified by a hunk
of meteorite) because of a prophecy inferred from the Sibylline Books
and confirmed by the oracle at Delphi that she would deliver victory
for Rome over Hannibal. Within months after her arrival in Rome, the
prophecy was fulfilled. Soon after, a temple was erected to Cybele on the
summit of the Palatine, the meteorite was set as the face in a silver statue

of the Goddess, she was officially recognized as one of the Gods of Rome, and she was worshipped there for more than five hundred years. Every March 27, the silver statue of Cybele was borne by a procession of her priests to a nearby tributary of the Tiber River and bathed, then carried back to the temple.

The Romans soon learned that having Cybele on their side was a very mixed blessing. Cybelene worship was a wild, disruptive affair. "The enthusiastic transports and somber fanaticism of [Cybelene worship] contrasted violently with the calm dignity and respectable reserve of the official religions."[110] Her priests, known as the *galli*, excelled at ecstatic frenzies. Not only did they castrate themselves during their initiation, subsequently they cross-dressed, wore makeup, frizzed their hair, drenched themselves in perfume, and acted like women. Although Romans were not offended by homosexuality, they were absolutely appalled by effeminacy. Yet they could not doubt the power of the Goddess—she had ended the Carthaginian threat. Hence came the decision to isolate the religion before it could infect the populace, but to permit the "barbaric" rites to continue on her behalf. Once a year Cybele was honored by all Romans, and her "priests marched the streets in procession, dressed in motley costumes, loaded with heavy jewelry, and beating tambourines."[111] During the rest of the year the priests were "segregated and inaccessible to the Romans, their cultic activities were confined to the temple."[112] Moreover, Roman citizens were prohibited by law from becoming Cybelene priests.

In time, Cybelene worship adjusted to Rome, and Rome adjusted to the Cybelenes. The legend of Attis was minimized, and Romans were allowed to become priests. Once freed of legal restrictions, Cybelene groups flourished, which points to the matter of central interest: the formation of religious groups of intense and very active devotees. They were not marked by a singular ethnicity or even social class, but depended upon voluntary affiliations. It was these groups that brought "the most radical changes to Roman religious life."[113]

Meanwhile, Cybele was not alone. A new Goddess from Egypt also was rapidly attracting followers and provoking Roman officialdom.

Isis Comes West

In the next chapter, Isis worship will be examined as an impressive attempt by Greco-Roman paganism to approximate monotheism. Here it is sufficient to note that she began as an Egyptian Nature Goddess who was responsible for the annual flooding of the Nile, and gained substantial followings throughout the Grecian world after Ptolemy I, a comrade of Alexander the Great and the first Greek ruler of Egypt, had her promoted to the Savior Goddess, "or more explicitly 'saviour of the human race.'"[114]

And, just as so many other Greek Gods had moved to Rome, soon it was Isis's turn to go West, transported by Greek merchants and sailors. By about 100 BCE, a temple dedicated to Isis was built in Pompeii, and soon after that came her first temple in Rome.

As with the other new religions, Isis inspired *congregations*. Her followers set themselves apart and gathered regularly; they did not disparage the other Gods and temples, but neither did they attend to them. This singularity did not escape official attention. In 58 BCE the Senate outlawed Isis and ordered her altars and statues torn down.[115] They repeated their ban ten years later, and Roman consuls around the empire responded by destroying Isiaic altars as "disgusting and pointless superstitions."[116] Next, Isiacism was "vigorously repressed by Augustus,"[117] and Tiberius had the Isiaic temple in Rome destroyed and its priests crucified.[118] Indeed, it was Caligula, hardly a paragon of tolerance, but who had a taste for the exotic, who first allowed a temple dedicated to Isis to be built on the Campus Martius, and it was not until the reign of Caracalla early in the third century that an Isiaic temple was allowed on the Capitol.[119]

So, when Isis came West she encountered considerable Roman opposition to foreign cults, especially those of Egyptian origins. Indeed, well after official intolerance of Isis had ceased, Roman intellectuals continued to rage against all things Egyptian, especially religion.[120]

Mithraism

Too often confused with the ancient Persian God Mitra,[121] Mithras was a new God, so closely associated with the sun that he sometimes was called "Mithras, the Invincible Sun." Mithraic worship took the form of a mystery cult that began in the city of Rome.[122] There is no record of its gradual development; evidence of the cult's existence suddenly appears in the historical record dating from about 90 CE. This has led scholars to agree with Martin Nilsson that Mithraism was created all at once by some "unknown religious genius."[123] Although some scholars continue to trace

Mithraism to Iran in the sixth century BCE, it "was an independent creation with its own unique value within a given historical, specifically Roman, context."[124] Some of the confusion over the cult's origins was caused by the fact that Mithraism represented itself as based on the wisdom of Zoroaster and of Persian origins. But this seems to have been a bogus attempt to gain credibility and prestige,[125] very similar to claims by many modern cults to be descended from various ancient groups such as the Druids.

Being a mystery cult, only initiated members were informed of the key elements of Mithraic faith or allowed to know and take part in its secret rituals—each was sworn to secrecy. That fact has inspired an immense amount of nonsense by writers who believe they have decoded the "Mithraic mysteries."[126] But the fact remains that we know very little about Mithraic doctrines, their mysteries, or what went on at their secret meetings. What we do know is largely based on archaeology. Scores of Mithraist sites have been discovered and studied, including a large number of Mithraea—the man-made caverns within which the groups met. These are remarkably uniform, the average Mithraeum being from sixteen to twenty-two feet long, and nine to twelve feet wide, which means, of course, that the average congregation could hardly have numbered fifty people.[127] Since these underground grottos had no windows, everything was done by the light of oil lamps or torches, creating a darkened room with flickering lights and shadows, which heightened the mysterious effect of the rituals. Access to a Mithraeum was through a maze of subterranean passages that seem to have played a role in the initiation ceremonies.[128]

Since a key aspect of Mithraic belief involved the God Mithras sacrificing a bull by leaping onto its back and severing the carotid artery, some scholars believe that (echoing Cybelene faith) a bull sacrifice was a part of the inner mysteries practiced at the secret ceremonies. Others doubt this, especially in light of the smallness of the sanctuary, and believe that the bull sacrifice took place only in a symbolic form. What is well known is that each Mithraeum was also a dining hall and that a sacred meal was served at each gathering. This meal was reported to be remarkably similar to the Christian Eucharist. Bread and wine were shared in the belief that members were thereby reborn and perhaps the words consecrating the "meal" were quite similar to those used by Christians (given when the

A typical underground Mithraeum reveals that the congregations could not have been large since they could meet in such a small space. Participants sat on the two stone benches located along each wall. The altar in the center is fronted by a bas-relief of the God Mithras sacrificing a bull. This mithraeum was discovered beneath the Church of San Clemente in Rome. (S. Clemente, Rome; Photo: Alinari/SEAT/Art Resource, New York)

cult began, they easily could have been copied from Christianity). Justin Martyr, who seems to have had firsthand knowledge of Mithraism dating from his pre-Christian days, was so concerned about the similarities between the two rites that he attributed this to the work of evil demons.[129] Tertullian offered a similar explanation.

Perhaps because these two distinguished early Christians paid attention to parallels with Mithraism, many modern scholars have concluded that it was the primary competitor of the early Church. The famous nineteenth-century French historian Ernest Renan wrote that "if Christianity had been arrested in its growth by some fatal malady, the world would have become Mithraist."[130] This has often been repeated: "In the 2nd and 3rd centuries this mystery cult competed with its slightly older rival, Christianity."[131] "The cult of Mithras was indeed one of Christianity's chief competitors."[132] Mithraism was "a religion which very nearly became the foundation of our modern world."[133] "Mithraism was in fact Christianity's most serious competitor during the critical years of the third century."[134]

But it's not so, and a glance at any map of known Mithraic sites reveals why.[135] The dots locating individual sites provide a very good outline of the borders of the Roman Empire! Why? Because, first and last, Mithraism was an army cult, and most of the sites are at old legionary camps and fortresses, which were, of course, mainly along the frontiers. By this time the Roman army was not composed of citizens-in-arms, but was primarily a professional force. It was not representative of the population (the army already had large numbers of Germanic recruits) and was quite deficient in social ties to civilians—no army cult was going to become a popular movement.

There probably were many reasons why soldiers were attracted to Mithraism. The initiations and services seem to have aroused deep emotions. There was much emphasis on being washed free of personal sins. Mithraism had written scriptures—although all of them have been lost. And it generated intensely committed, small congregations that met frequently and built strong attachments among members. Mithraism differed from the various imported faiths primarily in its total exclusion of women. This may have appealed to legionnaires, but it further doomed Mithraism to being only a peripheral movement.

Roman Anti-Semitism

Strange ideological commitments have driven some contemporary scholars, especially Rosemary Ruether,[136] Jules Isaac,[137] and John Gager,[138] to claim that Christians originated anti-Semitism. For this reason, they stress passages in the New Testament that criticize Jews for rejecting Christ and for persecuting Christian missionaries, although they know full well that deep hostility toward Jews was prevalent in Rome long before the birth of Jesus. To get around this obvious fact, these revisionists resort to word games. Thus, it is admitted that from time to time the ancients did feel some "antagonism" toward the Jews, but this can be attributed entirely to political conflicts such as the Maccabean Revolt—wars always breed hard feelings. These "occasional outbursts" of anger, it is claimed, are different both as to their basis and their virulence from true anti-Semitism, the latter being something entirely new, introduced by Christianity, and born of Christian arrogance and ambition. If this were so, then many leading Roman intellectuals must have been Christians, even some who wrote before the birth of Jesus!

It was the great Roman philosopher and statesman Lucius Annaeus Seneca who denounced Jews as an "accursed race"[139] and condemned their influence. It was Marcus Tullius Cicero, regarded as the greatest Roman orator, who complained that Jewish rites and observances were "at variance with the glory of our empire, [and] the dignity of our name."[140] It was the esteemed Roman historian Cornelius Tacitus who railed against the Jews because they "despise the gods," and who called their religious practices "sinister and revolting." Not only that, according to Tacitus the Jews had "entrenched themselves by their very wickedness" and they seek "increasing wealth" through "their stubborn loyalty" to one another. "But the rest of the world they confront with hatred reserved for enemies."[141] I am unable to detect how Tacitus's complaints differ from standard European anti-Semitism prevalent in the nineteenth and twentieth centuries.

Nor was it only a matter of words. The Jews were expelled from Rome in 139 BCE by an edict that charged them with attempting "to introduce their own rites" to the Romans and thereby "to infect Roman morals."[142] Then, in 19 CE the Emperor Tiberius ordered the Jews in Rome to burn all their religious vestments and assigned all Jewish males of military age to serve in Sardinia to suppress brigandage, where, according to Tacitus, "if they succumbed to the pestilential climate, it was a cheap loss."[143] In addition, all other Jews were banished not only from the city, but from Italy "on pain of slavery for life if they did not obey," as told by Paulinus Suetonius.[144] In 70 CE the Emperor Vespasian imposed a special tax on all Jews in the empire, thereby impounding the contributions that had been made annually to the Temple in Jerusalem. And in 95 CE Emperor Domitian executed his cousin Flavius Clemens and "many others" for having "drifted into Jewish ways," as Cassius Dio put it.[145]

No doubt many Romans did resent that Jews dismissed the Gods as illusions and their temples as blasphemous, but it seems likely that the most compelling objection on the part of the state was more generic: fear of and opposition to *all* tightly knit congregations. Hence, a major sin of the Jews was to be a strong, well-organized, separated community, which is consistent with the fact that the periodic persecutions of the Jews were not so different from persecutions of the Bacchanalians and followers of Isis. These aspects of Mithraism were ignored, no doubt only because emperors were unwilling to risk any needless conflicts with the army. As for Cybele, having invited her to Rome as an official state-sponsored religion, the Senate had to settle for merely isolating this Goddess from public access.

By the time Christianity presented Rome with intense, active, set-apart congregations of the sort sustained by Jews, Bacchanalians, and followers of Isis, the repressive response was quite predictable. As Gibbon reported, compared with such things as volunteer fire departments, Christian assemblies "appeared of a much less innocent nature: they were illegal in principle, and in their consequences might be dangerous . . ."[146] What Roman officials preferred were easygoing Gods whose clients were content to gather from time to time for a feast.

Christian Martyrs and Roman Revivals

And so it came to pass in the year 64, that scores of Christians died as human torches, crucified and set on fire in Nero's garden. Thereafter it was illegal to be a Christian, but the prohibition was only enforced from time to time, and then only here and there—for two centuries, all persecutions were local.[147] The various local persecutions sometimes took the form of mob violence and sometimes involved government antagonism against Christians for sustaining strong, relatively closed voluntary organizations, as noted above, or for refusing to sacrifice to the local deities. However, when the great, empire-wide persecutions began, they were different not only in their extent, but in their motivation as well.

Given the millions of words that have been written on the subject, it might seem idle to ask: Why were the Christians persecuted? Why, within several months of having gained the throne in 249, did Decius suddenly have the Bishop of Rome (Pope Fabian) and the Bishop of Antioch put to death and initiate a wave of torture and executions of Christians across the empire? Why did Valarian continue the persecution from 257 to 260? And why, after a lapse of forty peaceful years, was the persecution renewed by Diocletian, Galerius, and Maximinus in 303 through 313?

Unfortunately, non-Christian historians of the day regarded Decius's actions against the Christians as of so little importance that none of them even mentioned it.[148] The Christian writers all attributed the persecutions to imperial outrage in response to Christian unwillingness to obey orders that they acknowledge the pagan Gods. As Gibbon explained, Decius "was desirous of delivering the Empire from what he condemned as a recent and criminal superstition."[149] But more attention should be paid to Gibbon's qualifying remark in that same paragraph when he noted that Decius's "general design" was to restore the "purity" of Roman culture. Recently, some historians have pursued Gibbon's suggestion and now propose that it is far more plausible that initially Decius was not especially concerned with Christianity.[150] Rather, his real concern was the revival of traditional religion, made urgent, in his judgment, by the need to offset the many calamities afflicting the empire. Thus, his initial actions were meant merely to restore proper worship of the traditional Roman state Gods, and he may not even have anticipated that Christians would defy his edicts. Hence, from the Roman perspective, Decius's persecution of Christians may have been a matter of "collateral damage."

When Decius took the throne, the empire was in great peril.[151] Invaders were making frequent inroads all along the European frontiers: Saxons, Franks, Alamanni, Marcmanni, Quadi, Vandals, and Goths. Decius had spent much of his career fighting these enemies of the empire. Meanwhile, back in Rome legitimate governance had collapsed into a period of military anarchy when emperor after emperor was created by the army. Between 235 and 285, twenty-six men were elevated to the throne, and all but one of them died a violent death.[152] Decius was among those hailed into office by the army, and to secure the throne, he had to defeat his predecessor, Philip, in the Battle of Verona (in which Philip was killed). To defend the empire and to retain the support of the troops, each emperor was forced to create an ever-larger and more expensive army.[153] Even so, the Romans often were defeated in battles with invaders (which is how Decius died), and even the victories, being defensive, brought no significant booty to offset costs. Consequently, taxes grew increasingly oppressive, and citizen unrest and discontent rapidly rose. What was wrong? What could set things right?

Decius came to the conclusion that all Rome's troubles were of religious origin. His reasoning was as follows. For centuries the Gods had smiled on and sustained an expansive and invincible Rome. But with the arrival of the many new religions, the traditional Gods had been considerably neglected and, consequently, they had in turn been neglecting

Rome. The solution was obvious: a religious revival to regain the favor of the Gods who had made Rome great!

The method was equally obvious: stage an unprecedented display of piety. So the famous edict was issued requiring that "*all inhabitants of the Empire sacrifice to the Gods, taste the sacrificial meat, and swear that they had always sacrificed*"[154]—or that they regretted past neglect and promised future observance. In addition to seeking divine aid, Decius (and his successors) hoped that by returning to the traditional Gods they also could reestablish a religious basis for a renewal of patriotism and civic-mindedness, persuading the people to be more willing to pay taxes and otherwise support the state.

Decius was not content to send a message to the Senate or even to circulate an edict to the appropriate provincial governors. In a remarkable break with tradition, he directed his edict to all the people of the empire. Nor was he content with expressing his wishes; he demanded proof of fulfillment by requiring local magistrates to issue certificates to all persons and households verifying that the required sacrifice had been accomplished in their presence. Notice that Decius did not ask the people to pray, or to fast, or to confess, or to attend a praise meeting. In keeping with traditional Roman religious conceptions, his idea of a revival involved nothing but a quick, unemotional ritual—as is obvious when one reads this certificate of compliance, typical of the many that have survived from Roman Egypt:[155]

> To the Superintendents of Sacrifices, from Aurelius Akis, from the village of Theadelphia, with his children Aion and Heras, all being of the village of Theadelphia. It was always our practice to sacrifice to the gods and now in your presence, in accordance with the regulations, we have sacrificed, have made libations, and have tasted the offerings, and we request you certify this.
>
> [Below]
> We, Aurelius Serenus and Aurelius Hermas, saw you sacrificing.
> [Signed and dated]

Nothing was said about Christians in the edict, and many historians now believe that although Decius *may* have been aware of the implications of the edict in terms of Christian prohibitions, his motives were at

An ancient mosaic shows two Romans sacrificing at an altar by selecting pieces of meat dedicated to the Gods from the bowl and dropping them into the sacred flame. (Museo Nazionale Romano (Terme di Diocleziano), Rome; Photo: Erich Lessing/Art Resource, New York)

most incidentally anti-Christian, preferring "to emphasize [his] positive goal of ensuring that everyone in the empire, Christians included, perform a full and traditional sacrifice."[156] Indeed, the sacrifices could not be to just any God; rather Decius proposed that everyone now embrace a "religion of the empire," and this required worship of the ancient state Gods, being the traditional Gods of one's city or, alternatively, Jupiter, Hercules, Mars, and the other residents of Mount Olympus. But it was not appropriate to count sacrifices to foreign Gods such as Isis or Cybele. Thus, a recently discovered inscription hailed Decius as "Restorer of the Cults."[157]

It is one thing to decide to attack Christians; it is quite another to proclaim a universal revival of the state religion. Indeed, there is considerable evidence that Decius did not intend to prohibit Christianity per se. He did not seize church property. He did not ban worship services. He even allowed Christians to perform their religious rites while in prison awaiting trial. He simply "failed to understand why Christians could not offer a normal sacrifice in addition to worshipping their god in their own fashion."[158] It was only when Christians refused this "simple" request, and did so very loudly and in public, that the persecution began. At that point, Decius may well have come to "hate" Christians. Following the execution of Pope Fabian, Decius is quoted as saying, "I would far rather receive news of a rival to the throne, than another bishop in Rome."[159]

However, there was a second major factor in the conflict between Decius and the Christians that also is much overlooked. By the time Decius seized the throne, Christianity was no longer a tiny sect. As will be seen in Chapter 7, by the year 250 Christians probably made up about 2 percent of the imperial population, nearly all of them living in the major cities, where their presence was greatly magnified. Moreover, Christian membership was growing so rapidly that over the next fifty years, they increased fivefold, to make up 10 percent of the population by the time Diocletian renewed the persecutions. Nor were the Christians mostly recruiting slaves and poor people; they were doing best among the more privileged classes, which made their growth both more visible and more significant.[160] In fact, many (including Eusebius) have supposed that Philip, Decius's predecessor on the throne, was a Christian.[161] Hence, in Rome's pagan ruling circles, Christians no longer were merely the objects of scorn; increasingly they aroused fear and apprehension.

No doubt the rapidly growing Christian "threat" played a major role in Diocletian's decision to renew an empire-wide persecution of Christianity in 303. He had risen to the throne in 284 and for many years allowed Christianity to flourish in peace, even though it was an era of more rapid imperial decline and even greater peril than had been faced by Decius. Large areas were lost to barbarian invaders. As for internal affairs, Michael Rostovtzeff (1870–1952) offered this pithy summary:

> Hatred and envy reigned everywhere: the peasants hated the landowners and the officials, the city proletariat hated the city *bourgeoisie*, the army was hated by everybody. . . . Work was disorganized and productivity was declining; commerce was ruined by the insecurity of the sea and the roads; industry could not prosper, since the market for industrial products was steadily contracting and the purchasing power of the population was diminishing; agriculture passed through a

terrible crisis. . . . Prices constantly rose, and the value of the currency depreciated at an unprecedented rate. . . . The relations between the state and the taxpayer were based on more or less organized robbery: forced work, forced deliveries, forced loans and gifts were the order of the day. The administration was corrupt and demoralized. . . . The most terrible chaos thus reigned throughout the ruined Empire.[162]

What could be done? Like Decius, Diocletian decided that the salvation of Rome lay in the hands of the Gods. And, guided by Decius's prescription for revival, he issued an edict requiring a general sacrifice. Also like Decius, Diocletian "passed over the various oriental deities so popular in the Empire and put himself and his colleagues under the protection of Jupiter and Hercules—gods worshipped at Rome from prehistoric times."[163] But unlike Decius, who ignored Christians except as they refused to sacrifice, Diocletian attempted to root out that faith entirely, because "an old religion ought not be set aside for a new one. For it is the blackest of crimes to repudiate institutions . . . defined by the men of old."[164] Since all Christians had abandoned their traditional faith, whether by converting in the present generation or in generations past, they all were guilty of having repudiated an old religion. This also would seem to explain why there are no reports in either Roman or Jewish sources that Jews were persecuted by Decius or by a later emperor, although they, too, must have refused to sacrifice—they were "exempted" since they were merely observing their ancestral religion.[165]

Perhaps adding to the "sins" of Christians in the eyes of Diocletian, they had built a large new church directly facing his palace (Diocletian resided in Nicomedia). So it was that on February 23, 303, imperial soldiers marched into this church, looted the altar plates and chalices, burned all sacred scriptures, and then demolished the building.[166] The next day Diocletian issued an edict that banned all Christian gatherings, ordered the seizure or destruction of all churches, required that all Christian scriptures be burned, barred Christians from public office or from appearing in court, and prohibited anyone from freeing a Christian slave. In response, some Christians recanted their faith. Some bishops and priests went into hiding. Approximately 3,000 leaders and prominent members were executed, and thousands of others were sentenced to slavery and sent to the mines. Even so, the edicts against Christians were ignored in some cities and, even more remarkably, rapid Christian growth continued! By the end of this final great persecution, which lasted for ten years, there may have been about three million more Christians than there had been at the start (see Chapter 7).

But even Diocletian was not so much an enemy of Christianity as he was determined to cause a revival of the state religion. As Michael Grant (1914–2004) put it, Diocletian and his collaborators were motivated primarily by a "passionate enthusiasm for the old Roman religion and tradition and discipline, in the interests of imperial, patriotic unity."[167] That is, the emperors in this era were not merely against the Christian religion, they greatly favored one of its major competitors.

In the end, of course, the traditional temples proved incapable of holding their own in a free market. By 313, when the last persecution ended, Christians had grown to about 15 percent of the total population and probably made up majorities in many of the larger cities, inspiring Constantine to seek their support. By mid-century they numbered about half of the total population, dominated the cities, and were consolidating their position as the state church, with the result that Rome's dynamic and competitive religious economy withered away.

In any event, these sketches of religious conflict and persecution offer a needed rebuttal to several centuries of unfounded and often disingenuous claims about the inherent tolerance of paganism. This nonsense probably began with Gibbon, who celebrated the "mild spirit of antiquity" in contrast with the "narrow and unsocial spirit . . . [and] sullen obstinacy of the Jews"[168] and the "intolerant zeal"[169] of Christianity. Similar claims about tolerant pagans and intolerant Christians and Jews have been made again and again. As recently as 1990 a distinguished historian could write that "polytheism is by definition tolerant and accommodating."[170] Even more recently, Jonathan Kirsch explained: "Nowhere in the ancient world was the open-mindedness [of paganism] more apparent than in imperial Rome."[171] In support, Kirsch quoted Ramsay MacMullen to the effect that paganism was "no more than a spongy mass of tolerance and tradition."[172] Kirsch continued by regretting the failure of the Emperor Julian to undo Constantine's boost of Christianity and restore the empire to paganism: "It is tantalizing to consider how close he [Julian] came to bringing the spirit of respect and tolerance back into Roman government and thus back into the roots of Western civilization, and even more tantalizing to consider how different our benighted world might have been if he had succeeded."[173] And just who was it who threw Christians to the lions, crucified priests of Isis, or executed converts to Judaism?

COMMITMENT

The market theory of religion proposes that religious competition increases the overall religiousness of a population. It follows that because subsidized monopoly religions gain no benefits from popular support, they will not exert themselves to engage the public (how the energy and effort of Christianity declined following its becoming the official religion is traced in Chapter 7). In fact, in many societies with state temples, most people were not even permitted to see, let alone take part in, the sacred rituals. This does not mean that most Sumerians or Egyptians, for example, were irreligious. But as was evident in the previous chapter, it does mean that they were abandoned by the state temples to seek satisfaction from undemanding and not very fulfilling folk religions. In Egypt, for example, "the common people played little or no role" in the temple religions. They patronized public shrines devoted to local Gods, but their primary emphasis was on "the veneration of personal or local gods honoured in even smaller household shrines. Homes excavated at Dier-el-Medina contained niches in which were kept the images of departed relatives and also of household gods."[174] The same was true wherever state temples ruled the religious scene. Oppenheim noted that the influence of the state religion "on the individual . . . was unimportant in Mesopotamia . . . the participation of the individual in the cult of the city deity was restricted in the extreme; he was simply an onlooker in certain public ceremonies of rejoicing or communal mourning. He lived in a quite tepid religious climate . . ."[175]

In contrast, Romans had the opportunity to be involved in relatively intense, competitive religious groups eager to enlist their support. But *did* they respond? Was the average Roman more involved in religion than were people in societies served by monopoly state temples? Lacking public opinion polls, that is a very difficult question to answer. Nevertheless, although only a few pertinent facts are available, all of them support the prediction that there were relatively high levels of religiousness among *ordinary* Romans.

Perhaps the most obvious indication of unusually high religious participation on the part of the Roman public is that both Decius and Diocletian thought it important to have *everyone* take part in their revival campaigns. No Sumerian king or Egyptian pharaoh would have seen any reason to involve the general public in an appeal to the Gods—they didn't even allow the public to see the Gods or to take part in temple ceremonies. It seems reasonable that the inclusive policy of the emperors reflected a different religious outlook in which it was not enough that priests conducted the appropriate rituals, but that the *extent* of participation mattered, too—that for society as a whole to deserve divine aid, *everyone* should have participated in the sacrifices.

That leads directly to a second reason to suppose that Rome excelled in religiousness: that Greek intellectuals remarked on it. Writing in the middle of the second century BCE, Polybius[176] claimed that "the cohesion of the Roman state" was because members of the ruling class were meticulous in their public piety and thereby aroused intense religious feelings in the "common people." This was necessitated, according to Polybius, because Romans, unlike the Greeks, had been unable to form a state ruled by "wise men" and therefore had to hold the "unreasoned passion and violent anger" of the masses in check through the "invisible terrors" of religion. According to J. H. W. G. Liebeschuetz, such piety among the Romans "had no parallel among comparable circles in Greece."[177]

A third indication of a relatively high level of public piety is the presence of a number of successful religious mass movements. Cybele and Isis did not merely gather a priesthood, nor did Bacchus. Each attracted significant numbers of committed, active lay devotees. So did Mithras. That alone sets the Roman religious economy much apart from those served by monopoly state temples. In addition, of course, there was the presence of millions of Jews and, eventually, millions of Christians. By the first century CE, there were from six to ten million Jews living in the empire outside Palestine, much of this growth coming through conversion.[178] And although early Christianity was very attractive to the upper classes and was not primarily a religion of the poor and dispossessed, it attracted a substantial following among these social strata, too, thus contributing greatly to the overall religious mobilization of the general population of Rome.

Of course, to cite the success of these mass movements as evidence of a high level of religious involvement on the part of the imperial public approaches circularity—to say that pluralism and competition resulted in greater involvement because of the presence of a variety of competing movements. But this is not simply true by definition: these competing movements *could* have languished, failing to mobilize public support. That they did not seems of compelling significance.

There also are fragments of physical evidence to be cited. The most persuasive "hard" evidence of unusual religious involvement by non-elite Romans is that many ordinary Romans, and even many poor people and slaves, pooled their resources to build temples, as is frequently attested in temple inscriptions listing the donors.[179] A very early study of inscriptions found that 16 percent of those contributing to the "oriental cults" in Rome were identifiable as freedmen or slaves.[180] Obviously, such people made up a somewhat larger percentage than this of the total population of the city. But given their circumstances, this seems like a very substantial representation. Nothing comparable is known from the ancient societies with state temples.

In addition, beneath the ruins of a temple devoted to Cybele (Magna Mater), archaeologists found a large cache of terra-cotta images of her companion, Attis, brought as offerings to the Goddess. Significantly, "the poor quality of the terracottas suggests . . . [the] offerings . . . [came from] poor devotees of the cult."[181] Surviving records also show that once it became legal for Romans to serve as priests and priestesses of Cybele, most who did so were ex-slaves.[182] As important negative evidence, men of the Senatorial class are "conspicuously absent" from lists of members or donors to the "new" religions,[183] which suggests that they were mainly funded by the less affluent.

Admittedly, the evidence is not abundant. But perhaps it is enough, since there is nothing obvious to offset it.

CONCLUSION

One of the handicaps of social science is that theories meant to have universal application often have only been tested against contemporary data—too often only with current data from the United States! It is exceptionally important to make use of any practical opportunities to apply such theories to very different eras and cultures. That gives this chapter unusual significance—that the market theory of religious economies jibes so well with the religious life of Rome. A free religious market did result in pluralism, and the competition among faiths did increase the overall level of Roman religiousness as well as spelling the decline of less energetic faiths.

There also is a specific finding of, perhaps, even more importance vis-à-vis this particular time and place: the common bases for repression and persecution—not just of the Jews and the Christians, but of many of the "new" pagan religious movements. It wasn't just their monotheism or in retaliation for rejecting Roman polytheism that got the Jews and Christians in trouble with Rome, because the followers of Cybele, Isis, and Bacchus got in serious trouble, too. What all these groups had in common were high levels of commitment to closely knit religious congregations.

It was "too much" religious commitment that upset the ruling Roman elite, and that has remained a primary cause of religious conflict ever since. Groups committed to more intense religion often provoke fear and retaliation from less demanding religious organizations and from governments that favor them. As will be seen in the next chapter, monotheistic movements always engender conflict and sometimes violence, not only between these movements and their social and political surroundings, but also *within* any given monotheism because feuding internal factions always develop.

THE "REBIRTH" OF
MONOTHEISM

THE IDEA OF ONE SUPREME GOD seemed to vanish with
the advent of civilization, but it had merely gone out of fashion.
Then, after several millennia of polytheism, renewed interest in
monotheism appeared in Egypt, Iran, Israel, Greece, and Rome.

All successful new religions are founded by gifted individuals. But,
gifted or not, priests serving state temple religions rarely introduce even
tiny changes and almost always try to squelch anything new. Ruling elites
also usually attempt to suppress religious innovations, if only because
they already have everything going their way. As a result, significant religious innovations are the work of people who are in some important
ways *outsiders*—even when they are members of the elite. Hence, in order to succeed, founders of new religions must attract sufficient support
to withstand the substantial opposition they invariably arouse—they
must create effective social movements. In the end, nearly everyone who
greatly reformulates a religion, or initiates a new one, fails. A few change
the world.

Of course, even the Gods and rituals of the state temples of Sumer,
Egypt, Greece, and Mesoamerica originated with religious innovators
who initially provided what then became the "unchanging" truths sustained by the priesthoods. The handiwork of innovators was even more
fully on display in the many new faiths that crowded the Roman religious

economy. In this chapter religious innovators come to the fore, a series of historical figures and their efforts on behalf of monotheism.

THE PHARAOH'S GOD

In 1379 BCE Amenhoptep IV succeeded his father to the throne of Egypt. We know little about him because after his death extreme efforts were made to excise his existence from all records. Official lists of pharaohs omit his name and, although he ruled for seventeen years, his successor's reign is listed as beginning upon the death of Amenhoptep's father. These efforts to conceal him from history were so successful that it required a triumph of archaeology to rediscover Amenhoptep's existence and to re-cover the fundamental story of his reign—including the immense heresy that caused the militant efforts to erase him from all records and the de-struction of all the temples he built.

At first the young pharaoh fulfilled his many ritual obligations, includ-ing one each morning to insure that the sun rose, but he became increas-ingly focused on the God Re and soon he became convinced that there was only one God. So, about six years after taking the throne, the pharaoh changed his name to Akhenaten (the glorious spirit of Aten) and, in a "Great Hymn," proclaimed **Rē-Herakhte**, whose symbol is Aten, the solar disk, to be the "Sole God, like unto whom there is no other!" The hymn continues:

> *Thou didst fashion the earth according to thy desire when thou wast*
> *alone . . .*
> *Thou appointest every man to his place and satisfiest his needs.*
> *Everyone receives his sustenance and his days are numbered.*
> *Their tongues are diverse in speech and their qualities likewise, and*
> *their colour is differentiated for thou hast distinguished the nations.*
> *All distant foreign lands also, thou created their life.*[1]

Rē-Herakhte was not just a Supreme God ruling over a pantheon of lesser divinities, but the One God. Consequently, Akhenaten took pains to suppress all references to the plural form of "God" from texts and in-scriptions.[2] According to Karl Richard Lepsius (1810–1884), the founder of modern Egyptology, Akhenaten commanded that "the names of all the deities be hacked away from all public monuments, and even from the

This bas-relief found at Amarna shows Pharaoh Akhenaten, Queen Nefertiti, and three daughters being blessed by the rays of the Sun (Aten)—the symbol of the Only God. (Egyptian Musem, Cairo; Photo: Erich Lessing/Art Resource, New York)

accessible private tombs, and that their images be destroyed to the extent possible"[3] on grounds that it is absurd to suppose that a real God can be created by human craftsmen.[4] No longer were priests assigned to tend, feed, clothe, or bathe the Gods. Instead, the temples of all these "false" Gods were closed, their priesthoods disbanded, and Egypt was commanded to worship "an abstract and intangible god."[5] A God utterly lacking in "mythology." A God who could not be depicted, only symbolized.[6]

A surviving proclamation by Akhenaten attributes the new faith to a revelation given to him by God himself. As Akhenaten expressed it in his Great Hymn, "there is none other who knows thee save thy son Akhenaten. Thou hast made him wise in thy plans and thy power."[7]

Then, according to the proclamation, the pharaoh called all his courtiers and other great men of Egypt to him and explained that God had directed him to create a temple in "a virgin site," whereupon Akhenaten commenced to build a lavish new city in the desert at a place now called

Amarna. Here he raised a magnificent new temple to God that was unlike any of the other temples in Egypt, being open to the sun and to public view—Akhenaten, his wife, and his six daughters could be seen at worship. It also was here in Amarna that the royal family and the courtiers had their tombs carved in the rock cliffs at the edge of the city.

Like the city itself, the tombs (many of which have survived) were filled with remarkably lively art—quite distinct from the standard Egyptian forms and styles, both earlier and later. This is easily appreciated in the surviving bust of Akhenaten's wife Nefertiti, which is so much more naturalistic than usual Egyptian art that it is able to reveal her extraordinary beauty. This new spirit was embodied in the architecture as well as the art—reconstructions based on twentieth-century archaeology reveal "spacious villas, with trees, pools, and gardens. Indoors the walls were painted in the free flowing new art. . . . Everything was lively. . . . The present-day viewer of this ancient art feels as though he were there."[8]

This portrait bust of Queen Nefertiti was as different from conventional Egyptian art as her husband's monotheism differed from Egyptian polytheism. Consequently, modern viewers can fully appreciate her remarkable beauty. (Aegyptiches Museum, Staatliche Museum zu Berlin, Berlin; Photo: Vanni/Art Resource, New York)

Akhenaten's new theology is only partly known, but what survives "goes back to the man himself"[9] and is free of any later emendations or distortions, since it was effectively sealed in a "time capsule" until rediscovered in the nineteenth century. What we know of his monotheism stresses God's goodness and his blessings. The Great Hymn, quoted above, has often been compared with the 110th Psalm for its celebration of God's bounties.[10] So far as can be determined, this was a happy religion without an ethical code: "Men were asked only to be grateful."[11] Nothing seems to have been said about the problem of evil, but the existence even of minor deities was so utterly rejected that it seems unlikely that Akhenaten posited the existence of any satanic power. Absolute monotheism was slightly compromised, however, because in keeping with the traditional Egyptian view that pharaoh was a God, Akhenaten styled himself as the "son of God" who was "issued from thy rays" and who was to be prayed to as the "source of blessings for people after death."[12]

But even as a God, Akhenaten was the ultimate outsider.[13] He seems not to have been trained to take the throne, having succeeded his father only because of the untimely death of his older brother. Controversy has long raged over his physical characteristics, some artwork having depicted him as a strange creature having very narrow shoulders, pendulous breasts, and wide hips. However, this probably was some strange artistic convention, since in other portraits he appears normal. In any event, Akhenaten abandoned the Egyptian capital city, leaving behind most of the elite families and setting up in Amarna accompanied only by his family and a small inner circle. He also left much to be desired in his management of secular affairs—during his reign most of Egypt's colonies were lost to the Hittites and their allies. An extraordinary cache of more than 300 clay tablets sent to Akhenaten by his puppet rulers in Palestine were discovered in 1887 amid the ruins of the palace in Amarna (they have come to be known as the Amarna Letters).[14] Again and again they plead for help in the face of impending defeat. It appears that Akhenaten did not bother to answer.[15]

Akhenaten surely displayed a lack of political sensitivity when he shut down all of the other temples. Even though he vigorously advocated the new monotheism, it is not clear that much of anyone besides his inner circle actually became a committed convert—and most of them probably did not convert either, as is evident in their actions to suppress his new religion and restore the old ones after Akhenaten's death. Indeed, archaeologists have found many figurines of various traditional Gods in ruins of private homes at Amarna, revealing that during the time when all the old Gods and their images were banned, many of Akhenaten's officials continued to worship them in secret.[16]

As for the "people," they had always been shut out of the temples and ignored by the priests. Granted that commoners in many parts of Egypt could now see into the open, sunny temples of Rē-Herakhte that Akhenaten had built, but even so the people could not now see God, because he was never depicted—an invisible God was offered in place of hidden Gods. Perhaps the major impact of the new religion on the average Egyptian was the termination of the many religious festivals, which had provided frequent "public holidays."[17] Had Akhenaten simply transformed these into festivals on behalf of Rē-Herakhte, he might have attracted some popular support to his cause. Instead, by doing away with many holidays, he alienated the public as well as the elites.

This first attempt to establish monotheism was doomed from the start because the pharaoh failed to grasp that he needed to *enlist* support, rather than to simply order it done. His failure was to not have tried to build a social movement of committed believers. So long as he lived, the pharaoh's edicts against the Gods were obeyed, but when Akhenaten died without a son, he was succeeded briefly by Tutankhaten, who soon changed his name to Tutankhamen, honoring Amen (Amon) rather than Aten. He moved the court to Memphis and began to restore the old Gods. On his "Restoration Stele" Tutankhamen noted that he had come to the throne "at a time when the temples of the gods and goddesses . . . had fallen into ruin, and their shrines become dilapidated . . . [meanwhile] this land had been struck by catastrophe: the gods had turned their backs upon it."[18] Tutankhamen's efforts to restore the old religions were continued by his successor, Akhenaten's former grand vizier, Aye. Hence, the "images of the proscribed gods were fashioned anew, their shrines were refurbished, their priesthoods restored, the old worship re-established, and the traditional eschatology fervently embraced."[19] And there was no significant group of converts to monotheism to oppose these revivals.

Soon thereafter, Horemheb, commander of the army, seized the throne. Then came revenge. The great temple at Amarna was destroyed, and all the stones and bricks used in its construction were taken away and reused in other public buildings. Since each was marked with Akhenaten's *car-touche* (a royal trademark), after immense effort modern archaeologists have recovered large numbers of them and have made hypothetical reconstructions of some of the original murals and inscriptions.[20] Also in ancient times, Akhenaten's tomb was entered, and his granite sarcophagus was smashed into such small pieces that it cannot be reconstructed and his mummy was taken away—probably destroyed so as to deny him an afterlife. Everywhere they could be found, likenesses of the pharaoh and his family were obliterated or at least defaced. Akhenaten was lost from all memory for more than three millennia.

That fact alone would seem to refute the many efforts to trace Jewish monotheism to Egyptian origins, Sigmund Freud's peculiar *Moses and Monotheism* being the most notorious example. Granted, a period of Egyptian slavery played a significant part in the history of the Israelites, but if we accept the traditional date of the Exodus as around 1440 BCE, then the Jews left long before Akhenaten was born. On the other hand, if we accept the far more plausible date for the Exodus as occuring in the middle of the thirteenth century BCE,[21] then the Jews were present in Egypt during Akhenaten's reign and for some time afterward. That still does not encourage the conclusion that Jewish monotheism originated with Akhenaten because for many centuries after the Exodus, as will be seen, the religion that prevailed among the Israelites involved a number of Gods, and it is silly to compare the Jewish faith that took many centuries slowly to develop into a brilliant monotheism with the monotheism that had appeared so many centuries before and so briefly in Egypt, and then vanished.[22]

ZOROASTRIANISM

The next appearance of monotheism may have been in what today is eastern Iran and western Afghanistan. Whether Zoroastrianism was the second major manifestation of monotheism, or the third, depends upon the dates assigned to Zoroaster as well as upon judgments as to when Jewish monotheism actually began. Until well into the twentieth century, it was agreed that Zoroaster lived in the sixth century BCE. Then, some prominent scholars began to insist that he lived many centuries earlier, somewhere between 1700 and 1200 BCE, and a bitter debate ensued.[23] The basis for this and many other disputes about Zoroastrianism is the lack of original sources. Only about a fourth of the original **Avesta**, the Zoroastrian holy text, survives, and even this fragment was greatly reworked between the fourth and ninth centuries CE and now reveals substantial Christian and Muslim influences.[24] Some additional scriptures referred to as the "Younger Avesta"[25] seem to have been written in the fourth century BCE and "flatly contradict the prophet's own doctrines," being openly polytheistic.[26] Only the **Gāthās**, hymns attributed to Zoroaster, are thought to be relatively authentic. Unfortunately, rather than indicating when Zoroaster lived, the "date of the Gāthās depends upon the date that is assigned to Zoroaster."[27] Some of what has been believed about Zoroaster and his religious movement comes from various ancient Greek writers, and questions arise as to their biases and the reliability of their sources. Finally, because Zoroastrianism is still a living faith, especially as sustained by the Parsis in India, it has generated a much more recent religious literature of unknown validity vis-à-vis ancient events.

Zoroaster's dates matter. If he lived sometime between 1700 and 1200 BCE, then Mary Boyce[28] was probably correct to situate him among Stone Age nomads. The later dates place him at the edge of the emerging Persian Empire and make him a contemporary of Cyrus the Great. The early date also falsifies many traditions concerning Zoroaster—that, for example, he met and influenced Pythagoras,[29] and that he was known to the Jews as the Prophet Ezekiel.[30] Neither of these very old traditions may be true, but both require Zoroaster to have lived in the sixth century. Consequently, I must choose sides in a debate that involves very technical evidence.

The first draft of this section favored the early dates. Then I was fortunate enough to obtain a new book by Gherardo Gnoli, the distinguished scholar of ancient Near Eastern religions.[31] In it Gnoli retracted his many years of vigorous support for the early dating of Zoroaster and carefully detailed what has become a compelling case in favor of the later dates. Gnoli fully convinced me that Zoroaster's dates are approximately 618–541 BCE. Hence, the ancient Greeks may have been right in claiming that Pythagoras met Zoroaster, and although it seems implausible that Zoroaster was Ezekiel, the leaders of the increasingly powerful monotheistic Jewish faction did encounter a new, robust Zoroastrianism during their stay in Babylon. A later section is devoted to this matter.

The Prophet

Although his name literally means "he who manages camels,"[32] a highly respected occupation at that time, it appears that Zoroaster was trained as a priest and a chanter in the prevailing polytheism. This was an established temple religion typical of the time and place, served by professional priests who opposed all innovations (and soon became Zoroaster's bitter enemies). They worshipped the usual collection of nature and functional Gods (sky, moon, rain, war, fertility, wisdom, etc.) and devoted their time and energy to performing rites.[33]

Biographical details are scanty, but it appears that Zoroaster was initiated into the priesthood at about age fifteen and five years later took up a wandering life, devoting the next decade to intense spiritual reflection and searching.[34] When he was about thirty, Zoroaster had a revelation. While attending a spring festival, he went to the river for water. Having waded to midstream, he had begun to return when he suddenly had a vision in which he saw a shining "being" who then led Zoroaster into the presence of **Ahura Mazdā** (also Mazdāh) and five other subordinate radiant figures.

Accounts of Zoroaster's revelation do not claim that Ahura Mazdā and the other shining beings were actually present at the river, but only that this is where Zoroaster had his vision of them. Although the discussion of revelations in Chapter 1 demonstrated that entirely normal people can, and do, have visions such as this in quite normal ways, modern scholars have been quick to attribute such events to abnormal mental states produced by psychosis or chemistry. True to form, Henrik Nyberg (1889–1974) gained international attention by depicting Zoroaster's visions as the work of an ignorant Stone Age witch doctor, chronically intoxicated on hemp. Nyberg buttressed his claims by citing the ambiguity of the Gāthās.[35] True, the Gāthās are ambiguous and extremely difficult, but they also are brilliant in ways unlikely to have been produced by a drugged ignoramus.

Having summoned Zoroaster to serve him, Ahura Mazdā revealed that there is only One God—that he, Ahura Mazdā, is the eternal creator and ruler of the universe and that the other shining beings are his servants. Unlike the monotheism of Akhenaten, Zoroaster's revelation confronted the problem of evil—God is engaged in a battle with the inferior **Angra**

Mainyu, the "Fiendish Spirit," who causes calamities and leads humans into evil. Each human is required to choose between good and evil, and the outcome of the battle "rests on mankind: the support which each man lends to the side he has chosen will add permanent strength to it; in the long run, therefore, the acts of man will weigh the scales in favor of the one side or the other."[36] No more powerful doctrine of "free will" and its implications has ever been stated.

Many regard dualistic monotheism as the most important contribution made by Zoroastrianism to the evolution of religion. The influential Walter Bruno Henning (1908–1967) explained that whenever a "purely monotheistic" religion is proposed, it must "provoke the question why the world, in the outcome, is so very far from good. Zoroaster's answer, that the world had been created by a good god" and that an "evil spirit" is attempting "to spoil the good work, is a complete answer: it is a logical answer." To fully "appreciate Zoroaster," we must acknowledge him as the "first to put forward" the dualistic solution to the problem of evil and monotheism, and recognize what a "great achievement" it was.[37] Whether Zoroaster was the first dualistic monotheist, or whether the Jews preceded him, is impossible to determine. What we know is that from no later than the sixth century BCE, some human beings conceived of the One God as consistently loving and virtuous (although vindictive in response to sin), and also as a God who places full responsibility for our fate on each of us.

Having accepted the mission to lead humanity into righteousness, Zoroaster began to proselytize on behalf of an explicitly dualistic monotheism. In doing so, he enjoyed the advantage of continuity with the prevailing Iranian religious culture, which allowed his converts to *minimize their expenditure of religious* (or spiritual) *capital.*

Religious capital consists of the *degree of mastery and attachment to a particular body of religious culture.*[38] In any society most people are socialized into a religion. They learn the beliefs, the rites, the norms, and the traditions of some faith. For example, young Christians learn the meaning of the cross, whether and when to say "Amen," the words of liturgies and prayers, passages of scripture, stories and history, music, even jokes. Moreover, through practice and social reinforcement people come to value their religious culture, to invest in it emotionally.

When confronted with new Gods within a polytheistic context, people may accept them simply by adding to their existing stock of religious capital. But when faced with claims of exclusive religious truth, for people to change their religion puts their religious capital at risk of becoming worthless, which is why converts typically are those having had relatively little religious capital to lose—most people drawn to new religions grew up in irreligious or religiously inactive homes.[39] Put another way, *people will more readily join an exclusive religion to the degree that it minimizes their loss of religious capital.* Therefore, relatively exclusive new religions will be more successful to the extent that they retain *cultural continuity* with the relevant old religions.

Cultural continuity refers to *similarities and correspondences* between two cultures. As an example, consider Christians deciding whether to become Mormons or Hindus. To become Mormons, Christians retain all (or nearly all) of their religious capital, needing merely to add to it: they already possess two of the three scriptures, needing only to add the *Book of Mormon*: *Another Testament of Jesus Christ*. But to become Hindus, Christians must discard their Bible and all their other religious capital, rush out and buy a copy of the *Bhagavad-gītā*, and invest the time and energy needed to build a whole new cultural stake. So, most would choose to become Mormons.

Ancient Iranians could retain much of their religious capital when they embraced Zoroastrianism. Ahura had long been known to Iranians as a major God. Zoroastrianism simply added Mazdā (meaning "wise") to his name. Many other traditional deities reappeared within Zoroastrianism as subordinate supernatural creatures, and even many familiar rituals were retained. Iranian polytheists believed in life after death, albeit in a somewhat shadowy underworld. Upon this foundation, Zoroastrianism offered a far more attractive, if conditional, version: the souls of the virtuous will reach heaven, while those of evildoers will fall into hell.

Based on these new notions about the afterlife, Zoroastrianism rejected the standard ancient cosmology of eternal historical cycles and replaced it with a linear view of history leading to an apocalyptic last judgment when the righteous dead will be resurrected and given indestructible bodies and evil will be banished forever. Norman Cohn hailed this as one of the greatest of all religious innovations, one that has repeatedly animated Jewish and, subsequently, Christian religious movements ever since.[40] Whether this was, in fact, the origin of apocalypticism is difficult to say.

The Movement

Following his revelation, Zoroaster began his career as a prophet and organizer, but virtually without success. If tradition is to be believed, during the first ten years of his mission Zoroaster made only one convert: his cousin Maidhyōimāh. Then he converted his wife's uncle[41] (nothing is said about whether his wife believed him, but that would seem likely). There may well have been a few additional converts, and they could also have been relatives, but very little about Zoroaster and his movement has survived. We do know, however, that Zoroaster's efforts to found a new religion aroused such angry opposition that he feared for his life. For, not only did Zoroaster challenge the prevailing temple priesthood, he denounced them as utterly evil. He was the prophet of Truth. They were the followers of the Lie—to whom he declared himself to be "a true enemy." Indeed, Zoroaster referred to his priestly opponents as "mumblers," in reference to their endless "recitation of a traditional liturgy."[42]

Faced with militant opposition and his failure to attract a significant following, in desperation Zoroaster fled north to the nearby kingdom of Chorasmia (in modern Uzbekistan). Here, as an inspired *outsider*, he made his mark. Somehow he gained the ear of Queen Hutaosā and she helped him convert her husband, King Kavi Vīštāspa. With royal testimonials, the new faith quickly spread through the nobility. Holy wars soon ensued with neighboring polytheists—this may have been the first historical manifestation of the conflict inherent in the belief that there is only One True God and that it is sinful to worship others.[43] Their enemies were nearby rulers, supported by the traditional priesthood. For Zoroaster there could "be no question of compromise with . . . evil: the enemy must either be vanquished or converted."[44] King Vīštāspa's forces were victorious, and soon the new monotheistic faith had gained sufficient momentum so that Zoroaster was no longer essential to keep things going. Now he found time to take two additional wives and father at least six children.

According to tradition, Zoroaster was murdered at age seventy-seven by an assassin who probably was a priest of the old religion. Mary Boyce, one of the foremost historians of Zoroastrianism (although probably wrong about his dates), reflected "that in the end a fanatic should have slain the prophet seems wholly credible in light of the fierce religious controversies and holy wars depicted in the Avesta."[45]

Then came Cyrus the Great (c. 590–529 BCE), who defeated King Vīštāspa and submerged his kingdom into the immense, new Persian Empire. Initially, having been reduced from the official religion to a relatively powerless minority, the Zoroastrians moderated their attitudes toward nonbelievers. For example, as R. C. Zaehner (1913–1974), the distinguished Oxford orientalist, noted, the "formula 'good thoughts, good words, good deeds' appears for the first time, the Prophet's injunction to render evil for evil is passed over in silence."[46] However, once Darius I (550–486 BCE) gained the Persian throne, Zoroastrianism regained power—Darius having embraced the new monotheism.[47] His son Xerxes (c. 519–465 BCE), famous for having been routed by the Greeks at Salamis, also was a committed Zoroastrian, albeit he lacked the theological sophistication of his father. Some still dispute whether Darius and Xerxes were Zoroastrians, but I judge that Ilya Gershevitch (1914–2001), another distinguished Oxford don, has fully demonstrated that they were.

In any event, the initial commitment of Persian emperors to Zoroastrian monotheism was soon followed by a relapse into polytheism. Artaxerxes II (405–359 BCE) expressed his devotion to three Gods: Ahura Mazdā, Mithras, and Anāhitā. More remarkably, the Zoroastrian priesthood went along—the Younger Avestan texts, written at this time, are "strangely contaminated with . . . 'pagan' polytheism. Beside Ahura Mazdā numerous other gods are worshipped. . . . There are passages in the hymns to these gods in which Ahura Mazdā himself is represented as worshipping them."[48] As Zaehner put it, "A host of gods, fetched up from an older tradition . . . now share his glory."[49] Indeed, there is evidence that Zoroaster himself was worshipped as a God in this era[50]—a fate that also befell Buddha, Lao-Tzu, and Confucius.

This was but one of the many examples of how difficult it is to maintain uncompromised monotheism in the face of the constant and obvious attractions of polytheism. These pressures are especially acute when a ruler seeks to merge "nations" honoring different Gods into an empire (as in the case of the Israelite kings as well). But, once revealed, the concept of an Only God has demonstrated the ability to persist and win out, at least in the long run. Thus, even in the Younger Avesta, dualism remained the primary tenet, and eventually Zoroastrian monotheism regained its full authority. This seems to have occurred late in the fourth century BCE, when the *Magi* became Zoroastrians.

The Magi were professional priests who apparently knew and performed all of the rites and rituals of all the various Gods and faiths prevalent in the area that eventually came under Persian rule. They also were astrologers of note, who probably taught that art to the Greeks (who sometimes referred to them as Chaldeans). For several centuries there seems not to have been a traditional Magi faith,[51] rather they "ministered [for] payment, much as a professional musician earns his living by performing the works of different composers."[52] However, the Magi did believe the dead should be exposed rather than buried (a practice later adopted by Zoroastrians), and they preferred incestuous marriages.[53] During the lapse of Zoroastrianism into polytheism, it appears that the Magi conducted Zoroastrian rites as well as those of the traditional religions, but eventually they "acknowledged Zoroaster as their prophet."[54] Of course, the conversion of the Magi has been disputed by various scholars,[55] but many others[56] have joined the inimitable Arthur Darby Nock[57] to agree with a long list of famous ancient authors, including Plato, Pliny the Elder, and Plutarch,[58] as well as Clement of Alexandria, Origen, and Saint Augustine, that the Magi did become Zoroastrians. Moreover, by doing so "they ensured the preservation down to the present day of its Avestan scripture. Without this scripture the bright dawn of Iranian thought would be hidden from us."[59]

Thus does Zoroaster stand as the founder of an impressive and surviving monotheism. As Henning summed up: "A great nation revered him as its prophet. Long after Iranians had forgotten Cyrus and Darius and all their crowd, they continued to accord nearly divine honours to Zoroaster."[60]

JUDAISM

Judaism is preeminently a "religion of the book." The scriptures included in the **Tanakh** (which Christians refer to as the Old Testament) play the authoritative role in the religious life of observant Jews. The Tanakh consists of the **Torah** (the first five books, attributed to Moses), the writings of the prophets, known as the **Nevi'im**, and the literary books (such as Psalms), which are known as the **Kethuvim** (the writings). The word *Tanakh* is an acronym of the titles of these three parts. In addition, there is an immense body of commentary on scripture, and particularly on the

Torah, written over the centuries by learned rabbis and known as the **Tal-mud**, which consists of two parts, the **Mishnah** and the **Gemara**.

What most distinguishes the Tanakh from other scriptures of its time is that it includes a great deal of history—so much so that some even have proposed that the Jews "invented" the writing of history.[61] In contrast with the religious writings of Sumer or of Egypt, for example, the Tanakh tells very little about events in a "divine world" and nothing at all as to a biography of God. Instead, it devotes a good deal of text to the relationship between Israel and God, and far more to the history of the Israelites. Being history, questions necessarily arise as to its accuracy. This has increasingly become an issue because of the rapidly growing mass of archaeological data, as well as the discovery and translation of records from Israel's neighbors: Egypt, Mesopotamia, Babylon, Persia, and even Greece and Rome.

Consequently, biblical scholarship is wracked by disputes over the fit between these other sources, especially archaeological data, and the scriptural accounts. Some militant extremists from several minor universities even claim none of it ever happened: That the Bible deals with "a people who never existed."[62] That the prophets are fictional characters. That the whole Torah was made up sometime about 200 BCE as "pious propaganda"[63] by Hellenized Jews in the Diaspora wishing to impress their Greek and Roman neighbors.[64]

Sad to say, these so-called minimalists are much quoted in the media, partly because outrageous statements about religion are thought to be "news," but also because respectable scholars have been forced by substantial archaeological and textual evidence to reject *some* portions of early Jewish history as it is told in *some* scriptural passages, although these revisions often are in accord with other parts of the Bible. Of considerable importance is that scholars have detected many late scriptural insertions and revisions involved in what has come to be known as "Deuteronomistic History."[65] At issue are Deuteronomy, Joshua, Judges, 1 and 2 Samuel, and 1 and 2 Kings, now thought to be a unified work, as well as revisions and insertions in other scriptures (especially Exodus and Leviticus). Although much of this can be traced to a Book of Laws reportedly found when the Temple in Jerusalem was being renovated in the seventh century BCE, the work of the Deuteronomists seems to have taken place later, during the middle of the sixth century BCE.[66]

The Deuteronomists will be discussed at length in a subsequent section. Here it is sufficient to point out that merely because some portions of scripture were produced at a later date does not necessarily mean that they are spurious—most respectable scholars accept that the Deuteronomists worked with far older texts and, probably, with oral traditions as well.[67] That so much scripture is written in poetry is indicative of having been passed along orally,[68] and, as will be demonstrated in Chapter 5, oral transmission even over several millennia can be remarkably precise. Moreover, all discrepancies with earlier scriptures could reflect that by the sixth century, human recipients were better able to understand God's words. Keep in mind the doctrine that *all revelations* are limited by the capacity of humans to comprehend, and that on these grounds, John Calvin dismissed Genesis as an account of Creation told in "baby talk" in order to penetrate the ignorance of Israel. Remember, too, that even if the source is divine, all revelations become subject to human foibles and frailties, to misunderstanding, distortion, and exaggeration. Besides, the major emphasis in what follows is not on early Jewish history per se, but on the development of Jewish conceptions of God and how these were embodied in religious institutions. Within this context, the long struggle to convert Israel to full-fledged monotheism in the face of traditions and temptations favoring polytheism will be assessed. I will then turn to the Diaspora and to the spread of Jewish monotheism—especially Jewish missionary efforts among Greeks and Romans.

Whatever its defects, considering its age, the Tanakh is remarkably reliable as to many important matters. Its lists of kings of Israel and Judea are solidly confirmed by outside sources from Egypt, Assyria, Babylon, and elsewhere. Its references to wars, to various "captivities," and its essential geography also jibe with these sources.[69] Its frequent denunciations of persistent polytheism is well supported by archaeology. Moreover, historical errors do not *necessarily* challenge religious tenets. Consider this example.

The best of the archaeologically informed historians[70] now believe that the Jews did not conquer Israel after their long stay in the wilderness, but settled peacefully. For example, Jericho is the oldest known Neolithic (New Stone Age) town site, having first been settled in about 10,000 BCE.[71] Recent archaeology shows that it was destroyed in about 1500 BCE by the Egyptians and lay in abandoned ruins at the time Joshua was said to have brought down its walls.[72] What now seems most likely is that a small band (or bands) of Israelite slaves did leave Egypt.[73] Having settled in the rural hill country of Palestine, their numbers subsequently were increased many times over by locals, most of them Canaanites, but also various malcontents and rebels, all of whom fled repressive rule in the corrupt and collapsing cities of Egyptian-controlled Palestine. After all, the Bible reports that not only did Midianites and Moabites accompany the Israelites, but that they were joined in the wilderness by Jebusites, Gibeonites, Hebrews, Kenites, and others. Soon there was a large population up in the hills, and few people were left in the cities, some of which had become virtual ghost towns. At this point, rather than having overwhelmed and sacked these cities, as Egyptian control waned, the hill people gradually and *peacefully* resettled the cities. This historical reconstruction is consistent with the archaeological record.[74]

But it also is consistent with *some portions* of the Bible, which also contradict the tradition of conquest under Joshua. As pointed out by the eminent Gösta Ahlström[75] (1918–1992), even in Joshua (13:2) there is the acknowledgment that "there remains yet very much land to be possessed," and in Judges (1:21, 27–36), there is a long list of cities that the Israelites had been unable to conquer. Gradual settlement also fits with 1 Samuel (12:8), which, as interpreted by Ahlström, suggests that Moses and Aaron led Israel to settle in the hill country, and makes no mention of the "Joshua conquest," it being "probable that had there been a glorious entry and conquest, [Samuel] would have recorded them as mighty 'deeds' of Yahweh . . . [and] since no 'promise of the land' is included in this text, we must assume that the material found [in Genesis and Deuteronomy] was unknown [then]." Ahlström continued: "Because this Moses tradition is unaware of a conquest of Canaan under Joshua . . . any historical reconstruction of an Israelite settlement that is founded on the conquest material must fail."[76]

Clearly, then, whether the archaeological evidence is contrary to the Bible in this instance depends upon which scriptural passages one chooses—albeit that the Joshua conquest is the traditional Jewish and Christian account. In any event, historical errors as such do not challenge the validity of the Jewish vision of God—their monotheism is not contingent on there having been a Battle of Jericho, or even on the Parting of the Red Sea. It is the Jewish discovery of Yahweh that brings us here.

However, even some aspects of the nature of early Jewish monotheism are surrounded by controversies, too. One of these disputes is not only over what Moses taught, but whether or not he even existed.

Moses

The first thing that needs to be acknowledged about whether or not Moses actually existed is that, beginning in the nineteenth century, revisionist scholars have attracted considerable notice by denying the existence of many major religious figures, not only Moses, but Buddha, Confucius, Lao-Tzu, Zoroaster, and even Jesus, as well as many less prominent figures including Orpheus, Pythagoras, and Gilgamesh, as was discussed in Chapter 2. Indeed, some of the current biblical "minimalists" even deny the existence of David and Solomon, let alone Moses. Although this fad is now in retreat, it seems worthwhile to deal with the existence of major religious figures as they enter the narrative—as Moses does now.

According to the Torah, there are five major aspects to the Moses story: his revelations from God; the Exodus; receiving the Law; marking time in the wilderness; and preparing for the conquest of the Land of Canaan. These often are summarized as Moses the prophet, Moses the Lawgiver, and Moses the leader. This epic is said to have taken about 120 years. But even if we suppose Moses's life to have been of more conventional duration and dismiss some of the miracles as having literary origins, the story poses problems that vex many serious modern scholars. As to Moses the Lawgiver, the many subsequent prophets deny that Israel in the wilderness possessed the extensive laws credited to Moses—indeed, only Jeremiah (15:1) and Micah (6:4) even mention Moses by name.[77] As to Moses the leader, he also is unmentioned in the oldest biblical reference to the Exodus, Miriam's "Song of the Sea" (Exodus 15). In fact, even though Moses is a towering presence in Exodus and Deuteronomy, he is surprisingly unattested in most of the Bible. This is of concern because much of the emphasis on Moses seems to have been added by the Deuteronomists.

A second basis for concern about the existence of Moses is that there is no direct extra-biblical evidence of his existence. The extensive Egyptian histories do not mention either him or the Exodus. Of course, most figures, religious or secular, mentioned in ancient sources left no independent traces. That does not mean they should therefore be dismissed as fictive. Indeed, for a long time scholars assumed that Gilgamesh was only a "mythical" figure—then his name turned up on a list of real Sumerian kings.[78] That doesn't vouch for the truth of Gilgamesh's many great deeds or his interactions with the Gods, but it does alert us that his narrative is based on someone regarded as remarkable by his contemporaries. Nevertheless, Moses's name, as such, does not appear anywhere other than in the Bible.

One "outside" fact favoring that there was a real person underneath the biblical accounts of Moses, is that his name is Egyptian, not Semitic. Another is that *someone* had revelations and founded the Israelite religion, since many of the truly distinctive features of Judaism appear at this time. Consequently, as William Dever has acknowledged, "even some rather radical scholars would take seriously the notion . . . [that] the tribal peoples who became early Israel . . . may indeed have been guided through the desert by a charismatic, sheikh-like leader with the Egyptian name of 'Moses' . . . [who was subsequently] incorporated into the national epic."[79]

There also is an interesting circumstantial factor that gives credence to accounts of Moses as prophet. Recall from Chapter 1 that it is typical for religious innovators to depend upon their families to offer initial ratification of their claims—even Zoroaster's first converts were his cousin (and, perhaps, his wife) and then his wife's uncle. Half of the first twenty-two converts to Mormonism were from the immediate family of Joseph Smith, and the rest were neighbors. Buddha also began by converting his immediate family, and the same applies to Jesus (Chapter 7) and Muhammad (Chapter 8). In this regard, Moses ran true to type. His father-in-law and his wife seem to have been his first loyal supporters, followed by his brother, Aaron, and his sister, Miriam. Then came Moses's sons and nephews.[80] If the Moses story were made up, there is no reason for the composers to detail this family recruitment pattern. It seems far more likely that they would simply have presumed that Moses rapidly converted the Jews en masse, merely by revealing his powerful new truths. But no. The Bible tells that the first to accept Moses's revelations were his immediate family, which has, from the standpoint of social science, the profound ring of truth.

All things considered, it seems reasonable to assume that Moses did exist and that he played a major role in establishing **Yahweh** as the God of Israel. Written without vowels as YHWH, the original pronunciation is lost and the pronunciation "Ya Way" "is a scholarly guess."[81] The Christian form of the word as *Jehovah* has been traced to Pope Leo X's confessor in 1518.[82]

Scholars are uncertain as to the actual meaning of the word *Yahweh*, and most of the modern translations evade the issue by substituting the word *Lord* for *Yahweh* and are content with the amplification in Exodus 3:13: "*I am who I am.*" The earliest appearance of the name *Yahweh* would seem to be in the Song of Deborah (Judges 5), which has been dated to the eleventh century BCE. Some suggest that Moses derived the name *Yahweh* from the Egyptians, others that he adopted it from the Midianites through his father-in-law,[83] and hundreds of millions believe that God himself told Moses: *I am Yahweh.*

Early Israelite Polytheism

Discussion of the fully developed Jewish conception of Yahweh is deferred until a later section because it took many centuries before the Israelites actually became Jews—a people who observe the Law and embrace authentic monotheism. There is no indication that Abraham believed there was only One God, nor does it appear that the conception of One God even began with Moses. The voice from the burning bush did not say, "I am the only God." And later, when God is quoted as commanding the Israelites to "*have no other Gods before me,*" the *existence* of other Gods is implicit. As recorded in scripture Yahweh did not tell the Israelites that Baal and the many other Gods associated with the surrounding peoples were fantasies, but that they were off limits. In fact, monotheistic claims are rarely expressed in the Tanakh, and these "relatively few instances" are to be found in those portions attributed to the Deuteronomists and especially in the additions made by the writer known as "Second Isaiah."[84]

Thus, it is not surprising that for many centuries after Moses, most Israelites seem to have cheerfully broken the First Commandment, if they even knew of it. The prevailing religion of Israel far more closely resembled those faiths that gave particular emphasis to a High God or a Father of the Gods, than it did monotheism.[85] There is a great deal of archaeological evidence in support of this claim.[86] Many inscriptions combine other Gods with Yahweh. Any number of figurines, votives, and "graven images" have been found in Israelite sites—many of these are of the Goddess Asherah, who seems to have been widely acknowledged as Yahweh's wife.[87] All of this "hard" evidence attests that Yahweh was regarded as the highest God by many, that some even worshipped "Yahweh alone" as Israel's exclusive God, but that the existence of other Gods and Goddesses—including Baal, Astarte, Chemosh, and Molech, as well as Asherah—was generally accepted.[88]

Although abundant and convincing, this archaeological evidence is, in many ways, superfluous since the Bible abounds in passages that acknowledge the widespread worship of other Gods by the Israelites.[89] For example:

> The people of Israel did what was evil in the sight of the LORD, forgetting the LORD their God, and serving the Ba'als and the Ashe'roth. (Judges 3:7)

Such "idolatry" was not limited to very early times, but flourished at the height of Israel's national power, when idols were set up and worshipped even in the famous Temple built by Solomon. That is a principal theme of 1 and 2 Kings.

Temple Judaism

When Saul established the Jewish monarchy, he placed his capital in Jerusalem. David made it the religious capital as well by having the Ark of the Covenant placed there, and then Solomon built up the city in accordance with the "standard" acropolis model. That is, the lower city was dominated by a palace-temple complex atop Temple Mount. In keeping with the diversity of Gods and rites that soon existed within Solomon's Temple, the building itself was designed and constructed by Phoenicians who were the descendants of Canaanites and who worshipped Baal. This is reported in 1 Kings and is confirmed by archaeological evidence.[90]

Not only did Solomon's Temple closely resemble other Near Eastern temples of the day, but it served the same primary function: to impose a centralized state-sponsored religion to replace the local religious shrines and associations and thereby transfer the "locus of primary religious life from family and clan to the *royal* cultus in Jerusalem, under priestly supervision."[91] Considerable pressure was applied to discontinue use of local shrines and to force everyone wishing to worship to "go up to Jerusalem." Even so, as in Sumer and Egypt, the public was barred from the Temple and could only stand in "the outer court in front of the temple, and had

These three figurines of the Goddess Astarte are typical of the large numbers of such figurines found in Israelite sites, dating from around 1000 BCE. This is but a fragment of the evidence that strongly supports the biblical claim that polytheism was widespread in Israel until the return from Babylon. (Israel Museum [IDAM], Jerusalem; Photo: Erich Lessing/Art Resource, New York)

no access to the temple itself. . . . For the people, Yahweh . . . disappeared behind thick walls in the semi-darkness of the royal temple."[92] Despite being excluded, as was also the case in Egypt and Sumer, the "people" had no doubt been conscripted to build the Temple, and they paid for and continued to support it through "huge levies of taxes."[93]

Moreover, as with polytheistic temples of the era, the Temple in Jerusalem also was considered to be a "divine dwelling place." Although there was no image of Yahweh in the Temple, there was an enormous throne supported by cherubs, upon which he was believed to sit invisibly.[94] In addition, the Temple contained various "idols," including the bronze serpent attributed to Moses and which received offerings.[95] The religious diversity of the Temple reflected the religious diversity of Solomon's realm and of his imperial aspirations as demonstrated in his choice of wives. Many of his marriages represented foreign alliances, and these brides brought their national Gods with them. And as 1 Kings 11:3–8 tells us, "*His wives turned his heart after other gods.*" The passage continues:

> *For Solomon went after Ash'toreth the goddess of the Sido'nians, and after Milcom the abomination of the Ammonites. . . . Then Solomon*

*built a high place for Chemosh the abomination of Moab, and for
Molech the abomination of the Ammonites, on the mountain east of
Jerusalem. And so he did for all his foreign wives, who burned incense
and sacrificed to their gods.*

Granted that this passage is one of the sections added or revised by the
Deuteronomists, but that in no way compromises these reports of royal
"idolatry." Since the Deuteronomists were militant monotheists, there
seems little reason for them to have made up accounts of the unfaithfulness of one of Israel's greatest heroes; it seems more likely that if they had
falsified the record, it would have been to claim Solomon as a model of
orthodoxy. In addition to plausibility, we have a very large and rapidly
growing trove of archaeological evidence in support of widespread polytheism in this era.[96]

Polytheism became even more pronounced when, upon Solomon's
death, the kingdom was divided with Rehoboam reigning as King of
Judah in the south (922–915 BCE), while Jeroboam became King of Israel
in the north (922–911 BCE). As can be seen in Map 4–1, the border between the two realms ran east and west just south of Jericho and Bethel,
thus placing Jerusalem in Judah. Rehoboam may have built shrines to
many Gods and even sustained temple prostitutes, although historians
dispute the matter. Jeroboam is reported to have constructed two golden
calves, appointed non-Levitic priests, and made sacrificial offerings to
other Gods. Some historians dismiss all of this as propaganda inserted
in Kings by the Deuteronomists,[97] but the more plausible case is made by
scholars[98] who regard it as a reliable account, probably "drawn from the
annals of the kings of Israel."[99] Moreover, it, too, is consistent with a substantial body of archaeological evidence.[100]

Mention once again of the Deuteronomists brings us to the major dynamic behind the evolution of Israelite monotheism—centuries of bitter
conflict between a group committed to the worship of Yahweh Only, and
the majority who worshipped Yahweh and Others.

THE YAHWEH-ONLY SECT

Israel did not finally embrace monotheism because this conception of
God had such obvious merit or compelling attraction. Granted that ideas

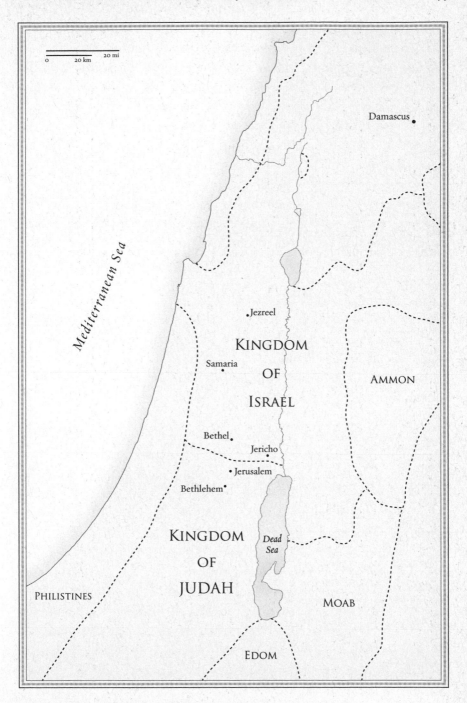

Map 4–1: Map of Israel's Divided Kingdom, 900 BCE.

differ greatly in their attractiveness and plausibility, but even attractive and very plausible ideas win out *only* when they are pursuasively advocated or are imposed by force. Therefore, to explain how the Israelites became monotheists, it is necessary to search for an organized faction of devoted monotheists and to examine the means by which they won out. Such a search quickly leads to the discovery of a dedicated sect movement that, over the course of many centuries of effort and agitation, finally established one God in the stead of many.

A **sect** is a *religious group that sustains a relatively intense level of religious commitment, thereby maintaining a substantial degree of tension with its cultural environment.*[101] Tension refers to the degree of distinctiveness, separation, and antagonism between a religious group and the "outside" world. A **sect movement** is *a sect that actively promotes social change in accord with its religion.*

Fleeting glimpses of a monotheistic Jewish sect movement can be seen in many biblical passages, and several scholars have noted its role in the transformation of Israel during and after the Babylonian exile. But a far more satisfactory "history" can be constructed if these glimpses are assembled into a coherent account, informed by the very well-developed sociology of religious economies, especially the formation and transformation of sects.[102]

The starting point is the observation, clarified in Chapter 3, that members of any society vary in terms of their religious tastes and preferences. Sects are formed by, and appeal to, those *persons who desire a relatively intense form of religion.* However, sect formation also is shaped by the social situation. Within strong states committed to an official religious culture, as in Sumer and Egypt, sects are marginalized and may engender serious repression, although if they remain small and attract only socially insignificant followers, they probably will be ignored, as was the case for the various "folk" religions that existed in these societies. Unlike Egypt or Mesopotamia, through much of its history Israel lacked a state, and even while they reigned, Israelite kings were relatively weak. Eventually, of course, Israel was ruled by cultural outsiders who usually took little or no interest in its religious controversies. As a result, Israel enjoyed a relatively unregulated religious economy. There lay the key to unique contours of Jewish history: *unregulated religious economies always abound in sect movements, and when they enjoy sufficient freedom, sects sometimes achieve dra-*

matic religious changes. Thus, sects abounded throughout Jewish history, including at least one devoted to the exclusive worship of Yahweh.

That this faction has not previously been identified as a sect movement probably is because for many decades sociologists mistakenly assumed that sects primarily enlist the lower classes and shape their theology to compensate the poor and powerless for their deprivations and discontents. The term *sect* was first used in this sense by the German sociologist Ernst Troeltsch (1865–1923), who asserted that all such movements are the work of the lower classes. Subsequently, the American theologian H. Richard Niebuhr (1894–1962), once regarded as the leading sociological authority on sects, explained, "The sect has ever been the child of an outcast minority, taking its rise in the religious revolts of the poor."[103]

If it were true that sects arise from lower-class misery and protest, the Yahweh-Only Movement was no sect. But this sociological tradition is unfounded. Perhaps some sects have been primarily lower-class movements, but it is quite clear that *most* sects, including extremely ascetic ones, primarily have been movements based on the privileged. Those who form and sustain sects may not hold the reins of power, but they often are the wealthy sons and daughters of those who do, and *their grievances stem from the failure of power and privilege to satisfy spiritual concerns.*[104] Recall the Orphics and the Pythagorans, the very ascetic Greek sects discussed in Chapter 2. Ancient Greek writers including Plato reported them to be wealthy and literate. Or consider the Essenes, the very ascetic Jewish sect from Roman times. Rather than being the lower-class dissidents that too many sociologists have assumed them to be,[105] they primarily drew their members from the "economic, social, and educational elite . . . who could afford the 'luxury' of indulgence in affairs of the spirit."[106] There have been many similar upper-class sects, including such famous medieval movements as the Cathars (Albigensians) and the Waldensians.[107] As for the appeal of high-tension religion to the upper classes in general, 75 percent of ascetic medieval Catholic saints were members of the nobility.[108] Of course, the most famous sect movements to have been sustained in their formative days by the more privileged classes were Buddhism and Christianity, as will be seen. The same sort of people formed the Yahweh-Only Movement in ancient Israel.

Much has been written about the Deuteronomists and their efforts during the late seventh and sixth centuries BCE to convert Israel to monotheism and how they "wrote" and revised many parts of the Bible to reflect their views. They have been described as everything from a conspiracy to a political party, but not as what they so obviously were: a sect movement. Moreover, remarkably little attention has been paid to the fact that this sect existed for many centuries before being identified as Deuteronomists. The controversial Morton Smith (1915–1991) wrote an excellent monograph on this movement (calling it a political party), but he began his story late in the seventh century, just prior to the Babylonian exile.[109] Bernard Lang's brief monograph paid a bit of attention to the early days of what he called the "Yahweh-alone movement," but quickly shifted to the exilic era, and his subsequent essay followed the same pattern.[110] William F. Albright attempted to sketch the start of the "prophetic movement," but only in connection with Samuel.[111] Frankly, the best single work on this subject is a five-page article written by Ira M. Price (1856–1939) in 1889: "The Schools of the Sons of the Prophet." As far as I can tell, aside from some passing mentions in several reference works, that's the entire literature. This is a major omission because ignoring the Yahweh-Only Sect fails to properly situate the Old Testament prophets and treats the Deuteronomists as innovative newcomers rather than as representatives of a well-organized movement with a very long history during which many of its activists took up an ascetic life and everyone involved demanded the repudiation of all other Gods and idols, lest Israel be destroyed.

Precisely when this sect movement appeared cannot be determined, but it seems to have been well developed before the establishment of the monarchy, embodied in the various bands of prophets led by Samuel.[112] According to Price, these groups formed "the beginnings of the prophetic order, whose continuous existence can be traced down through Old Testament times, and whose influence is felt in all subsequent Old Testament history and literature."[113] Although committed to calling Israel to repentance, these bands do not seem to have been collections of outsiders or of the underprivileged, but to have constituted a sect drawing its adherents mainly from the upper classes. Samuel probably came from an affluent family, was raised to be a priest, and enjoyed such high prestige that he was chosen to anoint Saul as the first king of Israel. Indeed, as Bernard Lang noted, "All the prophets belong[ed] to the landowning nobility and so to the social stratum from which highly placed state officials [we]re recruited."[114] Rainer Albertz attributed successive efforts for monotheistic reforms to a segment "of the Jerusalem upper class . . . [as these were] reform[s] from above."[115] And Morton Smith identified some specific "great families, as the backbone"[116] of this militant group.

In the beginning, this sect movement seems not to have advocated strict monotheism, but merely to have proposed that although there were other Gods, Israelites should worship Yahweh only. That is, Yahweh was deemed the national God to whom Israel owed exclusive allegiance, a message proclaimed by a series of prophets who preached that the fate of Israel rose and fell depending upon the prevalence of the exclusive worship of Yahweh. Hence, when Elijah confronted King Ahab (ruled c. 874–853 BCE) with a prophecy of his doom for offending Yahweh and consorting with Jezebel,[117] he spoke on behalf of the Yahweh-Only Sect, as is obvious in 2 Kings 2. Here we read that as Elijah prepared to be taken into heaven, there appeared a number of his followers, referred to as "*the sons of the prophets*" (2 Kings 2:3). The first to come forth was a group from Bethel. They were followed by a group from Jericho. When Elijah and Elisha reached the Jordan River, "*Fifty men of the sons of the prophets also went, and stood at some distance from them*" (2 Kings 2:7). Later in 2 Kings 4:43, when a farmer is told to set his contribution to Elisha before the sons of the prophets, he replied, "*How am I to set this before a hundred men?*" Indeed, in 2 Kings 6:1 the sons of the prophets tell Elisha that they have become so numerous that they need larger living quarters. Clearly, "the sons of the prophets . . . consisted of considerable numbers."[118] And they may well have been far more numerous than these passages suggest if this was a *dual movement* involving full-time ascetics (those referred to as the sons) and a much larger association of lay supporters, as was the case with the medieval Cathars and many other sect movements.[119]

Nevertheless, it was not until Hezekiah ascended to the throne of Judah (c. 715–687 BCE) that the sons of the prophets were able to gain substantial and sustained support for their efforts to purge the land of the worship of other Gods. According to 2 Kings 18:3–4, Hezekiah was the king who "*did what was right in the eyes of the LORD. . . . He removed the high places, and broke the pillars, and cut down the Ashe'rah. And he broke in pieces the bronze serpent that Moses had made, for until those days the people of Israel had burned incense to it; it was called Nehush'tan.*" Apparently having recovered the support of Yahweh, Hezekiah was able to hold

out against a siege laid against Jerusalem by Sennacherib when he led his
Assyrian hosts across Israel and into Judah. Soon after, during the reign
of Josiah (640–609 BCE), came even more vigorous and far-reaching reforms in accord with the aims of the Yahweh-Only Sect. As is reported in
2 Kings 23:4–6:

> *The king commanded . . . the priests . . . to bring out of the temple of*
> *the* LORD *all the vessels made for Ba'al, for Ashe'rah . . . he deposed the*
> *idolatrous priests . . . those also who burned incense to Ba'al, to the sun,*
> *and the moon, and the constellations, and all the host of the heavens.*
> *And he brought out the Ashe'rah from the house of the* LORD *. . . burned*
> *it at the brook Kidron, and beat it to dust . . .*

King Josiah also commissioned a major renovation of the Temple, during which there was a stunning discovery—enter the Deuteronomists.
According to 2 Kings 22:8 the High Priest Hilkiah found hidden away in
the Temple a Book of Law, attributed directly to Moses and portions of
which came to be known as the Book of Deuteronomy, while other portions probably constitute Leviticus.[120] It would seem that prior to the discovery of this book, Israelites knew very little of what became the core of
Judaism—the Law. Along with Genesis, Exodus, and Numbers, these five
books became the Torah. Although Jews revere the entire Tanakh, it is the
Torah that is treated as the truly sacred document. Written on a scroll,
it is read and revered in every synagogue, for not only is it attributed to
Moses, but it contains the entire Law. Before the discovery of the book
in the Temple, members of the Yahweh-Only Sect may already have been
aware of some portions of the Law, but there is no surviving evidence
that anyone knew such elementary aspects of Jewish life as how to observe the Sabbath, or to celebrate Passover, or even what to eat, when, or
with whom. It is agreed that the Deuteronomists were the first Israelites
who rightfully can be called Jews.

Although *Deuteronomy* clearly precipitated a religious revolution,
there has been enormous controversy about its authenticity because it
contains obvious insertions and revisions by the Yahweh-Only Sect.[121]
Consequently, some scholars[122] have claimed that it is a complete forgery,
composed during the seventh century BCE. But careful analysis supports
the view that Deuteronomy consists of several quite independent docu-

ments, some of which are of far earlier origins. Referring to the scriptures concerning Samuel, Albright noted that "the Deuteronomic editor and his precursors were unusually careful not to omit conflicting traditions in order to produce a uniform narrative. . . . They treated the discrepant traditions with respect, though they must sometimes have been just as puzzled as we are."[123] That the Deuteronomists sometimes revised and often added material to augment their case for pristine monotheism is clear. But it is equally clear that they began with far earlier documents.[124] Where would such documents have been kept other than in the Temple? And in an age of oral culture, is it surprising that scrolls may have lain forgotten and unread for generations? Moreover, if the Deuteronomists had their own revelations to add, who is to say that these were not superior to those given in earlier times to less sophisticated recipients?

When King Josiah was killed in battle, there soon was a general resumption of polytheism for, as in Egypt during the reign of Akhenaten, all during Josiah's campaign against "false" gods many Israelites must have continued in the old ways, albeit somewhat circumspectly. Faith in familiar, humanoid, nearby, permissive Gods is not easily overcome. So, once again, leaders of the Yahweh-Only Sect assumed the role of critics committed to predicting dire consequences for the nation should it continue in these heathen ways. The most outspoken among them was the Prophet Jeremiah.

As appropriate for a sect based on the privileged classes, Jeremiah descended from a priestly family who owned a considerable amount of land, and it appears that he had a substantial income.[125] Shortly after the Book of Law was discovered in the Temple, Jeremiah felt called to become a prophet and began by agitating for reinstatement of the reforms made by Josiah and by calling the people to embrace Yahweh and to observe the Law: "*For your gods have become as many as your cities, O Judah; and as many as the streets of Jerusalem are the altars you have set up to shame, altars to burn incense to Ba'al*" (11:13).

When his preaching failed to result in reform, Jeremiah turned to far more dire prophecies of Yahweh's impending judgment against the nation as punishment for its flagrant sins: "*I will make void the plans of Judah and Jerusalem, and will cause their people to fall by the sword before their enemies, and by the hand of those who seek their life. I will give their dead bodies for food to the birds of the air and to the beasts of the earth*" (19:7).

Throughout the history of Israel, such prophecies were entirely plausible because the nation's existence always was so precarious. As a case in point, Jeremiah's prophecies took place at a time when an overwhelming Babylonian threat loomed in the north, as did an Egyptian threat from the south. Consequently, Jeremiah's sermons aroused so much anguish in the court that many called for him to be put to death. But his prophecies came true.

Once King Nebuchadnezzar had defeated the Egyptians, in 597 BCE he turned his Babylonian forces against Jerusalem, which quickly surrendered, thus avoiding its destruction. To ensure his new territory, Nebuchadnezzar appointed his young son as his vassal king. He also took somewhere between eight and ten thousand high officials, military leaders, priests, and other members of the upper class back to Babylon as captives.[126] For the rest of his life, Jeremiah prophesied that these exiles would be returned and the nation repossessed. That, too, came to pass, but only several generations later and long after an abortive rebellion against Babylonian rule had prompted the total destruction of Jerusalem in 586 BCE. Meanwhile, it was in Babylon that the Yahweh-Only Sect became dominant, and, consequently, it was not Israelites, but authentic Jews who returned from exile.

Monotheism and Exile

Nebuchadnezzar took the political, military, and religious elite of Israel off to Babylon in order to deny leadership to potential rebels and to create an expatriate elite with a considerable stake in maintaining order back home, lest their property be forfeited—the exiles retained much of their status back in Israel. The king went even further; rather than forcing the exiles into unattractive circumstances in Babylon, every effort was made to "assimilate the [exiles], and to cause them to strike roots in their new homeland."[127] To this end, Israelites soon were "serving in the royal court and attaining high rank."[128]

Clearly many of the exiles did assimilate, and their sons and daughters became Babylonians with no interest in a "return." For example, many exiles—"even members of the royal family of Judah"—gave their children Babylonian names.[129] Moreover, many born in Babylon grew up speaking Aramaic, not Hebrew.[130] But some stood firm and refused to intermarry or otherwise assimilate, and the key to their steadfastness was religion.

Those who observed the newly discovered Law did not take Babylonian wives or give their sons and daughters in marriage to outsiders—they didn't even invite their Babylonian neighbors to dinner. Nor did these exiles embrace Babylonian Gods; they were committed ever more strongly to Yahweh, to the belief that their exile was punishment for having forsaken the One True God, and that if they were steadfast in their faith, one day this punishment would end and their nation would be reborn.

The steadfast exiles were, of course, members of the Yahweh-Only Sect. As Morton Smith pointed out, "Most of the leaders of the Yahweh-alone party were probably among the upper classes of Jerusalem whom Nebuchadnezzer carried off to Babylon."[131] Although they had been only a minority at the beginning of the exile, the temptations to assimilate served as a very efficient selection mechanism that, over several generations, would have filtered out the less committed, with the result that the self-conscious Israelite exile community came to consist almost entirely of sect members with unwavering faith that Yahweh was the Only God.[132] Two great prophets shaped the religious life of the exilic community: Ezekiel, and an equally remarkable figure known to us only as the author of chapters 40–55 of the Book of Isaiah, and referred to by historians as Second Isaiah (or Deutero-Isaiah).

Ezekiel came first, being active from about 593 BCE until about 571. Typical of the exiles, Ezekiel was well-off, possessing a spacious house and having considerable leisure.[133] He was the son of a priest, married, and well educated.[134] He claimed that, at age thirty, God had opened the heavens and granted him a vision. On that basis, prior to the Babylonian conquest, Ezekiel preached impending doom because Israel had "*played the harlot*" (16:26) to false Gods. Scholars accept that these were not "after-the-fact" insertions, since the Babylonian threat was obvious well ahead of time. When the Babylonians came as predicted, Ezekiel was among those taken into exile. Once there, his message shifted. While he continued to blaze away at Israel's sins, he also began to preach hope and deliverance if Israel abandoned wickedness, observed the Law, and made an exclusive commitment to Yahweh. In anticipation of a return, Ezekiel gave detailed attention to such things as building a new Temple. As will be discussed later, some of Ezekiel's prophecies seem to reflect strong Zoroastrian influences (especially his famous passage about the resurrection of the dry bones).

The Book of Ezekiel makes "no references to events subsequent to the reign of [Nebuchadnezzar]," who died in 562, which not only dates the author, but helps demonstrate the lack of "editing" by later hands.[135] Consequently, Ezekiel's witness was to the first generation of exiles and their older children. It was Second Isaiah who guided the later exilic period and provided the blueprint for a Jewish nation. We know nothing about this prophet except that he lived in Babylon and was a master of language. It has been suggested that the anonymity of the prophet was a deliberate attempt to maximize the connection between these chapters and the traditional prophecies of Isaiah.[136] However, Second Isaiah knew that Cyrus had recently risen to power in Persia and was likely soon to overwhelm Babylon—he quoted God as saying "*of Cyrus, 'He is my shepherd, and he shall fulfil all of my purpose'*" (44:28). But Second Isaiah did not report Cyrus's conquest of Babylon in 539 BCE and thus is thought to have completed his work in 540.[137] Nonetheless, Second Isaiah assumes that his readers (or hearers) know that the fall of Babylon to Cyrus is imminent and that this will make a new Exodus possible: "*Go forth from Babylon, flee from Chalde'a, declare this with a shout of joy, proclaim it, send it forth to the end of the earth; say, 'The LORD has redeemed his servant Jacob!'*" (48:20).

The final eleven chapters of the Book of Isaiah were written after Cyrus had conquered Babylon and freed all the exiles to return to their various homelands. The experts accept that these chapters were the work of still another author, who is sometimes referred to as Third Isaiah. It exhorts the Jews to be faithful and observe the Law as they rebuild their Zion.

Before following the Jews home from Babylon, it is important to consider a difficult and controversial matter. What impact, if any, did Babylonian culture, especially the new and vigorous Zoroastrian religion, have on Judaism?

Zoroastrian Influences?

The Middle East is not a very large area, and there was a substantial amount of travel, trade, and migration back and forth across the region from very early times. Consequently, historians have found many striking similarities in the religions of the region—nearly everyone had a flood "myth," for example. However, the Babylonian captivity provided a circumstance for long and very close contact between Israel and Zoroastrianism, during a very formative period of the former and a very vigorous, early period in the history of the latter. As a result, enough apparent mutual influence can be seen by comparing scriptures that several Greek and early Christian writers, including Clement of Alexandria, presumed that Ezekiel and Zoroaster were one and the same person.[138] Subsequently, many influential Jewish writers claimed that Zoroastrianism was borrowed from Judaism: several suggested that Abraham was Zoroaster's teacher, while others claimed that Zoroaster was a Jew born in Palestine.[139]

Then, beginning in the sixteenth century, both Christian and Jewish scholars proposed that there had been substantial Zoroastrian influences on Judaism. As A. H. Sayce (1845–1893) put it in his 1887 Hibbert Lectures, "The Jews did not live in the midst of the Babylonians for seventy years without borrowing from them something more than the names of the months."[140] Sayce went on to cite belief in the resurrection and a large number of other Jewish doctrines and rites that he believed originated in Babylon. This view prevailed well into the twentieth century, and a quite persuasive case was assembled. For, as Peter Kingsley explained, "The parallels between Zoroaster and Ezekiel—note for example Ezekiel's emphasis on fire and his reference to physical resurrection—are obvious and striking to anyone prepared to look for them."[141] But then many scholars dismissed this whole literature when it was "discovered" that rather than being a contemporary of the exilic Jews, Zoroaster had lived many centuries earlier.[142] Recently, however, this position became untenable when scholars restored Zoroaster's dates to the sixth century BCE. Of course, the dismissal of Zoroastrian influence on Judaism based on redating Zoroaster always was irrelevant except as "proof" that Zoroaster personally did not meet Ezekiel or other Israelite prophets. Merely to claim that Zoroastrianism influenced Judaism, all that is necessary is that the doctrines and practices of the former predated the latter (which they may), that Zoroastrianism was a vigorous presence in Babylon when the Jewish exiles were there (which it was), and to discover significant *changes* in their religious culture sustained by members of the Yahweh-Only Sect during their stay in Babylon, changes that closely resemble prior Zoroastrian ideas or practices. There seem to have been a number of such changes.

A strong case can be made that contact with Zoroastrian notions of heaven and hell explains the sudden appearance of similar doctrines in post-exilic Judaism, replacing the previous concept of "*Sheol*, a shadowy and depersonalized existence which is the lot of all men irrespective of what they had done on earth."[143] Or, as summarized by the distinguished Ronald Hendel, Sheol "is dark, dusty, and wormy (Job 17:13–16). Its inhabitants are ghosts, and if the shade of Samuel is any indication, they are not in a very good mood (1 Samuel 28:15). They cannot praise God (Psalm 30:10 [Hebrew]), and they exist in silence (Psalm 31:18 [Hebrew], 94:17). It is not a very desireable place to spend eternity."[144]

Then suddenly, Judaism embraced a dual conception of life after death. As Daniel 12:2 reveals: "*Many of those who sleep in the dust of the earth shall awake, some to everlasting life, and some to shame and everlasting contempt.*" When did this new doctrine arise? During, or immediately after, the sojourn in Babylon. Moreover, the eventual Jewish depiction of hell's everlasting fires can be compared with the centrality of fire in Zoroastrianism. It also seems of interest that some scholars believe that Second Isaiah's attack on "*all who kindle a fire*" (50:11) was aimed at exilic Jews who were dabbling in Zoroastrianism.[145] Another impressive correspondence involves the exilic elaboration of Satan as the dualistic opponent of God, and Zoroaster's Angra Mainyu, the "Fiendish Spirit" who causes calamities and leads humans into evil.

But perhaps the most persuasive similarity between Zoroastrianism and Judaism involves the resurrection, as proclaimed in the quotation from Daniel above. Zoroaster taught that the time will come when the dead will be reassembled and everyone who ever lived will be gathered and judged, whereupon the wicked will then be destroyed and the good will be given everlasting life. The Jewish version not only is very similar, but it did not appear in scripture until the encounter with Babylon.[146] The key figure is Ezekiel, and the critical passage is Chapter 37, in which God commands him to resurrect a field of dry bones.

The Zoroastrians did not bury the dead, but exposed them in the open air, soon to become bare bones. In contrast, as Bernard Lang pointed out, Jews regard an unburied human bone as extremely defiling. Thus, the fact that Ezekiel is so "matter-of-fact [in] speaking of bones lying on the ground . . . betrays his Zoroastrian connection. It seems plausible to assume that Ezekiel had visited, or heard of, Zoroastrian funeral grounds—areas full of dry bones lying in the ground. His vision echoes the Zoroastrian belief that one day the dry bones would be reassembled and restored to life."[147]

Finally, most scholars agree that there also are obvious Zoroastrian influences in the Dead Sea Scrolls, the recently discovered Jewish scriptures associated with the community at Qumran, which many regard as having belonged to the Essenes.[148] Albright suggests that this was the result of a "second" return from Babylon by some members of the Yahweh-Only Sect whose ancestors had remained behind.[149] Be that as it may, it seems reasonable to conclude that, at the very least, there are significant traces of the Jewish encounter with Zorostrianism.

Jewish Pluralism

Having defeated Babylon and declared himself as the God Marduk's choice to be "king of the world, even though he had not conquered Egypt,"[150] Cyrus gave all of the exiled peoples permission to return to their native lands and rebuild their temples. So the Jews departed. "Obviously, a considerable number of exiles decided to remain in Babylon, despite the enthusiastic urging of Deutero-Isaiah that they depart immediately from the 'land of the Chaldeans.' . . . [They] had struck roots in Babylon and their economic situation was sound." We must realize, too, that by this time many did not regard themselves as "exiles" since they had been born in Babylon and were not attracted to "a distant homeland that they had never seen."[151] Thus it was that the exiles who returned were primarily those deeply committed to the Yahweh-Only Sect.

Even so, those who came back were very wealthy. Ezra (1:4–6) tells us that the returnees brought large numbers of servants, singers, and livestock back with them. They also reclaimed their original high status in Israel and reaffirmed it by providing large sums to rebuild the Temple. But, most of all, they launched vigorous efforts to impose true monotheism on the entire society.

There have been many attempts to cram various conceptions of Yahweh into an evolutionary scheme, starting with the rather undefined deity in the burning bush and arriving at the elegantly conceived One True God of post-exilic Judaism: "Israel's religion passed gradually through an elementary stage of animism, totemism, fetishism, through the stage of tribal deity, to the stage represented by the religion of the prophets."[152] Such a claim is very inconsistent with the historical record, at least as we possess it. There is nothing other then the prior assumption that it "must have done so" to suggest that Israel's religion ever resembled animism, totemism, or fetishism. Moreover, the Bible clearly reports that the Patriarchs had a rather more sophisticated image of God than did Moses.[153] Indeed, if scripture is our guide, Solomon's establishment of the Temple was accompanied, at least implicitly, by a substantial decline in the scope and powers accorded to Yahweh. If so, then the Israelites traced the pattern of decline from early belief in a High God to the worship of an array of small, less demanding Gods—the same decline that took place with the advent of other "civilizations." In any event, all previous conceptions of Yahweh paled in comparison with the One True God embraced by the Yahweh-Only Sect. Gone were notions about a national God deserving of Israel's exclusive worship; Yahweh was the Only God, deserving of universal worship. Moreover, although the Jews were forbidden from creating any images of Yahweh, they were not forced to conceive of him as a vast being without shape or appearance. Instead, they took comfort in the doctrine that God had created humans in his own image.

Thus it was that after the exiles returned from Babylon, Israel once again had an "official" faith that eventually was centered in a restored and well-subsidized Temple. And as would be predicted and explained by the market model of religious economies, because of the inability of any one religious institution to satisfy the full range of religious niches, Israel soon abounded in disputatious sects.

Recall from Chapter 3 that pluralism is the natural state of any religious economy. This follows from the existence in all societies variations in individual religious tastes. Consequently, there will exist a set of market niches ranging from a group with little or no interest in religion to one with very intense religious concerns. No single institution can serve this full spectrum of religious market niches, as no one institution simultaneously can be worldly and otherworldly or lax and strict. It follows that religious monopolies can exist only to the extent that coercion is able to keep dissenting groups tiny and circumspect and that whenever coercion falters, competing religious groups will arise. Because erstwhile monopoly religions inevitably are relatively lax, lazy, and worldly, most of their opposition will come from groups promoting a far more intense faith—from sects. This is true even when the monopoly was first established by those committed to an intense faith. One reason that a monopoly religion drifts toward laxity and low tension is that religious intensity is never transmitted very efficiently from one generation to the next. Inevitably, many of the sons and daughters of sect members prefer a lower tension faith than did their parents.[154] So long as leadership positions in a sect are restricted to those who are committed to the original standards, a sect can sustain a relatively high level of tension. But when these positions are hereditary, and when they are highly rewarding as well (so that the less "religious" seldom depart for other careers), the institution will soon be dominated by those favoring a lower level of intensity. This process has long been referred to as the transformation of sects into churches, the social process that causes successful sects to become lower tension religious groups.[155] This process is also speeded by the involvement of the leadership in worldly affairs, both political and economic. Finally, if such a religious institution lacks the coercive power to muffle competitive impulses, it soon will be surrounded by sect movements mounted by those wanting a higher tension faith. This is what happened in Israel, beginning soon after the return from exile.

The Judaism put in place by the Yahweh-Only Sect leaders upon their return from exile required strict observance of the Law and absolute intolerance of polytheism. But authority over this new orthodoxy was centralized in Jerusalem and placed in the hands of a professional, hereditary priesthood. Initially, plans to rebuild the Temple were delayed, apparently by factional conflicts between the returned exiles and those descended from the majority of Israelites who had not gone into exile.[156] But soon it was rebuilt and, as reported in *Nehemiah*, the Temple Mount was fully re-walled in accord with the standard acropolis model.[157]

As had been the practice in Mesopotamia, a universal tithe was imposed on the entire Jewish population to support the Temple and subsidize the hereditary priesthood.[158] Of perhaps even greater significance, the Temple became the dominant financial institution, acting as the state treasury as well as an investment bank—"a depository for capital sums, such as money belonging to widows and orphans or to the rich, who feared for their capital under the often insecure conditions that prevailed."[159] Consequently, the priests became "the wealthiest class and the strongest political group among the Jews of Jerusalem,"[160] given that Israel was ruled as a province by outsiders. Consequently, the High Priest was not only "the religious head but also the political leader of the nation."[161] Membership in the priesthood was entirely hereditary, and even the office of High Priest passed from father to son—and priests tended to only marry the daughters of other priests. Not surprisingly, the priests demanded and enjoyed a high level of public deference. As Ben Sira advised in about 180 BCE:

> Fear God with all thy heart
> And Revere his priests . . .
> Glorify God and honour the priests
> And provide their portion as has been commanded.[162]

Although many priests did not live in Jerusalem, they went there to serve in the Temple when their turn came, as well as for "the three festivals of Passover, Pentecost and Tabernacles."[163] Thus, the official Jewish religion was a centralized Temple religion, and the observance of any organized rites elsewhere was frowned upon. Centralization was also served by the fact that the tithes were gathered in Jerusalem and dispersed from there.

It was this combination of a rich, relatively worldly priesthood controlling a subsidized state Temple, on the one hand, and "outsider" political rulers reluctant to coerce religious conformity on the other, that gave rise to the abundance of Jewish sects as well as to several more moderate Jewish groups. Following the lead of Josephus (37–95 CE), modern historians have paid close attention to three main organized religious groups in post-exilic Israel, while acknowledging the existence of many others—the Talmud notes an additional twenty-four sects.[164] Among the many other significant Jewish sects were the community at Qumran, the Fourth Philosophy (Sicarii), the Zealots, the followers of the hermit Bannus, those gathered by John the Baptist, and the earliest Christians.[165]

The three well-known Jewish religious groups were: the Sadducees, the Pharisees, and the Essenes. Members of each of these three groups kept themselves apart from other Jews and probably numbered no more than 20,000 members altogether out of a population of perhaps one million.[166] But they played the determining influence on religious life, as the three spanned the spectrum of religious tastes from very low to very high intensity. All three were recruited primarily from among the wealthy and privileged.

The *Sadducees* represented the "official" Temple Judaism and drew their support mainly from the aristocracy—primarily the hereditary priestly families.[167] Despite their conflicts with the more powerful Pharisees, the Sadducees were able to maintain their monopoly on the right to serve as priests in the Temple (it was a Sadducee High Priest who judged Jesus).[168] And, typical of all such temple priesthoods, their theology was quite worldly. For example, they rejected the idea that "fate" determines human affairs, postulating that humans had the power and responsibility to determine their actions. They also denied both the immortality of the soul and the resurrection of the body and taught that God's rewards are gained only in this life. Perhaps their most controversial position was to assert that "only those laws written in the Pentateuch were to be regarded as binding, while those that were not written down [those that were only "oral" traditions] were not to be observed."[169]

The *Pharisees* believed in an immortal soul, in the resurrection of the good, and in the condemnation of the wicked to "eternal torment."[170] In their view the "good" were those who obeyed the Law, both written and oral. The Pharisees probably originated as a sect movement, generated by the increasing worldliness and accommodation of the restored Temple religion. If so, they, too, soon became a relatively lower tension movement, the equivalent of a "mainstream" denomination, representing the large, moderate portion of the Jewish religious spectrum—having "the multitude on their side," according to Josephus.[171] In keeping with their moderate stance, the Pharisees "formulated the doctrine of two realms, secular and divine, with respect to the state." Consequently, when the first Roman procurator initiated a census in order to fix the amount of Jewish taxes, "the Pharisees urged the people to cooperate, since the Romans were not interfering in the religious sphere,"[172] thereby anticipating Jesus's counsel to "render unto Caesar." Perhaps the most significant single contribution of the Pharisees was the establishment of synagogues in Israel. The word *synagogue* refers both to a building used for local worship and to the congregation that gathers there to worship. Synagogues had of necessity existed in Babylon, but when they were instituted in Israel, they posed a direct challenge to the centralized Temple Judaism. The Pharisees held that synagogues could "be established wherever there were enough men to constitute a *minyan* (quorum)," which was ten.[173] Initially this practice was opposed by the Sadducees, but having the numbers on their side, the Pharisees prevailed, and after the destruction of the Temple once again—this time by the Romans in the year 70 CE—the synagogue became the primary institution of Jewish religious life.

The *Essenes* were typical of the many high tension, ascetic sect movements that abounded in Israel. Josephus reported that the Essenes condemned "pleasures as evil," rejected marriage, embraced abstinence, and that their piety was "very extraordinary."[174] Many authors suggest that the community at Qumran, from whose library the Dead Sea Scrolls probably came, were Essenes.[175] John the Essene was one of the Jewish generals in the Great Revolt against Rome (66–74), and Josephus indicated that rebellious Essenes were tortured by the Romans. Following the revolt, "the Essenes disappear from the stage of history,"[176] but there were many other high intensity groups to take their place.[177]

Jewish pluralism was not limited to Israel. As sizeable Jewish communities spread around the Mediterranean, forming the Diaspora, the diversity of Jewish religion went along. Something else went along, too—the conviction that Yahweh was not simply the God of the Jews, but the One and Only God of all, hence the Jews had a duty to spread their faith.

Diasporan Missionizing

It recently has become fashionable for many secular Jews, being eager to prohibit all religious proselytizing, to deny that Judaism ever was a missionizing faith.[178] But as every orthodox Jewish scholar agrees,[179] the historical facts are clear: Judaism was the "first great missionary religion."[180] As reported in Chapter 3, the Romans sometimes persecuted the Jews for proselytizing and even executed some members of the Roman nobility because they converted. For, as Maimonides (1135–1204), the famous medieval Jewish scholar, explained: "Moses our teacher was commanded by the Almighty to compel all the inhabitants of the world to accept the commandments."[181]

It could hardly have been otherwise. The obligation to missionize is always implicit in monotheism, and is explicit in the Tanakh. Isaiah (49:6) reads: "*I will give you as a light to the nations, that my salvation may reach to the end of the earth.*" Later in Isaiah (66:18–19) God reveals his plan to "*gather all nations and tongues*" and to send missionaries "*to the coastlands afar off, that have not heard my fame or seen my glory; and they shall*

The rapid growth of sizeable Jewish communities in many cities of the Roman Empire is well documented by burial plaques such as this one from the Vigna-Randanini catacomb in Rome. (The Jewish Museum, New York; Photo: The Jewish Musem, NY/Art Resource, New York)

declare my glory among the nations." And in Psalm 117:1: *"Praise the* Lord, *all nations! Extol him, all peoples!"*

These and similar verses inspired the renowned third-century ce rabbi, Eleazar ben Pedat, to assert that "God sent Israel into Exile among the nations only for the purpose of acquiring converts."[182] Some of Pedat's contemporaries even claimed that "converts are dearer to God than born Jews."[183] Nor was it only rabbis who praised Jewish missions or noted their success. Writing in the first century ce, Josephus reported the very widespread impact of Judaism on the host cultures of the Diaspora: "[T]he multitude of mankind itself have had a great inclination for a long time to follow our religious observances."[184] That same century Philo, the great Jewish philosopher in Alexandria, wrote at length about converts and missions to the Gentiles, even claiming that many converts left Egypt as part of the Exodus.[185] Like Josephus, Philo also described the widespread observance of Jewish customs, and both of them confirmed that it was common for Jews to invite Gentiles to attend services in the synagogues. This was facilitated by the fact that the language of the Diasporan synagogues was not Hebrew, but Greek, and therefore comprehensible not only to everyone residing in Hellenic regions, but also to all educated Romans, since they more frequently spoke Greek than Latin.

As the practice of inviting guests to worship makes clear, Jews in the Diaspora sought converts, and they seem to have been quite successful in doing so.[186] The best estimate is that by the first century, Jews made up from 10 to 15 percent of the population of the Roman Empire, nearly 90 percent of them living in cities outside Palestine.[187] This would have amounted to from six to nine million people. To achieve these numbers, a considerable amount of conversion would have been required. As Adolf von Harnack recognized, "It is utterly impossible to explain the large total of Jews in the Diaspora by the mere fact of the fertility of Jewish families. We must assume . . . that a very large number of pagans . . . trooped over to Yahweh."[188] Thus, Josephus was probably accurate when he claimed that: "All the time they [the Jews] were attracting to their worship a great number of Greeks, making them virtually members of their own community."[189]

Christian sources also acknowledge the existence of many "God-fearers" in the synagogues, as in the case of Lydia and the women at Philippi.[190] Paul began his sermon in the synagogue in Antioch, "*Men of Israel, and you that fear God, listen.*"[191] Later in the sermon he repeated this distinction: "*Brethren, sons of the family of Abraham, and those among you that fear God . . .*"[192] The God-fearers were Greeks and Romans, like the Roman soldier Cornelius,[193] who had embraced Jewish monotheism, but who remained marginal to Jewish life because they were unwilling to fully embrace Jewish ethnicity—not only adult circumcision, but some other aspects of the Law as well.[194] For the fact was that *religious* conversion wasn't sufficient. Rather than letting other "nations" extol Him, the Jewish leadership demanded that all "nations" become fully Jewish; there was no room for Egyptian-Jews or Roman-Jews, let alone Germanic- or British-Jews, but only for Jewish-Jews. Given the remarkable success they achieved, this ethnic barrier to conversion probably was the sole reason that the Roman Empire did not embrace the God of Abraham, as perhaps demonstrated by the subsequent conversion of the empire to Christianity.

Given this discussion of conversion to Judaism in the Greco-Roman world, this is the appropriate place to give greater attention to the sociology of conversion.

On Conversion

For generations it was assumed that religious conversions were the result of doctrinal appeal—that people embraced a new faith because they found its teachings particularly appealing, especially if these teachings seemed to solve serious problems or dissatisfactions that afflicted them. On this, both theologians and social scientists agreed. So much so, that "everyone" was content to "discover" how a particular religious movement gained adherents by inspecting its doctrines and then *deducing* who converted to this group on the basis of who most needed what was offered.

This is precisely how so many scholars concluded that, in the words of Friedrich Engels, "Christianity was originally a movement of oppressed peoples: it first appeared as the religion of slaves and emancipated slaves, of poor people deprived of all rights, of peoples subjugated or dispersed by Rome."[195] After all, the Bible often directly addresses the poor and downhearted and promises that they will be compensated in heaven, where the "*first will be last, and the last first.*"[196] Despite this "evidence," as previously noted a consensus has formed among historians of the early Church that regardless of biblical assurances to the lower classes, the early Christians were drawn mainly from the ranks of the privileged.[197]

Nevertheless, the method of correlating doctrinal appeals with a target population remained popular so long as no one ventured out of the library to watch people actually undergo conversions in order to discover what really was involved. Then someone did.[198] What they discovered was that doctrines are of very secondary importance in the initial decision to convert. One must, of course, leave room for those rare conversions resulting from mystical experiences such as Paul's on the road to Damascus. But these instances aside, conversion is primarily about bringing one's religious behavior into alignment with that of one's friends and relatives, not about encountering attractive doctrines. Put more formally: *people tend to convert to a religious group when their social ties to members outweigh their ties to outsiders who might oppose the conversion, and this often occurs before a convert knows much about what the group believes.* Of course, one can easily imagine doctrines so bizarre as to keep most people from joining. But, barring that, *conversion primarily is an act of conformity*; but so is nonconversion. In the end it is a matter of the relative strength of social ties. This principle has, by now, been examined by dozens of close-up studies of conversion, all of which confirm that social networks are the basic mechanism through which conversion takes place.[199] To convert someone, you must first become their close and trusted friend.

Clearly, these same principles applied as fully in the Greco-Roman world as in modern times. Indeed, as will be seen in Chapter 7, the portrayal in Acts of Paul's missionary career, as well as his letters to various congregations, all testify to the centrality of friendship and social networks in conversions to Christianity. Paul's tactics seem to have been modeled upon those of the Diasporan Jews, for not only were converts gained through social ties, they were thereby linked not merely to some individual members, but to an intense and highly integrated religious group—a synagogue or congregation. That is, potential converts to Judaism were immersed in a group of people prepared to shower them with attention and affection, and to manifest the benefits of belonging. Of course, this was only possible because, for all their sense of solidarity, Jewish congregations in the Diaspora remained *open* communities, willing and able to form strong bonds to Gentiles. Of course, this not only facilitated the conversion of Gentiles, but also the defection of Jews.

Just as had happened in Babylon, large numbers of Jews in the Diaspora embraced the prevailing culture to a very considerable degree. After several generations, most of them spoke and thought in Greek—Philo referred to Greek as "our language."[200] Most had taken Greek names, and "intermarriage was frequent."[201] All but a very few had so entirely lost their Hebrew that they worshipped in Greek and their scripture had to be translated into Greek—the **Septuagint**. Many Diasporan Jews, probably the majority of them, had abandoned some provisions of the Law. For example, the rules that made it very difficult to eat with non-Jews probably were widely ignored.[202] It seems equally likely that many took part in feasts and festivals having polytheistic significance, since toleration of the "Gods" had even crept into their scripture. In the Septuagint, Exodus 22:27[203] was not translated as "You shall not revile God," but as "You shall not revile the gods." Calvin Roetzel is surely right that this was an open declaration of tolerance, utterly "alien to Hebrew Scriptures."[204] Equally dramatic evidence of a tolerant attitude toward Greco-Roman Gods comes from the fact that the Diasporan Jews "did not even hesitate to [adopt] names derived from those of Greek deities, such as Apollonius,

Heracleides and Dionysus" or those of Egyptian Gods—Horus was especially popular among the Diasporan Jews.[205]

The net result of all this assimilation was to enable Jews to develop strong social ties to Greeks and Romans, and these provided the linkages along which substantial rates of conversion were achieved. Soon Jewish monotheism was no longer found only in a tiny society on the edge of the empire; it was beginning to play a major part in the religious life of Rome. But only because it continued to produce sect movements!

All the while Greeks and Romans were becoming Jews, a substantial number of Jews were taking up with the Greco-Roman Gods, followed by extensive conversion by Jews to Christianity (see Chapter 7). These defections involved precisely the same process that had gone on in Babylon: many of those born in the Diaspora and for whom Israel was an increasingly unfamiliar, faraway land, found it attractive to shed the "outsider" status imposed on them by their observance of the Law. As they became increasingly assimilated, whatever remnants of Jewishness they retained seemed less satisfying, and the attractions of other religions beckoned. That is, whenever Jews have drifted away from a very serious commitment to their religious heritage, the attractions of assimilation have often come to outweigh those of remaining a Jew. This has happened many times, in many other places. Many Jews became Christians in medieval Europe. Although it took centuries, finally all the Jews in China became Confucianists. Following "emancipation" of the Jews in Western Europe early in the nineteenth century, large numbers of Jewish parents gave their children Gentile names, and intermarriage rates soared, reaching almost 25 percent in Germany by 1929. Not surprisingly, rates of conversion to Christianity soared as well.[206]

The only reason the Jews did not end up like Babylonians, as just another extinct ancient people, is because each time assimilation began to make serious inroads into the Jewish community, some Jews responded with renewed commitment to high tension versions of the faith—they sustained Jewish sect movements. These were the Jews who drove the Apostle Paul from the synagogues where he had preached that the messiah had already come. It was they who adopted strict rules ostracizing those who fraternized too freely with Gentiles, even as Christianity became the official Church of Rome. It was they who chose death rather than conversion when Count Emich of Leisinger "cleansed" the lower

Rhine Valley of "unbelievers" in 1096. It was they who continued to worship in deepest secrecy when ordered to become Muslims or leave Spain, on pain of death—the esteemed Maimonides (1135–1204) among them. It was they who reenacted this strategem, becoming "crypto-Jews" when ordered to become Christians or leave Spain in 1492 by Ferdinand and Isabella. It was they, during the nineteenth century, who adopted the distinctive clothing and grooming we now associate with orthodox Jews, precisely in order to be very visibly set apart.

In contrast, a national study conducted in 1991 found that a third of self-identified American Jews put up a Christmas tree in their homes. Hence, it is no surprise that recent studies show that about 20 percent of living Americans who were born into a Jewish home have become Christians. However, orthodox Jews do not buy Christmas trees, and very few, if any, of the many recent Jewish converts to Christianity were born into orthodox Jewish homes.[207] Indeed, contrary to the received wisdom concerning modernization and religiousness, in the past decade orthodox Jews have at least doubled their percentage of the population of self-identified American Jews.[208]

The moral of this story is that most religious history is written by sect movements. It is they who establish new faiths, and it is they who renew and preserve old ones. It was an Israelite sect that gave the world Jewish monotheism, and Jewish sects have preserved this faith for more than 2000 years. Indeed, it was a Jewish sect that gave rise to Christianity.

POLYTHEISTIC APPROACHES
TO MONOTHEISM

The Greco-Roman Gods were of many sizes, shapes, and species. But none was supremely powerful, and most were of dubious worth to humans, being unreliable and of doubtful virtue—"charming figures [but] . . . unedifying examples."[209] Eventually, the lack of character of the Gods, their great number, and their modest powers drew intellectual scorn. Consequently, and perhaps stimulated by the presence of Diasporan Jews in their midst and by contacts with Zoroastrianism, many Greek and Roman philosophers began to entertain monotheistic ideas, while several pagan groups attempted to transform one of their Gods into as close an approximation of monotheism as was possible within the limiting assumptions of polytheism.

Inventing Serapis

Many sophisticated people in the Greco-Roman world were deeply troubled by the sheer chaos that existed because the number of Gods had grown so enormous, as well as the confusion as to their names and functions. To deal with these matters, around 300 BCE, Ptolemy I, a comrade of Alexander the Great and the first Greek ruler of Egypt, commissioned two distinguished priests to impose some order.[210] Manetho was an Egyptian historian[211] with ties to Isiacism. Timotheus was an Athenian who had settled in Egypt after being involved in the mysteries at Eleusis. Their major innovation was to organize the Gods into a hierarchy ruled by a *supreme God*: creator, rule-giver, all-powerful. Rather than refer to this supreme God as Zeus or by another traditional name, Manetho and Timotheus named him **Serapis**. Although Serapis was immediately popular in Egypt (especially because his introduction was accompanied by the reopening of the traditional temples that had been shut by the Persians), he "was deliberately created by the Ptolemaic theologians for export abroad. He had powers of assimilation to the leading Gods of Greece and in time won international acceptance."[212] In addition, Manetho and Timotheus paired Serapis with a female divinity, **Isis**. For centuries, Isis had reigned as the Goddess in charge of the annual inundations of the Nile, as a healer, and as a patron of lovers and married couples. As temples to Serapis proliferated, a section always was devoted to Isis. However, Isis soon became far more important than Serapis, and many temples devoted exclusively to her were built—eventually there were eleven of them in the city of Rome alone.[213]

Isis: The "Savior" Goddess

Although Isis came west in conjunction with Serapis, she soon shed those ties and was hailed as the Goddess Supreme, the Queen of the Sky, the Mother of the Stars, and often was referred to as the Savior Goddess, "or more explicitly 'saviour of the human race.' "[214] As Plutarch explained: "Isis is the female principle in nature, which is the receiver of every act of creation; wherefore she is called 'nurse' and 'receiver of all' by Plato, and by mankind in general 'the goddess of ten thousand names.' "[215]

The many surviving inscriptions and scriptures in praise of Isis[216] include such claims as:

It was Isis "who separated earth from heaven, showed the stars their courses, ordained the path of sun and moon."

Isis is "sole ruler of eternity," and "all call me the highest goddess, greatest of all the gods in heaven," and "nothing happens apart from me."

Isis is "ruler of the world . . . greatest of the gods, the . . . ruler of heavenly things and immeasurable. . . . You are the ruler of all forever."

In his classic novel *The Golden Ass*, Apuleius (second century CE) offered this hymn to Isis: "The gods above worship you; the gods below reverence you; you turn the earth and give light to the sun, you rule the world. . . . The stars respond to you, the seasons return, the gods rejoice, the elements give service. By your will the winds blow, the clouds give nourishment, seeds sprout, fruits grow. . . . My voice lacks the strength to express what I think of your majesty, nor would a thousand mouths or tongues continuing to speak forever."[217]

Not bad for a female divinity who had spent several thousand years as no more than a respected Egyptian Goddess. The original Isis "myth" is typical of its Egyptian origin. As was frequently the case among Egyptians, commoners as well as royalty,[218] Isis was believed to have married her twin brother, Osiris—their initial mating having taken place within the womb of their mother, Nut, Goddess of the Sky. Osiris and Isis had a brother, Seth, and a sister, Nephthys, and they, too, married. Seth turned out to be evil and jealous and eventually he murdered Osiris, tore his body into fourteen pieces, and flung them all over the earth. A mourning Isis searched far and wide for the pieces of her beloved Osiris's corpse. Having found everything but his penis, she carefully reassembled his body, placed him in a tomb, and then raised him from the dead. Subsequently, Osiris became the judge of the dead. At this point Isis became pregnant with Horus. In some accounts she is impregnated rather miraculously by Osiris after his resurrection (sans penis). In others, she is impregnated by a flash of lightning. After Horus was born, he, too, became the target of Seth's jealousy, and Isis was forced to flee into the marshes to prevent her son from being murdered. When Horus grew up he defeated Seth— reminiscent of Moses having been hidden in the bulrushes and living to

This white marble statue of the Goddess Isis still has traces of gold-plating and was found in her temple in Pompeii. Isis was so popular that eleven temples were built for her in Rome, in comparison with only four devoted to either Venus or Jupiter. (Museo Archeologico Nazionale, Naples, Italy; Photo: Erich Lessing/Art Resource, New York)

defeat the pharaoh. From these beginnings, Isis next became paired with Serapis, and then soon left him far behind to emerge as a Supreme God.

Although Isis sometimes was referred to as the "one True and Living God,"[219] she could not escape the limitations of polytheism. She could be recognized as a Supreme God, but not as an Only God because the existence of a whole pantheon of other Gods, including her offspring, could not be denied within the context of polytheism. Moreover, hers was entirely an "otherworldly tale," in contrast to the manifest historicity of Judaism. As the influential Cyril Bailey (1871–1957) put it: "On the one side were the legendary figures, unhistorical and mere puppets in a story . . . on the other side there were indeed historical personages."[220] God was believed to have revealed himself to mortal Jews, and the Bible tells the history of a real people and occurs on this earth. In contrast, Isis's "biography" took place entirely within the invisible world of the Gods.

No human ever clasped her hand or joined her at table. Isis simply could not be freed from the fundamental shortcomings of "mythology."

SOL INVICTUS

Isis was not the only Greco-Roman effort to approximate monotheism. Late in the day, as the exponential curve of conversions to Christianity began to accelerate, two emperors tried to establish Sol Invictus (the invincible Sun God) as the Supreme God of Rome. Their failure to do so is instructive since it reaffirms the reasons why Isis also failed to serve as an adequate approach to monotheism.

Sol Invictus may have originated in Canaan, but gained prominence as Sol Invictus Elagabal, the major God of Syria with an immense and popular temple in Emesa, a small city on the Orontes River, south of Apamea.[221] Like Cybele, Sol Invictus was physically represented by a meteorite, this one being conical, black, and marked by mysterious signs thought to symbolize the sun. Herodotus reported that the "god is not worshipped by natives alone. All the barbarian kings and satraps in the neighborhood annually send him as many magnificent offerings as he could desire."[222]

In 218 CE the High Priest of this temple in Syria was the fourteen-year-old Varius Avitus Bassianus—it was an hereditary office previously held by his grandfather. Young Bassianus also was the "natural" son of the recently slain emperor Caracalla (reigned 211–217 CE). As a result of an elaborate intrigue involving his mother, aunt, and grandmother, the legions stationed in the area rose against Emperor Macrinus, killed him and his son, and installed the teenage High Priest on the throne. He took the name Emperor Elagabalus (alternatively Heliogabalus) in honor of his God and ruled from 218 to 222, whereupon he was murdered, along with his mother, by rebellious Praetorian Guards.[223]

While he ruled Rome, Elagabalus had two sumptuous temples constructed for Sol Invictus, one upon the Palatine (where the meteorite representing the God was installed) and the other in the lower city. Next he declared Sol Invictus to be the supreme God of Rome, elevating him above Jupiter and all of the other traditional Roman Gods. To this end he sponsored a full identification of all the traditional Gods of Rome that they might officially be declared servants of Sol Invictus, and Elagabalus even declared the God of the Jews and the Christians as among the sub-ordinate Gods.[224] Elagabalus also created a college of priests to supervise this new ecclesiastical structure, breaking with tradition by making his new faith a state-supported temple religion. To force conformity to the new religion, Elagabalus appointed only those who embraced his religion to high offices and dismissed all who refused to conform.

The most striking aspect of this new religion was a "pronounced ten-dency toward monotheism."[225] Although no claim was made that Sol Invic-tus was the *only* God, he was presented as far superior to all others, and his adherents were expected to devote "themselves entirely to his service."[226] As to specific doctrines, far less knowledge has survived than for Isis and Cybele. But we do know that of central importance was the promise that each adherent would gain eternal bliss upon death. Although we lack de-tails, we also know that the cult featured complex mysteries and elaborate rites—Elagabalus appeared each morning "to slaughter bulls and a vast quantity of sheep."[227] Obviously, this was not a religion whipped up over-night by a teenager, but reflected the pressures toward monotheism that had long been building up, presumably in response to the same tendencies that sustained the many conversions to Judaism, to the God-fearers, and to emerging Christianity. However, the new faith soon suffered a setback due to Elagabalus's scandalous reign and bloody end.

Scholars disagree as to the trustworthiness of ancient accounts of Elagabalus's misdeeds, but it is agreed that they were many and that they deeply shocked Roman sensibilities—itself a remarkable feat.[228] It is agreed that he often impersonated women. That he staged all manner of orgies. That he married and then divorced an upper-class Roman woman and quickly took a Vestal Virgin as his second wife—a woman sworn to chastity.[229] He may even have consulted the entrails of young children who had been sacrificed during the mysteries.[230] However, on the eve-ning of March 21, 222, when rebellious Praetorians murdered Elagabalus, his mother, and a group of his supporters in the garden of the imperial palace, it wasn't to punish him for his various offenses, but because he stood in the way of his grandmother's plans to exert greater control over the throne.

The cult of Sol Invictus did not die with Elagabalus. Although reduced greatly as to both influence and affluence (being shorn of state support), and even having its symbolic meteorite taken back to the temple in Emesa, the cult lived on to once again take center stage fifty years later.

In 274 the Emperor Aurelian consecrated a lavish new temple in Rome dedicated to Sol Invictus. Some scholars[231] claim that this was not the same God as had been brought to Rome by Elagabalus, even though the name was unchanged and Aurelian had fought and won the most important battle of his life at Emesa, where he afterward visited (and later refurbished) the great temple there, from which Sol Invictus had been brought to Rome. In any event, Aurelian decreed that Sol Invictus was the Supreme Deity of Rome and that his worship was the official state religion. He also declared December 25 to be a festival celebrating the birth of the "Unconquered Sun." Many modern writers have mistakenly claimed that Christmas was set on this same date as an overlay to this festival. But that's backward. Aurelian picked this day because it was already being celebrated as Christmas by Rome's growing Christian Movement.[232] The emperor also inaugurated games in Sol's honor, and provided public funds to support his priesthood. Then Aurelian had statues of the other primary Gods of Rome placed in the new temple, not to share in the glory of Sol Invictus, but to demonstrate their very inferior and subordinate status. In fact, Sol Invictus was given primacy in all the attributes and special functions of all the other Gods. In this way, Mars, for example, became merely a "helper" God of War.

The cult of Sol Invictus retained the allegiance of most Roman emperors who followed Aurelian—even Constantine featured him on his coins until he decided that Sol was not the supreme God and instead embraced Christianity.

CONCLUSION

For all that the cult of Sol Invictus probably represented a growing taste for monotheism among the Romans, his cult was doomed to fall short, just as had that of Isis. Both were far too rooted in "mythical" origins and actions, surrounded with too many other (if subordinate) Gods, and each was conceived of in all too human terms—Isis was often portrayed as nursing the infant Horus. Contrast them with Yahweh, whose origins, if any, were utterly unknown, whose motives and character were regarded as mainly beyond human comprehension, and whose splendor and magnitude precluded depiction. Of course, that also was Yahweh's main vulnerability, as was demonstrated by Israel's chronic reversions to idolatry.

Even so, long before the fall of Rome, monotheism had arrived in the West to stay. Meanwhile, the evolution of religion was tracing a quite different course in the East.

· 5 ·

INDIAN INSPIRATIONS

MUCH OF THE RELIGIOUS HISTORY of India is little remembered. Consider that it was not until early in the nineteenth century, when some stubborn Englishmen dug into
various ruins and bribed several members of the hereditary Brahman
priesthood to teach them the secret, sacred language of Sanskrit, that it
was discovered that Buddhism had originated in India and initially had
attracted a substantial following there. The Indians had forgotten a millennium of extensive and active Buddhism so completely that the large
shrine marking Buddha's birthplace was not rediscovered until 1896.[1]
This was not exceptional. Rather, as Arthur Llewellyn Basham (1914–
1986), the very influential historian of India, put it: "It is perhaps unjust
to maintain that India had no sense of history whatever, but what interest
she had in her own past was generally concentrated on the fabulous kings
of a legendary golden age, rather than the great empires which had risen
and fallen in historical times. Thus our knowledge of the . . . history of
ancient India is tantalizingly vague and uncertain."[2]

   This uncertainty fully applies to the origins of Hinduism. Scholars
have determined that it arose in India about 1500 BCE, but whether it was
brought by outsiders or was of local origin is the basis of a bitter dispute.
Far more reliable information has survived concerning the remarkable
events of the sixth century BCE, when Hinduism underwent a theological revolution at the very same time and in the same area that Siddhartha
Gautama was founding Buddhism and that Vardhamāna Mahāvīra was
perfecting Jainism. As will be seen, none of these faiths seem to have been

based on revelations, and initially each greatly minimized the significance of any Gods. Thus it can be proposed that these faiths were regressive as to the "discovery" of God, even though lush polytheism eventually
emerged within each.

Why a major revision of Hinduism, and the rise of Buddhism and of
Jainism, all happened at the same time will be examined, but primary
attention will be given to the origins of these faiths. Of course, Islam has
long been a major religion in India, too, but since this is not a history
of places, but of religions, it will be more coherent to deal with Islam in
Chapter 8. Although the story of the founding, early success, and then
the collapse of Buddhism in India is told in this chapter, the story will
conclude in the next, since Buddhism lives on in the Far East. The appropriate place to begin this account of Indian religion is with the early and
long-forgotten civilization that arose in the Indus River Valley before any
of these great faiths had yet appeared.

RELIGION IN THE INDUS VALLEY

The existence of an ancient and very impressive civilization in the Indus
Valley (now in Pakistan) was discovered in the 1920s by English and Indian archaeologists, led by Sir John Marshall (1876–1958).[3] What they un-
covered was an immense urban society that flourished from about 2500
BCE until about 1500 BCE. Here towns and villages were crowded together
along the Indus River and its principal tributaries, which originate in the
Himalayan Mountains and run south to the Arabian Sea, creating a valley
about 1,000 miles long. In ancient times the Indus Valley was much more
densely occupied than either the Nile or the Tigris-Euphrates Valleys,
made possible by the rich soil deposits brought by the mighty annual tor-
rent, which amounts to twice the flow of the Nile.[4]

As shown on Map 5–1, all of this was ruled by two major cities, Harappa
in the north and Mohenjo-daro in the south, named by archaeologists
for the modern village nearest to each, and the society itself is called the
Harappan Civilization. These two major cities were remarkably similar,
indicative of a centralized regime. There were no signs in the ruins of
gradual development or growth—each city was built initially in its final
form, which was in accord with the *acropolis model* wherein a large lower
city was dominated by an elevated and fortified elite complex. In most

acropolis cities the upper complex was built on a hill, but since both of these cities were built on flat ground, the elevated area was sited on a platform made of brick, about 40 feet high, 500 yards long, and 300 yards wide.[5] The lower city was laid out in a rectangular grid of streets dividing the city into blocks. "All the buildings remained unchanged in basic plan

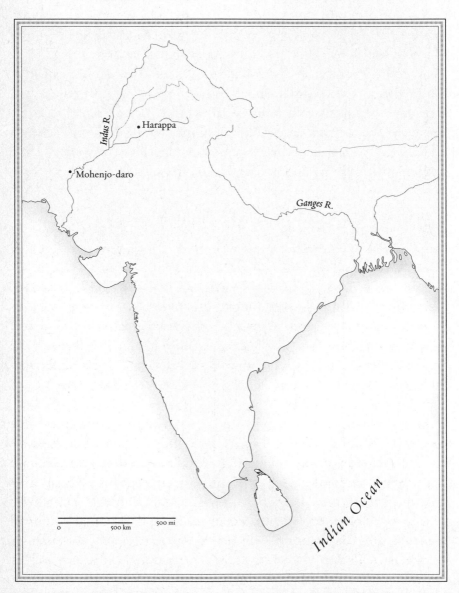

Map 5–1: Indus Valley civilization.

over the centuries; when units were rebuilt, old walls served as foundations for new construction."[6]

Although it was typical of cities built on the acropolis model for one of the major buildings on the elevated section to be a temple, there is no conclusive evidence of temples at either Harappa or Mohenjo-daro, which there may not have been since subsequently early Hinduism was opposed to temples. Nevertheless, some evidence concerning the religion practiced by this civilization has survived—keeping in mind "the notorious incapacity of material objects to represent the true content and affinity of a religion or belief."[7] We will learn much more about the religion of the Harappan Civilization if anyone is ever able to decipher its script—large numbers of inscriptions and seals with writing on them have survived. But the most prevalent surviving objects seeming to have religious significance are terra-cotta figurines of a nearly nude female that some scholars believe represented a Mother Goddess.[8] In addition, many "polished stones, mostly small but up to 2 ft. or more in height, have been correctly identified with the *linga* [penis]."[9] Indeed, many seals display a God with an erect penis, which "seems to pre-figure the Rudra-Shiva of later times."[10] This interpretation is "reinforced by the prevalence of the bull (the vehicle of Shiva) or of bull-like animals amongst the seal symbols."[11] Many other deities and scenes depicted on the seals found in the Indus Valley ruins are "reminiscent" of Sumerian culture, especially the Gilgamesh story.[12] Usually, this similarity has been dismissed as coincidence, but the fact remains that there is solid evidence of contact between these two early civilizations: "seals and other knick-knacks" of Harappan origin having been found in Sumer, and some Sumerian objects having been found along the Indus.[13]

But by around 1500 BCE it was all gone. The two great cities were mostly abandoned, occupied only by people who built rude huts on top of the ruins. Scholars disagree about what happened. Some propose that changes in the river, especially its silting up in various places, led to devastating floods and abandonment of the area. Others, especially Sir Mortimer Wheeler (1890–1976), one of the great archaeologists to work on Indus sites, claim that it was overwhelmed by Aryan invaders from northeastern Europe. More recently, however, despite apparent references to such an invasion in Vedic scriptures, many scholars now doubt that it took place, believing that Aryans had long been resident in India. In any event, the demise of this Harappan Civilization coincided with the arrival of Hinduism.

HINDUISM

Today, anyone who would write of Hinduism must first defend their use of the word and the assumption that there is a unified Indian religious tradition to which "Hinduism" might accurately refer. A number of recent scholars, most of them in the grip of Postmodernism, have charged that "Hinduism" was "invented" by Western colonialists.[14] Their case rests on two points. First, and most trivial, is their claim that Western colonials coined the word *Hindu*, or *Hindoo* as it was often spelled early in the nineteenth century. Second, they condemn "Hinduism" as a false "construction" imposed on "the extravagant variety"[15] of Indian sects, doctrines, Gods, and rituals—an array that Indians themselves are said not to have regarded as having any common core until "educated" in this view by British imperialists and missionaries.[16]

As to the first claim, although Westerners named the oceans and the continents, that doesn't falsify geography. More to the point, the word *Hindu* occurred in Muslim texts before the British even knew where India was.[17] The word actually derives from *Sindhu*, the local name for the Indus River, which "became 'Hind' or 'Hindu' in Persian languages and then reentered Indian languages as 'Hindu.'"[18] As to the second claim, the variations within Hinduism do not exceed those within Judaism, Christianity, or Islam. Like the multitude of disputatious groups within these three faiths, the Hindu variations are clearly and explicitly based on a common core of scripture, doctrine, and practice. All groups usually included as Hindu have "one sacred literature, accepted and revered by all adherents,"[19] a common set of doctrines (including transmigration of the soul), the same array of deities (even if they differ in emphasis and preference), and similar restrictions and rituals. As the respected Jan Gonda (1905–1991) summed up, "Despite the utmost variety and complexity of its ethnic and social composition . . . [Hinduism] is characterized by an almost complete integration of heterogeneous elements."[20] Without apology I turn now to the origins and development of Hinduism.

Recently, a distinguished Indian historian wrote that "Hinduism is perhaps the only major religion in the world that has not been started by a prophet. . . . [As a] religion that originated with the people [it] has really no beginning . . ."[21] While much remains unknown about the origins of Hinduism, one thing is certain: it was *not* originated by "the people." New culture, including religion, always originates with individuals or very small groups, although their identity is often lost, as it was in the case of those who produced the **Vedas**, the scriptures on which early Hinduism was based, as well as of those responsible for Upaniṣads, the scriptures that revolutionized Hinduism. But given the content of these works, their authors should be called prophets.

These scriptures define the two major stages in the development of Hinduism and provide an appropriate framework for analyzing the rise of this great faith.

VEDAS AND BRAHMANS

The earliest form of Hinduism, based on scriptures known as the Vedas, and the caste system intrinsic to the religion, arose in India during the fifteenth century BCE. As noted, raging controversy exists as to whether this new culture was brought to India by Aryan, or Indo-Aryan, conquerors or whether both religion and caste originated with an indigenous people.[22] In many ways, it doesn't matter nearly so much who originated Hinduism as what it was that they gave to the world, and that was a faith that recognized many "Nature" Gods and stressed that humans must frequently and perfectly perform certain rituals in order "to ensure the orderly functioning of the world."[23]

Scriptures and Ritual

For more than three millennia, the Vedas were regarded as so secret that not a line of them was ever written down. This immense text was transmitted orally from one generation to the next, and only male members of the upper classes were ever allowed to hear it—should a lower-class person or a woman happen to hear any portion of the Vedas being recited, his or her ears were to be filled with molten lead.[24] Not until British colonial administrators managed to bribe several *Brahmans* (the priestly upper class) to divulge portions of the Vedas, was anything ever written down. Once this had occurred, other Brahmans from many distant parts of India also divulged the scriptures they had memorized. The remarkable fact is that when the various versions were collected and compared, they were virtually identical—these lengthy scriptures had been transmitted for three thousand years "with hardly an error." This despite the fact that many of those who had memorized portions of the Vedas "had only the vaguest notions of its meaning, because its language is so archaic that it is almost unintelligible" today.[25]

Like the Bible, the Vedas are not a single scripture, but an anthology. They are divided into four major parts. The first is known as the **Rgveda** (also Rig Veda), and is a collection of 1,028 hymns directed to various Gods. It is divided into ten sections called *mandalas*. The second part is the **Sāmaveda**, "a collection of extracts from the [Rgveda] with appropriate musical instructions for recitation."[26] The third part of the Vedas is the **Yajurveda**. It is devoted to rituals and ceremonies. The fourth part is known as the **Atharvaveda**, and is a "collection of hymns and spells."[27] Of these four, the Rgveda is regarded as by far the most important and so much stress is placed on the exact wording of its hymns and even the sounds given to syllables, that this has generated an additional literature known as the **Vedāngas**, which consists of five parts. The **Śīkṣa** deals with precise pronunciation. The **Vyākarana** deals with grammar and philology. **Nirukta** "treats the etymology of unusual and rare words." The **Chanda** explains and offers practice in verse meters, and the **Jyotiṣa** "teaches planetary science, astronomy and astrology together, which was (and is) the instrument for determining the right moment for religious acts."[28]

And knowing the right moment was crucial since the continued existence of the world depended upon the correct and frequent performance of a sacrifice that reenacted the original Creation. Sometimes identified as the *Fire Sacrifice*, it was thought that unless it was conducted regularly, "all cosmic processes would cease, and chaos would come again."[29] The Fire Sacrifice exalted the power of the Brahmans in that the existence of the world did not depend primarily on the Gods, but on Brahmans "who by the magic of the sacrifice compelled [the Gods]." Hence the Brahmans were "more powerful than any earthly king, or any god . . . and . . . therefore the most dangerous of enemies."[30] Three classes of Brahmans took part in the sacrifice, often numbering as many as seventeen. The *rtvij* performed the actual sacrifice. The *hotr* intoned the hymns that accompanied the sacrifice. And the *purohita* ("he who is placed in front") supervised everything.

Of course, the Brahmans preformed many other rituals seeking to gain various benefits from the Gods, "success in war, progeny, increase of cattle, and long life."[31] Most of these rituals also involved fire. Thus professional Brahman poet-priests of Vedic Hinduism placed offerings of food and other gifts to various Gods in a large sacrificial fire while chanting hymns of praise that, among other things, directed the God of Fire to convey an offering to a specific God. It is these hymns that make up the Rgveda. During the rituals it was believed that the Gods came down invisibly, sat around the sacred fire, and "drank and ate with the worshippers."[32] Near the end of a sacrifice, the presiding priest would say, "The god hath accepted the offering; he hath become strengthened; he hath won greater might." At which point the client would respond, "May I prosper in accordance with the prospering of the god." Thus, as was pointed out in Chapter 2, sacrifice usually involves exchange. As Arthur Berriedale Keith (1879–1944), the distinguished Scottish Orientalist, put it: the Vedic "theory of the sacrifice and its result as an exchange of gifts, strength for strength, is the fundamental fact of the whole Vedic religion."[33]

At complete variance with modern Hinduism's view of cattle, and especially cows, as sacred animals, the eating of which is considered the equivalent of cannibalism, in Vedic times cattle not only were sacrificed, but their roasted carcasses were pulled from the fire and eaten by the priests! Indeed, human sacrifice was sometimes practiced, being "considered necessary to make impregnable such strong points as bastions and city gates . . . the victim[s] had to be buried in the foundations of the new construction."[34] Some Hindu sects such as the Maraya and Thugs continued to engage in human sacrifices until very recent times.[35]

Castes

In Vedic times, Indian society consisted of four primary castes or *varnas*: the priestly elite of Brahmans (*brāhmanas*), the warrior elite (*kṣatriyas*) from whence came kings and princes, the "middle class" of farmers and merchants (*vaiśyas*), and the mass of "unpropertied laborers, servants, and menials" (*śūdra*).[36] Slaves were sometimes distinguished separately as the *dāsa*. These castes were hereditary and fully sanctified by the Rgveda, which taught that at the Creation the primal being known as the *puruṣa-sūkta* was sacrificed by the gods "and dismembered, and from the parts of his body the universe, including its human inhabitants, was fashioned."[37] From his mouth came the Brahmans, from his arms the *kṣatriyas*, from his thighs came the *vaiśyas*, and the *śūdra* came from his feet.[38] Thus, in early days Vedic Hinduism was mainly by and for the two (and sometimes three) elite castes.

So, what of the people? Where did the *śūdra* and the *dāsa* turn for religion, since they were not allowed even to hear the Rgveda or attend the Fire Sacrifice? As in Sumer and Egypt, they seem to have had the services of shamans (*munis*), a collection of wonder-workers and holy men who operated outside the priestly fraternity.[39] Even so, it appears that at least in the beginning the common people in Vedic India were mainly on their own religiously—they were identified in scripture as "devoid of any direct relation to religion."[40] Just as in the early civilizations with temple religions, the Indian masses depended on rituals and ceremonies that they could conduct for themselves, such as keeping a sacred fire burning in their homes.[41] The people also conducted their own wedding ceremonies and probably some sort of funeral rites—it appears that at that time "only the rich were cremated."[42] Although the common people acknowledged the great Gods, they also worshipped many lesser Gods "of a functional type who helped them in their daily lives and who were worshipped in simple rituals and offerings that did not need the mediation of priests."[43]

Over time, however, the original four-caste system proliferated into a very complex set of "more than 3,000 subdivisions"[44] (or *jātis*), based mainly on hereditary occupations, but also with the "absorption of new tribes or regional groups."[45] Various of these caste groups soon came to identify with certain deities and eventually many formed and sustained their own Hindu sects. Faced with competition from a host of lower-caste holy men, the Brahmans "eventually agreed to serve all castes as priests and to adapt new worships to old forms in order to gain [their] livelihood[s]."[46] Thus, Hinduism was extended down the caste system until it embraced virtually all social groups.[47]

Competition and Pluralism

As true professionals, the Brahmans only performed sacrifices in exchange for payment. This prompted intense competition among them, not only to expand their clientele to include everyone, but for elite patronage as "[t]hose who could afford it thus sought far and wide for priests whose skill was generally acknowledged and whose sacrificial services would most likely be effective. . . . It was common practice for . . . the most renowned priests to travel long distances to serve such patrons."[48] As would be expected, competition spurred innovation. New hymns and new ritual "embellishments . . . were readily adopted by fellow professionals to increase the effectiveness and value of their own services," and the most prominent priests drew multitudes of students.[49]

Priestly competition was greatly facilitated by the fact that Vedic Hinduism functioned without any temples.[50] The priests only built temporary sacrificial altars as needed for a specific sacrifice—Vedic texts "pour contempt on the image worshippers and temple builders."[51] Lack of temples meant lack of central control, which, of course, unleashed impulses toward *pluralism*. These impulses were greatly facilitated by the fact that through most of history, and especially during the Vedic era, India has been "a land of weak states."[52] Hence, within their relatively unregulated religious market, Vedic priests not only competed for clients and students, but formed a number of "schools." These schools differed not only in the relative emphasis given to various Gods, but also in their versions of "myths" concerning such basic matters as the Creation. It is this proliferation of schools and theologies that makes the reconstruction of Vedic Hinduism so difficult. In effect, there were many Vedic Hinduisms. But all of them accepted essentially the same group of Gods.

Vedic Gods

During the Vedic era, Hindus worshipped at least thirty-three Gods, or *devas*. It is difficult to present a coherent and accurate portrayal of this Vedic pantheon because contradictions abound, given that different hymns in the Rgveda were composed by different priestly schools. An additional complication is a habit of mind that best can be described as polytheistic monotheism—often enough any given God was regarded as an Only God by worshippers.[53] Although published nearly 150 years ago, Max Müller's description of this phenomenon has not been surpassed. When Hindus invoke "individual gods . . . they are not conceived as limited by the power of others, as superior or inferior in rank. Each god . . . is felt at the time as . . . supreme and absolute despite the necessary limitation which, to our mind, a plurality of gods must entail on every single god. All the rest disappear from vision ... and only [the God] who is to fulfill their desires stands in full light before the eyes of the worshippers."[54] Keep in mind, too, that not all of the major Gods of later Hinduism were known in the Vedic era, that some Gods of major standing in modern Hinduism were minor figures back then, while some major Vedic Gods were later reduced to minor deities.

The Vedic Gods were overwhelmingly portrayed as male. Few Goddesses appear in the Rgveda, those who do are mostly "mothers" of various Gods, and none is given much attention.[55] However, all of the Vedic Gods, male and female, were "Nature" Gods, divided into three fundamental classes or "worlds": celestial, atmospheric, and terrestrial. It was this set of categories that prompted Max Müller to propose (incorrectly) that *all* of the *earliest* religions worshipped Nature Gods (Chapter 1). Of course, the Vedic Gods were far from being the earliest Gods, even in India.

Celestial Gods were associated with various heavenly bodies. The oldest of these Gods was a "Sky Father," but the most important of them was **Varuna** who was believed to rule over the night, although he also was said to make the sun shine.[56] In some scriptures Varuna was credited as the Creator (although "there is no clearly defined creator-god in the main body of the Rgveda"[57]),and in most he was regarded as guardian of the cosmic order, providing "the basis for what is true and in its proper place, for proper movement and for what is correctly said or done."[58] As conceived by the Brahmans, Varuna was "a king—not a boisterous tribal warlord ... but a mighty emperor, sitting in a great palace in the heavens, often with associated gods around him."[59] One of these was the God **Mitra**, thought to correspond "to the Iranian sun god Mithra."[60] But the most important celestial God was **Vishnu**, who also was associated with the sun, although it was only centuries later that he became such a major Hindu God—in the Vedic era Vishnu was only a subordinate figure, "largely overshadowed by his friend and ally" Indra.[61]

Indra was among the *atmospheric* Gods, being the God of Thunder, along with **Vāyu**, the God of Wind; **Parjanya**, the God of Rain; and a cluster of Storm Gods known as the **Maruts**. **Rudra**, the "Red One" or "Howler," was the father of the Maruts and greatly feared for his angry and destructive nature, being "depicted as a ruddy, swarthy man with a

J.M. 363—1923.

Davaindram on White Elephant

The rowdy God Indra is depicted riding into battle on his elephant. (Victoria and Albert Museum, London; Photo: Victoria and Albert Museum, London/ Art Resource, New York)

wild temper and the murderous temperament of a wild beast."[62] He was only a minor God early in Vedic times, but eventually he evolved into a major deity.

Meanwhile, Indra not only was by far the most important atmospheric God, he was perhaps the most important of all the Vedic Gods, since he was essentially the God of Warriors, too. "He was a rowdy amoral deity, fond of feasting and drinking."[63] As Thomas Hopkins described him: "The tawny Indra, belly full of exhilarating Soma Juice, beard agitated, brandishing his glittering thunderbolt, boasting of his prowess and eager to join battle with the enemy, clearly reflects the . . . warrior's self image."[64]

Even so, the greatest emphasis in the Rgveda scriptures is given to the *terrestrial* Gods because they were the active agents in all the sacrifice rituals: **Agni**, the Fire God; **Brihaspati**, teacher of the Gods and Lord of Prayer; and **Soma**, the God who "represents and animates the juice of the Soma plant,"[65] an hallucinogen that was consumed only at sacrifices.

Soma probably was hemp, and in liquid form it would have been very similar to the modern Indian drink known as *bhang*.[66] Thus, the central aspect of Vedic Hinduism occurred when priests, filled with Soma juice, gathered around sacred fires to burn offerings and offer prayers in strict adherence to prescribed words, intonations, and gestures.

Some readers may be wondering why Brahmā, whom some Hindus regard as the Supreme God, has yet to be discussed.[67] In the Vedic era the priests were known as Brahmans, not because they served Brahmā, but because they served an impersonal, magical force or spirit, known as *Brahman* (also known as *Prajāpatu*). This impersonal force was involved in the Creation and gave supernatural power to the hymns and prayers of the Brahmans, but it was not personified. Only later did it evolve into the God Brahmā.[68]

It is from these beginnings that the complex pantheon of Hindu Gods developed.

Major Vedic "Myths"

The Rgveda is as remarkable for its poetic beauty as for its profundity. Nowhere are both more evident than in the *Hymn of Creation*,[69] one of the oldest of Vedic scriptures. The lack of active deities and the fundamental uncertainty expressed in the last two verses may suggest to some that this is more of a philosophical poem than a "myth." No matter.

Then even nothingness was not, nor existence.
There was no air then, nor the heavens beyond it.
What covered it? Where was it? In whose keeping?
Was there then cosmic water, in depths unfathomed?

Then there were neither death nor immortality,
nor was there then the torch of night and day.
The One Wind breathed windlessly and self-sustaining.
There was that One then, and there was no other.

At first there was only darkness wrapped in darkness.
All this was only unillumined water.
That One which came to be, enclosed in nothing,
arose at last, born of the power of heat.

In the beginning desire descended on it—
that was the primal seed, born of the mind.
The sages who have searched their hearts with wisdom
know that which is its kin to that which is not.

And they stretched their cord across the void,
and know what was above, and what below.
Seminal powers made fertile mighty forces.
Below was strength, and over it was impulse.

But, after all, who knows, and who can say
whence it all came, and how creation happened?
The gods themselves are later than creation,
so who knows truly whence it had arisen?

Whence all creation had its origin,
he, whether he fashioned it or whether he did not,
he, who surveys it all from highest heaven,
he knows—or maybe even he does not know.

The uncertainty expressed in this scripture was not the prevailing Vedic view of Creation, for there wasn't one. Instead, there existed "a bewildering variety of speculations and theories on the origin of the universe."[70] Many of these proposed a First Person of divine proportions who, out of loneliness, created a wife from his own flesh and they then created and populated the universe, including all of the animals. But the doubt expressed in this hymn lingered as an important counterpoint and, as will be seen, during the great religious revolution of the sixth century BCE, the Hymn of Creation prompted new interpretations of Brahman.

Most of the "myths" recounted in the Vedas are neither so philosophical nor so abstract as the Hymn of Creation. As would be expected, many involve deities doing great deeds, and the most popular of these involves *Indra's battle with the evil Vrtra.*

Recall that Indra was an atmospheric God of Thunder. Vrtra was a powerful demon in the form of a serpentine monster who was blocking the flow of earth's streams and rivers. To restore the flow of life-giving waters, Indra went out to do battle, armed with thunderbolts and after drinking three cups of Soma. As for Vrtra: "Like an enraged coward he called a challenge." But Indra blasted him with a thunderbolt. Now both "footless and handless, he still gave Indra battle" but another thunderbolt finished him off, whereupon "the waters suddenly, like bellowing cattle, descended and flowed on, down to the ocean."[71] At this point Indra also raised up the sky, which until then had been lying on the earth, and in so doing he inaugurated the contrast between light and darkness, heaven and earth.[72]

However, Indra was not to remain the favorite Hindu God. The sages who produced the Upaniṣads pushed him into the background and characterized him as an enthusiastic adulterer and the primary impediment to enlightenment, as a deity who sends visions of beautiful women to distract those attempting to meditate.[73]

AN OUTBREAK OF PLURALISM

During the sixth century BCE, an enormous number of disputatious holy men and the many competing sects that formed around them swept over northern India. To most Indians at the time, especially to those living in the Ganges Valley, it must have seemed that anywhere they turned, there stood ascetic beggars holding out their bowls and reciting new religious slogans and principles.[74] Among the literally hundreds of new sects, the *Ājīvaka* taught that there is no such thing as free will and that each person's life follows the course of preordained fate, hence good or evil deeds have no bearing on one's circumstances. Despite this, the Ājīvaka were extreme ascetics who went naked and often intentionally starved themselves to death.[75] In contrast, the *Cārvāka* proposed that since there is neither rebirth nor any afterlife, "the only wise course is to grasp life now . . . [being] concerned with the pleasures of this life alone."[76] The *Pāśupata* worshipped Shiva, bathed in ashes, went naked, were celibate, and engaged in minor forms of public antisocial behavior, such as shouting nonsense, in order to cause others to abuse them.[77] However, most sects advocated a middle way, proposing that good deeds are rewarded and evil deeds are punished, albeit in a rather roundabout way as one manages to escape the endless transmigration of one's soul through countless rebirths. This was the view promulgated by a radically new form of Hinduism, as well as by the two sects that rose to become major new faiths: *Jainism* and *Buddhism*.

Why did all this religious turmoil occur at this particular time and place? The answer is to be found in a rapid shift toward a far more urban society, the rise of "self-made" kings ruling over much larger political units—with the consequent erosion of Brahman power—and the emergence of a relatively unregulated religious economy that facilitated extensive pluralism.

Keep in mind that the Brahmans never established themselves as a subsidized, monopoly temple religion as did the Sumerian and Egyptian priesthoods. Instead, the Brahmans of the Vedic era were but a loose network of priests who disdained "indoor" worship, let alone temples; who were segmented into many "schools" and followings, and who engaged in a great deal of competition. Indeed, non-Brahman holy men (*shramana*) were always active on the religious fringes. Moreover, for more than a millennium, Vedic Brahmanism's relative domination of the religious scene rested on its hereditary connections to the ruling elites of the small rural kingdoms that dominated Indian life. Most of these kingdoms were based on a single tribe and were so small that they are best described as "statelets."

By the start of the sixth century, these rural statelets were disappearing, submerged by an urban-centered society that developed along the Ganges Valley—often referred to by historians as the "second urbanization" to distinguish it from the previous Harappan Civilization along the Indus Valley.[78] However, these new cities were not built on the acropolis model, although they did have moats and walls, the latter serving not only as defensive ramparts but also as levees against the frequent flooding by the Ganges. Indeed, it was the river that gave these cities life, not only by sustaining a productive agriculture capable of feeding urbanites, but by enabling the development of extensive trade via water transport.

These new cities arose amid the huge mosaic of tiny rural kingdoms, and the two modes of life and sovereignty were quite incompatible. The advent of the new urbanism thus entailed a long and bloody struggle for political supremacy, during which the weakened and distracted kings and princes ruling small rural kingdoms had neither the will nor the means to suppress unorthodox religious expression, even had they been so inclined, nor were the new urban regimes interested in doing so. In these circumstances, what already was a relatively open religious economy became almost completely unregulated and, as would be expected, lush pluralism quickly emerged as many religions fashioned their appeals to specific "market" niches. The extremes to which some groups went may have reflected the difficulty any new group had in attracting attention amid this extraordinary cacophony.

Meanwhile, the many small kingdoms were quickly incorporated into much larger states, and eventually all were merged into the Magadhan kingdom ruled by Bimbisāra (558–491 BCE). Given the extensive and energetic religious diversity that had arisen, it would have been very difficult for Bimbisāra to reimpose any meaningful Brahman control, and he had no motives for doing so. For one thing, Bimbisāra was a "self-made" man of modest origins who had no ties to the Brahmans. For another, once set in motion, pluralism would have been very difficult to suppress, for the "limitless Gangetic forest could have sheltered" all religious dissenters.[79] Moreover, King Bimbisāra himself embraced dissent, offering considerable support to Buddha, in which he was joined by the two most influential Brahmans in his court.[80] Eventually Bimbisāra was murdered by his son Ajatashatru, who then seized the throne, only to be murdered and replaced by his own son, as were the next four Magadhan kings after him.[81] Each of these kings was far more interested in conquest and consumption than in defining any religious orthodoxy. Hence, a relatively unregulated, innovative, and competitive Indian religious economy became firmly embedded in the culture, and nothing was ever the same again.[82]

Upaniṣads and the New Hinduism

The revolution that swept through Hinduism in the sixth century BCE was so profound that some reputable scholars have suggested that this was the first authentic form of Hinduism—that the religion of the Vedic era was a different faith.[83] The basis for this view is the extensive reconceptualization of the Gods and the introduction of a radically different belief system as presented in a whole new body of more than 200 scriptures known as the **Upaniṣads**.[84] As with the Vedas, the Upaniṣads "do not represent a coherent body of information or one particular belief system,"[85] although a general perspective can be distilled from them. Often, a Upaniṣad takes the form of a dialogue, frequently involving several sages and their students or some other audience, and some of the sages are "famous" because they appear in a number of scriptures.

Recall that the Vedas were regarded as so secret that they only could be communicated to upper-caste males. So, too, were the Upaniṣads to be imparted only from Brahman fathers to sons or to the pupils of a Brahman who had studied with him for at least a year. The secret nature of these scriptures is reinforced in the texts as well. Whenever the most important part of a discussion arrives, the most senior sages taking part in the dialogue step away to converse in private.[86]

Of course, the dialogue format often involves fictional participants, and because there is no very convincing evidence that the sages portrayed in the Upaniṣads actually existed, the best guess is that they were written by prominent sages whose names are forgotten, but probably not by the ones named in the texts. Even if we don't know who actually wrote any of the Upaniṣads, internal evidence suggests that many were written in the Panchala region, located within the Ganges Valley and only several hundred miles west of the birthplaces of Buddha and Mahāvīra! In the final analysis, of course, the names and even the biographies of those who wrote Upaniṣads are of far less importance than what they revealed, which was the primacy of self and the existence of "sin" and "salvation." Moreover, even though the actual words of these new scriptures were, in early days, kept secret, the primary new doctrines concerning sin and salvation were widely promulgated.

Sin and Salvation

Vedic era Hinduism had little to say about death or an afterlife; some passages in the Rgveda suggest that the dead go to a shadowy existence. But the Upaniṣads changed all that by introducing the doctrine of the **transmigration of souls**: that upon each death we are reborn (*samsara*) and that our situation in each life is determined by our *karma*,[87] which translates as "deeds," and refers to our behavior in our previous life or lives. Thus arose the concept of *sin*, although the Hindus did not use this term. At issue here is the revolutionary idea that our behavior has transcendent or supernatural implications—that immoral behavior is punished and that good behavior is rewarded! Somewhat similar ideas had risen at about this same time in Zoroastrianism and Judaism—albeit these were experienced not in the next life, but in the afterlife.

The concept of sin and the doctrine of transmigration sanctified the rigid caste system and the marked inequalities of Indian life. They justified the exalted status of the Brahmans as well as that of kings and princes as having been *earned* in past lives. By the same token, those born at the very bottom of the caste system were getting only what they *deserve*—there is, quite literally, a hell on earth and one should feel no sympathy for those born into such straits. In this fashion, the doctrine of karma "provided a satisfactory explanation of the mystery of suffering."[88]

Significantly, those on the bottom rungs of the status pyramid could find considerable comfort in this doctrine, since they could strive to be reborn into far greater privilege by living righteously. However, it was much less appealing to the privileged, many of whom found far less satisfaction in their exalted status than those beneath them could imagine. Even for kings and princes, as for the most admired Brahmans, there was no escape from life's many disappointments and sorrows and there was no more satisfying life to strive for—the future could only be more of the same, or worse. Thus, the goal of many Brahmans and other upper-caste Indians became **release**—an escape from the cycle of birth, death, and rebirth into an ultimate state of unconscious, everlasting bliss: **Nirvana**. But how to do it?

Self and Transformation

The central feature of the New Hinduism was an intense focus on the "self," or *ātman*, and how it was linked to Brahman, the unifying spiritual force that underlies all existence and empowers all rituals. Eventually, the ātman was identified as an aspect of Brahman, that within each person there is a fragment of the eternal. Initially, both ātman and Brahman were defined in such indefinite ways as to deepen the mysteries. In a famous Upaniṣads, it is said that the "self is not this, not that. It is incomprehensible for it is not comprehended. It is indestructible for it is never destroyed. It is unattached for it does not attach itself. It is unfettered. It does not suffer. It is not injured."[89] But what *is it*? In some ways, the ātman is like what Christians define as the soul. The body is mortal, but the ātman is eternal and "is essentially free of the body, although supported by the body while incarnate; in its freed state it is bodiless."[90] However, it would be incorrect simply to equate the ātman with the soul because the latter consists primarily of consciousness, while the most desirable state of the ātman is a very unaware sort of consciousness, an intelligence without desire that blissfully returns to and becomes one with Brahman. For it is desire that traps humans in endless existence, hence the New Hinduism taught, "the man who does not desire, who is without desire, whose desire is satisfied, whose desire is self"[91] escapes and "goes to Brahman at his death. When desire is eliminated, rebirth is eliminated; there is no further embodiment of the self."[92]

How then to overcome desire? Through "much meditation and asceticism."[93] The key players in the spread of the New Hinduism were not the traditional Brahman priests, but wandering ascetics, whose numbers grew exponentially at this time. Even though many of these new "holy men" came from privileged backgrounds, they served the entire religious market, not just a wealthy elite. Many were accessible to everyone; others were associated with various sects serving particular castes, and the number of such sects expanded rapidly, too. Some holy men validated their claims to possess remarkable magical and spiritual powers by their visible and dramatic suffering, such as lying on beds of thorns or nails or by holding their arms raised until they atrophied. Others devoted most of their waking hours to meditation and the rest of their time to wandering "often in large groups, begging alms, [and] proclaiming their doctrines to all who wished to listen."[94] Most wore simple garments, but Ājīvakas went naked, followed severe dietary rules, and "often ended their lives by self-starvation."[95] Together, these ascetic holy men revolutionized Hinduism.

From the start, however, the New Hinduism was of two minds about the Gods. While some of the Upaniṣads are concerned with the Gods, by far the greater number are relatively "Godless" in that they reduce divinity to a subjective state—"All the gods are within me," according to one Upaniṣads. Another teaches: "The highest *brahman*, which is all forms, which is the supreme reality of the universe, which is the most subtle of the subtle and which is eternal, *is nothing but yourself.*"[96] The Brahman is the active force of the universe, but it is immaterial, cosmic, impersonal, and unaware. However, rather than define *Brahman* as "unreal," most of the Upaniṣads teach that it is the material world that is unreal, and this is why the basis of salvation, of release from the cycle of rebirths, is to recognize this unreality and surrender all attachments to the illusions of "reality."[97] That was, of course, the propellant for the extraordinary explosion of asceticism—that the world must be utterly rejected in all its works and ways.

Eventually the Brahmans could not ignore the explosion of asceticism, so they instituted a series of priesthood levels and began to incorporate various hermit meditators and wandering ascetics into their lower ranks.[98] Soon formal priestly roles were sustained "within virtually every caste or even subcaste,"[99] and this expanded Brahmanical system reasserted itself by taking far greater "concern for the ongoing life of society, largely ignored by . . . ascetic groups."[100] Soon, too, the Brahmans broke with their long tradition of opposition to temples. In a relatively short period of time, Indians had erected what might well be the greatest density of temples of any place on earth.[101] This did not, however, transform Hinduism into a traditional temple religion. The temples were neither exclusive nor subsidized. They lived by donations, were frequented by both rich and poor, and were served by priests representing all levels of social status.[102]

Restoring the Gods and Approximating Monotheism

The Brahmans were not content merely to build temples and expand their clientele. They also responded to the proliferation of new sects and holy men by attacking the New Hinduism of the Upaniṣads at its most vulnerable point, its "Godlessness." For people confronted with the vicissitudes of life, of what use is a nonconscious, divine essence? It is all well and good that full-time ascetics can occupy themselves with meditation and seek "God" within themselves, but "Godless" religions offer neither hope nor meaning, and the popular form of such faiths always involves a restoration of conscious, active Gods—as will be seen later, as well as in several subsequent chapters. That is precisely what happened here.

With Brahmans leading the way, the "Godless" Hinduism of the Upaniṣads was transformed into a very God-filled Hinduism, culminating in a remarkable new scripture known as the **Bhagavad-gītā**. This beautiful and poetic work, which most Western admirers of Hinduism take to be the primary Hindu scripture, appeared in perhaps the third century BCE. It stresses "theism and devotion to a supreme deity" by *personifying* the abstract Brahman.[103] Moreover, the Gītā, as it often is referred to, agrees with the earlier New Hinduism that within the self of every individual is a "minute part of God,"[104] and therefore the self is immortal. It expands the New Hinduism by proposing that self-realization involves the full integration of one's consciousness with one's God "particle," which is taken to involve a conscious, caring God.

Thus, not only did the Gods regain their centrality in Hinduism, this new era involved extensive reconceptualization of them all. Keep in mind that any attempt to identify and characterize the Hindu Gods must be an approximation, since contradictions, confusions, and ambiguities abound, partly because so many different "schools" and sects of Hinduism are involved, and partly because all scriptural discussions of the Gods are extremely mystical and vague.

Brahmā (the Creator) is the personification of Brahman. No longer merely an impersonal spiritual force, Brahmā is often characterized as the Supreme Being and the God of the Gods for having been their Creator.[105] Indeed, Brahmā created the world and every living thing. He is portrayed as an old man with four arms and four heads, which face in four directions, and sometimes he is shown riding a swan or a goose. He often is linked to an Earth Goddess **Sarasvati** who, in some versions of the creation story, is said to have sprung from Brahmā's forehead. Together they created all creatures as she first took the form of a cow, and he of a bull, then she of a ewe, he of a ram, and so on. Despite the fact that Brahmā appears in more myths than any other Hindu God,[106] with his work of creation done, he is but a background figure and is very "seldom worshipped in India."[107] Although he is recognized as one of the three Gods making up Hinduism's **Divine Trinity**, this is mostly a formality.

Vishnu (the Preserver) is the second God of the trinity, having emerged from a relatively minor position in the Vedic days of the faith, to become the "preserver and protector of the world, lord and ruler of all."[108] The name *Vishnu* comes from the root *visr* which means to spread in all directions, and Vishnu is believed to pervade existence and hold everything together.[109] Reflective of his role as protector and preserver, Indian culture abounds in reports of Vishnu's intervention into earthly affairs on behalf of individual supplicants. He is depicted as having dark blue skin and, like Brahmā, is believed to have four arms—but Vishnu rides an eagle, not a goose or a swan. He, too, is inseparably paired with a Goddess, **Lakshmi**, and their respective duties reflect male and female principles. Vishnu is believed to take an additional ten distinct Godly forms, or *avatars*—the term literally means a "descent," a coming down to earth, and it is understood that an avatar is only a partial manifestation or inferior form of the deity who takes this form.[110] Hence, when one worships one of Vishnu's avatars, such as **Krishna**, one is, in effect, worshipping Vishnu, although some devotees of Krishna regard him as the supreme God and Vishnu as one of Krishna's avatars.

The Hindu Divine Trinity is portrayed in this sculpture of the heads of Brahma, Vishnu, and Shiva wearing identical crowns. (Musee des Arts Asiatiques-Guimet, Paris; Photo: Erich Lessing/Art Resource, New York)

Shiva (the Destroyer) is the third God of the Trinity. Here, too, is a case of the evolution of a God. Recall Rudra, the "howler," the terrifying Vedic God. In early Upaniṣads, he was known as Rudra-Shiva, and finally, Shiva came to the fore and Rudra was demoted to being one of his avatars. Shiva is the Lord of Sleep who governs the end of all existence and who takes pleasure in destruction. He, too, has a female companion, the beautiful **Parvati**. Once when he was resting, Parvati snuck up from behind and put her hands over Shiva's eyes, whereupon darkness covered the entire world. Then a huge tongue of flame burst from Shiva's forehead and a third eye appeared, which lit up the world again. Usually he keeps this third eye turned inward, but when he turns it outward, it burns everything in sight. Shiva is depicted as chalk white in color, he wears a snake around his neck, and in his hair is a garland of skulls. He often rides on Nandi the bull.

This, then, is the Divine Trinity representing the three primary forces: creation, preservation, and destruction. However, for all the elaborate personifications of Brahmā, Vishnu, and Shiva, most Hindu teachers do not regard them as separate Gods, but as three aspects of Brahman. When asked the number of the Gods, the sage Yajnvalka (frequently portrayed in Upaniṣads) replied, "One." The others are said to be merely personifications of the various powers of the single divine being.[111] Claims about an underlying Hindu monotheism have attracted much favorable attention from Western scholars.[112] The highly respected Ninian Smart (1927–2001) noted that Brahmā, Shiva, and Vishnu "form a threefold symbol of the one Being." But, Smart continued, "the Hindus have never rejected . . . other gods."[113] One need only point to the extraordinary proliferation of Gods one encounters in any Hindu temple. Most individual Indians may, as many have claimed, tend to worship only one of these Gods or only one of them at a time, but most seem to freely agree to the existence of all the others. This may be a somewhat muted form of polytheism; it is not monotheism. Indeed, what is revealed here is a difference between what some Indian scholars and philosophers believe and what is (and was) believed by everyone else in India.

Most Indians not only embrace the Divine Trinity and the many avatars, but also a host of lesser Gods, including: **Durga**, the invincible Mother Goddess; **Ganesha**, the elephantine God of Wisdom; **Hanuman**, the celibate monkey-God; **Indra**, once the fearsome God of Thunder of the Vedas, then reduced to a boozing God of the senses; **Kali**, the frightening Goddess of Destruction; **Soma**, God of the Moon and the nectar of the Gods; **Vishvarkman**, son of Brahmā and Architect of the Universe; and, of course, the three Goddesses who are the consorts of Brahmā, Vishnu, and Shiva.

This New Hinduism was not simply an instance of theological evolution; it was a true revolution that grew out of the intense competition among various emerging sects and disputatious holy men who "set religious goals that stood outside, and in direct opposition to, the religious and social order of the . . . brahmans."[114] Some of these sects stretched the common heritage so far as to become new religions. Most of these new faiths believed in the transmigration of souls, but the two that achieved lasting historical significance both began by rejecting the Creation and demoting the Gods to relative unimportance, as had most of the Upaniṣads—both having arisen before the era of the Bhagavad-gītā, when the Gods were fully restored. The Jains took asceticism to its theological and practical limits; Buddhists rejected self-mortification, opting for meditation as the path to Nirvana. Both were primarily monastic movements, but the Jains were far more successful in building a substantial lay following, while the Buddhists mainly depended upon subsidies and favors from the nobility, a dependency that eventually proved to be a fatal weakness.

JAINISM

Vardhamāna Mahāvīra was born in about the middle of the sixth century BCE in Kundagrāma, a village in the Ganges Valley about one hundred miles east of where Buddha was born at approximately the same time (see Map 5–2). Although elaborate legends now surround his conception and birth, there is a strong and plausible tradition that Mahāvīra was born into the nobility. He "received a princely education,"[115] and his family seems to have followed the teachings of Pārśva, an eighth-century ascetic and the son of the Queen of Benares.[116] It was Pārśva's teachings that Mahāvīra revised and extended as the basis for Jainism—the name identifying them as followers of *Jinas*, a series of "Tirthamkaras or 'Ford-makers' who enable the faithful to cross [ford] the stream of existence to the other shore—to liberation, Nirvana."[117] The Jains posit a chain of twenty-four *Jinas*, beginning in a legendary long ago time and culminating in Pārśva and Mahāvīra.

Mahāvīra is believed to have married a princess named Yashoda who bore him a daughter, Anoja. When he was about thirty, Mahāvīra's parents died, and his older brother took over as head of household, whereupon Mahāvīra obtained his brother's consent to leave the family and become a wandering ascetic. First, he plucked out all his hair, then he shed all of his clothing and went naked, begging for his food and shelter, and engaging in extreme forms of self-inflicted penance. Along the way he gained some disciples from among the other wandering holy men.

Mahāvīra spent nearly thirteen years in this fashion until one summer night, seated on a riverbank, he is believed to have attained true omniscience—"full knowledge of the world (and nonworld), and of the past, present, and future of its inhabitants, whether divine, infernal, animal, or human."[118] He now began to proselytize and organize in earnest, and soon was able to build a sect movement having four groups of members: monks, nuns, and male and female laity. These converts came primarily from among "the wealthy and influential," in keeping with Mahāvīra's

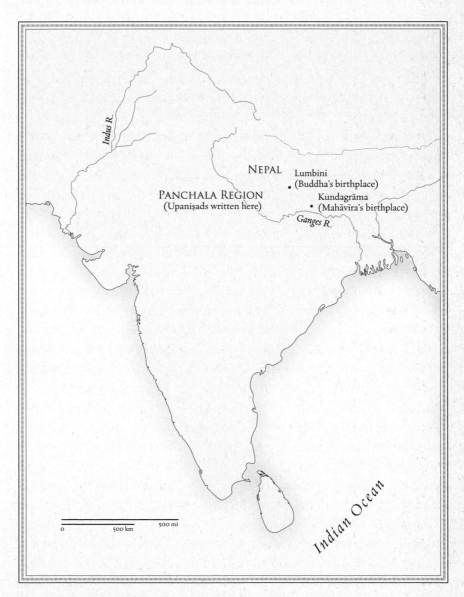

Map 5–2: New Indian faiths, sixth century BCE.

own origins.[119] While the monks and nuns busied themselves with seeking Nirvana, the laity provided funds to build many beautiful temples. Finally, perhaps at the age of seventy-two, Mahāvīra died in a village about fifty miles from his birthplace, and is believed to have entered Nirvana.[120]

As might be expected with the founder gone, a serious factional fight broke out over the proper and tolerable level of asceticism. The focus was on clothing: the Digambaras practiced complete nudity while the Shvetambaras believed it was appropriate to wear clothing so long as it was white (recall that the Pythagorans also wore only white and that Pythagoras had traveled in the East). The Shvetambaras faction soon took control, although small groups of nude Digambaras have continued through the centuries.

Even though they decided to wear clothing, the Jains have remained a very ascetic religion. Many of their most unusual practices derive from their extreme reverence for life. Not only are they vegetarians, Jains avoid fruits with seeds, reject anything fermented (since yeasts are living), and spurn honey since this may deprive the bees. Jains always strain their water so as not to swallow any organisms, they wear masks to prevent breathing in "innocent" insects, and they never eat after sunset for fear of harming the many insects that become active in the dark. Jains also use a feather whisk to sweep insects off the ground ahead of them, and they tread as softly as possible. In addition, Jain monks and nuns renounce all sexual pleasures—indeed, they renounce all attachments to others. Monks and nuns vow to beg for all their food, not to use umbrellas to ward off sun or rain, and to walk everywhere—without sandals. As to fasting, the ideal is that when they become elderly they will fast to death, which is referred to as the "wise man's death."[121] Given their extreme emphasis on not taking life, the Jains are not able to pursue most occupations. For example, they cannot farm because they cannot uproot weeds or kill insects or pests. Eventually, the Jains drifted into commerce, with a strong "preference for financial transactions."[122] Consequently, nearly all Jains are urbanites.

Most Jain doctrines are quite similar to the New Hinduism of the Upaniṣads, except that Jains do not believe in a Creator God because they believe the universe had no beginning and will have no end, passing through "an infinite number of cosmic cycles,"[123] during each of which civilization rises and falls. Thus, the entire aim of human existence is to escape the succession of rebirths. Hence, during every cosmic cycle, twenty-four Tirthamkaras (sages) appear one after another and "not only attain liberation for themselves but also teach the path of salvation to others."[124]

Although Mahāvīra denied the existence of a Creator God, he did admit the existence of the many Hindu divinities. But he dismissed them as minor spirits, lacking power and irrelevant to the fate of the individual in that they can offer no release from the cycle of rebirths.[125] In this sense, the Jainism taught by Mahāvīra is relatively Godless; no forms of worship are acknowledged nor are the Gods worthy of worship. But if monotheism has often been found to be too austere and demanding a faith, plagued by "backsliding" into polytheism, Mahāvīra's Godless spirituality would seem to be even less satisfying to most humans. Thus it was that the Jains did not sustain their initial "Godlessness." Jain temples contain large statues of the twenty-four Tirthamkaras (including Mahāvīra), and the Jains conduct elaborate ceremonies in front of these statues that surely *resemble* worship. That is, in addition to participating in various rituals, the faithful bring offerings, including rice, and place them on the plates and planks that are in front of a statue for that purpose.[126] These practices not withstanding, some claim that no worship actually is involved. However, Jain temples also frequently contain images of various "folk" Gods, "secondary divinities" that are very popular and often appealed to for blessings and benefits.[127] It is rather more difficult to explain these traditional "idols" away.

BUDDHISM

The biographies of Siddhartha Gautama, who came to be known as Buddha ("the Awakened One"), and Mahāvīra are remarkably similar. Buddha was born in Lumbini, a tiny village on the border of Nepal and about one hundred miles west of Kundagrāma where Mahāvīra was born (see Map 5–2). Both were sons of the nobility—Buddha's father may have been the Raja of Kapilavastu, a city about twenty miles northwest of Lumbini. Both married and fathered one child—Buddah's was a son, Rahula. When they were about thirty, each abandoned his family to become a wandering ascetic holy man—Gautama took one last look at his sleeping wife and son and then left without saying good-bye.[128]

Not only were Buddha and Mahāvīra contemporaries, but they also built their movements close to home in the same rather small area—the esteemed Sukumar Dutt (1891–1970) estimated that most of Buddha's missionary career took place within the "Eastern Tract" (*Puratthima*), a roughly square area having sides about thirty miles in length,[129] and he probably never journeyed more than seventy-five miles from his birthplace. Both Buddha and Mahāvīra drew their initial followers from among the same set of local wandering holy men. Consequently, both men would have been very aware of one another—three Buddhist scriptures mention Mahāvīra.[130] Given that the New Hinduism also was developing nearby, not surprisingly both men were greatly influenced by early Upaniṣads and both proclaimed that the goal of all spirituality was release from the cycle of rebirth. Therefore both deemphasized the Gods. The primary difference between them was that Mahāvīra believed salvation was to be gained through extreme self-mortification, while Buddha eventually abandoned severe asceticism in favor of meditation. Finally, both died within a few miles of their birthplaces—Mahāvīra in about 477 BCE,[131] and Buddha perhaps in 483 BCE—a date that is supported by Chinese records.[132]

Having become a wandering holy man, Gautama began to practice intense forms of asceticism. After a few years, and having reduced himself to skin and bones and being near death, he decided that this was not the way to enlightenment and turned instead to meditation. Leaving his ascetic associates, Gautama found a place on the bank of a tributary to the Ganges River and, sitting beneath a bo-tree, he began to meditate, planning to stay at it until he found enlightenment. After several weeks of meditation, it is believed that he was disturbed by Māra, the evil tempter who is Lord of the World of Passion, who tried to prevent him from attaining enlightenment. But Gautama was unmoved. Having defeated Māra, he spent the rest of the night in meditation, and at dawn he became Awakened, having entered a transcendent realm and become the Buddha.

Buddha remained in meditation for another week, during which Māra intruded on him again, tempting him to shed all concerns about humanity and to remain within the blissful, spiritual realm. But Buddha felt obligated to help humanity discover the way to release, so he launched his preaching mission and began to organize a monastic order.

Scripture and Doctrines

Just as the Bible is our only source of knowledge about Moses, so, too, we only know of Buddha through scripture. Hence, as with Moses, some Western historians denied that Buddha ever existed, but the conflict never became nearly so heated as that concerning Moses because Buddhism engenders far less concern among Western scholars, even those bitterly opposed to religion. In any event, that dispute now seems to have been settled in favor of a historical Buddha, if for no other reason than, as the eminent Étienne Lamotte (1903–1983) put it, "Buddhism would remain inexplicable if one did not place at its beginning a strong personality who was its founder."[133]

Buddhist scriptures are known collectively as **Tipitaka**. The name means Three Baskets and was applied because when, after generations of oral transmission the scriptures finally were written down, they were kept in three separate containers on the basis of their primary emphasis. The first basket is known as the **Sutta Pitaka,** known also as the Basket of Discourse. It includes more than 200 sermons (*suttas*) believed to have been delivered by Buddha and which lay out his doctrines in detail. The second is the **Vinaya Pitaka**, the Basket of Discipline, which is devoted to rules governing Buddhist monastic life. The third is the **Abhidhamma Pitaka**, the Basket of Scholasticism, and consists of seven philosophical and theological analyses. It is believed that these works originated with Buddha and were taken down by those who heard them, and that there was relatively little doctrinal innovation after Buddha's death,[134] albeit there were profound disagreements as to interpretation.

In many ways, Buddhism is nothing but the New Hinduism of the Upaniṣad era. The central Buddhist doctrines of reincarnation and how to escape to Nirvana were basic to the religious outlook of the multitude of holy men, inspired by the New Hinduism, with whom both Buddha and Mahāvīra spent long apprenticeships. However, like Mahāvīra, Buddha greatly expanded on these themes, providing an elaborate doctrinal tapestry.

The *Three Jewels* govern all Buddhists. These consist of faith 1) in Buddha; 2) in the law (doctrine) taught by him; and 3) in the community that is the depository of his teaching. Hence, devout Buddhists frequently affirm: "I take refuge in Buddha, I take refuge in the law, I take refuge in the community."[135]

As to what constitutes the law that Buddha taught, it begins with the *Four Noble Truths*. First is the *truth of misery*, that life consists of sorrows, tragedies, pain, old age, and hopelessness. Second is the *truth of desire*, that our misery originates within us from our craving for happiness and pleasure. Third is the *truth that desire may be overcome*. Fourth is the *true method for eliminating desire*. This method involves following the *Eightfold Path*,[136] whereby to escape the cycle of birth and rebirth, one must adopt:

1. Right *vision*—to perceive that the human experience is intolerable.

2. Right *aims*—not to be lost in luxury, not to exploit others, but to love them.

3. Right *speech*—to hold one's tongue, to be truthful.

4. Right *action*—to never kill, steal, or fornicate, but to do positive things that benefit others.

5. Right *livelihood*—to make one's living without harming others or society. Pure and honest practices should be followed.

6. Right *mindfulness*—to abjure all evil thoughts and focus only on good thoughts.

7. Right *awareness*—to constantly avoid attachments to body and desires.

8. Right *meditation*—to adopt the elaborate mental procedures worked out by Buddha.

Each of these aspects of the Eightfold Path has prompted a considerable literature, both by Buddha and his successors, spelling out many details about each "right" way and how one can follow this "Path" to Nirvana. Remarkably, Buddha had very little to say about Nirvana, other than it is where rebirth ceases—beyond this he was silent other than to note that Nirvana is indefinable and inexpressible.[137]

Godless Buddhism?

As noted in the Introductory Chapter, the famous French sociologist Emile Durkheim (1858–1917) excluded Gods from his definition of religion. A primary reason he did so was because he believed that although Buddhism clearly is a religion, it is Godless. It must be said on Durkheim's behalf that he cited a number of experts in support of this claim, among them Eugene Burnouf (1801–1852), who asserted that "[Buddhism is] a morality without god and an atheism without Nature," and Auguste Barth (1834–1916), who wrote that "its doctrine is absolutely atheist."[138] Durkheim knew that Godlessness did not apply to the popular form of Buddhism, although he did his best to minimize the significance of Gods and worship among the "masses," too. But he, and those he cited, were certain that the elite form of Buddhism, as pursued by Buddhist monks and philosophers, and as embraced and advocated by Western intellectuals, was, as the German scholar Hermann Oldenberg (1854–1920) put it, "a religion without god."[139]

Unfortunately, Durkheim's experts paid far too much attention to scripture and far too little to practice. Buddhist scriptures echo Mahāvīra,

A rediscovered and restored Buddhist stupa in India. Initially there were eight stupas, each containing a fragment of Buddha's body. (Sanchi, Madhya Pradesh, India; Photo: Borromeo/Art Resource, New York)

dismissing the Gods as rather trivial spirits, irrelevant to the quest for Nirvana. Indeed, Buddha referred to himself as the "teacher of Gods." However, as with the Jains, Buddhism's disregard for the Gods was not sustained, and even the elite form is infused with such a reverence for Buddha that it appears to constitute worship. As for popular Buddhism, it abounds in Gods, a major one of whom is Buddha himself.

When Buddha died, his body was cremated, but this process only destroyed flesh, not bones, and so these were divided among eight different groups to be treated as holy relics. These relics were placed in eight *stupas* (literally "mounds"), which are round, domed shrines. As time passed, the relics of Buddha were further divided (a tooth here, a fragment of bone there), and stupas proliferated—in Asia, pagodas were built for the same purpose. Stupas also were erected at places believed to have been associated with various events in the life of Buddha, such as his birthplace, where he was Awakened, and where he died—and some of these also contained fragments of bone thought to be his. From early days, Buddhist stupas drew large numbers of pilgrims whose behavior soon shifted from a "commemorative ritual associated with the stupa . . . to the ritual of worship and devotion associated with the Buddha image."[140] Despite their many centuries of popularity, the significance of the stupas in India was forgotten by about the tenth century CE until they were excavated by the British at the end of the nineteenth century.[141]

Soon after Buddha's death, his followers became deeply involved in temple-building, and these came to be dominated by increasingly large statues of Buddha. Contrary to the expert opinion quoted above, Buddhist intellectuals (especially those in Western universities) often claim that these statues are not worshipped, but only serve as a reminder of the Buddha and his teachings. However, "[p]opular practice often ascribes a living presence to the statue, whether by placing a relic within it or by a ritual of consecration that infuses it with 'life.' "[142] Indeed, there has arisen a specific Buddhist belief that statues of Buddha come to life when the eyes are painted on or carved into a statue. Once this has occurred, the statue becomes "an object of worship," not "a mere reminder of the Buddha."[143] There simply is no getting around the fact that many Buddhists worship the Buddha.[144] In addition, most Buddhist temples are chock-full of lesser Gods, for Buddhism became "an extremely theistic religion."[145]

Nevertheless there is some truth in the Godlessness claim. The original core of Buddhism, as with Jainism, is not a *revelation*—neither Buddha nor Mahāvīra reported any visions or communications from a God (other than from Māra). All their "truths" were gained by introspection, by searching their own consciousness, so both religions are admittedly of human origins. Perhaps of even greater importance, both teach that salvation does not come from God or Gods, but from one's own efforts. It is a doctrine of salvation by works alone! In this sense these are remarkably egocentric and effectively Godless religions in which the self is the all and the only. But since salvation (Nirvana) seems not to involve consciousness, to see the supreme goal of life as release is, in effect, to equate salvation with suicide. Combined with the doctrine that life is inevitably a succession of sufferings and sorrows and that in addition one must strive to frustrate all desires, to become a true follower of Buddha or Mahāvīra is to embrace unrelieved pessimism. Such pessimism seems to have attracted some alienated members of the elite to become monks or nuns, but it surely "could not attract the minds of the laity."[146] No wonder that the initial Godlessness of these faiths could not be sustained. Gods provide comfort in the face of life's tragedies and can give meaning and hope to what Buddha and Mahāvīra judged to be a pointless existence. Consequently, as Wilhelm Schmidt noted, "everywhere that [Buddhism] has become a popular religion, it has included . . . innumerable personal deities, brought in by a thousand back doors."[147]

Building Buddhism

Setting out on his mission to spread his newly found truths, Buddha went back to the five ascetics with whom he had lived and suffered for six years in the forest. In keeping with the network process of conversion, they became his first followers. Soon they were joined by another fifty-five of their fellow holy men. Thus, the first sixty Buddhists were all avowed ascetics, and as a result, the first settled Buddhist community was a monastery; thus monasticism became the defining feature of Buddhism. Although Buddha soon attracted some lay followers, his movement remained primarily an organization of monks (and nuns) with loose attachments to a laity—many of whom, in fact, never came to regard themselves as Buddhists.[148]

The first sixty converts had something else in common: fifty-five of them came from "prominent families," and the other five may well have been from privileged backgrounds, too.[149] Many other early converts came from the ranks of Brahman priests who were, necessarily, members of the upper class.[150] This, too, set a lasting precedent. Indian Buddhism remained an elite movement.

Buddha's "Holy Family"

When Buddha first turned to the laity, he continued to focus on the elite. He also did something else that has significance well beyond this particular instance—just as Zoroaster and Moses recruited their immediate families, so, too, did Buddha. Returning home for the first time since leaving to become an ascetic, Buddha revealed the story of his Awakening and gained his first lay converts: his wife, Yasodharā; his father, Suddhodana; his stepmother, Mahaprajapati; his son, Rahula; his half brother, Nanda; his cousin, Ananda; his brother-in-law, Devadatta; and Devadatta's attendant, Upali.[151] However, these converts did not help establish a Buddhist laity for they, too, entered the monastic life.

Monasteries

The Ganges Valley is subject to three months of pounding monsoon rains beginning every June. Consequently, all the wandering holy men took shelter as best they could during this period and resumed their travels when the rainy months had ended. As would be expected, over time groups of holy men tended each year to return to the same shelters. Buddha continued this practice, but with a difference. His affluent supporters, including King Bimbisāra and a rich banker named Anāthapindika, built fine permanent shelters for Buddha and his monks and provided them with ample subsistence during each monsoon. Then, following Buddha's death, many of his monks began to spend more of their time at these and many similar permanent settlements, and eventually large numbers abandoned the wandering life and initiated monasticism.

Although ascetic holy men abounded in India, the Buddhists seem to have invented monasticism, wherein people sharing an intense religious commitment choose to live together in a single-sex, celibate community in accordance with a formal discipline, or set of rules that define a relatively austere lifestyle. The Buddhists referred to their monastic rules as the Vinaya Pitaka, the Basket of Discipline. Initially there were 227 rules in this basket—the number was expanded to 250 in China and 253 in Tibet.[152] Every fortnight the monks gathered for a confessional ceremony during which each rule was recited, and after each there was a pause for anyone present to confess to that fault. Punishments ranged from minor penances to permanent expulsion from the group. The list of offenses includes all of the obvious things: murder, stealing, sexuality, and taking intoxicants. The rules also proposed that monks live in personal poverty, beg for all of their food, and have no personal property beyond three robes and a begging bowl—all other property belonged to the community.

Not so obvious, and of lasting and harmful consequences, were rules prohibiting monks from engaging in agriculture or, indeed, performing any manual labor. This probably was meant to prevent the monks from acting like peasants and very clearly reflected the upper-class origins of the movement and its subsequent recruits. Combined with the ability of the monks to attract wealthy and powerful patrons, the result was to transform an ascetic movement into a pampered elite, much like the subsidized temple priesthoods. As Princeton's Martin Collcutt put it, "As Buddhism flourished and patrons lavished gifts of buildings, lands, statues, gold, slaves, and other items on the [monks and nuns], the ideal of poverty was sometimes abandoned . . ."[153] Or, according to the distinguished Joseph Kitagawa (1915–1992), "Some monasteries became wealthy enough to have slaves and hired labourers to care for the monks and tend the lands they owned."[154]

Some of this lavish support came from "wealthy lay devotees," but many monasteries were built by and endowed by kings and princes.[155] One of the largest monasteries in India not only was built by and added to by a series of Gupta kings, but was given the taxes from "more than 100 villages" for its support.[156] Consequently, as with all subsidized religions, Buddhists in India did not bother to gather "broad popular support but . . . relied exclusively on royal patronage," which isolated "the monasteries from life in the village community" and encouraged them "to look inward and to lose interest in proselytizing and serving the surrounding communities."[157] What began as privilege, ended in disaster.

COMPETITION AND FAILURE

The decline of Buddhism in India was poorly recorded by Indians, who eventually forgot that it ever had existed, but was progressively documented by Chinese Buddhists who visited India as the birthplace of their faith.[158] When Fa-hien came around 400 CE, Buddhist monasteries were flourishing in some parts of India, but he also found abandoned ruins in other parts. When Song-yun and Tao-sheng came in the first half of the sixth century CE, they found that many Buddhist temples had neither monks nor nuns in residence, although some were occupied by Brahmans. In the seventh century Hiuen-tsang found many abandoned temples, and was disappointed to discover that the monks had drifted far from Buddha's teachings and were far more interested in magical exorcisms. And so it went. More and more deserted temples falling into ruins. Fewer and fewer monks and nuns. By the twelfth century, "Buddhism ha[d] disappeared altogether from India."[159]

Why did Buddhism fail in India? Many have blamed the Muslims, depicting a pacifist Buddhist community as having been annihilated by brutal Islamic hordes. This explanation fails for several reasons. First of all, when Muslims first invaded and settled in India, they established relatively tolerant relationships with the Indians and their culture. Later, when Turkish Muslims did attack the few remaining Buddhist centers, Buddhism had already nearly disappeared. More importantly, Hinduism and Jainism survived all Islamic efforts to suppress or replace them! Why didn't Buddhism?

Briefly put, Buddhism failed because it could not survive in a competitive religious economy once it was forced to do so on a level playing field. That was when Buddhism's centuries of failure to compete for popular support came home to roost. In the words of the distinguished Edward Conze (1904–1979), "The monks [were] . . . the only Buddhists in the proper sense of the word."[160] This was all well and good as long as Buddhism enjoyed the support of kings, princes, and wealthy families. Eventually, however, as newcomers ascended to power, and in the face of mass support for the newly revived Hinduism of the Bhagavad-gītā, Buddhism lost its elite position, and the loss of subsidies was fatal.

But that was not all. When its privileges ended, Buddhism was confronted by a militant and united Hinduism. "[W]ith its firm roots in In-

By the twelfth century, all that remained of Indian Buddhism were the ruins of monasteries like these—the remains of a stupa are to the left. (Guldara, Afghanistan; Photo: Borromeo/ Art Resource, New York)

dian society and freedom from the costly institution of the monastery, [Hinduism] offered a colossal challenge to Buddhism."[161] This challenge took several dimensions. First of all, Hinduism had the *numbers*. As Jan Gonda explained, the general public had all along "largely continued adhering to Hindu belief and Hindu practices." Even as they gave alms to the Buddhist monks, "the masses doubtless always remained Hinduist."[162] Second, Hinduism had the *intense levels* of popular commitment. There were scores of Hindu sects and movements, each of which was aimed at a relatively narrow market segment, often one of the several thousand *jātis* (sub-castes). In contrast, Buddhism offered only a general appeal, drawing monks and nuns from the elite, but even when it began to offer an array of Gods, it lacked market specialization when compared with Hinduism. Third, Hinduism *incorporated* Buddhism, proclaiming that Buddha was, in fact, an avatar of Vishnu whose purpose was to spread a false religion as a test of the faithful. Thus was Buddhism assimilated into Hinduism, and for many centuries, when all knowledge of Buddhism per se was lost in India, Buddha lived on as the ninth incarnation of Vishnu.

CONCLUSION

The primary lesson to be taken from the early religious history of India is how very religious a whole society can become when there are large numbers of aggressive and motivated religious groups seeking adherents. Since the earliest Vedic period, India has enjoyed a relatively unregulated religious economy, and, as a result, Hinduism has been as pluralistic as has Christianity in the United States, with very similar consequences. Granted that the caste system placed some constraints on competition in the sense that most Hindu sects were based on only one or a very limited group of *jātis*. This was offset by several other factors. First, there often was some degree of competitive rivalry (pluralism) *within* any given sect, thus motivating efforts to arouse and sustain support. Second, any sect's membership base often was threatened by potential outside competitors. Third, and perhaps most important, religious commitment has been inseparable from caste loyalty and has given special symbolic focus to inter-caste conflicts. Anyone who appears to be lacking in piety, falls under suspicion of lacking loyalty to her or his caste peers. Finally, when a religious marketplace is sufficiently crowded, some groups will be driven to remarkable lengths in order to differentiate themselves from their competitors—hence the clutter of extreme ascetics.

These are the reasons that people so often speak of "Holy India."

· 6 ·

CHINESE GODS AND "GODLESS" FAITHS

EVERY TEXTBOOK in comparative religion addresses itself to the "big three" religions of China: Taoism, Confucianism, and Buddhism.[1] That approach displays a remarkably narrow grasp of Chinese religious culture and history. For one thing, the textbooks focus on the elite form of each of these three faiths—the religion of monks, intellectuals, and upper-class adherents—thereby stressing the philosophical nature and relative "Godlessness" of each. That sort of "religion" seems to appeal to those who write Western textbooks and teach comparative religion, but it has had little appeal to most Chinese. Far more significant are the popular forms of each of these three faiths, which not only embrace a substantial pantheon of Gods, but also have elevated Confucius, Lao-Tzu, and Buddha into Godhood. However, even when expanded to six "religions," the actual religious life of *most* Chinese through the centuries is ignored: the lush polytheism often referred to as Folk Religion.

Consequently, I shall explore the origins of all seven of these faiths and examine how they influenced one another—how the elite forms of Taoism, Confucianism, and Buddhism gave rise to popular versions and how even their popular versions lacked sufficient popularity to displace the Folk Religion. The latter consists of a relatively unsophisticated polytheism dominated by ancestor worship and amoral Nature Gods—the religion that originated in ancient times and continues to flourish in

China (and the Far East) long after such faiths were supplanted in the West.[2] The chapter is focused on China because religion in the rest of Asia largely derives from Chinese origins.

RELIGION IN ANCIENT CHINA

For thousands of years, the area that became China was a land of Neolithic villages and small tribal societies. Eventually, one of the local chiefs amassed sufficient power to merge these many groups into an organized state, thus founding the Shang Dynasty (c. 1766–1122 BCE). The prevailing religion of Shang China very closely resembled the religions that flourished at that same time in Sumer and Egypt—the religious economy was dominated by subsidized temples. As in Sumer and Egypt, in China, too, only the elite (knights and above) "ha[d] the right of attendance at [religious] ceremonies." According to law "the ritual d[id] not extend down to the common people," and the general public "was prohibited from taking part in religious ceremonies" conducted in the temples.[3]

At this time, the "urban" cores of China consisted primarily of towns and cities located in the basin of the Yellow River (see Map 6–1), with a secondary center along the Yangtze River to the south. Local areas were ruled by "clans of noble families [that] were held together by an elaborate system of rights, privileges and relationships which were already sacrosanct by tradition and made obligatory by a fixed obedience to the will of a tribal ancestor."[4] These were, however, ritual obligations, not a matter of morality—there is little trace that any notions of moral responsibility existed among the Chinese elite in this era.[5] Moreover, even these obligations did not apply to relations with the common people, large numbers of whom were held in slavery.

GODS AND ANCESTORS

Gods and ancestors formed a supernatural confederacy in the elite religion of the Shang Dynasty, which Li Chi, the celebrated Chinese archaeologist, characterized as a theocratic society "dominated by excessive devotion to ancestor worship."[6] It was extremely important to please and placate ancestors since they were able to "persuade the Supreme Ruler to send

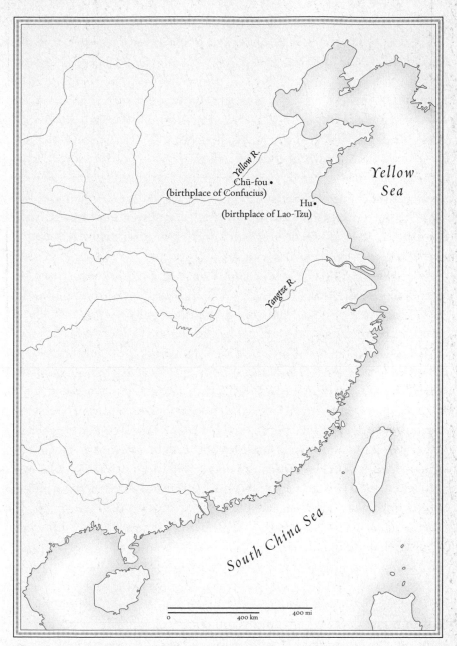

Map 6–1: Map of birthplaces of Chinese founders Confucius and Lao-Tzu, 600 BCE.

down blessings" or, if the ancestors were displeased, to cause calamities.[7] When a ruler died he became an ancestral spirit, and the eldest ancestor spirit was known as **Shang-ti**, the "High God, or God Above."[8] Hence, Shang-ti was worshipped as "the lord over other gods, spirits and deified ancestors."[9] He was "thought of as a cosmic god, dwelling in or above the sky at the apex of the rotating heavens. Indeed, [he] might have been a deified embodiment of the pole star itself."[10] Because the ruler could intercede with Shang-ti "through divination" as well as "through prayer and sacrifice, the will of the ancestral spirits legitimated the concentration of political power in his person."[11] Moreover, the "awesome power of the ancestors" was demonstrated by the "magnificence of the royal sacrifices—which could involve several hundred head of cattle."[12] Shang-ti also is known as the **Jade Emperor.**

The other traditional Gods of China include the usual array of Function and Nature Gods. The list is very long, but these are some of the more important ones. **Ch'eng-Huang** is the God of Moats and Walls, who protects communities from attack. **Chu Jung** is the God of Fire, who punishes those who break the laws of heaven. **Erh-Lang** is the Protector God, who drives away evil spirits. **Fu-Hsing** is the God of Happiness. **Hou-chi** is the God of Agriculture. **I-ti** is the God of Wine. **Kuan Ti** is the God of War, and he probably was an actual historical figure, a general during the Han Dynasty. **Kwan Yin** is the Goddess of Mercy and is depicted as a lady dressed in white, sitting on a lotus, holding a baby. **Lei Kun** is the God of Thunder. He has the head of a bird and his chariot is pulled by six boys. **P'an-Chin-Lein** is the Goddess of Prostitutes. **Shi-Tien Yen-Wang** refers to the ten Gods of the Underworld. **Ti-Tsan Wang** is the God of Mercy. He patrols the caverns of Hell. **T'Shai-Shen** is the God of Wealth. **Tsao Wang** is the God of the Hearth. Every household has its own image of Tsao Wang. **Yeng-Wang-Yeh** is the greatest of the Lords of Death.

In addition to these many Gods, two dominant spiritual representations played an important role in Chinese religious culture: the *dragon* and the *ogre mask*, or *T'ao t'ieh*. Both were meant to be awesome. Associated with storms and with the power of the throne, the dragon "can only be approached with abject mien and downcast eyes."[13] However, the dragon also was the source of many blessings, including rain. The ogre mask is a blend of creatures, but predominately the tiger. It was revered for guarding graves and driving away evil spirits and often was depicted at the entryway of homes and on the shields of soldiers.

PRIESTS AND RITUALS

During the Shang Dynasty, there emerged a professional priesthood, re-cruited from the best families and given substantial training. The *shih* were priest-scribes and "were selected from the royal family itself."[14] They recorded and interpreted significant events as influenced by the spirit world. The *chu* were masters of ritual and in charge of composing and compiling prayers. The *wu* were experts in divination. These priests served in the ancestral temples built by each local ruling clan, each sited on a mound and surrounded by a sacred grove. Some have claimed that this temple design reflected Mesopotamian influences.[15] Whether or not this is true, it remains that there were many other similarities with Sume-rian, Egyptian, and even Roman religions in terms of rituals, sacrifices, and funereal practices.

For one thing, as in Rome, very little took place unless the omens were favorable. "The most important government officials were those who were gifted with the power of communicating with the spirits and recording their commands and wishes for the guidance of the king."[16] At the begin-ning of the seventh century BCE, divination was codified into the still-famous work, the **I-Ching** (or *Book of Changes*). The I-Ching supposes that all human situations can be characterized on the basis of sixty-four sets of six horizontal lines (hexagrams). These are represented by sticks having numerical values corresponding to the hexagrams. By casting the sticks and following the proper procedures one can create a hexagram believed to reflect one's present situation. Study of this hexagram was (and is) thought to reveal the future. Other methods of divination that were in use long before as well as after the appearance of the I-Ching, in-volved heating turtle shells or the shoulder bones of sheep and oxen, then plunging them into cold water to produce cracks, and then interpreting the cracks.

Another similarity with Sumer, Egypt, and the traditional Roman re-ligion, as well as with Vedic Hinduism, was the immense "emphasis on precision in sacrifice; the correct objects offered in the right way were believed to obligate the spirits to respond." Here, too, "reciprocity . . . [was and] has remained a fundamental pattern of interaction throughout the history of Chinese religions."[17]

As to the sacrifices, they often were of huge proportions, "sometimes even hundreds of animals were sacrificed" at once.[18] Nor did the Shang Chinese settle for livestock. Humans frequently were made into sacrificial offerings.[19] Indeed, as in Sumer, early Egypt, and Mesoamerica, the tombs of the great were often stuffed with human attendants: servants, wives, slaves, and numerous horses (sometimes still hitched to chariots)[20] were usually buried with a king. "About four hundred victims were discovered in each of the larger tombs at Anyang."[21]

So much for the elite. But what did most people do for religion? Again, as in Sumer and Egypt, they were left to their own devices to such an extent that the "[e]ducated religious leaders tended to despise the beliefs and rituals of the common people."[22] Even so, in this era the "popular" religion and the religion of the elite were far more similar than in later times. Both stressed ancestor worship and performed elaborate rituals to please their predecessors. Many commoners maintained a small ancestral shrine in their homes and offered food and other gifts to their ancestral spirits, especially those of their parents and grandparents. All classes believed in divination and called upon various Nature Gods, according to their needs. In contrast with the modest religious resources of the general public, the elite sponsored immense feasts to honor their ancestors and employed professional priests to perform the other religious functions, including divination, in subsidized temples from which everyone else was excluded.

DISORGANIZATION AND INNOVATION

In about 1100 BCE the Shang emperors were succeeded by the Chou Dynasty. These new rulers continued the Shang's imperial and religious traditions without interruption for more than three hundred years, but then came a long era of civil war and social disorganization. It all began in 771 BCE when a Chou emperor was assassinated, "after which the real power passed into the hands of the lord who was strongest at any given time. Soon civil wars broke out among the many small states . . . [and this] lasted for several hundred years."[23] At the start, there were about two hundred feudal states making up China. By the sixth century there were only eleven.[24] Throughout the era, "war was endemic. Territories . . . were constantly changing hands. High ranking and noble families were being reduced to penury."[25] The breakdown of central authority resulted in a substantial amount of social mobility. Just as in India at this same time, where self-made outsiders often managed to usurp thrones, so, too, in China military prowess often was the road to power, regardless of background, and during this period of disorganization, even peasants were able to flee one master for another. And just as this era was marked by substantial "urbanization" in India, in China this, too, was a time of "increase in the number and size of cities, and in the circulation of goods between states."[26] By the end of the fourth century BCE, "several Chinese cities had a population exceeding 100,000."[27]

Perhaps it should not be surprising that just as very weak governance and social disruption had prompted an era of religious innovation in India, so, too, in China similar circumstances prompted efforts to provide for new religious needs—especially among the elite. Lacking a tradition of pluralism, however, the Chinese religious innovations of the sixth century BCE were, by comparison with India, tepid and limited: enter Taoism and Confucianism.

TAOISM

According to tradition, Lao-Tzu (the name translates as "old master") lived in the sixth century BCE, and many written accounts have been passed down concerning a meeting between him and Confucius, in which the latter comes off a decidedly second best. Nevertheless, beginning early in the twentieth century, a group of young Chinese scholars rejected the existence of Lao-Tzu and redated the **Tao-Te Ching** (*Sacred Book of the Tao and the Te*), which had been attributed to him, as written some centuries after the time of Confucius.[28] Western scholars quickly accepted this new view, and many textbooks now either dismiss Lao-Tzu as at best "a quasi-historical figure"[29] (whatever that might mean), as the "legendary founder of Taoism,"[30] or they make no mention of him at all in lengthy accounts of Taoism.[31] Even so, the inimitable Karl Jaspers (1883–1969) got to the heart of the matter when he acknowledged that Lao-Tzu's authorship and even his existence are "contested," but "one cannot doubt that

the [Tao-Te Ching] was created by a thinker of the highest rank,"[32] whatever his name.

And indeed, it now appears that this was but another of the many episodes of misguided skepticism about the existence of a religious founder.
Here, too, Chinese scholars recently have led the way, basing their rever-
sion to the traditional account of Lao-Tzu on the basis of a discovery in
1993 of a far earlier manuscript of his book in a tomb that itself dates
from about 300 BCE.[33] Let us therefore meet Lao-Tzu as he was presented
in various Chinese writings, especially a "biography" included in *Shih chi*
(Records of the Historian) written in about 90 BCE by Ssu-ma Ch'ien.
This account was expanded upon in the *Lieh-hsien chuan* (Lives of the
Immortals), attributed to Liu Hsiang, which appeared a few years later.[34]

The *Shih chi* gives Lao-Tzu's name as Li Erh or Li Tan and identifies his
birthplace as Hu (Map 6–1). Three important claims are made about his
life. First, that he served as the archivist for the Chou emperor. Second,
that after his retirement from that position he was consulted by Confucius—reports of this meeting suggest that Lao-Tzu was a rather testy
character. Third, having become disgusted with the decadence of the
Chou court, Lao-Tzu headed west, stopping at the Han-ku Pass to compose the Tao-Te Ching, which he left in the care of the gatekeeper Yin Hsi,
and then traveled on, and out of history.

It seems appropriate to reserve for later the reported encounter with
Confucius. Here the focus is on the initial scripture of Taoism, the Tao-
Te Ching—whether written by Lao-Tzu or someone else, it gave rise to a
religion that has influenced Asian thinking ever since. Indeed, it greatly
influenced Confucianism and then, too, Buddhism after it arrived from
India.

The Tao-Te Ching is either extremely subtle or pretentiously empty,
fully in keeping with its warning that "he who knows does not speak. He
who speaks does not know." Perhaps this explains why translations differ so radically. As Karl Jaspers explained: "The text does not speak to us
directly in its own language, but through a medium which clouds and
muffles it. . . . The differences in meaning between one translation and
another are sometimes enormous."[35] In any event, the book consists of a
series of maxims arranged in eighty-one brief chapters. The central concepts are the *Tao* and the *Te*, hence the title.

The **Tao** can be translated as the "way," the "pathway," or the "teaching," and more specifically, "the way the whole universe operates."[36] As might be expected of something so fundamental, it is beyond being, and is inexpressible: "The Tao that can be told is not the eternal Tao; the name that can be named is not the eternal name. The Nameless is the origin of Heaven and Earth."[37] In a sense, the Tao is nothing, having neither image nor form, but "it is not nothing in the sense of not-at-all, but in the sense of more-than-being . . . [n]onbeing is the source and aim of all being."[38] Thus, the Tao is the basis of all being, the uncaused cause, the origin of everything. It has both natural and supernatural aspects.

A drawing of Lao-Tzu riding a water buffalo. Of course, there are no surviving portraits of the "old master" done from life, so no one knows what he really looked like. (Religions Collection, Castle, Marburg, Germany; Photo: Erich Lessing/Art Resource, New York)

The **Te** is best translated as "virtue." It, too, is discussed in terms of negatives and contradictions. All efforts to gain Te must fail since it can only be gained by trying to avoid it. As the Tao-Te Ching (chapter 38) explains: "*The one [with] the highest te does not seek te; therefore he has te.*" Just as is true of the New Hinduism, Jainism, and Buddhism, Taoism identifies overcoming the self as the key to virtue. Thus, the Tao-Te Ching (chapter 47) advises: "*Therefore the Sage arrives without going, Sees all without looking, Does nothing, yet achieves everything.*"

Taoism soon developed an organized community, complete with temples and staffed by professional priests, obviously patterned on those of the ancient religion. But after several centuries, in response to the arrival of Buddhism (itself quite transformed), Taoism added doctrines of sin and salvation.

Sin and Salvation

The concept of "sin" was absent from the religion of ancient China,[39] as it was from so many other early religions. The Gods imposed no moral standards, and one need only fear offending them by failing to offer sufficient sacrifices in the correct manner. Eventually (probably after the arrival of a new form of Buddhism), Taoism adopted the notion of sin—that certain immoral actions offend the Gods. Taoism balanced this innovation with another, the promise of "salvation."

According to Lao-Tzu, all the ills of humanity arose because of a fall from the Tao as humans became preoccupied with self. In addition, humans fell into the great error of intervening in the course of events. It is far preferable to do nothing, to be content with *wu-wei*, or inaction. In this way, Taoism began as a religion that encourages resignation and passivity. However, unlike the pessimistic faiths of India, Taoism did not regard release into unconscious nonbeing as the ultimate goal. Instead, Taoism began to offer the prospect of Paradise. For elite practitioners of the faith, those able to fully live the life of the Tao, Lao-Tzu believed they would rise to a heaven where they would forever enjoy one another's company. Eventually, coincidental with competition from Buddhism, the doctrine arose that after death some will forever linger in a drab underworld while others, having gained greater Te, will eventually rise from the underworld to immortality in Paradise. Hence, the Taoist faithful are encouraged to "pray for the souls of the dead, who, through the merit of the living, might finally gain release from the underworld and entrance to paradise."[40] Subsequently, Taoism embraced the notion of hell, indeed, of a multi-level hell wherein the very sinful suffer forever.[41] This seems a far more compelling deterrent than to be reborn, just as eternal life in Paradise surely is a far more attractive goal than the promise of "release."

Gods

The Tao is not a God, although some believe it occasionally takes on "human" form. Generally, however, it is a supernatural essence, lacking consciousness and intention. This might suggest that Taoism is a Godless religion, but in fact Taoism venerates a huge cast of Gods, so many that it is quite impossible to list them all. For example, it is claimed that there are 36,000 Gods associated with the human body, each charged with some part or function.[42] As for more traditional Gods, most of them populate an elaborate "divine bureaucracy" although there also exists "a rambunctious group of unruly deities."[43] Those included in the bureaucracy are quite similar to earthly functionaries. Each has a position that is defined by a set of duties. Many of these Gods originated in the ancient religion. In addition, there has been a great deal of borrowing of Gods back and forth, among Taoism, Confucianism, Buddhism, and the Folk Religion.[44] The divine bureaucracy is ruled by the **Jade Emperor**, who is the supreme God in traditional Chinese religion and is the supreme Taoist deity as well—his statue occupies "a central place in the main hall of Taoist temples."[45] Beneath the Jade Emperor are "a whole series of celestial ministries: A ministry of Thunder and Wind, of the Waters, of Fire, of Time, of the Five Peaks, of Literature, of War, of Wealth, of Works . . . and so on. Each has its presiding officer, with his assistants and his army of subordinates . . ."[46] These ministries are headed by the traditional Gods, many of whom were listed earlier in the chapter.

In addition, Lao-Tzu was himself divinized. When this first occurred is unknown, but it was taken for granted by 165 CE when the Emperor Huan ordered that rituals be performed at the birthplace of Lao-Tzu and erected a stele at the site that acknowledged him as a God.[47] Many Taoists believe that Lao-Tzu emerged from the primordial chaos and, after several "cosmic metamorphoses . . . achieved an incarnate form and thus [descended] as savior to the mortal realm."[48] Eventually there were many variations on this messianic conception of Lao-Tzu, including one in which his mother is said to have carried him in her womb for seventy-two years.[49] As an additional variant, in response to the arrival of Buddhism in China, some Taoists claimed that Lao-Tzu transformed himself into the Buddha, having gone on to India after leaving the Tao-Te Ching with the gatekeeper at Han-ku Pass. This is an interesting parallel to the Hindu claim that Buddha is an avatar of Vishnu.

Popular Taoism

Through the centuries there have arisen dozens of Taoist sects—one of which (the Yellow Turbans[50]) even attempted to overthrow the emperor. These sects can be distinguished into two major groups. The first group involves the elite form of Taoism, which emphasizes theological concerns. These sects have more closely resembled philosophical "schools,"[51] than true religious movements, thereby remaining closer to what Lao-Tzu probably had in mind. The second group represents Popular Taoism. These are intense sect movements that have exhibited an activism that probably would have shocked Lao-Tzu—each has attempted to arouse the public to a religious awakening.

The pioneering French sinologist Henri Maspero (born in 1883 and murdered by the Nazis at Buchenwald in 1945) pointed out that "Taoism was the Chinese attempt to create a personal religion . . . a salvation religion which aims to lead the faithful to Life Eternal."[52] Of course, both the elite and the popular forms of Taoism are salvational. What differs is that the popular sects have always been energetically conversionist and created well-organized temples, featuring emotionally charged ceremonies, conducted by a highly professional, inspirational priesthood.

Popular Taoism burst forth to achieve "prodigious success" during the Han Dynasty (200 BCE–220 CE) and peaked during the Six Dynasties (220–581 CE).[53] Subsequently, the elite version of Taoism increasingly withdrew into monasticism, while the popular form has mostly blended into what today constitutes the Folk Religion of China. But amid Taoism's energetic outburst came a new revelation in 142 CE to Chang Tao-ling, who styled himself as the Celestial Master and who introduced both a more elaborate doctrine of salvation and new rituals and techniques for being saved. His revelation consisted of books and alchemical formulas that were given to him by the Most High Lord atop Mount Ho-ming in Szechuan.[54] It is believed that Chang Tao-ling succeeded in making a drug for immortality, which he finally drank and then "mounted to heaven in full daylight upon a five-colored dragon, taking with him his wife and his disciples."[55]

Chang Tao-ling's revelations are but a tiny fragment of the immense Taoist literature that has piled up over the years. Late in the fifth century, a catalog of Taoist scriptures, compiled for the Emperor Ming, listed 1,228 texts.[56] Each of these scriptures was presented as a revelation dictated by a God or an Immortal, that was received and taken down by a "medium" having the ability to go into a trance and communicate with the world beyond. As would be expected given the sources and the quantity, Taoist scripture is incredibly confused and contradictory. Nevertheless, common themes can be identified. Thus, for example, as Taoism developed into a popular religion, its theology became increasingly focused on *ch'i*, "the vital breath out of which nature, gods, and humans evolve."[57] This "breath" is created by the Tao. The Gods are "personified manifestations of *ch'i*, symbolizing astral powers of the cosmos and organs of the human body with which they are correlated." As life proceeds, the *ch'i* loses its potency and must be renewed through proper rituals, which are said to heal and to revitalize the bodies of supplicants. Indeed, concern for health and for curing sickness is central to both elite and Popular Taoism, since, as illustrated by the story of Chang Tao-ling's ascension, the dominating focus had become the search for Eternal Life, not merely in a spiritual sense, but physically.[58] Indeed, Popular Taoism celebrates **Eight Immortals**, ordinary people whose virtues were rewarded by **Hsi Wang Mu**, the Queen Mother Goddess, who gave them peaches of everlasting life to eat. These immortals include: **Chang-Kuo Lao**, a hermit with a donkey that could reach incredible speeds; **Chung-Li Ch'uan**, a smiling, acsetic old man; **Han Hsiang-Tzu**, who chose to study magic rather than cram for civil service exams; **Ho Hsien-Ku**, a girl who became immortal by eating mother of pearl; **Lan Ts'ai-Ho**, an inspired flute player; **Li Tieh-Kuai**, a begger who sold wonderful drugs that could revive the dead; **Lu Tung-Pin**, a hero of early Chinese storytelling who slew dragons with a magic sword; and **Ts'ao Kuo-Chiu**, who tried to reform his brother, the emperor.

Although it was believed that these and some other elite practitioners of Taoism achieved immortality by passing directly into heaven, it was evident that they, too, seemed to die just like everyone else. However, this was said to be merely an illusion. That, to avoid upsetting others, those who passed over into immediate immortality gave "the appearance of having died" and were "buried according to ordinary rite," while the real bodies of such persons rose "to live among the immortals."[59] Notice that this was not a spiritual ascension, but involved the actual body. Consequently, it was believed to be necessary to physically transform the body to make it immortal—recall that Chang Tao-ling had invented a drug that gave immortality. Thus developed an elaborate and a strict regimen "of dietary practices, breathing control, sexual disciplines and the like"[60] meant to Nourish the Body into immortality. As to diet, one must abstain from eating all grains such as wheat and rice, as well as avoid all "wine, meat, and plants with a strong flavor" (such as onions and garlic).[61] Elite Taoists also took a substantial variety of herbs and "alchemical elixirs" in order to transform their bodies. That some of these were in fact poisonous did "not deter the experimenters; those who died were believed by devotees to have transferred themselves to another plane of existence."[62]

Had the Taoists settled for Nourishing the Body, theirs would have been best described as "a hygiene, or medical system, but not a religion."[63] But they also believed that immortality required them to Nourish the Spirit. This involved entering into a relationship with the Gods. But it was believed that one could not simply approach the Gods, no matter with what degree of reverence; the Gods must consent to a relationship and this depends upon good works, and especially on an overwhelming *ratio* of good works to evil deeds. A Taoist rule of life presented an elaborately quantified system of misdeeds and punishments. When evil actions outnumber the good by 120, a person falls ill. An excess of 530 will cause one's children to be born dead. When the excess reaches 1,800, there will occur a catastrophe that will afflict five generations of the family. On the other hand, an excess of 1,200 good deeds over evil deeds will result in Heavenly Immortality.[64]

Fortunately for most people, many rituals of penitence were developed to erase evil deeds from one's account and thereby create a favorable ratio of good to evil deeds. Consequently, one did not need to be a saint to have hope of heaven, as atonement rites provided a plausible and feasible path by which ordinary people could aspire to immortality. It was the pursuit of penitence that served as the cornerstone of popular support for the Taoist churches and clergy.

By the end of the fourth century CE, elite Taoism had largely become a monastic faith, catering to both men and women seeking a withdrawn, celibate life of meditation and philosophizing. Entry was particularly attractive since monks were exempted from military service, mandatory labor (*courvée*), and most taxes.[65] In contrast, Popular Taoism was served by a lay clergy who married and were supported by donations. Their role was (and is) more similar to that of sorcerers and exorcists than to that of a traditional priest. Moreover, there always have tended to be more clergy than can be supported, thus creating intense competition, which favors the more entrepreneurial divines whose energy and ambition have produced the proliferation of sects. As will be seen, it was by mobilizing popular support that Taoism periodically came into conflict with the faith that usually prevailed among the Chinese ruling classes: Confucianism.

CONFUCIANISM

K'ung Fu-tzu (or Master K'ung), who came to be known in the West as Confucius,[66] was born in about 551 BCE. Just as Buddha and Mahāvīra were born only about one hundred miles apart, so Confucius is believed to have lived in Chü-fou, about ninety-five miles northwest of Hu, where Lao-Tzu was said to have been born.[67] If this is true, and if both of them lived at about the same time, then there is no reason to doubt the reports about Confucius having consulted Lao-Tzu.

The meeting between the two is said to have occurred when Confucius decided he would like to deposit his writings in the Chou imperial archives. His disciple Tzu-lu told him that there was a wise scholar named Lao-Tzu who had been the archivist, but was now retired and that it would be appropriate to visit him in order to gain access to the archives. So Confucius called upon Lao-Tzu, who refused his request, denounced his teachings, and dismissed him saying, "Get rid of that arrogance of yours, all those desires, that self-sufficient air, that overweening zeal; all that is of no use to you. That is all I can say to you." Confucius then withdrew and said to his disciple, "Today I have seen Lao-Tzu, and he is like a dragon."[68] If it is true, as tradition insists, that Lao-Tzu had retired because he was disgusted with the corruption and decadence of the Chou regime and that Confucius was dedicated to reforming the regime, then

A stone stele and burial mound mark what is believed to be the tomb of Confucius in Qufu, China. (Qufu, Shandong Province, China; Photo: Werner Forman/Art Resource, New York)

this account has a ring of authenticity—a man of action could hardly have pleased a proponent of inaction.

As is typical of religious figures from this era, it is difficult to determine which portions of Confucius's traditional biography are trustworthy. It seems probable that his father, Shu-liang Ho, was a military commander in service to the state of Lu and was celebrated for his skill as well as his heroic conduct. However, although his family may have belonged to the nobility at one time, Shu-liang Ho belonged to the emerging class of "able and ambitious men, ready to seize the opportunities which patronage or chance placed in their hands."[69] Hence Confucius was not of the nobility, but the patronage earned by his father seems to have allowed him to obtain a first-rate education, which may have helped him develop his life-long love of music. Little is known of his private life, but it is believed that he married at nineteen and fathered a son and a daughter. Tradition has it that he was unusually tall and of striking appearance, although he has come to be depicted as "of ungainly appearance and decidedly unattractive, with a prominent bump on his forehead, large pendulous ears and prominent front teeth."[70] Of course, this depiction was first made long after the fact and seems to have been a composite of the most striking feature of each of various famous figures.[71]

Early on, Confucius became a minor official in the state of Lu, with a salary sufficient to allow him to live as a gentleman. Soon his experience in office convinced him that good government only could be achieved if it were administered in accord with the principles he was working out. However, Confucius was somewhat frustrated by the fact that he could not expect an appointment to the highest offices—although men of his class bore the burden of state administration, the Great Offices were hereditary and reserved for the nobility. Apparently, Confucius did reach the highest rank immediately below those offices reserved for the nobility, but this fell well short of those providing him with the power to which he aspired.[72] Keep in mind that Confucius was no ascetic. "He certainly enjoyed the good things of life. Rank and wealth must be refused only if their acceptance is incompatible with righteousness."[73]

Nor was Confucius the sort of man to keep his dissatisfactions a secret, and during an interlude of particularly irresponsible governance, he found it expedient to withdraw from Lu. Eventually he set himself up as a teacher and began to surround himself with disciples—both his students and his disciples were of his own class, and most sought education to prepare them for public administration (being the forerunner of the system in which such offices were awarded to Confucian scholars on the basis of competitive exams). Pupils gathered around Confucius not only because of his immense learning and great wisdom, but also because of his geniality and sense of humor,[74] something not often found in a sage. For example, Analects 17:4: "*When the master went to the walled town of Wu, he heard the sound of stringed instruments and singing. Our master said with a gentle smile, 'To kill a chicken one does not use an ox-cleaver.'* "

When he was fifty, Confucius was made "chief magistrate of the town of Chung-tu in Lu,"[75] and eventually he may have been appointed as minister of crime. Shortly thereafter, however, Confucius became convinced that he could not reform governance in Lu in accord with his ideals, so he gathered some of his disciples and went on a long tour of Chinese courts, traveling in a convoy of carriages in search of an enlightened prince. In the end he was disappointed as each of the courts he visited turned out to be corrupt.[76] So, at age sixty-nine Confucius returned to Lu and spent his last years with a new set of disciples. It was not a happy time, being marked by the deaths of loved ones and the rejection of his philosophy by the powerful. As he put it (Analects 14:37): "*The truth is, no one knows me!*" Then he added: "*But the studies of men here below are felt on high, and perhaps after all I am known; not here, but in heaven.*"

Teachings

Tradition credits Confucius with having edited various ancient texts, including the I-Ching, but modern scholars reject these attributions.[77] That leaves only the **Analects** as an authentic Confucian scripture. But just as the New Testament was not written by Jesus, the Analects was not written by Confucius. The word itself means "literary gleanings," and the book consists of short sayings attributed to Confucius and probably written down by his students after his death.[78] In addition to the Analects, our knowledge of Confucianism is dependent on his greatest interpreter, Mēng K'o (c. 390–305 BCE), known in the West as Mencius. He regarded it as his mission to transmit the teachings of Confucius as taught to him: "From Confucius down to the present day there has been more than one hundred years. Thus I am not yet far from the generation of that sage, and am extremely close to the place where he lived. Under these circumstances is there no one [to transmit his doctrines]?"[79] Hence, he wrote what came to be known as the *Works of Mencius*, in which he often quoted from the Analects, but appears also to have had access to an additional collection of Confucius's sayings. How much is an accurate report of what Confucius taught and how much may have originated with Mencius or with those who had transmitted the teachings to him, cannot be known.

In any event, everyone agrees that Confucius's teachings are dominated by the aim "to devise a set of moral and political beliefs which, if widely and consistently acted on in human society, would produce the greatest good of which he could conceive, namely a stable social and political order in which human beings could flourish. . . . It [was] intended to be a working solution to some of the most urgent human concerns: to identify the nature of moral goodness, and to trace its implications in both private morality and the theory of government."[80] To exemplify his philosophy, Confucius introduced the concept of the perfect, or morally superior man—*chün-tzu*. Such a being must display in abundance at least three primary virtues.

The first is *jên*. Confucius never defined this term, but he associated many synonyms with it and thus it has been translated a number of ways, as love, benevolence, kindness, or goodness.[81] The essence of *jên* is to love, honor, and respect others. "Of all the virtues that *jên* generates, filial piety and brotherly respect are the greatest, for it is on these that humanity is founded."[82] In Analects 12:21 Confucius advised: "*Attack the evil that is within yourself; do not attack the evil that is in others,*" and in Analects 12:1 he warned: "*Do not do to others what you would not like yourself.*"

The second great virtue is *li*, which refers to the proper observance of ceremonies and the duty to always carefully and reverently observe the correct forms of behavior. Thus, in Analects 12:1–2: "*He who can submit himself to ritual is good . . . to look at nothing in defiance of ritual, to listen to nothing in defiance of ritual, to speak of nothing in defiance of ritual, never to stir hand or foot in defiance of ritual. . . . Behave when away from home as though you were in the presence of an important guest. Deal with the common people as though you were officiating at an important sacrifice.*" As Ninian Smart noted, in its origin, the term *li* "referred to specifically religious ritual, and in particular to the sacrificial cult. But [Confucius] gave it a meaning which extended far beyond ritual. Here was a norm which could govern the various kinds of social relationships."[83] As explained in Analects 12:5: "*If a gentleman attends to business and does not idle away his time, if he behaves with courtesy to others and observes the rules of ritual, then all within the Four Seas are his brothers.*"

The third great virtue is *i*, which, according to Confucius, is that which is "fitting, right, seemly." He offered no abstract definition, but proposed that it is "learned in the concrete situations of life,"[84] and follows from *jên* and *li*. Moreover, Confucius linked *i* to the "Way" (Tao). "*When the Way prevails under heaven, then show yourself; when it does not prevail, then hide*" (Analects 8:13). And what is the Way? It is "the righteous way of the ancient sages."[85] In fact, Confucius did not regard himself as an originator. As he put it: "*I have transmitted what was taught to me without making up anything of my own. I have been faithful to and loved the Ancients*" (Analects 7:1).

Thus, Confucius and his followers were regarded as members of the *ju*, the class of teachers and ritual specialists who were descended from ancient times. While they must excel in *jên*, their specialty was *li*—in guiding the "correct ritual deportment of aristocrats toward one another."[86] Indeed, Confucius did not address himself to ordinary people, except by the implication that "everyone" should manifest the virtues. Instead, the Analects outline a code of behavior for "gentlemen," with many specific admonishments to rulers. In this way the Analects has much the same aim as Machiavelli's *The Prince*, although it would be hard to find a more contrasting pair of documents, the one cynically amoral, the other urging the nobility to exemplary morality and propriety. However, Confucius's conception of nobility was quite revolutionary: "that true nobility is not a matter of blood, but of character, and hence is achievable by any man."[87] This proved to be an ideal philosophy for bureaucrats and administrators.

Han Confucianism

Confucian scholars soon became ascendant in the court and administrative bureaucracy during the Han Dynasty (200 BCE–220 CE). This development not only involved innovations in political administration, but so many new theological ideas were added to Confucian thought that scholars have found it appropriate to refer to "Han Confucianism."

The most fundamental premise of Han Confucianism is that all things belong to one of three spheres—heaven, earth, and humans. These are the basis of reality and are connected in "an orderly, predictable way."[88] Moreover, all phenomena are animated by two complementary, rather than opposite, modes of being or principles that are directed by heaven: **yin** and **yang**. Yin is the female principle: "the dark, the recessive, the moon, the west." The yang is the male principle: "the bright, the creative, the sun, the east."[89] In addition, Han Confucian scholars posited five elements and thereby classified "all phenomena in an ordered hierarchy" created by "the complementary oscillation of *yang* and *yin* and by the regular succession of the five elements."[90]

From this system, Han scholars derived an elaborate conception of the *duties* of the emperor as the Son of Heaven. He must ensure that proper rituals are performed at appropriate times, that astronomy and the calendar are kept current, that proper arrangements are made for agriculture, that land use and taxation are fair, and that all his subjects have an adequate means of livelihood. In addition, the emperor must educate and civilize his people, teaching everyone the proprieties, music, and morality. Finally, the emperor has an obligation to provide for the moral development and intellectual perfection of the gifted few and use them to administer the state. Thus were Confucian scholars provided with a heaven-sent right to study and to staff the entire state bureaucracy.[91] Eventually there were over thirty thousand students enrolled at any one time in the state university devoted to Confucian scholarship. From their ranks came all officials that staffed the Han state.

Meanwhile, of course, Confucian scholars began to break up into "schools" and to quarrel over the proper interpretation of texts—intellectuals always form factions and have such fallings out.[92] However, all of these disputes lost their significance when, upon the fall of the Han Dynasty, a period ensued during which Confucian scholars did not staff the bureaucracy and found themselves replaced by Taoists and Buddhists. Eventually they regained their control of the state and used their power to repress and persecute both Taoists and Buddhists, as will be seen.

But even at the height of their power during the Han Dynasty, the elite form of Confucianism consisted mainly of a highly educated literati, drilled in chapter and verse of an ever expanding literature of commentary. Despite their emphasis on conducting proper rituals, this elite did not constitute a priesthood—the rituals were not meant to propitiate or invoke the Gods, but to satisfy the highest standards of civilized behavior and diplomacy. Therefore, the question must arise: was Confucianism a religious movement?

A Religion?

For many centuries there has been a controversy over whether Confucius founded a philosophy or a religion. In recent times this has taken on rather intense political aspects as the Communist regime in China pronounced that Confucianism was not a religion so that they could claim that their ideology was in accord with Confucian principles, while at the same time continuing to condemn all religions.[93] Many Western intellectuals have expressed similar views, thereby affirming their commitment to morality while preserving their irreligiousness. Hence, Confucianism often is referred to as one of the "Godless" religions.

A learned German scholar noted that "it is only in a very unreal sense that Confucianism can be called a religion."[94] The esteemed Wu-Chi Liu (1907–2002) agreed: "Unlike Christianity, Buddhism or Mohammedanism, Confucianism is a pure philosophy, and is non-religious in nature. It is without any trace of the metaphysical or the supernatural."[95] And in the influential book *What Confucius Really Meant*, it is argued that Confucianism is a superior intellectual system precisely because it is not a religion![96]

It is true that many typical features of organized religion are absent from Confucianism. "It has never possessed a distinctively religious organization." It has never developed a professional priesthood. It has "frowned upon monasticism and asceticism."[97] As for Confucius himself, clearly he was not irreligious—he often referred to heaven. But equally clearly he was not much concerned with the Gods, and he often used the word *heaven* as a synonym for "fate." Nor did he invoke divine will or punishments to warrant his moral system—he did not classify wrong behavior as sin, but as impropriety. And he never, ever suggested that his wisdom came from heaven or had been in any sense revealed to him. Thus, it seems reasonable to suppose that Confucius regarded himself as merely a philosopher, and it is certain that he was not an *intentional* religious founder. However, despite the fact that the Confucian bureaucracy that ruled China for so many centuries stressed the secular, philosophical character of Confucianism, even a cursory examination of Popular Confucianism reveals that Confucius founded a religion!

As D. Howard Smith pointed out: "Throughout its history Confucianism has manifested a deep sense of man's dependence upon a supreme Deity, and of the intimate relationship between the spiritual world and the world of men. It has given expression to that sense of dependence in elaborate rituals and heartfelt prayers."[98] This aspect of Confucianism is fully confirmed by recent fieldwork. Even those who deny that Confucianism is a religion admit that there are Confucian sections in the thousands of ancestral temples found in China and elsewhere in Asia. The central focus of these temple areas is an imposing statue of Confucius. When my colleague Anna Xiao Dong Sun visited several of these temples in China, she observed people praying to the statues of Confucius.[99] They were not simply paying tribute to a great man, but were earnestly praying for his intervention in their affairs. Indeed, temple officials told Sun that huge crowds of young worshippers always gather in front of the statue of Confucius during the week of the national college entrance examinations. The religious character of Confucianism is equally overt in Korea: "A grand ceremony of worship of Confucius is held twice a year, including offering sacrifices."[100]

However it was that Confucius regarded himself, he soon was transformed into a God, thus making a mockery of all claims that his is a "Godless" philosophy.

BUDDHISM ARRIVES

Buddhism originated and grew powerful in the Ganges Valley of eastern India. But it did not travel on east into China—the way being blocked by the nearly impenetrable Himalayan Mountains. Hence, the passage of Buddhism to China was delayed until it had established a secure foundation in far western India and eastern Persia, from whence Buddhist monks and merchants had access to the "Silk Roads," the famous caravan routes that looped north of the Himalayans and led directly to the urban core of northern China.

The first evidence that Buddhism had reached China is a royal edict issued in 65 CE reporting that a prince in northern Kingsu Province "respectfully performs the gentle sacrifices to the Buddha."[101] Obviously, Buddhism must have been active in China well before this report, and most scholars assume that the first Buddhists arrived sometime between 100 BCE and the first century CE.[102] What is clear is that the most influential form of Buddhism *brought* to China was a radical departure from the Buddhist faith that was failing in India. This new Buddhism probably was greatly transformed by contact with Zoroastrianism as it passed through Persia on the way to China.

Pure Land and Ch'an Buddhism

Indian Buddhism regarded the world as an evil site of human suffering and located all hope in a psychological means of escape from the illusion of existence. In contrast, the preexisting Chinese religions and philosophies regarded the world as real, not illusory, and as essentially good. Because they stressed the need to harmonize with the forces of nature, for the Chinese, "enlightenment consist[ed] of identifying these forces, rather than being freed from them."[103] These basic assumptions were very compatible with a new and very compelling reconception of Nirvana.

As used by Buddha and his orthodox (or Theravāda Buddhist) disciples in India, Nirvana is a state of nonbeing, involving the final discovery that the world is mere appearance, lacking all point or purpose, and hence Nirvana affords an individual with release from the cycle of rebirths. Although he often was quizzed by his followers, Buddha steadfastly refused to define or describe Nirvana, but he did make it clear that only a few could hope to achieve it.[104] In contrast, the Buddhism that triumphed in China conceived of Nirvana, not as a psychological state, but as a heavenly *place*, a literal, physical Paradise known as the **Pure Land**, where the virtuous go after death and where "people get whatever they wish for, be it music, fine food, clothing, jewels, or palaces."[105] Moreover, salvation does not require a life of ascetic meditation; the Pure Land can be reached by ordinary people through faith and devotion alone.

This attractive reconception of Nirvana was spelled out in a new Buddhist scripture called the **Pure Land Sutra** that is identified with Mahāyāna Buddhism, which began in northwestern India and central Asia along the Silk Roads in about the first century BCE, coincident with the transmission of Buddhism to China.[106] It has been suggested that the Pure Land Sutra, and Mahāyāna Buddhism more generally, is the result of the exposure of Buddhism to Zoroastrian influences, a conclusion encouraged not only by doctrinal similarities, but by having apparently originated in Persia and by the tradition that the monk who introduced the Sutra to China was a Persian.[107] In addition to the Pure Land conception of Nirvana, Mahāyāna Buddhism explicitly deified Buddha as an eternal being who becomes incarnated from time to time.[108] This was a far more vivid and optimistic faith than was offered by the Buddhism that eventually failed in India, and these new doctrines enabled Chinese Buddhism to become a very successful popular movement, celebrated in thousands of temples, each with its "living" statue of Buddha ready to hear one's prayers.

Meanwhile, an elite version of Buddhism also developed in China. According to the distinguished Erik Zürcher, this was formulated by "cultured monks who, by a fruitful combination of Buddhist doctrine and traditional Chinese scholarship, were able to develop the particular type of Buddhism which spread among the upper classes." Zürcher designated this as "gentry Buddhism."[109]

Gentry Buddhism emerged at the end of the second century CE. It involved "gentlemen-monks" who could recruit effectively among the well-educated and affluent because they belonged to this class "by birth and education, [and] could preach their version of the [Buddhist] doctrine with the authority of a Chinese scholar and with ... polished eloquence."[110] Rapid growth continued until China abounded in "thousands of monasteries, many of them wealthy, with lots of land, servants, and golden images [of Buddha] donated by rich merchants and officials."[111]

That elite Buddhism remained primarily a monastic movement proved attractive to the gentry, especially as it offered a respectable, even distinguished, calling for "second" sons—those who were not heirs—and surplus daughters. Indeed, the monasteries took on a major educational function, and this resulted in the entry of novices at an early age, in keeping with the fact that, as Randall Collins pointed out, "Buddhism is an intellectual's religion. . . . Detached from family life and practical concerns, focusing on the analysis of inner experience ... the Buddhist monk might be regarded as living a life of philosophy to its extreme."[112] Consequently, while Popular Buddhism flourished as ordinary people embraced the promise of going to the Pure Land, many monks turned against worldly success, even on behalf of their faith, and demanded a return to the notion of Nirvana as release from existence and to meditation as the fundamental religious path. This became known as *Ch'an Buddhism*, better known in the West as *Zen Buddhism*.

Ch'an Buddhism originated in China around 1000 CE. The primary emphasis was placed upon meditation (the Chinese word *Ch'an* translates as "meditation"), but with a very original twist: that by fully realizing one's own inner potential and becoming "enlightened," one becomes a Buddha!

Like Taoism, Ch'an Buddhism was (and is) decidedly anti-intellectual. One does not make progress "from book knowledge," for words "are at best like pointers toward the supreme experience of illumination and release."[113] The most fundamental truths are "inaccessible to speech and rational thought," and can therefore be accessed only through intuition.[114] Thus, rather than pore over scriptures, one should "study" under a master who already has achieved enlightenment and who will run the candidate through a maze of meditation sessions (replete with physical abuse) until "the ultimate state of 'no-mind' has been realized, not gradually but as a sudden explosion."[115]

Nevertheless, Ch'an Buddhists did not utterly reject Popular Buddhism, welcoming the visibility it gave to their faith. Indeed, Ch'an monks even originated methods of meditation that could be practiced by lay people in their homes, and some even taught that the "eternal truth of Buddhism was the same as the cosmic [T]ao, so that one could seek enlightenment amid the beauties of nature."[116] Thus it was that Pure Land and Ch'an Buddhism were the only two "schools" of Buddhism to survive in China into modern times.

State Buddhism

In 220 CE the Han Dynasty fell, and during the subsequent period of disorganization, northern China suffered invasions by various non-Chinese groups from the north, eventuating in the sack of the capital in 311 and the flight of the court to the south. For nearly three hundred years thereafter, China was divided into the northern region around the Yellow River, ruled by a succession of non-Chinese regimes, and the southern region around the Yangtze River, ruled by a series of unstable Chinese regimes. Rulers of northern China welcomed close ties with both Buddhism and Taoism and provided "grandiose government patronage."[117] There came "a veritable orgy of temple-building, monasteries were heavily endowed, new Buddhist statues and paintings were commissioned."[118] And, of course, tens of thousands became monks and nuns. Buddhist monks were particularly favored, and many "became political, military and diplomatic advisers, and also gained a great reputation among the people through their skill in thaumaturgical and magical performances."[119] During this era, Buddhism was so popular that in the northern capital city of Loyang, having a population of about five hundred thousand, it is reported that "there were 1,367 temples."[120]

Even so, there were several outbreaks of vicious anti-Buddhist persecution in the north. In 424 a new ruler began his reign, as the Emperor Wu. Among the leading figures in his court were a devoted Taoist and a prominent Confucianist, both of them dedicated to the overthrow of Buddhism. In time they converted the emperor to Taoism—to such a degree that he conducted a Taoist service to "proclaim Taoism as the dominant faith of the empire."[121] Next the conspirators began to warn the emperor of Buddhist plots against him. So, in 438 Emperor Wu decreed that no one under fifty could become a Buddhist monk. Six years later he forbade anyone from privately supporting Buddhist monks, upon pain of death. Finally, in 446 he ordered the execution of all Buddhist monks and the destruction of all monasteries, temples, images of Buddha, and copies of the sutras. Many officials opposed these moves, and they were carried out slowly and haphazardly. This enabled most of the monks to go into hiding, taking copies of the sutras with them. But the temples were destroyed; how many monks were executed is unknown.[122] Eventually, the emperor regretted his actions, and the measures against Buddhism were relaxed. After Wu's death Buddhism quickly recovered its privileged position. Once again emperors built temples by the thousands and lavishly

In the third century, the new rulers of northern China initiated a massive building program in support of Buddhism. They not only built temples and monasteries, but had many colossal figures of Buddha carved into rock cliffs. This is the oldest known example of the genre. (Yungang Caves, Datong, China; Photo: Werner Forman/Art Resource, New York)

subsidized the faith with such extravagance that the price of gold rose substantially.[123]

But about a century later, persecution broke out again. Once again it was ordered by an emperor named Wu. This Emperor Wu seems to have been motivated by a prophecy suggesting that the Buddhists meant to usurp his throne. So in 574 the emperor outlawed Buddhism and ordered the destruction of the temples, the confiscation of the temple treasures, and their distribution among ministers and the upper nobility. All monks and nuns were ordered to return to the laity. But quite unexpectedly, he applied the edict not only to the Buddhists, but to the Taoists as well![124] Once again thousands of temples were destroyed and their treasures looted, both Buddhist and Taoist. When Emperor Wu died in 578, he was succeeded by an emperor more favorable to Buddhism. Then, three years later, China was reunified, and Buddhism (and Taoism) enjoyed an immense revival of fortune and influence. Once again thousands of temples were built. Once again tens of thousands became monks and nuns. Once again the monastery treasuries were full. But the extreme vulnerability of Buddhism, as well as Taoism, to autocratic rulers persisted.

While all this was going on up north, Buddhism consistently enjoyed great favor in southern China. Having lost half of the area of the empire and about 90 percent of the population,[125] the governing elite that had fled south seemed to have lost confidence in traditional Chinese ways. Therefore, the staffing of the bureaucracy with Confucian scholars came to an end as renewed emphasis was given to birth over achievement. Loss of commitment to Confucianism also opened the door to religious innovations. At first, a new variety of Taoism flourished, but it soon gave way to an even more energetic Buddhism.[126] "Buddhists worked hard and skillfully to win the favor of the southern rulers, offering them not only the hope of personal salvation but new, potent, and colorful rituals invoking the help of Buddhist divinities for the well-being of the realm, [and] for warding off of evil."[127]

Soon, in the south, too, the state provided generous subsidies, and huge numbers of temples and monasteries were built—by 400 CE, there were "more than 1,700 monasteries and 80,000 monks and nuns" in southern China alone.[128] Not content with lavish subsidies, the Buddhists even managed to persuade another Emperor Wu, this one in the south and the founder of the Liang Dynasty (502–549), to not only build many

Buddhist temples, but to abolish those dedicated to Taoism (the emperor later entered a Buddhist monastery).[129]

Chinese Buddhism is credited with originating two forms of fund-raising that have remained central features of Chinese life—the pawnshop and the lottery. "Pawnshops owned and operated by Buddhist monasteries can be traced back to the fifth century" as can the sale of lottery tickets.[130] However, funds provided by the state and a few wealthy donors were the main source of Buddhist wealth and, just as has been the case in India, dependence on subsidies proved the undoing of Chinese Buddhism, too.

Competition and Renewed Persecution

Buddhism enjoyed such a remarkable period of success in China for a number of reasons. Just as Buddhism benefited from political turmoil during its formative days in India, so, too, in China, Buddhism arose during the waning days of the Han Dynasty and achieved its greatest prominence during the perilous times when invaders ruled the north and an anxious regime held out in the south.

Of course, these unsettled conditions merely provided an opportunity for religious innovations. That it was Buddhism that filled the gap was due to its competitive advantages vis-à-vis other available options. These advantages fall into two overlapping categories: Buddhism's appeal to the general public and to the elite. For the public, Buddhism was the only religion that offered an attractive afterlife (with well-developed "conceptions of paradise and purgatory") that was available to everyone.[131] It also seems to have been the first religion in China to place divine "images" in its temples to provide a concrete focus for prayers[132]—prayers that were thought to bring various benefits, especially healing and protection from evil.

As for the elite, they also welcomed the prospect of spending eternity in the Pure Land, and in addition Buddhism offered them "a full-time religious vocation for both men and women in an organization largely independent of family and state."[133] It also offered them the intellectual satisfactions of a complex philosophy and the "challenge of attaining new states of consciousness in meditation."[134]

Moreover, Buddhism seemed quite compatible with other faiths. It complemented Confucianism by adding a spiritual dimension to its focus on the state and society, and it fit so well with fundamental Taoism that during the Han Dynasty, Buddhism was regarded as a form of Taoism. Even so, Taoism changed so substantially in response to Buddhist examples and competition, that historians apply the term *Neo-Taoism* to the version that developed. Indeed, many Neo-Taoist sages denied there were any significant differences between their faith and Buddhism, if one properly understood that sometimes different terms were used for the same thing. Even so, Neo-Taoism placed far greater emphasis on eternal life than had been the case in earlier forms of the faith. Neo-Taoism also greatly expanded its investment in monasticism, and in response to the Buddhist example, nunneries were added, with both monks and nuns adopting celibacy.[135] The Taoists even began to teach that Buddha was an incarnation of Lao-Tzu and "so it was quite proper for [them both] to be worshipped at the same altar."[136]

The privileged position of Buddhism was enhanced when in 581 Yang-chien reunited the North and the South, founding the Sui Dynasty. The new emperor acknowledged the support of Buddhism in unifying China and promoted Buddhism in various ways, including the founding and funding of monasteries "at the foot of each of the five sacred mountains, and also on the sites of famous battles."[137] The court remained generously favorable to Buddhism during the first two centuries of the T'ang Dynasty (618–907) as well. But opposition slowly grew.

For one thing, the enormous wealth of the Buddhist temples, with their extensive and tax-exempt land holdings, once again stirred forces of greed and envy. For another, the examination system for filling positions in the government bureaucracy was restored. Once again the examinations had an exclusively Confucian content, because it was "the only available corpus of political theory, ritual precedents, and normative rules of conduct of court and official affairs."[138] The restoration of Confucian scholars to power not only raised issues of authority, but the Confucian establishment also found many Buddhist teachings repugnant. Since their philosophy stressed the secular, the perfectibility of this life, the Confucianists rejected "the quest for purely individual salvation . . . as narrow-minded and selfish."[139] They were even more offended by monasticism, as it involved rejection and abandonment of the family. The Confucian elite branded the monastic life "as immoral [and] parasitical."[140]

Initial efforts by Confucian bureaucrats to control Buddhism began in the eighth century as a number of regulations were imposed. One of these prohibited monks and nuns from wandering about the country and from selling scriptures and other mementos. Several years later, entry to Buddhist monastic orders was taken under government control, with certificates being required. These new rules did not seriously impede Buddhism. A census in 739 revealed 3,245 Buddhist monasteries and 2,113 convents (compared with 1,137 Taoist monasteries and 550 convents).[141] But government interference was an omen of far worse to come. In 845, the worst occurred. A coalition of Confucian bureaucrats and Taoist masters at court led a wave of terror. The state seized Buddhist lands, emptied the temple treasuries, and more "than 40,000 temples were destroyed and 265,500 monks and nuns were forced to return to lay life."[142] It was a blow from which Buddhism never recovered. Nor was Neo-Taoism exempt from state usurpation and repression. Eventually, both faiths lived on primarily as major features of the prevailing Folk Religion.

FOLK RELIGION

Chinese Folk Religion retains many of the Gods, beliefs, and practices of the ancient religion of China—ancestor worship, the Jade Emperor, ghosts and demons, exorcism, and divination—and has blended all of this with elements of popular Buddhism, Taoism, and Confucianism. In keeping with this blend, these temples have "no specific name in Chinese—people merely speak of 'worshiping the deities.' "[143] Indeed, the folk temples are stuffed with traditional Gods, and most temples also house very large "idols" representing Lao-Tzu, Confucius, and Buddha.

Like the temples in Rome, the Chinese Folk Temples have no professional priests. Instead a caretaker "cleans the temple, sells incense and other ritual articles, and occasionally helps supplicants to read oracle slips."[144] The temples are funded and sustained by local people. A few temples are served by amateur clergy who perform special rituals, but often Taoist priests or Buddhist monks are hired for such occasions.[145] Mostly people do their own praying and worshipping in the temples, often bringing offerings of food and incense, which they place before the image of the God from whom they hope to receive blessings. Moreover, much Chinese Folk Religion takes place in the home before a family altar.

Just as the Folk Religion is an amalgamation of Gods and doctrines, its aims are those of "generic" religion as well:

1. Protection of life and property.

2. Control of natural forces.

3. Secure and harmonious family life.

4. Economic success and security.

5. Forgiveness of sins and salvation from hell.

6. Entry into heaven.[146]

Particular concern has to do with controlling demons, most of whom are spirits of "the restless dead who died unjustly or whose bodies were not properly cared for."[147] Demons are blamed for most illnesses, fires, and natural disasters, and a great deal of effort is devoted to keeping them under rein. A favorite method is to hire a medium or a Taoist priest to write a charm to thwart the demon of present concern. For example:

"I, the Jade Emperor, hereby order the evil and crooked forces causing this illness to leave immediately. This order has the power to smash and drive away all demons."[148]

Having read this charm aloud, the priest then burns it so that it rises to the Gods in the sky.

The strength of Chinese Folk Religion stems from its array of divine options and the comprehensiveness of the existential issues it addresses. Its primary weakness is its failure to generate and sustain congregations and the intense loyalty and commitment inherent in them. This lack of congregations seems to be a major factor in the rapid rates of Christian growth taking place in contemporary China and Taiwan.[149]

CONCLUSION

Although each founder of the three major Chinese religions was elevated into Godhood, it appears that none of them legitimated their teaching on the basis of a revelation. Buddha did not. It is doubtful that Lao-Tzu even meant to found a religion, and it seems most likely that Confucius never knew that he had done so. Can it then be said that any of these three founders was a participant in the discovery of God?

That question is addressed in the concluding chapter. Meanwhile, we now leave Asia and return to the Middle East to examine the origins of two faiths that claim to be based on revelations and which grew to become the two largest and most influential religions on earth today.

° 7 °

THE RISE OF CHRISTIANITY

I N TWO PREVIOUS BOOKS on the rise of Christianity I was careful to begin the story in the year 40, about a decade after the Crucifixion.[1] By doing so I avoided becoming involved in complex and contentious discussions about who Jesus really was, and I could focus instead on the religious movement led by Paul and the apostles. No longer. This chapter must begin with the controversial and often bizarre search for the "historical" Jesus. Then comes an analysis of the theological Christ to show why Greek and Roman pagans found him so familiar, reassuring, and appealing. That concluded, I very briefly summarize Christian doctrines and sacraments before turning to the task of assessing the militant debates concerning the New Testament, its origins, and its reliability.

Then, following a brief sketch of the role of Jesus's family in early Christianity and an assessment of Paul's missionary work, the chapter develops and validates an estimated growth curve that traces the number of confessing Christians in the Empire from the year 40 through the year 350. Next, these overall membership statistics are decomposed to estimate the number of Christians in five Greco-Roman cities at various times in order to bring many matters into sharper relief, including why some emperors became so fearful of the Christian Movement and why Constantine sought Christian support.

Having described the Christianization of the Empire in terms of plausible numbers, the chapter then asks why it happened. It won't do to attribute Christianization to a miracle since the task was consigned to human efforts (Matthew 28:19), and it is a task that remains to be fully achieved.

Thus, we should ask: what competitive advantages did Christianity possess in contrast with the other faiths of the time? Among these was its appeal to philosophers and intellectuals who had begun to prefer monotheistic solutions to the origins of the universe. Some of these speculations were very favorable to Christian theology; others set the stage for attempts to incorporate Christianity within a new form of paganism, which came to be known as Gnosticism.

Moving on, the chapter briefly traces the long decline of European Christianity that began as a response to its favored status as the monopoly Church. We see that the "empty" churches of Europe are not a new phenomenon, but have existed for more than a millennium. Then, the chapter turns to the rapid revival of Christian energy and commitment in response to the competitive American religious economy and how this unleashed a new era of foreign missionizing that has initiated the explosive growth of Christianity in the "Global South": Latin America, Africa, and Asia.[2]

THE HISTORICAL JESUS

During the past two centuries the "search" for the "Historical Jesus" has been carried to obsessive and often absurd lengths as soaring scholarly imaginations have created many new conceptions of Jesus: as a magician,[3] a Cynic sage,[4] a wicked priest,[5] a homeless charismatic,[6] a proletarian rebel,[7] a marginal Jew,[8] a mystical peasant,[9] a homosexual prophet,[10] a rabbi,[11] a revolutionary plotter,[12] the bastard offspring of a raped teenager,[13] a Galilean holy man,[14] the married founder of a family whose descendents live on in anonymity while pursuing a "Goddess" religion,[15] and on and on.[16]

Whatever else can be said of their notions about the historical Jesus, at least these writers agreed that he actually existed, in contrast with others who claimed that Jesus is but a figment of pious imaginations.[17] The charge that Jesus never lived became prominent among nineteenth-century German scholars such as Bruno Bauer (1809–1882)[18] and Albert Kalthoff (1850–1906)[19] and was continued early in the twentieth century by Arthur Drews (1865–1935)[20] and the Englishman John M. Robertson (1856–1933).[21] There is no sure evidence outside of New Testament scriptures that Jesus actually lived. But all reputable scholars now agree that the Gospel evidence is sufficient, not because the Bible is authoritative, but because it clearly reflects the common culture of first-generation Christians—their behavior makes absolutely no sense if there was no Jesus. To deny that Jesus existed, it is necessary to claim that the entire New Testament was made up at a later date. However, no one competent now doubts that most of Paul's letters are authentic. Granted that Paul never met the living Jesus, but he had long, close associations with people who had known him, including Jesus's brother James who, until he was executed by the Sanhedrin in 62 CE, led the Christian Movement. This not only is asserted in scripture,[22] but also by the Jewish historian Josephus, who reported the execution of "the brother of Jesus, who was called Christ, whose name was James."[23] Of course, Josephus may not have been informed by an independent source but may have only repeated the Christian tradition; the same can be said of Tacitus's mention of a religious group in Rome who worshipped a "Christ" who had been killed by Pontius Pilate during the reign of Tiberius.[24] But the concerns for independent, nonbiblical sources shrink to unimportant quibbles when weighed against the utter implausibility that, as the great Shirley Jackson Case (1872–1947) put it, "a company of people claiming to have been companions of a fictitious person [would continue] reverencing him even to the point of sacrificing their lives for his cause."[25] Hence, today only dedicated atheist writers cling to the notion that Jesus never existed.

But while scholars agree that there was an historic Jesus, they disagree substantially as to who he was, as noted above. And, underneath all of the academic skepticism about the credibility of the Gospel accounts of the life of Jesus lies the issue of miracles. It is these that are said to "prove" that the Gospels are but a compendium of mythology, a charge that began with the influential work of Hermann Samuel Reimarus[26] (1694–1768), was expanded by David Friederich Strauss[27] (1808–1874), and became a dominant scholarly thesis when ratified by Rudolph Bultmann[28] (1884–1976). Indeed, Bultmann argued that some of Jesus's sayings are the only authentic part of the Gospels,[29] a position leading to the current posturings of the Jesus Seminar (of whom, more later).[30] Thus, from the very start, most searchers for the historical Jesus have assumed that no intelligent modern person could credit tales involving healing, exorcism, or changing water into wine, let alone such an absolute impossibility as the claim that Jesus rose from the dead! Thus are miracles used to discredit the entire Jesus tale, just as accounts of the Parting of the Red Sea and the sun stopping in the heavens are said to fully discredit the Old Testament.

These attacks reveal nothing so much as remarkable ignorance about miracles. On the one side are the militant atheists who fill endless pages with "proof" that various miracles are "fairy tales" because they violate fundamental natural laws and are therefore "impossible." Thus, the movement of the sun across the sky could not have been stopped, because that would have required that the earth suddenly cease turning, which would have caused incredible natural disasters. On the other side are those seeking to defend their faith by trying to show how various miracles could have had natural causes. For example, it often has been proposed that astronomical anomalies such as the close passage of a rogue planet created gravitational effects that parted the Red Sea at just the right time.[31] Both approaches to miracles are equally absurd. To make miracles plausible, all that is needed is to postulate the existence of a God who created the universe, nothing more. Surely a God who created the natural laws could suspend them at will. Moreover, *unless* physical laws are violated, there is no miracle!

So, was Lazarus raised from the dead? Perhaps, and perhaps not. But if God exists, he *could* have been. Was Mary a virgin? She *could* have been. Did the resurrection occur? It *could* have. Some believe these things happened, some believe they didn't—and *both* positions are based on faith!

Ignoring miracles, what can be said about the historical Jesus beyond his mere existence? First of all, his family knew him as Joshua—Jesus being the Greek form of that name. He probably was born in about 4 BCE, at the very end of the reign of Herod the Great. He grew up in the village of Nazareth. He usually preached in Aramaic, but in Hebrew to more sophisticated audiences.[32] Some scholars believe that he also spoke Greek,[33] since Nazareth is only about five miles from Sepphoris, then the capital of Galilee and a Greek-speaking city.[34] Unfortunately, assuming that Jesus spoke three languages doesn't tell us much. Some biographical knowledge of Jesus also can be inferred from the fact that he was born and raised in Galilee. But these inferences must lack detail, being equally applicable to most young men of that time and place, a point well-made by Sean Freyne's admonition that the search for the historical Jesus is "in danger of becoming a quest for the historical Galilee."[35] All efforts to squeeze these "background" data to come closer to the historical Jesus

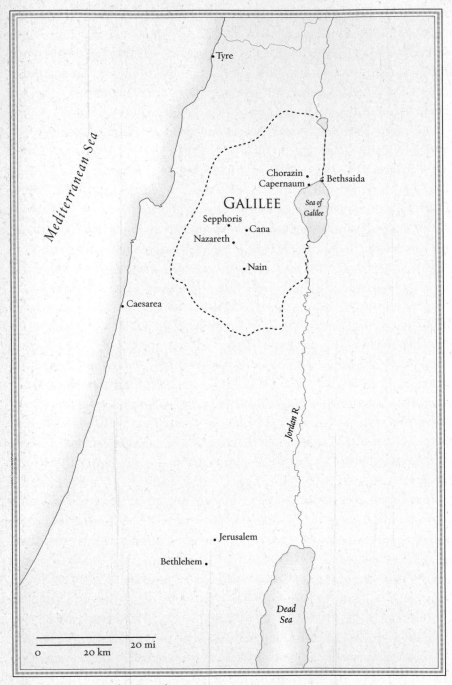

Map 7–1: Palestine in the time of Jesus.

necessitate risky assumptions as demonstrated by the many contradictory "inferences." Some scholars claim that the Galilean villagers deeply resented the more Hellenized Jews living in the cities and that Jesus shared their feelings.[36] But another well-known scholar "repositions the historical Jesus away from a specifically Jewish sectarian milieu and toward the Hellenistic ethos known to have prevailed in Galilee."[37]

When Jesus is identified more narrowly as a particular kind or category of Galilean, matters can very quickly get out of hand. In his book *The Historical Jesus: The Life of a Mediterranean Jewish Peasant*, John Dominic Crossan offers an extensive account of peasant life in Palestine. Even if his portrait of that culture is as well drawn as it is well written, it surely cannot support obvious inventions such as: "He [Jesus] comes as yet unknown into a hamlet of Lower Galilee. . . . He looks like a beggar, yet his eyes lack the proper cringe, his voice the proper whine, his walk the proper shuffle."[38] At least Crossan stopped short of reporting that Jesus had a hooked nose, a hairy chest, and calloused hands. But far more important is the fact that Crossan defines a "peasant" as an impoverished farmer.[39] There is no hint in the Gospels or anywhere else that Jesus ever lived on a farm or tilled the soil! Consequently, Crossan's entire undertaking is an immense irrelevancy. Similar problems arise when scholars infer what Jesus "must have been like" from the fact that he was a Galilean Jew. The results differ immensely depending on *what kind* of Jew the author assumes Jesus to have been[40] for, as usual, Israel was full of Jewish sects at the time. So much, then, for the many efforts to "situate" Jesus in order to dig up the truth.

Finally, the emphasis on the homeless itinerancy of Jesus and his disciples seems geographically naive. Although the *Gospel of John* has Jesus spending a substantial amount of time in Judea and Jerusalem, even *John* agrees he spent most of his time in Galilee, and the other three Gospels suggest that's where he spent nearly all his time, often preaching along the Sea of Galilee.[41] Galilee is so tiny that it is an easy two-day walk from north to south and only a day's walk from east to west at the widest point.

Specifically, it is less than twenty-five miles from Nazareth to Capernaum, where most of Jesus's ministry took place (it was "his own city" according to Matthew 9:1), and only about two miles north from Capernaum to Chorazin, and less than five miles from Capernaum along the shore of the Sea of Galilee to Bethsaida, home of Simon, Peter, and Andrew.

The "Sea" is, of course, a lake fed by the Jordan River and is only "about thirteen miles long and eight miles wide at its broadest point."[42] Shifting south, it is only about seven miles from Nazareth to Cana, and Nain is even closer. The only "long" trips reported in the Gospels were a journey from Capernaum to the Tyre area (about thirty miles), and one or several to Jerusalem, about seventy miles from Nazareth. Thus, almost nowhere is Jesus reported to have visited even "a full day's journey away from either Nazareth or Capernaum and . . . it would have been quite feasible to regularly return to a home base in either town."[43] In fact, Peter had a house in Capernaum,[44] and perhaps Jesus did, too (Mark 2:1–2). In any event, as E. P. Sanders noted, "After preaching elsewhere, Jesus would return [to Capernaum]."[45]

Aside from a probable year of birth, and where he grew up and preached, our few reasonably solid biographical facts about Jesus are these. He was the son of a woman named Mary, whose husband, Joseph, probably was a carpenter, although he might have been what today would be called a contractor.[46] Jesus had brothers and sisters, but did not marry. At about age thirty he responded to John the Baptist and had a vision:

> In those days Jesus came from Nazareth of Galilee and was baptized by John in the Jordan.
> And when he came up out of the water, immediately he saw the heavens opened and the Spirit descending upon him like a dove;
> and a voice came from heaven, "Thou art my beloved Son; with thee I am well pleased."[47]

It is believed that Jesus then went into the wilderness and after forty days returned to Galilee and began his ministry, which lasted only for about a year according to Matthew, Mark, and Luke, while John extends it to at least two years, and possibly three. Then he was tried by Jewish authorities and turned over to the Romans for crucifixion. After his death, he is believed to have been restored to life (the Resurrection), and a number of his supporters reported encountering him alive and in the flesh before he joined God in heaven (the Ascension).

And that's pretty much it. Indeed, scripture hardly mentions Jesus's life before his baptism by John, and nearly all of the text of each Gospel is devoted to his ministry. Indeed, half or more of each Gospel is devoted to the last week of his life![48] In any event, we know nothing of his appearance and little more about his personal style, although he clearly had no respect for the prevailing social distinctions, being quite willing to associate with stigmatized outsiders such as Samaritans, publicans, "fallen" women, beggars, and various other outcasts.

Details of Jesus's religious life also are rather remarkably lacking in the Gospels. We are told almost nothing about his relationship with God, other than that Jesus sometimes referred to him as "father dear." Jesus acknowledged that his message was God-given, but seems not to have shared specific revelations with his followers. Frankly, the search for the "Historic Jesus" is in many ways a fool's errand since scripture is the only direct source and it tells us so very little about his life. It is his death and resurrection that dominate Christian thought.

THE THEOLOGICAL CHRIST

A serious objection to the entire Christ story has been that it seems so fundamentally pagan. What purpose was served by the Crucifixion? Surely a God of miracles could simply have offered universal clemency to those who believed and thereby have dispensed with any need for a "blood sacrifice." Although such a sacrifice may have seemed plausible to pagans, it rings quite false in our more enlightened times.

But that's the whole point. Recall the discussion of divine accommodation from the introductory chapter—that God's revelations are always geared to the current capacity of humans to comprehend. Hence, the message to Greco-Roman pagans: *Christ died for your sins!* Forget offerings of a hundred or even a thousand cattle! The Christian *God so loved the world, that he gave his only begotten Son, that whosoever believeth in him should not perish, but have everlasting life.* That message spoke powerfully and eloquently to a culture that took sacrifice, especially blood sacrifice, as fundamental to pleasing the Gods.

The same can be said for other miracles reported in the Gospels. Many critics have mocked the Christ story as a compendium of pagan mythical elements. Mary's conception seems very like that of many women who were said to have been impregnated by pagan Gods. Zeus was believed to have fathered "more than a hundred children by human mothers, most often, though not always, by virgins."[49] These half-Gods, as Hesiod (700 BCE?) called them, include both Perseus and Dionysos as well as Helen of Troy.

In similar fashion, dramatic signs and portents were to be expected at any celebrity birth, and always at the arrival of a future divinity—it was believed that many prodigies and portents accompanied the births of both Alexander the Great and Caesar Augustus. For some born of women to have ascended into Godhood after gory deaths was commonplace—Fraser recounted many such "myths" in *The Golden Bough.*

But to claim that these similarities with pagan mythology discredit Christianity is to fail to see how these features played to the pagan world. There they were taken as compelling proof of Christ's divinity—the Christ story fulfilled every element of the classical Hero, of how a human rose to become a God.[50] The early church fathers fully understood this. Having told the Christ story to a Roman magistrate, Tertullian (c. 160–?) suggested that he "accept this story—it is similar to your own."[51] Indeed, it is entirely consistent with the theology of divine accommodation to propose that these events actually happened just as reported in the Gospels precisely to prove to pagans that Jesus was the Son of God.

All of this is fully in accord with the principles governing conversion that were introduced in Chapter 4. Recall that *religious capital* consists of the degree to which an individual has mastered the beliefs, rites, norms, and the traditions of a particular faith. Other things being equal, people are more likely to convert to a new faith to the degree that they are able to retain their religious capital. It follows that new religious movements will be more successful to the extent that they retain *cultural continuity* with the prevailing religious culture—so that converts can retain elements of the old faith(s) and mostly just add to, rather than replace, their religious capital. The "pagan elements" of the Christ story maximized cultural continuity between Greco-Roman paganism and Christianity. Pagan converts could retain many of their familiar conceptions about the Gods and miracles, while embracing the far more intense levels of commitment, more comprehensive morality, and the far more compelling message of salvation.

As will be seen, Christianity not only offered a far more attractive and accessible eternal life, but a remarkably improved life here and now: Christians lived longer, better, and more securely than did their pagan neighbors. Jews may have enjoyed these same benefits. But unlike converts to Judaism, those who became Christians did not need to entirely abandon the more comprehensible, more familiar, more "human" aspects of the

Gods and embrace the remote, far less comprehensible, and forbidding Yahweh. Instead, Christians could have it *both* ways! Indeed, Jews and Muslims often object that Christianity is not monotheistic because it acknowledges Jesus as a divinity in his own right. Be that as it may, Christ gives a comfortable, reassuring, and more comprehensible aspect to Christianity than either Judaism or Islam can provide. Christ is regarded as an understanding, forgiving *person* who not only died that all may be saved, but continues in the role of intercessor. Moreover, while Yahweh, Jehovah, and Allāh are invisible and indescribable, Christ is plausibly *depictable*—consider the extraordinary impact of Christian art.[52] It is because Jesus so fully humanizes divinity that there has been little tendency for Christians to relapse into polytheism. Thus it is entirely appropriate that this faith is known as Christianity, not as Jehovahism. And that, of course, forced the irrevocable break with Judaism.

Many of the same scholars who claim Jesus never existed, or that he was but a minor holy man, are equally convinced that the early followers of Jesus did not regard him as Christ. It is claimed that the "Easter religion," based on the resurrection of Jesus, came considerably later. This argument often takes a semi-syllogistic form: All religious Jews were strict monotheists. The early followers of Jesus were religious Jews. Therefore they did not worship Jesus. Consequently, Jesus's divinity must have been "invented" by Gentile Christians. With the publication of the magisterial *Kyrios Christos* in 1913 by Wilhelm Bousset (1865–1920), it became the standard academic view that the belief in Jesus as divine originated with "Hellenistic Gentile" communities, "a view influenced by pagan analogies of divine heroes and cult deities."[53] It was to this "secondary stage" of Christianity that Paul was said to have converted and that he espouses in his letters—thus shifting Paul from the missionary *to* the Gentiles to, in effect, the missionary *from* the Gentiles. The popularity of this revisionist view cannot be separated from the intense regrets expressed by many of the most outspoken contemporary religious scholars that such a shift occurred—they much prefer to imagine Jesus as just another small-time sage with a bit of talent for aphorisms. But wishing doesn't make things so, and recently their position was irretrievably overturned by Larry W. Hurtado[54] who demonstrated that from earliest times the Christian Movement employed a language of worship in which Jesus was explicitly acknowledged as divine.

What seems truly strange is that anyone ever thought otherwise. It was Jews who *knew* Jesus who gave initial momentum to the movement, for which some of them gave their lives. Followers of a local sage don't do such things. As for early Gentile influences on Paul, later in the chapter we shall see that for all the talk of his mission to the Gentiles, he seems to have spent most of his time missionizing to Jews. But before taking up such matters, it seems wise to first sketch the essentials of Christianity.

CHRISTIANITY

During the slightly more than 2000 years since the birth of Jesus, Christianity has inspired an enormous literature of theology, commentary, history, and interpretation. But despite that, its essential message is clear and quite brief, and its primary sacraments are few and simple.

Doctrines

The essence of Christianity is elegantly summed up in a statement of faith known as the *Apostle's Creed*.[55]

> *I believe in God the Father, Almighty, Maker of heaven and earth:*
> *And in Jesus Christ, his only begotten Son, our Lord:*
> *Who was conceived by the Holy Ghost, born of the Virgin Mary:*
> *Suffered under Pontius Pilate; was crucified, dead and buried: he de-*
> *scended into hell:*
> *The third day he rose again from the dead:*
> *He ascended into heaven, and sits at the right hand of God the Father*
> *Almighty:*
> *From thence he shall come to judge the quick and the dead:*
> *I believe in the Holy Ghost:*
> *I believe in the holy Christian church: the communion of saints:*
> *The forgiveness of sins:*
> *The resurrection of the body:*
> *And the life everlasting. Amen.*

Thus, Christians believe in an infinite, all-powerful Creator God (sometimes called **Jehovah**, which is simply another pronunciation of Yahweh). They also believe that God sent his son, **Jesus Christ**, into the world to atone for human sins through his death, thus providing everyone with the option to be saved—to enjoy eternal life. The emphasis always has been on belief as the essential for salvation, although all major theologians have made some room for virtue as expressed in good works—even Luther agreed that good works pleased God and that any sincere Christian would, of course, perform good works even if salvation is by faith alone. The **Holy Ghost** (or Holy Spirit) is the third "person" making up the **Holy Trinity** and is defined as a manifestation of God's abiding presence in the world, albeit all leading theologians have struggled to define the Holy Ghost and many frankly refer to it as a mystery.

As is evident, the principal Christian doctrine is that of the **Atonement,** that *Christ's death on the cross served as a sacrifice that reconciled humanity with God.*

Sacraments

To qualify as a Christian one must be *baptized.* This ritual takes two forms. *Infant baptism* involves a ceremony, usually held as a part of a regular Sunday service, in which the baby is sprinkled three times with water in the name of the Father, Son, and Holy Ghost. This sacrament also gives religious sanction to the infant's name, which is why it sometimes is referred to as *christening. Godparents* are a man and a woman (usually married) who take part in the baptism ritual in addition to the biological parents and who take an oath to be responsible for the infant's Christian education should that be necessary. *Adult baptism* is performed on persons in their teens or older—sometimes because they have just become Christians, but usually because they attend a Protestant church (such as the many Baptist groups) that withholds baptism until the individual is old enough to fully understand its implications. Adult baptism is not achieved by sprinkling, but by the full immersion of the individual—usually in a baptismal tank constructed for that purpose.

The second primary Christian sacrament is the *Eucharist,* or *Holy Communion,* also called the Lord's Supper. It is a reenactment of the Last Supper when Jesus sat at table with his disciples just prior to his arrest, identified bread as his body and wine as his blood, and advised the apostles to "*do this in remembrance of me*" (Luke 22:19). Consequently, in some Christian churches, periodically the qualified members are invited to come forward and to swallow a wafer of bread and drink a sip of wine in remembrance of Jesus's sacrifice for their sins.

A third sacrament is *confirmation* (also First Communion). It is a sort of second baptism that rededicates a young person (often around the age of twelve or thirteen) as a Christian and admits them to full membership in the Church after a period of formal instruction. The confirmation ceremony involves, among other things, serving the young people their first communion. Confirmation is not conducted by churches that perform adult baptism.

Additional sacraments are Christian *marriage* ceremonies, Christian *funerals* (including extreme unction for the dying), *ordination* into the ministry or holy orders, and in some denominations, *absolution* for confessed sins.

Christian Scriptures

The Christian **Bible** is divided into two major parts. By far the longer portion is known as the **Old Testament** and corresponds to the Hebrew Bible, known to Jews as the Tanakh. Being far older, the Old Testament has been studied far longer than has the **New Testament**. However, since the New Testament is the scriptural basis for Christianity, the largest religious group in the world, it may be the most-studied work ever written. It consists of twenty-seven short "books." The first four are known as the **Gospels** (Matthew, Mark, Luke, and John), and each is devoted to the story of Christ. The fifth book is the **Acts of the Apostles** and probably was written by the same author as the third Gospel—Luke, who was the companion of the Apostle Paul. Acts recounts the missionary activities of the early Church and especially Paul's missions to the West. The next twenty-one books are the **Epistles** (or letters), most of them written by the Apostle Paul. Last comes the apocalyptic work known as **Revelation** or as **The Apocalypse of Saint John the Divine.**

For much more than a millennium, people pored over the New Testament to better understand their faith or seeking to support alternative theological interpretations. But then, for the past several centuries, immense attention has been paid to the New Testament by scholars, many of whom seem to have been primarily concerned to discredit it. Appropriately, these various "schools" of Bible commentary are known as kinds of "Criticisms"—Form Criticism, Redaction Criticism, Source Criticism, and many others.[56] It should be noted that this skeptical activity began when New Testament scholarship became primarily an academic field. In order to enjoy academic success one must innovate; novelty at almost any cost is the key to a big reputation. This rule holds across the board and has often inflicted remarkably foolish new approaches on many fields.[57] This academic thirst for novelty has disfigured much modern writing about the New Testament. But even greater damage has been done by the very large number of Bible "scholars" who are motivated by angry atheism. Many of those participating in the Jesus Seminar, for example, were once very committed Christians, many having been clergy, who have lost their faith and are now bitter about ever having believed.[58]

In any event, there are four unavoidable concerns that have prompted these critical schools. First, like the Old Testament, the New is remarkably historical in character. And, as with the Old Testament, questions inevitably arise about the *historical reliability* of these scriptures. Secondly, questions are raised as to the *sources* of these accounts, especially of the Gospels and Acts. *When* were various books written? How reliable was the *transmission* of Christian material from earliest days until the New Testament accounts took their current form? A third issue has to do with the extent to which the scriptures might have been *falsified*, tampered with, rewritten or edited. Finally, why were some writings that also purport to be Christian scriptures *excluded* from the recognized canon? Since the excluded scriptures overwhelmingly are those often identified as Gnostic, this issue will be considered when Gnosticism is discussed later in the chapter.

Historical Reliability

It has suited many modern critics of the New Testament to take the position that unless something reported in scripture can be completely verified by nonbiblical sources, it must be rejected as mythical.[59] Over the years, Acts has been a very central focus, and it has sometimes seemed that a competition had been organized to determine who could discredit the most passages—a race seemingly won by Hans Conzelmann (1915–1989) with his claim that, from beginning to end, Acts is a made-up story.[60] Paul's' missionary voyages never happened! Paul's shipwreck is pure fantasy![61] In dismissing the Acts account of Paul's voyages and shipwreck, Conzelmann and others "proved" that the story must be a fantasy by demonstrating that it has the boat following "implausible" routes and otherwise goes against common sense. Knowledgable as they might have been about many esoteric subjects, these historians knew nothing about sailing. To them the Mediterranean is like an indoor swimming pool and one would, naturally, head directly to one's destination, giving no heed to currents or to the fact that it is impossible to sail directly into the wind. When it subsequently was shown that the Acts account is fully in accord with meteorological and nautical conditions and principles,[62] the response was to grudgingly accept the account in Acts as accurate, but to claim that it didn't happen to Paul—rather, that the account in Acts must have been lifted from another unknown, but unbiblical source![63]

As in the case above, the major result of the many unrelenting scholarly attacks on the historical reliability of the New Testament has been to frustrate the attackers because again and again scripture has stood up to their challenges. For one thing, the New Testament provides a very accurate geography, not only of Israel,[64] but of the Roman Empire. Places are where they are supposed to be. Reported travel times are consistent with the distances involved. The topography is accurately described and extends to tiny details such as the location of wells, streams, springs, gorges, cliffs, city gates, and the like.[65]

New Testament identifications and characterizations of a variety of individuals, both famous and obscure, also have frequently been confirmed. Commenting on the writings of Luke, the distinguished Frederick Fyvie Bruce (1910–1990) noted that a remarkable example of Luke's accuracy "is his sure familiarity with the proper titles of all the notable persons who are mentioned in his pages. This was by no means such an easy feat."[66] In fact, Luke used the term *politarchs* to identify the officers or magistrates in Thessalonica. If correct, this term would apply only in this city, as it is used nowhere else in ancient literature. And that turns out to be the case, since this usage has been "completely vindicated by . . . inscriptions."[67] Many similar instances have been reported.

Turning to more specific identifications, an inscription discovered at Delphi in 1905 revealed that Gallio, a brother of Seneca the philosopher, was, in fact, proconsul of Achaia from July 51 to August 52, during which time Acts 18:12–17 says Paul was taken before him in Corinth.[68] Acts 19:22 identifies Erastus as one of Paul's helpers in Corinth and Romans 16:23 identifies him further as "the city treasurer." That was deemed unlikely by scholars who were certain that the early Christians were recruited from the lower classes. But in 1929, archaeologists excavating a first-century street in Corinth unearthed an inscribed stone reading: "Erastus, Procurator and Aedile, laid this pavement at his own expense." Among the duties of an aedile was to supervise the financial affairs of the city.[69] A recently discovered ossuary identifies Caiaphas as the High Priest who presided over the Sanhedrin when it condemned Jesus, just as the Gospels and Josephus maintained. An inscription found in Caesarea Maritima in 1961 identifies Pontius Pilate as governor of Judea precisely when the New Testament places him there. Moreover, accounts both by the Jewish historian Josephus and the Jewish philosopher Philo characterize Pilate as the callous figure depicted in scripture.[70]

As a final example, Acts 18:2 tells that Paul met Aquila and his wife, Priscilla, in Corinth and that this couple had recently come from Rome because the Emperor Claudius had "*ordered all the Jews to leave.*" The Roman historian Suetonius had this to say in his section on Claudius (who ruled from 41 to 54 CE): "Because the Jews of Rome caused continuous disturbances at the instigation of Chrestus, he expelled them from the city."[71] "Chrestus" is "a slight misspelling of 'Christos,' the Greek word that translates into the Hebrew 'Messiah.' "[72] Whether rioting among Rome's Jews involved their attacks on some early Christian activity, or whether this was merely inferred by Suetonius (who was writing about a century later), cannot be determined. The account in Acts is confirmed either way.[73]

Over and above these many specific proofs of accuracy is the more general aspect, made so effectively by the great Harvard scholar Henry J. Cadbury (1883–1974). Referring to Acts he wrote: "In itself it often carries its own evidence of accuracy, of intelligent grasp of its theme, of fullness of information. Its stories are not thin and colorless but packed with variety and substance."[74] However, even though the New Testament has the proper feel for the places and the people of its time and it is quite reliable as to geography, topography, and Roman and Jewish history, that does not mean, of course, that it is accurate as to the life of Jesus. But it does mean that efforts by Conzelmann and other "critical" scholars to disparage the Gospels as nothing but ahistorical fantasies are themselves revealed as wishful thinking. As for the accounts of Christ's ministry, at least Paul's letters were written and the early Gospels appeared while eyewitnesses still lived.

Transmission

There has been much controversy as to when various books of the New Testament were written. To this outsider, it appears that the majority opinion as to when the Gospels were written and the order of their appearance rests on nothing more substantial than that is it the majority view,[75] for the persuasive analyses are offered by a few recent writers who urge much earlier dates.[76] Nearly everyone agrees that Paul's letters were written during the 50s. The majority view takes Mark as the earliest Gospel, dating from about 70 CE, and proposes that Matthew and Luke appeared about ten years later. The two later Gospels are thought to have been based substantially on Mark, augmented with material taken from other sources. These three Gospels are very similar, which is why they are referred to as the "Synoptic" (or "look-alike") Gospels. They also contain some differences and contradictions, which have given rise to an enormous academic industry to deal with the "Synoptic Problem," which is: how can we possibly resolve these conflicts? The whole undertaking seems exceedingly overdone, even overwrought, unless one is seeking either to defend the absolute inerrancy of scripture or to advance radical skepticism, these points having been brilliantly demonstrated by Eta Linnemann.[77]

The Gospel of John is generally thought to have been written later than the other three and is dated around 90 CE.[78] Because it departs quite substantially from the Synoptic Gospels, many scholars have long dismissed it as mere affirmation of a later "orthodox" faith. However, John A. T. Robinson (1919–1983), the remarkable son of another famous Bible scholar,[79] not only regarded it as much the superior work, but argued brilliantly in favor of the less popular view that John predates the Synoptic Gospels.[80] Robinson noted that if John had been written as late as is typically assumed, one must wonder why it is infused with fear of and antagonism toward the Jews at a time when the Roman authorities had long since become the primary persecutors. This "problem" evaporates if one dates John to the period immediately following the Crucifixion, when it was the Sanhedrin, not the Romans, who were the primary threat: Paul confessed[81] that prior to his conversion in about 35 CE, he delivered Christians to the "high priest and council of elders" for punishment, and Stephen was stoned to death in about the year 37. Such a redating also fits exceedingly well with the general depiction of the social environment found in John, including the apparent lack of knowledge that Jerusalem had been destroyed by the Romans in the year 70 CE—John seems to assume that many places were currently existing that were razed by the Romans. Indeed, John displays far more detailed and accurate information about the city of Jerusalem than do the other three Gospels, which suggests he lived there (and before 70 CE).[82] Of additional importance is that John gives a far more likely account of the timing of the Crucifixion vis-à-vis the Passover, which also suggests he had first-hand knowledge.[83] The same can be said for the fact that John reports that Jesus's ministry lasted at least two and perhaps as long as three years, while the Synoptic Gospels limit his ministry to a year. As the very respected D. Moody Smith asked, "Did Jesus gather disciples, teach, gain fame as a miracle worker, and arouse opposition that led to his death in less than a year?" He answered, "Possibly, but the ... longer (Johnnine) time frame makes considerable sense."[84] This, too, suggests that John is better informed and that the author may have been an eyewitness, as he claims to have been (John 21:24).

Leaving aside the debate as to when John was written, many scholars have begun to recognize an abundance of evidence suggesting that the Synoptic Gospels also were written at an earlier date than has been allowed. One strong basis for dating the Synoptic Gospels earlier than the 70s and 80s is, as both Gerd Theissen and Richard Bauckham have noted,[85] the very frequent use of "protective anonymity" in many passages reporting actions that might have exposed the actors to prosecution had they been identified.[86] There are large numbers of people scattered through the Gospels who seem sufficiently significant to have been named, but who are not, such as the woman who anointed Jesus (Mark 14:3–9) and the man who took up a sword and wounded one of those who came to seize Jesus at Gethsemane (Mark 14:47). This frequent resort to anonymity suggests that the Gospels were written at a sufficiently early date that these people were alive and still at risk.

A second basis is that a number of very distinguished scholars recently have made a compelling case that most or all of the Gospels, including John, were originally written in Hebrew and predate or are contemporaneous with Paul's letters! Those who made this case include the Sorbonne's remarkable Claude Tresmontant[87] (1927–1997); Jean

Carmignac[88] (1914–1986), the celebrated translator of Dead Sea Scrolls; and Robert L. Lindsey [89] (1917–1995), founder of the Jerusalem School for the Study of the Synoptic Gospels. Their claim also is consistent with the earliest reports as to the origins of the Gospels. Thus, Irenaeus (c. 115–202) was quoted by Eusebius (c. 260–339): "Matthew published a Gospel in writing also, among the Hebrews in their own language, while Peter and Paul were preaching the Gospel and founding the church in Rome. But after their decease Mark, the disciple and interpreter of Peter—he also transmitted to us in writing the things which Peter used to preach."[90] Carmignac noted that seven other early Church fathers also reported that Matthew wrote his Gospel in Hebrew, while Eusebius quoted both Clement and Papias as reporting that Mark wrote his Gospel with Peter's help.[91] Why was such uniform and seemingly trustworthy testimony rejected? Partly because so many modern academics take the view that *no* ancient sources are trustworthy, and also because the earliest copies of the Gospels that have survived are in Greek, ergo that's the language in which they were written. But these copies date from the second and third century! To someone having no career interests in the matter, it strikes me that the case for the Gospels having been written in Hebrew is overwhelming.

Tresmontant's work rests on remarkable linguistic analyses, as well as common sense. Is it credible, he asked, that those who regularly heard Jesus preach never made any notes? Literacy was widespread in this time and place, and many of the apostles could read and write. Consider, too, that the words of many Old Testament prophets, including Amos, Hosea, Isaiah, and Jeremiah, were taken down by their listeners—surely this establishes a tradition. Indeed, would literate men who believed they were listening to the Son of God not have bothered to record anything he said or did? Tresmontant dismissed this possibility as "simply absurd."[92]

He also made a persuasive case that they would have written their notes in Hebrew. Tresmontant's triumph is to show that there are many unmistakable signs in the Greek versions of the Gospels that they have been *translated from* Hebrew—presumably so they could be read by Gentiles and by the Jews of the Diaspora, the latter having so lost their Hebrew that they depended on Greek translations of the Hebrew Bible. Indeed, the translated Hebrew Bible—the Septuagint—offers strong evidence as to the original language of the Gospels. Hebrew and Greek differ greatly in many respects, particularly in preferred word order—no one could mistake the one order for the other. Indeed, as Robert Lindsey pointed out, no writer proficient in Greek ever wrote Greek with a Hebrew word order—these differences pose a very major difficulty for any translator.[93] But those who translated the Old Testament into Greek to create the Septuagint were very careful to render the Greek strictly in accord with Hebrew word order—presumably because these were sacred texts and should be preserved as fully as possible. Precisely the same thing is true of the Gospels. The surviving Greek copies are very easily translated into Hebrew without any need to alter the word order—like the Septuagint, the word order already is Hebraic. In addition, a lexicon composed of Greek words selected to translate specific words in the translation of the Hebrew Bible is followed in the Gospels. That is, of several Greek terms that might have been used for a given Hebrew term, only the one already chosen by the translators of the Septuagint is used. Finally, the Gospels contain many idioms that "are peculiar to the Hebrew language"[94] and would never have been used by someone writing in Greek, but only by a careful translator.

If the Gospels were written in Hebrew, that would support a date for the original documents substantially earlier than the current "consensus" accepts. In fact, it encourages the view that the originals may well have been written during and immediately after Jesus's ministry by eyewitnesses— that Peter may very well have been involved in the composition of Mark, just as the early Church fathers believed. Indeed, several leading scholars argue that there is overwhelming internal evidence that Peter was the source of Mark.[95] If so, there remains little basis for claims that major problems of transmission occurred.

In fact, even if we accept the conventional dates for the Gospels and agree that they were not written by men who actually knew Jesus, the authors would have had access to people who had known him. Followers of Jesus who were in their twenties at the time of the Crucifixion would only have been in their sixties in the seventh decade CE.

Even most scholars primarily concerned with debunking the Gospels have accepted the idea that the Gospel writers must have drawn upon written source material. Predictably, they have turned the search for sources into an effort to further discredit scripture by postulating the existence of a hypothetical book containing some sayings attributed to Jesus, and

which is referred to as Q (from the German *Quelle*, "source").[96] Efforts to
reconstruct Q have gone on since the middle of the nineteenth century
and still constitute "a considerable industry."[97] A leading proponent of
the Q thesis is Burton Mack, the John Wesley Professor of Early Christianity at the Claremont School of Theology until his recent retirement. Mack
has published *The Lost Gospel: The Book of Q and Christian Origins*, in
which he provides a rendition of Q. According to Mack, Jesus actually
spoke only a few of the sayings attributed to him in the Gospels, and he
was neither a prophet nor a savior. It was not until long after his death
that groups "in northern Syria and Asia Minor" began to formulate "the
Christ cult," drawing heavily on Greek mythology. In contrast, the people
who heard Jesus and who recorded his sayings in Q, "were not Christians.
They did not think of Jesus as a messiah or the Christ. . . . They did not
regard his death as a divine, tragic, or saving event. And they did not
imagine that he had been raised from the dead. . . . Instead, they thought
of him as a teacher whose teachings made it possible to live with verve in
troubled times. They did not gather to worship in his name . . ."[98] Thus,
Mack dismisses the whole New Testament as an obvious work of fiction,
and thinks its only value is in having preserved a few authentic sayings of
Jesus. That said, Mack enthusiastically concludes: "It's over. We've had
enough apocalypses. We've had enough martyrs. Christianity has had a
two-thousand year run, and it's over."[99] Similar attitudes have animated
the highly publicized Jesus Seminar, whose members (Mack among
them) have been meeting annually to winnow the Gospels for sayings
that can be assigned to Q—their approved list becoming ever shorter and
more trivial. Fortunately, more objective scholars have begun to reject the
whole Q enterprise as misguided and futile.[100]

In summary: there are no compelling reasons to believe that "problems" of transmission distorted the Gospels. They may have been written
by actual participants in the events in question, and if not, the Gospels
certainly met the approval of such eyewitnesses. Hence, the reliability of
the Gospels really comes down to a question of truthfulness.

Falsification

Efforts to dismiss the New Testament as fraudulent occupied a number of scholars in Germany during the nineteenth century, led by Bruno
Bauer and his followers in the Tübingen School. Bauer first gained fame

for denying the historical existence of Jesus, and his tactic for discrediting the New Testament was to redate the Gospels as not having been written until well into the second century. If that were true, then they all could be revealed as inauthentic forgeries written to promote the authority of the clique that eventually came to rule the Church. In fact, Bauer could muster no significant evidence for his redating, and no qualified scholar accepts his views today, but the redating was popular because it suited the antireligious sentiments that dominated German and Dutch intellectuals during this period.[101] Indeed, once Bauer's attacks were discredited, the prominent German scholars simply shifted to other grounds for rejecting Christian scriptures as falsifications—as in the work of Rudolph Bultmann and Hans Conzelmann.

Such critics benefit from the fact that it is extremely difficult to prove a negative, to show that from early days scribes making copies of scriptures *did not* make changes to "enhance" the scriptures in various ways, either on their own or at the direction of those in charge of the Church. These critics also gain credibility from the fact that there *are* a substantial number of ancient writings that claim to be Gospels and that are obvious fakes and forgeries—the pile of so-called Gnostic and Apocryphal writings that were quite properly excluded from the New Testament. However, in logic as in law, the burden of proof must rest on those claiming that falsifications took place. To claim, for example, that Paul did not write the letters attributed to him requires some reasonable evidence, not mere assertion. Unfortunately, it has been possible to sell tens of millions of copies of a book that rests on an alleged falsification of the Christ story and the conspiracy that sustains it, based on nothing but bizarre fantasies that differ from those offered by the Tübingen School only by being more interesting. Thus, it seems useful to summarize here the evidence that the scriptures that have come down to us are exceedingly faithful renditions of versions dating from earliest days.

Compared with the most famous literary works from the same period, such as Julius Caesar's *The Gallic War* or Tacitus's *Histories*, we have many more and far older manuscripts of the New Testament.[102] The oldest known copy of Caesar's classic dates from about 900 CE, as does the oldest copy of Tacitus. Even so, no one supposes that they have been tampered with or that Caesar actually lost in Gaul. In comparison, many surviving papyrus copies of most of the New Testament date from the second and third centuries CE.[103] In addition, many writings by early Church fathers dating from as early at 96 CE include extensive quotations from most books of the New Testament. Assessing these and many other early New Testament manuscripts, Sir Frederic Kenyon (1863–1952), longtime director of the British Museum, explained that the interval "between the dates of the original composition and the earliest extant evidence [is] so small as to be in fact negligible and . . . any doubt that the Scriptures have come down to us substantially as they were written has now been removed. Both the *authenticity* and the *general integrity* of the books of the New Testament may be regarded as finally established."[104]

It turns out that at present, the major concern about scriptural transmission involves what is known as "Textual Criticism" and has to do partly with minor copyist errors, but mainly with claims of mistranslation.[105] Even were these major matters, they are known only by reference to older copies and/or the "original" Greek. That is, scholars can rant and rave over how a word or phrase *should* be rendered in English (or whatever the language in question), but *only* in comparison with a surviving Greek edition. Such are not transmission errors; indeed, they often have

A nearly complete copy of the Acts of the Apostles written sometime during the fifth century is one of many ancient copies of the New Testament that have survived. It is kept in the Pierpont Morgan Library in New York City. (The Pierpont Morgan Library, New York; Photo: The Pierpont Morgan Library, NY/Art Resource, New York)

far more to do with interpretation than translation, that is to say, with theology than with language.

The conclusion of this section: at the very least, the New Testament provides a truthful and reliable account of what the first generation of Christians believed to have taken place.

THE CHRISTIAN HOLY FAMILY

In previous chapters we have seen that, without exception, the founders of significant religions have begun by converting members of their immediate circle of relatives and friends. Contrary to the traditional teaching, but fully in keeping with the comments by Paul and many early Church fathers, the same applies to Jesus. Matthew (13:55–56) and Mark (6:3 and 15:40–47) both report that Jesus had four brothers (named James, Joses, Judas, and Simon according to Mark) and an unknown number of sisters. Paul (1 Corinthians 9:5) asked: "*Do we not have the right to be accompanied by a wife, as the other apostles and the brothers of the Lord and Cephas?*" The clear implication here is that the Lord's brothers traveled with Jesus. This is supported by John 7:3, wherein Jesus's brothers urge him to go to Judea "that your disciples may see the works you are doing." This prompted R. E. Brown to comment that "it is curious to find the 'brothers' of Jesus following him along with his mother and disciples."[106] Jesus's uncle Cleopas also was one of the disciples, although not one of the twelve.[107] Not only did the family often travel with Jesus, they were counted as equal to the apostles and remained well known and active in the early Church.[108] Indeed, according to Clement of Alexandria (c. 160–215), following the Ascension, none of the apostles claimed leadership of the Church, but deferred to the Lord's brother, "James the Righteous."[109] As mentioned, Josephus also identified James as the brother of Jesus and head of the Church until his execution in 62 CE.

As for the famous denial of his family by Jesus as reported in Mark 3:33, the early Church father Tertullian dismissed it as a misinterpretation. When told that "*Your mother and your brothers are outside, asking for you,*" Jesus is quoted as responding, "*Who are my mother and my brothers?*" Then, gesturing to those who sat listening to him, Jesus added, "*Here are my mother and my brothers! Whoever does the will of God is my brother, and sister, and mother.*" Tertullian explained that Jesus used this device to stress the kinship of faith, not to deny family feelings.[110] In addition, Origen (c. 185–251) dismissed as figurative the claim that "a prophet is not without honor, except in his own country, and among his own kin." If taken literally and generally, Origen noted, "it is not historically true," citing the many prophets of the Old Testament who were honored in their local communities. "But," he continued, "figuratively interpreted, it is absolutely true for we must think of Judea as their country, and . . . Israel as their kindred."[111] He then pointed out how different the history of Israel would have been had their "country" truly honored the prophets.

Although Jesus's family was prominent in the early Church, they soon went into eclipse because of the developing tradition that not only was Mary a virgin when she bore Jesus, but that she remained one for life. As this doctrine of the perpetual virginity of Mary emerged, the brothers and sisters of Jesus were at first transformed into cousins and eventually ignored altogether. Blood relations are unnecessary in order to constitute a Christian "holy family." All that is needed is that there have existed a close primary group around Jesus for him to recruit as early followers. And there was.

PAUL AND THE MISSION TO THE JEWS

Paul is regarded as such a towering figure in the rise of Christianity that some have claimed that he "invented" Christianity or that his letters provided the basis for the development of a "Christ cult" early in the second century.[112] Such claims ignore the obvious: Paul was surrounded by people who actually had known Jesus and who already were worshipping him as Christ,[113] which is what Paul had intended to punish Jews for doing in Damascus. In any event, unlike the historical Jesus, far less mystery surrounds the historical Paul.

There were five major components to Paul's identity. First, he was raised as a highly committed Jew, who probably became a Pharisee.[114] Acts 22:3–5 reports:

I am a Jew, born in Tarsus in Cili'cia, but brought up in this city [probably Jerusalem][115] *at the feet of Gama'li-el [a prominent Rabbi], educated according to the strict manner of the law of our fathers, being zealous for God as you all are this day. I persecuted this Way [Christianity] to the death, binding and delivering to prison both men and women, as the high priest and the whole council of elders bear me witness. From them I received letters to the brethren, and I journeyed to Damascus to take those also who were there and bring them in bonds to Jerusalem to be punished.*

Second, Paul was immersed in Hellenic culture. His everyday language was Greek, and he "must have had a good Hellenistic education" because he wrote first-rate Greek. His "letters—with their skillful rhetoric, careful composition, and elaborate theological argumentation—reflect an author who was in every way uniquely equipped to become the 'apostle to the Gentiles.' "[116] Third, his facilty in Greek is consistent with claims that Paul came from a quite privileged background.[117] Indeed, he was chosen by the Jewish priestly establishment to persecute Christians. Fourth, and also reflective of his upper-class background, Paul was a Roman citizen. This gave him a somewhat unusual standing and special privileges—he could not be tried in local courts, but only in Rome, a right that the Romans ultimately observed. Finally, of course, Paul was a Christian and spent most of his mature years surrounded by other Christians.

Following his conversion on the road to Damascus in about the year 35 BCE, Paul seems to have immediately begun to missionize on behalf of his new faith. First he went to Arabia, then to Syria and Cilicia, and then probably back to Damascus, with what results we don't know—these years in Paul's life are referred to by some scholars as the "hidden period." Then, in about the year 48 or 49, Paul went to Antioch, launching his mission in the West.

Even though Paul defined his mission to the West as focused on Gentiles, it is worthwhile to look more closely at *where* he went and *with whom* he associated when he got there. As noted in Chapter 4, in this era there were millions more Jews living in Diasporan communities around the Mediterranean than inhabited Palestine. Of the six major Greco-Roman cities missionized by Paul, four had large Jewish settlements, including Antioch and Corinth, the cities in which he spent by far the greatest amount of his time.[118] Moreover, it appears as though nearly all of Paul's missionary efforts took place among the Jews in these communities. As reported in Acts, Paul and his fellow missionaries "almost unfailingly go first to the Jewish synagogue and find opportunities to speak and debate at regular sabbath services."[119] In addition, most of his entourage was Jewish, he was welcomed by Jews, and most of those greeted in his letters seem to have been Jews. Having noted these facts, Wayne Meeks then reverted to tradition by pointing out that "the pattern of beginning always in synagogues accords ill with Paul's own declaration that he saw his mission as primarily or even exclusively to the Gentiles," and went on to suggest that "these statements are not to be taken absolutely."[120] But why not?

Put yourself in Paul's place. You have decided to lead a band of missionaries west from Jerusalem to spread the word. But where in the West? Who will receive you? The answer would have seemed obvious: you should go to your relatives, friends, and friends of friends in the Diasporan Jewish communities, for these are people to whom you can gain introductions and who are accustomed to visits by religious teachers from Jerusalem. So, Paul stayed in the homes of Jews and preached in Jewish homes and in the synagogues, none of these being places where he could have expected to encounter many Gentiles. In addition, if Paul really had devoted his efforts to the Gentiles, why did he continue to receive so many severe beatings (plus a stoning) from Jews?[121] Surely he would have been ignored by Diasporan Jewish leaders had he kept to Gentile circles. Perhaps, too, he would have been ignored had his arrival been little noticed and had his presence been less remarkable.

But that's not how it was. "Paul's missionary work . . . should not be thought of as the humble efforts of a lonely missionary. Rather, it was a well-planned, large-scale organization . . ."[122] He typically began a visit to a new community by holding "privately organized meetings under the patronage of eminent persons . . . who provided him with . . . an audience composed of their dependents."[123] Paul did not travel alone, but often took a retinue of as many as forty or fifty followers with him, sufficient to constitute an initial "congregation"[124] which made it possible to hold credible worship services immediately and to welcome and form bonds with newcomers. Among Paul's entourage there undoubtedly were scribes, as was typical in this day before typewriters, printing, or copy machines—most of the prolific early Church fathers had remarkably large staffs to write down and copy their words.[125] We even know the name of one of Paul's scribes since he revealed himself at the end of Romans (16:22). Paul was not content to merely appear in local synagogues to present his views, he took his mobile congregation along, probably including an admixture of

Gentile converts (there having already been Christian groups in most of these cities before Paul's visits). That puts his beatings by local Jews in a somewhat different perspective.

Chapter 4 detailed the many ways in which the Jews of the Diaspora were ripe for conversion to a faith that allowed them to retain most of their religious capital while freeing them from many of the "ethnic" limitations of Judaism. The entire Hebrew Bible was retained by the Christians, Jesus was presented as the promised messiah, and Christian services were modeled on the familiar routines of the synagogue. The only major innovation was to cease strict observance of the Law. It often has been noted how that eased conversion for Gentiles who could enter the new faith without being subject to such things as adult circumcision or encountering barriers against dining with their friends and relatives. But much too little has been made of the immense appeal this would have had for Hellenized Jews who were chafing under the Law's social limitations. Thus, despite the emphasis on missionizing the Gentiles, Paul's efforts may well have actually more often brought in Jewish converts. True enough, Paul's relaxation of the Law created a profound gap between Christianity and orthodox Judaism. But, as a practical matter, devoutly orthodox Jews were not going to convert to Christianity anyway. Which is why Palestine was not a rewarding mission area. Rather, as Nock explained, it was Hellenized Jews "who had lost their traditional piety . . . [who] were receptive of new convictions."[126]

Perhaps an even more significant question concerning Paul's missionary work is this: did his activities really play a direct, significant role in founding Christian congregations, whether they were made up largely of Hellenized Jews or of Gentiles? Keep in mind that before Paul arrived, there already were Christian congregations functioning in some of the cities he missionized, including Antioch and Corinth, as well as in some other cities of the Empire that he did not missionize, including Rome and Alexandria. Clearly, then, there were other effective Christian missionaries at work, as is supported by Paul's frequent complaints about interloping competitors—in addition to all of the rank-and-file Christians who were busy spreading their faith. Elsewhere I have analyzed quantitative data based on the larger Greco-Roman cities, including those missionized by Paul, and found that his missionizing had no independent effect on whether or not a city had a Christian congregation by the year

100. In contrast, the presence of a Diasporan Jewish community had a huge effect on the formation of Christian congregations.[127]

Thus it appears that Paul's missionizing role may have been considerably overplayed, partly because we know so much about it from his letters and Acts, while we do not even know the names of those "competitors" of whom he complained. But the major basis for error probably is that his importance as a missionary has been inferred from his immense theological importance. He did, after all, write much of the New Testament. But Paul may have been far more important as a trainer, organizer, and motivator of missionaries than as an actual founder of congregations.

CHRISTIANIZING THE EMPIRE

It is agreed that by 350 CE the Christian population of the Empire had grown very large.[128] As Lucian the Martyr put it early in the fourth century: "Almost the greater part of the world is now committed to this truth, even whole cities."[129] This probably was too optimistic if applied to the Empire as a whole (especially to the rural areas), but there is no disputing that Christians were everywhere and numbered many millions. At issue is how this was achieved: was Christianization the result of a relatively *constant rate* of growth as social scientists would expect, or was it produced by a *series of leaps* caused by mass conversions, as many historians and Bible scholars assume?

On Mass Conversions

Mass conversions are described in Acts and are ratified by many historians. For example, Acts 2:37–42 reports a sermon by Peter in Jerusalem on Pentecost after which "three thousand souls" came forward and were baptized. Even so, the result would not have been three thousand converts, only three thousand wet Jews and pagans. One sermon, no matter how dynamic, does not prompt the fundamental shift of identity essential to a religious conversion; even after being baptized there would have been a great deal of educating and socializing still to be done before any of these three thousand listeners could have been claimed as a Christian. The same points apply to Eusebius's report that the early Christian missionaries were so empowered by the "divine Spirit" that "at the first hearing whole multitudes in a body eagerly embraced in their souls piety towards the creator of the universe."[130]

Granted that the illustrious Adolf von Harnack (1851–1930) confirmed claims of mass conversions by quoting Augustine to the effect that the growth of the early Church was so rapid that "Christianity must have reproduced itself by means of miracles, for the greatest miracle of all would have been the extraordinary extension of the religion apart from any miracles."[131] And even the distinguished Ramsay MacMullen accepted that only "successes en masse"[132] could produce sufficiently rapid growth to meet the total number achieved in the time allowed. Nevertheless, modern social science rejects the possibility of mass conversions.

First of all, no one who has studied conversion has seen even one normal[133] person join up spontaneously immediately following initial exposure to a group's message. Recall that sociological studies have found that doctrine plays a very secondary role in conversion, that people convert when their social ties to members of a religious group outweigh their ties to nonmembers. But even people having strong social ties to a group take their time about converting and usually do so only after considerable introspection, playing an active role in "converting themselves."[134] As for conversions taking the form of "mass hysteria," "herd instincts," "mob psychology," "collective madness," or what Freud described as "psychical epidemics, of historical mass convulsions,"[135] the fact is that social scientists have relegated all such terms, and the behavior they postulate, to the dustbin of useless concepts.[136] Fully in keeping with this development is the fact that no one can cite any reliable historical cases of mass conversions. Most instances that have been offered as examples turn out to be revivals, not conversions. When the magnificent eighteenth-century evangelist George Whitefield caused Boston crowds to writhe upon the ground and beg their souls' forgiveness, he was not asking them to change their religious identity, merely to intensify their commitment. The Bostonians had been Christians when Whitefield arrived and were Christians when he left. Of even less relevance are the "mass conversions" of whole societies to Islam produced by treaty or conquest. As will be seen in Chapter 8, no change of heart was involved, and it often was centuries before most individuals in these societies actually embraced Islam, and when they did so it was through normal network processes.[137]

Finally, von Harnack, MacMullen, and all the rest erred in thinking the speed at which Christianity spread necessitated mass conversions. As is about to be seen, the Christianization of the Empire could easily have been achieved by an arithmetic of growth that is entirely compatible with the normal processes of network conversion.

Modeling Overall Growth

What follows is primarily an exercise in the arithmetic of the possible and plausible. Given realistic assumptions, how large *could* the Christian population of the Empire have become within various time limits? Projections of Christian growth require only an estimate of the total number of Christians at some specific time and an assumed rate of subsequent growth. The results can be tested against whatever independent estimates of the Christian population are available for various times.

Although Origen remarked, "Let it be granted that Christians were very few in the beginning,"[138] no one knows how many Christians there were in the early days. Paul claimed that following the Resurrection, Jesus appeared "*to more than five hundred brethren*," but it is hard to know whether that was meant as a real number or was a way to say "many."[139] Citing several of Paul's letters, Howard Clark Kee warned that "the gatherings of Christians took place in private homes . . . [which] suggests that participants in the Jesus movement in Gentile cities during the first generation numbered in the dozens, or scores at most."[140] Let us then be conservative, and assume there were 1,000 active Christians in the year 40. If so, at what rate would Christianity need to have grown in order for their number to have become as large as many historians estimate it to have been by the beginning of the fourth century? Approximately 3.4 percent per year. Projections based on a starting point of 1,000 Christians and this rate of growth are shown in Table 7–1 below.[141]

Notice that the growth is very slow in the beginning. By the year 150 there still aren't quite 40,000 Christians, which is in close accord with Robert L. Wilken's estimate that there were "less than fifty thousand Christians" at this time.[142] Even by the year 250 there are only slightly more than one million Christians, or 1.9 percent of the imperial population. This, too, matches an estimate by a distinguished historian—Robin Lane Fox proposed that Christians made up 2 percent of the population in 250.[143] During the next fifty years, the number shoots up dramatically,

Table 7–1: Christian Growth Projected at an Annual Rate of 3.4 Percent

YEAR	NUMBER OF CHRISTIANS	PERCENT OF POPULATION*
40	1,000	—
50	1,397	—
100	7,434	—
150	39,560	0.07
180	107,863	0.18
200	210,516	0.35
250	1,120,246	1.9
300	5,961,290	9.9
312	8,904,032	14.8
350	31,722,489	52.9

*Based on an estimated imperial population of 60 million[144]

and by the year 300 reaches slightly fewer than six million—this, too, is consistent with estimates made by many historians.[145] In 312, the year of Constantine's conversion, these projections show nearly nine million Christians, making up about 15 percent of the population.

When the projection is extended to the year 350, this rate of increase projects that 31.7 million (or about 53 percent of the population) had become Christians. No one would argue that the Christian population was larger than this in 350, and most would argue that it was rather smaller at that time,[146] which would be in keeping with the obvious principle that as the pool of potential recruits diminishes, at some point a rate of growth must slow down as well. But even if there were 31.7 million Christians in 350, these projections show that there need not have been anything miraculous about Christian growth. Rather, many contemporary religious bodies, including the Jehovah's Witnesses, the Mormons, and the Pentecostals, have sustained well-documented growth rates as high as or higher than 3.4 percent a year for many decades. As for objections that there were far more than a thousand Christians in the year 40,[147] if there were more, then the needed rate of growth would have been substantially lower. For example, had there been 10,000 Christians in the year 40, a rate of growth of only 2.5 percent would have sufficed. Thus, there was plenty of time for Christianity to achieve its growth by way of the conventional network process.

Even though these projections are hypothetical, they so closely match several bodies of actual data that they must be granted considerable credibility. For example, the projections agree very closely with estimates made by Roger S. Bagnall of the percent of Christians in the population from the year 239 though 315 based on an analysis of the percentage of Christian names among those appearing in Egyptian documents.[148] A second basis of comparison is even more compelling. Carlos R. Galvao-Sobrinho[149] has published data on the number of Christian epigraphs appearing on gravestones in the city of Rome, broken down into twenty-five-year groupings.[150] A time series analysis using the Roman data and the projections of the Christian population of the Empire, beginning in the year 200 and ending at 375, resulted in an incredibly close matchup. As can be seen in the graphed Z-scores shown in Figure 7–1, the two curves are virtually identical and produce an almost perfect correlation of .996.

It should be noted that, of course, this curve could not have kept rising indefinitely, and it soon must have decelerated as the number of potential converts declined. Furthermore, not only is it impossible to convert more than 100 percent of a population, in this instance significant numbers of

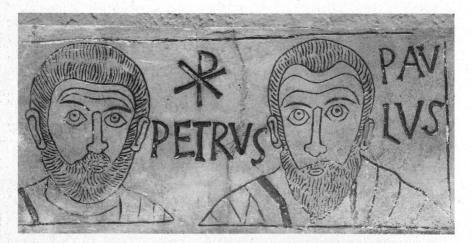

Images of the Apostles Peter and Paul incised on the tomb of a Roman child reveal that hers was a Christian family. The date (not shown) on this and similar gravestones made it possible to graph the increasing proportion of Christians in Rome. (Vatican Museum, Vatican State; Photo: Erich Lessing/Art Resource, New York)

Figure 7–1: Christian Epigraphs in Rome and Membership Projections

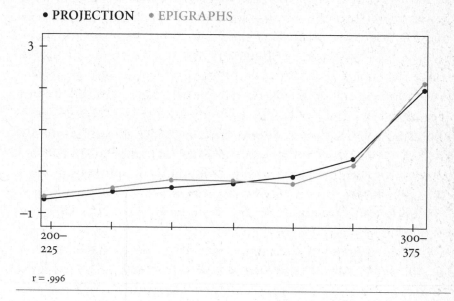

Z SCORES

• PROJECTION • EPIGRAPHS

r = .996

residents of the Empire never converted to Christianity. Many Jews did not; organized paganism lingered for centuries; and many people in rural areas seem never to have gone beyond merely adding Jesus to their pantheon of Gods. Consequently, the complete conversion curve would resemble the S-shaped or sigmoid curve that has been found to so typically apply to the diffusion of various phenomena through a population.[151]

Urban Christians

Although Jesus preached in the villages and from the hillsides in Galilee, within twenty years after the Crucifixion, early Christianity had become overwhelmingly an urban movement. Paul's missionary journeys took him to major cities such as Antioch, Corinth, and Athens, with occasional visits to smaller communities such as Iconium and Laodicea, but no mention is made of him ever preaching in the countryside. In fact, it was several centuries before the Christians devoted much effort to converting the rural peasantry. By then, of course, many rural people had been Christianized by friends and neighbors who had returned from a sojourn in a city where they had become Christians. However, for the first several centuries, it is important to assess the Christian growth curve as heavily weighted to the cities, for that fact maximized the visibility as well as the local impact of Christian communities. Both factors would have been enhanced by the intense congregational nature of Christianity—whatever their numbers, they gathered regularly and coordinated their participation in civic life. I have made this point in several previous publications, but without calculating more fully illuminating statistics.

Table 7–2 ends this neglect. Keep in mind, however, that these membership statistics for various cities in 180 and again in 250 and 300 are *only illustrative*, and are far less trustworthy than the overall growth curve. I have limited the calculations to only some of the more important cities, all of which had well-established Christian congregations by the year 100.[152] To avoid giving a false impression of precision, the totals have been rounded.

The following assumptions were involved in these calculations. First, that the population of the Empire was 60 million and remained stable

Table 7–2: Estimated Christian Population of Cities in Various Years

	180	250	300
Rome (450,000)*	11,000	84,000	295,000
Alexandria (250,000)	6,000	47,000	163,000
Antioch (100,000)	2,400	19,000	65,000
Athens (75,000)	1,800	14,000	49,000
Corinth (50,000)	1,200	9,000	33,000

*Estimated total population.[153]

during this time. Second, that about 3 million Greco-Romans (5 percent), lived in urban places. Then, by dividing the estimated population of a city by 3 million, its percentage of the urban population was calculated. Third, in early days when the Church was small, it was far more exclusively urban than later when the Church had grown large. Consequently, for the year 180 I assumed that two-thirds of Christians were urbanites. For the year 250, I cut this to half, and by 300 I assumed that about one-third of Christians were urbanites. Having thus estimated the total urban Christian population at three different times, Christians were parceled out to each city in accord with its percentage of the urban population.

In about the year 200, the early Church father Tertullian boasted that "nearly all the citizens of the cities are Christians."[154] This was an exaggeration, but only by about a century. In the year 250, of approximately 450,000 residents of Rome, 84,000 were Christians, but by the year 300 Christians were a substantial majority in Rome as well as in these other cities. But even in 200, in these cities Christianity was not just another insignificant sect! Unlike pagans, Christians were well organized. They belonged to relatively small, intense congregations, and they may even have had their own neighborhoods. They could easily be mobilized vis-à-vis local affairs, which greatly amplified their numbers. Thus, the size and effectiveness of the Christian communities may well have been a factor in the persecution that fell upon them in 250 at the hands of Emperor Decius. Half a century later, when Christians probably did make up a majority of the residents of Rome, Emperor Diocletian renewed the persecution.

It is not too surprising that these large and rapidly growing numbers of Christians caused some emperors to fear them. What is perhaps more surprising is that it was not until Constantine that anyone recognized what powerful political support the Christians could supply. Soon thereafter, most Greco-Romans were Christians, and theirs had become the official state Church.

WHY PAGANS BECAME CHRISTIANS

It already has been established that the conversion of the pagans to Christianity was greatly facilitated by the extensive cultural continuity between classical paganism and many elements of the Christ story. Of course, similarity per se does not cause people to adopt a new religion. That also requires novelty—the new faith must offer something attractive that one's prior religion lacks. The novel aspect of Christianity, what set it apart not only from classical paganism but also from the other new "oriental" religions, was the message that *all could be saved*, and that salvation entailed an *attractive afterlife*. Salvation was not reserved for an elite, but was easily within the reach of everyone willing to "believe and be baptized." Eternal life was not reserved for monks, nuns, or intense ascetics—ordinary, worldly folks could reach heaven. Nor was eternal life conceptualized as an unconscious Nirvana, or as a dull underworld. Heaven involved a conscious, attractive, fully human existence. In addition, the promise of "going to heaven" was given immense credibility by the fact that Christians enjoyed a substantially superior quality of life here and now, a fact that was highly visible to outsiders.

Benefits of the Christian Life

Congregations not only provide participants with intense religious experiences and very satisfying emotional ties, but they also generate an immense amount of social energy. And the Christian congregations used this energy to improve the daily lives of their members. It often has been suggested that Christianity compensated people for their lives of misery by promising them a glorious life to come (often denigrated as "pie in the sky"). Possibly so, but it seems far more significant that Christianity actually made life much less miserable in the "here and now"!

A truly revolutionary aspect of Christianity lay in moral imperatives such as "loving one's neighbor as oneself," "do unto others as you would have them do unto you," "it is more blessed to give than to receive," and "when you did it to the least of my brethren, you did it unto me." These were not just slogans. Members did support orphans, widows, the elderly, and the poor; they did concern themselves with the lot of slaves. In short, Christians created "a miniature welfare state in an empire which for the most part lacked social services."[155] Consequently, according to data assembled from monuments and gravestones, Christians even lived longer than their pagan neighbors.[156] It was this *response* to the long-standing misery of life in antiquity that offered people obvious and compelling "material" reasons to convert.

The Christian capacity for good works depended in part on the ability of congregations to generate large numbers of volunteers. But the fact that from early days Christianity was an elite movement with considerable financial means was very significant, too.[157] Nevertheless, these material benefits were entirely spiritual in origin, as is evident in the inability of pagan groups to meet this challenge. In 362, when the Emperor Julian launched a campaign to revive paganism, he recognized that to do so it would be necessary to match Christian "benevolence." In a letter to a prominent pagan priest, Julian wrote: "I think that when the poor happened to be neglected and overlooked by the priests, the impious Galileans observed this and devoted themselves to benevolence. . . . [They] support not only their poor, but ours as well, everyone can see that our people lack aid from us."[158] But his challenge to the temples, to match Christian benevolence, asked the impossible. Paganism was utterly incapable of generating the commitment needed to motivate such behavior. Not only were many of its Gods and Goddesses of dubious character, they offered nothing that could motivate humans to go beyond self-interested acts of propitiation. Indeed, many pagan temples were essentially "eating clubs," where a host furnished an animal to be sacrificed to the Gods, after which the beast was cooked and eaten by his many invited guests (temples employed skilled chefs).

Perhaps nothing demonstrates these contrasts so vividly as the ways in which Christians and pagans responded when plagues struck the empire, as they did in the year 165 and again in 251. The pagan response was panic and retreat. Those who could, fled to refuge in the countryside—even Galen, the most famous physician of classical times, left Rome and stayed at his country estate until the danger passed, as did most rich people, political leaders, and even the pagan priests. Ordinary Greeks and Romans who could not flee attempted to avoid all contact with victims. Hence, when their first symptom appeared, victims were thrown into the streets by their own families to join the piles of dead and dying. But this was not how the Christians responded. Neither wealthy Christians nor the clergy fled, but took part in efforts to nurse the sick, not only their own kind, but many pagans as well. Some of those who nursed the sick lost their lives as a result. But perhaps as many as two-thirds of those who were nursed, and who would otherwise have died, lived—modern epidemiologists suggest that simply by providing food, and especially water, to plague victims, huge numbers of deaths can be averted. The fact that large numbers of Christians survived did not go unnoticed, lending immense credibility to Christian "miracle-working."[159]

But these were not the only ways in which Christianity surpassed the competition. The faith was especially appealing to women and to intellectuals.

Gender

Given the times, women played a remarkably prominent role in the early Church. The Gospels frequently report women among those traveling with Jesus,[160] and women often appear in Acts as well as in Paul's letters—frequently they are upper-class women, and they often appear in leadership roles. Thus Paul commended Phoebe to the Romans as a deaconess in the Church and his patroness.[161] In Corinth, Chloe headed a substantial household of Christians.[162] Acts reported that among converts in Thessalonica, "*not a few*" were "*leading women.*"[163] In addition, von Harnack noted that in his Epistle to the Romans, Paul sent personal greetings to fifteen women and eighteen men.[164] If, as seems most likely, in proportion to their numbers in the Roman congregation, there probably were more men than women in leadership roles, this would suggest that women made up the majority of members. Thus von Harnack concluded that "the percentage of Christian women, especially among the upper classes, was larger than that of men."[165] And the august Oxfordian Henry Chadwick agreed: "Christianity seems to have been especially successful among women. It often was through the wives that it penetrated the upper classes."[166] Why?

In a Greco-Roman world where women were severely disadvantaged and many upper-class women even were relegated to nearly complete seclusion,[167] Christianity (like the other "oriental" faiths) accorded women considerable status and an opportunity to lead. Beyond that, Christianity made life far more attractive for *all* female members.

The advantages of Christian females began at birth. Infanticide was widely practiced by Greco-Romans, and it was especially female infants who were dispatched.[168] A study of inscriptions at Delphi made it possible to reconstruct six hundred families. Of these, only six had raised more than one daughter. As would be expected, the bias against female infants showed up dramatically in the sex ratios of the imperial population. It is estimated that there were 131 males per 100 females in the city of Rome, and 140 males per 100 females elsewhere in the Empire.[169]

The advantages of Christian women continued into the teens. Roman law suggested that girls not marry until age twelve, but there were no restrictions on earlier marriage (always to a far older man). A study based on inscriptions determined that about 20 percent of pagan girls married before the age of thirteen, compared with 7 percent of Christian girls. Only a third of pagan girls married at age eighteen or older, compared with half of Christian girls.[170] Once married, pagan girls had a substantially lower life expectancy, much of the difference being due to the great prevalence of abortion, which involved barbaric methods in an age without soap, let alone antibiotics.[171] Given the very significant threat to life and the agony of the procedure, one might wonder why pagan women took such risks. They didn't do so voluntarily. It was men—husbands, lovers, and fathers—who made the decision to abort. It isn't surprising that a world that gave husbands the right to demand that infant girls be done away with would also give men the right to order their wives, mistresses, or daughters to abort. Indeed, both Plato[172] and Aristotle[173] advocated mandatory abortions to limit family size and for various other reasons.

Christian wives did not have abortions (nor did Jewish wives).[174] According to the *Didache*, a first-century manual of Church teachings, "Thou shalt not murder a child by abortion nor kill them when born."

Christian women also enjoyed very important advantages in terms of a secure marriage and family life. Although rules prohibiting divorce and remarriage evolved slowly, the earliest Church councils ruled that "twice-married" Christians could not hold church offices.[175] Like pagans, early Christians prized female chastity, but unlike pagans they rejected the double standard that gave men sexual license.[176] Christian men were urged to remain virgins until marriage, and extramarital sex was denounced as adultery. Henry Chadwick noted that Christianity "regarded unchastity in a husband as no less serious a breach of loyalty and trust than unfaithfulness in a wife."[177] However, this was not paired with opposition to marital sexual expression. Indeed, in his first letter to the *Corinthians* (7:3–5), Paul specifically advised: *"The husband should give to his wife her conjugal rights, and likewise the wife to her husband. For the wife does not rule over her own body, but the husband does; likewise the husband does not rule over his own body, but the wife does. Do not refuse one another except perhaps by agreement for a season, that you may devote yourselves to prayer; but then come together again, lest Satan tempt you through lack of self-control."*

These are some of the reasons why women were especially attracted to Christianity. And as I have pursued at length elsewhere, a major factor in the rapid growth of the early Church was that after a woman became a Christian, she often went to work at converting her husband.[178] Her task was greatly facilitated to the extent that her husband was well educated.

Intellectualism and Monotheism

Early Christianity was not only a religion of the book, it was a *theological* religion. It did not merely rely on stories, on the sermons and sayings of Jesus, or even on accounts of miracles. It stood foursquare on *general principles* concerning morality, reality, and the nature of God. Indeed, early Christianity was so deeply rooted in the formal reasoning and logic of Greek *philosophy* that there is a huge literature devoted to Christian Platonism.[179]

From earliest days, Christians directed their appeals toward the head as well as the heart, as illustrated by Paul's lecture to the philosophers in Athens. This was continued by other leading early Christian theologians, especially Justin Martyr. Justin (c. 100–165) was trained in Greek philosophy before he encountered Christianity, and converted, as he put it, "not because the teachings of Plato are different from those of Christ, but because they are not in all respects similar,"[180] and these differences are crucial. In Greek philosophy, *Logos* refers to the "rational order of the universe, an immanent natural law, a life-giving force hidden in things" to which the Stoic philosophers even were willing to apply the name "God."[181] So conceived, "God" is at best an unconscious divine essence, and Justin found this unsatisfying, opting instead to interpret Jesus as the embodiment of the *Logos*. In this and in many other ways, Justin embedded central Christian doctrines in a Platonic vocabulary. Similar theological works measuring up in terms of Greek philosophy were produced by Clement of Alexandria and Origen. But in addition to offering a philosophically sophisticated theology, Christianity appealed to the intellect by its commitment to monotheism, for by this time, polytheism had become an embarrassment in many pagan philosophical circles.

Possibly the first philosophical monotheist among the Greeks was Xenophanes (560–480 BCE), who dismissed Homer's portrayal of the Gods as immoral nonsense. Writing at the start of the remarkable sixth century BCE, which saw such an outburst of new religions and new religious ideas, Xenophanes wrote that "there is one God," and "neither in shape nor in thought [does this God] resemble mortals." As for the abundant Gods of Greek polytheism, Xenophanes noted that "men imagine gods to be born and to have raiment and voice and body, like themselves . . . [but, these are] fictions of the earlier people." He then pointed out that "oxen, lions, and horses, if they had hands wherewith to grave images, would fashion gods after their own shapes and make them bodies like their own."[182] But Xenophanes said nothing about what God was really like, except to doubt that anyone knew or could know.

Soon after Xenophanes raised the possibility that there is only one God, the great Greek playwright Aeschylus (525–456 BCE) attributed immense stature to Zeus as a Master Mind "who alone controls the outcome of events and the fulfillment of human expectations."[183] There were other Gods, but they were minor players in a universe directed by Zeus. Hence, Aeschylus could be considered "not exactly a monotheist, but as a noble heathen straining towards enlightenment that would culminate in monotheism."[184] Moreover, given that Aeschylus was not a philosopher, but a very popular playwright, it seems reasonable to suppose that he reflected a significant intellectual current. Indeed, Anaxagoras (500–428 BCE) soon postulated a single controlling Mind that rules the universe. Some have proposed this as the first instance of monotheism in Greek philosophy, but Anaxagoras failed to make it clear whether this Mind is conscious, nor did he ever refer to the Mind as God. The Mind was at best a divine essence.

As noted in the introductory chapter, one of the attractions of an impersonal conception of God is that a divine essence bears no responsibility for evil or tragedy. But, of course, that also is the fatal weakness of essences and explains why such faiths have never prevailed as a popular religion. For, of what use is a God that does nothing? Where is the comfort in a God that neither hears nor sees? Any statue is every bit as Godlike as a divine essence. Hence, given the commitment to unconscious

Gods, much of the quasi-monotheism that arose in Greek philosophy was largely irrelevant as a religious factor in antiquity[185] except as it set a tone in favor of embracing a Supreme *Being*.

Enter Plato. This immensely influential Greek philosopher (428–347 BCE) was quite willing to identify the Mind as God—one who "must be perfectly good, changeless, and the maker of the best possible world."[186] Although his God was a rather inert essence, Plato also postulated the existence of a conscious, active, lower divine being he called the *Demiurge*, who was the personification of reason. Plato proposed that it was the Demiurge, not God, who actually did the work of constructing the world. Plato viewed the Demiurge as a divine being having only limited powers, who could only construct the world from already available materials and in accord with an already-given set of ideas. In addition, the Demiurge was to blame for the existence of evil.

As subsequent Greek philosophers echoed Plato's notion of a higher and lower God, some considered the Demiurge to be the equivalent of Satan: a "fallen" lesser divinity of evil intent. This was, of course, similar to how Judaism and Christianity solved the problem of evil and, having been given a long-standing Greek philosophical blessing, the concept of one supreme God and an "evil" creator predisposed Hellenic intellectuals to accept both Christian and Jewish monotheism.

But some intellectuals interpreted the "greater and lesser God thesis" in a far more radical way. They reasoned that if the Demiurge created the world and everything in it, and if the Demiurge were responsible for evil, too, then everything on earth was hopelessly corrupt and ultra-asceticism was the only valid religious option. It was a strange amalgam of philosophy, paganism, Judaism, and Christianity. It appeared in the many forms and varieties that have come to be known collectively as Gnosticism.

GNOSTICISM: THE PAGAN RESPONSE

It wasn't only suspicious emperors or those seeking the throne who noticed the rapid growth of Christianity. Long before Christians were all that numerous, some pagan intellectuals began to perceive them as a threat, especially given the philosophical weaknesses of polytheism. The response by these pagan intellectuals was to create a species of new religious perspectives combining Plato's notions about the Demiurge with standard features of pagan mythology, to which they added major elements of the Christ story and a considerable dose of anti-Semitism. Seeking legitimacy, this new paganism was typically manifested in "secret" Gospels falsely attributed to famous figures of first-generation Christianity—Peter, James, Pilate, Judas, or Mary Magdalene, for example—or to someone claiming extraordinary status, such as Didymus Jude Thomas, Apostle of the East, and twin brother of Jesus.

These works began to appear early in the second century and straggled out for several more centuries. Although until very recently there were no known copies of these writings, we have been aware of many of them and have had lengthy extracts from some since the publication of *Against Heresies* by Irenaeus, Bishop of Lyon, in the year 180. It has long been charged by scholars that Irenaeus greatly misrepresented these "heretics," the better to discredit them, which seemed a reasonable judgment when one read the absurd views he attributed to each author. Then, late in the nineteenth century, several of these "lost Gospels" were discovered in the Middle East, and in 1945 several dozen Gnostic manuscripts were found buried in a large earthenware pot at Nag Hammadi in Egypt. Although written in Coptic during the fourth century, these were translations of Greek manuscripts, many of which had been attacked and excerpted by Irenaeus. Guess what? The good bishop had followed the original texts essentially word for word, distorting nothing, perhaps thinking that they "were so contorted and ludicrous that the heretics were best condemned out of their own mouths."[187] Even so, some scholars continue to pretend that the summaries and quotations offered by the early churchmen "are biased and apparently distort many features of gnostic religion."[188]

In addition to the amazing cache discovered at Nag Hammadi, other Gnostic scriptures have also come to light—most recently a Gospel of Judas was purchased from an antiquities dealer for a reported $1 million by the National Geographic Society and released with a huge publicity campaign in May 2006. Remarkably enough, these "lost" scriptures enjoy much greater credibility today than they ever did back when they were written. According to the prominent scholar Marvin Meyer, these newly recovered Gospels are "just as precious, and perhaps even more precious" than the texts in the New Testament.[189]

In spite of such claims, the early Church fathers were correct to dismiss these texts as ill-conceived heresies. And for all the sensational tales told recently about how these works were suppressed, it is closer to the truth to say that they were ignored and discarded. I have dealt with these matters at great length very recently.[190] Here I shall be brief.

Elaine Pagels, Princeton's well-known admirer of Gnosticism, is incensed that Bishop Irenaeus identified the authors of these Gospels as "heretics." According to Pagels, the word *heretic* "means people who make choices about what to think. Irenaeus didn't want people making choices. He wanted them to think what the bishop told them to think."[191] Although she carefully avoids the topic, presumably Pagels is willing to accept the doctrine that God is the epitome of evil and the gleeful cause of human suffering, as merely a choice, and not a heresy—for *that* is the most fundamental message of the lost Gospels!

Turning to The Secret Book of John (the most central of Gnostic "Gospels"), we learn that the world and everything in it is totally corrupt because it was created by an inferior and utterly evil, renegade Godling. This depraved creature is identified as none other than Plato's Demiurge, who has long defiled humanity in his role as the God of the Jews! In fact, most Gnostic scriptures "portray the Old Testament God as vain, ignorant, envious, and jealous—a malicious Creator who uses every means at his disposal to keep humanity from attaining true perfection."[192] Hence, the Creation is but the bizarre plaything of this Satanic rebel named *Ialtabaōth*. Jesus was not the son of this evil creature, but was a teacher, or a sage, or an inspired being who taught how an initiated elite could escape from the grasp of Ialtabaōth. Thus, Jesus is reported to have imparted the various "secrets" concerning the evil God noted above, and then, rather than instruct John to go forth and tell the nations, Jesus says: "For my part, I have told you these things, so you might write them down and transmit them secretly to those who are like you in spirit." That's why these works are called *Gnostic*—the term "refers to 'revealed knowledge' available only to those who have received secret teachings from a heavenly revealer."[193]

In addition to their strange cosmology, unlike either the New or Old Testaments, the representative Gnostic works include almost no historical or geographical content and take place in an "enchanted" setting typical of pagan "mythology." As Pheme Perkins explained, "Gnostics reject gods and religious traditions that are tied to this cosmos in any way at all! Thus, Gnostic mythology often seems devoid of ties to place or time."[194]

This is no surprise given that the authors were attempting to assimilate Christianity into paganism.

It should be obvious that these works were not excluded from the Bible because the early Church fathers were malicious dogmatists, but because they were fully aware that the Gnostic scriptures are not Christian. And the Roman authorities agreed! As Kurt Rudolph noted, the "Gnostic sects" enjoyed "complete immunity" from the Roman persecution of Christians.[195]

Unfortunately, we are far from done with the Gnostics. New manuscripts will be found (others will be quoted at length but never produced),[196] and, as with the Gospel of Judas, the press will hail each as a major find that overthrows conventional Christian doctrines. Granted, the Gospel of Judas, which claims that Jesus instructed Judas to betray him, would cause major theological revisions *if* it were accepted as part of the New Testament. But that will never happen because it bears all the disqualifying marks of its Gnostic origins, which is why Irenaeus dismissed this very same "gospel" as fiction nearly 2000 years ago. He wrote: "They declare that Judas the traitor was thoroughly acquainted with these things, and that he alone, knowing the truth as no others did, accomplished the mystery of betrayal; by him all things were thus thrown into confusion. They produce a fictitious history of this kind, which they style the Gospel of Judas."[197] Today, their modern counterparts style their fictitious histories as *Holy Blood, Holy Grail* or as *The Da Vinci Code*.

MONOPOLY AND DECLINE

Christianity was by far the most successful sect movement in history. Beginning as a tiny group at the far eastern edge of the Empire, it surged across cultural and political boundaries building a massive following as rank-and-file converts spread the faith to others. By the start of the fourth century, there were large Christian communities in most of the cities and towns. All of this took place within the highly competitive Roman religious economy, which, despite several eras of repression and persecution, energized the Christians by exposing them to serious challenges from other active faiths. It was at this point that Constantine embraced Christianity.

Constantine was not responsible for the triumph of Christianity. Rather, Christianity played a leading role in the triumph of Constantine, providing him with substantial and well-organized urban support for his struggle to gain the throne. Unfortunately, although that surely was not his intent, Constantine pointed the potent Christian sect movement down the road to laxity and negligence, the profoundly negative effects of which continue to shape European religious life even today.

Constantine does not bear all the blame for transforming Christianity from a sect to a lower tension faith (a Church), because religious movements are always somewhat moderated if they grow large enough.[198] As it became increasingly conventional to be a Christian, inevitably the movement became increasingly accommodating—less set apart, less critical of society, and requiring less intense commitment. But it would have remained a far different, more energetic, and responsible institution had it continued to operate within a pluralist religious economy. Instead, Christianity was designated as the official state religion.

Overnight Christianity became "the most favoured recipient of the near-limitless resources of imperial favour."[199] A faith that had been meeting in homes and humble structures was suddenly housed in magnificent public buildings—the new Church of Saint Peter built by Constantine in Rome was modeled on the basilican form used by imperial throne halls. A clergy recruited from the people and modestly sustained by member contributions suddenly gained immense power, status, and wealth as part of the imperial civil service. Bishops "now became grandees on a par with the wealthiest senators."[200] Consequently, in the words of Richard Fletcher, the "privileges and exemptions granted the Christian clergy precipitated a stampede into the priesthood."[201]

As Christian offices became another form of imperial preferment, they were soon filled by the sons of the aristocracy. As with the professional priesthoods in Sumer and Egypt, there was no obligation that one be morally qualified, let alone that one be "called." Gaining a Church position was mainly a matter of influence, commerce, and eventually of heredity. Simony became rife—an extensive and very expensive traffic in religious offices developed, involving not only the sale of high offices such as bishoprics but even of lowly parish placements. There soon arose great clerical families, whose sons followed their fathers, uncles, and grandfathers into holy office.[202] Indeed, women often enrolled in religious orders headed by their mothers and aunts—both men and women often entered holy orders later in life. The extent to which these families dominated the

Church is revealed by the fact that nearly 20 percent of medieval saints had another saint in their immediate family;[203] this was especially common among female saints (37 percent). The saints were, of course, the exceptions to the lack of clerical commitment. The vast majority of clergy from clerical families were more than willing to, as Adam Smith put it so well, "repos[e] themselves upon their benefices"[204] and pursue luxury and ease.

Given their monopoly situation, the privileged Christian clergy were content to recreate a Church very similar to the subsidized temple religions of the ancient civilizations, especially in terms of ignoring the religious needs of the general public. They were so lacking in energy that it took many centuries to expand the Church beyond the old boundaries of the Roman Empire, and even then the "Christanization" of the North amounted to little more than becoming the monopoly state Church, collecting the tithes, and leaving the population unmissionized.

Meanwhile, even in the old imperial areas, Christian fervor was allowed to wither. Indeed, most prominent historians of medieval religion now agree that medieval Europeans, both clergy and lay, were even less religious than is the case today. According to the eminent historian Keith Thomas, "[I]t is problematical as to whether certain sections of the population [of Britain] at this time had any religion at all."[205] Alexander Murray reported the same for medieval Italy:[206] "[S]ubstantial sections of thirteenth-century society hardly attended church at all." Even when medieval people did go to church, they often went unwillingly—often having been ordered to do so by their lord—and behaved very inappropriately while there. According to Thomas, when the common people did show up in church they often so misbehaved "as to turn the service into a travesty of what was intended. . . . Members of the population jostled for pews, nudged their neighbours, hawked and spat, knitted, made course remarks, told jokes, fell asleep, and even let off guns."[207] We know of this behavior from presentations before ecclesiastical courts and from scores of memoirs written by clergy. Court records tell of a man in Cambridgeshire who was charged with misbehaving in church in 1598 after his "most loathsome farting, striking, and scoffing speeches" had resulted in "the great offence of the good and the great rejoicing of the bad."[208] Surely no such behavior would draw cheers even from a minority in attendance at any Anglican church today.

As Europe passed out of medieval times, religious participation seems not to have improved—although statistics on religious behavior do. Some

It often is claimed that the many magnificent medieval cathedrals that exist all over Europe, like this one in Spain, prove that people must have loved the Church and been very religious back then. But Europe also is dotted with hundreds of castles. Do they prove that the people must have loved the nobility? In fact, "the people" were not consulted when either castles or cathedrals were built, they only were forced to pay for them. (Cathedral, Burgos, Spain; Photo: Vanni/Art Resource, New York)

of the most enlightening of these can be found in reports written by various Anglican bishops and archbishops following visitations to their parishes. Thus the Oxford Diocesan Visitations for 1738 report that in thirty parishes in Oxfordshire, fewer than 5 percent of the total population had taken communion in that particular year. Other visitation reports yield similarly low rates of taking communion over the remainder of the eighteenth century.[209] Were these twentieth-century statistics, they would be cited routinely as proof of widespread secularization.

Note that the communion data cited above were subsequent to the Reformation. That great upheaval in European Christianity had many consequences, but it failed to restore any meaningful religious competition. Instead, Protestant state churches replaced Catholicism in northern Europe. These, too, were fully subsidized monoplies served by a privileged clergy—albeit these Protestant churches were more subject to the whims of the state than was the Catholic Church in the south. Indeed, the Protestant establishments proved to be even less energetic and effective than the Catholics. Thus, the Protestant churches today are nearly empty while the Catholic churches in Southern Europe are only poorly attended.

Of course, most European intellectuals think it is silly to blame the low levels of religious participation in Europe on lack of competition. They note that their societies enjoy complete religious freedom, so that if there were any demand for alternatives to the state-subsidized churches, where are they? In fact, European claims to religious freedom are false. For one thing, the governments and especially the bureaucrats work hard at impeding religious competition. Elsewhere I have written at length about these European practices, including how difficult it is to get a building permit for a church or a license to hold public religious meetings in an existing structure.[210]

Fortunately, it no longer is necessary to rely on anecdotal evidence. Brian Grim and Roger Finke[211] have completed an exhaustive study of governmental practices vis-á-vis religious groups and created an index measuring the extent of government favoritism toward a single, often the official, faith. The index is not based on subjective judgments, but on official policies and practices. What Grim and Finke found is definitive, and all claims about European religious freedom simply vanish. The Grim and Finke favoritism scale varies from 0 (absolute lack of favoritism) to 10 (total favoritism) and is based on objective measures. The United States, Australia, and Taiwan score 0, meaning there is no government bias in favor of any particular religious group. In contrast, Afghanistan, where anyone who converts from Islam to Christianity risks execution, has a score of 7.8 on this scale. Now consider this: Iceland and Spain also score 7.8, Belgium and Greece score 7.5, Denmark gets a 6.7, and Finland 7.5. In fact, *every* Western European nation scores well above the score achieved by Syria. And that's that!

Keep in mind, too, that Europe's lack of religiousness is primarily a matter of the lack of participation in Church. Because most people in Europe still affirm religious beliefs and the majority of them pray, Grace Davie refers to them as "believing non-belongers."[212] To recognize that this strange state of affairs reflects lazy churches without serious competition, one need only look beyond Europe.

REVIVAL AND GLOBAL GROWTH

It is instructive to realize that, contrary to popular misconceptions, during the early days of the American colonies, organized religion was as weak there as it was in Europe. The vast majority of early settlers were not Pilgrims, not even in Massachusetts, and they brought European traditions of little religious participation with them. Prior to the Revolution, Church participation remained low because nearly every colony had an established Church: Congregationalist in New England, Anglican in most other colonies. Indeed, the negative effects of establishment already were recognized by perceptive colonists. Thus, the former colonial governor of New Jersey, having retired in New York, wrote to a friend that "if by force the salary is taken from [the people] and paid to ministers of the church, it may be a means of subsisting those Ministers, but they won't make many converts."[213] He went on to note that religion was far stronger in colonies having no establishment. He was quite correct. In 1776 only about 17 percent of colonial Americans actually belonged to a local church congregation, but New Jersey and Pennsylvania, the only large colonies without an established church, had the highest membership rates of 26 and 24 percent respectively (compared with 15 percent in Anglican New York).[214]

The United States Constitution prohibited the establishment of religion, not mainly from philosophical objections, but from the fact that no denomination was sufficiently dominant—even the Congregationalists had only 20 percent of the congregations and the Anglicans had but 15 percent. Hence, American churches were placed on equal footing and all had to compete for members. The benefits of pluralism quickly began to appear. By 1860 more than a third (37 percent) of all Americans belonged to a specific local congregation. The 50 percent mark was passed by 1900, and for the past thirty years, slightly more than 60 percent have belonged, which is probably about as high a rate as can be sustained (90 percent of Americans claim a denominational affiliation, but many do not actually maintain a local membership).[215] It is significant that not all American denominations benefited from this great increase in membership rates. Those denominations, such as the Episcopalians, United Church of Christ, Methodists, and Presbyterians, that drifted away from traditional Christianity have been shrinking quite rapidly, while Evangelical Protestant groups, including the Church of God in Christ, the Assemblies of God, and the Foursquare Gospel, have enjoyed rapid growth. Even the huge Southern Baptist Convention has sustained significant growth.[216]

Competition not only built strong American churches, in doing so it renewed the impulse to: "*Go therefore and make disciples of all nations*" (Matthew 28:19). Because sending missionaries abroad was a normal part of building a colonial empire, a substantial mission movement had begun in Europe by the start of the nineteenth century. Very soon American missionaries also played a role, even without imperial considerations. By 1900, the majority of Christian foreign missionaries were Americans, and since the end of World War II, foreign missions have become almost exclusively American. Thus, in 2001, American denominations were spending $3.7 billion a year to support more than 44,386 full-time, long-term missionaries abroad, augmented by 346,225 Americans serving short-term missions of a year or less.[217] Because these amazing totals are based entirely on missionaries offically dispatched by denominational mission boards, they actually far underestimate the total effort. In 2005 Robert Wuthnow conducted a national survey that allowed him to project that 1.6 million Americans go abroad on short-term missions every year at their own expense.[218]

What has all this effort produced? Obviously American missionaries cannot take full credit for the rapid growth of Christianity in the "Global South," but they surely have played a significant role.

Latin America

The southern hemisphere was long said to be a Catholic continent. In truth it was only legally Catholic, while in actuality, Latin America was quite unconverted. Outside of the cities there were few churches and fewer priests. Thus, in 1965 according to official Roman Catholic statistics, one priest served an average of 9,881 Catholics in Guatemala, 6,486 in Brazil, 5,630 in Peru, 4,927 in Mexico, and 4,486 in Colombia. These ratios revealed the long-standing weakness of the Latin Church, not only because of its inability to attract priests (despite their small numbers, most Latin American priests have been sent there from abroad), but for lack of complaints about too few clergy. These implications are clear when compared with the fact that in that same year, there was one priest for every 602 Catholics in Canada and 782 in the United States. Moreover, by 1965 a major missionary effort by American Protestant groups was well underway all across Latin America. It was not too long before there were more full-time American missionaries active in most Latin American nations than there were local Catholic priests![219] Soon, however, there were far more *local* Protestant clergy and evangelists than there were American Protestant missionaries, and it is they who have been largely responsible for the fact that in most Latin nations today, the majority of those in church on a Sunday morning are Protestants. Of perhaps even greater significance is the fact that results have not been limited to rapid Protestant growth. Competition has energized the Catholic Church to such an extent that it is growing, too—as measured by church attendance and seminary enrollments.[220] Soon, Latin America will be a Christian continent.

Africa

Sub-Saharan Africa has been a major Christian mission field for several centuries, especially by European missions to their colonies. At present, Africa is second only to Asia in terms of the number of full-time American missionaries stationed there. However, missionaries have played a very secondary role in the rapid Christianization taking place in Africa. The major factor has been intense Christian sects founded by native Africans. There are thousands of them.[221] And as in Latin America these Protestant sects have greatly energized Catholic missions in Africa. By now at least half of the population in sub-Saharan Africa is Christian.[222]

Asia

Asia, especially China, has long been the premier American mission area. Throughout the first half of the twentieth century, there was scarcely an American Protestant congregation that was not visited every year or two by a returned missionary from China, seeking funds to sustain the massive mission presence. Of course, these mission activities were attacked and often ridiculed by intellectuals and various leftists who proclaimed that the Chinese were immune to religion—an immunity that long preceded the Communist rise to power. When, in 1937, Edgar Snow quipped that "in China, opium is the religion of the people," the media "experts" chuckled in agreement. And when Mao Tse Tung seized power in 1949, sophisticated opinion agreed that the several million Chinese claimed as converts by Christian missionaries were nothing but "rice

Christians"—cynical souls who frequented the missions for the benefits they provided—and that China soon would be a model of the fully secularized, post-religious society.

But it wasn't to be. Instead, the faith in a forthcoming post-religious China turned out to be the opium of Western intellectuals and media experts. After many decades of extraordinary efforts to root out all religion, China today is far more religious than before the revolution, perhaps more religious than ever before in its history. The two million "rice Christians" have somehow grown into anywhere from 40 to 50 million devoted followers of Christ. Nor is it primarily peasants or the poor who are converting. Christians abound on university faculties and among the sons and daughters of party officials.

Thus it is that, even without counting any Chinese converts, Christianity is now the largest religion in the world. Christians outnumber Muslims by more than three to two, Hindus by more than two to one, and Buddhists by more than five to one.[223] Given the continuing rapid growth of the faith, one might anticipate that Christianity will soon claim an even greater proportion of humanity. But that overlooks the very tight connection between Christianity and modernity, and the marked effects of the latter on fertility. A strong case has been made that Christianity played the vital role in the birth of modernity—in the rise of the West.[224] Subsequently, Christianization has tended to accompany modernization in other parts of the world.[225] Modernization, in turn, is highly correlated with reduced fertility, to such an extent that most European nations now have fertility rates far below the level needed merely to replace their existing populations. Consequently, the number of Christians in Europe is declining quite rapidly, not mainly because of defections from the faith, but from ever-smaller generations. Meanwhile, Muslim fertility everywhere remains well above replacement levels, including among Muslims living in Europe and among the substantial and continuing stream of Muslims immigrating to Europe. It is conceivable that a century from now, the religious map of the world will show a Muslim Europe and a Christian China.

These prospects underline the fact that change has been the singular constant in Christian history. Who among the apostles could possibly have anticipated the Roman Catholic Church? What medieval pope could have foretold the Southern Baptist Convention? And what Baptist

preacher could have imagined that early in the twenty-first century, formal ties would be sustained between Baylor University and the University
of Beijing?

CONCLUSION

Beginning with Chapter 3 on Rome, considerable attention has been paid
to the positive effects of pluralism for sustaining high levels of religious
commitment as faiths vie with one another for followers. However, an
unfortunate side effect of such competition has largely been neglected
thus far: religious conflict. A brief discussion of this aspect of pluralism
serves as an appropriate conclusion to this chapter and an introduction
to the next.

Unfortunately, sociologists have popularized two very misleading
claims about religious conflicts and the formation of *sects*—groups that
sustain relatively intense levels of religiousness. The first is the false notion
that sects always arise from lower-class protest. As was discussed in Chapter 4, the great majority of sects originate among the upper classes and
seemingly grow out of the inability of power and privilege to satisfy spiritual and existential concerns, especially among those who inherit their
advantages. The second false claim builds upon the first, and proposes
the equally spurious notion that the proliferation of religious groups and
the conflicts among them, including those between sects and more moderate religious groups, are never really about beliefs and doctrines, but
always are rooted in material differences.

Oddly enough, the most vociferous proponent of this claim was an
American theologian-turned-sociologist named H. Richard Niebuhr
(1894–1962). In his classic work *The Social Sources of Denominationalism*
(1929), Niebuhr undertook to answer the question: why is Christianity
fractured into so many different groups, or denominations? Why is it
that, wherever free to do so, new sect groups constantly form? And even
when faced with a repressive state and the prospect of terrible vengeance,
why have so many people through the centuries risked everything on
behalf of dissident sects?

To answer these questions, Niebuhr first proposed a cyclical account of
the proliferation of sects within Christianity. Religious groups begin with
a high level of intensity, as sects. Over time successful sects accommodate

to their social environment by reducing their initial level of intensity, becoming ever more respectable, whereupon dissenters break away and found a new sect. Thus did the Methodist sect split away from the Church of England only to eventually become today's low-intensity liberal denomination, which has, consequently, produced dozens of breakaway sects.[226] So far, so good. But then Niebuhr proposed that this cycle rests upon a Marxist dynamic whereupon sects are created by the poor and disinherited but, if they succeed, sects are always captured by the privileged who then modify them, thus forcing the poor to depart and begin again. From this class-based model Niebuhr derived his primary point: that the basis for denominationalism is social, not theological.

From his Marxist perspective, Niebuhr assumed that all social conflicts arise from material causes. Thus, although various religious groups always assert that doctrinal differences set them apart from other groups, and while battles for control of growing sects always are fought in the name of doctrine, this is but a smokescreen of false consciousness. According to Niebuhr and several subsequent generations of sociologists, the reality is that it is never doctrinal disagreement, but class conflicts that sunder Christianity—these are "the social sources of denominationalism." Hence, according to Niebuhr, the "effort to distinguish churches primarily by reference to their doctrines ... [and] from a purely theological point of view ... [is] artificial and fruitless."[227]

But just as he was wrong about sects always or usually being the product of lower class protest, Niebuhr was equally wrong about the unimportance of doctrinal differences. Most of the time doctrines *are* the real grounds for dispute, not a cover for class interests, if for no other reason than that class differences so often are lacking! John Wesley (1703–1791) and his colleagues did not depart from the Church of England and found Methodism because they were lower-class dissidents who wanted religious compensations for their economic deprivations. They were themselves young men of privilege who began to assert their preference for a higher intensity faith while at Oxford. Eventually they were driven from the Anglican faith over specific issues of piety and doctrine. Nor does the schism emerging within the Episcopalian Church in the United States pit the rich versus the poor; it is confrontation between people of considerable privilege on both sides over what it means to be a Christian. This is not peculiar to disputes within Christianity. Jewish sects also have typically originated with the upper classes, and there was and is nothing illusory about their conflicts over doctrine. Indeed, Zoroaster, Buddha, Mahāvīra, Confucius, Lao-Tzu, and other founders discussed in previous chapters also were from the upper classes and so were those who opposed them.

Furthermore, even when religious disputes do involve less privileged factions, doctrinal differences are not a smokescreen for class interests, but are real issues. The Anabaptists truly believed that infant baptism was invalid, Calvinists did embrace predestinarianism, and scores of Protestant groups have separated over specific issues of worldliness. So, rather than continuing to conduct futile searches for "real" material bases of religious disputes, it is past time that sociologists realize that people can care as much about ideas as about material benefits and that sincere religious innovations are what they claim to be: *attempts to discover and refine conceptions of God*, even when it is proposed that the Gods are many and unimportant.

Obviously, rather different religious notions exist within most polytheistic faiths, but because no claim is made to exclusive truth, these differences are not very divisive. Religious differences are far more volatile when they occur within monotheism, for these faiths arouse much higher levels of individual commitment and their claims to exclusive truth imply invidious judgments of others. The people who pursue another faith are not merely different, they are wrong. And when such people persist in their errors, they often will be defined as evil! From here it often is but a short step to repression and violence. Frequently, these have been internal conflicts—as not only Christianity, but Judaism and Islam have been abundant in bitter and aggressive factions. But over the centuries vicious external conflicts have broken out among the great monotheisms, especially between Christians and Muslims, inherent in the fact that each group believes it knows far more about God than does the other.

I have written on the evolution of norms of religious tolerance at some length elsewhere, suggesting that over time tolerance also is inherent in pluralism, and that the greatest dangers exist when religious differences coincide with national or regional boundaries.[228] But in this book my emphasis is on the "discoveries" about God that provide the basis for conflicts within and among monotheistic faiths. And so, on to Muhammad.

· 8 ·

ISLAM:
GOD AND STATE

IN ABOUT 570 CE a boy was born to Āminah, newly widowed from Abdullah ibn Abd-al-Muttalib, a small-time merchant-trader, and she named her infant Muhammad. The birth occurred in the town of Mecca, located forty-five miles from the Red Sea and situated in a narrow, rocky valley along the western part of the Arabian Peninsula. Mecca had long been regarded as a holy city by Arab tribes in the surrounding area as it contained a sacred building, the *Ka'bah*, which was a sanctuary and the object of annual pilgrimages. Thus, Mecca was a very appropriate birthplace for a Prophet who would radically change world history.

Most biographies of Muhammad focus nearly exclusively on him as a religious founder, paying little attention to his role in creating an Arab State and as a military leader.[1] A few biographies give almost no attention to religion and focus on Muhammad's "worldly" achievements in politics and war.[2] But as Fred McGraw Donner demonstrated in a brilliant study, the two facets of Muhammad's life are inseparable.[3] Without the political and military achievements, Muhammad might have remained such an obscure religious figure as to have escaped historical notice. Without the religion, there probably would have been no state-building or victories.

To put Muhammad fully in perspective it is necessary to comprehend the isolated, disorganized, and tribal world into which he was born—pagan Arabia. With the stage thus set, the chapter turns to a concise biography of

Muhammad. Then, to more fully explore his religious contributions, comes an assessment of the primary features of Islam, of the Qur'an (Koran), and of the Muslim conception of Allāh. To appreciate Muhammad's political and military gifts, the chapter traces how he successfully forged an Arab State, using military campaigns not only to impose his rule, but especially to attract allies. Next, the chapter sketches the spread of Islam throughout the Middle East, then across North Africa, and east into India, drawing a careful distinction between conquest and conversion. However, not even an authoritarian state could prevent the repeated fracturing of Islam into numerous sects. The chapter concludes with a brief assessment of Islamic sectarianism to demonstrate the fact that Islam incorporates as much diversity as do Judaism and Christianity.

ARABIA

Most of the Arabian Peninsula is a desert, often designated on maps as the "Empty Quarter." Only the southwestern corner, now Yemen, has sufficient rainfall to support farming without irrigation. In the sixth and seventh centuries, most of the Peninsula was very thinly occupied by nomadic and semi-nomadic Bedouin tribes. However, there was a strip along the Red Sea, about two hundred miles across at its widest point, known as the *Hijāz*, where a few small communities managed to exist, even though this, too, was a barren landscape.

The nomads and semi-nomads lived primarily by herding and force of arms. Even though they were very greatly outnumbered by residents of the towns and villages, the desert Arabs so excelled in fighting that they supplemented their income by raids on the settlements—some tribes being able to impose regular "protection" fees on a community or two. For the desert tribes, military adventures not only were essential to their economies, but as Donner so aptly put it, fighting was also "a form of entertainment, a challenging and exciting game . . . that reduced the monotony of desert life."[4]

The desert herds mainly consisted of sheep or goats, but a few tribes specialized in raising camels. The nomads kept on the move all year, following a traditional route from one small watered area to another, staying only until the grazing had been exhausted. Usually their bands were very small "tenting groups" including only several dozen people—the tribe only assembled periodically. The semi-nomads occupied settled communities where they practiced some agriculture (using water from springs or wells) and then went out during the grassy season to graze their flocks.

In addition to robbery and protection fees, both nomads and semi-nomads depended on trade with the settled communities for many

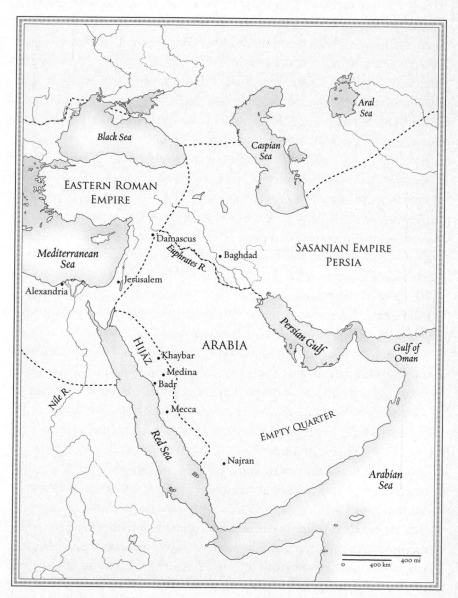

Map 8–1: Ancient Arabia.

necessities—trading leather, cloth woven from wool and from goat and camel hair, and livestock in exchange for additional foodstuffs and metal items such as weapons. The towns and villages were sustained by springs, by local gardens and date palms, and supported by commerce: some of it with the desert tribes, some of it involving caravans. To the extent that Arabia had any contact with the outside world, it was via long-distance caravans that crossed the desert because it was the most direct route linking Asia and the Mediterranean. Townspeople profited from these caravans by resupplying them as they passed through and by participating directly in some of these commercial ventures, especially in those having a more local scope. The desert tribes profited by selling camels to the caravans, by hiring on as drivers, by selling safe passage and their services as guards, and by robbing a caravan from time to time.

As is obvious, Arabia in this era was a stateless region. Power relations among the desert tribes were constantly shifting, and no central authority existed. Consequently, relations among the tribes and between desert tribes and settled communities depended in part on the recognition of a degree of mutual self-interest. This involved an additional aspect of Arabian life that empowered the settled communities vis-à-vis the desert-dwellers: *religion*.

There were substantial communities of Arabs who had converted to Judaism and others who embraced various kinds of Christianity, but most Arabs were pagans who believed in a large number of Gods, both great and small. Apparently, many acknowledged *Allāh* as the Creator God, but as in many early religions, he was a withdrawn "High God" and not worshipped.[5] As would be expected, Nature Gods predominated among those who were worshipped. Of special importance were local Gods associated with a specific shrine sited by a spring, an outcrop of rock, or even an unusual tree. Each shrine was controlled by a "devout" family, made up of descendants of the person who first established the religious character of the site, and some sites took on major importance when they were established as a *haram*. A *haram* was a sacred place where overt conflict was forbidden—especially murder. It thus served as a sanctuary, providing neutral ground where feuding tribes could negotiate in safety. In addition, a *haram* often provided the site for trade fairs, because merchants and desert Arabs could go there without fear. Indeed, what no existing political power could provide, the Gods furnished since everyone believed that violation of a *haram*'s sanctuary would bring divine punishment.[6] As a result, the family in charge of a *haram* acquired substantial power, especially as the head of the family (the *mansib*) often served as a mediator for tribal disputes. A *mansib* not only could invoke divine threats, but could deny a given tribe or faction access to the *haram* or its trade fairs.[7] However, the families controlling shrines were not the most influential religious figures in Arabia. These were the *Kāhins*, "shamanistic seers who [it was believed] could enter a trance state and through visionary means locate lost relatives, camels, or other objects."[8] Moreover, because poetry was the primary art form in Arabia, to such an extent that poets gathered to hold competitions, the *Kāhins* presented their sacred formulas in rhymes.[9]

MECCA

Tradition has it that because of "its admirable situation,"[10] Mecca was the center of an extensive commercial empire,[11] a place where many caravan routes crossed as part of a long-distance trading network linking the sea routes to India and China with the Mediterranean.[12] It also has been accepted that Meccan traders specialized in light, easily transported luxury goods, especially incense, spices, and silk, as well as slaves, and thereby Mecca became a city of considerable wealth. According to the prominent Scottish Arabist W. Montgomery Watt (1909–2006), "the great merchants of Mecca had obtained a monopoly control of this trade. Mecca was thus prosperous, but most of the wealth was in a few hands."[13] This inequality, in turn, is said to have undercut tribal solidarity and led to the neglect of "traditional duties to the unfortunate."[14] Hence, according to Watt and many other historians of Islam, sudden new wealth created social tensions and a general malaise in Mecca that set the stage for the sudden rise of Islam, which was able to restore a sense of community and of mutual obligations.

Or perhaps not, for what has just been sketched is an application of the standard social-scientific explanation for *all* social movements, which holds that *whenever* people organize to do something new, it *must be* in reaction to strains created by *material stresses*, although sometimes one must dig very deep to find them. At most, this is a very partial truth. No doubt when people form movements aimed at changing things, they do believe that "something is wrong in their social environment" that needs fixing. It follows that "some form of strain must be present if an episode of collective behavior is to occur."[15] What is not true is the nearly universal assumption that these must be *material* strains.[16] No convincing evidence of material strains, of conflict caused by sudden wealth and extremes of inequality, can be unearthed to explain the origins of Islam. Rather, Muhammad and his earliest followers seem to have experienced an acute sense of cultural and spiritual inferiority, as will be seen.

As for "material strains," Mecca was not situated at a major crossroads,[17] nor was it a harbor. This makes the traditional assumption that Mecca grew rich as a center for international trade in precious commodities seem unlikely. True enough, some caravans did originate in Mecca and go somewhere with some kinds of goods. What modern historiography reveals is that these were not long-distance caravans, and they did not carry light, precious cargos.[18] Instead, Mecca dealt in modest products and transported them over relatively short distances. Leather goods seem to have been the city's major export. In addition, its caravans dealt in "clothing, animals, [and] miscellaneous foodstuffs."[19] Such trade was unlikely to have created sudden large fortunes or to have unsettled traditional social life. Nor was it a recent development. When Muhammad began to pursue a career with the commercial caravans, he was simply doing what his father and grandfather had done before him—as their ancestors probably had also done for generations. Continuity does not typically result in a crisis.

Although it was not a major hub of caravans, Mecca was prominent because of its religious significance as a *haram*. Inside its boundaries was the *Ka'bah* (literally "the cube"), an ancient temple said to have housed some 360 idols,[20] including all the Gods of all the tribes[21] and "perhaps including crudely painted images of Jesus and his virgin mother," and an odd black stone that might be a meteorite.[22] The stone was associated with the God Hubal—possibly a War God. Three "Daughters of Allāh" were central to worship at the *Ka'bah*: the Goddesses Al-Lāt, al-'Uzzah, and Manāt, the latter may have been the Goddess of Love. The *Ka'bah* also played a central role in Arabian poetry contests, it being the highest honor to have one's verses inscribed and placed inside.[23]

Because Mecca was a *haram* sanctuary, it benefited from trade fairs to which members of the feuding nomadic tribes could come without risk. Moreover, some Arabs had long made an annual pilgrimage to Mecca to worship at the *Ka'bah*, doing so at a time of year they referred to as *Ramadan*. There was nothing sudden about any of this, things had been this way for as long as anyone could remember, without prompting social "strains."

So what did unsettle Meccan life? Why were the "times" ripe for Muhammad?

Pagan Arabs were not the only occupants of their region. Many kinds of Christians and large numbers of Jews lived among them, both as enclaves within Arab settlements and in communities of their own. Contact was close and constant, and significant numbers of Arabs had converted to each of these faiths—some entire nomadic groups had turned Christian[24] and other tribes were Jewish converts.[25] This caused some Arabs to feel "an acute sense of inferiority: it seemed as though God had left the Arabs out of His divine plan."[26] Indeed, not only the desert but even the *Hijāz* was a stateless region that counted for little in comparison with the neighboring societies—the Eastern Roman Empire and Persia. Some of the more sophisticated among the Arabs wondered whether God had overlooked them because they lacked culture. Although the Arabs were probably not the simple polytheistic idolaters depicted in the Qur'an, the fact remains that theirs was the only area in the Near East that was not dominated by monotheism, whether by several varieties of Christianity, by Judaism, or, indeed, by Zoroastrianism.

This situation led some to predict the coming of an Arabian prophet. Among those making such predictions was Waraqa ibn Naufal, a cousin of Muhammad's wife Khadījah. Waraqa was an educated man and a member of a small group of Arabs known as *hanifs* ("pious ones") who "accepted the ethical monotheism of Judaism and Christianity but did not join either of these two religious communities"[27] while seeking a deeper spiritual experience than Arab paganism could provide.[28] Waraqa seems to have known Muhammad from childhood,[29] and some scholars believe that by his mid-thirties, Muhammad had become a *hanif*.[30] It was within this social and religious context that Muhammad began to have visions.

THE PROPHET

Unlike the other religious founders discussed in previous chapters, Muhammad's life seems to have been recorded in detail—even an extensive physical description and quite candid accounts of his personal style and mannerisms have come down to us. Thus we possess a rich tapestry of details compared with all other founders, *if* the sources are trustworthy. Unfortunately, as Muslim scholars candidly admit, Muhammad is not nearly so well attested as might be supposed from the rather uncritical biographies, many of them by Western authors, currently in circulation.[31] The oldest surviving biographies (*sira*) were written "at least 125 years after Muhammad's death."[32] These *sira* probably utilized older sources—we know the names of a number of persons credited with having written very early biographies of Muhammad, but none of their work survived.[33] In any event, medieval Muslim scholars[34] detected that some fabrications and rearrangements of events had been introduced in the surviving *sira*, done to further the cause of various Muslim factions—Islam always has been riddled with disputatious and ambitious sects. Consequently, as with Jesus, there has been a long search for the "historical" Muhammad, albeit most of these searchers have been rather more responsible.[35] The consensus is that the main outlines of the traditional biography are accurate enough. It may well be that the extensive descriptions of Muhammad's appearance and demeanor are, too, but I shall not include them.

I must emphasize that I have followed the traditional biography of Muhammad, the one that is presented in Muslim schools and accepted by the faithful. As will be seen, this traditional biography includes incidents that many Western apologists for Islam find so embarrassing that they ignore or try to minimize them. But these incidents are taken for granted in the Muslim world and are regarded as central to the life of the prophet.

Because his father had died before he was born, Muhammad came under the guardianship of his grandfather. Soon after his birth, he was sent to be wet-nursed by Bedouins in the desert. Then, having returned to his mother's care sometime after his first birthday, Muhammad was orphaned when she died five years later. Two years after that, his guardian grandfather died, and Muhammad became a charge of his uncle, who succeeded to the headship of the *Hāshim* clan.

When he was old enough, Muhammad began to participate in trading caravans as did his male relatives. Because he had no capital of his own, however, he was limited to the role of hired helper. This way of life continued until he met and married Khadījah, a somewhat older woman of property who had been commissioning caravans on her own behalf. It seems to have been an unusually strong marriage. She bore him two sons (who died very young) and four daughters, and so long as she lived, Muhammad took no other wives. Khadījah also played a major role in Muhammad's religious development. But before his religious activities began, Muhammad led the life of a successful merchant and father.

First Visions

When he was about forty, consistent with his participation among the *hanifs*, Muhammad began to engage in annual periods of solitary religious contemplation. Each year, during the month of Ramadan, he secluded himself in a cave on Mount Hira. There "Muhammad spent his days and nights in contemplation and worship."[36] Eventually he began to have vivid dreams involving angels and to experience mysterious phenomena such as lights and sounds having no source.[37] These upset him, and he feared he was losing his sanity or that he had been possessed by an evil spirit. So he confided in his wife, Khadījah. She gave him immediate reassurance. She also hurried to consult her cousin Waraqa, who accepted these as signs that greater revelations would be forthcoming.[38] Subsequently, when Khadījah brought Muhammad to consult him, Waraqa cried out, "If you have spoken the truth to me, O Khadījah . . . he is the prophet of his people."[39] Later, when he encountered Muhammad in the marketplace, Waraqa kissed him on the forehead as a mark of his mission as the "new prophet of the one God."[40] Indeed, Waraqa served "as a kind of John the Baptist in the accounts of Muhammad's early revelations."[41] Thus reassured, Muhammad now accepted his mission and expected to receive major new revelations—and soon did so.

Of these, by far the most dramatic and important is known as Muhammad's "Night Journey."[42] It occurred in 620 CE, about ten years after his first visions. While sleeping at the home of his cousin in Mecca, he was awakened by the Angel Gabriel who led him by the hand to a winged horse, whereupon the two were quickly transported to Jerusalem. There he was introduced to Adam, Abraham, Moses, and Jesus, after which he was taken through each of the seven heavens, and then beyond where he was allowed to see Allāh who appeared as divine light. On his way back down through the seven heavens, Muhammad had a series of interactions with Moses concerning the number of times Muslims would be required to pray each day, the number gradually being reduced from fifty to five times. By morning, Muhammad was safely back in bed. The Dome of the Rock eventually was built to mark the place in Jerusalem from which it is believed Muhammad rose into the heavens on his Night Journey.

It is nearly impossible to accurately date most of the various revelations as they appear in the Qur'an, although it is generally believed that some of the earliest ones appear toward the end of the volume. Even so, the same primary themes dominate throughout. First, that Muhammad has been sent to institute true monotheism: "*Allāh! There is no God save Him, the Alive, the Eternal*" (II: 255). Muhammad also vigorously denied his own divinity, claiming instead to be the last of 124,000 prophets sent by God, first to the Jews, then to Christians, and now to Arabs and all the rest of humanity.

The second major theme is that as "People of Scripture" it is time for unity among the three faiths based on their common tradition. "[I]n the beginning of his career Muhammad expected to be warmly received by [these] two previous scriptural communities."[43] To this end, his revelations retell many accounts from both the Old and New Testaments, all of them meant to demonstrate that Islam was the final fulfillment of Jewish and Christian scripture. Thus, for example, an entire revelation is devoted to Mary, to her virginal conception and to the birth of Jesus—the latter occurs at an oasis, beneath a date palm tree, and within moments of his birth, Jesus is able to speak and informs his mother's relatives that Allāh "*hath given me the Scripture and hath appointed me a prophet*" (XIX:30). In addition to these revelations, in pursuit of unity Muhammad initially instructed that his followers should face Jerusalem when they prayed and that they should fast at the Day of Atonement.[44] But Jews and Christians persisted in rejecting Muhammad's new teachings and criticized the Qur'an's retelling of their scriptures. In response, Muhammad established that one should face Mecca when one prays, and he replaced the Jewish fast with a fast during the month of Ramadan.

The third consistent theme of Muhammad's revelations is that everyone will be bodily resurrected at Judgment Day, whereupon believers will enter Paradise and all others will suffer eternity in Hell. Although this view was shared with the Christians, Jews, and Zoroastrians in the region, it was new among the Arabs, who were fatalists and did not believe in an afterlife.[45] Consequently, of course, the Arabs also lacked notions of sin and this, in turn, encouraged hedonism.[46] By promising an extremely attractive Paradise awaiting believers, and a merciless Hell for unbelievers, Muhammad was able to link morality to divine will. Although Muhammad allowed that women, too, would enter Paradise, all descriptions of it involve very masculine joys—sitting in a cool, upland oasis; drinking a wine that neither muddles nor leaves a hangover; and served hand and foot by beautiful virgins.

The fourth primary theme is concerned with leading the moral life and obeying divine authority, predicated, of course, on the doctrine of divine judgment and the afterlife. The importance of obedience to God proved invaluable when Muhammad sought to create an Arab State. Long before such matters could arise, however, came the challenge to convince others that he was truly hearing the voice of the Angel Gabriel—that Allāh had chosen to have his actual words spoken to a small-time Meccan merchant.

The Holy Family

As with the other major religious founders, Muhammad's first followers were his family members and close associates. His wife, Khadījah, was his first and probably his most important convert. Next, of course, came Waraqa. Because both of their sons had died in infancy, Muhammad and Khadījah had adopted two young boys: one of them Muhammad's cousin Ali and the other Zayd ibn-Hārithah, whom they had originally purchased as a slave. Both became converts, as did Muhammad and Khadījah's four daughters: Fātimah, Zaynab, Ruqayya, and Um Kulthūm. Next came three male cousins of Muhammad and one of their wives. Muhammad's aunt also was an early convert, as was his freed slave, Umm Ayman, a woman who had cared for him in infancy. In addition to relatives, Muhammad's oldest and closest friend (and eventual successor), Abū-Bakr soon converted. He, in turn, converted "a group of

five men who became the mainstay of the young [movement]."[47] These
five were close friends, and all of them were successful young merchant
traders. One of them was Abū-Bakr's cousin and another was a cousin
of Khadījah. In addition, two servants of Abū-Bakr whom he had freed
from slavery also converted, including Bilāl, who gained lasting fame as
the first muezzin (or crier) to call the faithful to prayer. So, there we have
Muhammad's first twenty-two converts. In fact, the "names of 70 [of the
earliest] followers are known. . . . Most were young men under 30 when
they joined Muhammad. They included sons and brothers of the richest
men in Mecca."[48]

To Medina

The new faith soon began to arouse antagonism in Mecca, for it not
only claimed to possess new truths, it condemned the traditional religious
institutions and practices. Worse yet, when Muhammad attacked paganism and called for "the end of idolatry in Mecca," the community leaders
saw this "as a real threat to their livelihoods."[49] If the idols were destroyed,
the Ka'bah would become merely an empty building, and there no longer
would be any basis for Mecca as a haram. No haram, no trade fairs. So
opposition grew. But Muhammad and his followers were protected by
his clan, the Hāshim, even though his uncle heading the clan was not a
convert—it was enough that Muhammad was a fellow clansman. However, when this uncle died and was replaced by another uncle as head of
the clan, amid growing opposition to Muhammad, clan support became
undependable. It was at this time, too, that Khadījah died.

Meanwhile, in the summer of 621, twelve men from Medina (then
known as Yathrib) had come on a pilgrimage to the Ka'bah. They accepted instruction from Muhammad and then returned to Medina very
deeply impressed by him as well as his message. The next year a party of
seventy-five persons came from Medina, ostensibly on a pilgrimage, but
actually to consult Muhammad. Although the Medinans seem to have
found Muhammad's monotheism of considerable interest, their primary
concern was to recruit him to arbitrate the bloody feuds that had beset
Medina for a number of years—involving the dozen Arab clans resident
in Medina as well as several quite powerful Jewish clans. In pursuit of this
aim, the group from Medina took an oath "to defend Muhammad as they
would their own kin,"[50] thereby providing a substitute for the wavering

support of Muhammad's own clan. Consequently, in the face of growing opposition in Mecca, Muhammad encouraged his followers to withdraw to Medina, a few at a time. Eventually about seventy Meccans did so,[51] journeying about 250 miles north. As this took place there was a plot to murder Muhammad, but he and Abū-Bakr escaped their Meccan enemies and made their way safely to Medina. The emigration to Medina is famous in Muslim history as the *hijirah* (also *hegira*).

Once in Medina, Muhammad did agree to arbitrate all disputes among the clans, and eventually this role evolved into the first approximation of an Arab State. Muhammad also quickly settled in and had a house built in Medina, where he lived for the rest of his days. It had adjacent small houses for his new wives—how many he eventually married is uncertain, but he left at least nine widows.[52] Meanwhile, his fellow emigrants from Mecca had a more difficult time gaining a livelihood in their new home, so Muhammad organized them to rob caravans.

To Arms

Traditional Islamic biographies of Muhammad give considerable coverage to the raids he directed against Meccan caravans, but many recent historians go to great lengths to justify or evade these matters. Karen Armstrong described raids on caravans as "a sort of national sport in Arabia and an accepted way of making ends meet when times were hard . . . a rough and ready way of securing a fair circulation of wealth."[53] Reza Aslan echoed Armstrong, claiming that these were not robberies, because in Arabia at this time, "caravan raiding was a legitimate means for small clans to benefit from the wealth of larger ones. It was in no way considered stealing."[54] M. A. Salahi would not even share these visions of Arab Robin Hoods, refusing to acknowledge these as raids on caravans, carefully describing them instead as "expeditions" to "learn about their enemies" and as training "manoeuvres [that] enhanced the Muslims' fighting ability and enriched their knowledge of the surrounding area."[55] All this, despite the fact that traditional Muslim sources take considerable pride in listing all the booty.

In any event, the early efforts by Muslim raiders from Medina to ambush caravans surely did not involve stealing—as they were utter failures! The first attempt involved thirty men on camels who set out to capture a caravan returning to Mecca from Syria. It isn't clear why they did not attack, but the best surmise is that the caravan was too well-guarded.[56] Soon after that, a force of sixty Muslims shot some arrows at another caravan, but also failed to capture it. Next, Muhammad led several groups of raiders, but they, too, were unsuccessful. Apparently, Muhammad's opponents in Medina were warning the Meccan merchants.[57] Perhaps that's why the first successful raid involved such a small caravan and so few raiders that the informants probably failed to notice anything. This caravan originated in Mecca and was escorted by only four merchants. Muhammad sent a raiding party of fewer than a dozen men led by Abdallāh ibn Jahsh to set up an ambush south of Mecca. The raiders captured the caravan intact as well as taking two of the four merchants prisoner, another merchant was killed, and the fourth escaped. No raider was hurt. The booty and prisoners were taken back to Medina, where Muhammad set his share of the profits at 20 percent, including the large ransoms paid by the two prisoners' families. Even so small a caravan made the Meccans in Medina quite affluent. But the raid aroused bitter demands for revenge in Mecca.[58]

Several months later a very large caravan set out for Mecca from Gaza, accompanied by seventy merchants. Upon learning of this enterprise, Muhammad called for volunteers to participate in a raid. Approximately three hundred men responded, and Muhammad led them forth to lie in wait near the wells at Badr. Meanwhile, the leader of the caravan seems either to have been warned or to have guessed that an attack was planned, and he sent word to his partners in Mecca to come and defend their merchandise—nearly every family in Mecca had some stake in this huge caravan. An army of nearly a thousand men came out from Mecca.[59] In the interests of speed the caravan did not turn aside to water at Badr, but pushed on toward Mecca and soon was far out of danger, whereupon many Meccans returned home. But those who had suffered from the first raid agitated for an attack against Muhammad's forces, who still lay in wait for the convoy, not knowing it had sped past them. So a substantial force of Meccans pushed on. Muhammad learned of their approach at the last minute and drew up his forces on favorable ground. Muhammad's army was badly outnumbered, but his followers displayed far superior discipline and tactics as well as ardor, and by noon the Battle of Badr was over. About seventy-five Meccans lay dead, and the winners went back to Medina in triumph loaded with booty stripped from the corpses (especially armor) and herding several hundred prisoners—most of whom brought substantial ransoms.[60]

Far more than wealth was gained at Badr. As the French scholar Maxime Rodinson (1915–2004) explained, "The effects of the victory were especially noticeable on Muhammad himself. He had suffered and struggled, a butt for mockery and disbelief. He may even have doubted himself. And now Allāh was giving him a clear sign of his support. An army bigger than his own had been overcome. The hand of Allāh was clearly at work."[61]

Now there were scores to settle in Medina, and Muhammad's revenge began with assassinations. The first to die was a woman, "Asimā" bint Marwān, who had written scurrilous verses attacking the Prophet, such as:

Fucked men of Mālik and of Nabit
And of 'Awf, fucked men of Khazraj:[62]
You obey a stranger who does not belong among you,
Who is not of Murād, nor of Madh'hij.
Do you, when your own chiefs have been murdered, put your hope
*   in him*
Like men greedy for meal soup when it is cooking?
Is there no man of honour who will take advantage of an unguarded
*   moment*
And cut off the gulls' hopes.[63]

Having returned to Medina, and learning that "Asimā" had written new verses in opposition to him, the Prophet said, "Will no one rid me of this daughter of Marwān?" That night one of Muhammad's supporters came upon her asleep with a babe in her arms and drove his sword through her. In the morning he reported his accomplishment to Muhammad, who praised him as having done a service to Allāh.[64] A month later an aged poet who also had written critical verses was murdered in his sleep, in response to an appeal by the Prophet that someone should avenge him "on this scoundrel."[65] A third poet who wrote against Muhammad now made the mistake of moving from Mecca to Medina. Although the poet was protected by the most powerful of the Jewish clans in Medina, once again the Prophet suggested assassination, and once again his followers complied. Luring the poet from his safe quarters, they killed him, and took his head back to Muhammad.[66]

At this point, Muhammad began to express increased hostility toward Jews and Christians in response to the frustration of his early expectations that the other people of the book would embrace the new faith. Thus, the Qur'an:

> O People of Scripture! Why confound ye truth with falsehood and knowingly conceal the truth? (III.71).

> O People of the Scripture! Do not exaggerate your religion or utter aught concerning Allāh save the truth. The Messiah,[67] Jesus son of Mary, was only a messenger of Allāh (IV.171).

> O People of Scripture! Now hath our messenger come unto you, expounding unto you much of that which ye used to hide in Scripture, and forgiving much (V.15).

> The Jews and Christians say: We are sons of Allāh and His loved ones. Say: Why then doth He chastise you for your sins? (V.18).

> The only rewards of those who make war upon Allāh and his messenger and strive after corruption of the land will be that they will be killed or crucified, or have their hands and feet on alternative sides cut off, or will be expelled out of the land. Such will be their degradation in the world, and in the Hereafter theirs will be an awful doom (V.33).

> O Prophet! Strive against the disbelievers and the hypocrites! Be harsh with them. Their ultimate abode is hell, a hapless journey's-end (IX:73).

However, due to their far greater proximity and opposition, it was the Jews who became the primary targets of Muhammad's wrath. There were three powerful Jewish clans in Medina. They probably were not the descendents of settlers from Palestine, but of Arabs who had been converted to Judaism.[68] These Jewish clans had been the earliest settlers of Medina, owned the most fertile land, and specialized in the most valuable crop: dates. They also dominated skilled crafts, especially as jewelers and goldsmiths.[69] Moreover, the Jews in Medina were a literate group, able to sustain some local religious scholars, and it was they who stirred Muhammad's wrath because they not only criticized his interpretations of the Old Testament (revealing many conflicts), but mocked his claims to divine access.[70] Even before the Battle of Badr, Muhammad had responded to Jewish criticisms by ending the practice of praying toward Jerusalem. When no Jews had joined his expedition that eventuated in the battle, Muhammad's attitude toward them grew increasingly bitter. So, during the same month when the "scoundrel" poet was murdered, Muhammad decided to attack the *Qaynuqā*, weakest of the Jewish clans in Medina. The *Qaynuqā* withdrew into their fortified tower, and Muhammad's troops took it under siege. After fifteen days the Jews surrendered. Muhammad wanted them all killed, but gave in to pressure from his allies and agreed to spare the *Qaynuqā* if they abandoned all their property in Medina and left within three days. "The spoils were enormous and Muhammad kept a fifth."[71]

Meanwhile, the Meccans tried to secretly send a caravan to Mesopotamia. But word leaked out, and Muhammad sent a force of a hundred men to waylay it. The raid was a success, and more riches were added to Muhammad's treasury. In celebration, Muhammad took a third wife.[72]

By now the Meccans realized that Muhammad was far more than a nuisance. He must be destroyed. They assembled an army including many fighters from desert tribes, a total of about 3,000 well-armed men.[73] The Medinans responded by withdrawing into their strong fortifications. From there they looked on helplessly while the Meccans destroyed their ripening crops. This caused some younger men to demand battle.[74] Reluctantly, Muhammad and other leaders agreed. A force of about a thousand men was assembled, virtually none of them from the Jewish clans. Looking over the ranks, Muhammad ordered a number of young boys to go back to Medina, and so an army of about seven hundred camped that night on a rocky hillside. The next morning the far larger Meccan force overwhelmed Muhammad's troops. Many Medinans were killed, many others were wounded (including Muhammad), and after dark the survivors made their way back to the shelter of the Medinan fortress. Foolishly, the Meccans wasted their opportunity for a more complete victory by turning away to mutilate the corpses on the battlefield, while their surviving enemies escaped.[75] In the morning the Medinans were securely holed up in their fortifications, where they should have stayed in the first place. Faced with these dim prospects, the Meccan forces headed for home. So, who won? The Meccans won the tactical encounter, but they utterly failed to achieve their strategic goals: Medina was still under Muhammad's rule.[76]

With the immediate Meccan threat ended, the Prophet now took his revenge upon the second major Jewish clan in Medina, the *Banū n-Nadīr*. Again there was a short siege and again the Jews were ordered to leave, taking only what they could load on their camels. The extensive Jewish lands were divided among Medinans and the emigrants who had followed Muhammad from Mecca. Muhammad took some of the best fields for himself and found time to marry two more wives.[77]

Knowing that they must do something final about Muhammad, the leaders in Mecca began to enlist the support of the various desert tribes. Muhammad responded, and a bidding war ensued, in addition to which Muhammad had several desert chieftains assassinated to prevent them from supporting Mecca. But the Meccans persisted and assembled a large army of perhaps 10,000 men and marched on Medina.

Because of natural barriers, the only feasible place to attack Medina was from the north. Muhammad strengthened the northern defensive system by having a deep ditch dug—everyone, including the remaining Jewish clan, took part in the digging. The ditch prevented cavalry charges, and the excavated earth formed a strong palisade on the Medinan side of the ditch. What followed was a lengthy period of remarkably pointless posturing. Weeks were spent with the Meccans shouting insults from the outer side of the ditch, with the Medinans shouting back. A few arrows were shot. Finally, with three dead among the attackers and five dead defenders, the desert Arabs began to defect. Soon the entire Meccan army left.[78]

Even as the Meccans disappeared over the horizon, Muhammad turned his troops against the fortified enclave of the *Banū Qurayza*, the last Jewish clan in Medina. Some accounts claim they favored the Meccans; others bring no such charges. Whatever the case, after a short siege they, too, asked for surrender terms, but this time there would be no mercy.[79] Great trenches were dug, all the Jewish men were lined up along them and beheaded—from six to nine hundred of them.[80] The Jewish women and children were sold into slavery—Muhammad took one of the widows as a concubine.[81]

The massacre of the *Banū Qurayza* has greatly troubled those recent Western writers who are most favorably disposed toward Muhammad and Islam. Ironically, their efforts to put a better face on the event would seem to make matters worse. Everyone agrees that the fate of the *Banū Qurayza* was entirely in Muhammad's hands—that had he wished to spare them, they would have lived. So, to explain why Muhammad did it, these writers blame the barbaric Arab culture. Thus, Karen Armstrong warned that this event should not be associated with "Nazi atrocities" because "[t]his was a very primitive society—far more primitive than the Jewish society in which Jesus had lived and promulgated his gospel of mercy and love some 600 years earlier."[82] Similarly, W. Montgomery Watt reminded his readers that "in the Arabia of that day . . . [the tribes lacked] what we would call common decency. The enemy and the complete stranger had no rights whatsoever."[83] In framing this "excuse" these Western authors implicitly deny Muhammad's divine inspiration, reducing him to just another primitive Arab having no greater moral comprehension than the average Bedouin warrior. This is an amazing "slip," given the admiring tone of their biographies. On this event the traditional Islamic authors are far more consistent, holding that the fate of the *Banū Qurayza* was ordained by God as revealed to Muhammad, and that they obviously deserved what they got.[84] It is true, of course, that Muhammad had a civilizing influence on the assorted Arab tribes. As he managed to unite them, he imposed a more inclusive definition of community as embracing all believers, thus causing a considerable reduction in the bloodshed caused by inter-tribal aggression—as will be discussed. But this innovation offered no protection to outsiders such as Jews.

Having dealt with the *Banū Qurayza*, Muhammad sent his forces against an even greater prize, the rich Jewish community of Khaybar—a vast date palm plantation ninety miles south of Medina. The Jews' desert allies betrayed them (probably having been bribed), and they had to stand alone against the army of about sixteen hundred men that Muhammad led against them. The Jewish forts quickly fell to the far superior forces, and large numbers of Jews were taken prisoner and sold. Muhammad took two of the young Jewish women for wives, one of them the same day he had her husband executed for trying to conceal his goods.[85] All the other Jewish communities in the region quickly agreed to pay regular tributes to Muhammad.

Now it was Mecca's turn. As Muhammad began to march with ten thousand men, many of them from newly allied desert tribes, he was joined by many additional contingents along the way,[86] some of them even from Mecca. Facing reality, the city fathers quickly negotiated a settlement. In return for no resistance, Muhammad offered amnesty to all. After marching into Mecca peacefully, the Prophet kept his word, except for ten men and women who had once mocked him in public. These he had executed. Of course, the *Ka'bah* was cleansed of idols, but the black stone was kept and the *Ka'bah* was rededicated as a Muslim shrine (the Qur'an says that the *Ka'bah* originally was built by Abraham).

With Mecca finally in his fold, Muhammad launched an expedition against those desert tribes that still remained apart. That accomplished, Muhammad stood unchallenged as head of an Arab State that controlled nearly all of the Arabian Peninsula and was able to send military expeditions probing to the north and the east, especially into Syria. This was not yet a Muslim army—most of his tribal allies did not embrace the new faith, as will be seen. But it was Muhammad's army, so it might as well have been a Muslim army in that it fought battles that extended the Prophet's rule.

Muhammad was now in his sixties, but he continued to be very active and to take new wives. Then, in May 632, he fell ill. After several weeks he seemed to be getting better, and everyone looked forward to his recovery. But he soon relapsed, and on June 8 he died, his head in the lap of his favorite wife 'Ā'ishah, daughter of Abū-Bakr, whom he had married when she was nine. Muhammad was buried under the floor of 'Ā'ishah's bedroom, on the very spot where he had died. Since then, a mosque has arisen over the Prophet's humble grave in Medina, and it has been "adorned with gold, silver, marble, mosaics and diamonds" as the "rulers of Islam have heaped rich gifts upon it and vied with one another in embellishing it."[87]

Muhammad's death took everyone by surprise, and no arrangements had been made for his succession. This touched off a crisis of leadership, but eventually his old and trusted friend Abū-Bakr took over.

ISLAM

The great world faith founded by Muhammad came to be known as **Islam**, an Arabic term meaning "submission." Followers of this faith are called **Muslims**, which means "submitters" in Arabic.[88] Unlike the Eastern faiths, there is nothing very complex about its doctrines or practices. Indeed, that Islam is easy to learn and to follow greatly facilitated its spread.

The Five Pillars

Like Judaism, the religion that Muhammad left to the world has often been called a religion of ortho*praxy*, or correct practice, in contrast with Christianity's concern with ortho*doxy*, or correct beliefs or doctrine.[89] This difference is fully evident in the **Five Pillars**, which encompass the foundations of Islam, only the first of which concerns belief: the **Shahāda**, which is the Muslim confession of faith. It consists of but one sentence: "*I bear witness that 'There is no god but God'; I bear witness that 'Muhammad is the messenger of God.'*" All that is required to be fully accepted as a convert to Islam is to recite this sentence in the presence of two Muslim witnesses.

The second pillar is **Salāt**, or worship. It involves engaging in formal prayer five times a day (and at other occasions such as funerals and during eclipses). Muslim prayers involve recitation of a fixed set of words, at five specific times, beginning at just before daybreak and ending just after sunset. Prayer also requires a succession of body postures—bowing, prostrating, and sitting—while facing Mecca. Since there are no "priests" in Islam, all adult Muslim males are expected to be able to perform the role of *imām*, or prayer leader, although in practice "professional" specialists exist and some of these imāms gain immense respect and influence in both religious and secular affairs. Every Friday Muslim men (but not women) also must attend prayers at a *mosque*. *Mosque* is actually an English word based on the Arabic word *masjid*, which means "place of prostration."[90] Thus, any space dedicated to Muslim ritual is a mosque, but most often a mosque is a building, the Islamic equivalent of a church or temple. Before praying, Muslims wash their hands, face, and feet—preferably with running water.

The third pillar is **Zakāt**, or almsgiving. Muslims are required to give alms to support those in need, and to do so at the end of each year. *Zakāt* is not considered charity, but an obligation to Allāh—a sort of loan to God that will be paid back multifold.[91] **Sawm** identifies the duty to fast from dawn to dusk each day during the month of Ramadan. The fifth pillar is **Hajj**, which refers to the expectation that all Muslims will make a pilgrimage to Mecca during their lifetimes.

It could be argued that the requirement to obey holy law known as **Sharī'a** is a sixth pillar. The scope of *Sharī'a* is not limited to religious matters since Muslims have traditionally made no distinction between the religious and the secular and regard the *Sharī'a* as an adequate basis for the full legal system of a Muslim state. An additional sort of "professional" clergy are the specialists in *Sharī'a*, known as the "*ulamā*," or the "learned."[92] Their rulings, known as *ijtihād*, carry great force. Indeed, "ulamā" often rise to official government positions, and those who do have been known since the seventeenth century as *mullahs*.

Sharī'a is based on two sources: the Qur'an and *Sunnah* ("custom"), which derives from accounts of how Muhammad lived and his many sayings (see *Hadith*, below). Many matters of Muslim law are specified in the Qur'an, especially dealing with virtues and charity. But *Sunnah* is the basis for many of the practical aspects of day-to-day Muslim life. Examples include the dietary laws (which very closely approximate kosher as defined by Judaism); rules concerning defilement such as those limiting the use of the left hand (it being reserved for unclean matters); circumcision; and very strict rules concerning treatment of the Qur'an, such as never placing any object on top of this holy book.

The Qur'an

Islam is the third religion of "the book," but with a very great difference. The Old and New Testaments are *collections* of writing having many different authors. The **Qur'an** is a unitary work that consists of 114 *Sūras* (chapters) of varying length. It is not a history—only seven or eight actual places are mentioned. "Identifying what the Koran is talking about in a contemporary context is therefore usually impossible without interpretation. . . . We could not tell that the sanctuary was in Mecca, or that Muhammad himself came from there, and we could only guess that he established in Yathrib [Medina]."[93] The Qur'an is a series of messages or sermons, spoken in the first person (the more majestic "We" is often substituted for "I"), as is appropriate for a scripture that claims to consist of the actual words of Allāh that were repeated to Muhammad by the Angel Gabriel. Tradition holds that Muhammad could neither read nor write, although some modern scholars are convinced that he was literate.[94] If so, one must wonder why he seems not to have written down any of his revelations. Instead, he recited them repeatedly and encouraged followers to memorize them, although it is said that scribes sometimes wrote down what Muhammad recited.

When Muhammad died unexpectedly in 632, apparently there was no written Qur'an. This prompted an intensive search for any written portions that could be found, "many of them written on crude materials such as scraps of leather."[95] In addition, a great deal of material that had been memorized and transmitted orally was put in writing, probably for the first time, and an "official" Qur'an was assembled. Inevitably, this process caused a great deal of confusion and conflict as to what

A page from the Qur'an. For all that it is beautiful, this traditional Arabic script lacks short vowels, which often causes confusion as to which of several possible words actually is intended. (Musee du Quai Branly, Paris; Photo: Rèunion des Musées Mationaux/Art Resource, New York)

may have been overlooked, suppressed, or added. Muhammad himself contributed greatly to these problems since he never ceased to revise, to reorganize, and to add and delete material. Thus there are "indications that parts of earlier revelations were not included in the scripture. Early Muslims ... were aware that ... passages had been deliberately excluded by the Prophet, since [they] referred to them as what was 'abrogated,' 'lifted,' 'caused to be forgotten' or 'dropped.'"[96] Indeed, the Qur'an says this directly: "*Such of Our revelations as We abrogate or cause to be forgotten, we bring (in place) one better or the like thereof*" (II:106). The Qur'an (XXII:52) also apparently acknowledges the withdrawal of the so-called Satanic Verses. These are said to have been inserted by Muhammad as an appeal to Meccans by acknowledging the three pagan Goddesses worshipped at the *Ka'bah*. But it later was revealed to Muhammad that these verses did not originate with Allāh, but came from Satan, and hence were revoked. In any event, due to Muhammad's tendency to revise and rearrange, many sections of the Qur'an are "of a composite character, holding embedded in them fragments received by Muhammad at widely differing dates" often with somewhat "incongruous" results.[97]

Questions also persist because of the inherent ambiguities of Arabic script in this era—there are no short vowels and no diacritics in the earliest surviving texts. This has resulted in inevitable controversies as to the precise word that is meant in various places—albeit most words in the Qur'an are not in doubt. However, the ambiguities that do exist pose some significant questions of interpretation.[98]

In any event, all challenges to the authenticity of the Qur'an must confront the literary evidence that it all was "written" by the same "author." It is a matter of Muslim orthodoxy that the Qur'an is the most beautiful and powerful poetry ever written in Arabic. This claim, combined with the orthodox Muslim belief that God spoke to humanity in Arabic, which qualifies it as the divine language, makes it sinful to translate the Qur'an into other languages. Indeed, those Westerners who have ventured to render the Qur'an into their own languages have done so very circumspectly and have warned that no translation can provide more than a faint glimmering of the real thing. The eminent Cambridge Arabist A. J. Arberry (1905–1969), who translated a portion of the Qur'an into English, wrote that "the rhetoric and rhythm of the Arabic of the Koran are so characteristic, so powerful, so highly emotive, that any version whatever is bound in the nature of things to be but a poor copy of the glittering splendor of the original."[99] Similarly, the English convert to Islam and celebrated novelist Marmaduke Pickthall (1875–1936) flatly asserted that "the Koran cannot be translated," and qualified his "translation" with the title *The Meaning of the Glorious Koran* since no one could translate "that inimitable symphony, the very sounds of which move men to tears and ecstasy."[100] This may well be true, but a surprisingly large number of Muslim writers have long disputed the Qur'an's literary merits.[101] Those of us lacking command of Arabic cannot evaluate this issue, but we can notice that the claimed literary merits are entirely absent from English translations of the Qur'an as well as from translations into other European languages.[102] In Western languages, most readers will find the Qur'an "prosaic" and often "tedious."[103] However, this may be purely a matter of inadequate translations: to effectively translate good poetry requires a translator who is a good poet.

Be that as it may, clearly the Qur'an is not the work of some committee, nor can it be a collection gathered from various forgers and conspirators. Of course, this does not rule out substantial omissions or the fact that even slight alterations, even the changing of a single word, could have had a dramatic impact on meaning. Western scholars tend to accept the existing Qur'an as a reliable guide to Muhammad's teachings—disputes over authenticity are primarily among various Muslim sects and factions.

In addition to the Qur'an, Muslims also place great weight on collections of writings known as **Hadith**. These consist of three elements. The most important Hadith consist of sayings attributed to Muhammad and accounts of his actions—the biographies, or **sira**, as noted above. To a considerable degree these parts of the Hadith are akin to the Christian Gospels and the Book of Acts. They are Muhammad's teachings, not Allāh's revelations, and thus the source of *Sunnah* law. Second, the Hadith also include Muhammad's comments on the Qur'an (known as *tafsir*) and, third, his assessments of actions taken by others and his legal reasoning (known as *fīqh*). Examples of the latter:

The thing that is lawful but is disliked by Allāh is divorce.
Actions will be judged according to intentions.

All of the major branches of Islam accept the authority of the Hadith. The trouble is, they bitterly dispute which collections are authentic and which are not.

As already mentioned, many Sūras refer to characters and stories in both the Old and the New Testaments, and there often are very substantial differences between the Qur'an and the Bible. This is especially the case vis-á-vis the Old Testament since Muhammad had far more contact with Jews than with Christians. This is overwhelmingly reflected in the Qur'an, which includes far more Jewish than Christian material. Aside from retelling the birth of Jesus and acknowledging that Mary was virtuous, the Qur'an has very little overlap with the New Testament other than to deny that Jesus is anything more than "*a messenger, the like of whom had passed away before him*" (V:75) and quoting Jesus directly as saying, "*O children of Israel! Lo! I am the messenger of* Allāh *unto you*" (LXI:6). Consistent with this, on the side of the Dome of the Rock in Jerusalem, facing the Church of the Holy Sepulchre, it is written in Arabic: "God has no son."

To the extent that Muhammad's views about Jesus were influenced by his contacts with Christians, it is important to know that the Christians living in Arabia at that time were overwhelmingly members of various heretical groups. Many of them were Nestorians, a Christian group that began in the fifth century and was condemned as a heresy for teaching that Jesus was simply a man inspired by God, a position fully compatible with the one subsequently expressed in the Qur'an. The Qur'an also denies that Jesus was crucified, that it was only a "look-alike" of Jesus who was nailed to the cross (IV:157–158). This, too, is a common "heresy," known to the early Christian fathers as Docetism, and is very prominent in the Gnostic writings—Basilides, the second-century Alexandrian Gnostic teacher, even claimed that Jesus stood by and laughed while the wrong man suffered in his place.[104] Various Gnostic groups also were influential among the tribes in Arabia during Muhammad's time, particularly the Manichaeans with whom Muhammad may have had some contact.[105]

In contrast to the slim attention paid to Christianity, the Qur'an "retells" numerous Old Testament stories about Abraham, Moses, Solomon, David, and other leading figures. Often the character is abruptly brought into the discussion and the biblical account is simply alluded to and not retold, but when there are retellings they often depart greatly from the biblical "originals."[106] The Jewish scholars in Medina were quick to point out "the way in which the Koran distorted the Old Testament stories and the errors and anachronisms of which it was full."[107] It was partly in retaliation for these criticisms that Muhammad attacked Jewish groups and settlements in Arabia, and the issue remains as incendiary today as it was then. It seems unnecessary to summarize these disputes, but keep in mind that while Jews and Christians believe that the Qur'an is in error, thus reflecting Muhammad's misunderstandings about and ignorance of the Bible, Muslims believe that the Bible is wrong, that Allāh's original revelations were corrupted by Jews and Christians. This disagreement ultimately rests on faith, as does the ultimate point at issue: Are *Yahweh*, *Jehovah*, and *Allāh* different names for the same God?

Allāh

As would be expected, since Allāh was the name associated with the withdrawn High God of Arab paganism, the word itself is actually generic: *Ilāh* is the Arabic word for God, and *al-ilāh* means "the God," hence **Allāh**. However, despite the constant condemnations of anything less than absolute monotheism, like Judaism and Christianity, Islam is also a dualistic religion. Angels abound—some aid believers in battle; others known as *jinn* serve as guardian angels who record each person's deeds in preparation of the Last Reckoning, and huge numbers surround Allāh to everlastingly praise him. Islam also acknowledges **Shaytān**, that being the Arabic term for Satan (also known as **Iblīs**). As do the other two monotheisms, Muslims teach that this evil creature leads humans into error and sin after having fallen from high status among the angels, and that he will promote evil until held accountable at the Last Day.

Although traditional Muslims contend that *Yahweh* and *Jehovah* are simply other names for Allāh, they also believe that Jews and Christians have so corrupted their understanding of God, that in effect they worship different Gods. Indeed, when examined with care, Muslim conceptions of God not only differ considerably from Jewish and Christian doctrines, but differ quite significantly among the various Muslim groups. The most crucial of these various disagreements concerns the issue of free will versus predestination. Since the Qur'an sometimes affirms free will and sometimes asserts that all of one's life was predetermined by Allāh at the beginning of time, it is a never-ending dispute that divides Islam "into two distinct camps."[108]

Some Muslim sects, including the Shī'ah and the Mu'tazilīs, affirm free will—that humans are able to govern their actions and thus to choose between doing good and evil. This, then, is the basis for divine judgment as to entering Hell or Paradise. However, the Sunni majority holds otherwise: that despite the existence of Shaytān, God is responsible for both good and evil and all human actions are predetermined. The Sunni start from the assumption that Allāh has absolute freedom to act as he chooses. Hence, if God is just, it is only "because he wills to be just; were he to will otherwise his actions would still be right and good." Hence there is no intrinsic basis for good or evil; they are merely conventions. "Were God to stipulate in *shari'ah* that lying, adultery, and theft were good, they would be allowed in spite of the fact that human reason may judge them evil."[109] In any event, humans do not choose good or evil. Everything anyone does was already written in their book at the beginning of time:

> *Naught of disaster befalleth in the earth or in yourselves but it is in a Book before We bring it into being (LVII:22).*

> *Unto whomsoever of you willeth to walk straight.*
> *And ye will not unless (it be) that Allāh willeth (LXXXI:28–29).*

And finally:

> *Thus God misleadeth whom He will, and whom He will doth he guide aright (LXXIV:34).*[110]

Perhaps the single most important thing that sets Allāh apart from Yahweh and Jehovah is that Islam teaches that he utterly defies all understanding. It is impossible for human intellects to grasp any aspect of Allāh, nor can he reveal himself further since he is unknowable. Consequently, reasoning about the nature of God is regarded as impossible by some Muslim scholars and denounced as blasphemy by many.[111] Instead of concerning themselves with the sorts of questions about God that occupy Christian theologians, Muslim scholars devote their efforts to working out the intricacies of *Sharī'a*, or holy law.

Thus, the dominant Muslim conception of God is of a very intrusive, unpredictable, incomprehensible divinity.[112] Nothing may be assumed about Allāh, not even that he loves us, as that, too, might be a limiting factor. Whereas Christians assume that Jehovah is the epitome of rationality, Muslims deny that Allāh is rational or even virtuous, these being human judgments entirely—some Muslim thinkers even have denied the existence of "causality altogether," even in earthly matters, on grounds that it is contrary to God's unlimited freedom to act.[113] Indeed, elsewhere I have pointed out that such doctrines, including the "orthodox" claim that all attempts to formulate natural laws are blasphemous in that they, too, would limit Allāh's freedom, have played a major role in the failure of Islam to keep pace with the West.[114]

Finally, Allāh is without any physicality, and all references to his hands, or face, or to his sitting on a throne that occur in the Qur'an are to be taken as metaphorical. As so often happens, most Muslims find so distant and incomprehensible a God somewhat daunting. Thus, in an effort to humanize the supernatural, for most Muslims "religion consists above all in invoking the local saint and visiting his 'marabout' [tomb] . . . [reflecting] the irrepressible need for mediation which seems inherent in human nature."[115] Even so, what most Muslims believe about Allāh is that he is utterly inaccessible and fundamentally beyond all understanding. One simply submits.

BUILDING AN ARAB STATE

Submission to Allāh was the basis of the Arab State created by Muhammad, which was interpreted as submission to Muhammad's rule. Authoritarian states ruled by a king or an emperor were, of course, typical of the times. What was different about the new Arab State is that it was a true *theocracy*—the ruler was the actual head of the religion. That was to be expected during Muhammad's lifetime; he had created the state partly on the basis of his authority as Prophet (which drew to him a committed core of followers), and partly through treaties negotiated on the basis of his assembly of an army. Some desert tribes joined Muhammad's coalition only after he sent forces against them; others were drawn to Muhammad's banner through the promise of a share in future booty.

As for the urbanites, after Mecca set the example, other towns were allied through treaties specifying regular payments for "protection"—not only the Jewish communities, but also the Christian communities, such as Najrān at the southwestern tip of the peninsula, and pagan Arab communities, too.

The result was an Arab State embracing all of Arabia. Three logically related principles distinguished this state from anything seen before.[116] The first was the notion of *umma*, of a community defined and *set apart purely on religious grounds*. All other group characteristics were subordinated to this one feature—clan, tribe, language, and race were to be given no significance in defining members of the *umma* of Islam. It was purely a community of believers, and therefore the individual's bonds to the community were not those of kinship or proximity, but were *moral*! To betray the *umma* was to betray God. In this fashion all the traditional ties to communities were replaced by the contrast between believers and unbelievers. Hence, the principle was adopted (although soon to be ignored) that there must be no feuding within the *umma,* that conflicts were only legitimate with outsiders. The second principle was that the *authority of the state was God-given*. Hence it was claimed that laws were not enacted or proclaimed, but were *discovered* by close study of the Qur'an and the *Sunnah*. The third principle was that there could only be *one central authority*. Given Islam's strict monotheism—"the idea that there was but one locus of divine power in the universe—may have made it easier for Muslims to accept as well the idea of a single locus of political authority in the realm of worldly affairs."[117]

When the Prophet died and was succeeded by his close friend Abū-Bakr, the theocracy continued as Abū-Bakr's sole leadership was acknowledged. Of course, he was not Muhammad's successor as a prophet, that mission was now taken to be ended, but Abū-Bakr's role soon included interpretation of *Sharī'a* and an initial effort to gather up the Qur'an, as well as being head of the Arab State. Indeed, Abū-Bakr was the first to hold what became known as the office of *Caliph*, literally "successor" to the Prophet. Abū-Bakr's greatest achievement as Caliph was to hold the Arab State together when many of the desert tribes attempted to abandon the cause, as did some of the southern towns as well. Abū-Bakr dispatched armies at once to counteract these threats, and a series of victories in what are known as the *Ridda* wars settled the matter.

Of course, it took more than a Caliph to sustain an Arab State—it took a sophisticated and relatively united governing elite. Such an elite rapidly took shape during Muhammad's last years and, as might well be expected given the Prophet's background and that of many of his first converts, it consisted of "merchants and financiers of the *Hijāz*."[118] This elite quickly developed techniques for controlling and directing the warlike propensities of the desert tribes.

Two years after Muhammad's death, Abū-Bakr died, too, and was succeeded as Caliph by 'Unmar ibn-al-Khattāb, a former Meccan merchant who was one of the last converts Muhammad made in that city before the withdrawal to Medina. 'Unmar was well known for his asceticism and his lack of humor, and under his stern leadership the Arab State set out to conquer the world, in the name of Islam.

THE FAITH MILITANT

Before he died, Muhammad had gathered a military force not only able to dominate Arabia, but sufficient for him to contemplate expansion beyond. Incursions into the Fertile Crescent had become increasingly attractive because the rise of an Arab State greatly diminished the opportunities for the desert tribes to impose protection payments on the towns and villages, as well as ending their freedom to rob caravans. So, attention turned to the north and east where "rich spoils were to be won, and warriors could find glory and profit without risk to the peace and internal security of Arabia."[119] Raids by Muhammad's forces into Byzantine Syria and Persian (Sasanian) Iraq began during the last several years of the Prophet's life, and serious efforts ensued soon after his death.

Conquest

In typical fashion, many historians have urged entirely material, secular explanations for the Muslim conquests. Thus, the prominent Carl Heinrich Becker (1876–1933) explained that the "bursting of the Arabs beyond their native peninsula was . . . [entirely] due to economic necessities."[120] Specifically, it is said that a population explosion in Arabia, combined with a sudden decline in caravan trade, were the principal forces that drove the Arabs to suddenly begin a series of invasions and conquests at this time. Nonsense! The "population explosion" never happened, but was invented by authors who assumed that the "civilized" Byzantines and Persians could only have been overwhelmed by barbarian "Arab hordes."[121] The truth is quite contrary: the invasions were accomplished by remarkably small, very well led, and well-organized Arab armies. As for the caravan trade, if anything, it increased in the early days of the Arab State, probably because the caravans were now far more secure.

A fundamental reason that the Arabs attacked their neighbors at this particular time was because they finally had the power to do so. Having become a unified state rather than a collection of uncooperative tribes, the Arabs now had the ability to sustain military campaigns rather than the hit-and-run raids they had conducted for centuries. As for more specific motivations, as mentioned, Muhammad had seen expansion as a means to provide new opportunities, "in the form of booty and captured lands" for the desert tribes. And indeed, many desert Arabs were eager to attack, and some members of the ruling elite were attracted by the opportunity to rule new territories. But most important of all: the Arab invasions were planned and led by those committed to the spread of Islam.

The first conquest was Syria, then a province of the Eastern Roman Empire (Byzantium). It presented many attractions. Not only was it close, it was the most familiar foreign land—the merchants of the *Hijāz* had regularly dealt with Syrian merchants, some of whom came to the trade fairs at Mecca. Then, too, it was a more fertile region and had larger, more impressive cities, including Damascus. Not incidentally, in those days Jerusalem was also a Syrian city. Hence, Syria offered an attractive opportunity for both greed and creed!

Syria also presented a target of opportunity because of its unsettled political situation and the presence of many somewhat disaffected groups. After centuries of Byzantine rule, Syria had fallen to the Persians (Sasanians) in about 611 CE, only to be retaken by Byzantium in about 630 (two years before Muhammad's death). The Persians destroyed the institutional basis of Byzantine rule, and when they were driven out, a leadership vacuum developed. Moreover, Arabs had been migrating into Syria for centuries and had long been a primary source of recruits for the Byzantine forces. In addition, some Arab border tribes had long served as mercenaries to guard against their raiding kinsmen from the south. The Arabs in Syria had little love for their Roman rulers. Hence, when the Arab invasions came, many Arab defenders switched sides during the fighting.

The first Muslim forces entered Syria in 633 and took an area in the south without a major encounter with Byzantine forces. A second phase began the next year and met more determined resistance, but the Muslims won a series of battles, taking Damascus and some other cities in 635, and by 636 the Byzantine army abandoned Syria. Meanwhile, other Arab forces had moved against the Persian area known today as Iraq. The problem of unreliable Arab troops also beset the Persians just as it had the Byzantines—in several key battles, whole units of Persian cavalry, which consisted exclusively of Arab mercenaries, joined the Muslim side. By 637 the Persian army was routed, and the capital city of Ctesiphon had fallen to Arab forces.

Now, the Arab forces in Syria moved west and south, soon reaching the Mediterranean shore: Jerusalem was taken in 638, Caesarea Maritima in 640. The next year Arab armies invaded Egypt, taking Cairo; Alexandria fell to them in 642. Since they now were holding some major port cities, the Muslims began to build a fleet and in 649 sustained an invasion of Cyprus—Sicily and Rhodes were pillaged soon after. Then, in 655 the Muslim fleet shattered the Byzantine fleet off the Anatolian coast. A major Muslim Empire now ruled most of the Middle East and was spreading along the North African coast. Thirty years later the Empire stretched past Tangier and reached the Atlantic. By 714 much of Spain was occupied, and Muslim forces had expanded far to the east, occupying the Indus Valley. Shortly thereafter, Caliph Abu'l-Abbas al-Saffah moved the capital of the Muslim Empire from Damascus to a new city he built on the Tigris River in Iraq. Its official name was Madina al-Salam (City of Peace), but everyone called it Baghdad.

It was not until the battles had been won that civilians moved in to enjoy the status of ruling conquerors and a privileged lifestyle paid for by local taxes, these being the migrations that too many historians have confused with the invasions. This is obvious from the fact that the population of the Arabian Peninsula declined greatly *subsequent* to the Muslim conquests.[122] That the Arabs fled their arid, unproductive homeland for the far more favorable climates and easy living of the new areas is hardly surprising. Even so, the migrant Arabs were always very greatly

The Muslim conquest of the Middle East resulted in an Islamic overlay of Christianity, well illustrated by this mosque in Turkey. Originally built in the fourth century as a massive Christian church, it was converted into a mosque by painting over the Christian mosaics and adding a tall minaret at each corner. (Hagia Sophia, Istanbul, Turkey; Photo: Erich Lessing/Art Resource, New York)

outnumbered by the locals. Thus it was that the Muslim conquerers constituted a small elite who ruled over large populations of non-Muslims, most of whom remained unconverted for centuries, as will be seen.

How did the Arabs triumph so quickly and seemingly so easily? Many historians unfamiliar with military arts have found this inexplicable. They ask: how could a bunch of desert barbarians roll over the large, trained armies of the "civilized" empires? One must ask why these same scholars have not been similarly astounded by the victory of the Germanic barbarians over the "civilized" Romans on the other side of the Mediterranean? The two developments are relatively comparable, aside from the fact that the Arabs were better organized and better led than the Germanic tribes that took Rome.

The first thing to recognize is that the more "civilized" empires did not possess any superior military hardware, with the exception of siege engines, which were of no use in repelling attacks. *Everyone* depended on swords, lances, axes, and bows. Moreover, by this era there no longer were dedicated and highly disciplined "citizen soldiers" in the imperial forces— not in those Rome sent against the Germanic tribes, nor in those fielded by Byzantium or Persia. Instead, these forces were recruited from hither and yon, and mostly drew "foreigners" who served mainly for pay, which placed limits on their loyalty and their mettle. Indeed, as mentioned above, many of the rank and file in the Byzantine and Persian forces were Arabs, large numbers of whom ended up deserting to the Muslim side.

Nor were the "professional" armies of Persia and Byzantium better trained. The desert Arabs devoted themselves to arms from an early age, and when they went into battle, the individual Muslim fighters were part of a close-knit, small unit of men from the same tribe, who fought along-side their relatives and lifelong friends and thus were under extreme social pressure to be brave and aggressive. Because the Arab forces traveled by camel rather than on foot, they were far more mobile; they could always find and attack the most weakly held places and avoid the main Persian and Byzantine forces until they had them at a great disadvantage.

Contrary to what many would suppose, a very significant Arab ad-vantage lay in the *small* size of their field armies—they seldom gathered more than 10,000 men and often campaigned with armies of 2,000 to 4,000.[123] Their successes against the far larger imperial forces were simi-lar to those often enjoyed by small, well led, aggressive forces in the face of lumbering enemy hosts—consider the tiny Greek armies routing the Persians. In fact, due to their smaller numbers, the Arab invading forces often were able to far outnumber their opponents on a given battlefield because their much greater mobility allowed them to "git thar fustest, with the mostest," as the American Civil War commander so famously explained. The imperial forces either wore themselves out marching in fruitless pursuit of a battle or made themselves vulnerable by spreading out and trying to defend everywhere at once.

As should be clear, the Arab forces were very well led. Not by their tribal leaders, but by officers selected from "the new Islamic ruling elite of settled people from Mecca, Medina or al-Tā'if."[124] All of the middle to higher ranks were staffed from the elite by men who clearly under-stood administration, including the chain of command, and who were able to keep the larger strategic goals in mind while embroiled in tactical engagements. In fact, they were so aware of the need to "win the peace" that they imposed tight discipline on their forces vis-á-vis civilian populations, choosing instead to make very substantial, regular payments to their fighters in lieu of booty. Finally, of course, it was religion that bound the entire enterprise together—the Muslim Empire was the triumph of the *umma*!

Conversion

But it was a very long time before this empire was truly Muslim in anything but name. The reality of the Muslim Empire was that in the beginning very small Muslim elites ruled over non-Muslim (mostly Christian) populations in the newly conquered areas. This runs contrary to the widespread belief that early Muslims were uniformly a bunch of religious fanatics who demanded immediate conversion, and that, in addition, Islam aroused such intense and immediate appeal that voluntary mass conversions soon followed Muslim conquests. But, as noted in Chapter 7, mass conversions don't happen. As for widespread Muslim fanaticism, it seems to be a very recent phenomenon—a reaction both against modernity and anger over the lack of modernity. No doubt there always have been some Muslim fanatics, as there always have been fanatical Jews and Christians, as well as fanatical atheists, but it appears that most Muslims of, say, the seventh and eighth centuries, were as instrumental and lackadaisical vis-á-vis their faith as were most medieval European Christians. In any event, the conversion of the Muslim conquests took centuries.

Richard W. Bulliet[125] has provided superb data on conversion to Islam in the various conquered regions. For whatever reason, from earliest times, Muslims produced large numbers of very extensive biographical dictionaries listing all of the better-known people in a specific area, and new editions appeared for centuries—eventually Bulliet was able to assemble data on more than a million persons. The value of these data lies in the fact that Bulliet was able to distinguish Muslims from non-Muslims on the basis of their names. Then, by merging many dictionaries for a given area and sorting the tens of thousands of people listed by their years of birth, Bulliet was able to calculate the proportion of Muslims in the population at various dates and thus create curves of the progress of conversion in five major areas. Because only somewhat prominent people were included in the dictionaries, these results overestimate both the extent and the speed of conversions vis-á-vis the general populations in that elites began with a higher proportion of Muslims and Muslims would have continued to dominate. Consequently, Bulliet devised a very convincing procedure to convert these data into conversion curves for whole populations.

Table 8–1 shows the number of years required to convert 50 percent of the population to Islam in five major areas. In Iran it took 200 years from the date of the initial conquest by Muslim forces to the time when half of Iranians were Muslims. In the other four areas it took from 252 years in Syria to 264 years in Egypt and North Africa. At the bottom of the table we see that it took 310 years to convert 50 percent of the Roman Empire to Christianity, based on the projection presented in Chapter 7. And as was true for Christianity, conversion to Islam occurred rather more rapidly in the cities than in the rural areas.[126]

As to why things happened somewhat more rapidly in Iran, two things set it apart from the other areas. Probably the most important is that for more than a century after falling to Islamic invaders, the Iranians frequently revolted against Muslim rule and did so with sufficient success so that many very bloody battles ensued, as did brutal repressions. These conflicts would have resulted in substantial declines in the non-Muslim population, having nothing to do with conversion. Secondly, the climate of fear that must have accompanied the defeats of these rebellions likely would have prompted some Iranians to convert for safety's sake and probably caused others to flee.

That it took a bit longer to convert the Empire to Christianity than to convert these areas to Islam is also no surprise. Had the Christians begun their efforts in Rome under a Christian emperor and with control of all governmental functions, surely their task would have been somewhat eased—there would have been no persecutions, for one thing. That the Christians actually succeeded in a comparable time frame seems truly remarkable.

The most fundamental finding in Table 8–1 is consistency. From that, several important conclusions would seem to follow. First, the data strike another blow to the idea of mass conversions—it took a long time to convert the Islamic conquests. Second, the remarkable comparability of elapsed times, including the speed of the Christianization of the Empire, strongly suggests that there is statistical regularity to conversion—that

Table 8–1: Number of Years It Took to Convert
50 Percent of the Population

To Islam*

Syria	252 years
Western Persia (Iraq)	253 years
Eastern Persia (Iran)	200 years
Egypt & North Africa	264 years
Spain	247 years

To Christianity

Roman Empire	310 years

*Source: Calculated from Bulliet, *Conversion to Islam in the Medieval Period,* and
"Conversion to Islam and the Emergence of Muslim Society."

there may be something approaching a constant pattern at which conversion proceeds through any given social network. Indeed, conversion seems to be another phenonomenon best represented by the S-shaped or sigmoid curve, which has been found to characterize many other sorts of population-wide social changes, such as the diffusion of new technology and market penetration of new products.[127]

THE SPLINTERED "MONOLITH"

Not only did it take centuries to convert most of the conquered people to Islam, but even then significant non-Muslim minorities persisted within many parts of the Islamic world. To this was added, from early days, multitudes of Islamic sects. Both sources of pluralism often ignited angry and sometimes bloody conflicts.

Non-Muslim Minorities

For at least a century, many Western writers have praised the existence of tolerant, multireligious Muslim states. The most prominent example is Moorish Spain, which often has been hailed as "a shining example of civilized enlightenment"[128] and the "ornament of the world,"[129] in contrast with Christianity's repressive and prejudiced ways. In particular, enlightened treatment of Jews under Islam is compared with their often tragic persecution by Christians. This is pure fiction! Not that Muslims were more intolerant than Christians, but they surely were no less so. Consider these facts.

Not only did Muhammad initiate the banishment and murder of Jews, these practices have often been repeated by Muslim authorities.[130] Thus, 'Unmar, the second Caliph, expelled all Jews from the Arabian Peninsula. As for "enlightened" Moorish Spain, about 4,000 Jews were murdered there in 1066 and several thousand more in 1090.[131] Much is made of the fact that upon having reconquered Moorish Spain, in 1492 Ferdinand and Isabella ordered all Jews to convert to Christianity or to leave. But almost nowhere is it mentioned that in doing so, they merely repeated a prior Muslim policy: in 1148 all Christians and Jews were ordered to convert to Islam or leave Moorish Spain immediately, on pain of death.[132] Consequently, the great Jewish scholar Moses Maimonides (1135–1204) pretended to convert to Islam and lived many years in fear of being found out, even after having fled to Egypt.[133] The special Jewish vulnerability under Muslim rule stemmed in part from the fact that most of the new Muslim Empire consisted of societies that initially included large Christian majorities. This provided Christians with some protection as a matter of practicality.

But even when banishment or murder were not in the offing, Jews and Christians in Muslim societies were placed under severe restrictions and highly stigmatized. As the remarkable historian of Islam Marshall G. S. Hodgson (1922–1968) pointed out, from very early times Muslim authorities often went to great lengths to humiliate and punish *dhimmis*—these being Jews and Christians who refuse to convert to Islam. It was official policy that *dhimmis* should "feel inferior and to know 'their place' . . . [imposing such laws as] that Christians and Jews should not ride horses, for instance, but at most mules, or even that they should wear certain marks of their religion on their costume when among Muslims."[134] In other places non-Muslims were prohibited from wearing clothing similar to that of Muslims, nor could they be armed.[135] In addition, non-Muslims were invariably severely taxed compared with Muslims.[136]

Let me reiterate that I am not suggesting that Islam was more intolerant than Christianity. But it is important to refute the politically correct nonsense that medieval Muslims were possessed of a modern sense of inclusiveness.

Muslim Sectarianism

The most persistent mistake Westerners make about Islam is to think of it as monolithic. Like Christianity and Judaism, Islam has always spawned large numbers of disputatious sects and sustains many bitter factions even within various sects.[137] In fact, serious sect movements began during the Prophet's lifetime in the sense that at least three other Arabs also claimed to be prophets and successfully founded significant competing monotheistic movements.[138]

One of these was Musaylima who also "recited revelations in rhymed prose" and who, some sources suggest, began to do so before Muhammad began having visions.[139] A "sura" attributed to Musaylima has survived: "*God has been gracious to the pregnant woman; He has brought forth from her a living being that can move; from her very midst.*"[140] Like Muhammad, Musaylima also was influenced by Christianity and gained the support of a major Arab tribe.[141] Hence, in about 631, Musaylima sent envoys with a message to Muhammad proposing that they share authority. Muhammad replied that "if it were not that envoys must not be slain I would cut off your heads." He then dictated an angry response to Musaylima "the liar."[142] Shortly before his death, Muhammad sent troops against Musaylima, who was killed in the battle.

Another competitor was Al-Aswad al-Ansi, who rose to power in Yeman. He was known as the "veiled one" because he normally wore a mask in public. Like Muhammad he organized an army, conducted raids on caravans and towns, and established a large political base. Muhammad sent a select group of ten of his companions to infiltrate Al-Aswad's court. Having gained the support of one of Al-Aswad's wives (whose previous husband had died opposing Al-Aswad), two of Muhammad's supporters gained access to Al-Aswad's bedroom and stabbed him to death while he slept. Tradition has it that the murder took place only hours before Muhammad's own death, but that he learned of it through a revelation while still alive.[143]

A third prophetic challenger was a woman named Sajāh, who gained the support of a northern nomadic border tribe that had previously accepted Nestorian Christianity. She, too, had revelations in rhymed prose. Muhammad died before he could take action against her, but Abū-Bakr crushed her dissenting movement during the *Ridda* wars.[144] Sajāh's fate following the defeat of her army is unknown.

The existence of competing prophets is an aspect of the origins of Islam that would seem worthy of serious study, especially in connection with the apparently widespread expectations that an Arabian prophet was coming. But very few of the leading modern studies even mention any of them,[145] and those that do settle for a sentence or two[146]—only Rodinson devoted most of a page to the matter even though he omitted Al-Aswad.

Muhammad's unexpected death was the principal cause of the most important and longest-lasting schism in Islam, between the Shī'ah and the Sunni. Not having officially designated his successor, tensions arose over who should lead. One party believed Muhammad should be succeeded by his closest heir; the other party believed his successor ought to be selected by the group who had served as Muhammad's primary assistants and confidants. Since Muhammad did not leave a biological son, his cousin and son-in-law, Ali, was proposed as the true heir. Ali's claim was supported by most of Muhammad's relatives, but opposed by some of Muhammad's longtime companions and by the Medinan leadership, who united behind Abū-Bakr, Muhammad's old friend and father-in-law. Ali did not contest the selection. Just before his death, Abū-Bakr appointed 'Unmar as his successor. Again Ali went along. But when 'Unmar was murdered and the Companions of the Prophet (as his old friends now were known) once again passed over Ali, selecting another of Muhammad's sons-in-law 'Uthmān as Caliph, this not only greatly offended Ali, but angered Medinans because 'Uthmān favored the Meccans. When 'Uthmān also was murdered in 656, the people of Medina proclaimed Ali as Caliph. But they were opposed by 'Ā'ishah, daughter of Abū-Bakr and Muhammad's favored child bride, along with the leading Meccans, and they (probably falsely) accused Ali of complicity in 'Uthmān's death. This led to the Battle of the Camel, a bloody confrontation that ended with the defeat of Ali's forces and his withdrawal to a garrison town in Iraq, later to be assassinated.

Thus was the unity of the *umma* destroyed forever. "Henceforth no caliph would be able to rule without an army."[147] Perhaps an even more significant result was that never again would there be *an* "Islam." To say someone is a Muslim necessarily raises the question: what kind of Muslim? There are scores of possible answers.

Ali's supporters came to be known as the "Seceders" and lived on as the *Shī'ah* (or Shi'ites), and those from whom they broke away are known as the *Sunni*. The Sunni are by far the largest group of Muslims today, being dominant in most Islamic nations; the Shī'ah are the dominant group in Iran, and they also are the majority in Iraq where they were long suppressed by a Sunni minority and by Saddam Hussein..

Since this initial split, many sects have emerged within both the Shī'ah and the Sunni—in fact, the famous mystical Sufi movement seems to have broken off from both of them. There is no authoritative catalogue of Islamic sects, nor are there available membership statistics for the various Muslim groups within specific nations. Thus the most cited source on the religious profiles of the nations of the world[148] is able only to report

This Iranian fresco shows Sunni soldiers beheading dead Shī'ah fallen in battle sometime in the seventh century. The wives of the Shī'ah are being forced to watch the dismemberment from behind their veils. (Imam zadeh Shah Zaid, Isfahan, Iran; Photo: SEF/Art Resource, New York)

the total number of Muslims within a nation, and can only list the various Muslim groups active in a nation without a statistical breakdown. Even so, the lists suggest a very diverse and often bitterly divided Islam. Consider Saudi Arabia. It is reported to be 93.7 percent Muslim, or just over 20 million Saudis. The Saudi Muslims are said to be almost entirely Sunni, with only 130,000 Shī'ah. But the Wahhabis, a militant sect within Sunnism, make up the dominant group, and the other Saudis mainly belong to other sects including Shafiite, Hanafiite, Malikite, Hanbalites, and 60,000 Ismailis.[149] In contrast with Saudi Arabia, Iran is said to be 97 percent Shī'ah, with only 2.6 million Sunnis. Of course, there are many different kinds of Shī'ah in Iran, including Imamites and Ahl-i-Haqq. Even these lists of various Muslim sects within a country greatly minimize the extent of Islamic diversity because there are bitter divisions within most sect groups. Even so, the very recent World Values Surveys of Muslim nations did not bother to use the opportunity to ask respondents their particular affiliation or preference. Instead, we learn that 98.5 percent of those surveyed in Iran are "Muslims," and we must turn elsewhere even to learn that the majority of them probably are Shī'ah. It is the same for the other Islamic nations in the surveys—everyone is coded as part of an undifferentiated Muslim "monolith," which doesn't exist. My friend Mansoor Moaddel, a distinguished expert on Islam, has told me that in any given Islamic city there is as much variation among the local mosques as there is among Protestant churches in American communities.

CONCLUSION

Competition among its many sects has helped Islam avoid the centuries of weakness inflicted on Christianity by its having become an uncontested monopoly faith. Of course, here and there, and from time to time, a particular Islamic sect would manage to abolish its competitors, and whenever that took place, the average level of individual Muslim commitment declined. However, from earliest days, Islam has often displayed the immense competitive advantage of monotheism: the capacity to inspire unwavering commitment among rank-and-file believers. Like their Christian and Jewish counterparts, ordinary Muslims were ready to make great sacrifices for their faith and eager to convert others to believe in the One True God. That belief can, of course, be a two-edged sword. If it made the Jews in Arabia willing to be slaughtered rather than to recant their faith in Yahweh, it made the Muslim Arabs equally willing to slaughter them for not embracing Allāh. Fortunately, that kind of intolerance can be overcome without any corresponding loss in fervor, as it has been in many modern situations.[150]

However, it also must be acknowledged that thoughout history, much that is read as Muslim religious intolerance has often had less to do with religious zeal and more to do with the unwillingess of tyrannical states to abide nonconformity, religious or otherwise. And there lies the great historical burden of Islam: taken as in keeping with the will of Allāh, the Arab State established by Muhammad has persisted through the centuries in Muslim nations, with its fundamental tyranny unmodified and rarely challenged.

DISCOVERING GOD?

IS IT TRUE THAT ALL RELIGIONS offer a valid, if quite different glimpse of God? If not, do any religions offer any truths about God? If so, which ones? And how are we to decide? Indeed, how are we to know that God isn't an illusion, conjured up by humans desperate to comprehend and give purpose to a meaningless universe? Although the entire book has been leading to these questions, they are no less daunting.

To begin, the chapter considers the religious revolution that occurred in the sixth century BCE—the so-called **Axial Age**. How can we account for the appearance of so many founders of new faiths at approximately the same time? Was this an age of widespread revelations? In pursuit of an answer, I will attempt to trace the probable interactions among these new religions, attempting to identify what may have diffused from whence to where. Then, having recognized the fundamental incompatibility of some major religions, I consider whether a common core of faiths can be isolated—a succession of religions that trace either the progressive *discovery* of God, or the *evolution* of our image of God. That is, can we identify which of the world's religions seem to reflect real discoveries about God? Obviously, no certain answer is possible, but some simple criteria can be applied to suggest which religions could be divinely inspired. Finally, the chapter confronts *the* question: have we discovered God, or have we invented him?

EXPLORING THE AXIAL AGE

Although the German philosopher Karl Jaspers (1883–1969) was the first to refer to the religious events of the sixth century BCE as the Axial Age and attempted (rather unsuccessfully) to promote interest in it, apparently the first scholar to notice the simultaneous appearance of so many founders was the influential German scholar Ernst von Lasaulx (1805–1861). He wrote in 1856: "It cannot possibly be an accident that, six hundred years before Christ, Zarathustra in Persia, Gautama Buddha in India, Confucius in China, the prophets in Israel . . . all made their appearance pretty well simultaneously."[1] Fourteen years later, his fellow countryman Viktor von Strauss (1809–1899) expanded on Lasaulx: "During the centuries when Lao-tse and Confucius were living in China, a strange movement of the spirit passed through all civilized peoples. In Israel Jeremiah, Habakkuk, Daniel and Ezekiel were prophesying and in a renewed generation the second temple was erected in Jerusalem. . . . In Persia an important reformation of Zarathustra's ancient teaching seems to have been carried through, and India produced . . . the founder of Buddhism."[2]

What was the common element? How did all of this come to pass at once? There has been very little effort to answer either question, and those few scholars who have paid any attention to the matter have either limited themselves to purely "material" sources and consequences of these religious changes,[3] or they have gone to the other extreme and treated these religious developments as a relatively disembodied contest of ideas.[4] Obviously, there was a clash of ideas *and* there were significant social aspects of these religious changes. But it is vital to focus on the primary fact: these were *religious* revolutions initiated by *individuals*!

Perhaps the most important thing to understand about the Axial Age is that it did *not* reflect the nearly simultaneous occurrence of revelations since many founders dismissed the Gods as of little or no importance. The dominant theme of the New Hinduism conceived of the Gods in purely subjective terms—"All the gods are in me." Subjective Gods are incompatible with revelations. Buddha and Mahāvīra also minimized the Gods and claimed to have found the truth within themselves. As for Lao-Tzu and Confucius, they were not even aware that they were founding religions. In Greece, too, there was no tradition of founding revelations among either the Orphics or Pythagorans. The only apparent revelations in this era involved Zoroaster and the Hebrew prophets. Clearly, then, the common aspect of this outbreak of new religions did not involve God, at least not directly.

The revolutionary religious outlook that appeared in the Axial Age was, as Jaspers put it, that "religion was rendered ethical."[5] Prior to that era, religion revolved around efforts to propitiate the Gods (lest they punish us) and to obtain favors from them. Since the Gods were not thought to be especially moral or much concerned about human behavior per se, no link existed between religion and morality. Of course, human groups had moral codes, but these were not reinforced by religious sanctions.[6] Suddenly, in the Axial Age that changed. The idea rapidly spread that we earn our fates, whether from the Gods or from an impersonal universe, on the basis of our behavior—the connected concepts of sin and salvation had been invented or discovered.

The New Hinduism proposed that, through the process of reincarnation, individuals earn their situation in their next life by their *karma*, by the extent of their sins in their current life. The "good" are reborn into a higher social position; the "wicked" into a lower status. Indeed, if one sufficiently overcomes desire and attachment to self, one can escape the cycle of rebirths entirely, gaining release into a benign unconsciousness. Mahāvīra accepted these ideas and proposed that escape from the cycle of reincarnation required a heroic level of asceticism. Similarly, in Greece the Orphics and the Pythagorans pursued favorable reincarnation through an extensive, ascetic code of behavior. In contrast, Buddha dismissed asceticism, proposing that one achieved Nirvana through meditation. But the fact that he spelled out an extensive moral code made it clear that he believed that sinful living obviated any fruits of meditation. Admittedly the concept of sin did not become prominent in China at this time; both Taoism and Confucianism became concerned about sin only when Pure Land Buddhism (probably shaped by Zoroastrianism) arrived about five centuries later.[7]

The Zoroastrians and Jews advocated especially strong conceptions of sin and salvation that departed sharply from those embraced further east or in Greece. Most importantly, they were not pessimists seeking to escape. They believed in a Paradise where their fully self-aware and conscious individual souls would enjoy everlasting life. As for the wicked, they did not simply face a less attractive next incarnation, but were doomed to suffer forever in hell.

Ignoring the great variations in ideas about salvation, a truly interesting question about the Axial Age is, why did a link between religion and

In contrast with faiths dedicated to escaping from conscious existence, Zoroastrians, Jews, and subsequently Christians believe in an attractive, conscious life after death as illustrated here by Lucas van Leyden's (1526) painting of the dead rising from their graves at Judgment Day. (Stedelijk Museum de Lakenhal, Leiden, The Netherlands; Photo: Erich Lessing/Art Resource, New York)

morality become so important at this time? Notice that I have not asked how the idea of sin originated. That is a question that extends far beyond the information available. One might suggest that the idea of sin originated with Zoroaster's revelations. But if this were the origin of the idea of sin, it spread east without his notion of Paradise. Nor did he originate the idea of reincarnation. That seems to have arisen among the founders of the New Hinduism, about whom we know virtually nothing. As for the ancient Hebrews, we simply don't know what they actually taught, although it appears that their knowledge of the Law dates from the era of the Deuteronomists and that Jewish belief in an attractive afterlife arose during their days in Babylon. Hence, it seems well advised to admit that the origins of the idea of sin and of some kinds of salvation must remain mysterious. But it is quite feasible to ask why these notions were embraced so eagerly.

Social Control

As I sketch how the link between religion and morality helped solve an increasingly acute social problem, keep in mind that although most social scientists would argue that the idea of sin was developed to meet this need, I do not. The need existed for a considerable time before this solution arose. What I am attempting is to explain why, once the "answer" appeared, it proved so popular.

Social life is only possible to the extent that groups exert *social control—collective efforts to ensure conformity to the moral standards of the group.* Lacking social control, humans would need to be hermits because the behavior of others would be too dangerously unpredictable. So, from infancy humans are raised to believe that the norms of their group are the "right" way to behave and are trained to conform. In addition, *informal* methods of social control consist of *pressures to conform imposed by those in our immediate social environment.* That is, even if they have no inner inhibitions against misbehavior, most people conform most of the time in order to avoid offending those around them—misbehavior can cost us the respect and goodwill of others. In extreme cases, misbehavior can cost us our lives. In small, very settled societies, informal social control usually suffices to sustain an adequate level of moral conformity; hence it rarely is necessary even to resort to force to keep people within acceptable limits. But as societies become larger and social life becomes increasingly impersonal, it is necessary to resort to *formal* means of social control: these are *organized and often quite impersonal methods of deterring and punishing moral violations.* Enter specialists in detecting and punishing miscreants.

Formal social control is expensive—contrast the cost of dirty looks from neighbors with that of maintaining a police officer. It also is rather less effective than informal control, if for no other reason than it is not nearly as capable of detecting violations. Indeed, even informal means of social control are of no avail against misdeeds done in secret. But sin is never invisible! Nor does it ever go unpunished! Hence, as societies encounter increasing problems of nonconformity and social disorder, the concept of sin provides a powerful means of social control.

A rapidly increasing need for more effective means of social control clearly took place in India during the sixth century BCE. During this century hundreds of small rural "statelets" were merged into far larger, far more urban states and eventually into the single Magadhan kingdom. As these changes took place, many found themselves living amid strangers, which left them relatively free from informal social control. Thus, the informal basis of social order began to collapse.[8] Even the authority of rulers no longer was based on respected traditions—most rulers were usurpers. For example, once the Magadhan kingdom was in place, the first six successions to the throne involved a royal heir murdering his father. Such social pathologies stemming from this new era of "urbanization" meant that nearly *everyone* had a great deal to gain from a new basis for social control—one that could detect and punish each and every moral lapse. The concept of sin filled this urgent need. In similar fashion, both Zoroaster and the Deuteronomists confronted substantial levels of social conflict and disorganization as they promoted a very strong link between religion and morality. In Zoroaster's time, many small kingdoms, including the one that elevated him to prominence, were being submerged in the new and rapidly growing Persian Empire. The Deuteronomists endured conflicts within Israel, the constant threat of invasion from both north and south, and eventually the Babylonian Captivity. Recall, too, that later when Pure Land Buddhism swept across China, it was during the disorders produced by the conquest of the North and the displaced rulers of the South.

Let me repeat, I am not suggesting that a growing need for enhanced social control caused the "discovery" of the idea of sin. All I am suggesting is that when this idea appeared, the times were especially ripe for its rapid adoption.

But not everywhere! Axial Age or not, the concepts of sin and salvation were not embraced in the most imposing of the early civilizations, such as Egypt and Sumer (Mesopotamia). Why did they not "awaken" to the new concepts? Because they were, as the celebrated Arnoldo Momigliano (1908–1987) put it, already "spiritually stagnant,"[9] being tightly in the grip of subsidized temple religions impervious to anything new. As Jaspers noted, any culture that did not soon embrace the innovations radiating from the regions involved in the Axial Age became peripheral to history—even if history did begin at Sumer. Because these once-great civilizations took no part in this historical turning point, "We are infinitely closer [culturally and religiously] to the Chinese and the Indians" than to Egyptians and Mesopotamians of that era.[10] In fact, the most dramatic doctrines of sin and salvation arose in areas peripheral to Egypt and Mesopotamia—in Palestine and at the edge of Persia, places where there was sufficient latitude for innovation. By the same token, India was nothing but a huge collection of effectively "peripheral" states when the New Hinduism, Jainism, and Buddhism arose. Meanwhile, as noted, the concept of sin made no headway in China at this time, and became important only in a later era of disorganization.[11]

Diffusion

The entire discussion above assumes the diffusion of the idea of sin across many societies. Sad to say, at present this is not a very popular assumption. Despite the fact that we now possess overwhelming physical evidence of extensive trade and travel linking Asia and Europe far earlier than the era in question,[12] many scholars seem to object to all claims that anything came to any particular society from elsewhere, and especially to the slightest suggestion that anything of any value diffused from the West to the East.[13] Even so thoughtful a scholar as Eric Weil (1904–1977) dismissed all possibility of contact or mutual influence among the faiths that arose in the sixth century BCE—even among those in India—referring instead to them as "astonishingly parallel developments."[14] Astonishing, indeed!

The facts are entirely against these denials. As noted in Chapter 5, many Sumerian artifacts were found in the Indus civilization in India, and Indus objects have been unearthed in Sumer. Students of ancient pottery trace several major varieties of Chinese pottery, dating from around 2000 BCE, to Persia.[15] Indeed, it is regarded as established fact that the wheel reached China from Sumer more than a thousand years before the Axial Age, incidental to the introduction of horse-drawn war chariots.[16] Ideas would seem to be far more easily transported.

Within India, of course, the notions developed by the New Hinduism had to travel only a very short distance to reach Mahāvīra and Buddha, and these two founders lived only a rather short stroll from one another. Given that Pythagoras is believed to have traveled in the East, the transmission of the principles of the New Hinduism to Greece and southern Italy is easily assumed. Although it would have been quite feasible for Zoroastrian and Jewish ideas to have diffused to India, this need not be presumed since there is no convincing trace of them in the Indian inspirations—unless it was merely the notion that individual misbehavior has transcendent meaning. As for the link between China and India, we possess very plausible details of how Pure Land Buddhism was transported over the Silk Roads.

So much then for the Axial Age. A far larger question has to do with the connections among faiths more generally. Can we grant all religions some degree of divine inspiration?

CRITERIA OF DIVINE INSPIRATION

The idea that all religions are somewhat true is popular among students of comparative religions. John Hick has long campaigned in support of the proposition that all the major faiths are equally valid, although it is not clear that he actually finds much validity in any religion.[17] Nicholas F. Gier has heaped contempt on everyone who fails to grasp the essential equivalence of the major faiths.[18] As for the popular Huston Smith, he claims to be a practicing believer in all the world's great religions—a lifelong Christian, he prays to Allāh five times a day and practices yoga, among other things.[19] Even such an ardent Christian as C. S. Lewis (1898–1963) made allowance for the validity of other faiths: "I can't say for certain which bits came into Christianity from earlier religions. An enormous amount did. I should find it hard to believe in Christianity if that were not so. I couldn't believe that nine-hundred and ninety-nine religions were completely false and the remaining one true."[20] Be that as it may, the question persists: *have all religions contributed to the discovery of God?*

Assuming for the moment that God exists, the answer must be "no." I am fully sensitive to the controversial aspects of that answer, but to answer "yes" is certainly as controversial and, in my judgment, far less plausible. I suggest three criteria by which it is possible to separate faiths into those that could reflect actual divine inspiration in that they increased our understanding of God, and those that seem not to have been inspired.

The first criterion assumes that *God reveals himself*. If that is not so, then there is nothing further to discuss because all faiths are entirely of human origins. But if God does reveal himself, some religions cannot claim divine inspiration. That is, some of the great founders based their teachings on what they perceived as revelations, but other religious founders rejected the possibility of revelations and presented their doctrines as their own creations—albeit sometimes these were "discovered" through deep meditation. It would seem appropriate to take the founders at their word and assume that those who reported no revelations lacked the means to contribute to the discovery of God.

The second criterion is *consistency*. It is all well and good to suppose that God limits his revelations to the prevailing level of human understanding, but it is not plausible to suppose that his revelations are utterly contradictory. Granted that variations can arise from the transmission and interpretation of revelations, but there still should be substantial compatibility among any religions that are based on divine inspirations. Hence, faiths that greatly depart from a consistent core can be relegated to human origins. The third criterion is *progressive complexity*. Ordered as to when they appeared, authentic religions should reveal an increasingly sophisticated and complex understanding of God—they should form a developmental or evolutionary sequence. Put another way, revelations should not regress—less sophisticated revelations should not follow the more complex, not even by being directed to less sophisticated societies. Presumably, once material of a particular level of complexity has been revealed, it is to be communicated to less sophisticated cultures by missionizing and conversion.

I now apply these criteria to the religions discussed in the previous chapters, attempting to assemble a central core of faiths. What follows assumes familiarity with the previous chapters; major aspects of various faiths will merely be cited, not spelled out at length.

Revelations

Karen Armstrong proposed that "if the Buddha or Confucius had been asked whether he believed in God, he would probably have winced slightly and explained—with great courtesy—that this was not an appropriate question."[21] She offered this as evidence of their superior wisdom and virtue. Perhaps. But it also demonstrates that they could not have made any contribution to the discovery of God.

It is on these grounds that, at least in their *initial* forms, Hinduism, Buddhism, Jainism, Taoism, and Confucianism can be excluded from the category of inspired faiths. I have italicized *initial* because some of these faiths were later substantially transformed in ways that may reflect revelations, at least indirectly. In the case of the "restored" New Hinduism represented by the Bhagavad-gītā, we do not know whether it originated with revelations to an unknown Indian sage (or sages), was prompted by a surviving popular commitment to the traditions of the Vedas, or was inspired by the diffusion of ideas from the West. As for direct revelations, no important revelatory tradition has survived within Hinduism. As for "diffusion," although there were substantial numbers of Jews and Persians on hand in India at this time, there is little in the New Hinduism that could reflect their influence. Thus it would seem that the impetus for the return of the Gods to the New Hinduism reflected the continuing popular attachment to Gods.

Turning to China, a case can be made that Pure Land Buddhism was a new religion, traditional Buddhism having been fundamentally reshaped by Zoroaster's revelations. If so, this in turn gave a revelatory basis to Taoism and Confucianism, albeit at "third hand." These possibilities suggest that there may be aspects of inspired religion present in these faiths. But to the extent that these were derivative of revealed religion, they made no *independent* contribution to human knowledge of God. Of course, some will seek to restore the "authenticity" of all these faiths by proposing that although the founder did not consciously experience a revelation, his teachings were divinely "inspired."[22]

Consistency

As a group, the leading world religions examined in this book are not logically compatible. Some religions propose the existence of a conscious life after death. Others offer no such prospects and idealize an escape into an eternal, unconscious bliss. These views are utterly incompatible and, unless we conceive of God as irrational or wicked, at least one of them must be false. Some religious founders acknowledged the existence of many Gods, albeit they placed little importance on any of them. Other founders were enthusiastic monotheists. Which ones have it right? Some founders taught that the universe was created by God. Others claimed that the universe is uncreated and eternal. Notice that in all these comparisons, the "revealed" religions are compatible.

Progressive Complexity

The principle of divine accommodation teaches that God reveals himself within the current limits of the human capacity to comprehend. Applied to the materials at hand, that means that over the course of history, God's revelations should progress from the simple to the more complex. Hence, we should not discover that some Stone Age tribes had full knowledge of Mosaic Law. Nor should later conceptions of God be less complex than earlier ones; when the Israelites turned from Yahweh to Baal, Astarte, Molech, and Asherah, this did not reflect divine inspiration.

This assumption leads to the conclusion that if faiths are ordered on the basis of when they began, the inspired faiths will exhibit a pattern of progress—later faiths will tell us more about God than will earlier faiths. The best way to apply this criterion is to attempt to order the faiths not already excluded from the inspired core by the first two criteria.

AN INSPIRED CORE?

It would seem legitimate to begin with the belief in *High Gods* that existed in so many early societies. Contrary to the dogmas of social evolution, very early humanity did not embrace crude superstitions of the kind Tylor called animism. Rather, as Giambattista Vico (1668–1744) explained, "Primitive religion was not nonsense, idiotic babbling, but man's first striving toward the divine truth."[23] Although they were not monotheists, many primitive groups embraced a High God who presided over a collection of lesser Gods and who was believed to be the Creator not only of the universe, but often of the lesser Gods as well. Moreover, unlike the Gods of subsequent pagan pantheons, many of the High Gods of the prehistoric times were linked to human morality! Of course, we know nothing of any revelations from this era, but it would not stretch plausibility to assume with Father Schmidt that God had revealed himself in earliest times.

The subsequent rise of polytheistic temple religions was regressive— the religions of Sumer, Egypt, Greece, early Rome, and Mesoamerica have no place within the progressive core of inspired faiths.

It is difficult to evaluate the monotheism founded by *Akhenaten*. In favor of inclusion in the inspired core are three factors. First, this religion appears to have been based on revelations. Second, it was considerably more sophisticated than the early conceptions of High Gods. Third, it was not incompatible with either the prior High Gods or with the subsequent monotheisms. The basis for rejecting it as inauthentic is its failure to have had any lasting effects. Perhaps that is irrelevant. Perhaps, too, it is inaccurate. The monotheism that flourished during Akhenaten's reign might have contributed to a trend toward monotheism that seemed to be building in the region, even though no direct links have been discovered.

Next come the *ancient Hebrews*. Clearly they contributed to the discovery of God even though they did not begin as full-fledged monotheists. From very early days many influential voices were raised to proclaim the exclusive worship of Yahweh, and eventually this evolved into the celebrated *Jewish monotheism*—although how much of this came prior to the Deuteronomists is very difficult to assess. In any event, the evolution of Jewish monotheism involved a series of revelations. It also involved some interaction with *Zoroastrianism* during the Jewish sojourn in Babylon. To the extent that the reconstructed biography of Zoroaster is accurate, the religion he founded deserves a place in the common core. It involved a revelation. It was unflinchingly monotheistic. It may even have been the origin of the idea of sin, in the sense that moral lapses have transcendent significance.

Christianity epitomizes revealed religion and offers a substantially more complex and nuanced vision of God as is appropriate for a faith that fulfills the Old Testament and presents a more comprehensive doctrine of salvation. Of course, Jews disagree and remain convinced that the promised messiah is still to come. So, too, the Parsis in India believe that Zoroaster was the last authentic prophet. And, of course, Muslims disagree with them all.

Thus we confront the most difficult aspect of identifying an inspired religious core: does *Islam* qualify? The most fundamental claim made by Muhammad and enshrined in the Qur'an is that Islam is God's final word to humanity: God never promised to send a messiah, all faiths other than Judaism and Christianity are entirely false, and even the Jews and the Christians have so corrupted God's truths that Muhammad was sent as the final prophet from God to lead humanity out of error. If we accept these claims, then Islam takes its place as the fulfillment of the inspired core of faiths. Perhaps the best way to resolve the matter is to ask whether

Islam is progressive or regressive vis-à-vis our understanding of God. It is quite unnecessary to doubt Muhammad's sincerity to conclude that the faith revealed in the Qur'an, having originated centuries after the other great monotheisms, is morally and theologically regressive. In sustaining theocracies and by repressing innovations, Islam resembles the temple religions of the ancient civilizations. As for discovering God, the prevailing conceptions of Allāh present him as so unpredictable and unknowable that it may not even be assumed that he is rational or virtuous, which has pretty much prevented the development of an Islamic theology—it is futile to reason about the unreasonable. Some Western apologists for Islam explain these apparent "deficiencies" are due to the fact that Arab culture was so "primitive"[24] that a more sophisticated message would have been inappropriate. But why would God have sent a regressive message to Arab tribes that were in the process of converting to Judaism and Christianity?

Therefore, in accord with criterion three, I think it inappropriate to include Islam in the inspired core of faiths. I accept that Muslims will condemn this judgment. And of course, it *is* merely my judgment, upon which matters of faith and taste inevitably intrude.

Be reminded, too, that this entire discussion of a common core is based on the *assumption* that God exists. If God does not exist, then *no* religion is inspired!

DOES GOD EXIST?

Through the millennia, many Gods have been invented, and many religious founders were either deluded or charlatans.[25] It could not be otherwise when the matters involved are so important and so impossible to fully verify. But it does not necessarily follow that all religions are rooted in fraud, illusions, or wishful thinking. To conclude this study I shall suggest that, quite aside from any and all traditional religious claims, there are objective grounds for accepting the existence of God as the more rational conclusion.

To begin at the beginning: in agreement with Eastern religious founders, for a long time Western opponents of religion claimed that all notions of a Creation were "fairy tales" because the universe had no beginning. It is difficult to grasp how the notion of an eternal universe is less of a fairy tale than the notion of an eternal Creator, other than that the former is purely material and the latter spiritual. Nevertheless, the assumption that the universe is eternal was routinely used by opponents of religion to "prove" that there is no need to assume the existence of God—because there is nothing to "explain."[26] The overwhelming evidence supporting the "Big Bang" came as a stunning blow to these irreligious presumptions—the universe did have a beginning! So, now what? It may have been feasible to argue that an eternal universe posed no question of origins, but that no longer applies. How *did* it all begin? *What* existed before the Big Bang? Of even greater significance is that, Big Bang or not, a compelling case for Intelligent Design[27] can be made—not only as demonstrated by science, but in the very existence of science!

Real science arose only once: in Europe, not in China, Islam, India, Ancient Greece, or Rome.[28] All of these societies had a highly developed alchemy, but only in Europe did alchemy develop into chemistry. By the same token, many societies developed elaborate systems of astrology based on excellent observations of the stars, but only in Europe did astrology lead to scientific astronomy. Why? Again, the answer has to do with images of God. I have written on this matter at length in two previous books[29]; here it is sufficient to summarize.

As noted, most non-Christian religions do not posit a Creation at all: the universe is eternal and, while it may pursue cycles, it is without beginning or purpose, and, most important of all, having never been created, it has no Creator. Consequently, the universe is thought to be a supreme mystery, inconsistent, unpredictable, and arbitrary. For those holding these religious premises, the path to wisdom is through meditation and mystical insights; there is no occasion to celebrate reason, and the scientific quest is absurd. As the distinguished Joseph Needham (1900–1995), lifelong student of Chinese technology, explained: in China "the conception of a divine celestial lawgiver imposing ordinances on non-human Nature never developed . . . [hence] there was no conviction that rational personal beings would be able to spell out in their lesser earthly languages the divine code of laws. . . . Indeed, [the Chinese] would have scorned such an idea as being too naïve for the subtlety and complexity of the universe as they intuited it."[30]

In contrast, based on their commitment to Judeo-Christian theology, Europeans assumed not only that the universe was created, but that its workings are logical and consistent, thereby being susceptible to reason and inquiry. As the great, if neglected, medieval theologian-scientist Nicole Oreseme (1320–1382) put it, God's creation "is much like that of a man making a clock and letting it run and continue its own motion by itself."[31] Consequently, science arose only in Christian Europe primarily because only Europeans *believed* it *could* be done, and *should* be done.

As Alfred North Whitehead (1861–1947) explained during one of his Lowell lectures at Harvard in 1925, science arose in Europe because of the widespread "faith in the possibility of science ... derivative from medieval theology."[32] Whitehead's pronouncement shocked not only his distinguished audience, but Western intellectuals in general, once his lectures had been published. How could this great philosopher and mathematician, coauthor with Bertrand Russell of the landmark *Principia Mathematica* (1910–1913), make such an outlandish claim? Did he not know that religion is the mortal enemy of scientific inquiry?

Whitehead knew better. He had grasped that Christian theology was essential for the rise of science in the West, just as surely as non-Christian theologies had stifled the scientific quest everywhere else. As he explained: "The greatest contribution of medievalism to the formation of the scientific movement [was] the inexpugnable belief that ... there is a secret, a secret which can be unveiled. How has this conviction been so vividly implanted in the European mind? ... It must come from the medieval insistence on the rationality of God, conceived as with the personal energy of Jehovah and with the rationality of a Greek philosopher. Every detail was supervised and ordered: the search into nature could only result in the vindication of the faith in rationality."[33]

Whitehead ended with the remark that the images of Gods found in other religions, especially in Asia, are too impersonal or too irrational to have sustained science. Any particular "occurrence might be due to the fiat of an irrational despot" God, or might be produced by "some impersonal, inscrutable origin of things. There is not the same confidence as in the intelligible rationality of a personal being."[34]

It was only because they believed in God as the Intelligent Designer of a rational universe that Europeans pursued the secrets of the Creation: Newton, Kepler, Galileo, and all the other stalwarts of the extraordinary flowering of science in the sixteenth and seventeenth centuries regarded the Creation itself as a *book*[35] that was to be read and comprehended. In the words of Johannes Kepler (1571–1630), "The chief aim of all investigations of the external world should be to discover the rational order and harmony which has been imposed on it by God and which He revealed to us in the language of mathematics."[36] And the French scientific genius René Descartes (1596–1650) justified his search for natural "laws" on grounds that such laws must exist because God is perfect and therefore "acts in a manner as constant and immutable as possible."[37] Descartes's statement is a virtual cliché in the writings of these early scientific "giants." Moreover, these great scientists not only searched for natural laws, confident that they existed, but *they found them!*

Again and again, science has revealed that the universe and all that it contains is not only immensely complex, but is utterly lawful. And that is the essential point, for, as Albert Einstein (1879–1955) once remarked, the most incomprehensible thing about the universe is that it is comprehensible: "*a priori* one should expect a chaotic world which cannot be grasped by the mind in any way." He went on to note that scientific theories assume "a high degree of ordering of the objective world, and this could not be expected *a priori*. That is the 'miracle' which is constantly being reinforced as our knowledge expands."[38] And that is the "miracle" that has prompted the recent renaissance of arguments in support of Intelligent Design.

The new supporters of Intelligent Design are very sophisticated, some of them having distinguished scientific careers.[39] Their case for design rests on two primary points. First, that infinitesimal variations in any of the basic features of the universe, such as Planck's constant, the speed of light, the gravity force constant, and the like, would produce the chaos that Einstein mentioned. The odds against all of these taking their present values by sheer accident seem far more than prohibitive. Second, many basic building blocks of life cannot have arisen helter-skelter, one tiny increment at a time. In the case of the eye, or indeed of organic molecules as such, no early or intermediate stage has any survival value to sustain development. Rather, the finished product seems to have appeared without antecedents, so there is no plausible "natural" explanation of its origin.

Finally, there is an even more basic and fundamental "proof" of Intelligent Design. Let us assume that the militant "scientific" materialists are right and that eventually we can identify sets of scientific rules sufficient to explain everything in the universe. These questions would still persist: Where did the rules come from? Why is the universe rational and orderly? It seems to me that the most remarkable "retreat" from reason is to cling to the belief that the principles that underlie the universe came out of nowhere, that everything is one big, meaningless accident.

I am no longer sufficiently arrogant or gullible to make that leap of faith. Instead, I find it far more rational to regard the universe itself as the ultimate revelation of God and to agree with Kepler that in the most fundamental sense, science *is* theology and thereby serves as another method for the discovery of God.

ANCIENT RELIGIOUS HISTORY

TIMELINE

As is explained in the text, many of these dates are in dispute, as is the existence of some of the persons listed.

Pre-History

−200,000 to	• Some burials include grave goods.
−10,000	• Possible altars found in some caves occupied by humans.
	• Figurines of an obese female have been found at many sites. Do they represent a Mother Goddess? A fertility charm?
	• Worship of High Gods and doctrines of Creation are inferred from observations of eighteenth- and nineteenth-century "primitive" societies.
−10,000	• First towns appear, including Jericho.

History begins

−4000	• Rise of Sumerian civilization: subsidized temple religions with professional priests, many Gods, little or no public access.
−2700	• Founding of the Old Kingdom of Egypt and development of Egyptian temple religions.
	• Cheops builds his pyramid.
	• Many retainers are buried with each pharaoh.
−2600 to −1801	• Gilgamesh reigns as King of Uruk.
	• Indus Civilization begins in India.
−1800 to −1701	• Founding of Shang Dynasty in China. Subsidized temple religions exclude commoners.
−1500 to −1401	• Vedic Hinduism arises in India. A religious "free market" ensues.
−1400 to −1301	• Pharaoh Akhenaten imposes monotheism on Egypt; his successor restores the old temple religions.
−1300 to −1201	• The Israelites leave Egypt.

−1100 to −1001	• Chou Dynasty comes to power in China.
	• Rise of Greek civilization.
−1000 to −901	• David crowned as King of a united Israel.
	• King Solomon builds the first Temple in Jerusalem (includes "pagan" Gods).
	• The Yahweh-Only Sect emerges.
	• Israel is divided into two kingdoms.
−900 to −801	• Elijah thunders against idolatry in Israel.
−800 to −701	• The founding of Rome.
	• The *I-Ching* appears in China.
−700 to −601	• "Lost" book containing Mosaic Law is discovered in the Temple in Jerusalem, prompting the Deuteronomists to reformulate Judaism.

The Axial Age

−600 to −501	• Zoroaster has revelations and introduces a new monotheism in Persia.
	• Pythagoras and Orpheus (?) initiate ascetic sects in Greece.
	• The *Upaniṣads* are written in India, revolutionizing Hinduism.
	• Mahāvīra perfects Jainism in India.
	• Buddha founds a new faith in India.
	• Lao-Tzu writes the *Tao-Te Ching*, which soon results in a new religion (Taoism) in China.
	• Confucius founds a Chinese movement that soon becomes a religion.
	• Jewish elite taken as captives to Babylon: Jeremiah, Ezekiel, and Isaiah are active.
	• Upon the return of the Jews from Babylon, a new Temple is built in Jerusalem.
	• The Roman Republic is established.
	• Rise of Mayan civilization.

The Classical Era

−400 to −301	• The *Bhagavad-gītā* appears.
	• Aristotle tutors Alexander the Great.
	• Alexander the Great declares himself a God.
−300 to −201	• The *Septuagint*, a translation of the Hebrew scripture into Greek, appears in Egypt.

- Also in Egypt, Manetho and Timotheus invent the God Serapis and pair him with the Goddess Isis.
- Popular Taoism arises in China.
- Han Confucianism dominates Chinese bureaucracy.
- Cult of Cybele (Magna Mater) arrives in Rome.

−200 to −101
- Cult of Bacchus is suppressed in Rome.
- Jews expelled from Rome.

−100 to −4
- Pure Land Buddhism arrives in China.
- Cult of Isis arrives in Rome.

The Common Era

−4
- The birth of Jesus.

1 to 19
- Emperor Tiberius expels Jews from Rome.

30 to 34
- Jesus's ministry occurs.
- Jesus is crucified.
- Christian missionizing begins.

35 to 99
- Paul is converted and begins his mission.
- The Gospels and Acts appear (probably in Hebrew).
- Emperor Tiberius outlaws Cult of Isis and has her priests crucified.
- James, brother of Jesus, is executed in Jerusalem.
- Peter and Paul are executed in Rome.
- Nero persecutes Christians.
- Jerusalem destroyed by Romans.
- Christian congregations are established in Alexandria, Antioch, Athens, Caesarea Maritima, Corinth, Damascus, Ephesus, Pergamum, Rome, Salamis, Sardis, Smyrna, and Thessalonica.
- The Cult of Mithraism is founded in Rome.

100 to 199
- Gnostic schools begin to form and produce "heretical" Gospels.
- Bar Kokhba revolt by Jews is ruthlessly suppressed by Romans.
- Chang Tao-ling's revelations encourage search for secrets of immortality in China.
- Christians number at least 200,000 by the end of the century.

200 to 299
- Emperor Decius initiates an empire-wide persecution of Christians, and the persecution is continued by Emperor Valerian.
- Emperor Elagabalus (also Heliogabalus) introduces Sol Invictus as the supreme Roman God.

300 to 399
- Persecution of Christians is resumed by Emperor Diocletian and is continued by Emperors Galerius and Maximinus.
- Emperor Constantine ends persecution and extends special status to Christianity.
- Half or more of residents of the Empire are now Christians.
- Emperor Julian briefly attempts to restore paganism and suppress Christianity.

400 to 499
- Persecution of both Buddhism and Taoism initiated by Emperor Wu in China. Thousands of monasteries are closed and their wealth confiscated while tens of thousands of monks and nuns are ordered to return to normal life.
- After death of the Emperor Wu, Buddhism regains its wealth and power.
- Rome falls.

500 to 599
- Massive persecution of Buddhists begins again in China.
- Emperor Justinian closes the Academy in Athens, the last major bastion of paganism.
- Birth of Muhammad.

600 to 699
- Muhammad "receives" the Qur'an.
- Muhammad and about seventy followers flee Mecca for Medina.
- Victorious Muhammad returns to Mecca.
- Muhammad dies in Medina.
- Islamic conquests begin.

GLOSSARY

Gods and Goddesses

Gods and **Goddesses** are supernatural beings having consciousness and intentions.
Supernatural refers to somewhat mysterious forces or entities that are above, beyond, or
  outside nature and which may be able to influence reality.

Major Sumerian Gods and Goddesses

An is a withdrawn High God.
Enki is the Ruler of the Abyss, and did the actual work of creation.
Enlil is the father of the Gods who produces dawn and blesses the king.
Ishtar is the Goddess of Carnal Love.
Nanna is the Moon God.
Ninmah is the Mother Goddess.
Nintura is the God of Storms.
Nipper is the God of Wind.
Utu is the Sun God.

Major Egyptian Gods and Goddesses

Amon is the King of the Gods.
Hathor is the most important Goddess and may have been the wife of Horus.
Horus is the Sun God.
Isis is the Goddess of the Nile and eventually became a High Goddess.
Khonsu is the Moon God who also eats other Gods.
Min is the God of Fertility.
Montu is the God of War.
Mut is the Great Mother and wife of Amon.
Nut is the Goddess of the Sky and consort of Ra.
Osiris is brother and husband of Isis, and Judge of the Dead.
Ra is a withdrawn High God.
Thoth is the Moon God who rules the earth.

Major Greek Gods and Goddesses

Aphrodite is the Goddess of Love and Sex.
Apollo is the God of the Sun and of Learning.

Ares is the God of War.
Artemis is the Goddess of Animals and Hunting.
Athena is the Goddess of War.
Cronus is a terrible Creator God who ate his children.
Demeter is the Earth Mother.
Dionysos is the God of Drunkenness.
Hades is the God of the Underworld.
Hephaistos is the God of Fire and of Crafts.
Hera is the wife of Zeus.
Hermes is the Divine Trickster.
Persephone is the Goddess of the Underworld.
Poseidon is the God of the Ocean.
Prometheus is the cousin of Zeus who stole fire and gave it to humans.
Rhea is the mother of Zeus and wife of Cronus.
Zeus is the King of the Gods.

Major Aztec Gods and Goddesses

Coatlicue is the Mother Goddess who bore four hundred Gods.
Huaxtec is the Love Goddess.
Huitzilopochtli is the God of War.
Itzpapalotl is the Goddess of Fertility.
Nanauatzin is the God known as the pimply one who sacrificed himself so the sun
    would rise again.
Omeciuatl is Ometecuhtli's wife.
Ometecuhtli is a semi-withdrawn Creator God.
Otontecuhtl is the Fire God.
Tepoztécatl is the God of Drunkenness.
Texcatlipoca is the God of Night.
Tlaloc is the God of Rain and Lightning.

Major Mayan Gods and Goddesses

Ah Puch is the Lord of Hell.
Chac is the Rain God.
Ek Chuah is the God of War.
Hunab Ku is the Creator of the present universe, but he was semi-withdrawn.
Hurakan is the God of Lightning.
Itzamná is Hunab Ku's son and ruler of the Mayan pantheon.
Ixchel is the Moon Goddess.
Kisin is the God of Earthquakes.
Yum Kaax is the God of Corn and of the Forest.

Major Roman Gods and Goddesses (Greek counterparts in parentheses)

Aesculapius is the God of Healing (Asklepios).
Apollo is the God of Prophecy, Medicine, and the Arts (also known as Apollo
    in Greece).

Ceres is the Goddess of Grain and Nature (Demeter).
Diana is the Goddess of the Moon and of Fertility (Artemis).
Fortuna is the Goddess of Luck (Tyche).
Hercules is the risen great hero (Herakles).
Janus is the guardian of doorways and custodian of the universe and is usually represented as two-faced.
Juno is the wife of Jupiter (Hera).
Jupiter is the Supreme Father of the Gods (Zeus).
Liber is the God of Fertility (Dionysos).
Mars is second only to Jupiter in the early Roman pantheon, a God of Agriculture, father of Romulus, and eventually worshipped as the God of War (Ares).
Mercury is the Messenger God (Hermes).
Minerva is the daughter of Jupiter (Athena).
Neptune is the God of the Sea (Poseidon).
Quirinus is the ascended Romulus, legendary founder of Rome.
Saturn is the father of Jupiter (Cronus).
Venus is the Goddess of Gardens and Beauty (Aphrodite).
Vesta is the Goddess of the Hearth, served by the six Vestal Virgins (Hestia).
Vulcan is the God of Fire and Craftsmen (Hephaistos).

Major "Foreign" Gods and Goddesses in Rome

Attis is the consort of Cybele (from Asia Minor).
Bacchus is the God of Dionysian Mysteries (from Greece).
Cybele is the Mother Goddess known in Rome as Magna Mater (from Phrygia).
Isis is the Supreme Savior Goddess, a pagan approximation of monotheism (from Egypt).
Mithras is the God of the Sun (falsely claimed to be from Persia, he was a Roman invention).
Serapis is the consort of Isis (from Egypt).
Sol Invictus is represented by the Sun and, like Isis, was introduced as a pagan attempt at monotheism (from Syria).

Major Hindu Gods and Goddesses

VEDIC ERA

Agni is the Fire God.
Brihaspati is the teacher of the Gods and the Lord of Prayer.
Indra is the God of Thunder, as well as the God of Warriors, and is therefore the most important of all the Vedic Gods. He is depicted as rowdy and immoral.
Maruts refers to a cluster of Storm Gods.
Mitra is a solar diety who personifies the day, closely associated with Varuna.
Parjanya is the God of Rain.
Rudra, the "Red One" or "Howler," is the father of the Maruts and greatly feared for his angry and destructive nature. He was only a minor God early in Vedic times, but eventually he evolved into a major deity.
Soma is the God of the Soma plant, which provided an hallucinogen that was consumed only at sacrifices.

Varuna rules over the night and is regarded as guardian of the cosmic order.

Vāyu is the God of Wind.

Vishnu is associated with the sun during this era and only later evolved into a major God.

Upanişad Era

Divine Trinity is comprised of the Gods Brahmā, Shiva, and Vishnu.

> **Brahmā** is the God of the Gods, the Creator God, one of the Gods of the Divine Trinity.
>
> **Shiva** is the Destroyer God and evolved from Rudra, one of the Gods of the Divine Trinity.
>
> **Vishnu** is the Preserver God and protector of the world, one of the Gods of the Divine Trinity.

Durga is the Mother Goddess.

Ganesha is the elephantine God of wisdom.

Hanuman is the celibate monkey-God.

Indra is a drunken God of the senses.

Kali is the Goddess of Destruction.

Krishna is an avatar of Vishnu.

Lakshmi is the Goddess paired with Vishnu.

Parvati is Shiva's female companion.

Sarasvati is an Earth Goddess and wife of Brahmā.

Soma is the God of the Moon and the nectar of the Gods.

Vishvarkman is the son of Brahmā and Architect of the Universe.

Chinese Gods and Goddesses

Traditional Deities

Ch'eng-Huang is the God of Moats and Walls, who protects communities from attack.

Chu Jung is the God of Fire, who punishes those who break the laws of heaven.

Erh-Lang is the Protector God, who drives away evil spirits.

Fu-Hsing is the God of Happiness.

Hou-chi is the God of Agriculture.

I-ti is the God of Wine.

Jade Emperor: see Shang-ti.

Kuan Ti is the God of War. He probably was an actual historical figure, a general during the Han Dynasty.

Kwan Yin is the Goddess of Mercy and is depicted as a lady dressed in white, sitting on a lotus, holding a baby.

Lei Kun is the God of Thunder. He has the head of a bird, and his chariot is pulled by six boys.

P'an-Chin-Lein is the Goddess of Prostitutes.

Shang-ti is the eldest ancestor spirit and the Supreme God. He also is known as the **Jade Emperor**.

Shi-Tien Yen-Wang refers to the ten Gods of the Underworld.

Ti-Tsan Wang is the God of Mercy. He patrols the caverns of Hell.

T'Shai-Shen is the God of Wealth.

Tsao Wang is the God of the Hearth. Every household has its own image of Tsao Wang.
Yeng-Wang-Yeh is the greatest of the Lords of Death.

TAOIST DEITIES

Hsi Wang Mu is the Queen Mother Goddess.

The Eight Immortals are ordinary people whose virtues were rewarded by Hsi Wang Mu, who gave them peaches of everlasting life to eat.

> **Chang-Kuo Lao** is a hermit with a donkey that could reach incredible speeds.
> **Chung-Li Ch'uan** is a smiling, ascetic old man.
> **Han Hsiang-Tzu** chose to study magic rather than cram for civil service exams.
> **Ho Hsien-Ku** is a girl who became immortal by eating mother of pearl.
> **Lan Ts'ai-Ho** is an inspired flute player.
> **Li Tieh-Kuai** is a begger who sold wonderful drugs that could revive the dead.
> **Lu Tung-Pin** is a hero of early Chinese storytelling who slew dragons with a magic sword.
> **Ts'ao Kuo-Chiu** tried to reform his brother, the emperor.

Gods and Evil Spirits of Monotheistic Systems

Egyptian

Rē-Herakhte is the only God, and his symbol is Aten, the solar disk.
No known evil spirit.

Zoroastrianism

Ahura Mazdā (also Mazdāh) is the One True God.
Angra Mainyu is the "Fiendish Spirit," who causes calamities and leads humans into evil.

Judaism

Satan is a fallen angel who rules Hell and tempts people to sin.
Yahweh is the One True God.

Christianity

The Holy Trinity is comprised of Jehovah, Jesus Christ, and the Holy Ghost.
> **Jehovah** is the Christian form of the word *Yahweh*, the One True God.
> **Jesus Christ** is the son of God, who died for humanity's sins.
> **Holy Ghost** (or Holy Spirit) is a manifestation of God's abiding presence in the world.
Satan is a fallen angel who rules Hell and tempts people to sin.

Islam

Allāh is the One True God.
Shaytān (also Iblīs) is a fallen angel who rules Hell and tempts people to sin.

Scriptures

Zoroastrianism

Avesta is the sacred text.
Gāthās are the hymns attributed to Zoroaster.

Judaism

Septuagint is the Greek translation of the Tanakh.
Talmud is an immense body of commentary on scripture, and particularly on the Torah, written over the centuries by learned rabbis. It consists of two parts, the **Mishnah** and the **Gemara**.
Tanakh (which Christians refer to as the Old Testament) is the scriptural basis of Judaism and plays the authoritative role in the religious life of observant Jews. It consists of three parts: the Kethuvim, the Nevi'im, and the Torah.
>**Kethuvim** contains the literary books (such as *Psalms*).
>**Nevi'im** refers to the writings of the prophets.
>**Torah** includes the first five books, which are attributed to Moses.

Hinduism

Bhagavad-gītā is the scripture that most Western admirers of Hinduism take to be the primary Hindu scripture. It appeared in perhaps the third century BCE as a central feature of the recommitment of Hinduism to the Gods.
Upaniṣads are the scriptures that revolutionized Hindusim during the sixth century BCE. They consist of more than 200 separate scriptures, most of them in the form of a dialogue.
Vedāngas refers to a literature devoted to the exact wording, pronunciation, and emphasis for recitations of the Rgveda. It consists of five parts: the Chanda, Jyotiṣa, Nirkuta, Śīkṣa, and the Vyākarana.
>**Chanda** explains and offers practice in verse meters.
>**Jyotiṣa** deals with determining the proper time to perform various rites, based on complex astronomy and astrology.
>**Nirukta** treats the etymology of words.
>**Śīkṣa** deals with precise pronunciation.
>**Vyākarana** deals with grammar and philology.
Vedas are the scriptures that defined Hinduism from about 1500 BCE until the sixth century BCE. They are divided into four major parts: the Artharveda, Rgveda, Sāmaveda, and the Yajurveda.
>**Atharvaveda** is a collection of hymns and spells.
>**Rgveda** (also Rig Veda) is the most important part of the Vedas and is a collection of 1,028 hymns directed to various Gods. It is divided into ten sections called *mandalas*.
>**Sāmaveda** is the second part of the Vedas and consists of portions of the Rgveda with musical instructions for recitation.
>**Yajurveda** is devoted to rituals and ceremonies.

Buddhism

Pure Land Sutra is a revisionist scripture that appeared in the first or second century BCE and serves as the primary scripture for the form of Buddhism that triumphed in China—which is known as Pure Land or Mahāyāna Buddhism.

Tipitaka is the collective name of Buddhist scriptures. It means "Three Baskets" and was applied because when, after generations of oral transmission, the scriptures finally were written down, they were kept in three separate containers. The Three Baskets include Abhidhamma Pitaka, Sutta Pitaka, and Vinaya Pitaka.

> **Abhidhamma Pitaka** is the Basket of Scholasticism, and consists of seven philosophical and theological analyses.

> **Sutta Pitaka** is known also as the Basket of Discourse. It includes more than 200 sermons (*suttas*) believed to have been delivered by Buddha and which lay out his doctrines in detail.

> **Vinaya Pitaka** is the Basket of Discipline, which is devoted to rules governing Buddhist monastic life.

Chinese Folk Religion

I-Ching (*Book of Changes*) is the basis for divination.

Taoism

Tao-Te Ching (*Sacred Book of the Tao and the Te*) is attributed to Lao-Tzu.

Confucianism

Analects is a collection of teachings attributed to Confucius.

Christianity

Acts of the Apostles is the fifth book of the New Testament and probably was written by the same author as the third Gospel—Luke, who was the companion of the Apostle Paul. Acts recounts the missionary activities of the early Church and especially Paul's missions to the West.

Bible is the collective name of the Christian scriptures. The Bible is divided into two major parts: the New Testament and the Old Testament.

> **New Testament** is the primary scriptural basis for Christianity. It consists of twenty-seven short "books."

> **Old Testament** refers to those scriptures included in the Hebrew Bible, known to Jews as the Tanakh.

Epistles (or letters) make up twenty-one books, most of them written by the Apostle Paul.

Gospels (Matthew, Mark, Luke, and John) refer to the first four books of the New Testament, each of which is devoted to the story of Christ.

Revelation or **The Apocalypse of Saint John the Divine** is the last book of the New Testament.

Islam

Hadith are collections of writings that enjoy semi-sacred standing in Islam. There are three different elements to these writings: the Fīqh, Sira and the Tafsir.

> **Fīqh** are writings that include Muhammad's legal reasoning.
>
> **Sira** are biographies of Muhammad and serve a purpose similar to the Christian Gospels and Acts. They also are the primary source of Sharī'a, or Muslim law.
>
> **Tafsir** are believed to be Muhammad's comments on the Qur'an.

Qur'an (also Koran) is the book of Muslim scriptures, consisting of 114 Sūras believed to have been revealed to Muhammad by Allāh.

Social-Science Concepts

Axial Age is the name given to the sixth century BCE, reflecting the nearly simultaneous appearance of major religious leaders along an axis from southern Italy to northern China.

Animism consists of the belief that literally everything is inhabited by a spirit, not only animate things, but inanimate things as well.

Congregations are communities of religious participants whose religious life is of substantial importance for their social relationships and self-conceptions. People *belong* to congregations.

Conversion refers to a major change in one's religious identity, a switch from one religious tradition to another, as from Christian to Jew. A less dramatic change in one's religion, as from one Christian denomination to another, is referred to as *reaffiliation*.

Cultural continuity refers to similarities and correspondences between two cultures.

Diffusion is the process by which cultural innovations spread from one society to others.

Durkheim's theory of totemism proposed that all religious rites constitute society worshipping itself in order to sustain social solidarity, and the most primitive form of this collective self-worship is Totemism.

Freud's incestuous theory of totemism imagined that once upon a time a group of young males killed their father, ate him, and possessed his women, and that ever after this event has been reenacted, albeit subconsciously, in totem ceremonies. Hence, religion is but a manifestation of the Oedipus Complex.

Ghost Theory addresses the question where do people get the idea that spirits exist? This idea arises because primitives, lacking a proper awareness of their own mental functioning, are puzzled by the difference between the living and the dead and between when they are dreaming and when they are awake, especially when their dreams involve people who are dead. To solve these mysteries, primitive people assume that all things are dualistic and possess a sort of inner phantom that is capable of detached movement so as to appear in one's dreams. Or, as in the case of death, the spirit departs to lead an independent existence.

High Gods are eternal beings who created the universe and are superior to (and may have created) a group of Gods of smaller scope. Some High Gods remain *active*. Others have *withdrawn* from any interest in their creation.

Idols are images of Gods, often very large and ornate, and usually assumed to be alive.

Magic is limited to efforts to manipulate the supernatural to obtain desired outcomes, without reference to a God or Gods and without general statements about existence or ultimate meaning.

"Myth" is an account that may happen in this world or in "another" world, but which includes active supernatural participants. Some "myths" involve only Gods; some tell of extensive interactions between Gods and humans; and in some the focus is on humans, with Gods in the background.

Naturism proposes that religions have their origins in the personification of natural forces and objects and the "myths" that arise from these personifications.

Pluralism consists of the existence of an array of independent religious suppliers.

Priests are persons who serve in a relatively formal role as an intermediary between humans and God(s).

Religion consists of explanations of existence (or ultimate meaning) based on supernatural assumptions and including statements about the nature of the supernatural, which may specify methods or procedures for exchanging with the supernatural.

Religious capital consists of the degree of mastery and attachment to a particular body of religious culture.

Religious economy encompasses all the religious activity going on in a society: a "market" of current and potential adherents, a set of one or more organizations seeking to attract or maintain adherents, and the religious culture offered by the organization(s).

Religious innovators are very gifted individuals who appear from time to time and introduce new religious culture. The source of this culture may be attributed to revelations or to introspection.

Revelation is a communication believed to come from a supernatural source, usually from a God, or to be divinely inspired knowledge.

Rites and rituals are measures and procedures for exchanging with the supernatural.

Sacrifices are things given up or foregone so that they may be offered to God(s).

Sect refers to a religious group that sustains a relatively intense level of religious commitment, thereby maintaining a substantial degree of tension with its cultural environment.

Sect movement refers to a sect that actively promotes social change in accord with its religion.

Temple religions are based on a structure devoted entirely to religious activities, are staffed by an exclusive priesthood, and serve a clientele rather than a membership. People *go* to temples; they do not *belong* to them.

Totemism holds that all religions originated in the practice of each primitive tribe, or of each clan within a tribe, to identify with a particular animal species (a totem) that is held to be sacred and not to be harmed. However, during certain festivals or at times of dire need, the group conducts a solemn rite during which the totemic animal is sacrificed and eaten. This is the origin of all rites and practices associated with sacrifice, especially of blood sacrifices, and from these humble beginnings came all of the more advanced religions.

Theological Concepts and Principles

Atonement refers to the Christian doctrine that Christ's death on the cross served as a sacrifice that reconciled humanity with God.

Divine Accommodation is the Judeo-Christian doctrine that God's revelations are always limited to the current capacity of humans to comprehend.

Five Pillars of Islam encompasses the foundations of islam: Hajj, Salāt, Sawm, Shahāda, and Zakāt.

> **Hajj** refers to the expectation that all Muslims will make a pilgrimage to Mecca during their lifetimes.
>
> **Salāt** concerns worship. Muslim men are required to engage in formal prayer five times a day (and at other occasions such as funerals and during eclipses).
>
> **Sawm** identifies the duty to fast from dawn to dusk each day during the month of Ramadan.
>
> **Shahāda** is the Muslim confession of faith. It consists of but one sentence: "*I bear witness that 'There is no god but God'; I bear witness that 'Muhammad is the messenger of God.'*"
>
> **Zakāt** is almsgiving. Muslims are required to give alms to support those in need.

Islam is an Arabic term meaning "submission." Followers of this faith are called **Muslims**, which means "submitters" in Arabic.

Nirvana is the primary aim of Buddhism, an ultimate state of unconscious, everlasting bliss that ends one's cycle of rebirths.

Pure Land is *Paradise* as conceived by the form of Buddhism that triumphed in China.

Release is a Hindu concept meaning to escape from the cycle of rebirths and deaths.

Sharī'a is *Muslim law*. The scope of *Sharī'a* is not limited to religious matters since Muslims have traditionally made no distinction between the religious and the secular and regard the *Sharī'a* as an adequate basis for the full legal system of a Muslim state.

Tao is the "way," the "pathway," or the "teaching," hence Taoism.

Te is a Taoist concept best translated as *virtue*.

Theology involves formal reasoning about God. The emphasis is on discovering God's nature, intentions, and demands, and on understanding how these define the relationship between human beings and God.

Three Confucian Virtues consitst of i, Jên, and Li.

> **i** means righteousness, which, according to Confucius, is that which is fitting, right, seemly.
>
> **Jên** has been translated a number of ways, as love, benevolence, kindness, or goodness.
>
> **Li** refers to the proper observance of ceremonies and the duty to always carefully and reverently observe the correct forms of behavior.

Transmigration of souls is the Hindu and Buddhist doctrine that upon each death we are reborn and that the circumstances in our next lives are determined by our behavior in our previous life (or lives).

Yang is the *male principle* in Han Confucianism: the bright, the creative, the sun, the east.

Yin is the *female principle* in Han Confucianism: the dark, the recessive, the moon, the west.

NOTES

Introduction: Revelation and Cultural Evolution

1. See Boyer, *Religion Explained*; Dawkins, *A Devil's Chaplain*, "Is Science a Religion?" *The Extended Phenotype*, *The Selfish Gene*, and *The God Delusion*; Dennett, *Breaking the Spell* and *Darwin's Dangerous Idea*.

2. After reading a draft of this chapter, a young professor of classics carefully instructed me that I must not capitalize the word *Gods*. Citing the dictionary, she explained that according to proper usage, *God* may be capitalized, but the plural form may not (nor can the word *Goddess*). According to my unabridged Webster's, she is correct. When associated with polytheistic systems, the word *gods* (or *a god*) is not capitalized, but in reference to monotheistic systems, the word *God* is capitalized. Hence, one should write, "Yahweh was the God of the Jews, while Baal was the primary god of the Philistines." I knowingly and unapologetically violated this convention, having capitalized *God*, *Gods*, *Goddess*, and *Goddesses*. I did so because, especially in a work of comparative religions, to adhere to the pedantic convention is unacceptably ethnocentric. By the same token I have used BCE (Before the Common Era) rather than BC (Before Christ). All years not identified as BCE belong to that era that once was designated as AD, but now as CE (Common Era).

3. In Preus, *Explaining Religion*, 8.

4. Brian Morris, *Anthropological Studies of Religion*, 103.

5. Frazer, *The Golden Bough*, III:120.

6. Frazer, *The Golden Bough*, III:188.

7. Frazer, *The Golden Bough*, III:189.

8. Frazer, *The Golden Bough*, III:190.

9. Frazer, *The Golden Bough*, III:196.

10. Frazer, *The Golden Bough*, III:198. It should be noted that Frazer moved the entire section devoted to Jesus to an appendix in his third edition, and it is missing entirely from the single-volume abridged edition done under his supervision, which is the only edition that has been readily available since 1922. The excision of the Jesus material was done for marketing purposes only; Frazer did not recant.

11. See Eisenstadt, *Origins and Diversity of Axial Age Civilizations*.

12. Stark and Bainbridge, *A Theory of Religion*.

13. *City of God*, 5.1.

14. In Lindberg, "Science and the Early Church," 27.

15. *The Confessions*, 12.

16. *The Confessions*, 12.

17. Some have claimed that *Shaddai* means "mountain," but most scholars regard the meaning of the word as unknown.

18. This is the traditional Torah version. Also see Alter, *The Five Books of Moses*, 339.

19. Matthew 13:13; also Mark 4 and Luke 8.

20. In Benin, *The Footprints of God*, 11.

21. In Benin, *The Footprints of God*, 183.

22. Calvin, *Sermons of the Ten Commandments*, 52–3.

23. In Benin, *The Footprints of God*, 173–74.

24. In Benin, *The Footprints of God*, 195.

25. Notwithstanding Richard Dawkins's (*A Devil's Chaplain*, *The Extended Phenotype*, and *The Selfish Gene*) "magical" construct, the "meme." More on this in Chapter 1.

26. Tylor, *Primitive Culture*, 8.

27. When Darwin adopted the term (in the sixth edition of *The Origin of Species*), he gave Spencer full credit: "I have called this principle . . . by the term natural selection . . . [b]ut the expression often used by Mr. Herbert Spencer, of the Survival of the Fittest, is more accurate . . ."

28. Spencer, *Social Statics*.

29. De Moor, *The Rise of Yahwism*.

30. Pagels, *The Origin of Satan*; Jeffrey Burton Russell, *The Devil*.

31. Job 1:6–12.

32. Durkheim, "Review of Part VI of the *Principles of Sociology*," 19.

33. Durkheim, "Review of Part VI of the *Principles of Sociology*," 19.

34. Durkheim, *The Elementary Forms of Religious Life*, 227.

35. Beattie, "Ritual and Social Change"; S. R. F. Price, *Rituals and Power*; Sperber, *Rethinking Symbolism*.

36. Needham, *Science and Civilization*.

37. This term was adopted by early Christians to identify the polytheistic religions of that era. Originally the word *pagan* referred to rural residents, *paganus* being a demeaning term equivalent to "rube" or "country hick." It came to have religious meaning because, after Christianity triumphed in the cities, most rural people remained unconverted, hence those who were neither Christians nor Jews were "country hicks." Scholars now use the term *pagan* without pejorative connotations as a convenient way to identify traditional polytheism.

38. Parrinder, *World Religions*, 192.

39. Jaspers, *The Origin and Goal of History*.

40. This led several scholars to call this the "age of transcendence." See Schwartz, "The Age of Transcendence."

Chapter 1: Gods in Primitive Societies

1. There is some opposition these days to the word *primitive* as applied to cultures or societies on grounds that it is a pejorative term that implies "inferior." Those making these objections seem unaware that the term *primitive* was adopted at the end of the nineteenth century by scholars who proposed it as a nonpejorative substitute for the terms then in use including *pre-logical*, *barbarian*, *savage*, *lower races*, and *sociétés inferieùrs*. To now prohibit *primitive* will merely require that we coin or discover a new term to identify that set of cultures lacking such things as domesticated animals, agriculture, metal-working, weaving, and writing. And whatever term we substitute will quickly take on negative connotations, too, for the truth of the matter is that pejorative implications inhere in what these societies lack. I see no point in seeking a new term.

2. Hodder, *The Leopard's Tale*.

3. Goodison and Morris, *Ancient Goddesses*; Hamilton, "The Figurines."

4. Albright, *From the Stone Age to Christianity*; Dickson, *The Dawn of Belief*; Eliade, *A History of Religious Ideas*; Narr, "Approaches to the Religion of Early Paleolithic Man."

5. Lewis, *God in the Dark*, 54.

6. Narr, "Approaches to the Religion of Early Paleolithic Man," 4.

7. Schmidt, *The Origin and Growth of Religion*, 29.

8. Girardot, *Myth and Meaning*, 215.

9. Müller, *The Hibbert Lectures*, 129.

10. Müller, *The Hibbert Lectures*, 130.

11. Müller, *The Hibbert Lectures*, 131–2.

12. Evans-Pritchard, *Theories of Primitive Religion*, 21.

13. The entire paragraph is based on Evans-Pritchard, *Theories of Primitive Religion*, 20–3.

14. David Frederich Strauss, *The Life of Jesus Critically Examined*.

15. Schmidt, *The Origin and Growth of Religion*.

16. Evans-Pritchard, *Theories of Primitive Religion*, 54.

17. Tylor, *Primitive Culture*; *Religion in Primitive Culture*.

18. Tylor, *Religion in Primitive Culture*, 10.

19. Tylor, *Religion in Primitive Culture*, 10.

20. Tylor, *Primitive Culture*, 8.

21. Tylor, "Limits of Savage Religion."

22. Tylor, *Religion in Primitive Culture*, 9.

23. Tylor, *Primitive Culture*, 89.

24. Stark and Finke, *Acts of Faith*, 7.

25. De Vries, *Perspectives in the History of Religions*, 163.

26. In Stark and Finke, *Acts of Faith*, 7.

27. Evans-Pritchard, *Theories of Primitive Religion*, 15.

28. Street, "Tylor, Sir Edward Burnett," 808.

29. Baker, "The Races of the Nile Basin," 231.

30. Spencer, *The Principles of Sociology*, 134–5.

31. Spencer, *The Principles of Sociology*, 136.

32. Spencer, *The Principles of Sociology*, 137.

33. Spencer, *The Principles of Sociology*, 137.

34. Quoted in Schmidt, *The Origin and Growth of Religion*, 63.

35. Schmidt, *The Origin and Growth of Religion*, 63.

36. Evans-Pritchard, *Theories of Primitive Religion*, 23.

37. Evans-Pritchard, *Theories of Primitive Religion*, 24.

38. W. Robertson Smith, *The Religion of the Semites*, 117.

39. Evans-Pritchard, *Theories of Primitive Religion*, 52.

40. Durkheim, *The Elementary Forms of Religious Life*, 420–1.

41. Evans-Pritchard, *Theories of Primitive Religion*, 58.

42. Durkheim, *The Elementary Forms of Religious Life*, 189.

43. Durkheim, *The Elementary Forms of Religious Life*, 208.

44. Durkheim, *The Elementary Forms of Religious Life*, 191.

45. Durkheim, *The Elementary Forms of Religious Life*, 299.

46. Durkheim, *The Elementary Forms of Religious Life*, 208.

47. Durkheim, *The Elementary Forms of Religious Life*, 418.

48. Stark, "Putting an End to Ancestor Worship."

49. Durkheim, *The Elementary Forms of Religious Life*, 44.

50. Richard, "Dogmatic atheism."

51. Stark and Bainbridge, *Religion, Deviance, and Social Control*.

52. Freud, *Totem and Taboo*.

53. Freud, *Totem and Taboo*, 154–5.

54. See Crews, *Unauthorized Freud*.

55. See Brian Morris, *Anthropological Studies of Religion*; Pals, *Seven Theories*; Wallace, *Religion*.

56. Darwin, *The Origin of Species*, 470. "The feeling of religious devotion is a highly complex one. . . . Nevertheless, we see some distant approach to this state of mind in the deep love of a dog for his master, associated with complete submission, some fear, and perhaps other feelings."

57. Hardy, *The Biology of God*, 170–1. His italics.

58. Hardy, *The Biology of God*, 168.

59. Hardy, *The Biology of God*, 172.

60. Admittedly, throughout his book Hardy indicates that he believes in God, but despite two long chapters devoted to the matter, it remains entirely unclear what he means by that term, and most of those whom he quotes expressed very vague notions about God as well, all of this being quite consistent with Hardy's involvement with psychic research groups.

61. Jaynes, *The Origin of Consciousness*.

62. Stark and Finke, *Acts of Faith*.

63. Boyer, *Religion Explained*.

64. Boyer, *Religion Explained*, 145.

65. Boyer, *Religion Explained*, 28.

66. Boyer, *Religion Explained*, 7.

67. Dawkins, *The Selfish Gene*, 192.

68. Dawkins, *The Extended Phenotype*.

69. Dawkins, "Is Science a Religion?" His fellow biologist Daniel C. Dennett (*Darwin's Dangerous Idea*, 515) proposed that "safety demands that religions be put in cages."

70. Dawkins, *A Devil's Chaplain*, 145.

71. For an excellent summary, see McGrath, *Dawkins' God*.

72. Dennett, *Breaking the Spell*, 21.

73. Lawson and McCauley, *Rethinking Religion.*
74. Lessa and Vogt, *Reader in Comparitive Religion,* 63.
75. Radin, *Primitive Religion,* chap. 2.
76. Quoted in Andrew Lang, *The Making of Religion,* 184.
77. Quoted in Radin, *Primitive Man,* 285.
78. Tillich, *Systematic Theology.*
79. Malinowski, *Magic, Science, and Religion,* 70.
80. Benedict, "Religion," 631–2.
81. Levack, *The Witch-Hunt,* 6.
82. Benedict, "Religion," 637, 647.
83. Max Weber, *The Sociology of Religion,* 28.
84. Stark, "A Theory of Revelations," *Exploring the Religious Life,* and "Normal Revelations."
85. Underhill, *Mysticism,* 95, 105.
86. Peyser, *The Memory of All That,* 80.
87. In William James, *The Varieties of Religious Experience,* 364.
88. Underhill, *Mysticism,* 63.
89. Wallace, *Religion.*
90. Wallace, *Religion,* 32.
91. Mooney, *The Ghost Shirt Religion.*
92. Sharot, *Messianism, Mysticism, and Magic.*
93. Bastide, *African Religions;* Simpson, *Black Religion.*
94. Stark and Bainbridge, *The Future of Religion;* Stark and Finke, *Acts of Faith.*
95. Stark, *Exploring the Religious Life.*
96. Stark, *One True God.*
97. Benz, "The Theological Meaning of the History of Religions," 9.
98. Eliade, "The Quest for the 'Origins' of Religion;" Grafton, "Protestant versus Prophet."
99. Eliade, "The Quest for the 'Origins' of Religion," 155.
100. Quoted in Robert Irwin, *Dangerous Knowledge,* 58.
101. Benz, "The Theological Meaning of the History of Religions," 11.
102. All quotations from the Revised Standard Version.
103. Mackintosh, "Does the Historical Study of Religion Yield a Dogmatic Theology?" 514.
104. Stark, *For the Glory of God,* 2.
105. Andrew Lang, *Myth, Ritual, and Religion,* 36–8.
106. Andrew Lang, *The Making of Religion,* 161–2.
107. Andrew Lang, *The Making of Religion,* 190–1.
108. The Greek *heno* meaning "one," plus *theos* meaning "God."
109. Schmidt, *The Origin and Growth of Religion,* 169.
110. Schmidt, *The Origin and Growth of Religion,* 170–1.
111. Eliade, "The Quest for the Origins of Religion," 161.
112. Quoted in Schmidt, *The Origin and Growth of Religion,* 174.
113. Best, "The Cult of Io," 98.
114. Man, "On the Aboriginal Inhabitants of the Andaman Islands," 157–8.
115. Radin, *Monotheism,* 21.
116. Eliade, "Australian Religions," 108.
117. Eliade, *Patterns in Comparative Religion,* 41.
118. Eliade, "South American High Gods, Part 1," "South American High Gods, Part 2."
119. O'Connell, "The Withdrawal of the High Gods in West African Religion."
120. Smart, *The Religious Experience of Mankind,* 33.
121. Hultkrantz, "North American Indian Religion."
122. Andrew Lang, *The Making of Religion,* 206.
123. O'Connell, "The Withdrawal of the High Gods in West African Religion."
124. Quoted in Radin, *Primitive Man as Philosopher,* 361–2.
125. I have used the MicroCase electronic version, available from Wadsworth Publishers.
126. Radin, *Primitive Religion.*
127. Wallace, *Religion,* 12.
128. Schmidt, *The Origin and Growth of Religion,* 262.
129. Goode, *Religion among the Primitives,* 22.

130. Davis, *Human Society*, 515–6.
131. Smart, *The Religious Experience of Mankind*, 27.

Chapter 2: Temple Religions of Ancient Civilizations

1. Kramer, *History Begins at Sumer*.
2. Hallo, "Before Tea Leaves," 39.
3. Michalowski, "Sumerians."
4. Soustelle, "Aztec Religion," "Sumerian Religion," and *Daily Life of the Aztecs*; J. Eric S. Thompson, *Maya History*.
5. Roux, *Ancient Iraq*, 85.
6. Oates, *Babylon*, 47.
7. Roux, *Ancient Iraq*, 70.
8. Kramer, "The 'Babel of Tongues' "; Parrot, *The Tower of Babel*.
9. Ghirshman, "The Ziggurat of Cogha-Zanbil."
10. Ghirshman, "The Ziggurat of Cogha-Zanbil."
11. Hodder, *The Leopard's Tale*.
12. Ghirshman, "The Ziggurat of Cogha-Zanbil," 262.
13. Margueron, "Temples," 165.
14. Oppenheim, *Ancient Mesopotamia*, 184.
15. Oppenheim, *Ancient Mesopotamia*, 184.
16. Until recently I knew no better and often repeated the spurious claim that the idols were merely symbols.
17. Pollard, "Greek Religion," 409.
18. Mettinger, *No Graven Images*.
19. Oppenheim, *Ancient Mesopotamia*, 186.
20. Oppenheim, *Ancient Mesopotamia*, 186.
21. Walker and Dick, "The Induction of the Cult Image."
22. Stevens, *Temples, Tithes, and Taxes*, 86.
23. Stevens, *Temples, Tithes, and Taxes*, 86.
24. Frankfort, *Kingship and the Gods*, 221.
25. Roaf, *Cultural Atlas*, 104.
26. Mendelssohn, *The Riddle of the Pyramids*, 175.
27. Stark and Bainbridge, *A Theory of Religion*.
28. *Statesman*.
29. There is a needless concern in the literature that definitions based on intercession will fail to identify the "professionals," as opposed to laity. See Beard and North, "Introduction" in *Pagan Priests*.
30. Roux, *Ancient Iraq*, 214.
31. Soustelle, "Aztec Religion," 551.
32. Carrasco, *Religions of Mesoamerica*.
33. Coe, *The Maya*, 209.
34. Breasted, "The Development of the Priesthood," 21.
35. Breasted, "The Development of the Priesthood," 23.
36. Burkert, *Greek Religion*, 98.
37. Garland, "Priests and Power," 77.
38. Garland, "Priests and Power," 77.
39. Parker, "Controlling Religion," 573.
40. Simon Price, *Religions of the Ancient Greeks*, 64–5.
41. Oppenheim, *Ancient Mesopotamia*, 175.
42. Kramer, *The Sumerians*, 100.
43. Oppenheim, *Ancient Mesopotamia*, 178–9.
44. Breasted, "The Development of the Priesthood," 22.
45. Martens, "Music," 415.
46. Kramer, *The Sumerians*, 140.
47. Roux, *Ancient Iraq*, 210.
48. Roux, *Ancient Iraq*, 212.
49. Kramer, *The Sumerians*, 34.

50. Spalinger, "The Limitations of Formal Egyptian Religion," 241.
51. Beaulieu, "Greece," 267.
52. Hollinshead, "'Adyton,' 'Ophisthodomos,' and the Inner Room."
53. B. F. Cook, *Reading the Past*, 36.
54. Carrasco, *City of Sacrifice*; Soustelle, "Aztec Religion."
55. Coe, *The Maya*, 210.
56. Roux, *Ancient Iraq*, 87.
57. Oates, *Babylon*, 171.
58. Roux, *Ancient Iraq*, 88.
59. Kramer, *The Sumerians*, 119.
60. Roaf, *Cutural Atlas*, 81.
61. Kramer, *The Sumerians*, 122.
62. Kramer, *The Sumerians*, 122.
63. Foster, *From Distant Days*, 349.
64. Black and Green, *Gods, Demons and Symbols*, 151–2.
65. Kramer, *The Sumerians*, 123.
66. Roaf, *Cultural Atlas*, 76.
67. Frankfort, *Kingship and the Gods*, 145.
68. Stark, *The Rise of Christianity*.
69. Griffiths, "The Orders of Gods in Ancient Greece and Egypt."
70. Burkert, *Babylon, Memphis, Persepolis*, chap. 2.
71. Clive Barrett, *The Egyptian Gods and Goddesses*, 120.
72. Clive Barrett, *The Egyptian Gods and Goddesses*.
73. Hornung, *Conceptions of God*.
74. Richard Wilkinson, *The Complete Gods and Goddesses*.
75. Richard Wilkinson, *The Complete Gods and Goddesses*, 139.
76. Richard Wilkinson, *The Complete Gods and Goddesses*, 113.
77. *The History*, 2.43.
78. Burkert, *Greek Religion*, 119; Simon Price, *Religions of the Ancient Greeks*, 3.
79. Burkert, *Greek Religion*, chap. 3.
80. Lefkowitz, *Greek Gods, Human Lives*, 13.
81. Pollard, "Greek Religion."
82. Simon Price, *Religions of the Ancient Greeks*, 11.
83. Soustelle, "Mayan Religion."
84. Carrasco, *City of Sacrifice*, 78.
85. Unfortunately, there are various spellings used for Aztec and Mayan words and names. *Ometecuhtli* also is spelled *Ometeotl*, while *Huitzilopochtli* is also spelled *Uitzilopochtli*.
86. Soustelle, *Daily Life*, 96.
87. Carrasco, *City of Sacrifice*, 79.
88. Coe, *Breaking the Maya Code*.
89. Soustelle, "Mayan Religion."
90. Percy S. Cohen, "Theories of Myth," 337.
91. Bain, "Man, the Myth-Maker," 61. Bain proceeded to rage against many current myths, including "free enterprise" and "free trade."
92. Weinfeld, "Israelite Religion," 481.
93. Oppenheim, *Ancient Mesopotamia*, 172.
94. Carroll, "A New Look at Freud on Myth," 199.
95. Carroll, "A New Look at Freud on Myth."
96. Campbell, *The Hero*.
97. Carroll, "A New Look at Freud on Myth," 199.
98. See the nice discussion by Lefkowitz, *Greek Gods, Human Lives*, 8–9.
99. According to the Baylor Survey of American Religion, as of 2005, 19 percent of adult Americans had read at least one *Left Behind* novel.
100. By Tim LaHaye and Jerry B. Jenkins.
101. Bidney, "Myth, Symbolism, and Truth," 379.
102. Kramer, *The Sumerians*, 163.
103. Roux, *Ancient Iraq*, 110.

104. Dundes, *The Flood Myth.*
105. Peschel, "Structural Parallels in Two Flood Myths."
106. Horcasitas, "An Analysis."
107. Parrot, *The Flood and Noah's Ark.*
108. Róheim, *The Gates of the Dream.*
109. Dundes, "The Flood."
110. Jacobsen, *The Treasures*, 195; Roux, *Ancient Iraq*, 116; von Soden, *The Ancient Orient*, 215.
111. As quoted in Roux, *Ancient Iraq*, 119. This entire account owes much to Roux.
112. Gladstone, *Landmarks of Homeric Studies.*
113. Abusch, "The Development and Meaning of the Epic of Gilgamesh."
114. Bowra, *Heroic Poetry*; Burkert, *Babylon, Memphis, Persepolis*; Gresseth, "The Gilgamesh Epic"; Held, "Parallels"; West, *The East Face of Helicon.*
115. Quoted in Carrasco, *City of Sacrifice*, 61.
116. Carrasco, *Religions of Mesoamerica*, 75.
117. Carrasco, *City of Sacrifice*, 64.
118. Stark, *Exploring the Religious Life.*
119. Burkert, *Greek Religion*, 248.
120. Albright, *From the Stone Age to Christianity*, 265.
121. She went on to note that "mortals cannot look to the gods for comfort," and in this she found reason to express her contempt for Christianity and Judaism, by calling Greek polytheism "a religion for adults." Lefkowitz, *Greek Gods, Human Lives*, 239.
122. Carrasco, *Religions of Mesoamerica*, 65.
123. Black and Green, *Gods, Demons, and Symbols*, 27–8.
124. Roux, *Ancient Iraq*, 101.
125. Clifford Herschel Moore, *The Religious Thought of the Greeks*, 39.
126. Clifford Herschel Moore, *The Religious Thought of the Greeks*, 39.
127. Carrasco, *Religions of Mesoamerica*, 65.
128. Mendelssohn, *The Riddle of the Pyramids.*
129. Black and Green, *Gods, Demons, and Symbols*, 104–5; Woolley, *Discovering the Royal Tombs.*
130. Kramer, *The Sumerians*, 130.
131. Mendelssohn, *The Riddle of the Pyramids*, chap. 7; Carrasco, *Religions of Mesoamerica.*
132. Wilford, "Maya Tomb Tells Tale of Two Women."
133. Bard, "The Emergence of the Egyptian State," 72.
134. Eliade, *Patterns in Comparative Religion*, 43.
135. Baly, "The Geography of Monotheism," 255.
136. McNeill, *The Rise of the West*, 41.
137. McNeill, *The Rise of the West*, 40–1.
138. Oppenheim, *Ancient Mesopotamia*, 182.
139. Frankfort, "Heresy in a Theocratic State," 152.
140. Burkert, *Greek Religion*; Detienne, "Orpheus"; Bennett Ramsey, "Pythagoras."
141. Walker, "Orpheus the Theologian and the Renaissance Platonists."
142. In Burkert, *Greek Religion*, 296
143. William V. Harris, *Ancient Literacy.*
144. LaCocque, "Sin and Guilt," 329.
145. In Burkert, *Greek Religion*, 303.
146. Simon Price, *Religions of the Ancient Greeks*, 119.
147. Kahn, *Pythagoras*, 6.
148. Bennett Ramsey, "Pythagoras," 114.
149. Gnoli, *Zoroaster*; Kahn, *Pythagoras*; Zaehner, *The Dawn and Twilight of Zoroastrianism.*
150. Alfred Weber, *History of Philosophy*, 22.
151. Alfred Weber, *History of Philosophy*, 22.
152. Ahlström, *Royal Administration and National Religions in Ancient Palestine*, 2–4.
153. Frankfort, *Kingship and the Gods*, 237
154. Frankfort, *Kingship and the Gods*, 237.
155. Frankfort, *Kingship and the Gods*, 243.
156. Frankfort, *Kingship and the Gods*, 253.
157. Frankfort, *Kingship and the Gods*, 279.

158. Adkins, *Empires of the Plain.*
159. Sahlins, *Stone Age Economics.*
160. Adam Smith, *An Inquiry into the Nature and Causes of the Wealth of Nations,* 190.
161. Mauss, *The Gift,* 37.
162. In MacMullen, *Roman Social Relations,* 62.
163. David P. Wright, "Anatolia," 192.
164. Simon Price, "Sacrifice, Offerings, and Votives," 344.
165. Freud, *Totem and Taboo;* also Money-Kyrle, *The Meaning of Sacrifice.*
166. Stark and Finke, *Acts of Faith,* 100.
167. Stark and Finke, *Acts of Faith,* 100–2.
168. Firth, "Offering and Sacrifice," 20.
169. Bottéro, *Religion in Ancient Mesopotamia,* 125.
170. Willems, "Sacrifice, Offerings, and Votives," 326.
171. Simon Price, *Religions of the Ancient Greeks,* 32–40.
172. Simon Price, *Religions of the Ancient Greeks,* 35.
173. E. O. James, *Origins of Sacrifice;* Yerkes, *Sacrifice.*
174. Hughes, *Human Sacrifice.*
175. Díaz, *The Discovery and Conquest of Mexico,* 119.
176. Carrasco, *City of Sacrifice,* 2.
177. Carrasco, *City of Sacrifice,* 3.
178. Carrasco, *City of Sacrifice,* 83.
179. Carrasco, *City of Sacrifice,* 192.
180. Clendinnen, *Aztecs,* 91.
181. Carrasco, *City of Sacrifice,* 76, 81.
182. For a full critique, see Stark, *Exploring the Religious Life,* chap. 2.
183. Clendinnen, *Aztecs;* Harner, "The Ecological Basis for Aztec Sacrifice"; Harris, *Cannibals and Kings;* Read, *Time and Sacrifice.*
184. Sherburne F. Cook, "Human Sacrifice"; Barbara J. Price, "Demystification."
185. Ingham, "Human Sacrifice," 380.

Chapter 3: Rome: An Ancient Religious Marketplace

1. In Augustine, *The City of God* IV.31.
2. Bailey, *Phases in the Religion of Ancient Rome;* Boak and Sinnigen, *A History of Rome.*
3. Beard, North, and Price, *Religions of Rome,* I:12.
4. Beard, North, and Price, *Religions of Rome,* I.
5. Liebeschuetz, *Continuity and Change in Roman Religion,* 1.
6. North, "Conservatism and Change," 1.
7. Beard, North, and Price, *Religions of Rome,* II:129.
8. Rives, *Religion and Authority,* 559.
9. Liebeschuetz, *Continuity and Change in Roman Religion,* 7.
10. Liebeschuetz, *Continuity and Change in Roman Religion,* 3.
11. Liebeschuetz, *Continuity and Change in Roman Religion,* 8.
12. Liebeschuetz, *Continuity and Change in Roman Religion,* 4.
13. Lang, Chan, and Ragvald, "Temples and the Religious Economy."
14. See Allport, *The Individual and His Religion;* Nock, *Conversion;* MacMullen, *Paganism in the Roman Empire,* chap. 2.
15. Finke and Stark, *The Churching of America;* Stark, "From Church-Sect to Religious Economies," "Religious Economies," "Spiegare le Variazioni," and *The Rise of Christianity;* Stark and Finke, *Acts of Faith;* Stark and Iannaccone, "Recent Religious Declines."
16. Bruce, *Choice and Religion,* 2. In his attack on "rational choice" theories, Bruce proposed to drive "the stake through the vampire's chest."
17. Heath, *Rational Choice.*
18. Coleman, "Social Cleavage and Religious Conflict," 18.
19. Hobbes, *Leviathan,* I:98.
20. Hume, *Inquiry Concerning Human Understanding,* 123.
21. Comte, *The Positive Philosophy,* II:554.

22. Feuerbach, *The Essence of Christianity.*

23. Durkheim, *The Elementary Forms of Religious Life,* 206.

24. Freud, *The Future of an Illusion,* 88.

25. Scharfstein, *Mystical Experience,* 1, 45.

26. Carroll, "Praying the Rosary," 491.

27. Bergin, "Religiosity and Mental Health"; Ellison, "Religious Involvement and Subjective Well-Being"; Hackney and Sanders, "Religiosity and Mental Health"; Pargament and Park, "Merely a Defense?"

28. Stark, *For the Glory of God;* Stark and Finke, *Acts of Faith;* Wuthnow, "Science and the Sacred."

29. Stark, *Exploring the Religious Life.*

30. Stark and Finke, *Acts of Faith.*

31. Bader and Froese, "Images of God."

32. Introvigne, "Niches in the Islamic Religious Market."

33. Lang, Chan, and Ragvald, "Temples and the Religious Economy."

34. Beard, North, and Price, *Religions of Rome,* I:42.

35. Saggs, *The Encounter with the Divine in Mesopotamia and Israel,* 67.

36. Geertz, "Religion as a Cultural System."

37. Douglas, "The Effects of Modernization," 29.

38. MacMullen, *Paganism in the Roman Empire,* 63.

39. Saggs, *The Encounter with the Divine in Mesopotamia and Israel,* 162.

40. Finke and Stark, *The Churching of America;* Stark and Finke, *Acts of Faith;* Stark, *For the Glory of God.*

41. Adam Smith, *An Inquiry into the Nature and Causes of the Wealth of Nations,* II:788–9.

42. Schmidt, *The Origin and Growth of Religion,* 289.

43. Spalinger, "The Limitations of Formal Egyptian Religion."

44. Oppenheim, *Ancient Mesopotamia,* 176.

45. Goody, "A Kernel of Doubt."

46. Douglas, "The Effects of Modernization," 29.

47. Spalinger, "The Limitations," 242.

48. Beard, North, and Price, *Religions of Rome,* I: 88.

49. Beard, North, and Price, *Religions of Rome,* I:88.

50. Beard, "Priesthood," 27.

51. Beard, North, and Price, *Religions of Rome,* I:87.

52. Beard, North, and Price, *Religions of Rome,* I:88.

53. Beard, North, and Price, *Religions of Rome,* I:196–7.

54. Peter Brown, *The Making of Late Antiquity,* 28.

55. Peter Brown, *The Making of Late Antiquity;* Rostovtzeff, *The Social and Economic History.*

56. Stark, *Cities of God,* chap. 7.

57. MacMullen, *Paganism in the Roman Empire,* 107.

58. Scheid, "Graeco Ritu," 17.

59. Barclay, *Jews in the Mediterranean Diaspora.*

60. Harnack, *The Expansion of Christianity in the First Three Centuries,* vol. 1; Stark, *The Rise of Christianity* and *Cities of God.*

61. Clauss, *The Roman Cult of Mithras.*

62. Cumont, *Oriental Religions,* 20–45.

63. Beard, North, and Price, *Religions of Rome,* I:287.

64. *The Stromata,* book 7, chap. 6.

65. Burkert, *Greek Religion,* 109.

66. In Burkert, *Ancient Mystery Cults,* 113.

67. Cumont, *Oriental Religions,* 30.

68. Pettazzoni, *Essays on the History of Religions,* 208.

69. Liebeschuetz, *Continuity and Change in Roman Religion,* 40.

70. Cumont, *Oriental Religions,* 39.

71. Pettazzoni, *Essays on the History of Religions,* 62.

72. Beard, North, and Price, *Religions of Rome,* I:284.

73. Cumont, *Oriental Religions,* 44.

74. Beard, North, and Price, *Religions of Rome,* I: 286.

75. Cumont, *Oriental Religions*, 43–4.

76. Beard, North, and Price, *Religions of Rome*, I: 297.

77. Kraemer, *Her Share of the Blessings*.

78. Beard, North, and Price, *Religions of Rome*, I: 96.

79. Kraemer, *Her Share of the Blessings*; also, for Cybele: Roller, *In Search of God*; for Isis: Donalson, *The Cult of Isis*; Heyob, *The Cult of Isis*.

80. Brooten, *Women Leaders*; Kraemer, *Her Share of the Blessings*; Tribilco, *Jewish Communities*.

81. Michael Grant, *The History of Rome*, 23.

82. Beard, North, and Price, *Religions of Rome*, I:287.

83. Beard, North, and Price, *Religions of Rome*, I:42.

84. Beard, North, and Price, *Religions of Rome*, I:287.

85. John North, "Religious Toleration."

86. Nock, *St. Paul*, 59.

87. John North, "Rome," 231.

88. Stark and Finke, *Acts of Faith*, chap. 6.

89. Beard, North, and Price, *Religions of Rome*, II:275.

90. Gierke, *Associations and Law*.

91. *The Letters of Pliny the Younger* (edited by Betty Radice), Book X:33–4.

92. Lucian, *Decorum Concilium*, 14.

93. Beard, North, and Price, *Religions of Rome*, I:92.

94. Beard, North, and Price, *Religions of Rome*, I; Klauck, *The Religious Context of Early Christianity*.

95. For the relevant extracts, see Beard, *Religions of Rome*, II:288–90, and Warrior, *Roman Religion*, 99–105.

96. Keith Hopkins, "Controlling Religion," 573; also Warrior, *Roman Religion*.

97. Beard, North, and Price, *Religions of Rome*, II:290–1.

98. John North, "Religious Toleration in Republican Rome," 87.

99. John North, "Religious Toleration in Republican Rome"; Beard, North, and Price, *Religions of Rome*, I:92–6; Burkert, *Babylon, Memphis, Persepolis*.

100. John North, "Religious Toleration in Republican Rome," 86.

101. Burkert, *Babylon, Memphis, Persepolis*, chap. 4.

102. In Burkert, *Babylon, Memphis, Persepolis*, 77.

103. In Burkert, *Babylon, Memphis, Persepolis*, 80.

104. John North, "Religious Toleration in Republican Rome."

105. Beard, North, and Price, *Religions of Rome*, I:95.

106. Roller, *In Search of God*.

107. Roller, *In Search of God*, 108.

108. Roller, *In Search of God*, 113.

109. Ferguson, *The Religions of the Roman Empire*, 27.

110. Cumont, *Oriental Religions*, 52.

111. Cumont, *Oriental Religions*, 53.

112. Beard, North, and Price, *Religions of Rome*, I:97.

113. Beard, North, and Price, *Religions of Rome*, I:98.

114. Bailey, *Phases in the Religion of Ancient Rome*, 258.

115. Bailey, *Phases in the Religion of Ancient Rome*, 186.

116. Robert M. Grant, *Augustus to Constantine*, 34.

117. Bailey, *Phases in the Religion of Ancient Rome*, 186.

118. Josephus, *Antiquities of the Jews*, 18:Chapter III.

119. Bailey, *Phases in the Religion of Ancient Rome*, 186.

120. Donalson, *The Cult of Isis*, 132–3.

121. Cumont, *Oriental Religions*.

122. Clauss, *The Roman Cult of Mithras*; Merkelbach, "Mithra, Mithraism."

123. M. P. Nilsson, quoted in Clauss, *The Roman Cult of Mithras*, 7.

124. Clauss, *The Roman Cult of Mithras*, 7

125. Beard, North, and Price, *Religions of Rome*, I:280.

126. For example, Cooper, *Mithras*.

127. Merkelbach, "Mithra, Mithraism," 877.

128. Merkelbach, "Mithra, Mithraism," 290.

129. *First Apology*, 66.

130. In Clauss, *The Roman Cult of Mithras*, 168.

131. Merkelbach, "Mithra, Mithraism," 878.

132. L. Michael White, "Mithraism," 609.

133. Cooper, *Mithras*, ix.

134. Gager, *Kingdom and Community*, 133.

135. A superb example is included in Manfred Clauss's fine study, *The Roman Cult of Mithras*, 26–7.

136. Ruether, *Faith and Fratricide*.

137. Isaac, *Jesus and Israel* and *The Teaching of Contempt*.

138. Gager, *The Origins of Anti-Semitism*.

139. Quoted in Augustine, *City of God*, 6:11.

140. Cicero, *Pro Flacco*, 28:69.

141. Tacitus, *The Histories*, 5:1–13 (The Jews).

142. Smallwood, *The Jews*, 129.

143. Tacitus, *Annales*, 2:85.

144. Suetonius, *Tiberius*, 36.

145. Cassius Dio, *Historia Romana* 67:14.

146. Gibbon, *The Decline and Fall of the Roman Empire*, book I, chap. XVI.

147. De Ste. Croix, "Why Were the Early Christians Persecuted," 7; Rives, "The Decree of Decius," 135.

148. Rives, "The Decree of Decius," 151.

149. Gibbon, *The Decline and Fall of the Roman Empire*, book I, chap. XVI.

150. Frend, *Martyrdom and Persecution in the Early Church*; Michael Grant, *The History of Rome*; Rives, "The Decree of Decius."

151. Boak and Sinnigen, *A History of Rome*; Michael Grant, *The History of Rome*.

152. Boak and Sinnigen, *A History of Rome*.

153. Stephen Williams, *Diocletian*, 18.

154. Rives, "The Decree of Decius," 137.

155. Boak and Sinnigen, *A History of Rome*, 415.

156. Rives, "The Decree of Decius," 142.

157. Michael Grant, *The History of Rome*, 307.

158. Rives, "The Decree of Decius," 142.

159. Quoted in Frend, *Martyrdom and Persecution in the Early Church*, 405.

160. For a summary of evidence, see Stark, *The Rise of Christianity*.

161. Sordi, *The Christians*.

162. Rostovtzeff, *The Social and Economic History*, 453–4.

163. Van Sickle, "Conservative and Philosophical Influence in the Reign of Diocletian," 52.

164. Quoted in Van Sickle, "Conservative and Philosophical Influence in the Reign of Diocletian," 51.

165. De Ste. Croix, "Why Were the Early Christians Persecuted," 25; Rives, "The Decree of Decius," 138.

166. Frend, *Martyrdom and Persecution in the Early Church*, 491.

167. Michael Grant, *The History of Rome*, 308.

168. Gibbon, *The Decline and Fall of the Roman Empire*, I:2,14.

169. Gibbon, *The Decline and Fall of the Roman Empire*, I:15.

170. Bowersock, *Hellenism*, 6.

171. Kirsch, *God against the Gods*, 9.

172. MacMullen, *Christianity and Paganism*, 2.

173. Kirsch, *God against the Gods*, 18

174. Richard H. Wilkinson, *The Complete Gods and Goddesses*, 46–8.

175. Oppenheim, *Ancient Mesopotamians*, 176.

176. In Liebeschuetz, *Continuity and Change in Roman Religion*, 4.

177. Liebeschuetz, *Continuity and Change in Roman Religion*, 4.

178. Stark, *The Rise of Christianity* and *Cities of God*; Harnack, *The Expansion of Christianity in the First Three Centuries*, vol. 1.

179. MacMullen, *Paganism in the Roman Empire*, 109.

180. Dwight Nelson Robinson, "A Study of the Social Position of the Devotees of Oriental Cults in the Western World," table 1.

181. Beard, North, and Price, *Religions of Rome*, I:98.

182. Beard, North, and Price, *Religions of Rome*, I:261.

183. Beard, North, and Price, *Religions of Rome*, I:291.

Chapter 4: The "Rebirth" of Monotheism

1. In Aldred, *Akhenaten*, 242.

2. Aldred, *Akhenaten*, 240.

3. In Hornung, *Akhenaten*, 4.

4. Dick, "Prophetic Parodies of Making the Cult Image."

5. Aldred, *Akhenaten*, 245.

6. Redford, *Akhenaten*, 169.

7. Aldred, *Akhenaten*, 243.

8. John Wilson, "Akhenaten," 402.

9. Hornung, *Akhenaten*, 17.

10. John Wilson, "Akhenaten," 402.

11. John Wilson, "Akhenaten," 402.

12. John Wilson, "Akhenaten," 402.

13. Redford, *Akhenaten*.

14. Dever, *Who Were the Early Israelites*; Aldred, *Akhenaten*.

15. Dever, *Who Were the Early Israelites*, 170.

16. Hornung, *Akhenaten*, 111.

17. Van Dijk, "The Armana Period," 311.

18. In Redford, *Akhenaten*, 208.

19. Aldred, *Akhenaten*, 245.

20. Smith and Redford, *The Akhenaten Temple Period*.

21. Kitchen, "Exodus," 703.

22. Redford, *Egypt, Canaan, and Israel*, 377–94.

23. For the new dates: Boyce, *A History of Zoroastrianism* and *Zoroastrianism: A Shadowy but Powerful Presence*; Kingsley, "The Greek Origin"; Nock, "The Problem of Zoroaster"; Shahbazi, "The 'Traditional Date of Zoroaster' Explained." For the old dates: Gershevitch, "Zoroaster's Own Contribution"; Henning, *Zoroaster*; Herzfeld, *Zoroaster*; Yamauchi, *Persia and the Bible*; Zaehner, *The Dawn and Twilight of Zoroastrianism*.

24. Gnoli, "Zoroastrianism," 586.

25. Gershevitch, "Zoroaster's Own Contribution."

26. Gershevitch, "Zoroaster's Own Contribution," 14.

27. Yamauchi, *Persia and the Bible*, 404.

28. Boyce, *A History of Zoroastrianism*, *Zoroastrianism: A Shadowy but Powerful Presence*, and *Zoroastrians*.

29. Porphyry, *Vita Pythagorae*, 11–2.

30. Gnoli, *Zoroaster*; Kingsley, "The Greek Origin."

31. Gnoli, *Zoroaster*.

32. Boyce, *Zoroastrianism*, 182.

33. Boyce, *Zoroastrians*; Zaehner, *The Dawn and Twilight of Zoroastrianism*.

34. Boyce, *Zoroastrianism*, 184.

35. Nyberg, *Die Religionen*.

36. Gershevitch, "Zoroaster's Own Contribution," 14.

37. Henning, *Zoroaster*, 35.

38. Stark, "From Church-Sect to Religious Economies," "Religious Economies," *The Rise of Christianity*, "Why Religious Movements"; Stark and Finke, *Acts of Faith*.

39. Stark and Bainbridge, *The Future of Religion*; Stark, *The Rise of Christianity*; Stark and Finke, *Acts of Faith*.

40. Cohn, *Cosmos, Chaos and the World*.

41. Yamauchi, *Persia and the Bible*, 417.

42. Zaehner, *The Dawn and Twilight of Zoroastrianism*, 36–7.

43. Stark, *One True God.*

44. Zaehner, *The Dawn and Twilight of Zoroastrianism*, 36.

45. Boyce, *Zoroastrianism*, 191.

46. Zaehner, *The Dawn and Twilight of Zoroastrianism*, 74.

47. Gershevitch, "Zoroaster's Own Contribution."

48. Gershevitch, "Zoroaster's Own Contribution," 14.

49. Zaehner, *The Dawn and Twilight of Zoroastrianism*, 80.

50. Darrow, "Zoroaster."

51. Gnoli, "Magi."

52. Gershevitch, "Zoroaster's Own Contribution," 25.

53. Gnoli, "Magi."

54. Gershevitch, "Zoroaster's Own Contribution," 28.

55. Boyce, *Zoroastrianism*; Yamauchi, *Persia and the Bible.*

56. Gershevitch, "Zoroaster's Own Contribution"; Gnoli, "Magi."

57. Nock, "The Problem of Zoroaster," 277.

58. Yamauchi, *Persia and the Bible*, 469.

59. Gershevitch, "Zoroaster's Own Contribution," 31.

60. In Zaehner, *The Dawn and Twilight of Zoroastrianism*, 359.

61. Halpern, *The First Historians.*

62. Thomas Thompson, *The Mythic Past*, 34.

63. Lemche, *The Israelites.*

64. Philip R. Davies, *In Search of "Ancient Israel"*; Lemche, *The Israelites*; Thomas Thompson, *The Mythic Past*; Whitelam, *The Invention of Ancient Israel.*

65. Noth, *A History of Pentateuchal Traditions.*

66. McKenzie, "Deuteronomistic History."

67. Albertz, *A History of Israelite Religion in the Old Testament Period*; Halpern, *The First Historians*; McKenzie, "Deuteronomistic History"; Weinfeld, "Deuteronomy."

68. Baumgarten, *The Flourishing of Jewish Sects in the Maccabean Era.*

69. See the remarkable study by Kitchen, *On the Reliability of the Old Testament.*

70. Dever, *Who Were the Early Israelites*; Finkelstein, "The Great Transformation"; Redford, *Egypt, Canaan, and Israel.*

71. Kathleen Kenyon, *Digging Up Jericho.*

72. For an excellent summary, see Dever, *Who Were the Early Israelites.*

73. Hoffmeier, "Out of Egypt."

74. Ahlström, "Another Moses Tradition," *Who Were the Israelites*; Callaway, "Village Subsistence"; de Geus, *The Tribes*; Gnuse, *No Other Gods.*

75. Ahlström, "Another Moses Tradition," *Who Were the Israelites.*

76. Ahlström, "Another Moses Tradition," 66–7.

77. Dever, *Who Were the Early Israelites*, 236.

78. Jacobsen, *The Treasures of Darkness*, 209; also Oppenheim, *Ancient Mesopotamia*, 266; von Soden, *The Ancient Orient.*

79. Dever, *Who Were the Early Israelites*, 237.

80. Stark, "A Theory of Revelations."

81. Henry Thompson, "Yahweh," 1011.

82. Henry Thompson, "Yahweh."

83. Henry Thompson, "Yahweh."

84. Mark S. Smith, *The Origins of Biblical Monotheism*, 154.

85. De Moor, *The Rise of Yahwism*; Dever, *Did God Have a Wife?*; Geller, "The God of the Covenant"; Gnuse, *No Other Gods*; Mettinger, *No Graven Images?*; Mark S. Smith, *The Origins of Biblical Monotheism* and *The Early History of God.*

86. Dever, *Did God Have a Wife?*; Gnuse, *No Other Gods*; Mettinger, *No Graven Images?*; Miller, *The Religion of Ancient Israel.*

87. Dever, *Did God Have a Wife?*

88. Zevit, *The Religions of Ancient Israel.*

89. For an excellent summary, see Gnuse, *No Other Gods*, 180–94.

90. Dever, *Did God Have a Wife?* 277.

91. Dever, *Did God Have a Wife?* 278.

92. Albertz, *A History of Israelite Religion in the Old Testament Period*, I:131.

93. Dever, *Did God Have a Wife?* 277.

94. Albertz, *A History of Israelite Religion in the Old Testament Period*, I:131.

95. Gnuse, *No Other Gods*, 186.

96. Dever, *Did God Have a Wife?*; Zevit, *The Religions of Ancient Israel*.

97. Van Seters, *In Search of History*.

98. Carl D. Evans, "Jeroboam"; Zevit, *The Religions of Ancient Israel*.

99. Carl D. Evans, "Jeroboam," 743.

100. Philip J. King, *Amos, Hosea, Micah*; Zevit, *The Religions of Ancient Israel*.

101. Benton Johnson, "On Church and Sect"; Stark and Bainbridge, "Of Churches, Sects, and Cults"; Stark and Finke, *Acts of Faith*.

102. For an up-to-date version, see Stark and Finke, *Acts of Faith*, chap. 8.

103. Niebuhr, *The Social Sources of Denominationalism*, 19.

104. Stark, *Exploring the Religious Life*.

105. Shaye J. D. Cohen, *From the Maccabees to the Mishna*; Niebuhr, *The Social Sources of Denominationalism*; Saldarini, *Pharisees, Scribes, and Sadducees*.

106. Baumgarten, *The Flourishing of Jewish Sects in the Maccabean Era*, 47.

107. Stark, *For the Glory of God* and *Exploring the Religious Life*.

108. Stark, *Exploring the Religious Life*, 56.

109. Morton Smith, *Palestinian Parties and Politics that Shaped the Old Testament*.

110. Bernard Lang, *Monotheism and the Prophetic Minority*, and "No God but Yahweh!"

111. Albright, *Samuel and the Beginnings of the Prophetic Movement*.

112. See 1 Samuel 10:2–5 and 19:20.

113. Ira M. Price, "The Schools of the Sons of the Prophets," 244.

114. Bernard Lang, *Monotheism and the Prophetic Minority*, 68.

115. Albertz, *A History of Israelite Religion in the Old Testament Period*, 202.

116. Morton Smith, *Palestinian Parties and Politics that Shaped the Old Testament*, 34.

117. 1 Kings 21:17–26

118. Ira M. Price, "The Schools of the Sons of the Prophets," 245.

119. Stark, *Exploring the Religious Life*.

120. W. A. Irwin, "An Objective Criterion for the Dating of Deuteronomy."

121. Noth, *A History of Pentateuchal Traditions*.

122. Van Seters, *In Search of History*.

123. Albright, *Samuel and the Beginnings of the Prophetic Movement*, 10.

124. Albright, *Samuel and the Beginnings of the Prophetic Movement*; Halpern, *The First Historians*; Noth, *A History of Pentateuchal Traditions*; Zevit, *The Religions of Ancient Israel*.

125. Bernard Lang, *Monotheism and the Prophetic Minority*, 68; Lundbom, "Jeremiah," 686; Sperling, "Jeremiah," 1.

126. Ahlström, *The History of Ancient Palestine*, 786.

127. Kaufmann, *The Babylonian Captivity and Deutero-Isaiah*, 7.

128. Kaufmann, *The Babylonian Captivity and Deutero-Isaiah*, 9. See the *Book of Daniel*.

129. Tadmor, "The Period of the First Temple," 163–4.

130. Kaufmann, *The Babylonian Captivity and Deutero-Isaiah*, 14.

131. Morton Smith, *Palestinian Parties and Politics that Shaped the Old Testament*, 75.

132. Kaufmann, *The Babylonian Captivity and Deutero-Isaiah*; Bernard Lang, *Monotheism and the Prophetic Minority*; Morton Smith, *Palestinian Parties and Politics that Shaped the Old Testament*.

133. Kaufmann, *The Babylonian Captivity and Deutero-Isaiah*, 8.

134. Boadt, "Ezekiel, Book of," 711.

135. Greenberg, "Ezekiel," 239.

136. Clifford, "Isaiah, Book of," 493.

137. Clifford, "Isaiah, Book of," 492.

138. Gnoli, *Zoroaster*, 111–8.

139. Winston, "The Iranian Component in the Bible, Apocrypha, and the Qumran," 184–5.

140. Sayce, *Lectures on the Origin and Growth of Religion*, 40.

141. Kingsley, "The Greek Origin," 258.

142. Kingsley, "The Greek Origin"; Yamauchi, *Persia and the Bible*.

143. Zaehner, *The Dawn and Twilight of Zoroastrianism*, 58.

144. Hendel, "Them Dry Bones," 26.

145. Winston, "The Iranian Component in the Bible, Apocrypha, and the Qumran," 187.

146. Boyce, *Zoroastrianism: A Shadowy but Powerful Presence*, 193; Cohn, *Cosmos, Chaos and the World.*

147. Bernard Lang, "Street Theater," 310–2.

148. Winston, "The Iranian Component in the Bible, Apocrypha, and the Qumran," 209–10.

149. Albright, "New Light on Early Recensions in the Hebrew Bible."

150. Ahlström, *The History of Ancient Palestine*, 814.

151. Tadmor, "The Period of the First Temple," 168.

152. W. L. Wardle, quoted in Baly, "The Geography of Monotheism," 257.

153. Saggs, *The Encounter with the Divine in Mesopotamia and Israel*, 36.

154. Stark and Bainbridge, *The Future of Religion*, ch. 7.

155. For a recent statement of the theory, see Stark and Finke, *Acts of Faith.*

156. Tadmor, "The Period of the First Temple," 170.

157. Geva, "Small City, Few People," 66.

158. Stevens, *Temples, Tithes, and Taxes*, 93–6.

159. Stern, "The Period of the First Temple," 194.

160. Feldman, "Judaism," 310.

161. Stern, "The Period of the First Temple," 192.

162. *The Wisdom of Ben Sira* 7:29–31.

163. Stern, "The Period of the First Temple," 194.

164. Shaye J. D. Cohen, *From the Maccabees to the Mishna*; Georgi, "The Early Church."

165. Baumgarten, *The Flourishing of Jewish Sects in the Maccabean Era.*

166. Baumgarten, *The Flourishing of Jewish Sects in the Maccabean Era*, 42–3.

167. Rivkin, "Sadducees," 563.

168. Rivkin, "Sadducees," 564.

169. Rivkin, "Sadducees," 563.

170. Rivkin, "Essenes," 269.

171. Josephus, *Antiquities of the Jews*, 13:10:7.

172. Both quotes from Rivkin, "Essenes," 271.

173. Shaye J. D. Cohen, *From the Maccabees to the Mishna*, 210.

174. Josephus, *Wars of the Jews*, 2:8:2–5.

175. Rivkin, "Essenes," 163.

176. Schiffman, "Essenes," 164.

177. Baumgarten, *The Flourishing of Jewish Sects in the Maccabean Era.*

178. See Cohen, "Was Judaism in Antiquity"; Goodman, *Mission and Conversion.*

179. See Feldman, "Was Judaism a Missionary Religion"; for an extensive summary, see Stark, *One True God*, 52.

180. George Foot Moore, *Judaism in the First Centuries of the Christian Era*, 324.

181. In Berger, *The Jewish-Christian Debate*, 107.

182. In Robert M. Grant, *The Jews in the Roman World*, 61.

183. In Bamberger, *Proselytism in the Talmudic Period*, 153.

184. *Against Apion*, 2.40.

185. *On the Life of Moses* 1.27.247.

186. George Foot Moore, *Judaism in the First Centuries of the Christian Era*, 324.

187. Frend, *Martyrdom and Persecution in the Early Church*, 133; Meeks, *The First Urban Christians.*

188. Harnack, *The Expansion of Christianity in the First Three Centuries*, 1:10–1.

189. *The Jewish War*, 7.44.

190. Acts 16:13–5.

191. Acts 13:16.

192. Acts 13:26.

193. Acts 10:22.

194. Reynolds and Tannenbaum, *Jews and God-Fearers*; Zetterholm, "The Covenant for Gentiles."

195. Engels, "On the History of Early Christianity," 316.

196. Mark 10:31.

197. For a summary, see Stark, *The Rise of Christianity.*

198. Lofland and Stark, "Becoming a World-Saver."

199. Kox, Meeus, and t'Hart, "Religious Conversion"; Smilde, "A Qualitative Comparative Analysis"; Stark and Finke, *Acts of Faith*.

200. Tcherikover, *Hellenistic Civilization*, 346–7.

201. Tcherikover, *Hellenistic Civilization*, 353.

202. Barclay, *Jews in the Mediterranean Diaspora*; Zetterholm, "The Covenant for Gentiles," 176.

203. As numbered in the Torah. It is 28:28 in the Old Testament.

204. Roetzel, *The World Shaped by the New Testament*, 80.

205. Tcherikover, *Hellenistic Civilization*, 346.

206. Stark, *One True God*, chap. 4.

207. Abel, "Retention Strategies and Religious Success"; Stark, *One True God*.

208. Based on the National Jewish Population Surveys of 1990 and 2001. It is assumed that orthodox Jews always are substantially undercounted because of their unwillingness to discuss religion with a telephone interviewer.

209. Albright, *From the Stone Age to Christianity*, 265.

210. Witt, *Isis in the Ancient World*.

211. His history of Egypt was the first to present a scheme of the succeeding dynasties and is still in use.

212. Witt, *Isis in the Ancient World*, 52–5.

213. Stark, *Cities of God*.

214. Bailey, *Phases in the Religion of Ancient Rome*, 258.

215. Bailey, *Phases in the Religion of Ancient Rome*, 258.

216. Robert M. Grant, *Gods and the One God*, 103.

217. Apuleius, *The Golden Ass*, 11.25.

218. Working from fragmentary census forms dating from the first several centuries CE, Hopkins ("Brother-Sister Marriage") found that from 15 to 21 percent of marriages were between brothers and sisters.

219. Witt, *Isis in the Ancient World*, 129.

220. Bailey, *Phases in the Religion of Ancient Rome*, 271.

221. Halsberghe, *The Cult of Sol Invictus*.

222. *The History*, V, 3, 5.

223. Halsberghe, *The Cult of Sol Invictus*; Hay, *The Amazing Emperor of Heliogabalus*.

224. Halsberghe, *The Cult of Sol Invictus*, 76.

225. Halsberghe, *The Cult of Sol Invictus*, 79.

226. Halsberghe, *The Cult of Sol Invictus*, 80.

227. Turcan, *The Cults of the Roman Empire*, 179.

228. Halsberghe, *The Cult of Sol Invictus*; Hay, *The Amazing Emperor of Heliogabalus*; Turcan, *The Cults of the Roman Empire*.

229. Hay, *The Amazing Emperor of Heliogabalus*.

230. Halsberghe, *The Cult of Sol Invictus*, 84.

231. Watson, *Aurelian*, 194–5.

232. Talley, *The Origins of the Liturgical Year*; Tighe, "Calculating Christmas."

Chapter 5: Indian Inspirations

1. Charles Allen, *The Search for Buddha*.

2. Basham, *The Wonder That Was India*, 44.

3. Hopkins and Hiltebeitel, "Indus Valley Religion," 223; Wheeler, *The Indus Civilization*.

4. Fairservis, *The Roots of Ancient India*, 228.

5. Wheeler, *The Indus Civilization*, 16.

6. Thomas J. Hopkins, *The Hindu Religious Tradition*, 4–5.

7. Wheeler, *The Indus Civilization*, 82.

8. Basham, *The Origins and Development of Classical Hinduism*, 3; Wheeler, *The Indus Civilization*, 68, 83; Zaehner, *Hinduism*, 16.

9. Wheeler, *The Indus Civilization*, 83.

10. Zaehner, *Hinduism*, 16; also Thomas J. Hopkins, *The Hindu Religious Tradition*.

11. Wheeler, *The Indus Civilization*, 83.

12. Wheeler, *The Indus Civilization*, 80; also Fairservis, *The Roots of Ancient India*, 292.
13. Wheeler, *The Indus Civilization*, 94.
14. For a summary, see Lorenzen, "Who Invented Hinduism?"
15. Wilfred Cantwell Smith, *The Meaning and End of Religion*, 144.
16. Some of those making this claim also have tried to redefine the term *Orientalist* from a term applied to scholars who study Eastern culture and history to one meaning a colonialist oppresser of the East.
17. Ernst, *Eternal Garden*.
18. Lorenzen, "Who Invented Hinduism?" 635; Chattopadhyaya, *Evolution of Hindu Sects*, 1.
19. Monier-Williams, *Hinduism*, 11.
20. Gonda, "Indian Religions," 169.
21. Chattopadhyaya, *Evolution of Hindu Sects*, 1.
22. D. K. Chakrabarti, quoted in Edwin Bryant, *The Quest for the Origins of Vedic Culture*, 3.
23. Gonda, "Indian Religions," 169.
24. Basham, *The Origins and Development of Classical Hinduism*, 10.
25. Basham, *The Origins and Development of Classical Hinduism*, 7.
26. Klostermaier, *A Survey of Hinduism*, 67.
27. Klostermaier, *A Survey of Hinduism*, 67.
28. Klostermaier, *A Survey of Hinduism*, 67.
29. Basham, *The Wonder That Was India*, 241.
30. Basham, *The Wonder That Was India*, 241.
31. Basham, *The Wonder That Was India*, 239.
32. Basham, *The Wonder That Was India*, 239.
33. Keith, *The Religion and Philosophy of the Veda Upanishads*, 279.
34. Kosambi, *Ancient India*, 102.
35. Basham, *The Wonder That Was India*, 336.
36. Klostermaier, *A Survey of Hinduism*, 334.
37. Basham, *The Origins and Development of Classical Hinduism*, 24.
38. *Rgveda* 10.90.
39. Basham, *The Origins and Development of Classical Hinduism*, 16.
40. Klostermaier, *A Survey of Hinduism*, 336.
41. Thomas J. Hopkins, *The Hindu Religious Tradition*, 16.
42. Basham, *The Origins and Development of Classical Hinduism*, 18.
43. Basham, *The Origins and Development of Classical Hinduism*, 18.
44. Klostermaier, *A Survey of Hinduism*, 335.
45. Thomas J. Hopkins, *The Hindu Religious Tradition*, 84.
46. Kosambi, *Ancient India*, 104.
47. Dumont, *Homo Hierarchicus*.
48. Thomas J. Hopkins, *The Hindu Religious Tradition*, 15.
49. Thomas J. Hopkins, *The Hindu Religious Tradition*, 15.
50. Klostermaier, *A Survey of Hinduism*, 311.
51. Klostermaier, *A Survey of Hinduism*, 311.
52. Collins, *The Sociology of Philosophies*, 178.
53. Wilkins, *Hindu Gods and Goddesses*, 10.
54. Müller, *History of Ancient Sanskrit*, 532; also Gonda, "Indian Religions," 172.
55. Basham, *The Wonder That Was India*, 233.
56. Wilkins, *Hindu Gods and Goddesses*, 38.
57. Basham, *The Wonder That Was India*, 240.
58. Thomas J. Hopkins, *The Hindu Religious Tradition*, 12.
59. Basham, *The Wonder That Was India*, 236.
60. Thomas J. Hopkins, *The Hindu Religious Tradition*, 12.
61. Thomas J. Hopkins, *The Hindu Religious Tradition*, 12.
62. Fowler, *Hinduism*, 102.
63. Basham, *The Wonder That Was India*, 234.
64. Thomas J. Hopkins, *The Hindu Religious Tradition*, 12.
65. Wilkins, *Hindu Gods and Goddesses*, 69.

66. Basham, *The Wonder That Was India*, 236.
67. Wilkins, *Hindu Gods and Goddesses*, 93.
68. Basham, *The Origins and Development of Classical Hinduism*, 29.
69. *Rgveda X*, 129.
70. Basham, *The Wonder That Was India*, 249.
71. *Rgdeva I*, 32.
72. W. Norman Brown, "Theories of Creation in the Rig Veda," 24; Kuiper, "The Basic Concept of Vedic Religion," 110.
73. Hemenway, *Hindu Gods*, 78.
74. Tinker, "Indian Subcontinent," 349.
75. Hopkins, *The Hindu Religious Tradition*, 54.
76. Bowker, *The Oxford Dictionary*, 36, 197.
77. Bowker, *The Oxford Dictionary*, 739.
78. Thapar, *Early India*, 141.
79. Kosambi, *Ancient India*, 103.
80. Rāhula, "Buddha," 372.
81. Thapar, *Early India*, 155.
82. Meanwhile King Cyrus not only expanded his Persian Empire to the west, incorporating Babylon, but to the east, by establishing a province in western India. There is not much to suggest that religious ideas flowed east into India in this era, but much evidence of a flow west, as in the case of both the Pythagorans and the Orphics (see Chapter 2).
83. Basham, *The Wonder That Was India*, 233.
84. Radhakrishnan and Moore, *A Sourcebook in Indian Philosophy*.
85. Fowler, *Hinduism*, 110.
86. Keith, *The Religion and Philosophy of the Veda Upanishads*, II:489.
87. Literally our "deeds," Basham, *The Wonder That Was India*, 243.
88. Basham, *The Wonder That Was India*, 243.
89. *Brihadāranyaka* 3.9.26.
90. Thomas J. Hopkins, *The Hindu Religious Tradition*, 39.
91. *Brihadāranyaka* 4.4.15.
92. Thomas J. Hopkins, *The Hindu Religious Tradition*, 42.
93. Basham, *The Wonder That Was India*, 243.
94. Basham, *The Wonder That Was India*, 244.
95. Thomas J. Hopkins, *The Hindu Religious Tradition*, 54.
96. Quoted in Mahony, "Upaniṣads."
97. Mahony, "Upaniṣads."
98. Basham, *The Wonder That Was India*, 246.
99. Knipe, "Priesthood," 541.
100. Thomas J. Hopkins, *The Hindu Religious Tradition*, 63.
101. Klostermaier, *A Survey of Hinduism*, 312.
102. Knipe, "Priesthood," 541.
103. Basham, *The Origins and Development of Classical Hinduism*, 106.
104. Zaehner, *The Bhagavad-Gita*.
105. Wilkins, *Hindu Gods and Goddesses*, 93.
106. O'Flaherty, "Brahmā," 293.
107. O'Flaherty, "Brahmā," 293.
108. Gonda, "Visnu," 289.
109. Hemenway, *Hindu Gods*, 28.
110. Kinsley, "Avatara," 14.
111. See Smart, *The Religious Experience of Mankind*, 107.
112. Smart, *The Religious Experience of Mankind*; Huston Smith, *The World's Religions*; Weightman, "Hinduism."
113. Smart, *The Religious Experience of Mankind*, 136.
114. Gómez, "Buddhism," 351–2.
115. Caillat, "Mahāvīra," 128–9.
116. Bowker, *The Oxford Dictionary*, 737.

117. Smart, *The Religious Experience of Mankind*, 89.
118. Caillat, "Mahāvīra," 129.
119. Gonda, "Indian Religions," 173.
120. Caillat, "Mahāvīra," 129.
121. Caillat, "Jainism," 509.
122. Thapar, *Early India*, 167.
123. Parrinder, *World Religions*, 241.
124. Parrinder, *World Religions*, 241.
125. Caillat, "Jainism," 510; Smart, *The Religious Experience of Mankind*, 89.
126. Caillat, "Jainism," 512.
127. Caillat, "Jainism," 512.
128. Rāhula, "Buddha," 370.
129. Dutt, *Buddhist Monks*, 101.
130. Keith, "Mahavira and Buddha."
131. Caillat, "Mahāvīra," 129.
132. Kosambi, *Ancient India*, 109.
133. Lamotte, *History of Indian Buddhism*, 707.
134. Reynolds and Hallisey, "Buddhism," 345.
135. Tucci, "Buddhism," 376.
136. Following Kosambi, *Ancient India*, 106.
137. Tucci, "Buddhism," 375–6.
138. Durkheim, *The Elementary Forms of Religious Life*, 28.
139. Durkheim, *The Elementary Forms of Religious Life*, 28.
140. Gómez, "Buddhism," 363; Lester, "Buddhism," 873–4.
141. Charles Allen, *The Search for Buddhism*.
142. Reynolds and Hallisey, "Buddha," 327.
143. Gombrich, "The Consecration of a Buddhist Image," 24.
144. Lester, "Buddhism," 853.
145. Bowker, *The Oxford Dictionary*, 172.
146. Hazra, *The Rise and Decline of Buddhism*, 388.
147. Schmidt, *The Origin and Growth of Religion*, 2.
148. Gonda, "Indian Religions," 173.
149. Lester, "Buddhism," 867.
150. Lester, "Buddhism," 867.
151. Lester, "Buddhism," 867; Rāhula, "Buddha," 372.
152. Collcutt, "Monasticism," 42.
153. Collcutt, "Monasticism," 43.
154. Kitagawa, "Buddhism, History of," 407.
155. Dutt, *Buddhist Monks*, 27.
156. Lester, "Buddhism," 882.
157. Gómez, "Buddhism," 380.
158. Hazra, *The Rise and Decline of Buddhism*, 371–3.
159. Parrinder, *World Religions*, 286.
160. Conze, *Buddhism*, 12.
161. Gómez, "Buddhism in India," 380.
162. Gonda, "Indian Religions," 173.

Chapter 6: Chinese Gods and "Godless" Faiths

1. See Parrinder, *World Religions*; Smart, *The Religious Experience of Mankind*.
2. Overmyer, "Chinese Religion," 257.
3. Kaizuka, *Confucius*, 34–5.
4. D. Howard Smith, *Confucius*, 3.
5. Eberhard, *Guilt and Sin in Traditional China*.
6. Li, *The Beginnings of Chinese Civilization*, 20.
7. Lawrence G. Thompson, "Chinese Religion," 22.

8. Major, "Shang-Ti," 223.

9. D. Howard Smith, *Confucius*, 6.

10. Major, "Shang-Ti," 422.

11. Keightley, "The Religious Commitment," 213.

12. Keightley, "The Religious Commitment," 213.

13. D. Howard Smith, *Confucius*, 9.

14. D. Howard Smith, *Confucius*, 26.

15. Wales, *The Mountain of God*.

16. D. Howard Smith, *Confucius*, 7.

17. Overmyer, "Chinese Religion," 258.

18. D. Howard Smith, *Confucius*, 7.

19. Overmyer, "Religions of China," 986.

20. Overmyer, "Chinese Religion," 258.

21. D. Howard Smith, *Confucius*, 7.

22. Overmyer, "Religions of China," 990.

23. Overmyer, "Religions of China."

24. D. Howard Smith, *Confucius*, 36.

25. D. Howard Smith, *Confucius*, 37.

26. Overmyer, "Chinese Religion," 261.

27. D. Howard Smith, *Confucius*, 39; also see Chandler, *Four Thousand Years of Urban Growth*.

28. For a summary, see Chan, *The Way of Lao Tzu*; Shih, "A Criticism of Some Recent Methods Used in Dating Lao Tzu"; and Dubbs, "The Date and Circumstances of the Philosopher Lao-Tzu."

29. Boltz, "Lao-Tzu," 454.

30. "Lao-Tzu," *Encyclopaedia Britannica* 15th ed.

31. Overmyer, "Religions of China," 994–7.

32. Jaspers, *Anaximander*.

33. Hendricks, *Lao-Tzu's Tao Te Ching*.

34. Boltz, "Lao-Tzu."

35. Jaspers, *Anaximander*, 88.

36. Nivison, "Tao and Te."

37. Quoted in Jaspers, *Anaximander*, 88.

38. Jaspers, *Anaximander*, 88.

39. Eberhard, *Guilt and Sin in Traditional China*.

40. Parrinder, *World Religions*, 339.

41. Eberhard, *Guilt and Sin in Traditional China*.

42. Maspero, *Taoism and Chinese Religion*, 347.

43. Shahar and Weller, *Unruly Gods*, 2.

44. Shahar and Weller, *Unruly Gods*, 3.

45. D. Howard Smith, *Confucius*, 110.

46. Maspero, *Taoism and Chinese Religion*, 92.

47. Baldrian, "Taoism," 293.

48. Boltz, "Lao-Tzu," 455.

49. Baldrian, "Taoism," 293–4.

50. D. Howard Smith, *Confucius*, 105.

51. Collins, *The Sociology of Philosophies*.

52. Maspero, *Taoism and Chinese Religion*, 265–6.

53. Maspero, *Taoism and Chinese Religion*, 266.

54. See Maspero, *Taoism and Chinese Religion*, 83, and Overmyer, "Chinese Religion," 272.

55. Maspero, *Taoism and Chinese Religion*, 83.

56. Yu, *History of Chinese Daoism*, 466.

57. Overmyer, "Chinese Religion," 272.

58. Maspero, *Taoism and Chinese Religion*, 266.

59. Maspero, *Taoism and Chinese Religion*, 267.

60. Parrinder, *World Religions*, 339.

61. Maspero, *Taoism and Chinese Religion*, 269.

62. Overmyer, "Chinese Religions," 264.

63. Maspero, *Taoism and Chinese Religion*, 272.

64. Maspero, *Taoism and Chinese Religion*, 273–4.

65. D. Howard Smith, *Confucius*, 109.

66. Ching, "Confucius," 38.

67. Dubbs, "The Date and Circumstances of the Philosopher Lao-Tzu," 217.

68. Based on Bodde, "The New Identification of Lao Tzu," and Kaltenmark, *Lao Tzu and Taoism*.

69. D. Howard Smith, *Confucius*, 40.

70. D. Howard Smith, *Confucius*, 54.

71. Ching, "Confucius," 39.

72. D. Howard Smith, *Confucius*, 48.

73. D. Howard Smith, *Confucius*, 69.

74. Harbsmeier, "Confucius Ridens."

75. D. Howard Smith, *Confucius*, 51.

76. Ching, "Confucius," 40.

77. Ching, "Confucius," 41.

78. Robert Wilkinson, "Introduction."

79. Quoted in D. Howard Smith, *Confucius*, 96.

80. Robert Wilkinson, "Introduction," ix.

81. D. Howard Smith, *Confucius*, 66.

82. Chan, "Confucian Thought," 18.

83. Smart, *The Religious Experience of Mankind*, 167.

84. D. Howard Smith, *Confucius*, 68.

85. D. Howard Smith, *Confucius*, 68.

86. Ching, "Confucian Thought," 37.

87. Ching, "Confucian Thought," 37.

88. Arthur F. Wright, *Buddhism*, 11.

89. Arthur F. Wright, *Buddhism*, 12.

90. Arthur F. Wright, *Buddhism*, 12.

91. Arthur F. Wright, *Buddhism*, 13.

92. Collins, *The Sociology of Philosophies*.

93. Sun, "The Fate of Confucianism."

94. Reichelt, *Religion in Chinese Garments*, 34.

95. Liu, *A Short History*, 9.

96. Chang, *What Confucius Really Meant*, 129.

97. D. Howard Smith, *Confucius*, 243.

98. D. Howard Smith, *Confucius*, 243.

99. Sun, "The Fate of Confucianism."

100. Yao, "Who Is a Confucian," 323.

101. Overmyer, "Chinese Religion," 270.

102. Overmyer, "Chinese Religion," "Religions of China"; D. Howard Smith, *Confucius*; Zürcher, "Buddhism," *Buddhism*, and *The Buddhist Conquest of China*.

103. Overmyer, "Chinese Religion," 271.

104. Ch'en, *Buddhism in China*, 10–11.

105. Overmyer, "Chinese Religion," 1007.

106. Hajime, "Buddhism, Schools of," 457.

107. Ch'en, *Buddhism in China*, 16.

108. Ch'en, *Buddhism in China*, 13.

109. Zürcher, *The Buddhist Conquest of China*, 6.

110. Zürcher, *The Buddhist Conquest of China*, 8.

111. Overmyer, "Religions of China," 1008.

112. Collins, *The Sociology of the Philosophies*, 272.

113. Smart, *The Religious Experience of Mankind*, 197.

114. Zürcher, "Buddhism," 419.

115. Zürcher, "Buddhism," 419.

116. Overmyer, "Religions of China," 1009.

117. Zürcher, "Buddhism," 418.
118. Arthur F. Wright, *Buddhism*, 58.
119. D. Howard Smith, *Confucius*, 115.
120. D. Howard Smith, *Confucius*, 120. The Chinese regularly and frequently conducted an official census from which these statistics and others reported in this chapter derive. The oldest surviving Chinese census documents date from 2 CE, but statistics from earlier reports were included in surviving documents from much earlier.
121. Ch'en, *Buddhism in China*, 148.
122. Ch'en, *Buddhism in China*, 150.
123. Ch'en, *Buddhism in China*, 163.
124. Ch'en, *Buddhism in China*, 191.
125. Arthur F. Wright, *Buddhism*, 44.
126. Ch'en, *Buddhism in China*, 57.
127. Arthur F. Wright, *Buddhism*, 50.
128. Zürcher, "Buddhism," 418.
129. Overmyer, "Chinese Religions," 271.
130. Lien-Sheng Yang, "Buddhist Monasteries."
131. Overmyer, "Chinese Religions," 270.
132. Overmyer, "Religions of China," 1005.
133. Overmyer, "Chinese Religions," 270.
134. Overmyer, "Chinese Religions," 270.
135. D. Howard Smith, *Chinese Religions*, 109.
136. Ch'en, *Buddhism in China*, 50.
137. D. Howard Smith, *Chinese Religions*, 121.
138. Arthur F. Wright, *Buddhism*, 86.
139. Zürcher, "Buddhism," 415.
140. Zürcher, "Buddhism," 416.
141. Lagerwey, "Taoism," 312.
142. Zürcher, "Buddhism," 419.
143. Cohen, *From the Maccabees to the Mishna*, 289.
144. Cohen, *From the Maccabees to the Mishna*, 292.
145. Overmyer, "Religions of China," 1011.
146. See Cohen, *From the Maccabees to the Mishna*, 290.
147. Overmyer, "Religions of China," 1012.
148. Overmyer, "Religions of China," 1012.
149. Lu, Johnson, and Stark, "Deregulation and the Religious Market in Taiwan."

Chapter 7: The Rise of Christianity

1. Stark, *Cities of God* and *The Rise of Christianity*.
2. Jenkins, *The Next Christendom*.
3. Morton Smith, *Jesus the Magician*.
4. Mack, *A Myth of Innocence*.
5. Thiering, *Jesus and the Riddle of the Dead Sea Scrolls*.
6. Theissen, *The Shadow of the Galilean*.
7. Kautsky, *Foundations of Christianity*.
8. Meier, *A Marginal Jew*.
9. Crossan, *The Historical Jesus*.
10. Morton Smith, *The Secret Gospel*.
11. Baldet, *Jesus, the Rabbi Prophet*.
12. Schonfield, *The Passover Plot*.
13. Spong, *Born of a Woman*.
14. Vermes, *Jesus the Jew*.
15. Baigent, Lincoln, and Leigh, *Holy Blood, Holy Grail*.
16. For a reliable and well-written summary, see Charlotte Allen, *The Human Christ*.

17. For a summary, see Case, "Is Jesus a Historical Character?," "The Historicity of Jesus"; and Kloppenborg, "The Sayings Gospel Q and the Quest for the Historical Jesus."

18. Bauer, *Christ and the Caesars.*

19. Kalthoff, *The Rise of Christianity.*

20. Drews, *The Myth of Christ.*

21. John M. Robertson, *Christianity and Mythology.*

22. Galatians 1:19, 2:9, and Acts 12:17.

23. Josephus, *The Antiquities of the Jews*, 20.9.1.

24. Case, "Is Jesus a Historical Character?" 207–8.

25. Case, "Is Jesus a Historical Character?" 210.

26. Reimarus, *Reimarus: Fragments.*

27. David Frederich Strauss, *The Life of Jesus Critically Examined.*

28. Bultmann, *Jesus and the Word* and *Jesus Christ and Mythology.*

29. N. T. Wright, "Jesus, Quest for the Historical," 798.

30. Sheler, *Is the Bible True?*

31. Velikovsky, *Ages in Chaos* and *Worlds in Collision.*

32. Tresmontant, *The Hebrew Christ.*

33. Witherington, *The Jesus Quest*, 26–7.

34. Batey, *Jesus and the Forgotten City.*

35. Freyne, "The Geography, Politics and Economics of Galilee," 76.

36. Freyne, "Urban-Rural Relations in First-Century Galilee."

37. Mack, *A Myth of Innocence*, 73.

38. Crossan, *The Historical Jesus*, xi.

39. Crossan, *The Historical Jesus*, 125–7.

40. For extreme variation in conclusions, see Vermes, *Jesus and the World of Judaism* and *Jesus the Jew*; and Casey, *From Jewish Prophet to Gentile God.*

41. Sanders, *The Historical Figure of Jesus*, 12.

42. Sanders, *The Historical Figure of Jesus*, 102.

43. Witherington, *The Jesus Quest*, 90–91.

44. Sanders, *The Historical Figure of Jesus*, 98.

45. Sanders, *The Historical Figure of Jesus*, 98.

46. Edwards, *Is Jesus the Only Savior?* 29.

47. Mark 1:9–11.

48. Witherington, *The Jesus Quest*, 92.

49. Riley, *One Jesus, Many Christs*, 39.

50. Riley, *One Jesus, Many Christs.*

51. *Apologeticus*, 21.15.

52. Pelikan, *Whose Bible Is It?*

53. Hurtado, *Lord Jesus Christ*, 14.

54. Hurtado, *Lord Jesus Christ.*

55. There are several versions, with slight differences in wording. I use the version that I grew up reciting every Sunday in the Lutheran Church.

56. Baird, "Biblical Criticism."

57. Consider the damage done to the social sciences recently by Postmodernism or to physics by String Theory.

58. Charlotte Allen, *The Human Christ*; Evans, *Fabricating Jesus.*

59. Gasque, *A History of the Interpretation of the Acts of the Apostles.*

60. Conzelmann, *Acts of the Apostles.*

61. Gasque, *A History of the Interpretation of the Acts of the Apostles*, 249; Hanson, *The Acts.*

62. Hanson, *The Acts*; Jefferson White, *Evidence and Paul's Journeys.*

63. Jefferson White, *Evidence and Paul's Journeys.*

64. Baly, *The Geography of Monotheism.*

65. Baly, *The Geography of Monotheism*; Frederick Fyvie Bruce, *The New Testament Documents.*

66. Frederick Fyvie Bruce, *The New Testament Documents*, 82.

67. Cadbury, *The Book of Acts*, 41.

68. Edwards, *Is Jesus the Only Savior?* 40–43.

69. Frederick Fyvie Bruce, *The Epistle of Paul*; Cadbury, *The Book of Acts*; Hemer, *The Book of Acts*; Jefferson White, *Evidence and Paul's Journeys*.

70. Edwards, *Is Jesus the Only Savior?* 42.

71. *Claudius*, 25.

72. Sanders, *The Historical Figure of Jesus,* 49–50.

73. Habermas, *The Historical Jesus*, 191.

74. Cadbury, *The Book of Acts*, 3.

75. To paraphrase Tresmontant, *The Hebrew Christ*, 9.

76. Especially John A. T. Robinson, *Redating the New Testament* and *The Priority of John*; and Tresmontant, *The Hebrew Christ*.

77. Linnemann, *Is There a Synoptic Problem?*

78. Kümmel, *Introduction to the New Testament*; Robinson, *Redating the New Testament* and *The Priority of John*.

79. Arthur William Robinson.

80. Robinson, *Redating the New Testament* and *The Priority of John*.

81. Acts 22:4–5.

82. Shanks, "How Historical Is the Gospel of John?"

83. D. Moody Smith, *John Among the Gospels*, 212–41.

84. D. Moody Smith, *John Among the Gospels*, 203–4.

85. Bauckham, *Jesus and the Eyewitnesses*; Theissen, *The Gospels in Context*, chap. 4.

86. Theissen, *The Gospels in Context*, chap. 4.

87. Tresmontant, *The Hebrew Christ*.

88. Carmignac, *The Birth of the Synoptics*.

89. Lindsey, *Jesus Rabbi and Lord*.

90. Quoted in Eusebius, *The Ecclesiastical History*:V:8:2–4.

91. Quoted in Eusebius, *The Ecclesiastical History*:II:15.

92. Tresmontant, *The Hebrew Christ*, 4.

93. Lindsey, *Jesus Rabbi and Lord*, 19.

94. Biven and Blizzard, *Understanding the Difficult Words of Jesus*, 53.

95. Bauckham, *Jesus and the Eyewitnesses*, chap. 7; Boomershine, "Peter's Denial as Polemic or Confession."

96. Mack, *The Lost Gospel*.

97. Goulder, "Is Q a Juggernaut?" 667.

98. Mack *The Lost Gospel*, 2, 4.

99. Quoted in Charlotte Allen, "The Search for the No-Frills Jesus," 67.

100. Goulder, "Is Q a Juggernaut?" 668.

101. Kenyon, *The Bible and Modern Scholarship*.

102. Frederick Fyvie Bruce, *The New Testament*, 11–13.

103. Hurtado, *The Earliest Christian Artifacts*.

104. Kenyon, *The Bible and Archeology*, 288–9.

105. Metzger and Ehrman, *The Text of the New Testament*.

106. R. E. Brown, "The Gospel According to John I–XII," 112.

107. Bauckham, *Jesus and the Eyewitnesses*, 130.

108. For a superb summary, see Bauckham, *Jude and the Relatives of Jesus*.

109. Quoted in Eusebius, *The Ecclesiastical History*, 2:I.

110. *Against Marcion*, 4.19.

111. *Commentary on Matthew*, 10.18.

112. Bousset, *Kyrios Christos*; Drews, *The Myth of Christ*.

113. Hurtado, *Lord Jesus Christ*.

114. Saldarini, *Pharisees, Scribes, and Sadducees*, 134–43.

115. Betz, "Paul," 187.

116. Betz, "Paul," 187.

117. Hock, *The Social Contex of Paul's Ministry*.

118. Stark, *Cities of God*.

119. Meeks, *The First Urban Christians*, 26.

120. Meeks, *The First Urban Christians*, 26.

121. 2 Corinthians 11:24–5.

122. Koester, *Introduction to the New Testament*, 110.

123. Malherbe, *Social Aspects of Early Christianity*, 47. Also Judge, "The Early Christians as a Scholastic Community."

124. Judge, "The Early Christians as a Scholastic Community," 134; Malherbe, *Social Aspects of Early Christianity*, 47.

125. MacMullen, *Christianity and Paganism*, 5.

126. Nock, *St. Paul*, 121.

127. Stark, *Cities of God*, chap. 5.

128. MacMullen, *Christianity and Paganism*, 151.

129. Quoted in Gager, *Kingdom and Community*, 142.

130. Quoted in Eusebius, *Ecclesiastical History*, 3.37.3.

131. Harnack, *The Expansion of Christianity in the First Three Centuries*, 466.

132. MacMullen, *Christianizing the Roman Empire*, 29.

133. During their early days in San Francisco, the Unificationists encountered a young man who "converted" within the first half hour of missionizing. Unfortunately for them, he turned out to be very psychotic and caused them no end of difficulty before they managed to be free of him.

134. John Lofland, "Becoming a World-Saver," 817. Also see Bainbridge, *Satan's Power*, and Barker, *The Making of a Moonie*.

135. In Jones, *Life and Works of Sigmund Freud*, 184.

136. Turner and Killian, *Collective Behavior*.

137. Bulliet, *Conversion to Islam in the Medieval Period*; Stark, *One True God*, 83–5.

138. *Against Celsus*, 3.10.

139. 1 Corinthians 15:6.

140. Kee, *What Can We Know*, 6.

141. For a more complete discussion, see Stark, *The Rise of Christianity*.

142. Wilken, *The Christians as the Romans Saw Them*, 31.

143. Fox, *Pagans and Christians*, 317.

144. J. C. Russell, *Late Ancient and Medieval Population*; MacMullen, *Christianizing the Roman Empire*; Wilken, *The Christians as the Romans Saw Them*.

145. Goodenough, *The Church in the Roman Empire*; Michael Grant, *The History of Rome*; Mac-Mullen, *Christianizing the Roman Empire*.

146. Chuvin, *A Chronicle of the Last Pagans*; MacMullen, *Christianity and Paganism*; McKechnie, *The First Christian Centuries*.

147. McKechnie, *The First Christian Centuries*, 57.

148. (r = .86); Bagnall, "Conversion and Onomastics" and "Religious Conversion."

149. I am grateful to Professor Galvao-Sobrinho for graciously providing me with his raw data.

150. Galvao-Sobrinho, "Funerary Epigraphy and the Spread of Christianity in the West."

151. Rogers, *Diffusion of Innovations*; Hamblin, Jacobson, and Miller, *A Mathematical Theory of Social Change*.

152. Stark, *Cities of God*.

153. Stark, *Cities of God*.

154. *Apologetics*, 37.8.

155. Paul Johnson, *A History of Christianity*, 75.

156. Burn, "Hic breve vivitur."

157. Stark, *The Rise of Christianity*.

158. In Ayerst and Fisher, *Records of Christianity*, 179–81.

159. Stark, *The Rise of Christianity*.

160. See Luke 8:1–3; Matthew 27:55; Luke 22:49; Mark 15:40–41.

161. Romans 16:1–2.

162. 1 Corinthians 1:11.

163. Acts 17:4.

164. Harnack, *The Expansion of Christianity in the First Three Centuries*, vol. 2, 220.

165. Harnack, *The Expansion of Christianity in the First Three Centuries*, vol. 2, 227.

166. Henry Chadwick, *The Early Church*, 56.

167. Pomeroy, *Goddesses, Whores, Wives, and Slaves*.

168. Fox, *Pagans and Christians*; Pomeroy, *Goddesses, Whores, Wives, and Slaves*; J. C. Russell, *Late Ancient and Medieval Population*.

169. J. C. Russell, *Late Ancient and Medieval Population*.

170. Keith Hopkins, "The Age of Roman Girls at Marriage."

171. Gorman, *Abortion and the Early Church*.

172. *Republic*, 5.9.

173. *Politics*, 7.14.10.

174. See Stark, *The Rise of Christianity*, chap. 5.

175. Fox, *Pagans and Christians*.

176. Sandison, "Sexual Behavior in Ancient Societies."

177. Henry Chadwick, *The Early Church*, 59.

178. Stark, *The Rise of Christianity*.

179. Dillon, "Platonism"; Whittaker, *Studies in Platonism and Patristic Thought*.

180. Hinson, "Justin Martyr," 221.

181. Pépin, "Logos," 9.

182. "Xenophanes," *Encyclopaedia Britannica*, 15th ed.

183. West, "Towards Monotheism," 28.

184. West, "Towards Monotheism," 27.

185. And such views remain largely irrelevant, as demonstrated by the rapid decline of those Protestant denominations that followed radical theologians such as Immanuel Kant or Paul Tillich in proclaiming inert conceptions of God. (See Finke and Stark, *The Churching of America*; Stark, *Exploring the Religious Life*.)

186. Ludwig, "Monotheism," 69.

187. Jenkins, *Hidden Gospels*, 29.

188. Meyer, *The Gnostic Discoveries*, 2

189. Remarks made on a TV special and quoted in Jenkins, *Hidden Gospels*, 5.

190. Stark, *Cities of God*, chap. 6.

191. Quoted in Jenkins, *Hidden Gospels*, 110.

192. Perkins, *The Gnostic Dialogue*, 16.

193. Perkins, "Gnosticism," 371.

194. Perkins, *The Gnostic Dialogue*, 10.

195. Rudolph, *Gnosis*, 367.

196. Morton Smith's (*The Secret Gospel*) claim to have read a "secret Mark" that then mysteriously disappeared is now recognized as a hoax (Carlson, *The Gospel Hoax*), and Michael Baigent's (*The Jesus Papers*) report of two letters Jesus wrote to the Sanhedrin in which he denies he is the actual son of God, letters held in secret by a mysterious Israeli, is utterly incredible. See Shanks, "Review."

197. *Against Heresies*, I:31.1.

198. Stark and Finke, *Acts of Faith*.

199. Fletcher, *The Barbarian Conversions*, 19.

200. Duffy, *Saints and Sinners*, 27.

201. Fletcher, *The Barbarian Conversions*, 38.

202. For a summary, see Stark, *For the Glory of God*.

203. Stark, *Exploring the Religious Life*.

204. Adam Smith, *An Inquiry into the Nature and Causes of the Wealth of Nations*, II:789.

205. Thomas, *Religion and the Decline of Magic*, 159.

206. Murray, "Piety and Impiety," 92–94.

207. Thomas, *Religion and the Decline of Magic*, 161.

208. Quoted in Thomas, *Religion and the Decline of Magic*, 162.

209. Currie, Gilbert, and Horsley, *Churches and Churchgoers*.

210. Stark, "Secularization, R.I.P."

211. Grim and Finke, "International Religion Indexes."

212. Davie, *Religion in Britain*.

213. Quoted in Finke and Stark, *The Churching of America*, 39.

214. Finke and Stark, *The Churching of America*.

215. Finke and Stark, *The Churching of America*.

216. Stark, *Sociology*, table 14–6, 402.

217. Welliver and Northcutt, *Mission Handbook*.
218. Wuthnow, personal communication with author.
219. Stark, *One True God*, 95.
220. Gill, "The Struggle to Be Soul Provider."
221. David G. Barrett, *Schism and Renewal of Africa*; Gifford, *African Christianity*.
222. Jenkins, *The Next Christendom*.
223. Barrett, Kurian, and Johnson, *World Christian Encyclopedia*.
224. Stark, *The Victory of Reason*.
225. North and Gwin, "Religion, Corruption, and the Rule of Law."
226. Finke and Stark, *The Churching of America*.
227. Niebuhr, *The Social Sources of Denominationalism*, vii.
228. Stark, *One True God*.

Chapter 8: Islam: God and State

1. Armstrong, *Muhammad*; Lings, *Muhammad*; Salahi, *Muhammad*; Watt, *Muhammad: Prophet and Statesman*.
2. Bousquet, "Observations"; Shaban, *Islamic History*.
3. Donner, *The Early Islamic Conquests*.
4. Donner, *The Early Islamic Conquests*, 17.
5. Denny, "Islam," 620–21.
6. Donner, *The Early Islamic Conquests*, 34.
7. Donner, *The Early Islamic Conquests*, 35.
8. Denny, "Islam and the Muslim Community," 622.
9. Denny, "Islam and the Muslim Community," 622.
10. Rodinson, *Muhammad*, 39.
11. Hodgson, *The Venture of Islam*; Rodinson, *Muhammad*; Watt, *Muhammad: Prophet and Statesman*.
12. Nicolle, *Historical Atlas of the Islamic World*, 21.
13. Watt, "Muhammad," *Encyclopaedia Brittanica*, 606.
14. Watt, "Muhammad," *Encyclopaedia Brittanica*, 606.
15. Smelser, *Theory of Collective Behavior*, 47.
16. Stark, *Exploring the Religious Life*, chap. 2.
17. Bulliet, *The Camel and the Wheel*, 105.
18. Aslan, *No God but God*; Crone, *Meccan Trade*.
19. Crone, *Meccan Trade*, 87.
20. Denny, "Islam and the Muslim Community," 620.
21. Aslan, *No God but God*, 27.
22. Ayoub, "The Islamic Tradition," 355.
23. Denny, "Islam and the Muslim Community," 622.
24. Donner, *The Early Islamic Conquests*, 76.
25. Katsh, *Judaism in Islam*.
26. Armstrong, *Muhammad*, 45–46.
27. Ayoub, "The Islamic Tradition," 356.
28. Denny, "Islam and the Muslim Community," 624.
29. Farah, *Islam*; Peters, *Muhammad*; Rodinson, *Muhammad*; Salahi, *Muhammad*; Watt, *Muhammad: Prophet and Statesman*.
30. Ayoub, "The Islamic Tradition," 357; Denny, "Islam and the Muslim Community," 624.
31. W. Montgomery Watt's biography (*Muhammad: Prophet and Statesman*) has sold by far the most copies, despite being condemned even by many Muslim writers as naive and uncritical to the point of being patronizing. Karen Armstrong's (*Muhammad*) has been the most successful recent biography, and she continued to court Muslim approval in the same rather fawning manner as did Watt.
32. Rodinson, *Muhammad*, xi.
33. Warraq, "Studies on Muhammad," 38.
34. Rodinson, *Muhammad*, xi.
35. See the collection of essays in Warraq, *The Quest for the Historical Muhammad*.

36. Salahi, *Muhammad*, 62.
37. Salahi, *Muhammad*, 62.
38. Payne, *The History of Islam*, 16.
39. Salahi, *Muhammad*, 85.
40. Salahi, *Muhammad*, 85.
41. Peters, *Muhammad*, 123.
42. Lings, *Muhammad*; Peters, *Muhammad*; Salahi, *Muhammad*.
43. Adams, "Qur'an," 171–2.
44. Watt, "Muhammad," *The Encyclopedia of Religion*, 142.
45. Denny, "Islam and the Muslim Community," 621.
46. Ayoub, "The Islamic Tradition," 354.
47. Watt, *Muhammad: Prophet and Statesman*, 35.
48. Watt, "Muhammad," *Encyclopaedia Brittanica*, 606.
49. Denny, "Islam and the Muslim Community," 621.
50. Watt, "Muhammad," *Encyclopaedia Brittanica*, 607.
51. Hodgson, *The Venture of Islam*, 1:172; Watt, "Muhammad," *Encyclopaedia Brittanica*, 607.
52. Salahi, *Muhammad*, 448.
53. Armstrong, *Muhammad*, 169.
54. Aslan, *No God but God*, 82.
55. Salahi, *Muhammad*, 226.
56. Watt, *Muhammad: Prophet and Statesman*, 103.
57. Watt, *Muhammad: Prophet and Statesman*, 104.
58. Rodinson, *Muhammad*, 163.
59. Watt, *Muhammad: Prophet and Statesman*, 120.
60. Rodinson, *Muhammad*, 164–8.
61. Rodinson, *Muhammad*, 168.
62. These are clans and tribes of Medina.
63. Rodinson, *Muhammad*, 157.
64. Rodinson, *Muhammad*, 171.
65. Rodinson, *Muhammad*, 172.
66. Rodinson, *Muhammad*, 176.
67. Probably interpreted by Muhammad to mean "anointed," for, as Rodinson noted, the Jewish and Christian meaning of "messiah" was "obviously not understood" (*Muhammad*, 239).
68. Aslan, *No God but God*, 54.
69. Rodinson, *Muhammad*, 172.
70. Watt, *Muhammad: Prophet and Statesman*, 114–15.
71. Rodinson, *Muhammad*, 174.
72. Rodinson, *Muhammad*, 176.
73. Watt, *Muhammad: Prophet and Statesman*, 136.
74. Aslan, *No God but God*, 76.
75. Hodgson, *The Venture of Islam*, I:190.
76. Watt, *Muhammad: Prophet and Statesman*, 140–41.
77. Rodinson, *Muhammad*, 193–4.
78. Rodinson, *Muhammad*, 208–11.
79. Hodgson, *The Venture of Islam*, I:191.
80. Armstrong, *Muhammad*; Hodgson, *The Venture of Islam*; Kister, "The Massacre of the Banū Qurayza"; Rodinson, *Muhammad*; Watt, *Muhammad: Prophet and Statesman*.
81. Rodinson, *Muhammad*, 213.
82. Armstrong, *Muhammad*, 207–8.
83. Watt, *Muhammad: Prophet and Statesman*, 173.
84. For a summary, see Kister, "The Massacre of the Banū Qurayza." In an attempt to "minimize" the matter, Reza Aslan (*No God but God*, 94) pointed out that these deaths "still represent no more than a tiny fraction of the total population of Jews who resided in Medina and its environs."
85. Rodinson, *Muhammad*, 254.
86. Hodgson, *The Venture of Islam*, I:194.
87. Rodinson, *Muhammad*, 309.

88. Denny, "Islam and the Muslim Community."
89. Ayoub, "The Islamic Tradition," 376; Denny, "Islam and the Muslim Community," 612.
90. Denny, "Islam and the Muslim Community," 642.
91. Denny, "Islam and the Muslim Community," 644.
92. Denny, "Islam and the Muslim Community," 657.
93. Cook, *Muhammad*, 69–70.
94. Adams, "Qur'an," 157.
95. Adams, "Qur'an," 162.
96. Modarressi, "Early Debates on the Integrity of the Qur'an," 7.
97. Arberry, *The Koran Interpreted*, 25.
98. Bellamy, "Textual Criticism of Koran," 1.
99. Arberry, *The Koran Interpreted*, 24.
100. Pickthall, *The Meaning of the Glorious Koran*, vii.
101. Rodinson, *Muhammad*, 92–3.
102. Nöldeke, "The Koran."
103. Nöldeke, "The Koran," 44.
104. Stark, *Cities of God*, 158.
105. Hawting, *The Idea of Idolatry and the Emergence of Islam*, 15; Rodinson, *Muhammad*, 63–4.
106. Torrey, "The Jewish Foundation of Islam."
107. Rodinson, *Muhammad*, 161.
108. Ayoub, "The Islamic Tradition," 422–3.
109. Ayoub, "The Islamic Tradition," 422.
110. Rodwell's translation.
111. Caspar, "The Permanent Significance of Islam's Monotheism," 70.
112. Rodinson, *Muhammad*, 235.
113. Ayoub, "The Islamic Tradition," 422.
114. Stark, *The Victory of Reason*.
115. Caspar, "The Permanent Significance of Islam's Monotheism," 69.
116. Donner, *The Early Islamic Conquests*, 55–62.
117. Donner, *The Early Islamic Conquests*, 60.
118. Donner, *The Early Islamic Conquests*, 78.
119. Rodinson, *Muhammad*, 273.
120. Becker, "Carl Heinrich Becker," 2.
121. Becker, "Chapter XL," 329.
122. Bulliet, *Conversion to Islam in the Medieval Period*, 8.
123. Donner, *The Early Islamic Conquests*, 221.
124. Donner, *The Early Islamic Conquests*, 225.
125. Bulliet, *Conversion to Islam in the Medieval Period*
126. Bulliet, "Conversion to Islam and the Emergence of Muslim Society in Iran," 32.
127. See Rogers, *Diffusion of Innovations*; Hamblin, Jacobson, and Miller, *A Mathematical Theory of Social Change*. For an elegant application to conversion, see Hayward, "A Dynamic Model of Church Growth" and "Mathematical Modeling of Church Growth."
128. Stanley Lane-Pool, quoted in Fletcher, *Moorish Spain*, 172.
129. Menocal, *The Ornament of the World*.
130. For an extensive summary, see Stark, *One True God*.
131. Stark, *One True God*.
132. Stark, *One True God*.
133. Alroy, *Behind the Middle East Conflict*.
134. Hodgson, *The Venture of Islam*, I:268.
135. Payne, *The History of Islam*, 105.
136. Hodgson, *The Venture of Islam*; Payne, *The History of Islam*.
137. Introvigne, "Niches in the Islamic Religious Market."
138. Rodinson, *Muhammad*, 272.
139. Eickelman, "Musaylima."
140. In Guillaume, *The Life of Muhammad*, 649.
141. Rodinson, *Muhammad*, 272.

142. Both quotations from Lings, *Muhammad*, 336.

143. Ad-Daylami, *Sahaabah's Biographies*.

144. Rodinson, *Muhammad*, 272.

145. Those making no mention of either include Armstrong, *Muhammad*; Aslan, *No God but God*; Peters, *Muhammad*; Salahi, *Muhammad*; Watt, *Muhammad: Prophet and Statesman*.

146. Hodgson (*The Venture of Islam*, I:197) devoted two sentences to Musaylima; Lings (*Muhammad*, 335–6) gave a short paragraph to Musaylima and a sentence to Sajāh; Crone (*Meccan Trade*, 248) squeezed all three into a sentence.

147. John Alden Williams, "Islam, History of," 929.

148. Barrett, Kurian, and Johnson, *World Christian Encyclopedia*.

149. Barrett, Kurian, and Johnson, *World Christian Encyclopedia*, 649.

150. Stark, *One True God*, chap. 5.

Conclusion: Discovering God?

1. Lasaulx, *Neuer Versuch*, 115.

2. Quoted in Jaspers, *The Origin and Goal of History*, 8–9.

3. See the collection edited by S. N. Eisenstadt, *The Origins and Diversity of Axial Age Civilizations*.

4. See the papers in *Dædalus* (Spring, 1975); also Jaspers, *The Origin and Goal of History*.

5. Jaspers, *The Origin and Goal of History*, 3. Having rendered this single sentence, Jaspers did not pursue the matter.

6. For a summary of the anthropological literature, see Stark, *Exploring the Religious Life*, chap. 7.

7. Eberhard, *Guilt and Sin in Traditional China*.

8. See Thapar, "Ethics, Religion, and Social Protest."

9. Momigliano, "The Fault of the Greeks," 10.

10. Jaspers, *The Origin and Goal of History*, 52.

11. Eberhard, *Guilt and Sin in Traditional China*, 16.

12. Bentley, "Beyond Modernocentrism."

13. Mair, "Kinesis versus Statis."

14. Weil, "What Is a Breakthrough in History?" 21.

15. Goodrich, "China, History of."

16. Piggott, "Chinese Chariotry."

17. Hick, *Problems of Religious Pluralism*.

18. Gier, *God, Reason, and the Evangelicals*.

19. Known for his best-selling textbook *The World's Religions*, his professions of faith in all religions have been made into a number of television and magazine interviews.

20. Lewis, *God in the Dock*, 54.

21. Armstrong, *The Great Transformation*.

22. Armstrong, *The Great Transformation*; Huston Smith, *The World's Religions*.

23. In Benin, *The Footprints of God*, 202

24. Armstrong, *Muhammad*, 207; Watt, *Muhammad: Prophet and Statesman*, 173.

25. I would estimate that at least 500 people have founded religious movements in the United States during the past century based on their claims of having been sent by God.

26. This theme was basic to Carl Sagan's public television series *Cosmos*.

27. For a long time Intelligent Design was dismissed by philosophers because of very complex and apparently irrefutable arguments against it formulated by Immanuel Kant (1724–1804) and by David Hume (1711–1776). But these arguments are now passé in light of current scientific knowledge. For example, Kant argued that the universe could not be finite because then there would be an edge or boundary, and it must follow that there is something beyond any boundary—ergo the universe is infinite, which suggests, too, that it is eternal. It was a clever argument, but it was completely undermined by Einstein's theory of relativity, which postulates that space is curved, and it also was refuted empirically by the Big Bang Theory.

28. Stark, *For the Glory of God* and *The Victory of Reason*.

29. Stark, *For the Glory of God* and *The Victory of Reason*.

30. Needham, *Science and Civilization in China*, 581.

31. In Crosby, *The Measure of Reality*, 83.

32. Whitehead, *Science and the Modern World*, 13.

33. Whitehead, *Science and the Modern World*, 12.

34. Whitehead, *Science and the Modern World*, 13.

35. Jeffrey, *By Things Seen*, 14.

36. Kepler, in Bradley, "The 'Just So' Universe," 160.

37. *Oeuvres* 8:61.

38. Einstein, *Letters to Solovine*, 131.

39. Behe, *Darwin's Black Box*; Bradley, "The 'Just So' Universe"; Paul Davies, *God and the New Physics*; Dembski, *The Design Revolution* and *Intelligent Design*; Polkinghorne, *Science and Creation*.

BIBLIOGRAPHY

Abel, Michael A. "Retention Strategies and Religious Success: A Regional Comparison of American Jews." *Interdisciplinary Journal of Research on Religion* (1990): article 12. http://www.religjournal. com.

Abusch, Tzvi. "The Development and Meaning of the Epic of Gilgamesh: An Interpretive Essay." *Journal of the American Oriental Society* 121 (2001): 614–22.

Adams, Charles J. "Qur'an: The Text and Its History." In *The Encyclopedia of Religion*, edited by Mircea Eliade. New York: Macmillan, 1987.

Ad-Daylami, Fayruz. *Sahaabah's Biographies*. Univ. of Southern California and the Muslim Student Association Online Database, 2006.

Adkins, Lesley. *Empires of the Plain: Henry Rawlinson and the Lost Languages of Babylon*. New York: St. Martin's Press, 2003.

Ahlström, Gösta W. "Another Moses Tradition." *Journal of Near Eastern Studies* 39 (1980): 65–9.

———. *The History of Ancient Palestine*. Minneapolis: Fortress Press, 1993.

———. *Royal Administration and National Religion in Ancient Palestine*. Leiden: E. J. Brill, 1982.

———. *Who Were the Israelites?* Winona Lake, IN: Eisenbrauns, 1986.

Albertz, Rainer. *A History of Israelite Religion in the Old Testament Period*. 2 vols. Louisville, KY: Westminster/John Knox Press, 1994.

Albright, William Foxwell. *From the Stone Age to Christianity: Monotheism and the Historical Process*. New York: Doubleday Anchor Books, 1957.

———. "New Light on Early Recensions in the Hebrew Bible." *Bulletin of the American Schools of Oriental Research* 140 (1955): 27–33.

———. *Samuel and the Beginnings of the Prophetic Movement* (The Goldenson Lecture for 1961). Cincinnati: Hebrew Union College Press, 1961.

Al-Buldan, Kitab Futuh. *The Origins of the Islamic State*. New York: Columbia Univ. Press, [1866] 1916.

Aldred, Cyril. *Akhenaten: King of Egypt*. London: Thames and Hudson, 1988.

Allen, Charles. *The Search for Buddha: The Men Who Discovered India's Lost Religion*. New York: Carroll and Graf, 2003.

Allen, Charlotte. *The Human Christ: The Search for the Historical Jesus*. New York: The Free Press, 1988.

———. "The Search for the No-Frills Jesus: Q." *Atlantic Monthly* Dec. (1996): 51–68.

Allen, Diogenes. *Christian Belief in a Postmodern World*. Louisville: Westminster/John Knox Press, 1989.

Allport, Gordon W. *The Individual and His Religion*. New York: Macmillan, 1960.

Alroy, Gil Carl. *Behind the Middle East Conflict: The Real Impasse Between Arab and Jew*. New York: G. P. Putnam's Sons, 1975.

Alter, Robert. *The Five Books of Moses: A Translation with Commentary*. New York: W. W. Norton, 2004.

Arberry, A. J. *The Koran Interpreted*. New York: Macmillan, 1955.

Armstrong, Karen. *Buddha*. New York: Viking Books, 2001.

———. *The Great Transformation: The Beginning of Our Religious Traditions*. New York: Knopf, 2006.

———. *Muhammad: A Biography of a Prophet*. San Francisco: HarperSanFrancisco, 1992.

Arnold, Dieter. "Temples: Egyptian Temples." In *The Oxford Encyclopedia of Archaeology in the Near East*. New York: Oxford Univ. Press, 1997.

Arnott, Peter. *The Romans and Their World*. New York: St. Martin's Press, 1970.

Aslan, Reza. *No God but God: The Origins, Evolution, and Future of Islam*. New York: Random House, 2006.

Assmann, Jan. *Moses the Egyptian: The Memory of Egypt in Western Monotheism*. Cambridge: Harvard Univ. Press, 1997.

Ayerst, David, and A. S. T. Fisher. *Records of Christianity*. Vol.1. Oxford: Basil Blackwell, 1971.
Ayoub, Mahmoud M. "The Islamic Tradition." In *World Religions: Western Traditions*, edited by Willard G. Oxtoby. Oxford: Oxford Univ. Press, 1996.
Bader, Christopher, and Paul Froese. "Images of God: The Effect of Personal Theologies on Moral Attitudes, Political Affiliation and Religious Behavior." *Interdisciplinary Journal of Religious Research* I (2005): 11. http:// www.religjournal.com.
Bagnall, Roger S. "Conversion and Onomastics: A Reply." *Zeitschrift für Papyrologies und Epigraphik* 69 (1987): 243–50.
———. *Egypt in Late Antiquity*. Princeton: Univ. of Princeton Press, 1993.
———. "Religious Conversion and Onomastic Change in Early Byzantine Egypt." *Bulletin of the American Society of Papyrologists* 19 (1982): 105–24.
Baigent, Michael. *The Jesus Papers*. San Francisco: HarperSanFrancisco, 2006.
Baigent, Michael, Henry Lincoln, and Richard Leigh. *Holy Blood, Holy Grail*. New York: Bantam, 1983.
Bailey, Cyril. *Phases in the Religion of Ancient Rome*. Berkeley: Univ. of California Press, 1932.
Bain, Read. "Man, the Myth-Maker." *The Scientific Monthly* 65 (1947): 61–9.
Bainbridge, William Sims. *Satan's Power: A Deviant Psychotherapy Cult*. Berkeley: Univ. of California Press, 1978.
Baird, William. "Biblical Criticism." In *The Anchor Bible Dictionary*, edited by David Noel Freedman. New York: Doubleday, 1992.
Baker, Samuel W. 1867. "The Races of the Nile Basin." *Transactions of the Ethnological Society of London* 5 (1867): 228–238..
Baldet, Jacques. *Jesus, the Rabbi Prophet*. Rochester, VT: Inner Traditions, 2003.
Baldrian, Farzeen. "Taoism: An Overview." In *The Encyclopedia of Religion*, edited by Mircea Eliade. New York: Macmillan, 1987.
Baldwin, Stephen L. *Foreign Missions and Protestant Churches*. Chicago: Missionary Campaign Library, 1900.
Baly, Denis. "The Geography of Monotheism." In *Translating and Understanding the Old Testament: Essays in Honor of Herbert Gordon May*, edited by Harry Frank Thomas and William L. Reed, 253–278. Nashville: Abingdon Press, 1970.
———. *The Geography of the Bible*. New York: Harper & Brothers, 1957.
Bamberger, Bernard J. *Proselytism in the Talmudic Period*. New York: Hebrew Union College Press, 1939.
Barclay, John M. *Jews in the Mediterranean Diaspora*. Berkeley: Univ. of California Press, 1996.
Bard, Kathryn A. "The Emergence of the Egyptian State." In *The Oxford History of Ancient Egypt*, edited by Ian Shaw, 61–88. Oxford: Oxford Univ. Press, 2000.
Barker, Eileen. *The Making of a Moonie: Brainwashing or Choice*. Oxford: Basil Blackwell, 1984.
Barlow, R. H. "Anales de Tula, Hidaldo." *Tlalocan* 3 (1949): 2–13.
Barrett, Clive. *The Egyptian Gods and Goddesses*. London: Diamond Books, 1996.
Barrett, David B. *Schism and Renewal in Africa*. Nairobi, Kenya: Oxford Univ. Press, 1968.
Barrett, David B., George T. Kurian, and Todd M. Johnson. *World Christian Encyclopedia*. 2 vols. Oxford: Oxford Univ. Press, 2001.
Barrett, T. H. "Taoism: History of Study." In *The Encyclopedia of Religion*, edited by Mircea Eliade. New York: Macmillan, 1987.
Bartos, F. G. *The Hussite Revolution, 1424–37*. New York: Eastern European Monographs, 1986.
Basham, Arthur Llewellyn. "Hinduism, History of." In *The Encyclopaedia Britannica*. Chicago: Univ. of Chicago Press, 1981.
———. *The Origins and Development of Classical Hinduism*. Oxford: Oxford Univ. Press, 1991.
———. *The Wonder That Was India*, 3rd edition. New Delhi: Rupa & Co., 1967.
Bastide, Roger. *African Religions in Brazil*. Baltimore: Johns Hopkins Univ. Press, 1978.
Batey, Richard A. *Jesus and the Forgotten City*. Grand Rapids, MI: Baker Book House, 1991.
Bauckham, Richard. *Jesus and the Eyewitnesses*. Grand Rapids, MI: William B. Eerdmans, 2006.
———. *Jude and the Relatives of Jesus in the Early Church*. Edinburgh: T & T Clark, 1990.
Bauer, Bruno. *Christ and the Caesars: The Origins of Christianity from Romanized Greek Culture*. Charleston, SC: Clareston House, [1877] 1999.
Baumgarten, Albert I. *The Flourishing of Jewish Sects in the Maccabean Era: An Intrepetation*. Leiden: Brill, 1997.

Beard, Mary. "Priesthood in the Roman Republic." In *Pagan Priests*, edited by Mary Beard and John North, 19–48. London: Duckworth, 1990.

Beard, Mary and John North. "Introduction." In *Pagan Priests*, edited by Mary Beard and John North, 1–14. London: Duckworth, 1990.

Beard, Mary, John North, and Simon Price. *Religions of Rome: A History*. Vol. 1. Cambridge: Cambridge Univ. Press, 1998.

———. *Religions of Rome: A Sourcebook*. Vol. 2. Cambridge: Cambridge Univ. Press, 1998.

Beattie, John. "Ritual and Social Exchange." *Man* I (1966): 60–70.

Beaulieu, Paul-Alain. "Greece." In *Religions of the Ancient World: A Guide*, edited by Sarah Iles Johnston. Cambridge: Belknap Press of Harvard Univ. Press, 2004.

Becker, Carl Heinrich. "Carl Heinrich Becker." In *Wikipedia*, the free encyclopedia, 2006. http://en.wikipedia.org/wiki/Main_Page.

———. "Chapter XL: The Expansion of the Saracens." In *The Cambridge Medieval History*. Vol. 2, edited by J. B. Bury, H. M. Gwatkin, and J. P. Whitney, 329–389. New York: Macmillan, 1926.

———. *Christianity and Islam*. Boston: IndyPublish, [1909] 2006.

Behe, Michael J. *Darwin's Black Box: The Biochemical Challenge to Evolution*. New York: The Free Press, 1996.

Bellamy, James A. "Textual Criticism of the Koran." *Journal of the American Oriental Society* 121 (2001): 1–6.

Benedict, Ruth. "Religion." In *General Anthropology*, edited by Franz Boas, 627–665. New York: C. D. Heath, 1938.

Benin, Stephen D. *The Footprints of God: Divine Accommodation in Jewish and Christian Thought*. Albany: State Univ. of New York Press, 1993.

Bentley, Jerry H. "Beyond Modernocentrism: Toward Fresh Visions of the Global Past." In *Contact and Exchange in the Ancient World*. Victor H. Mair, 17–61. Honolulu: Univ. of Hawaii Press, 2006.

Benz, Ernst. "The Theological Meaning of the History of Religions." *The Journal of Religion* 41 (1961): 1–16.

Berger, David, ed. *The Jewish-Christian Debate in the High Middle Ages*. Philadelphia: Jewish Publication Society, 1979.

Bergin, Allen E. "Religiosity and Mental Health." *Professional Psychology: Research and Practice* 14 (1983): 170–184.

Berkey, Jonathan P. *The Formation of Islam*. Cambridge: Cambridge Univ. Press, 2003.

Berrelleza, Juan Alberto Román. "Offering 48 of the Templo Major: A Case of Child Sacrifice." In *The Aztec Templo Major*, edited by Elizabeth Hill Boone, 131–143. Washington, DC: Dumbarton Oaks Research Library and Collection, 1987.

Best, Elsdon. "The Cult of Io, the Concept of a Supreme Deity as Evolved by the Ancestors of the Polynesians." *Man* 13 (1913): 98–103.

Betz, Hans Dieter. "Paul." In *The Anchor Bible Dictionary*, edited by David Noel Freedman. New York: Doubleday, 1992.

Biale, David. "The God with Breasts: El Shaddai in the Bible." *History of Religions* 21 (1982): 240–56.

Bidney, David. "Myth, Symbolism, and Truth." *The Journal of American Folklore* 68 (1955): 379–92.

Bird-David, Nurit. "'Animism' Revisited: Personhood, Environment, and Relational Epistemology." *Current Anthropology* 40 (1999): S67–S91.

Biven, David, and Roy Blizzard. *Understanding the Difficult Words of Jesus*. Shippensburg, PA: Destiny Image, 1995.

Black, Jeremy, and Anthony Green. *Gods, Demons and Symbols of Ancient Mesopotamia*. Austin: Univ. of Texas Press, 1992.

Bloomberg, Craig. *The Historical Reliability of the Gospels*. Downers Grove, IL: InterVarsity Press Academic, 1987.

Boadt, Lawrence. "Ezekiel, Book of." In *The Anchor Bible Dictionary*, edited by David Noel Freedman. New York: Doubleday, 1992.

Boak, Arthur E. R., and William G. Sinnigen. *A History of Rome to AD 565*. 5th ed. New York: Macmillan, 1977.

Bodde, Derk. "The New Identification of Lao Tzu." *Journal of the American Oriental Society* 62 (1942): 8–13.

Boltz, Judith Mcgee. "Lao-Tzu." In *The Encyclopedia of Religion*, edited by Mircea Eliade. New York: Macmillan, 1987.

Boomershine, T. E. "Peter's Denial as Polemic or Confession." *Semeia* 39 (1987): 47–68.

Bossy, John. *Christianity in the West, 1400–1700*. New York: Oxford Univ. Press, 1985.

Bottéro, Jean. *Religion in Ancient Mesopotamia*. Chicago: Univ. of Chicago Press, 2001.

Bousquet, Georges Henri. "Observations sur la nature et les causes de la conquête arabe." *Studia Islamica* 6 (1956): 37–53.

Bousset, Wilhelm. *Kyrios Christos: A History of the Belief in Christ from the Beginnings of Christianity to Irenaeus*. Nashville: Abingdon Press, [1913] 1970.

Bowersock, G. W. *Hellenism in Late Antiquity*. Ann Arbor, MI: Univ. of Michigan Press, 1990.

Bowker, John. *The Oxford Dictionary of World Religions*. Oxford: Oxford Univ. Press, 1997.

Bowra, C. M. *Heroic Poetry*. London: Macmillan, 1951.

Boyce, Mary. *A History of Zoroastrianism*. Leiden: E. J. Brill, [1975] 1996.

———. *Zoroastrianism: A Shadowy but Powerful Presence in the Judeo-Christian World*. London: Dr. Williams' Trust, 1987.

———. *Zoroastrians: Their Religious Beliefs and Practices*. London: Routledge & Kegan Paul, 1979.

Boyer, Pascal. *Religion Explained: The Evolutionary Origins of Religious Thought*. New York: Basic Books, 2001.

Bradley, Walter L. "The 'Just So' Universe: The Fine-Tuning of Constants and Conditions in the Cosmos." In *Signs of Intelligence: Understanding Intelligent Design*, edited by William A. Dembski and James M. Kushiner, 157–170. Grand Rapids: Brazos Press, 2001.

Brady, Thomas A. *Ruling Class, Regime and Reformation at Strasbourg, 1520–1555*. Leiden: Brill, 1978.

Bråkenhielm, Carl. *Världbild och mening: En empirisk studie av livsåskådningar i dagens Svrige*. Nora, Sweden, 2001.

Brandon, S. G. F. *The Judgement of the Dead*. New York: Charles Scribner's Sons, 1967.

Breasted, James Henry. "The Development of the Priesthood in Israel and Egypt—A Comparison." *The Biblical World* 2 (1893): 19–28.

Broadt, Lawrence. "Ezekiel, Book of." In *The Anchor Bible Dictionary*, edited by David Noel Freedman. New York: Doubleday, 1992.

Brøndsted, Johannes. *The Vikings*. Baltimore: Penguin Books, 1965.

Brooke, Rosalind and Christopher Brooke. *Popular Religion in the Middle Ages*. London: Thames & Hudson, 1984.

Brooten, Bernadette. *Women Leaders in the Ancient Synagogue*. Chico, CA: Scholars Press, 1982.

Brown, Peter. *The Making of Late Antiquity*. Cambridge: Harvard Univ. Press, 1978.

Brown, R. E. "The Gospel According to John I–XII." In *The Anchor Bible*, 29. Garden City, NY: Anchor Books, 1966.

Brown, W. Norman. "Theories of Creation in the Rig Veda." *Journal of the American Oriental Society* 85 (1965): 23–34.

Bruce, Frederick Fyvie. *The Epistle of Paul to the Romans*. Grand Rapids, MI: William B. Eerdmans, 1982.

———. *The New Testament Documents: Are They Reliable?* 6th ed. Grand Rapids, MI: William B. Eerdmans, 1981.

Bruce, Steve. *Choice and Religion: A Critic of Rational Choice Theory*. Oxford: Oxford Univ. Press, 1999.

Bryant, Edwin. *The Quest for the Origins of Vedic Culture: The Indo-Aryan Migration Debate*. Oxford: Oxford Univ. Press, 2001.

Bryant, Joseph M. "Intellectuals and Religion in Ancient Greece: Notes on a Weberian Theme." *The British Journal of Sociology* 37 (1986): 269–96.

Bulliet, Richard W. *The Camel and the Wheel*. Cambridge: Harvard Univ. Press, 1975.

———. *Conversion to Islam in the Medieval Period: An Essay in Quantitative History*. Cambridge: Harvard Univ. Press, 1979.

———. "Conversion to Islam and the Emergence of Muslim Society in Iran." In *Conversion to Islam*, edited by Nehemia Levtzion, 30–51. New York: Holmes & Meier, 1979.

Bultmann, Rudoph. *Jesus and the Word*. New York: Macmillan, [1934] 1975.

———. *Jesus Christ and Mythology*. Englewood Cliffs, NJ: Prentice-Hall, [1958] 1997.

Burkert, Walter. *Ancient Mystery Cults*. Cambridge: Harvard Univ. Press, 1987.

———. *Babylon, Memphis, Persepolis: Eastern Contexts of Greek Culture*. Cambridge: Harvard Univ. Press, 2004.

———. *Greek Religion*. Cambridge: Harvard Univ. Press, 1985.

Burn, A.R. "Hic breve vivitur." *Past and Present* 4 (1953): 2–31.

Byock, Jesse L. *Medieval Iceland: Society, Sages, and Power*. Berkeley: Univ. of California Press, 1988.

Cadbury, Henry J. *The Book of Acts in History*. London: Adam & Charles Black, 1955.

Caillat, Colette. "Jainism." In *The Encyclopedia of Religion*, edited by Mircea Eliade. New York: Macmillan, 1987.

———. "Mahāvīra." In *The Encyclopedia of Religion*, edited by Mircea Eliade. New York: Macmillan, 1987.

Caird, Edward. *The Evolution of Religion* 2 vols. Glasgow: James Maclehose and Sons, 1899.

Callaway, J. "Village Subsistence at Ai and Raddana in Iron Age I." In *The Answers Lie Below: Essays in Honor of Lawrence Edmund Toombs*, edited by Henry O. Thompson, 51–66. Lanham, MD: Univ. Press of America, 1984.

Calvin, John. *Sermons on the Ten Commandments*. Grand Rapids, MI: Baker Book House [c. 1555] 1980.

Campbell, Joseph. *The Hero with a Thousand Faces*. 2nd ed. Princeton: Princeton Univ. Press, 1968.

Carlson, Stephen C. *The Gospel Hoax: Morton Smith's Invention of Secret Mark*. Waco, TX: Baylor Univ. Press, 2005.

Carmignac, Jean. *The Birth of the Synoptics*. Chicago: Franciscan Herald Press, 1987.

Carrasco, David. *City of Sacrifice: The Aztec Empire and the Role of Violence in Civilization*. Boston: Beacon Press, 1999.

———. *Quetzalcoatl and the Irony of Empire*. Rev. ed. Boulder: Univ. of Colorado Press, 2000.

———. *Religions of Mesoamerica*. Long Grove, IL: Waveland Press, 1990.

Carroll, Michael P. "A New Look at Freud on Myth: Reanalyzing the Star-Husband Tale." *Ethos* 7 (1979): 189–205.

———. "Praying the Rosary: The Anal-Erotic Origins of a Popular Catholic Devotion." *Journal for the Scientific Study of Religion* 26 (1987): 486–98.

Case, Shirley Jackson. "The Historicity of Jesus: An Estimate of the Negative Argument." *The American Journal of Theology* 15 (1911): 20–42.

———. "Is Jesus a Historical Character?: Evidence for an Affirmative Opinion." *The American Journal of Theology* 15 (1911): 205–27.

Casey, Maurice. *From Jewish Prophet to Gentile God: The Origins and Development of New Testament Christology*. Louisville: Westminster/John Knox, 1991.

Caspar, Robert. "The Permanent Significance of Islam's Monotheism." In *Monotheism*, edited by Claude Geffré and Jean-Pierre Jossua, 67–78. Edinburgh: T & T Clark, 1985.

Chadwick, Henry. *The Early Church*. Harmondsworth, Middlesex: Penguin Books, 1967.

Chadwick, Owen. *The Reformation*. Rev. ed. London: Penguin, 1972.

Chan, Wing-tsit. "Confucian Thought: Foundations of the Tradition." In *The Encyclopedia of Religion*, edited by Mircea Eliade. New York: Macmillan, 1987.

———. *The Way of Lao Tzu*. Indianapolis: Bobbs-Merrill, 1963.

Chandler, Tertius. *Four Thousand Years of Urban Growth*. Lewiston, NY: Edwin Mellen Press, 1987.

Chang, Showbin W. *What Confucius Really Meant*. Singapore: Nan-Yang Confucian Association, 1960.

Chattopadhyaya, Sudhakar. *Evolution of Hindu Sects*. New Delhi: Munshiram Manoharlal, 2000.

Ch'en, Kenneth. *Buddhism in China: A Historical Survey*. Princeton: Princeton Univ. Press, 1972.

Ching, Julia. "Confucian Thought: The State Cult." In *The Encyclopedia of Religion*, edited by Mircea Eliade. New York: Macmillan, 1987.

———. "Confucius." In *The Encyclopedia of Religion*, edited by Mircea Eliade. New York: Macmillan, 1987.

———. "East Asian Religions." In *World Religions: Eastern Traditions*, edited by Willard G. Oxtoby, 316–429. Oxford: Oxford Univ. Press, 2002.

Chuvin, Pierre. *A Chronicle of the Last Pagans*. Cambridge: Harvard Univ. Press, 1990.

Clauss, Manfred. *The Roman Cult of Mithras*. New York: Routledge, 2000.

Clemen, Carl. "Missionary Activity in the Non-Christian Religions." *The Journal of Religion* 10 (1930): 107–26.

Clendinnen, Inga. *Aztecs: An Interpretation*. Cambridge: Cambridge Univ. Press, 1991.

———. "The Cost of Courage in Aztec Society." *Past and Present* 107 (1985): 44–89.

Clifford, Richard J. "Isaiah, Book of (Second Isaiah)." In *The Anchor Bible Dictionary*, edited by David Noel Freedman. New York: Doubleday, 1992.

Coe, Michael D. *Breaking the Maya Code*. New York: Thames & Hudson, 1992.

———. *The Maya*. 6th ed. London: Thames & Hudson, 1999.

Cohen, Alvin P. "Chinese Religion: Popular Religion." In *The Encyclopedia of Religion*, edited by Mircea Eliade. New York: Macmillan, 1987.

Cohen, Martin A. "Synagogue: History and Traditions." In *The Encyclopedia of Religion*, edited by Mircea Eliade. New York: Macmillan, 1987.

Cohen, Percy S. "Theories of Myth." *Man* 4 (1969): 337–53.

Cohen, Shaye J. D. *From the Maccabees to the Mishna*. Philadelphia: Westminster Press, 1987.

———. "Was Judaism in Antiquity a Missionary Religion?" In *Jewish Assimilation, Acculturation and Accomodation*, edited by Menachem Mor, 14–23. Lanham, MD: Univ. Press of America, 1992.

Cohn, Norman. *Cosmos, Chaos and the World to Come: The Ancient Roots of Apocalyptic Faith*. 2nd ed. New Haven: Yale Univ. Press, 2001.

Coleman. James S. "Social Cleavage and Religious Conflict." *Journal of Social Issues* 12 (1956): 44–50.

Collcutt, Martin. "Monasticism: Buddhist Monasticism." In *The Encyclopedia of Religion*, edited by Mircea Eliade. New York: Macmillan, 1987.

Collins, Randall. *The Sociology of Philosophies: A Global Theory of Intellectual Change*. Cambridge: Belknap Press, 1998.

Comte, Auguste. *The Positive Philosophy*. 2 vols. London: George Bell and Sons, [1830] 1896.

Conze, Edward. *Buddhism: Its Essence and Development*. New York: Harper Torchbooks, 1975.

———. *A Short History of Buddhism*. London: Unwin Paperbacks, 1980.

Conzelmann, Hans. *Acts of the Apostles: A Commentary on the Acts of the Apostles*. Minneapolis: Augsburg Fortress Publishers, 1987.

Cook, B. F. *Reading the Past: Greek Inscriptions*. Berkeley: Univ. of California Press, 1987.

Cook, Michael. *Muhammad*. Oxford: Oxford Univ. Press, 1983.

Cook, Sherburne F. "Human Sacrifice and Warfare as Factors in the Demography of Pre-Colonial Mexico." *Human Biology* 18 (1946): 81–102.

Cooper, D. Jason. *Mithras: Mysteries and Initiation Rediscovered*. York Beach, ME: Weiser Books, 1996.

Coulton, G. G. *Medieval Panorama*. Cambridge: Cambridge Univ. Press, 1938.

Crews, Frederick C., ed. *Unauthorized Freud: Doubters Confront a Legend*. New York: Viking, 1998.

Crone, Patricia. *Meccan Trade and the Rise of Islam*. Princeton: Princeton Univ. Press, 1987.

Crone, Patricia and Michael Cook. *Hagarism: The Making of the Islamic World*. Cambridge: Cambridge Univ. Press, 1977.

Crone, Patricia and Martin Hinds. *God's Caliph: Religious Authority in the First Centuries of Islam*. Cambridge: Cambridge Univ. Press, [1986] 2003.

Crosby, Alfred W. *The Measure of Reality: Quantification and Western Society, 1250–1600*. Cambridge: Cambridge Univ. Press, 1997.

Cross, Frank Moore. "Yaweh and the God of the Patriarchs." *Harvard Theological Review* 55 (1962): 244–50.

Crossan, John Dominic. *The Historical Jesus: The Life of a Mediterranean Jewish Peasant*. San Francisco: Harper Collins, 1991.

———. *Jesus: A Revolutionary Biography*. San Francisco: HarperSanFransico, 1994.

Cumont, Franz. *Oriental Religions in Roman Paganism*. New York: Dover, [1906] 1956.

Currie, Robert, Alan Gilbert, and Lee Horsley. *Churches and Chuchgoers: Patterns of Church Growth in the British Isles since 1700*. Oxford: Clarendon Press, 1977.

Daniélou, Alain. *The Myths and Gods of India*. Rochester, VT: Inner Traditions International, [1961] 1995.

Darrow, William R. "Zoroaster Amalgamated: Notes on Iranian Prophetology." *History of Religions* 27 (1987): 109–32.

Darwin, Charles. *The Origin of Species and the Descent of Man*. New York: Modern Library, [1871] 1936.

Davie, Grace. *Religion in Britain since 1945: Believing without Belonging*. Oxford: Blackwell, 1994.

Davies, Norman. *Europe: A History*. Oxford: Oxford Univ. Press, 1996.

Davies, Paul. *God and the New Physics*. New York: Simon & Schuster, 1983.

Davies, Philip R. *In Search of "Ancient Israel."* Sheffield: Sheffield Academic Press, 1995.

Davis, Kingsley. *Human Society*. New York: The Macmillan Company, 1949.

Dawkins, Richard. *A Devil's Chaplain*. London: Weidenfeld & Nicolson, 2003.

———. *The Extended Phenotype: The Gene as the Unit of Selection*. Oxford: Freeman, 1981.

————.*The God Delusion*. Boston: Houghton Mifflin Co, 2006.

————. "Is Science a Religion?" *The Humanist*. (Jan/Feb 1997). http://www.thehumanist.org/humanist/articles/dawkins.html.

————. *The Selfish Gene*. Oxford: Oxford Univ. Press, 1976.

De Geus, C. H. J. *The Tribes of Israel*. Amsterdam: Van Gorcum, 1976.

Delumeau, Jean. *Catholicism between Luther and Voltaire*. Philadelphia: Westminster Press, 1977.

————. *Christianisme va-t-il mourir?* Paris: Hachette, 1977.

Dembski, William A. *The Design Revolution*. Downer's Grove, IL: InterVarsity Press, 2004.

————. *Intelligent Design*. Downer's Grove, IL: InterVarsity Press, 1999.

De Moor, J. C. *The Rise of Yahwism: The Roots of Israelite Monotheism*. 2nd ed. Leuven, Belgium: Leuven Univ. Press, 1997.

Dennett, Daniel C. *Breaking the Spell: Religion as a Natural Phenomenon*. New York: Viking, 2006.

————. *Darwin's Dangerous Idea*. New York: Simon & Schuster, 1995.

Denny, Frederick M. "Islam and the Muslim Community." In *Religious Traditions of the World*, edited by H. Byron Earhart, 605–712. San Francisco: HarperSanFrancisco, 1993.

De Ste. Croix, G. E. M. "Why Were the Early Christians Persecuted?" *Past and Present* 26 (1963): 6–38.

Detienne, Marcel. "Orpheus." In *The Encyclopedia of Religion*, edited by Mircea Eliade. New York: Macmillan, 1987.

De Vaux, Roland. *Ancient Israel*. New York: McGraw-Hill, 1961.

Dever, William G. *Did God Have a Wife?* Grand Rapids, MI: William B. Eerdmans, 2005.

————. *Who Were the Early Israelites and Where Did They Come From?* Grand Rapids, MI: William B. Eerdmans, 2003.

De Vries, Jan. *Perspectives in the History of Religions*. Berkeley: Univ. of California Press, 1967.

Díaz, Bernal del Castillo. *The Discovery and Conquest of Mexico*. New York: Da Capo Press, [c. 1555] 1996.

Dick, Michael B. "Prophetic Parodies of Making the Cult Image." In *Born in Heaven, Made on Earth: The Making of the Cult Image in the Ancient Near East*, edited by Michael B. Dick, 1–53. Winona Lake, IN: Eisenbrauns, 1999.

Dickens, A. G. *The English Reformation*. 2nd ed. University Park: Pennsylvania State Univ. Press, 1991.

Dickson, D. Bruce. *The Dawn of Belief*. Tucson: Univ. of Arizona Press, 1990.

Dillon, John M. "Platonism." In *The Anchor Bible Dictionary*, edited by David Noel Freedman. New York: Doubleday, 1992.

Donald, Leland. *Aboriginal Slavery on the Northwest Coast of North America*. Berkeley and Los Angeles: Univ. of California Press, 1997.

Donalson, Malcolm Drew. *The Cult of Isis in the Roman Empire*. Lewiston, ME: Edwin Mellen Press, 2003.

Donner, Fred McGraw. *The Early Islamic Conquests*. Princeton: Princeton Univ. Press, 1981.

Douglas, Mary. "The Effects of Modernization on Religious Change." In *Religion and America: Spirituality in a Secular Age*, edited by Mary Douglas and Steven M. Tipton, 25–43. Boston: Beacon Press, 1982.

Drake, H. A. *Constantine and the Bishops: The Politics of Intolerance*. Baltimore: Johns Hopkins Press, 2000.

Drews, Arthur. *The Myth of Christ*. Amherst, NY: Prometheus Books, [1910–1911] 1998.

Dubbs, Homer H. "The Date and Circumstances of the Philosopher Lao-Tzu." *Journal of the American Oriental Society* 61 (1941): 215–21.

————. "The Political Career of Confucious." *Journal of the American Oriental Society* 66 (1942): 272–82.

Duby, Georges. *The Early Growth of the European Economy*. Ithaca, NY: Cornell Univ. Press, 1974.

Duffy, Eamon. "The Late Middle Ages: Vitality or Decline?" In *Atlas of the Christian Church*, edited by Henry Chadwic k and G. R. Evans, 86–95. New York: Facts on File, 1987.

————. *Saints and Sinners: A History of Popes*. New Haven: Yale Univ. Press, 1997.

————. *Stripping the Altars*. New Haven: Yale Univ. Press, 1992.

Dumont, Louis. *Homo Hierarchicus: The Caste System and Its Implications*, revised English edition. Chicago: Univ. of Chicago Press, 1980.

————. "On the Comparative Understanding of Non-Modern Civilizations." *Daedalus* 104:2 (1975): 153–72.

Dundes, Alan, ed. "The Flood as Male Myth of Creation." *Journal of Psychoanalytic Anthropology* 9 (1986): 359–72.

———. *The Flood Myth*. Berkeley: Univ. of California Press, 1988.

Durán, Fra Diego. *The History of the Indies of New Spain*. Norman: Univ. of Oklahoma Press, [1585] 1994.

Durant, Will. *The Reformation*. New York: Simon and Schuster, 1957.

Durkheim, Emile. *The Elementary Forms of Religious Life*. Translated by Karen E. Fields. New York: The Free Press, [1912] 1995.

———. "Review of Part VI of the *Principles of Sociology* by Herbert Spencer." In *Revue philosophique de la France et de l'étranger* 21 (1886): 61–69, translated and published by W. S. F. Pickering, *Durkheim on Religion*, 13–23. Atlanta: Scholars Press, 1994..

Dutt, Sukumar. *Buddhist Monks and Monasteries of India*. London: George Allen and Unwin Ltd, 1962.

Eberhard, Wolfram. *Guilt and Sin in Traditional China*. Berkeley: Univ. of California Press, 1967.

Edwards, James R. *Is Jesus the Only Savior?* Grand Rapids, MI: William B. Eerdmans Publishing, 2005.

Ehrman, Bart D. *Lost Christianities: The Battles for Scripture and Faiths We Never Knew*. Oxford: Oxford Univ. Press, 2003.

Eickelman, D. F. "Musaylima." *Journal of Economic and Social History of the Orient* 10 (1967): 17–52.

Einstein, Albert. *Letters to Solovine*. New York: Philosophical Library, 1987.

Eisenstadt, S. N. (editor). *The Origins and Diversity of Axial Age Civilizations*. Albany: State Univ. of New York Press, 1986.

Eliade, Mircea. "Australian Religions: An Introduction. Part 1." *History of Religions* 6 (1966): 108–34.

———. *A History of Religious Ideas*. Vol.1. Chicago: Univ. of Chicago Press, 1981.

———. *Patterns in Comparative Religion*. New York: New American Library, [1958] 1974.

———. "South American High Gods, Part 1." *History of Religions*. 8 (1969): 338–54.

———. "South American High Gods, Part 2." *History of Religions* 10 (1971): 234–66.

———. "The Quest for the 'Origins' of Religion." *History of Religions* 4 (1964): 154–69.

Ellison, Christopher G. "Religious Involvement and Subjective Well-Being." *Journal of Health and Social Behavior* 32 (1991): 80–99.

Ellwood, Robert S. "A Japanese Mythic Trickster Figure: Susa-no-o." In *Mythical Trickster Figures: Contours, Contexts, and Criticisms*, edited by William J. Hynes and William G. Doty, 141–158. Tuscaloosa: Univ. of Alabama Press, 1993.

Engels, Friedrich. "Dialectics of Nature." Reprinted in Karl Marx and Friedrich Engels, *On Religion*, 152–193. Atlanta: Scholars Press, [1873] 1964.

———. "On the History of Early Christianity." Reprinted in Karl Marx and Friedrich Engels, *On Religion*, 316–359. Atlanta: Scholars Press, [1894] 1964.

Ernst, Carl. *Eternal Garden: Mysticism, History, and Politics at a South Asian Sufi Center*. Albany: State Univ. of New York Press, 1992.

Evans, Carl D. "Jeroboam." In *The Anchor Bible Dictionary*, edited by David Noel Freedman. New York: Doubleday, 1992.

Evans, Craig A. *Fabricating Jesus: How Modern Scholars Distort the Gospel*. Downers Grove, IL: InterVarsity Press Books, 2006.

Evans-Pritchard, E. E. *Theories of Primitive Religion*. Oxford: Oxford Univ. Press, 1965.

Fairservis, Walter A., Jr. *The Roots of Ancient India: The Archaeology of Early Indian Civilization*. New York: Macmillan, 1971.

Farah, Caesar E. *Islam: Beliefs and Observances*. 5th ed. Hauppauge, NY: Barron's, 1994.

Fears, J. Rufus. "Sol Invictus." In *The Encyclopedia of Religion*, edited by Mircea Eliade. New York: Macmillan, 1987.

Feldman, Louis H. *Jew and Gentile in the Ancient World*. Princeton: Princeton Univ. Press, 1993.

———. "Judaism, History of, III, Hellenic Judaism." In *Encyclopaedia Britannica*. Chicago: Univ. of Chicago Press, 1981.

———. "Was Judaism a Missionary Religion in Ancient Times?" In *Jewish Assimilation, Acculturation and Accomodation*, edited by Menachem Mor, 23–37. Lanham, MD: Univ. Press of America, 1992.

Ferguson, John. *The Religions of the Roman Empire*. Ithaca, NY: Cornell Univ. Press, 1970.

Feuerbach, Ludwig von. *The Essence of Christianity*. New York: Harper Torchbooks, [1841] 1957.

Finke, Roger and Rodney Stark. *The Churching of America, 1776–1990: Winners and Losers in Our Religious Economy*. New Brunswick, NJ: Rutgers Univ. Press, 1992.

Finkelstein, Israel. "The Great Transformation: The 'Conquest' of the Highlands Frontier and the Rise of Territorial States." In *The Archaeology of Society in the Holy Land*, edited by T. E. Levy, 349–365. New York: Facts on File, 1995.

Firth, Raymond. "Offering and Sacrifice: Problems of Organization." *Journal of the Royal Anthropological Institute of Great Britain and Ireland* 93 (1963): 12–24.

Fishbane, Michael. "Judaism: Revelations and Tradition." In *Religious Traditions of the World*, edited by H. Byron Earhart, 375–483. San Francisco: HarperSanFrancisco, 1993.

Fletcher, Richard. *The Barbarian Conversions: From Paganism to Christianity*. New York: Henry Holt, 1997.

———. *Moorish Spain*. Berkeley: Univ. of California Press, 1992.

Foster, Benjamin R. *From Distant Days: Myths, Tales, and Poetry of Ancient Mesopotamia*. Bethesda, MD: Capital Decisions, 1995.

Fowler, Jeaneane. *Hinduism: Beliefs and Practices*. Brighton: Sussex Academic Press, 1997.

Fox, Robin Lane. *Pagans and Christians*. New York: Knopf, 1987.

Frankfort, Henri. "Heresy in a Theocratic State." *Journal of the Warburg and Courtauld Institutes* 21 (1958): 152–65.

———. *Kingship and the Gods: A Study of Ancient Near Eastern Religion as the Integration of Society and Nature*. Chicago: Univ. of Chicago Press, 1978.

———. "The Origin of Monumental Architecture in Egypt." *The American Journal of Semitic Languages and Literature*. 58 (1941): 329–58.

Frankiel, Sandra Sizer. "Christianity: A Way of Salvation." In *Religious Traditions of the World*, edited by H. Byron Earhart. San Francisco: HarperSanFrancisco, 1993.

Frazer, J. G. *The Golden Bough: A Study in Magic and Religion*. 2nd ed. 3 vols. London: Macmillan, 1900.

Frede, Michael. "Monotheism and Pagan Philosophy in Later Antiquity." In *Pagan Monotheism in Late Antiquity*, edited by Plymnia Athanassiadi and Michael Frede, 41–67. Oxford: Clarendon Press, 1999.

Freeman-Grenville, G. S. P. and Stuart C. Munro-Hay. *Historical Atlas of Islam*. New York: Continuum, 2002.

Frend, W. H. C. *Martyrdom and Persecution in the Early Church*. Grand Rapids, MI: Baker, [1965] 1981.

Freud, Sigmund. *The Future of an Illusion*. Garden City, NY: Doubleday, [1927] 1961.

———. *Moses and Monotheism*. New York: Vintage, [1939] 1955.

———. *Totem and Taboo*. New York: W. W. Norton, [1913] 1950.

Freyne, Sean. "The Geography, Politics and Economics of Galilee." In *Studying the Historical Jesus: Evaluations of the State of Current Research*, edited by Bruce Chilton and Craig Evans, 75–121. Leiden: Brill, 1994.

———. "Urban-Rural Relations in First Century Galilee." In *The Galilee of Late Antiquity*, edited by Lee I. Levine. New York: Jewish Theological Seminary, 1992.

Froese, Paul and Christopher Bader. "Religious Worldviews: The Bundling of Images of God, Moral Attitudes, and Political Identities in Eight Christian Societies." *Sociological Quarterly* (forthcoming).

Gager, John G. *Kingdom and Community: The Social World of Early Christianity*. Englewood Cliffs, NJ: Prentice-Hall, 1975.

———. *The Origins of Anti-Semitism: Attitudes towards Judaism in Pagan and Christian Antiquity*. New York: Oxford Univ. Press, 1983.

Galvao-Sobrinho, Carlos R. "Funerary Epigraphy and the Spread of Christianity in the West." *Athenaeum* 83 (1995): 431–66.

Garelli, Paul. "The Changing Face of Conservative Mesopotamian Thought." *Daedalus* 104:2 (1975): 47–56.

Garland, Robert. "Priests and Power in Classical Athens." In *Pagan Priests*, edited by Mary Beard and John North, 75–91. London: Duckworth, 1990.

Gasque, W. Ward. *A History of the Interpretation of the Acts of the Apostles*. Eugene, OR: Wipf and Stock, 2000.

Geertz, Clifford. "Religion as a Cultural System." In *Anthropological Approaches to the Study of Religion*, edited by Michael Banton, 1–46. London: Tavistock Publications, 1966.

Geffcken, Johannes. *The Last Days of Greco-Roman Paganism*. Amsterdam: North-Holland Publishing, [1920] 1978.

Geller, Stephen A. "The God of the Covenant." In *One God or Many: Concepts of Divinity in the Ancient World*, edited by Barbara Nevling Porter, 273–319. Casco Bay, ME: Transactions of the Casco Bay Assyriological Institute, 2000.

Gentilecore, David. *Bishop to Witch*. Manchester: Manchester Univ. Press, 1992.

Georgi, Dieter. "The Early Church: Internal Migration of New Religion." *Harvard Theological Review* 88 (1995): 35–68.

Gershevitch, Ilya. "Zoroaster's Own Contribution." *Journal of Near Eastern Studies* 23 (1964): 12–28.

Geva, Hillel. "Small City, Few People." *Biblical Archaeology Review* (May/June 2006):66–8.

Ghirshman, Roman. "The Ziggurat of Choga-Zanbil." *Archaeology* 8 (1955): 260–3.

Gier, Nicholas F. *God, Reason, and the Evangelicals*. Lanham, MD: Univ. Press of America, 1987.

Gierke, Otto. *Associations and Law: The Classical and Early Christian Stages*. Toronto: Univ. of Toronto Press, [1873] 1977.

Gifford, Paul. *African Christianity*. Bloomington: Indiana Univ. Press, 1998.

Gill, Anthony. "The Struggle to Be Soul Provider: Catholic Responses to Protestant Growth in Latin America." In *Latin American Religion in Motion*. Edited by Christian Smith and Joshua Prokopy. New York: Routledge, 1999, 14–42.

Girardot, N. J. *Myth and Meaning in Early Taoism*. Berkeley: Univ. of California Press, 1983.

Gladstone, William. *Landmarks of Homeric Studies*. London: Macmillan, 1890.

Gnoli, Gherardo. "Magi." In *The Encyclopedia of Religion*, edited by Mircea Eliade. New York: Macmillan, 1987.

———. *Zoroaster in History*. New York: Bibliotheca Persica Press, 2000.

———. "Zoroastrianism." In *The Encyclopedia of Religion*, edited by Mircea Eliade. New York: Macmillan, 1987.

Gnuse, Karl. *No Other Gods: Emergent Monotheism in Israel*. Sheffield: Sheffield Academic Press, 1997.

Goldenweiser, Alexander A. "Religion and Society: A Critique of Emile Durkheim's Theory of the Origin and Nature of Religion." *The Journal of Philosophy, Psychology and Scientific Methods* 14 (1917): 113–24.

———. "Review: 'Emile Durkheim—Les Formes élémentaires de la religieuse. 1912.'" *American Anthropologist* 17 (1915): 719–35.

Gombrich, Richard. "The Consecration of a Buddhist Image." *The Journal of Asian Studies* 26 (1966): 23–26.

Gombrich, Richard F. *Precept and Practice: Traditional Buddhism in the Rural Highlands of Ceylon*. Oxford: Clarendon Press, 1971.

Gómez, Luis O. "Buddhism in India." In *The Encyclopedia of Religion*, edited by Mircea Eliade. New York: Macmillan, 1987.

Gonda, Jan. "Indian Religions: An Overview." In *The Encyclopedia of Religion*, edited by Mircea Eliade. New York: Macmillan, 1987.

———. "Visnu." In *The Encyclopedia of Religion*, edited by Mircea Eliade. New York: Macmillan, 1987.

Goode, William J. *Religion among the Primitives*. Glencoe, IL: The Free Press, 1951.

Goodenough, Erwin R. *The Church in the Roman Empire*. New York: Henry Holt, 1931.

Goodison, Lucy, and Christine Morris, eds. *Ancient Goddesses: The Myths and the Evidence*. London: British Museum Press, 1998.

Goodman, Martin. *Mission and Conversion: Proselytizing in the Religious History of the Roman Empire*. Oxford: Clarendon Press, 1994.

Goodrich, L. Carrington. "China, History of," part 1. In *The Encyclopaedia Britannica*. Chicago: Univ. of Chicago Press, 1981.

Goody, Jack. "A Kernel of Doubt." *The Journal of the Royal Anthropological Institute* 2 (1996): 667–81.

Gorman, Michael J. *Abortion and the Early Church*. Downers Grove, IL: InterVarsity Press, 1982.

Goulder, Michael D. "Is Q a Juggernaut?" *Journal of Biblical Literature* 115 (1996): 667–81.

Grafton, Anthony. "Protestant versus Prophet: Isaac Casaubon on Hermes Trismegistus." *Journal of the Warburg and Courtauld Institutes* 46 (1983): 78–93.

Grant, Michael. *The History of Rome*. New York and London: Faber and Faber, 1978.

Grant, Robert M. *Augustus to Constantine: The Rise and Triumph of Christianity in the Roman World*. San Francisco: HarperSanFrancisco, [1970] 1990.

———. *Gods and the One God*. Philadelphia: Westminster Press, 1986.

———. *The Jews in the Roman World*. New York: Charles Scribner's Sons, 1973.

Grasser, Erich. "Norman Perrin's Contribution to the Question of the Historical Jesus." *The Journal of Religion* 64 (1984): 484–500.

Greeley, Andrew. *Religion as Poetry*. New Brunswick, NJ: Transaction Publishers, 1995.

Greenberg, Moshe. "Ezekiel." In *The Encyclopedia of Religion,* edited by Mircea Eliade. New York: Macmillan, 1987.

———. "Judaism, History of, II, The Ancient Near Eastern Setting." In *Encyclopaedia Britannica*. Chicago: Univ. of Chicago Press, 1981.

Gresseth, Gerald K. "The Gilgamesh Epic and Homer." *The Cultural Journal* 70 (1975): 1–18.

Griffiths, J. Gwyn. "The Orders of Gods in Greece and Egypt (According to Herodotus)." *The Journal of Hellenic Studies* 75 (1955): 21–3.

Grim, Brian J., and Roger Finke, "International Religion Idexes." *Interdisciplinary Journal of Research on Religion* 2: article 1. http://www.religjournal.com

Guillaume, A. *The Life of Muhammad, a translation of Ishaq's Sirat Rasul Allah*. Oxford: Oxford Univ. Press, 1967.

Gustafsson, Göran. "Politicization of State Churches—A Welfare State Model." *Social Compass* 37 (1990): 107–16.

Guthrie, Stewart. "A Cognitive Theory of Religion." *Current Anthropology* 21 (1980): 181–203.

Habermas, Gary R. *The Historical Jesus: Ancient Evidence for the Life of Christ*. Joplin, MO: College Press Publishing, 1996.

Hackney, Charles H., and Glenn S. Sanders. "Religiosity and Mental Health: A Meta-Analysis of Recent Studies." *Journal for the Scientific Study of Religion* 42 (2003): 43–55.

Hahm, David E. "Roman Nobility and the Three Major Priesthoods, 218–167 BC." *Transactions and Proceedings of the American Philological Association* 94 (1963): 73–85.

Hajime, Nakamura. "Buddhism, Schools of: Mahayana Buddhism." In *The Encyclopedia of Religion,* edited by Mircea Eliade. New York: Macmillan, 1987.

Hallo, William W. "Before Tea Leaves: Divination in Ancient Babylon." *Biblical Archaeology Review* 31 (March/April 2005):32–9.

Halpern, Baruch. "The Exodus from Egypt: Myth or Reality?" In *The Rise of Ancient Israel*, edited by Hershel Shanks, et al., 86–117. Washington, DC: Biblical Archaeology Society, 1992.

———. *The First Historians: The Hebrew Bible and History*. University Park, PA: Pennsylvania State Univ. Press, 1996.

Halsberghe, Gaston H. *The Cult of Sol Invictus*. Leiden: E. J. Brill, 1972.

Hamberg, Eva. *Studies in the Prevalence of Religious Beliefs and Religious Practices in Contemporary Sweden*. Uppsala, Sweden: Act Universitatis Upsaliensis, 1990.

Hamblin, Robert L., R. Brooke Jacobson, and Jerry L. L.Miller. *A Mathematical Theory of Social Change*. New York: Wiley, 1973.

Hamilton, Naomi. "The Figurines." In *Changing Materialities at Çatalhöyük: Reports from the 1995–99 Seasons,* edited by Ian Hodder. Ankara: McDondal Institute/British Institute of Archaeology, 2006.

Hannah, Ian C. *Christian Monasticism: A Great Force in History*. London: George Allen & Unwin, 1924.

Hanson, R. P. C. *The Acts*. Oxford: Clarendon Press, 1968.

Harbsmeier, Christoph. "Confucius Ridens: Humor in the Analects." *Harvard Journal of Asiatic Studies* 50 (1990): 131–61.

Hardy, Alister. *The Biology of God*. New York: Taplinger Publishing, 1976.

Harnack, Adolf von. *The Expansion of Christianity in the First Three Centuries*. Vol. 1. New York: G. P. Putnam's Sons, 1904.

———. *The Expansion of Christianity in the First Three Centuries*. Vol. 2. New York: G. P. Putnam's Sons, 1905.

———. *Marcion: The Gospel of the Alien God*. Durham, NC: Labyrinth Press, [1924] 1990.

Harner, Michael. "The Ecological Basis for Aztec Sacrifice." *American Ethnologist* 4 (1977): 117–35.

Harris, Marvin. *Cannibals and Kings: The Origins of Cultures*. New York: Random House, 1977.

Harris, William V. *Ancient Literacy*. Cambridge: Harvard Univ. Press, 1989.

Hawting, G. R. *The Idea of Idolatry and the Emergence of Islam*. Cambridge: Cambridge Univ. Press, 1999.

Hay, J. Stuart. *The Amazing Emperor Heliogabalus*. London: Macmillan, 1911.

Hayward, John. "A Dynamic Model of Church Growth and Its Application to Contemporary Revivals." *Review of Religious Research* 43 (2002): 218–41.

————. "Mathematical Modeling of Church Growth." *Journal of Mathematical Sociology* 23 (1999): 255–92.

Hazra, Kanai Lal. *The Rise and Decline of Buddhism in India*. New Delhi: Munshiram Manoharlal Publishers, 1995.

Heath, Anthony. *Rational Choice and Social Exchange*. Cambridge: Cambridge Univ. Press, 1976.

Heesterman, Jan C. "Brahman." In *The Encyclopedia of Religion*, edited by Mircea Eliade. New York: Macmillan, 1987.

Held, George F. "Parallels between the Gilgamesh Epic and Plato's Symposium." *Journal of Near Eastern Studies* 42 (1983): 133–41.

Hemenway, Priya. *Hindu Gods: The Spirit of the Divine*. San Francisco: Chronicle Books, 2003.

Hemer, Colin J. *The Book of Acts in the Setting of Hellenistic History*. Winona Lake, IN: Eisenbrauns, 1990.

Hendel, Ronald S. "Them Dry Bones." *Biblical Archaeology Review* 33:1 (2006): 26, 79.

Hendricks, Robert G. *Lao-Tzu's Tao Te Ching: A Translation of Startling New Documents Found at Guodian*. New York: Columbia Univ. Press, 2000.

Henning, Walter Bruno. *Zoroaster: Politician or Witch-doctor?* (The 1949 Ratanbai Katrak Lectures.) Oxford: Oxford Univ. Press, 1951.

Herzfeld, Ernt. *Zoroaster and His World*. 2 vols. Princeton: Princeton Univ. Press, 1947.

Heyob, Sharon Kelly. *The Cult of Isis among Women in the Greco-Roman World*. Leiden: E. J. Brill, 1975.

Hick, John. *Problems of Religious Pluralism*. London: Macmillan, 1985.

Hiltebeitel, Alf. "Hinduism." In *The Encyclopedia of Religion*, edited by Mircea Eliade. New York: Macmillan, 1987.

Hinson, E. Glenn. "Justin Martyr." In *The Encyclopedia of Religion*, edited by Mircea Eliade. New York: Macmillan, 1987.

Hobbes, Thomas. *Leviathan*. Vol. I. Chicago: Henry Regnery, [1651] 1956.

Hock, Ronald F. *The Social Context of Paul's Ministry: Tentmaking and Apostleship*. Philadelphia: Fortress Press, 1980.

Hodder, Ian. *The Leopard's Tale*. London: Thames & Hudson, 2006.

Hodgson, Marshall G. S. *The Venture of Islam: Conscience and History in a World Civilization*. 3 vols. Chicago: Univ. of Chicago Press, 1974.

Hoffmeier, James K. "Out of Egypt." *Biblical Archaeology Review* 33:1 (2006): 30–41.

Hollinshead, Mary B. "'Adyton,' 'Ophisthodomos,' and the Inner Room of the Greek Temples." *Hesperia* 68 (1999): 189–218.

Hopkins, Keith. "The Age of Roman Girls at Marriage." *Population Studies* 18 (1965): 309–27.

————. "Brother-Sister Marriage in Roman Egypt." *Comparative Studies in Society and History* 22 (1980): 303–54.

————. "Controlling Religion: Rome." In *Religions of the Ancient World: A Guide*, edited by Sarah Iles Johnston, 572–575. Cambridge: Belknap Press of Harvard Univ. Press, 2004.

————. "On the Probable Age Structure of the Roman Population." *Population Studies* 20 (1966): 245–64.

Hopkins, Thomas J. *The Hindu Religious Tradition*. Belmont, CA: Wadsworth, 1971.

Hopkins, Thomas J. and Alf Hiltebeitel. "Indus Valley Religion." In *The Encyclopedia of Religion*, edited by Mircea Eliade.. New York: Macmillan, 1987.

Horcasitas, Fernando. "An Analysis of the Deluge Myth in Mesoamerica." In *The Flood Myth*, edited by Alan Dundes, 183–219. Berkeley: Univ. of California Press, 1988.

Hornung, Erik. *Akhenaten and the Religion of Light*. Ithaca, NY: Cornell Univ. Press, 1999.

————. *Conceptions of God in Ancient Egypt: The One and the Many*. London: Routledge, 1982.

Hughes, Dennis D. *Human Sacrifice in Ancient Greece*. London: Routledge, 1991.

Hultkrantz, Ake. "The Concept of the Supernatural in Primal Religion." *History of Religions* 22 (1983): 231–53.

————. "North American Indian Religion in the History of Research: A General Survey, Part III." *History of Religions* 7 (1967): 13–34.

Hume, David. *Inquiry Concerning Human Understanding*. New York: Macmillan, [1748] 1962.

Humphries, S. C. "'Transcendence' and Intellectual Roles: The Ancient Greek Case." *Daedalus* 104:2 (1975): 91–118.

Hurtado, Larry W. *The Earliest Christian Artifacts: Manuscripts and Christian Origins*. Grand Rapids, MI: Eerdmans, 2006.

———. *Lord Jesus Christ: Devotion to Jesus in Earliest Christianity*. Grand Rapids, MI: Eerdmans, 2003.

Hwang, Philip Ho. "A New Interpretation of Confucius." *Philosophy East and West* 30 (1980): 45–55.

Ingham, John M. "Human Sacrifice at Tenochtitlan." *Comparative Studies in Society and History* 26 (1984): 379–400.

Introvigne, Massimo. "Niches in the Islamic Religious Market and Fundamentalism." *Interdisciplinary Journal of Research on Religion* 1 (2005): article 3. http://www.religjournal.com.

Irwin, Robert. *Dangerous Knowledge: Orientalism and Its Discontents*. Woodstock, NY: Overlook Press, 2006.

Irwin, W. A. "An Objective Criterion for the Dating of Deuteronomy." *The American Journal of Semitic Languages and Literatures* 56 (1939): 337–49.

Isaac, Jules. *Jesus and Israel*. New York: Holt, Rinehart, and Winston, 1971.

———. *The Teaching of Contempt: Christian Roots of Anti-Semitism*. New York: Holt, Rinehart, and Winston, 1964.

Jacobsen, Thorkild. *The Treasures of Darkness: A History of Mesopotamian Religion*. New Haven: Yale Univ. Press, 1976.

James, E. O. *Origins of Sacrifice: A Study in Comparative Religion*. London: John Murray, 1933.

James, William. *The Varieties of Religious Experience*. New York: Mentor Books, [1902] 1958.

Jaspers, Karl. *Anaximander, Heraclitus, Parmenides, Plotinus, Lao-Tzu, Nagarjuna*. New York: Harcourt Brace Jovanovich, 1966.

———. *The Origin and Goal of History*. New Haven: Yale Univ. Press, 1953.

Jaynes, Julian. *The Origin of Consciousness in the Breakdown of the Bicameral Mind*. Boston: Houghton Mifflin Company, 1976.

Jeffrey, David Lyle. *By Things Seen: Reference and Recognition in Medieval Thought*. Ottawa: Univ. of Ottawa Press, 1979.

Jenkins, Philip. *Hidden Gospels: How the Search for Jesus Lost Its Way*. Oxford: Oxford Univ. Press, 2001.

———. *The Next Christendom: The Coming of Global Christianity*. Oxford: Oxford Univ. Press, 2002.

Johnson, Benton. "On Church and Sect." *American Sociological Review* 28 (1963): 539–49.

Johnson, Luke Timothy. *The Real Jesus: The Misguided Quest for the Historical Jesus and the Truth of the Traditional Gospels*. San Franciso: HarperSanFrancisco, 1996.

Johnson, Paul. *A History of Christianity*. New York: Atheneum, 1976.

Johnstone, Patrick. *Operation World*. Carlisle, PA: OM Publishing, 1993.

Jonas, Hans. "Delimitation of the Gnostic Phenomenon—Typological and Historical." In *Le Origini Dello Gnosticismo*, edited by U. Bianchi, 90–108. Leiden: E. J. Brill, 1967.

———. *The Gnostic Religion*. 3rd ed. Boston: Beacon Press, 2001.

Jones, Ernest. *Life and Works of Sigmund Freud*. Vol. 1. New York: Hogarth Press, 1953.

Judge, E. A. "The Early Christians as a Scholastic Community." *Journal of Religious History* 1 (1960–1961): 125–41.

———. *The Social Pattern of Christian Groups in the First Century*. London: Tyndale, 1960.

Kahn, Charles H. *Pythagoras and the Pythagoreans*. Indianapolis: Hackett, 2001.

Kaizuka, Shigeki. *Confucius: His Life and Thought*. New York: Macmillan, 1956.

Kaltenmark, Max. *Lao Tzu and Taoism*. Stanford, CA: Stanford Univ. Press, 1969.

Kalthoff, Albert. *The Rise of Christianity*. London: Watts & Co., 1907.

Katsh, Abraham I. *Judaism in Islam*. New York: Sepher-Hermon Press, [1954] 1980.

Kaufmann, Yehazkel. *The Babylonian Captivity and Deutero-Isaiah*. New York: Union of American Hebrew Congregations, 1970.

Kautsky, Karl. *Foundations of Christianity*. New York: Russell & Russell, [1908] 1952.

Kee, Howard Clark. *Jesus in History*. New York: Harcourt, Brace, & World, 1970.

———. *What Can We Know about Jesus?* Cambridge: Cambridge Univ. Press, 1990.

Keightley, David N. "The Religious Commitment: Shang Theology and the Genesis of Chinese Political Culture." *History of Religions* 17 (1978): 211–25.

Keith, Arthur Berriedale. "Mahavira and Buddha." *Bulletin of the School of Oriental Studies, University of London* 6 (1932): 859–66.

———. *The Religion and Philosophy of the Veda and Upanishads*. 2 vols. Delhi: Motilal Banarsidass Publishers, [1925] 1998.

Kenyon, Sir Frederic George. *The Bible and Modern Scholarship*. London: John Murray, 1948.

———. *The Bible and Archeology*. New York: Harpers, 1949.

Kenyon, Kathleen. *Digging Up Jericho*. New York: Praeger, 1957.

King, Irving. "Some Notes on the Evolution of Religion." *The Philosophical Review* 18 (1909): 38–47.

King, Karen L. *The Gospel of Mary of Magdala: Jesus and the First Woman Apostle*. Santa Rose, CA: Polebridge Press, 2003.

———. *What Is Gnosticism?* Cambridge: Belknap Press, 2003.

King, Philip J. *Amos, Hosea, Micah—An Archaeological Commentary*. Philadelphia: The Westminster Press, 1988.

Kingsley, Peter. "The Greek Origin of the Sixth-Century Dating of Zoroaster." *Bulletin of the School of Oriental and African Studies, University of London* 53 (1990): 245–65.

Kinsley, David. "Avatara." In *The Encyclopedia of Religion*, edited by Mircea Eliade. New York: Macmillan, 1987.

Kirsch, Jonathan. *God against the Gods: The History of the War between Monotheism and Polytheism*. New York: Viking, 2004.

Kister, M. J. "The Massacre of the Banū Qurayza: A Re-Examination of a Tradition." *Jerusalem Studies of Arabic and Islam* 8 (1986): 61–96.

Kitagawa, Joseph M. "Buddhism, History of." In *The Encyclopaedia Britannica*. Chicago: Univ. of Chicago Press, 1981.

Kitchen, K. A. "Exodus, the." In *The Anchor Bible Dictionary*, edited by David Noel Freedman. New York: Doubleday, 1992.

———. *On the Reliability of the Old Testament*. Grand Rapids, MI: William B. Eerdmans, 2003.

Klauck, Hans-Josef. *The Religious Context of Early Christianity*. Minneapolis: Fortress Press, 2003.

Kloppenborg, John S. "The Sayings Gospel Q and the Quest for the Historical Jesus." *The Harvard Theological Review* 89 (1996): 307–44.

Klostermaier, Klaus K. *A Survey of Hinduism*, 2nd edition. Albany: State Univ. of New York Press, 1994.

———. *Hindusim: A Short Introduction*. Oxford: Oneworld Publications, 2000.

Knipe, David M. "Hinduism: Experiments in the Sacred." In *Religious Traditions of the World*, edited by H. Byron Earhart, 713–846. San Francisco: HarperSanFrancisco, 1993.

———. "Priesthood: Hindu Priesthood." In *The Encyclopedia of Religion*, edited by Mircea Eliade. New York: Macmillan, 1987.

Koester, Helmut. *Introduction to the New Testament, Volume One: History, Culture, and Religion in the Hellenistic Age*. Philadelphia and Berlin: Fortress Press/Walter De Gruyter, 1982.

———. *Introduction to the New Testament, Volume Two: History and Literature of Early Christianity*. Philadelphia and Berlin: Fortress Press/Walter De Gruyter, 1982.

Kohn, Livia. "Laozi: Ancient Philosopher, Master of Immortality, and God." In *Religions of China in Practice*, edited by Donald S. Lopez, Jr., 52–63. Princeton: Princeton Univ. Press, 1996.

Kosambi, D. D. *Ancient India: A History of Its Culture and Civilization*. New York: Meridian Books, 1969.

Kox, Willem, Wim Meeus, and Harm t'Hart. "Religious Conversion of Adolescents: Testing the Lofland and Stark Model of Religious Conversion." *Sociological Analysis* 52 (1991): 227–40.

Kraemer, Ross Sherpard. *Her Share of the Blessings: Women's Religions among Pagans, Jews, and Christians in the Greco-Roman World*. Oxford: Oxford Univ. Press, 1992.

Kramer, Samuel Noah. "The 'Babel of Tongues': A Sumerian Version." *Journal of the Oriental Society* 88 (1968): 108–11.

———. *History Begins at Sumer*, 3rd ed. Philadelphia: Univ. of Pennsylvania Press, [1956] 1981.

———. *The Sumerians: Their History, Culture, and Character*. Chicago: Univ. of Chicago Press, [1963] 1971.

Kuhrt, Amélie. "Nabonidus and the Babylonian Priesthood." In *Pagan Priests*, edited by Mary Beard and John North, 119–155. London: Duckworth, 1990.

Kuiper, F. B. J. "The Basic Concept of Vedic Religion." *History of Religions* 15 (1975): 107–20.

Kümmel, Werner Georg. *Introduction to the New Testament*. Nashville: Abingdon Press, 1996.

———. *The New Testament: The History of the Investigation of Its Problems*. Nashville: Abingdon Press, 1970.

LaCocque, André. "Sin and Guilt." In *The Encyclopedia of Religion*, edited by Mircea Eliade. New York: Macmillan, 1987.

Ladurie, Emmanuel LeRoy. *The Peasants of Languedoc*. Urbana: Univ. of Illinois Press, 1974.

Lagerwey, John. "Taoism: The Taoist Religious Community." In *The Encyclopedia of Religion*, edited by Mircea Eliade. New York: Macmillan, 1987.

Lambert, Malcolm. *Medieval History: Popular Movements from the Gregorian Reform to the Reformation*. 2nd ed. Oxford: Basil Blackwell, 1992.

Lamotte, Étienne. *History of Indian Buddhism*. Louvain: Publications Universitaires, 1988.

Lang, Andrew. *The Making of Religion*. London: Longmans, Green, and Co., 1898.

———. *Myth, Ritual, and Religion*. 2 vols. London: Longmans, Green, and Co., 1887.

Lang, Bernard. *Monotheism and the Prophetic Minority*. Sheffield, UK: The Almond Press, 1983.

———. "No God but Yahweh! The Origin and Character of Biblical Monotheism." In *Monotheism*, edited by Claude Geffré and Jean-Pierre Jossua, 41–49. Edinburgh: T & T Clark, 1985.

———. "Street Theater, Raising the Dead, and the Zoroastrian Connection in Ezekiel's Prophecy." In *Ezekiel and His Book*, edited by Johan Lust, 297–316. Leuven, Belgium: Leuven Univ. Press, 1986.

Lang, Graeme, Selina Ching Chan, and Lars Ragvald. "Temples and the Religious Economy." *Interdisciplinary Journal of Religious Research* 1 (2005): article 4. http://www.religjournal.com.

Lasaulx, Ernst von. *Neuer Versuch einer Philosophie der Geschechte*. Munich: J. G. Cotta, 1856.

Lash, Nicholas. *The Beginning of the End of "Religion."* Cambridge: Cambridge Univ. Press, 1996.

Latourette, Kenneth Scott. *A History of Christianity*. Rev.ed. Vol 2. San Francisco: HarperSanFrancisco, 1975.

Lawson, E. Thomas and Robert N. McCauley. *Rethinking Religion: Connecting Cognition and Culture*. Cambridge: Cambridge Univ. Press, 1990.

Layton, Bentley. *The Gnostic Scriptures*. Garden City, NY: Doubleday, 1987.

Lefkowitz, Mary. *Greek Gods, Human Lives: What We Can Learn from Myths*. New Haven: Yale Univ. Press, 2003.

Lemche, Niels Peter. *The Israelites in History and Tradition*. Louisville: Westminster/John Knox, 1998.

Lessa, William A. and Evon Z. Vogt. *Reader in Comparative Religion*. 3rd ed. New York: Harper & Row, 1972.

Lester, Robert C. "Buddhism: The Path to Nirvana." In *Religious Traditions of the World*, edited by H. Byron Earhart, 849–971. San Francisco: HarperSanFrancisco, 1993.

Levack, Brian P. *The Witch-Hunt in Early Modern Europe*. 2nd ed. London: Longman, 1995.

Lewis, C. S. *God in the Dock*. Grand Rapids, MI: William B. Eerdmans, 1970.

Li, Chi. *The Beginnings of Chinese Civilization*. Seattle: Univ. of Washington Press, 1957.

Lichtheim, Miriam. *Ancient Egyptian Literature: A Book of Readings*. Berkeley: Univ. of California Press, 1975.

Liebeschuetz, J. H. W. G. *Continuity and Change in Roman Religion*. Oxford: Clarendon Press, 1979.

Lindberg, David C. *The Beginnings of Western Science*. Chicago: Univ. of Chicago Press, 1992.

———. "Science and the Early Church." In *God and Nature: Historical Essays on the Encounter between Christianity and Science*, edited by David C. Lindberg and Ronald L. Numbers, 19–48. Berkeley: Univ. of California Press, 1986.

Lindsey, Robert L. *Jesus Rabbi and Lord: The Hebrew Story of Jesus behind the Gospels*. Oak Creek, WI: Cornerstone, 1989.

Lings, Martin. *Muhammad: His Life Based on the Earliest Sources*. Rochester, VT: Inner Traditions International, 1983.

Linnemann, Eta. *Is There a Synoptic Problem? Rethinking the Literary Dependence of the First Three Gospels*. Grand Rapids, MI: Baker Book House, 1992.

Liu, Wu-Chi. *A Short History of Confucian Philosophy*. London: Hyperion Press, 1955.

Lofland, John. "'Becoming a World-Saver' Revisited." *American Behavioral Scientist* 20 (1977): 805–18.

Lofland, John, and Rodney Stark. "Becoming a World-Saver: A Theory of Conversion to a Deviant Perspective." *American Sociological Review* 30 (1965): 862–75.

Lopez, Donald S., Jr., ed. *Religions of China in Practice*. Princeton: Princeton Univ. Press, 1996.

Lorenzen, David N. "Who Invented Hinduism?" *Comparative Studies in Society and History* 41 (1999): 630–59.

Lowie, Robert H. *Primitive Religion*. Rev. ed. New York: Liveright, 1948.

Lu, Yunfeng, Byron Johnson, and Rodney Stark. "Deregulation and the Religious Market in Taiwan." *Sociological Quarterly*, (forthcoming).

Ludwig, Theodore M. "Monotheism." In *The Encyclopedia of Religion*, edited by Mircea Eliade. New York: Macmillan, 1987.

Lundbom, Jack R. "Jeremiah." In *The Anchor Bible Dictionary*, edited by David Noel Freedman. New York: Doubleday, 1992.

Mack, Burton L. *The Lost Gospel: The Book of Q and Christian Origins*. San Francisco: HarperSanFrancisco, 1994.

———. *A Myth of Innocence: Mark and Christian Origins*. Philadelphia: Fortress Press, 1988.

Mackintosh, Hugh R. "Does the Historical Study of Religions Yield a Dogmatic Theology?" *The American Journal of Theology*. XIII (1908): 505–19.

MacMullen, Ramsay. *Christianity and Paganism in the Fourth to Eighth Centuries*. New Haven: Yale Univ. Press, 1997.

———. *Christianizing the Roman Empire*. New Haven: Yale Univ. Press, 1984.

———. *Paganism in the Roman Empire*. New Haven: Yale Univ. Press, 1981.

———. *Roman Social Relations*. New Haven: Yale Univ. Press, 1974.

Mahony, William K. "Upaniṣads." In Mircea Eliade, ed., *The Encyclopedia of Religion*. New York: Macmillan, 1987.

Mair, Victor H. "Kinesis versus Stasis, Interaction versus Independent Invention." In *Contact and Exchange in the Ancient World*, edited by Victor H. Mair, 1–16. Honolulu: University of Hawaii Press, 2006.

Major, John S. "Shang-Ti." In *The Encyclopedia of Religion*, edited by Mircea Eliade. New York: Macmillan, 1987.

Malandra, William W. *An Introduction to Ancient Iranian Religion*. Minneapolis: Univ. of Minnesota Press, 1983.

Malherbe, Abraham J. *Social Aspects of Early Christianity*. 2nd ed. Eugene, OR: Wipf and Stock Publishers, 2003.

Malinowski, Bronislaw. *Magic, Science, and Religion*. Propsect Heights, IL: Waveland Press, [1948] 1992.

Mallory, J. P. *In Search of the Indo-Europeans: Language, Archaeology and Myth*. London: Thames & Hudson, 1991.

Man, E. H. "On the Aboriginal Inhabitants of the Andaman Islands, Part 2." *The Journal of the Anthropological Institute of Great Britain and Ireland* 12 (1883): 117–75.

Margueron, Jean-Claude. "Temples: Mesopotamian Temples." In *The Oxford Encyclopedia of Archaeology in the Near East*. New York: Oxford Univ. Press, 1997.

Martens, Frederick H. "Music in the Life of the Aztecs." *The Musical Quarterly* 14 (1928): 413–37.

Maspero, Henri. *Taoism and Chinese Religion*. Amherst, MA: Univ. of Massachusetts Press, 1981.

Matthews, J. F. "Symmachus and the Oriental Cults." *The Journal of Roman Studies* 63 (1973): 175–95.

Mauss, Marcel. *The Gift: The Form and Reason for Exchange in Archaic Societies*. New York: W. W. Norton, [1923] 1990.

McDougall, William. *An Introduction to Social Psychology*. Boston: Luce, 1908.

McGrath, Alister. *Dawkin's God: Genes, Memes, and the Meaning of Life*. Oxford: Blackwell, 2005.

McKechnie, Paul. *The First Christian Centuries: Perspectives on the Early Church*. Downers Grove, IL: InterVarsity Press, 2001.

McKenzie, Steven L. "Deuteronomistic History." In *The Anchor Bible Dictionary*, edited by David Noel Freedman. New York: Doubleday, 1992.

McNeill, William H. *The Rise of the West*. Chicago: Univ. of Chicago Press, 1963.

McSheffrey, Shannon. *Gender and Heresy: Women and Men and Lollard Communities, 1420–1530*. Philadelphia: Univ. of Philadelphia Press, 1995.

Meeks, Wayne. *The First Urban Christians*. New Haven: Yale Univ. Press, 1983.

Meier, John P. *A Marginal Jew: Rethinking the Historical Jesus*. Garden City, NY: Doubleday, 1994.

Mendelssohn, Kurt. *The Riddle of the Pyramids*. New York: Praeger, 1974.

Menocal, María Rosa. *The Ornament of the World: How Muslims, Jews, and Christians Created a Culture of Tolerance in Medieval Spain*. New York: Little, Brown, 2002.

Merkelbach, R. "Mithra, Mithraism." In *The Anchor Bible Dictionary*, edited by David Noel Freedman. New York: Doubleday, 1992.

———. "Mithraism." In *Encyclopaedia Britannica*. Chicago: Univ. of Chicago Press, 1981.

Mettinger, Tryggve N. D. *No Graven Images?* Stockholm: Almquist & Wiksell, 1995.

Metzger, Bruce M., and Bart D. Ehrman. *The Text of the New Testament: Its Transmission, Corruption, and Restoration*. 4th ed. New York: Oxford Univ. Press, 2005.

Meyer, Ben F. "Jesus Christ." In *The Anchor Bible Dictionary*, edited by David Noel Freedman. New York: Doubleday, 1992.

Meyer, Marvin. *The Gnostic Discoveries: The Impact of the Nag Hammadi Library*. San Francisco: HarperSanFrancisco, 2005.

Michalowski, Piotr. "Sumerians." In *The Oxford Encyclopedia of Archaeology in the Near East*. New York: Oxford Univ. Press, 1997.

Miller, Patrick D. *The Religion of Ancient Israel*. Louisville, KY: Westminster/John Knox Press, 2000.

Moberly, R. W. L. "How Appropriate Is 'Monotheism' as a Category for Biblical Interpretation?" In *Early Jewish and Christian Monotheism*, edited by Loren T. Stuckenbruck and Wendy E. S. North, 216–234. London: T & T Clark, 2004.

Modarressi, Hossein. "Early Debates on the Integrity of the Qur'an: A Brief Survey." *Studia Islamica* 77 (1993): 5–39.

Momigliano, Arnoldo. "The Fault of the Greeks." *Daedalus* 104:2 (1975): 9–19.

Money-Kyrle, Roger. *The Meaning of Sacrifice*. London: Hogarth Press, 1929.

Monier-Williams, Monier. *Hinduism: Hinduism and Its Sources*. New Delhi: Orientalist [1919] 1993.

Mooney, James. *The Ghost Shirt Religion and the Sioux Outbreak of 1890*. Washington, DC: U.S. Government Printing Office, 1896.

Moore, Clifford Herschel. *The Religious Thought of the Greeks*. Cambridge: Harvard Univ. Press, 1916.

Moore, George Foot. *Judaism in the First Centuries of the Christian Era*. Vol.1. Cambridge: Harvard Univ. Press, 1927.

Morris, Brian. *Anthropological Studies of Religion: An Introductory Text*. Cambridge: Cambridge Univ. Press, 1987.

Morris, Colin. "Christian Civilization (1050–1400)." In *The Oxford History of Christianity*, edited by John McManners, 205–42. Oxford: Oxford Univ. Press, 1993.

Müller, Max. *The Hibbert Lectures 1878: Lectures on the Origin and Growth of Religion, as Illustrated by the Religions of India*. London: Longmans, Green, and Co., 1878.

———. *History of Ancient Sanskrit*. Columbia, MO: South Asia Books, [1859] 1993.

Murdock, George Peter. *Ethnographic Atlas*. Pittsburgh: Univ. of Pittsburgh Press, 1967.

Murray, Alexander. "Piety and Impiety in Thirteenth Century Italy." *Studies in Church History* 8 (1972): 83–106.

Narr, Karl J. "Approaches to the Religion of Early Paleolithic Man." *History of Religions* 4 (1964): 1–22.

Needham, Joseph. *Science and Civilization in China*. 6 vols. Cambridge: Cambridge Univ. Press, 1954–1984.

Neusner, Jacob. *First Century Judaism in Crisis*. Nashville: Abingdon Press, 1975.

Nicolle, David. *Historical Atlas of the Islamic World*. London: Mercury Books, 2004.

Niebuhr, H. Richard. *The Social Sources of Denominationalism*. New York: Henry Holt, 1929.

Niehr, Herbert. "The Rise of YHWH in Judahite and Israelite Religion: Methodological and Religi-Historical Aspects." In *The Triumph of Elohim: From Yahwisms to Judaisms*, edited by Diana Vikander Edelman. Grand Rapids, MI: William B. Eerdmans, 1996.

Nikiprowetzky, Valentin. "Ethical Monotheism." *Daedalus* 104:2 (1975): 69–89.

Nivison, David S. "Tao and Te." In *The Encyclopedia of Religion*, edited by Mircea Eliade. New York: Macmillan, 1987.

Nock, Arthur Darby. *Conversion*. London: Oxford Univ. Press, 1933.

———. "The Problem of Zoroaster." *American Journal of Archaeology* 53 (1949): 272–85.

———. *St. Paul*. New York: Harper and Brothers, 1938.

Nöldeke, Theodor. "The Koran." Originally published in the *Encyclopaedia Britannica*, 9th ed,. Reprinted in *The Origins of the Koran*, edited by Ibn Warraq, 36–63. Amherst, NY: Prometheus Books, [1891] 1998.

Norbeck, Edward. *Religion in Primitive Society*. New York: Harper, 1961.

North, Charles M. and Carl R. Gwin. "Religion, Corruption, and the Rule of Law." *Journal of Money, Credit, and Banking* (forthcoming).

North, John. "Conservatism and Change in Roman Religion." *Papers of the British School in Rome* 44 (1974): 1–12.

———. "Novelty and Choice in Roman Religion." *Journal of Roman Studies* 70 (1980): 186–91.

———. "Religious Toleration in Republican Rome." *Proceedings of the Cambridge Philological Society* 25 (1979): 85–103.

———. "Rome." In *Religions of the Ancient World: A Guide*, edited by Sarah Iles Johnston, 225–232. Cambridge: Belknap Press of Harvard Univ. Press, 2004.

Noth, Martin. *A History of Pentateuchal Traditions*. Englewood Cliffs, NJ: Prentice-Hall, [1948] 1972.

Nyberg, Henrik S. *Die Religionen des alten Iran*. Leipzig: J. C. Hinrichs, 1938.

Oates, Joan. *Babylon*, revised edition. London: Thames & Hudson, [1979] 2003.

Obelkevich, James. *Religion and the People, 800–1700*. Chapel Hill: Univ. of North Carolina Press, 1979.

O'Connell, James. "The Withdrawal of the High God in West African Religion: An Essay in Interpretation." *Man* 62 (1962): 67–9.

O'Flaherty, Wendy Doniger. "Brahmā." In *The Encyclopedia of Relgion*, edited by Mircea Eliade. New York: Macmillan, 1987.

Oppenheim, A. Leo. *Ancient Mesopotamia: Portrait of a Dead Civilization*. Rev. ed. Chicago: Univ. of Chicago Press, 1977.

———. "The Position of the Intellectual in Mesopotamian Society." *Daedalus* 104:2 (1975): 37–46.

Overmyer, Daniel L. "Chinese Religion: An Overview." In *The Encyclopedia of Religion*, edited by Mircea Eliade. New York: Macmillan, 1987.

———. "Religions of China." In *Religious Traditions of the World*, edited by H. Byron Earhart, 975–1073. San Francisco: HarperSanFrancisco, 1993.

Ozment, Steven. *The Age of Reform 1250–1550*. New Haven: Yale Univ. Press, 1980.

Pagels, Elaine. *Beyond Belief: The Secret Gospel of Thomas*. New York: Random House, 2005.

———. *The Gnostic Gospels*. New York: Random House, 1979.

———. *The Origin of Satan*. New York: Random House, 1995.

Pals, Daniel L. *Seven Theories of Religion*. Oxford: Oxford Univ. Press, 1996.

Pargament, K. I., and C. L. Park. "Merely a Defense? The Variety of Religious Ends and Means." *Journal of Social Issues* 51, no.2 (1995): 13–32.

Parker, Robert. "Controlling Religion: Greece." In *Religions of the Ancient World: A Guide*, edited by Sarah Iles Johnston, 570–572.Cambridge: Belknap Press of Harvard Univ. Press, 2004.

Parrinder, Geoffrey. *Jesus in the Qur'an*. Oxford: One World, [1965] 2003.

———. *World Religions: From Ancient History to the Present*. New York: Facts on File, 1983.

Parrot, André. *The Flood and Noah's Ark*. New York: Philosophical Library, 1953.

———. *The Tower of Babel*. New York: Philosophical Library, 1954.

Payne, Robert. *The History of Islam*. New York: Barnes & Noble, [1959] 1995.

Pelican, Jaroslav. *Whose Bible Is It?* New York: Viking, 2005.

Pell, George Cardinal. "Islam and Us." *First Things* 164 (June/July 2006): 33–6.

Pépin, Jean. "Logos." In *The Encyclopedia of Religion*,edited by Mircea Eliade. New York: Macmillan, 1987.

Perkins, Pheme. *The Gnostic Dialogue: The Early Church and the Crisis of Gnosticism*. New York: Paulist Press, 1980.

———. "Gnosticism." In *Encyclopedia of Early Christianity*, edited by Everett Ferhuson, 371–376. New York: Garland, 1990.

Perrin, Norman. "Jesus and the Theology of the New Testament." *The Journal of Religion* 64 (1984): 413–31.

Peschel, Enid Rhodes. "Structural Parallels in Two Flood Myths: Noah and the Maori." *Folklore* 82 (1971): 116–23.

Peters, F. E. *Muhammad and the Origins of Islam*. Albany, NY: State Univ. of New York Press, 1994.

Pettazzoni, Raffaele. *Essays on the History of Religions*. Leiden: E. J. Brill, 1954.

Peyser, Joan. *The Memory of All That: The Life of George Gershwin*. New York: Simon & Schuster, 1993.

Pickthall, Marmaduke. *The Meaning of the Glorious Koran*. New York: Alfred Knopf, [1930] 1992.

Piggott, Stewart. "Chinese Chariotry: An Outsider's View." In *The Arts of the Eurasian Steppelands*, edited by Philip Denwood, 32–51. London: Percival David Foundation of Chinese Art, 1978.

Pizan, Christine de. *The Writings of Christine de Pizan*. Edited by Charity Cannon Willard. New York: Persea Books, [1410] 1994.

Plott, John C. *Global History of Philosophy, Volume I: The Axial Age*. Delhi: Motilal Banarsidass, 1963.

Plumb, Derek. "The Social and Economic Spread of Rural Lollardy: A Reappraisal." *Studies in Church History* 23 (1986): 111–30.

Polkinghorn, John C. *Science and Creation*. Philadelphia: Templeton Foundation Press, 2006.

Pollard, John Richard Thornhill. "Greek Religion." In *Encyclopaedia Britannica*. Chicago: Univ. of Chicago Press, 1981.

Pollock, Susan. "Ur." In *The Oxford Encyclopedia of Archaeology in the Near East*. New York: Oxford Univ. Press, 1997.

Pomeroy, Sarah B. *Goddesses, Whores, Wives, and Slaves: Women in Classical Antiquity*. New York: Dorset Press. 1975.

Preus, J. Samuel. *Explaining Religion: Criticism and Theory from Bodin to Freud*. New Haven: Yale Univ. Press, 1987.

Price, Barbara J. "Demystification, Enriddlement, and Aztec Cannibalism: A Reply to Harner." *American Ethnologist* 5 (1978): 98–115.

Price, Ira M. "The Schools of the Sons of the Prophets." *The Old Testament Studies* 8 (1889): 244–49.

Price, S. R. F. *Rituals and Power: The Roman Imperial Cult in Asia Minor*. Cambridge: Cambridge University Press, 1984.

Price, Simon. *Religions of the Ancient Greeks*. Cambridge: Cambridge Univ. Press, 1999.

———. "Sacrifice, Offerings, and Votives." In *Religions of the Ancient World: A Guide*, edited by Sarah Iles Johnston, 344–346. Cambridge: Belknap Press of Harvard Univ. Press, 2004.

Radhakrishnan, Sarvepalli and Charles A. Moore. *A Sourcebook in Indian Philosophy*. Princeton: Princeton Univ. Press, 1957.

Radin, Paul. *Monotheism among Primitive Peoples*. London: George Allen & Unwin, 1924.

———. *Primitive Man as Philosopher*. New York: A. Appleton & Co., [1927] 1957.

———. *Primitive Religion: Its Nature and Origin*. New York: Dover Publications, [1937] 1957.

Rāhula, Walpola. "Buddha." In *The Encyclopaedia Britannica*. Chicago: Univ. of Chicago Press, 1981.

Ramsey, Bennett. "Pythagoras." In *The Encyclopedia of Religion*, edited by Mircea Eliade. New York: Macmillan, 1987.

Ramsey, George W. *The Quest for the Historical Israel*. Eugene, OR: Wipf and Stock, [1981] 1999.

Rawson, Elizabeth. "Scipio, Laelius, Furius and the Ancestral Religion." *The Journal of Roman Studies* 63 (1973): 161–74.

Read, Kay Almere. *Time and Sacrifice in the Aztec Cosmos*. Bloomington: Univ. of Indiana Press, 1998.

Reat, Noble Ross. *Buddhism: A History*. Fremont, CA: Jain Publishing, 1994.

Redford, Donald B. *Akhenaten: The Heretic King*. Princeton: Princeton Univ. Press, 1984.

———. *Egypt, Canaan, and Israel in Ancient Times*. Princeton: Princeton Univ. Press, 1992.

Reichelt, Karl Ludwig. *Religion in Chinese Garments*. London: James Clarke, [1951] 2004.

Reimarus, Hermann Samuel. *Reimarus: Fragments*. Philadelphia: Fortress Press, 1970.

Reynolds, Frank E., and Charles Hallisey. "Buddha." In *The Encyclopedia of Religion*, edited by Mircea Eliade. New York: Macmillan, 1987.

———. "Buddhism: An Overview." In *The Encyclopedia of Religion*, edited by Mircea Eliade. New York: Macmillan, 1987.

Reynolds, Joyce, and Robert Tannenbaum. *Jews and God-Fearers at Aphrodisias*. Cambridge: Cambridge Univ. Press, 1987.

Richard, Gaston. "Dogmatic atheism in the sociology of religion." In *Durkheim on Religion*, edited by W. S. F. Pickering, 228–276. Atlanta: Scholars Press, [1923] 1994.

Riley, Gregory J. *One Jesus, Many Christs*. San Franciso: HarperSanFrancisco, 1997.

Rives, J. B. "The Decree of Decius and the Religion of Rome." *The Journal of Roman Studies* 89 (1999): 135–54.

———. *Religion and Authority in Roman Carthage from Augustus to Constantine*. New York: Oxford Univ. Press, 1995.

Rivkin, Ellis. "Essenes." In *The Encyclopedia of Religion*, edited by Mircea Eliade. New York: Macmillan, 1987.

———. "Sadducees." In *The Encyclopedia of Religion*, edited by Mircea Eliade. New York: Macmillan, 1987.

Roaf, Michael. *Cultural Atlas of Mesopotamia and the Ancient Near East*. New York: Facts on File, 1990.

Roberts, Michael. *The Early Vasas: A History of Sweden, 1523–1611*. Cambridge: Cambridge Univ. Press, 1968.

Robertson, John M. *Christianity and Mythology*. London: Watts & Co., 1910.

Robinson, Dwight Nelson. "A Study of the Social Position of the Devotees of the Oriental Cults in the Western World, Based on the Inscriptions." *Transactions and Proceedings of the American Philological Association* 44 (1913): 151–61.

Robinson, John A. T. *The Priority of John*. Oak Park, IL: Meyer-Stone Books, 1985.

———. *Redating the New Testament*. Philadelphia: The Westminster Press, 1976.

Rodinson, Maxime. *Muhammad*. New York: Random House, 1980.

Roetz, Heiner. *Confucian Ethics of the Axial Age*. Albany: State Univ. of New York Press, 1993.

Roetzel, Calvin J. *The World Shaped by the New Testament*. Atlanta: John Knox Press, 1985.

Rogers, Everett M. *Diffusion of Innovations*. 5th ed. New York: The Free Press of Glencoe, [1962] 2003.

Róheim, Géza. *The Gates of the Dream*. New York: International Universities Press, 1952.

Roller, Lynn. *In Search of God the Mother: The Cult of Anatolian Cybele*. Berkeley: Univ. of California Press, 1999.

Rostovtzeff, Michael. *The Social and Economic History of the Roman Empire*. Oxford: Clarendon Press, 1926.

Roux, Georges. *Ancient Iraq*. London: Penguin Books, 1992.

Rudolph, Kurt. *Gnosis: The Nature and History of Gnosticism*. San Francisco: HarperSanFrancisco, 1987.

Ruether, Rosemary. *Faith and Fratricide: The Theological Roots of Anti-Semitism*. New York: Seabury Press, 1974.

Russell, J. C. *Late Ancient and Medieval Population*. Philadelphia: Transactions of the American Philosophical Society, 1958.

Russell, Jeffrey Burton. *The Devil: Perceptions of Evil from Antiquity to Primitive Christianity*. Ithaca, NY: Cornell Univ. Press, 1977.

Ruthven, Malise. *Historical Atlas of Islam*. Cambridge: Harvard Univ. Press, 2004.

Saggs, H. W. F. *The Encounter with the Divine in Mesopotamia and Israel*. London: The Athlone Press of the Univ. of London, 1978.

Sahlins, Marshall. *Stone Age Economics*. New York: Aldine, 1972.

Salahi, M. A. *Muhammad: Man and Prophet*. Shaftesbury, Dorset, UK: Element, 1995.

Saldarini, Anthony J. *Pharisees, Scribes, and Sadducees in Palestinian Society: A Sociological Approach*. Wilmington, DE: M. Glazier, 1988.

Sanders, E. P. *The Historical Figure of Jesus*. London: Penguin Books, 1995.

Sandison, A. T. "Sexual Behavior in Ancient Societies." In *Diseases in Antiquity*, edited by Don Brothwell and A.T. Sandison, 734–755. Springfield, IL: Charles C. Thomas, 1967.

Sawyer, P. H. *Kings and Vikings: Scandinavia and Europe, AD 700–1100*. London: Methuen, 1982.

Sayce, A. H. *Lectures on the Origin and Growth of Religion as Illustrated by the Religion of the Ancient Babylonians*, 3rd edition. London: Williams and Norgate, 1891.

Schäfer, Peter. *Judeophobia: Attitudes towards the Jews in the Ancient World*. Cambridge: Harvard Univ. Press, 1997.

Scharfstein, Ben-Ami. *Mystical Experience*. Indianapolis: Bobbs-Merrill, 1973.

Scheid, John. "Graeco Ritu: A Typically Roman Way of Honoring the Gods." *Harvard Studies in Classical Philology* 97 (1995): 15–31.

Schiffman, Lawrence H. "Essenes." In Mircea Eliade, ed., *The Encyclopedia of Religion*. New York: Macmillan, 1987.

Schmidt, Wilhelm. *The Origin and Growth of Religion: Facts and Theories*. London: Methuen and Co., 1931.

Schmied, Gerhard. "US-Televangelism on German TV." *Journal of Contemporary Religion* 11 (1996): 95–9.

Schmitt, John J. "Prophecy (Preexilic Hebrew)." In *The Anchor Bible Dictionary*, edited by David Noel Freedman. New York: Doubleday, 1992.

Schneider, Jane. "Spirits and the Spirit of Capitalism." In *Religious Orthodoxy and Popular Faith in European Society*, edited by Ellen Badone, 24–54. Princeton: Princeton Univ. Press, 1990.

Schonfield, Hugh J. *The Passover Plot: New Light on the History of Jesus*. New York: Bernard Geiss Associates, 1965.

Schwartz, Benjamin I. "The Age of Transcendence." *Daedalus* 104:2 (1975): 1–7.

———. "Transcendence in Ancient China." *Daedalus* 104:2 (1975): 57–68.

Shaban, Muhammad Abdulhayy. *Islamic History AD 600–750: A New Interpretation*. Cambridge: Cambridge Univ. Press, 1971.

Shahar, Meir, and Robert P. Weller. *Unruly Gods: Divinity and Society in China*. Honolulu: University of Hawaii Press, 1996.

Shahbazi, A. Shapur. "The 'Traditional Date of Zoroaster' Explained." *Bulletin of the School of Oriental and African Studies, University of London* 40 (1977): 25–35.

Shanks, Hershel. "How Historical Is the Gospel of John?" *Biblical Archaeology Review* 31:5 (2005): 23.

———."Review of Biagent's *The Jesus Papers*." *Biblical Archaeology Review* 32:5 (2006): 72–3.

Sharot, Stephen. *Messianism, Mysticism, and Magic: A Sociological Analysis of Jewish Religious Movements*. Chapel Hill: Univ. of North Carolina Press, 1982.

Sheler, Jeffry L. *Is the Bible True?* San Francisco: HarperSanFrancisco, 1999.

Shih, Hu. "A Criticism of Some Recent Methods Used in Dating Lao Tzu." *Harvard Journal of Asiatic Studies* 2 (1937): 373–97.

Simpson, George Eaton. *Black Religion in the New World*. New York: Columbia Univ. Press, 1978.

Smallwood, E. Mary. *The Jews under Roman Rule*. Leiden: E. J. Brill, 1981.

Smart, Ninian. *The Religious Experience of Mankind*, 3rd edition. New York: Charles Scribner's Sons, 1984.

Smelser, Neil J. *Theory of Collective Behavior*. New York: The Free Press, 1963.

Smilde, David. "A Qualitative Comparative Analysis of Conversion to Venezuelan Evangelicalism: How Networks Matter." *American Journal of Sociology* 111 (2005): 757–96.

Smith, Adam. *An Inquiry into the Nature and Causes of the Wealth of Nations*. 2 vols. Indianapolis: Liberty Fund, [1776] 1981.

Smith, D. Howard. *Chinese Religions: From 1000 BC to the Present Day*. New York: Holt, Rinehart and Winston, 1971.

———. *Confucius*. New York: Scribner's Sons, 1973.

———. "The Significance of Confucius for Religion." *History of Religions* 2 (1963): 242–55.

Smith, D. Moody. *John Among the Gospels*. 2nd ed. Columbia, SC: Univ. of South Carolina Press, 2001.

Smith, Huston. *The World's Religions*. San Francisco: HarperSanFranciso, 1991.

Smith, Mark S. *The Early History of God: Yahweh and Other Deities in Ancient Israel*. 2nd ed. Grand Rapids, MI: William B. Eerdmans, 2002.

———. *The Origins of Biblical Monotheism: Israel's Polytheistic Background and the Ugaritic Texts*. Oxford: Oxford Univ. Press, 2001.

Smith, Morton. "A Comparison of Early Christian and Early Rabbinic Tradition." *Journal of Biblical Literature* 82 (1963): 169–76.

———. *Jesus the Magician*. San Francisco: HarperSanFrancisco, 1978.

———. *Palestinian Parties and Politics that Shaped the Old Testament*. 2nd ed. London: SCM Press, 1987.

———. *The Secret Gospel: The Discovery and Interpretation of the Secret Gospel According to Mark*. New York: Harper and Row, 1973.

Smith, Ray Winfield and Donald B. Redford. *The Akhenaten Temple Project, Volume I: Initial Discoveries*. Philadelphia: The University Museum, Univ. of Pennsylvania, 1976.

Smith, W. Robertson. *The Religion of the Semites*. Edinburgh: Adam and Charles Black, 1889.

Smith, Wilfred Cantwell. *The Meaning and End of Religion*. Minneapolis: Fortress Press, [1962] 1991.

Sordi, Marta. *The Christians and the Roman Empire*. Norman: Univ. of Oklahoma Press, 1986.

Soustelle, Jacques. "Aztec Religion." In *Encyclopaedia Britannica*. Chicago: Univ. of Chicago Press, 1981.

———.*Daily Life of the Aztecs*. London: Phoenix Press, 1961.

———. "Mayan Religion." In *Encyclopaedia Britannica*. Chicago: Univ. of Chicago Press, 1981.

Spalinger, Anthony. "The Limitations of Formal Egyptian Religion." *Journal of Near Eastern Studies* 57 (1998): 241–60.

Spencer, Herbert. *Social Statics*. New York: Robert Schalkenbach Foundation, [1851] 1970.

———. *The Principles of Sociology*. Vol. 1. New York: D. Appleton and Co., [1876] 1896.

Sperber, Dan. *Rethinking Symbolism*. Cambridge: Cambridge University Press, 1975.

Sperling, S. David. "Jeremiah." In *The Encyclopedia of Religion*, edited by Mircea Eliade. New York: Macmillan, 1987.

Spiro, Melfrod E. "Religion: Problems in Definition and Explanation." In *Anthropological Approaches to the Study of Religion*, edited by Michael Banton, 85–126. London: Tavistock Publications, 1966.

Spong, John Shelby. *Born of a Woman: A Bishop Rethinks the Birth of Jesus*. San Francisco: Harper Collins, 1994.

Stark, Rodney. "A Theory of Revelations." *Journal for the Scientific Study of Religion* 38 (1999): 286–307.

———. *Cities of God: The Real Story of How Christianity Became an Urban Movement and Conquered Rome*. San Francisco: HarperSanFrancisco, 2006.

———. *Exploring the Religious Life*. Baltimore: Johns Hopkins Press, 2004.

———. *For the Glory of God: How Monotheism Led to Reformations, Science, Witch-Hunts, and the End of Slavery*. Princeton: Princeton Univ. Press, 2003.

———. "From Church-Sect to Religious Economies." In *The Sacred in a Post-Secular Age*, edited by Phillip E. Hammond, 139–149. Berkeley: Univ, of California Press, 1985.

———. "Micro Foundations of Religion: A Revised Theory." *Sociological Theory* 17 (1999): 264–89.

———. "Normal Revelations: A Rational Model of 'Mystical' Experiences." In David G. Bromley, ed., *Religion and the Social Order*, Volume 1. Greenwich: JAI Press, 1991.

———. *One True God: Historical Consequences of Monotheism*. Princeton: Princeton Univ. Press, 2001.

———. "Putting an End to Ancestor Worship." *Journal for the Scientific Study of Religion* 43 (2004): 465–75.

———. "Religious Economies: A New Perspective." Paper delivered at a conference on New Directions in Religious Research, University of Lethbridge, 1983.

———. "Secularization, R.I.P." *Sociology of Religion* 60 (1999): 249–73.

———. *Sociology*, 10th edition. Belmont, CA: Thomson/Wadsworth, 2007.

———. "Spiegare le Variazioni Della Religiosita: il Modello del Mercato" ("Explaining International Variations in Religiousness: The Market Model"), translation by Maurizio Pisati. *Polis: Ricerche e studi su società e politica in Italia* 12 (1998): 11–31.

———. *The Rise of Christianity*. Princeton: Princeton Univ. Press, 1996.

———. *The Rise of Mormonism*. New York: Columbia Univ. Press, 2005.

———. *The Victory of Reason: How Christianity Led to Freedom, Capitalism, and Western Success*. New York: Random House, 2005.

———. "Why Religious Movements Succeed or Fail: A Revised General Model." *Journal of Contemporary Religion* 11 (1996): 133–46.

Stark, Rodney, and William Sims Bainbridge. *The Future of Religion*. Berkeley: Univ. of California Press, 1985.

———. "Of Churches, Sects, and Cults: Preliminary Concepts for a Theory of Religious Movements." *Journal for the Scientific Study of Religion* 18 (1979): 117–31.

———. *Religion, Deviance, and Social Control*. New York: Routledge, 1997.

———. *A Theory of Religion*. New Brunswick, NJ: Rutgers Univ. Press, [1987] 1995.

Stark, Rodney, and Roger Finke. *Acts of Faith: Explaining the Human Side of Religion*. Berkeley: Univ. of California Press, 2000.

Stark, Rodney, Eva Hamberg, and Alan S. Miller. "Exploring Spirituality and Unchurched Religions in America, Sweden, and Japan." *Journal of Contemporary Religion* 20 (2005): 1–21.

Stark, Rodney, and Laurence Iannaccone. "Recent Religious Declines in Quebec, Poland, and the Netherlands: A Theory Vindicated." *Journal for the Scientific Study of Religion* 35 (1996): 265–71.

Stern, Menahem. "The Period of the Second Temple." In *A History of the Jewish People*, edited by Haim Hillel Ben-Sasson, 185–303. Cambridge: Harvard Univ. Press, 1976.

Stevens, Marty E. *Temples, Tithes, and Taxes: The Temple and Economic Life of Ancient Israel*. Peabody, MA: Hendrickson Publishers, 2006.

Stocking, George W., Jr. "Animism in Theory and Practice: E. B. Tylor's Unpublished Notes on 'Spiritualism.' " *Man* 6 (1971): 88–104.

Strauss, Barry. *The Trojan War: A New History*. New York: Simon & Schuster, 2006.

Strauss, David Frederich. *The Life of Jesus Critically Examined*. Bristol, UK: Thoemmes Continuum, [1833] 2006.

Street, Brian Vincent. "Tylor, Sir Edward Burnett." In *Encyclopaedia Britannica*. 15th ed. Chicago: Univ. of Chicago Press, 1981.

Sun, Anna Xiao Dong. "The Fate of Confucianism as a Religion in Socialist China: Controversies and Paradoxes." In *State, Market, and Religions in Chinese Societies*, edited by Fenggang Yang and Joseph B. Tamney, 229–253. Leiden: Brill, 2005.

Swanson, Guy E. *Religion and Regime: A Sociological Account of the Reformation*. Ann Arbor: Univ. of Michigan Press, 1967.

Tadmor, Hayim. "The Period of the First Temple." In *A History of the Jewish People*, edited by Haim Hillel Ben-Sasson, 91–182. Cambridge: Harvard Univ. Press, 1976.

Talley, Thomas J. *The Origins of the Liturgical Year*. Collegeville, MN: Liturgical Press, 1991.

Tcherikover, Victor. *Hellenistic Civilization and the Jews*. Peabody, MA: Hendrickson, [1959] 1999.

Thapar, Romila. *Early India: From the Origins to AD 1300*. Berkeley: Univ. of California Press, 2004.

————. "Ethics, Religion, and Social Protest in the First Millennium BC in Northern India." *Daedalus* 104:2 (1975): 119–32.

Theissen, Gerd. *Biblical Faith: An Evolutionary Approach.* Philadelphia: Fortress Press, 1985.

————. *The Gospels in Context.* Minneapolis: Fortress Press, 1991.

————. *The Shadow of the Galilean: The Quest for the Historical Jesus in Narrative Form.* Philadelphia: Fortress Press, 1987.

Thiering, Barbara. *Jesus and the Riddle of the Dead Sea Scrolls.* San Francisco: Harper Collins, 1992.

Thomas, Keith. *Religion and the Decline of Magic.* New York: Scribners, 1971.

Thompson, E. A. *The Visigoths in the Time of Ulfila.* Oxford: Clarendon Press, 1966.

Thompson, Henry. "Yaweh." In *The Anchor Bible Dictionary*, edited by David Noel Freedman. New York: Doubleday, 1992.

Thompson, J. Eric S. *Maya History and Religion.* Norman: Univ. of Oklahoma Press, 1970.

Thompson, Lawrence G. "Chinese Religion." In *The Encyclopaedia Britannica.* Chicago: Univ. of Chicago Press, 1981.

————. "Confucian Thought: The State Cult." In *The Encyclopedia of Religion*, edited by Mircea Eliade. New York: Macmillan, 1987.

Thompson, Thomas. *The Mythic Past: Biblical Archaeology's New Vision of Ancient Israel and the Origins of Its Sacred Texts.* New York: Basic Books, 1999.

Tighe, William J. "Calculating Christmas." *Touchstone* 6 (December 2003):12–4.

Tillich, Paul. *Systematic Theology.* Vol. 1. Chicago: Univ. of Chicago Press, 1951.

Tinker, Hugh Russell. "Indian Subcontinent, History of the." In *The Encyclopaedia Britannica.* Chicago: Univ. of Chicago Press, 1981.

Torrey, Charles Culter. "The Jewish Foundation of Islam." In *The Origins of the Koran*, edited by Ibn Warraq, 293–348. Amherst, NY: Prometheus Books, [1933] 1998.

Tracy, James D. *Europe's Reformations, 1450–1650.* Lanham, MD: Rowan & Littlefield, 1999.

Tresmontant, Claude. *The Hebrew Christ: Language in the Age of the Gospels.* Chicago: Franciscan Herald Press, 1989.

Tribilco, Paul. *Jewish Communities in Asia Minor.* Cambridge: Cambridge Univ. Press, 1991.

Trigger, Bruce G. "Monumental Architecture: A Thermodynamic Explanation of Symbolic Behaviour." *World Archaeology* 22 (1990): 119–312.

Tucci, Giuseppe. "Buddhism." In *The Encyclopaedia Britannica.* Chicago: Univ. of Chicago Press, 1981.

Turcan, Robert. *The Cults of the Roman Empire.* Oxford: Blackwell, 1996.

Turner, Ralph H. and Lewis M. Killian. *Collective Behavior.* 3rd. ed. Englewood Cliffs, NJ: Prentice-Hall, 1987.

Tylor, Edward Burnett. "Limits of Savage Religion." *Journal of the Anthropological Institute* 21 (1891): 283–301.

————. *Primitive Culture.* Vol. 1. New York: Harper and Row, [1871] 1958.

————. *Religion in Primitive Culture.* New York: Harper and Row, [1871] 1958.

Underhill, Evelyn. *Mysticism*, 14th edition. London: Methuen, [1911] 1942.

Van Dijk, Jacobus. "The Amarna Period and the Later New Kingdom." In *The Oxford History of Ancient Egypt*, edited by Ian Shaw, 272–313. Oxford: Oxford Univ. Press, 2000.

Van Seters, John. *In Search of History.* New Haven: Yale Univ. Press, 1983.

————. *The Life of Moses: The Yahwist as Historian in Exodus-Numbers.* Louisville: Westminister/John Knox Press, 1994.

Van Sickle, C. E. "Conservative and Philosophical Influence in the Reign of Diocletian." *Classical Philology* 27 (1932): 51–8.

Velikovsky, Immanuel. *Ages in Chaos.* Cutchogue, NY: Buccaneer Books, [1952] 1990.

————. *Worlds in Collision.* New York: Pocket Books, [1950] 1977.

Verkamp, Bernard J. "Concerning the Evolution of Religion." *The Journal of Religion* 71 (1991): 538–57.

Vermes, Geza. *Jesus and the World of Judaism.* Philadelphia: Fortress Press, 1984.

————. *Jesus the Jew: A Historian's Reading of the Gospel.* 2nd ed. New York: Macmillan, 1983.

Von Soden, Wolfram. *The Ancient Orient: An Introduction to the Study of the Ancient Near East.* Grand Rapids, MI: William B. Eerdmans, 1994.

Vorster, Willem S. "Gospel Genre." In *The Anchor Bible Dictionary*, edited by David Noel Freedman. New York: Doubleday, 1992.

Wales, H. G. Quaritch. *The Mountain of God.* London: Bernard Quaritch, 1936.

Walker, Christopher and Michael B. Dick. "The Induction of the Cult Image in Ancient Mesopotamia: The Mesopotamian *mīs pî* Ritual." In *Born in Heaven, Made on Earth: The Making of the Cult Image in the Ancient Near East*, edited by Michael B. Dick, 55–121. Winona Lake, IN: Eisenbrauns, 1999.

Walker, D. P. "Orpheus the Theologian and Renaissance Platonists." *Journal of the Warburg and Courtauld Institutes* 16 (1953): 100–20.

Wallace, Anthony F. C. *Religion: An Anthropological View*. New York: Random House, 1966.

Walsh, Jerome T. "Elijah." In *The Anchor Bible Dictionary*, edited by David Noel Freedman. New York: Doubleday, 1992.

Warraq, Ibn. "Studies on Muhammad and the Rise of Islam: A Critical Survey." In *The Quest for the Historical Muhammad*, edited by Ibn Warraq, 15–88. Amherst, NY: Prometheus Books, 2000.

Warrior, Valerie M. *Roman Religion: A Sourcebook*. Newburyport, MA: Focus Publishing, 2002.

Watson, Alaric. *Aurelian and the Third Century*. London: Routledge, 1999.

Watt, W. Montgomery. "Introduction." In *The Meaning of the Glorious Koran*, by Marmaduke Pickthall New York: Alfred Knopf, 1992.

———. "Muhammad." In *Encyclopaedia Britannica*. Chicago: Univ. of Chicago Press, 1981.

———. "Muhammad." In *The Encyclopedia of Religion*, edited by Mircea Eliade. New York: Macmillan, 1987.

———. *Muhammad in Mecca*. Oxford: Oxford Univ. Press, 1980.

———. *Muhammad: Prophet and Statesman*. Oxford: Oxford Univ. Press, 1961.

Weber, Alfred. *Das Tragische und die Geschichte*. Hamburg: Goverts, 1943.

———. *History of Philosophy*. New York: Charles Scribner's Sons, 1896.

Weber, Max. *The Protestant Ethic and the Spirit of Capitalism*. New York: Charles Scribner's Sons, [1904–1905] 1958.

———. *The Sociology of Religion*. Boston: Beacon Press, [1922] 1993.

Weightman, Simon. "Hinduism." In *A Handbook of Living Religions*, edited by John R. Hinnells. London: Penguin Books, 1984.

Weil, Eric. "What Is a Breakthrough in History?" *Daedalus* 104:2 (1975): 21–36.

Weinfeld, Moshe. "Deuteronomy, Book of." In *The Anchor Bible Dictionary*, edited by David Noel Freedman. New York: Doubleday, 1992.

———. "Israelite Religion." In *The Encyclopedia of Religion*, edited by Mircea Eliade. New York: Macmillan, 1987.

Welliver, Dotsey, and Minnette Northcutt. *Mission Handbook*. 19th edition. Wheaton IL: Billy Graham Center, 2004.

West, M. L. *The East Face of Helicon: West Asiatic Elements in Greek Poetry and Myth*. Oxford: Oxford Univ. Press, 1997.

———. "Towards Monotheism." In *Pagan Monotheism in Late Antiquity*, edited by Plymnia Athanassiadi and Michael Frede, 21–40. Oxford: Clarendon Press, 1999.

Wheeler, Sir Mortimer. *The Indus Civilization: Supplementary Volume to The Cambridge History of India*. Cambridge: Cambridge Univ. Press, 1953.

Whelan, Estelle. "Forgotten Witness: Evidence for the Early Codification of the Quran." *Journal of the American Oriental Society* 118 (1998): 1–14.

White, Jefferson. *Evidence and Paul's Journeys*. Hilliard, OH: Parsagard Press, 2001.

White, L. Michael. "Mithraism." In *Encyclopedia of Early Christianity*, edited by Everett Ferguson, 609–610. New York: Garland, 1990.

Whitehead, Alfred North. *Science and the Modern World*. New York: Free Press, [1925] 1967.

Whitelam, Keith W. *The Invention of Ancient Israel: The Silencing of Palestinian History*. New York: Routledge, 1996.

Whittaker, John. *Studies in Platonism and Patristic Thought*. London: Variorum Reprints, 1984.

Wilford, John Noble. "Maya Tomb Tells Tale of Two Women, Elite but Doomed." *New York Times*. June 14, 2005. http://www.nytimes.com.

Wilken, Robert L. *The Christians as the Romans Saw Them*. New Haven: Yale Univ. Press, 1984.

Wilkins, W. J. *Hindu Gods and Goddesses*. Mineoloa, NY: Dover Publications, [1900] 2003.

Wilkinson, Richard H. *The Complete Gods and Goddesses of Ancient Egypt*. New York: Thames & Hudson, 2003.

Wilkinson, Robert. "Introduction." In *The Analects*. Ware, Hertfordshire: Wadsworth Classics, 1996.

Willems, Harco. "Sacrifice, Offerings, and Votives." In *Religions of the Ancient World: A Guide*, edited by Sarah Iles Johnston, 326–330. Cambridge: Belknap Press of Harvard Univ. Press, 2004.

Williams, John Alden. "Islam, History of." In *Encyclopaedia Britannica*. Chicago: Univ. of Chicago Press, 1981.

Williams, Michael Allen. *Rethinking "Gnosticism": An Argument for Dismantling a Dubious Category*. Princeton: Princeton Univ. Press, 1996.

Williams, Stephen. *Diocletian and the Roman Recovery*. New York: Methuen, 1985.

Wilson, Bryan. *Magic and Millennium*. Frogmore, England: Paladin, 1975.

Wilson, John. "Akhenaten." In *Encyclopaedia Britannica*. Chicago: Univ. of Chicago Press, 1981.

Wilson, Robert R. "Prophecy: Biblical Prophecy." In *The Encyclopedia of Religion*, edited by Mircea Eliade. New York: Macmillan, 1987.

Wilson, Thomas A. "Sacrifice and the Imperial Cult of Confucius." *History of Religions* 41 (2002): 251–87.

Winston, David. "The Iranian Component in the Bible, Apocrypha, and Qumran: A Review of the Evidence." *History of Religions* 5 (1966): 183–216.

Witherington, Ben III. *The Jesus Quest: The Third Search for the Jew of Nazareth*. Downers Grove, IL: InterVarsity Press, 1997.

———. *The Paul Quest: The Renewed Search for the Jew of Tarsus*. Downers Grove, IL: InterVarsity Press, 1998.

Witt, R. E. *Isis in the Ancient World*. Baltimore: Johns Hopkins Univ. Press, 1997.

Woolley, Sir Leonard. *Discovering the Royal Tombs at Ur*. New York: Macmillan, [1954] 1969.

Wright, Arthur F. *Buddhism in Chinese History*. Stanford: Stanford Univ. Press, 1959.

Wright, David P. "Anatolia: Hittites." In Sarah Iles Johnston, ed., *Religions of the Ancient World: A Guide*. Cambridge: Belknap Press of Harvard Univ. Press, 2004.

Wright, N. T. "Jesus, Quest for the Historical." In *The Anchor Bible Dictionary*. David Noel Freedman, ed., New York: Doubleday, 1992.

———. *Judas and the Gospel of Jesus*. Grand Rapids, MI: Baker Books, 2006.

———. *The Resurrection of the Son of God*. Minneapolis: Fortress Press, 2003.

Wuthnow, Robert. *Communities of Discourse*. Cambridge: Harvard Univ. Press, 1989.

———. "Science and the Sacred." In *The Sacred in a Secular Age*, edited by Phillip E. Hammond, 187–203. Berkeley and Los Angeles: Univ. of California Press, 1985.

Yamauchi, Edwin M. *Persia and the Bible*. Grand Rapids, MI: Baker Books, 1996.

Yang, C. K. *Religion in Chinese Society*. Berkeley: Univ. of California Press, 1961.

Yang, Lien-sheng. "Buddhist Monasteries and Four Money-Raising Institutions in Chinese History." *Harvard Journal of Asiatic Studies* 13 (1950): 174–91.

Yao, Xinzhong. "Who Is a Confucian Today? A Critical Reflection on the Issues Concerning Confucian Identity in Modern Times." *Journal of Contemporary Religion* 16 (2001): 313–28.

Yerkes, Royden Keith. *Sacrifice: In Greek and Roman Religions and in Early Judaism*. New York: Charles Scribner's Sons, 1952.

Yu, David C. *History of Chinese Daoism*. Vol. 1. Lanham, MD: Univ. Press of America, 2000.

Zaehner, R. C. *The Bhagavad-Gita: With a Commentary Based on Original Sources*. Oxford: Oxford Univ. Press, 1969.

———. *The Dawn and Twilight of Zoroastrianism*. London: Phoenix Press, [1961] 2002.

———. *Hinduism*. Oxford: Oxford Univ. Press, 1966.

Zetterholm, Magnus. "The Covenant for Gentiles? Covenantal Nomism and the Incident at Antioch." In *The Ancient Synagogue from Its Origins until 200 CE*, edited by Birger Olsson and Magnus Zetterholm, 168–188. Stockholm: Amlqvist & Wiksell, 2003.

———. *The Formation of Christianity in Antioch*. London: Routledge, 2003.

Zevit, Ziony. *The Religions of Ancient Israel: A Synthesis of Paralactic Approaches*. London: Continuum, 2001.

Zürcher, Erik. "Buddhism: Buddhism in China." In *The Encyclopedia of Religion*, edited by Mircea Eliade. New York: Macmillan, 1987.

———. *Buddhism: Its Origin and Spread in Words, Maps and Pictures*. London: Routledge & Kegan Paul, 1962.

———. *The Buddhist Conquest of China*. Leiden: E. J. Brill, 1959.

INDEX

Page references followed by *fig* indicate photograph or illustration;
followed by *t* indicate a table; followed by *m* indicate a map.

Meriden Public Library
Meriden, CT 06450

A2090 4375Ll l

200
St

4375lll

Stark, Rodney.

Discovering God.

$25.95

FEB 29 2008

DATE			

BAKER & TAYLOR